THE OXFORD HANDBOOK OF

ETHICAL THEORY

THE OXFORD HANDBOOK OF

....

ETHICAL
THEORY

....

Edited by

DAVID COPP

OXFORD
UNIVERSITY PRESS
2006

OXFORD
UNIVERSITY PRESS

Oxford University Press, Inc., publishes works that further
Oxford University's objective of excellence
in research, scholarship, and education.

Oxford   New York
Auckland   Cape Town   Dar es Salaam   Hong Kong   Karachi
Kuala Lumpur   Madrid   Melbourne   Mexico City   Nairobi
New Delhi   Shanghai   Taipei   Toronto

With offices in
Argentina   Austria   Brazil   Chile   Czech Republic   France   Greece
Guatemala   Hungary   Italy   Japan   Poland   Portugal   Singapore
South Korea   Switzerland   Thailand   Turkey   Ukraine   Vietnam

Copyright © 2006 by Oxford University Press, Inc.

Published by Oxford University Press, Inc.
198 Madison Avenue, New York, New York 10016

www.oup.com

Oxford is a registered trademark of Oxford University Press

Library of Congress Cataloging-in-Publication Data
Copp, David.
The Oxford handbook of ethical theory / David Copp.
p. cm.
Includes bibliographical references and index.
ISBN-13 978-0-19-514779-7
ISBN 0-19-514779-0
1. Ethics.   I. Title.
BJ1012.C675 2005
171—dc22   2004065411

2 4 6 8 9 7 5 3 1

Printed in the United States of America
on acid-free paper

For Marina,
Margaret, and Cecil

PREFACE

....

THE twenty-two chapters of this book represent the current state of debate on the wide range of issues discussed in moral philosophy. The authors do not merely survey the field. They present and defend a point of view, sometimes a contentious point of view, and sometimes one that is disputed in another chapter in the volume. The chapters are demanding, and written at a professional level, but with the intention of being accessible to any sophisticated reader who has at least some background in philosophy. The introduction is intended to provide an overview of the field of ethical theory as well as an overview of the essays. I hope it will make the book more useful. My hope for the volume as a whole is that it will contribute to the continued flowering of moral philosophy.

I am grateful to many people for their help with the book and for their encouragement. My most important debt, of course, is to the authors of the essays, first for the very high quality of their work, but also for their patience. The volume took longer to put together than I had foreseen. For encouraging me to accept the challenge of doing the book, I thank Christopher Morris, Marina Oshana, and my editor at Oxford, Peter Ohlin. Tom Hurka gave me very helpful advice at several important points while I was working on the volume, as did John Fischer. I am sure that there are people who I have forgotten to mention, and I would like to thank them while apologizing for my memory. Many people gave me helpful advice about the introduction. I thank them by name in a note to that chapter.

Contents

PART II. NORMATIVE ETHICAL THEORY

CONTRIBUTORS

JULIA ANNAS is Regent's Professor, Department of Philosophy, University of Arizona.

SIMON BLACKBURN is professor in the Faculty of Philosophy at the University of Cambridge.

DAVID O. BRINK is professor of philosophy at the University of California, San Diego, and a director of the Institute for Law and Philosophy at the University of San Diego Law School.

JONATHAN DANCY spends two terms of each academic year at the University of Reading, England, where he is research professor of philosophy, and one semester at the University of Texas, Austin, where he is professor of philosophy.

JUSTIN D'ARMS is associate professor of philosophy at the Ohio State University.

STEPHEN DARWALL is John Dewey Collegiate Professor of Philosophy at the University of Michigan.

MICHAEL R. DEPAUL is professor of philosophy at the University of Notre Dame.

JAMES DREIER is professor of philosophy at Brown University.

GERALD DWORKIN is professor of philosophy at the University of California, Davis.

JOHN MARTIN FISCHER is professor of philosophy at the University of California, Riverside.

VIRGINIA HELD is Distinguished Professor, City University of New York, Graduate School.

THOMAS E. HILL, JR., is Kenan Professor of Philosophy at the University of North Carolina, Chapel Hill.

THOMAS HURKA is Henry N. R. Jackman Distinguished Professor of Philosophical Studies at the University of Toronto.

DANIEL JACOBSON is associate professor of philosophy and Senior Research Fellow of the Social Philosophy and Policy Center at Bowling Green State University.

PHILIP KITCHER is professor of philosophy at Columbia University.

MARK LANCE is professor of philosophy and in the Program on Justice and Peace, Georgetown University.

MARGARET LITTLE is associate professor of philosophy and senior research scholar, Kennedy Institute of Ethics, Georgetown University.

DAVID McNAUGHTON is professor of philosophy at Florida State University.

PHILIP L. QUINN, recently, sadly, deceased, was John A. O'Brien Professor of Philosophy, University of Notre Dame.

PETER RAILTON is John Stephenson Perrin Professor of Philosophy at the University of Michigan.

PIERS RAWLING is professor of philosophy at Florida State University.

GEOFFREY SAYRE-MCCORD is professor and chair of the Department of Philosophy at the University of North Carolina, Chapel Hill.

MICHAEL SLOTE is professor of philosophy at the University of Miami.

HILLEL STEINER is professor of political philosophy in the University of Manchester, England, and Fellow of the British Academy.

NICHOLAS L. STURGEON is professor of philosophy at Cornell University.

THE OXFORD HANDBOOK OF
ETHICAL THEORY

INTRODUCTION: METAETHICS AND NORMATIVE ETHICS

DAVID COPP

I UNDERTAKE two main tasks in this chapter. First, I aim to provide a brief overview of the chapters in this book and to show how they are related to one another. Second, I aim to introduce the issues in moral philosophy that are addressed in the book, and to do so in a way that is accessible to general readers with little background in philosophy. Because of my second aim, I discuss the chapters in the order that seems best pedagogically. My choice of which chapters to emphasize also reflects my pedagogical goal.

1. MORAL PHILOSOPHY

As we go about our lives, we face many decisions. Some of the decisions seem to concern only ourselves and people with whom we are intimate, such as decisions about behavior within the family. Other decisions concern our responsibilities in our jobs. Some concern our relationship to the state or the law, such as decisions about whether to abide by the tax code or whether to join the armed forces.

People who have governmental roles sometimes make decisions about controversial social issues, such as the morality of capital punishment or the justice of the tax system. All of us who live in democratic societies need to make decisions about such issues if we intend to vote responsibly. Moral philosophy addresses the many abstract ethical and philosophical issues that arise when we attempt to make such decisions in a reflective and responsible way.

Of course, some decisions have little moral import, but moral considerations have a bearing on a great many of our decisions. A person's decision-making can also be shaped, however, by considerations of self-interest, law, etiquette, custom, and tradition, and people in professional roles who are subject to codes of "ethics" may take such codes into account in their decisions. The question therefore arises: What distinguishes *moral* considerations from other kinds of consideration? What does *morality* require? Does morality determine what we ought to do, all things considered? These questions are addressed in various chapters in the volume.

For my purposes here, we can take a person's moral beliefs to be the beliefs she has about how to live her life when she takes into account in a sympathetic way the impact of her life and decisions on others. This statement is more vague than I would like, and it prejudges certain questions, but it is a place to begin. It is worth saying at the outset, moreover, that in this volume, "morality" and "ethics" are used interchangeably.

This book focuses on theoretical questions that can arise in thinking about any practical issue as well as general moral questions of theoretical importance. Applied ethics is an area of moral philosophy that focuses on concrete moral issues, including such matters as abortion, capital punishment, civil disobedience, drug use, family responsibilities, and professional ethics. Can war be just? Is euthanasia ever justifiable? This volume focuses, however, on questions that are more abstract than these. For example, what *kinds* of actions are right or wrong? These questions may seem far removed from concrete issues of everyday importance, but anyone who tries to think his way through a practical problem, such as the question whether euthanasia can ever be permitted, can eventually be led to the kinds of questions addressed in this book. The chapter by Gerald Dworkin is motivated by this point; Dworkin examines various philosophical moral theories in an effort to see how well they are suited to help us with practical questions. All of the chapters, however, deal with the abstract issues I am pointing to.

These issues can usefully be divided into two categories. First are *general moral issues*. What kinds of actions are right or wrong? What kind of person should one be? What are the moral virtues? What, in general, has moral value? What kinds of things make a person's life go well? What does justice require? Most generally, how should we live our lives? In answering any of these questions, one would be making a moral claim or a claim with moral implications. *Normative moral theory* aims to provide answers to the general moral questions that fall into this category.

Theories of this kind are sometimes called "first-order" in contrast with the "second-order" theories that deal with questions in the second category.

The second category includes issues or questions *about* morality and moral judgment. Are there moral truths? Do we simply have a variety of feelings and attitudes about moral issues, with there being nothing in virtue of which one side of a disagreement is correct and the other incorrect? Are there moral "properties"? For example, is there a property or characteristic that a kind of action can have of *being wrong* in the way that there is a property a kind of action can have of *being unpopular*? If so, is wrongness analogous to unpopularity, in that it is a relation between an action and the attitudes of a group of persons? Or is wrongness a more "objective" property? When a person makes a moral claim, is she expressing a belief or is she merely expressing a feeling or an attitude, such as approval or disapproval? Is it possible to have moral knowledge? What is the relation between morality and rationality? Would it be rational to commit oneself to morality? Answering such questions does not require making a moral claim. It requires making a claim *about* moral claims or *about* morality. This explains why the issues in this category are called "second-order" or "metaethical."

The chapters in this book defend a variety of positions in both normative moral theory and metaethics. The first part of the volume contains the chapters on metaethical issues, and the second part contains the chapters on normative issues. Issues in these two areas are much more closely connected than might seem to be the case, given what I say in this introduction. But it will be easier to introduce the material if I discuss the two areas separately.

2. METAETHICS

A philosophical study of morality is very different from a sociological or anthropological study, or a study from the perspective of biology or psychology. One important difference is that in moral philosophy we do not distance ourselves from our own moral views in the way we would if we were engaged in a study of one of these other kinds. We do not take the fact that people, including ourselves, have moral views as merely a datum to be explained. Our goal is not merely to explain data of this kind, whether it be the distribution of moral beliefs and attitudes, or the occurrence of selfish or altruistic actions. Rather, in moral philosophy, the correctness or cogency or defensibility of moral claims, convictions, and attitudes, and the probity of various behaviors, are among the things at issue. Normative ethics makes moral claims in its own right. Metaethics does not do this, yet, despite this, it is morally engaged. For among its central questions are the questions whether any moral claims are true, and whether it is rational to commit oneself to acting morally. One cannot answer such questions without taking a position on the correctness or cogency of people's moral convictions.

Moral realism takes an optimistic view on the issue of whether moral convictions can be correct or cogent. In the opening chapter, Geoffrey Sayre-McCord characterizes moral realism as the position that (1) there are *moral facts*, (2) people's moral judgments are made *true* or *false* by the moral facts, and (3) the mere fact that we have the moral beliefs we have is *not* what makes the moral facts be as they are. This is a highly abstract view that may be difficult to grasp. For this reason, I am going to begin with an example.

Many people find it plausible that the requirements of morality are determined by God's commands. This idea is a useful starting place because most people understand it immediately, and because it points the way to the divine command theory, which is generally regarded as a kind of moral realism. Philip Quinn defends a divine command theory in his chapter. The idea is, for example, that lying is morally wrong (if it is wrong) due simply and exactly to the fact that God has commanded that we not lie. More generally, Quinn holds that a kind of action is morally obligatory just in case God has commanded that actions of that kind be performed, and, he also holds, God's commanding that an action be performed is what *makes* it obligatory. So he holds that actions can have the properties of being obligatory, permissible, or forbidden—these are standardly called the "deontic" properties—and he holds that such properties *depend on* God's commands. God's commands bring it about that the wrong actions are wrong and the required actions are required.[1]

Views of this kind have been discussed by philosophers for centuries, and indeed the standard objection to them is derived from a discussion in Plato's dialogue *Euthyphro*. The objection takes the form of a dilemma. Either actions are commanded by God because they are obligatory, or they are obligatory because they are commanded by God. The first alternative is incompatible with Quinn's divine command theory, since the theory holds that what *makes* an action obligatory is God's commanding that it be performed. On this view, actions are not obligatory independently of God's commands, so God could not take an action's being obligatory as a reason to command it. But the second alternative seems unacceptable. For it seems to allow the possibility of God's commanding something arbitrary or horrible, and in that case, according to the theory, the action would be obligatory. Quinn discusses the story in *Genesis* (22:1–2) in which God orders Abraham to sacrifice his son, Isaac. The divine command theory seems to imply that in this case it was obligatory for Abraham to sacrifice Isaac, and indeed that *whatever* God commanded Abraham to do would be obligatory, no matter how arbitrary or horrible.

Quinn's answer to the challenge is that God's goodness ensures that his commands are not arbitrary. To make this reply work, however, Quinn cannot say that goodness depends on God's will in the way that the obligatoriness of an action depends on God's commands, for if he said this, the *Euthyphro* objection would come back to haunt him. (Is what God wills good because he wills it, or does he will it because it is good?) What Quinn says instead is that something is good just in case it *resembles* God in a relevant way. God is the standard of Goodness. Since God resembles himself, he is good. Deontic or duty-related properties depend on God's commands, but axiological or evaluative properties, such as goodness, do not.

The difficulty with Quinn's approach is that the fact that God is good does not seem to guarantee that his commands will not be horrible if his being good is simply a matter of his resembling himself. It is trivial that God resembles himself, but if God is perfectly good, this is a substantive and important moral fact. It would be different if there were an *independent* standard of goodness and if God qualified as perfectly good when measured against this standard. But if we added an independent standard of goodness to the theory, we would be leaving behind Quinn's idea that all moral statuses depend on God.

The chief problem with the divine command theory can be seen if we consider people who do not believe that there is a God. An atheist could accept that actions are obligatory just in case they are commanded by God, but since an atheist holds that there is no God, she would be committed to denying that any actions are obligatory. She would be committed to denying that any actions whatsoever are right or wrong. On Quinn's view about goodness, she would also be committed to denying that anything whatsoever is good or bad. Even a theist would be committed to holding that if God does not exist, then nothing is right or wrong, good or bad.[2] This implication of the divine command view is surely implausible. Even if there is no God, there are cases of harming others, coercing them, torturing them, and so on, and it is difficult to believe that such actions are not wrong, and that there is nothing bad about them, although this is implied by the divine command theory if God does not exist. Surely one would not accept this implication of the theory if one thought there were an alternative. And there are alternatives, as we shall see, including other kinds of moral realism.

For my purposes in exploring the kinds of moral realism and antirealism, it will be useful to define realism somewhat differently from the way Sayre-McCord defines it. I shall take moral realism to combine the following five doctrines.

(1) There are moral properties (and relations).[3] There is, for example, such a thing as wrongness. The divine command theory implies that actions have the property of *being wrong* when God has commanded that they not be performed. It implies that if God exists and has commanded that we not perform certain actions, those actions are wrong. Hence, on these assumptions, it also implies the second doctrine of moral realism: (2) Some moral properties are instantiated. For example, some actions are wrong. Moral realism also includes two doctrines about

moral thought and language: (3) Moral predicates are used to ascribe moral properties. And (4) moral assertions express moral beliefs. When we call an action "wrong" we are ascribing to it the property *wrongness,* and we are expressing the belief that the action is wrong. Finally, moral realism includes a doctrine designed to clarify its first thesis: (5) The moral properties, in that they are properties, have the metaphysical status that any other property has, whatever that status is.[4] This doctrine belongs in the list because some philosophers who reject moral realism think that we can call *wrongness* a "property" without misusing English, even though *wrongness* is not a property that would be recognized in an adequate metaphysics. An adequate metaphysics must give some account of the status of properties such as *redness* and *deciduous-ness.* These are not moral properties, of course, and they differ in a variety of ways from any moral property. Nevertheless, a moral realist insists that *wrongness* is like these properties in that it is also a *property*, and that, in this respect, it has the same metaphysical status as all other properties.

Moral realists disagree about various things, but they disagree chiefly about the nature of the moral properties. We can think of a realist theory as proposing a "model" that explains the nature of these properties. The divine command view sees *wrongness* as analogous to the property of *being unlawful.* It sees morality as, in effect, a divine legal system. Other versions of realism propose other models. There are both *naturalistic* and *nonnaturalistic* versions of realism, where naturalism treats moral properties as "natural" properties. Quinn's divine command theory is a kind of nonnaturalism, or it certainly appears to be. For Quinn holds that the goodness of something is a matter of its resembling God; God is the standard of goodness. As usually understood, however, God is not part of the natural world.

Naturalistic moral realism is defended in the chapter by Nicholas Sturgeon. Sturgeon holds that the moral properties are ordinary properties, akin to a variety of ordinary garden-variety properties, such as the property of *being a quarter dollar* or the property of *being deciduous.* He does not attempt to give an account in nonmoral terms of what *rightness* or *wrongness* are. He thinks that there is no adequate reason to suppose that moral properties are any more problematic or puzzling than are the properties that are theorized about in biology or in psychology, such as *being deciduous* or *being in pain.* The latter properties supervene on the basic physical natures of things in the sense that, roughly, any biological or psychological change in a thing depends on some underlying change in the physical nature of the thing. Similarly, Sturgeon holds, moral properties supervene on the basic nature of things. But just as we do not expect to be able to characterize the biology of a tree in nonbiological terms, we should not expect to be able to characterize the moral nature of an action or an institution or a person in nonmoral terms. We should not expect, that is, to be able to specify in nonmoral terms exactly which natural properties are the moral properties. On this point, Sturgeon disagrees with most philosophers who have thought about ethical naturalism. Most have thought that the viability of naturalism depends on there being, for each moral property, a true reductive identity statement that identifies that property with a natural property picked out in nonmoral terms. As Sturgeon says, they have thought that "ethical naturalism must be, in this sense, *reductive*." Sturgeon denies that this is so. He thinks, moreover, that to understand the moral properties, there is no substitute for normative theorizing. To understand what justice is, we need to think about what makes for just institutions. Metaethics, then, is continuous with normative moral theory.

Moral naturalism is attacked vigorously in the chapter by Jonathan Dancy. Dancy is a realist, but he thinks that naturalism is indefensible because it is unable to make sense of the *normativity* of moral judgment. There are, unfortunately, a variety of ways to understand normativity. The basic idea is that when all goes well, a person's moral judgments guide her actions. Suppose, for example, that a person thinks that she ought to help people in countries suffering from famine, and suppose that she receives a letter from CARE asking for a donation to help people suffering from famine. In this case, if all goes well, she will be motivated to make a donation (Smith, 1994, p. 7). Moral judgment, especially judgment about what one ought to do, has a kind of characteristic direct relevance to action or choice. This idea is unfortunately vague, and in an article on the topic, I distinguish three "grades" of normativity and argue that moral naturalism can accommodate all three (Copp, 2004).

Dancy disagrees. He thinks that, to understand the normativity of moral judgment, we must take the moral properties to be intrinsically normative. The problem for naturalism is, he thinks, that no natural property is intrinsically normative. We can express his argument in terms of the idea of a moral fact—a fact consisting of something's having a moral property. Naturalists claim that moral facts are natural facts. But Dancy argues that moral facts are normative and that no natural fact is normative. Why not? He holds that natural facts are not directly and immediately relevant to a decision about what to do in the way that normative facts are.

One might turn Dancy's argument into an argument against moral realism. J. L. Mackie argued for a position called the *error theory*, according to which there are no moral facts (Mackie, 1977, ch. 1; see also Joyce, 2001). The error theory says, in effect, that moral beliefs have the status of superstitious beliefs, such as beliefs in hobgoblins. Mackie offered several arguments for his view, including an argument something like Dancy's. Mackie held that the moral properties, if there were any, would be intrinsically normative. *Rightness* would have "to-be-doneness" built into it. He thought that such a property would be "queer," and unlike "anything else in the universe." He therefore concluded that there are no such properties. Accordingly, he held, all basic moral claims are false.[5] In effect, Mackie took Dancy's line of reasoning, added the premise that all properties are natural, and concluded that there are no moral properties. In so doing, he rejected one of the central doctrines of moral realism.

Mackie's error theory is highly controversial. It implies that nothing is morally wrong. This is as hard to accept as the implication of divine command theory that if God does not exist, nothing is wrong. There are cases of harming others, coercing them, torturing them, and so on. It is difficult to believe that such actions are not wrong, although this is implied by the error theory.

Three premises are on the table: first, that moral judgment is normative; second, that no natural property is normative; and third, that there are no non-natural properties. In arguing for nonnaturalism, Dancy accepted the first two of these premises but rejected the third. Assuming the truth of moral realism, he argued from the first premise to the conclusion that the moral properties are normative, and so he thought that, given the second premise, the moral properties must be nonnatural. Mackie was not prepared to assume the truth of moral realism. He accepted all three premises and was led to the error theory. But it is possible to accept all three premises without accepting the error theory. One can be led, instead, to *noncognitivism*, which is another form of moral antirealism. Like the error theory, it denies that there are moral properties, but it proposes to explain the normativity of moral judgment in another way.

The core idea of noncognitivism is the thesis that the state of mind of a person who accepts a (basic) moral claim is not a *belief* or any other kind of cognitive state, but is, instead, a *conative* state or a *motivational* state, akin to a desire. Any fully developed version of noncognitivism would need to say exactly what kind of state is involved, but we can neglect such details here. The view could be that the relevant state of mind is an "attitude." In his chapter, Simon Blackburn speaks of "stances." The root idea is that, for example, a person who accepts that capital punishment is wrong is in a state of mind that could most accurately be described as an attitude of disapproval of capital punishment or a stance of disapproval. Noncognitivists hold that moral assertions *express* such conative stances rather than beliefs. (Because it takes a thesis of this kind to explain the meaning of moral assertions, noncognitivism is often described as "expressivism.") What would lead one to accept this view?

Blackburn begins with the idea that cognitive states such as beliefs, and co-native states such as desires, have different "directions of fit." A belief represents the world as being a certain way and it tends to go out of existence, or should tend to go out of existence, when we have evidence that the world is not that way. Conative states are different. A desire need not go out of existence when we have evidence that the world is not the way we desire it to be. If my car fails to start one morning, my belief that it is reliable should tend to go out of existence, but I might still desire that it be reliable. If I do have this desire, I will be motivated to have the car repaired. In this sense, conative states such as desires have a different direction of fit from beliefs. They do not represent the world as being one way rather than another. Their function is to motivate action rather than to represent the world. Blackburn holds that moral states of mind have the direction of fit of desires and other conative states. They are "directive" rather than "representational." If a person holds that he ought to help the victims of famine, and if he receives a letter from CARE asking for a donation, then, if all goes well, he will be motivated to make a donation. For, according to the non-cognitivist, to hold that one ought to help is to have a stance that supports helping. It is, *inter alia*, to have an inclination or desire to help.

Philip Kitcher argues, in his chapter, that the best biological explanation of the existence of altruistic behavior supports noncognitivism. In his view, evolutionary biology supports the idea that the function of moral attitudes is to create motivation for the kinds of altruistic behavior that improve social cohesion. We accept a system of moral rules, but its content is not shaped by antecedently existing moral truths. As he says, "The criterion of success [of a system of moral rules] is not accurate representation, but the improvement of social cohesion in ways that promote the transmission of the system itself." One might combine Kitcher's view, according to which moral codes have the function of improving social cohesion, with the view that moral truths are "grounded in" the tendency of a system of moral rules to improve social cohesion. The result would be a cognitivist moral functionalism.[6] Kitcher holds, however, that there is no need to postulate the existence of moral truths in order to explain altruistic behavior.

A noncognitivist clearly would have difficulty accepting any of the doctrines that constitute moral realism. She denies that moral assertions express moral beliefs, for she holds that there are no moral beliefs to express. She will also want to deny that there are moral properties. For if there are moral properties, then surely it is possible to believe that something has a moral property, and presumably such a belief would qualify as a moral belief. For instance, there is a state of mind that we could express by saying "Torture is wrong," and if there are moral properties, including the property wrongness, it would be difficult to deny that this state of mind qualifies as a belief that ascribes wrongness to torture. So the noncognitivist will be led to deny that there are moral properties. Of course, if there are no moral properties, then there are no moral properties to be instantiated or to have any kind of metaphysical status, so she will deny two more realist doctrines. And, finally, she will deny that moral predicates are used to ascribe moral properties. For it would be odd to hold that moral predicates are used to ascribe moral properties while denying that an assertion, say, of the sentence "Torture is wrong" expresses the belief that torture has the property thereby ascribed. Accordingly, noncognitivism gives one reason to deny all five of the doctrines that constitute moral realism.

The problem is that moral thought and discourse at least *appear* to be cognitive in nature. As Blackburn says, everyday moralizing has a "realist surface." We speak of people as having moral beliefs. We speak of moral beliefs as true or false. A person who holds, say, that capital punishment is wrong would have difficulty denying that capital punishment has the characteristic or 'property' of *wrongness* or of *being wrong*. He would have difficulty denying that the term "wrong" is used to talk about wrongness and to express beliefs about things that are wrong. Accordingly, everyday moralizing seems to commit us to four of the realist doctrines. The missing doctrine is the récherché thesis that wrongness has the same metaphysical status as other properties. In everyday moralizing, we do not worry about metaphysical issues. Perhaps, then, the difference between realism and a plausible antirealism would boil down to this fifth doctrine.

Blackburn aims to develop a position that accepts and explains the realist surface of everyday moral discourse without abandoning the underlying, anti-realist doctrine of noncognitivism. He calls his view "quasi-realism." In his view, there are merely moral stances, such as moral approval and disapproval, but we have come to speak *as if* such stances are beliefs and *as if* there are properties such as wrongness. He sometimes calls his position "projectivism," drawing an analogy with the way a slide projector can make it seem as if there is, say, a tree in front of us when there is, in reality, only the play of light on a wall. His idea is that in doing metaphysics, we see that there are no moral properties, but, in ordinary moralizing, we speak as if there were, thereby projecting our moral stances out into the world. The trouble is that quasi-realist will be tempted by 'minimalism' about our use of the term "property"—a view that allows us to say a 'property' is 'expressed' by every predicate in the language, including moral predicates, but that denies this has any metaphysical significance. If Blackburn accepts such a minimalism, he would be forced to agree that so-called moral properties have the same metaphysical status as other so-called properties.

Where are we then? An anti-realist denies at least one of the five realist doctrines, but a quasi-realist may find it difficult to deny any of them, given the realist surface of moral discourse and the availability of minimalism. Yet Blackburn would deny that he is a realist. In the end, he distinguishes his position from realism on the ground that, as he says, whatever we *call* them, moral states of mind have the "directional" direction of fit rather than the "representational." That is, in effect, he denies that there are moral beliefs. Strictly speaking there are only stances.

Recent work by Blackburn and others has made it difficult to draw a clear and bright line between moral realism and antirealism. In his chapter, Sayre-McCord attempts to clarify matters. Blackburn and other noncognitivists and quasi-realists need to be clear about what they reject in moral realism. In some ways, moral realists face a more difficult burden, however. As Sayre-McCord explains, they need to explain the nature of the moral facts, how we can have knowledge of them, and why these facts give us reason to act in one way rather than another.

It is highly plausible that a person who has a moral conviction is in a relevant conative state of some kind, such as a state of approval or disapproval. A person with the conviction that capital punishment is wrong is naturally said to disapprove of capital punishment, and in saying that capital punishment is wrong, she would naturally be taken to express disapproval of it. This idea is fully compatible with moral realism, however (Copp, 2001). Many predicates in our language are "colored," to use Frege's term (Frege, 1984, pp. 161, 185, 357). For example, there are impolite terms for various ethnic groups that are used both to predicate membership in the group and to express an attitude of contempt. Moral predicates could be colored in a similar way. They could be used to predicate a moral property, such as wrongness, and also to express a corresponding attitude, such as disapproval. This idea is not a problem for moral realism.

Indeed, it is compatible with moral realism to go beyond this and treat moral judgment as concerned at root with the appropriateness of moral attitudes, such as approval and disapproval, disgust and shame. Blackburn's projectivism holds that moral judgment involves a potentially misleading projection of such attitudes onto a morally neutral reality. We might instead see the moral attitudes as responses to features of the world that make them appropriate. A moral property might then be understood as a "response-dependent" property, much as color properties are often taken to be properties whose nature is that they tend to cause certain associated visual experiences.[7] A number of research programs are exploring this idea. Justin D'Arms and Daniel Jacobson lay out the geography of the territory in their chapter. They distinguish projectivism from "perceptivism," which holds that the moral sentiments are responses to, or perceptions of, morally relevant features of the world. They distinguish a purely dispositional variety of perceptivism from the "sensibility theory" that has been proposed by John McDowell (1985). Ultimately they argue that the projectivist and perceptual metaphors are both misleading. What they find plausible is an idea that both views share—the sentimentalist idea that, as they say, "evaluation is to be understood by way of human emotional response."

Michael Slote explores a related idea. He sees moral sentimentalism as contrasting with rationalism, by which he means the view that reason rather than sentiment is the source of moral judgment and moral motivation. He sees sentimentalism as a position that straddles both normative and metaethical issues, since he thinks it goes hand in hand with a virtue theoretic approach in normative ethics and with a plausible account of the nature of moral properties. The chief moral sentiment, in his view, is empathic concern. He holds, for example, that moral goodness consists in empathic concern for others.

One might worry that sentimentalism supports a kind of relativism, since the empathic concern of different people might be engaged by different things. Slote thinks he can avoid this worry since, on his account, the reference of our moral terms is fixed by our *actual* empathic reactions, not by reactions we might have in merely possible circumstances. But it is not clear what *rationale* can be given for taking our actual empathic reactions to fix what counts as right and wrong. Perhaps our actual reactions can be improved morally. Moreover, it is possible that different people or cultures *actually* have very different empathic reactions to things. Given this, it is not clear how best to understand Slote's theory. Suppose that my empathic concern is engaged by thoughts of capital punishment but yours is not. In this case, Slote's account could be taken to imply that it is indeterminate whether capital punishment is wrong. Or it could be taken to imply that capital punishment is wrong-relative-to-me but is not wrong-relative-to-you. It is not clear, then, that Slote's sentimentalism can avoid a troubling relativism.

Notice that there is a kind of "normative relativism" that is highly plausible. For instance, it is plausible that whether telling a lie would be wrong depends on the circumstances. It might not be wrong to lie to Alice if telling her the truth would distract her while she is doing neurosurgery. The underlying idea could be expressed crudely by saying that any plausible moral evaluation depends on, or is "relative to," the circumstances. This thesis is surely highly plausible, but I want to focus on a kind of metaethical relativism that is much more interesting and controversial.

James Dreier advocates a relativism of this kind in his chapter. In his view, the moral "properties," such as rightness, are not monadic properties, but are actually *relations* to the moral standards of relevant person(s) or groups. For example, there may be rightness-relative-to-Alice as distinct from rightness-relative-to-Bill, and an action that is right-relative-to-Alice might not be right-relative-to-Bill. Here is an analogy. Weight is a *relation* between an object's mass and the local gravitational field. This is why an object has a different weight on the moon than it has on the earth. The relevant gravitational field must be specified or assumed before we can fully understand an assertion to the effect that something has a given weight. Similarly, in Dreier's view, a system of moral rules must be specified or assumed in order for us to understand what proposition is expressed by an assertion to the effect that something is right or wrong. In contexts in which different moral systems are at issue, assertions to the effect that something is "right" will express different propositions and different rightness-relations. Dreier proposes a "speaker relativism," according to which the moral system of the speaker is the relevant one. If Alice says, "Capital punishment is right," she expresses the proposition that capital punishment is permitted in her moral system, whereas if Bill says this, he expresses the different proposition that capital punishment is permitted in his moral system. Of course, it is possible that Alice and Bill accept different systems so that what Alice says is true but what Bill says is false.

Dreier thinks that this view is supported by the widely accepted thesis that there is an "internal connection" between moral judgment and moral motivation, the thesis that, necessarily, a person who believes she morally ought to do something is thereby motivated to some degree to do it. Stephen Darwall has called this thesis "judgment internalism" (Darwall, 1983, pp. 54–55). Judgment internalism figures in many arguments in metaethics. Blackburn invokes it in arguing for quasi-realism, and Mackie invoked it in arguing for the error theory. Dreier thinks that speaker relativism can explain judgment internalism without the counter-intuitive implications of these theories. If speaker-relativism is true, a person who asserts sincerely that he ought not to do something is thereby expressing a belief, and he presumably must also have motivations that incline him not to do the thing. For, in Dreier's view, accepting a moral system is a matter of having certain relevant attitudes and motivations. So it appears that speaker relativism explains the connection between moral belief and motivation that is postulated by judgment internalism.

Judgment internalism is controversial, however, as Sayre-McCord explains. Certain forms of moral realism conflict with it. The divine command theory does not ensure that there is a connection between moral belief and motivation. Sturgeon's moral naturalism and Dancy's nonnaturalism both reject it and are in this sense "externalist." Sturgeon argues that externalism is actually more plausible than internalism. And there are familiar objections to internalism. It seems possible, for example, for a depressed person to lose all motivation to do the right thing. Her beliefs about what is right could remain unchanged while her motivations waste away.

One serious objection to Dreier's relativism is the "disagreement argument." Speaker relativism seems to imply that if Alice says, "Capital punishment is right" and Bill says, "It is not the case that capital punishment is right," they have not disagreed. Alice has expressed the proposition that capital punishment is right-relative-to-Alice, and Bill has not denied this. He has expressed the proposition that it is not the case that capital punishment is right-relative-to-Bill. But this seems implausible. Surely Alice and Bill have disagreed in the imagined situation. Dreier would respond that there is a *pragmatic* disagreement between them; they would be expected, say, to vote in different ways in a referendum on capital punishment. But Dreier's view has odd implications. On his view, for example, if Alice says, "Capital punishment is right," Bill could reply, coherently and truly, by saying, "I agree with you, and, in addition, it is not the case that capital punishment is right." This would be a very puzzling conversation! Intuitively, what Alice says contradicts what Bill says in saying, "It is not the case that capital punishment is right."

A position that has counter-intuitive implications is difficult to defend, but we should not conclude that it is impossible to defend. I myself have attempted to support a kind of metaethical relativism against the disagreement argument (Copp, 1995, pp. 218–223).

Several of the authors I have discussed agree that morality is in some fundamental way the province of the *sentiments*. Blackburn, Kitcher, Slote, Dreier, and D'Arms and Jacobson agree about this, although they disagree about the details. An alternative view is that morality is fundamentally the province of *practical reason*. To understand this, we need to look at details.

Serious complications arise immediately, for there are theoretical issues about practical reason that are similar to the issues we have been discussing about morality. There are first-order, normative issues: What are the basic factors that determine which actions are rational and which are not? And there are second-order metatheoretical issues: Are there truths about rational behavior? Is there a property that an action can have of *being rational*? Do claims about the rationality of actions express beliefs or do they merely express noncognitive attitudes such as approval or disapproval? I will set aside most of these questions.

The essay by Peter Railton explores Humean and neo-Humean theories of practical reason and their relation to morality. A neo-Humean theory holds that rationality is basically a matter of efficiency in serving one's intrinsic ends or goals, where a person's intrinsic goals are taken as given—or as they would be if the person had more accurate information. On the standard neo-Humean view, it is a contingent matter whether a person has a good practical reason to be moral, for people's goals vary widely. A person who had no goal that would be well served by morally appropriate behavior would have no practical reason to act morally. True, most people have the goals of avoiding punishment and the disapproval of others, and it may be that these goals typically give them good practical reason to act morally. But this would be a purely instrumental reason to act morally, and the existence of such a reason would be a contingent matter.

As against this position, some philosophers hold that an adequate account of morality must show it to be a *necessary* truth that *every* person who is subject to morality has good practical reason to be moral. If we accept this claim, there are at least four ways to proceed. One is to concede that there may be rational agents who are not subject to morality because they lack good practical reason to be moral. This approach seems to embrace a skepticism about morality. A second strategy is to adopt the view that a person's goals, which, on the standard neo-Humean view, determine what she has reason to do, also determine what morality requires of her. This position is a version of ethical egoism, which I will discuss briefly when I turn to issues in normative ethics. A third strategy involves amending the neo-Humean account of practical reason in an attempt to avoid the skeptical result. The difficulty is to motivate such an amendment without giving up the basic idea that rationality is instrumental to serving one's intrinsic goals. A fourth strategy would involve abandoning the neo-Humean view by arguing that compliance with morality is partly *constitutive* of rationality. Aristotelian and Kantian theories take this approach.

Some theories of the latter kind have been called "constructivist" (Rawls, 1980). They can be seen as constructing ethics out of a theory of practical reason or as "reducing" morality to practical reason. Versions of the second and third strategies can also be seen this way.

David Gauthier took the third of these strategies in arguing for a contractarian moral theory (Gauthier, 1986). In much of life, we need to cooperate and coordinate our actions with other people. As Railton explains, however, even if each person acts rationally, according to a standard neo-Humean account, so that everyone serves his goals as well as possible *given* what everyone else is doing, it may be that *everyone* would have done better at serving his goals if *everyone* had acted differently. A situation that illustrates this possibility is a so-called prisoners' dilemma. In a prisoners' dilemma, no one can do better for himself, given what everyone else is doing, but everyone could do better for themselves if everyone were to act otherwise. To achieve the situation that is *better* for everyone, however, each must forego attempting to achieve what would be *best* for himself. Gauthier concludes from this that it is not always genuinely rational to attempt to maximize one's own advantage. He went on to argue, in effect, that morality exists to solve problems of cooperation and coordination that are modeled by the prisoners' dilemma.

Intuitively, rational persons ought to be able to cooperate. Gauthier thinks that a plausible account of rationality would dictate complying with agreements to cooperate, provided that the other parties to the agreement were also likely to comply. So, he concludes, rational persons would not be disposed to maximize their own advantage in general and without restriction. Instead, rational persons would be "constrained maximizers." They would be disposed to comply with systems of norms, mutual compliance with which would be mutually advantageous, in situations in which it is reasonable to believe that those with whom they are interacting are similarly disposed. This means that a rational person would comply with morality, provided that doing so promised to be mutually advantageous and provided that enough others were likely enough also to comply. This, in brief, is Gauthier's contractarianism.

There are two main objections. First, even in Gauthier's view, it is a contingent matter whether a given person has good practical reason to be moral. Whether she does will depend on whether enough others are likely to comply and on whether morality promises to benefit her in the circumstances, given her abilities and goals. It might seem that an adequate account would show morality to have a stronger and more internal connection to rationality than this. Second, Gauthier's view treats morality as merely of instrumental value. It might seem that it is intrinsically important to treat people fairly and that it is a mistake to view fairness as worthy of respect only to the degree that it serves our goals to adopt a disposition to be fair.

Kantian approaches are intended to show morality to have the intrinsic value and tight internal connection to rationality that, so far, has seemed elusive. Kantian moral theory is a fertile area of contemporary research that is especially interesting because of the way it seeks to link metaethical issues with issues in normative ethics. This book includes two chapters on Kantian theory. In one, Stephen Darwall develops and defends a Kantian connection between morality and rationality. In the other, Thomas E. Hill, Jr., explicates Kantian approaches to normative ethical theory. The volume also includes a chapter by Julia Annas that, among other things, outlines an Aristotelian account of the connection between morality and rationality.

The basic Kantian doctrine is that moral obligations are *categorical*. There are, however, different views about how best to spell out this idea. For Darwall, the idea is that it is necessarily the case that if an action is morally wrong, there is a reason not to do it; moreover, crucially, this reason has "genuine normative weight," such that anyone who is deliberating rationally will take it into account as appropriate and assign it conclusive weight. Darwall accepts this thesis, but he sees it as difficult to support. In summary, he argues that neo-Humean theories cannot accommodate it and that typical forms of moral realism also cannot accommodate it. He argues as well that Christine Korsgaard's recent neo-Kantian attempts to support it are unsuccessful (Korsgaard, 1996). Indeed Darwall thinks that Kant's arguments need to be supplemented.

Darwall's own argument begins from an idea of moral responsibility. A moral agent is responsible for complying with the demands of morality, and responsibility implies the capacity to respond to the moral demands placed on oneself. Moral agents view each other as responsible, moreover, in that they hold each other liable to respond to the demands placed on them.[8] Darwall holds that an assumption of "reciprocal accountability" of this kind is essential to the practice of holding people to be subject to moral obligations, and he argues that reciprocal accountability presupposes that other people can see the reasons for acting the way we say they are obligated to act. It also presupposes that the reasons in question are independent of the variable ends or goals these people might have, for we put forward claims of moral obligation to people merely as moral agents, not as people with special ends or goals. Moreover, in putting forward a demand, we assume the person addressed is capable of complying. Hence, in putting forward such demands we presuppose that people can act on reasons that are independent of their variable ends or goals. We presuppose that, in this sense, people are autonomous and capable of acting on moral reasons.

As we saw, Darwall begins with a conception of moral responsibility. In his chapter, John Fischer explores a variety of conceptions of moral responsibility and their connection to the idea of free will. His main focus is on the challenge of causal determinism. We typically take it that we have the freedom to choose what to do from a menu of alternatives, each of which is open to us. But the thesis of causal determinism says that everything we do is caused deterministically by events that happened in the past. It seems to follow from this that we do not have the freedom to choose. For it seems to follow that the "choice" we make from the "menu of alternatives" available to us at a given time was determined by events that happened prior to the choice. If so, it seems, we lacked the power to choose or to do otherwise than we did.

The thesis of causal determinism challenges moral theory in a variety of places. It seems to imply that we are not free to determine how we will act. It may even imply that we have no obligation to do anything other than what we actually do. For it is standardly assumed that we have an obligation to do something only if we can do it—"ought" implies "can"—and causal determinism seems to imply that we have no power to act differently from the way we actually act. Finally, the thesis of causal determinism appears to imply that we lack moral responsibility for our actions. For it is often assumed that we are morally responsible for doing something only if we could have done otherwise, and causal determinism seems to imply that we have no power to do other than we actually do. Fischer explores all of these worries.

3. Normative Ethics

In turning from metaethics to normative ethics, we turn from issues *about* ethics to issues *in* ethics. We turn to questions such as: What kinds of actions are right or wrong? What kind of person should one be? There are many theories about these issues. In thinking about the differences among them, it is helpful to consider the answers they give to two closely related questions. What is the basic matter of moral concern? And what are the fundamental or basic moral truths? The disputes posed by these questions are central to normative ethics.

First, what is the basic or fundamental matter of moral concern? Is it the kind of life we should live? Is it the kind of person we should be? Is it the actions we perform? Is it the kind of character we have? Is it our motivations or intentions? Is it goodness or value—either the goodness in a person's own life, or the overall goodness of the state of the world and the condition of people in the world? Second, what are the fundamental or basic moral truths? Are they propositions about the kind of life we should live? Are they propositions about the kind of person we should be? Are they about the kinds of actions we are required to perform, or about the kind of character we ought to have, or about our motivations or intentions? Or are they propositions about goodness or value? Typically, a theory that proposes or argues that certain moral truths are basic to ethics then attempts to support other moral propositions by deriving them in one way or another from the basic truths. But theories can differ in how they attempt to do this, and they can also differ in their views about the exact status of the truths they take to be basic. Of course, a theory could instead reject the idea that there are moral truths that are basic in any interesting sense. And a theory could take it that all or several of the matters of concern are equally fundamental, thereby denying that there is a basic matter of moral concern.

It is useful to categorize moral theories on the basis, *inter alia,* of the positions they take on these disputes. As we will see in what follows, there is a tendency for a theory to take the same position on both disputes. That is, there is a tendency to hold that the basic moral truths, if any, are propositions about the basic matter of concern. In classic virtue theories, for example, the basic concern is with the kind of person we should be, or with the kind of character we should have, and, in these theories, propositions about what kind of person to be or about what kind of character to have are treated as fundamental to morality. In the ethics of care, the basic concern is with relationships motivated by care, and the basic moral truths are about such relationships. In standard deontology, the basic concern is with right action or moral duty and the basic moral truths are propositions about our duties. In Kantian theory, the basic concern is with rational agency. The fundamental moral truths are judgments about rational agency, such as judgments about the maxims that a rational agent could will to be universal laws or judgments about the respect owed to rational agency. In rights-based theories, the basic concern is with rights, and the fundamental moral truths are propositions about the rights we have. Consequentialism presents a more complex situation, however. In consequentialism, the basic truths are or include propositions about intrinsic value or goodness. In different kinds of consequentialism, however, different things are taken to be matters of basic concern. In act consequentialism, the basic concern seems to be with right action, and the rightness of an action is a matter of the value of its consequences. In virtue consequentialism, the basic concern is with our character, and the best traits of character are those, the having of which tends to lead to the best consequences. In all forms of consequentialism, however, the basic truths are or include propositions about goodness.[9]

The two disputes I have been discussing may seem intractable, but they are in the background of a debate that has dominated normative moral theory, a debate about the theory of right action. The moral assessment of actions is a central concern in our moral life. In any situation, we can wonder what would be the right thing to do. A theory of right action attempts to answer the question, What are the basic factors that determine which actions are right and which are wrong? Or, what are the right-making properties of actions? A theory of right action is shaped by a conception of what is fundamental to morality. Theories that disagree about the content of the basic moral truths, or about the basic matter of moral concern, can be expected to disagree as well about right action. They will differ about the basic right-making properties.

To be sure, some normative theories do not aim to provide a theory of right action. Julia Annas proposes a kind of virtue ethics in her chapter, and Virginia Held defends an ethic of care; neither of them provides a theory of right action. They would deny that moral philosophy needs to provide such a theory, or perhaps that it can provide one. They would argue that disputes over right action have distracted moral theory from more central concerns.

Among approaches that *do* aim to provide a theory of right action, the central divide is between consequentialist and nonconsequentialist theories. Consequentialist theories share the basic idea that the rightness of an action depends in some way on the promotion of the good. Hence, consequentialism grounds the theory of right action in a theory of intrinsic good, or a theory of value. It is in this way that consequentialism takes propositions about the good to be basic or fundamental. It is difficult, however, to draw the distinction between consequentialism and nonconsequentialism in a precise way, and the distinction has sometimes been contested. The problem is that different kinds of consequentialism specify the right-making property in different ways, even if all specify that it is a function of the promotion of goodness. We can say that a consequentialist theory of right action proposes a criterion that takes the rightness of an action to be a function of the promotion of intrinsic goodness. But different theories propose different functions, and consequentialists also disagree about what things are intrinsically good.

Nonconsequentialist theories of right action include deontological theories, rights-based theories, and Kantian theories. The term "deontological" is often used to describe *any* such theory. But as I use the term, deontological theories are those that take the basic matter of moral concern and the fundamental moral truths to be about the rightness of actions or about our duties. Understood in this way, Kantian theories and rights-based theories are not best viewed as kinds of deontology. They are nonconsequentialist, but they share with consequentialism the idea that judgments about the rightness of action are derivative. In consequentialism, such judgments are derivative from judgments about value or goodness. In Kantian theories, they are derivative from judgments about rational agency. In rights-based theories, they are derivative from judgments about rights.[10]

It is convenient to begin with consequentialism because the best known consequentialist theories have a relatively simple structure and because other kinds of normative theory typically situate themselves in relation to consequentialism. I therefore turn to the chapter on value theory by Thomas Hurka. Value theory is important in its own right, which is sufficient reason to consider it, but consequentialism lacks content unless it is combined with a theory of value.

It is important to distinguish the idea of an intrinsic good from the idea of an instrumental or extrinsic good. Instrumental goods are good or valuable only because of something else they bring about—something that is good in itself—whereas intrinsic goods are good in themselves. It is plausible, for instance, that enjoyment and understanding are intrinsic goods, whereas money is good only instrumentally—because of the intrinsic goods it can perhaps buy. The distinction between the intrinsic and the instrumental can be drawn in different ways, as Hurka explains. The main point, however, is that our concern should be with intrinsic goods. The first step is to come to an understanding of what things are intrinsically good.

Hurka holds, very plausibly, that there is a great variety of intrinsic goods. He argues against hedonism, which is the view that only pleasure is intrinsically good, and against desire theories, which hold that the good in a person's life is her getting what she desires intrinsically—or what he would so desire if he were rational and informed. He favors a kind of perfectionism; that is, he favors a view according to which the good is not *determined* by desire but rather should *guide* desire, and according to which pleasure is not the only intrinsic good. Perfectionist theories set standards for our improvement or betterment, both with respect to what we desire and with respect to what gives us pleasure. Most perfectionist theories are pluralistic, listing a variety of goods, including such things as knowledge, friendship, creativity, and moral virtue. Hurka discusses strategies a perfectionist theory might follow to explain the unity in the set of intrinsic goods and to explain how various kinds of goods can be compared.

The most simple kind of consequentialist theory is "act consequentialism," according to which the morally required action in a situation is the action that, among the agent's options, produces, or would produce, the most good. But there is an enormous variety of consequentialist theories, and debates about their plausibility and formulation are astonishingly complex.

To begin with, consequentialists disagree about the theory of intrinsic good. Some are hedonists; some accept a desire theory; and some are perfectionists. A hedonist who accepted a simple act consequentialism would be committed to saying, for example, that a person is morally required to visit a friend in hospital just in case this is the option that would produce the most pleasure overall. Indeed, she would be committed to saying that a person is morally *permitted* to visit a friend in hospital only if there is no alternative that would produce more pleasure. But a perfectionist might hold that friendship is intrinsically good and, moreover, that the direct expression of friendship itself has great intrinsic value. Because of this, she might hold that there is always moral good to be gained by expressing friendship through such acts as visiting a friend in hospital. Hence, unless a person with a friend in hospital could do more good in some other way, she is permitted and indeed required to visit her friend.

Consequentialists disagree about other matters as well. Most important, they disagree about how to formulate the criterion of right action—about the precise relation between goodness and rightness. A modest amendment of act consequentialism would take into account the fact that the consequences of an action can be uncertain or unfixed. It would say that the rightness of an action depends on the *expected* value of its consequences rather than the actual value of its consequences—the *expected* value of an action is a measure constructed by taking the value of its consequences in different possible scenarios, weighing these values by the probability of the scenarios, and aggregating the weighted values into a measure of the overall value of the action.

Some consequentialists favor a simple and direct criterion, such as the act consequentialist criterion, but there are alternatives.[11] Some favor a much more indirect criterion. An example is "rule consequentialism," according to which an act is morally required if and only if it is required by the code of rules the currency of which in society would have the best consequences. There are varieties of rule consequentialism, depending on how precisely we understand such things as the currency of a code of rules. In principle, a rule consequentialist might think that a person is morally required to visit a friend in the hospital because treating friends this way is a generally beneficial practice—even if the consequences on a particular occasion are less good than the consequences would be of not visiting the friend.

So far I have been comparing direct and indirect criteria of right action. But consider the question of how such a criterion is to be used. The question is whether people ought to think about what to do by *applying* the criterion, or in some other way. There is a debate about this both among act consequentialists and between them and their critics. This debate is also sometimes described as concerned with a kind of indirection. The so-called direct view says to apply the criterion in moral decision-making. An act consequentialist who took this view would recommend that we decide what to do by considering which of our actions would have the best consequences. He would recommend, in effect, that we pursue the good directly. He would treat the act consequentialist principle as both a *decision procedure* and a *criterion* of rightness. McNaughton and Rawling discuss some of the problems with this approach. The so-called indirect view treats the principle simply as a criterion of rightness and rejects the idea that it is to be used in general as a decision procedure. It says that the question of how to decide is itself one that is to be determined by the criterion (Bales, 1971). On this view, a consequentialist theory recommends that we decide what to do in the way that the criterion implies is the right way. For act consequentialism, this is the way of deciding such that deciding in that way would have the best consequences. The right way to decide might not involve the direct pursuit of good consequences, for it might be best to decide what to do by following traditional moral rules without giving any thought to consequences. Perhaps, for example, it would be best to be moved directly by friendship, in visiting our friend in the hospital, rather than to worry about costs and benefits. The calculating attitude that weighs costs and benefits could have negative consequences for our friendships and for other intrinsic goods. In light of problems with the direct view, act consequentialists tend to favor this indirect view. McNaughton and Rawling and other critics argue that the indirect view is also problematic.

There are, then, many forms of consequentialism. Anyone defending consequentialism must choose his poison. Anyone attacking it as a general style of theorizing must attack every variety. She must find some underlying mistake or problem that is common to all kinds of consequentialism. In doing so, she must bear in mind the variety of theories of value as well as the variety of forms of direction and indirection.

The complexity among alternatives to consequentialism is at least as striking as the complexity among forms of consequentialism. The Ten Commandments offer a familiar deontological view. But even here we must remember that rule consequentialism might recommend the Ten Commandments as the best set of rules for our society.

In their chapter, David McNaughton and Piers Rawling aim to defend a "Rossian" deontology of the kind that was first articulated by David Ross (1930). Rossian deontology postulates a plurality of basic moral principles, such as the principle not to harm people and the principle of promise keeping. The duties postulated by these principles are prima facie, in that they can conflict with one another, and when they do, the relative importance of the conflicting duties must be weighed in order to determine what to do, all things considered.

A Rossian principle may seem to imply that a relevant corresponding property of actions is always right-making or wrong-making. For example, the principle that we ought not to lie may seem to imply that lying always at least tends to be wrong. Some "particularists" would argue, however, that *no* property of actions is *always* right-making or wrong-making in a way that would support the truth of a Rossian principle. In their chapter, Mark Lance and Margaret Little aim to clarify what is at issue in debates about particularism. On their account, particularism is the denial that there are true moral principles with all of the classical characteristics of being exceptionless, explanatory, and epistemically useful. On this showing, Rossian deontology may be a kind of particularism because it allows that there are exceptions to its basic moral principles.

Traditional deontology recognizes three significant moral statuses. First are *constraints*, such as the duty not to kill innocent people. These duties constrain us even when a prohibited action has good consequences. For example, to take a far-fetched example, the duty not to torture prohibits torturing Allan even if by doing so we could prevent someone else from torturing Bill and Carol. Second are *duties of special relationship*, such as duties of friendship and duties of family. And third are *options*. We normally think that there is a limit to how much good we are morally required to bring about. Traditional deontology agrees that there is a limit and gives us options to pursue our own projects even in circumstances where we could otherwise do more good. McNaughton and Rawling object to consequentialism mainly on the basis that it cannot account for options and the duties of special relationship. They think, for example, that duties of friendship are morally basic in a way that consequentialism misses, since it sees everything of moral significance as boiling down to issues about the impersonal good. Moreover, our concern for our own lives and personal projects is basic. Rule consequentialism may make room for options, but only if the currency of a system of rules with options works best overall. This makes room for options but without giving a fundamental significance to our own personal concerns.

The most surprising aspect of McNaughton and Rawling's view is that they reject constraints. Deontology has been bedeviled for thirty years by a line of argument according to which deontological constraints are paradoxical. The idea is basically as follows. If it is forbidden to torture Allan, then it must be a bad thing if Allan is tortured. But suppose that someone else will torture Bill and Carol unless I torture Allan. If it is forbidden to torture, it must be worse (other things being equal) if two people are tortured than if only one is tortured. So it is better (other things being equal) if I torture Allan, thereby ensuring that Bill and Carol are not tortured, than if I do not torture Allan, thereby ensuring that Bill and Carol are both tortured. Given this, it seems, it would be paradoxical if there were a constraint against torture that prohibits torturing one person to prevent the torturing of two. Yet the idea that my torturing one can be justified by the fact that I would be saving two from torture is a consequentialist idea. It appears, then, that instead of imposing constraints against torturing, a plausible view would treat torturing as a bad to be avoided. It would be a form of consequentialism.[12]

McNaughton and Rawling do not draw the consequentialist conclusion, but they find the argument against deontological constraints to be successful. They therefore adopt a deontology that rejects constraints of a traditional kind, such as constraints against lying and torture. They do hold, however, that there are a variety of proscriptions that are not constraints. For example, they hold that there is an absolute prohibition against killing someone when one's only motivation is personal gain and when there are no (other) reasons to kill. What they deny is that there are "proscriptions that admit the possibility of, and forbid, their own violation to good effect."

The defensibility of this overall position needs to be investigated. Part of the problem is that McNaughton and Rawling accept duties of special relationship even though such duties are a kind of constraint. I have a duty to care for my children even if, by neglecting them, I would set an example that would lead to an overall improvement in parents' caring for their children. It is not clear why we should think duties of this kind survive the critique of constraints if the duty not to torture does not. Moreover, intuitively, there *is* a constraint against torture. Intuitively, it *would* be morally wrong (other things being equal) to torture one person even if this is the only way to prevent two other people from being tortured.

McNaughton and Rawling hold that the Rossian principles are the most basic and fundamental normative moral truths. Accordingly, they reject a variety of attempts to derive or to ground deontology. It may be possible, however, to provide deontology with a kind of extra-moral grounding, even if McNaughton and Rawling are correct that the Rossian rules are the most fundamental *moral* truths. Such a grounding could perhaps embrace constraints. There is a view according to which, roughly, a system of moral rules is justified or authoritative just in case its currency in society would improve social cohesion and otherwise enable a society to meet its needs (Copp, 1995). It might be argued that a deontological moral code that includes constraints would be best suited to filling this role, and that this is sufficient to ground a deontology with constraints. This kind of grounding is structurally similar to the grounding that might be offered in rule consequentialism, but it is not consequentialist. Rule consequentialism depends on a view about the value of states of affairs and uses this view in justifying the code of rules the currency of which would have the best consequences. But the strategy at issue here does not depend on the idea that social cohesion is valuable. It proposes an extra-moral grounding of morality rather than a moral justification of a code of rules.[13]

The concept of a deontic constraint is closely related to the concept of a moral right. A right of the kind at issue—a claim-right—entails a constraint on others, an obligation not to treat the right-holder in a specified way. So understood, there is a right against being tortured only if there is a constraint against torture. Some philosophers have aspired to build a rights-based moral theory in which propositions about rights are taken to be basic (Mackie, 1978). But it is more natural to see rights as one element in a pluralistic deontology.

One of the central goals in the chapter by Hillel Steiner is to show what would be lost in a moral theory that failed to recognize claim-rights. Robert Nozick pointed out that it is possible to treat the minimization of rights-violations as an end to be achieved in a "utilitarianism of rights," a kind of consequentialism that treats the minimization of rights-violation as the central moral good. However, such a view does not treat rights as entailing the existence of constraints. So even if it recognizes a "right against torture," it does not recognize a claim-right against torture. Consequently, Steiner wants to argue, it fails to establish a proper moral status for persons. Nozick argued that claim-rights "reflect the underlying Kantian principle that individuals are ends and not merely means" (Nozick, 1974, pp. 28–32). Steiner agrees.

One might think that Nozick's Kantian approach answers the paradox of deontology, but this is unclear. For it can seem paradoxical that Allan's status as an end could preclude me from treating him as a mere means even if my doing so is the only way I can prevent Bill and Carol from being treated as mere means. The difficulty may only have been moved to a new level.

David Brink aims to defend a kind of perfectionist consequentialism in his chapter. He agrees in broad terms with McNaughton and Rawling that there are no traditional deontological constraints and that an adequate moral theory must give a plausible account of options and of duties of special relationship. He thinks, however, that an *agent-relative* consequentialism can do the trick. An agent-relative consequentialism can give special significance to the concerns and projects of the agent, thereby making room for options, and it can give special significance to the consequences of actions for those to whom the agent stands in special relationships, thereby making room for the duties of special relationship.

Traditional consequentialism is *agent-neutral*. It takes the consequences of an action—or of the currency of a rule, et cetera—for the good of *anyone* to matter, and to matter to the *same degree* (to the rightness of the action), provided that the degree of good effect is the same. There is also, however, an *agent-relative* form of consequentialism, called ethical egoism, according to which the right action is the action that would have the best consequences for the *agent*. Brink's view is a close relative of ethical egoism, if not a kind of egoism. Brink holds that the consequences of an action that determine whether it is right are consequences for the *agent's good*. Good consequences matter only if and to the extent that they are good for the agent.

Brink holds, however, that the good of an agent is not restricted to goods that "fall within" the agent's life. If you and I are related in certain ways, he thinks, it can be intrinsically good for me that a good falls in your life. For example, if you are a friend, an enjoyment experienced by you might be intrinsically good for me as well as for you.

To support this view, Brink takes up a line of argument about personal identity that is found in the work of Derek Parfit. As time goes by, I pass through a variety of psychological states. Many of these are continuous with other states or are connected to others in the way that a memory is connected to the event of which it is a memory, or in the way that an early childhood plan to become a firefighter can be continuous with one's later career as a teacher by means of a chain of decisions. Parfit proposed that a stream of psychological states over time constitutes a person just when—roughly, and ignoring certain complications—the events in the stream have a characteristic kind and degree of connectedness and continuity. He proposed that personal identity is best understood as depending on psychological connectedness and continuity (Parfit, 1984, pp. 204–209). Brink suggests that, since you and I can have interlocking plans and lives, there might be the same kind of psychological connectedness and continuity *between* our psychologies as there is *within* each of our psychologies. The difference is perhaps only a matter of degree. But if so, then perhaps the difference between distinct *persons* is no more significant morally than the difference between distinct *stages* in the life of *one* person. If personal identity boils down to psychological connectedness and continuity, then its moral significance boils down to the significance of psychological connectedness and continuity.

This line of reasoning suggests that the moral value to me of a good received by someone depends on the degree to which the person is psychologically connected to and continuous with me. An agent-relative consequentialism can hold that consequences of an action that determine its moral status are consequences for the good of those who are psychologically connected to and continuous with the agent, and that the degree to which such consequences affect the action's moral status depends, other things being equal, on the degree to which those affected are psychologically connected to and continuous with the agent.

The Parfitian account of personal identity raises issues in metaphysics that lie outside the realm of moral philosophy. But let me briefly raise a worry about Brink's use of it. Suppose that you and I are friends, and both of us have headaches. On Brink's view, your headache has the same *kind* of significance to my good as my own headache has, even though, since your headache is not as closely connected as my headache is to the psychological stream that is identical to me, your headache has a lesser *degree* of significance for my good than my headache does. This seems incorrect. Intuitively, my headache diminishes my good directly, by its very nature, while if yours diminishes my good, it does so only instrumentally or indirectly, because I care about you. On Brink's view, if I have one dose of painkiller, then my duty with respect to the use of it is determined by the effect it would have on each of the headaches weighted by the degree to which the person whose headache would be helped is psychologically related to me. So if our headaches are roughly equally bad and would benefit from the painkiller to roughly the same degree, I would be wrong to give it to you. This also seems incorrect. It illustrates the affinity between Brink's view and ethical egoism, for a standard kind of ethical egoism would have the same implication.

It may seem at this point that in order to make progress in the debate between deontology and consequentialism, we need to seek to ground in some way the approach we take to normative issues. It is time, then, to turn to Kantian moral theory. Kantian theory seeks to ground moral judgments in a metaethical doctrine about the relation between morality and rationality.

Thomas E. Hill, Jr., explores the variety of ways in which Kant, and contemporary philosophers who are applying and extending Kant's views, deal with normative issues. Kant holds that the fundamental principle of morality is the Categorical Imperative, but he offers several different formulations of it. Hill examines problems in the interpretation and application of each of these formulations. He begins with the formula of universal law: "Act only on that maxim by which you can at the same time will that it should become a universal law" (Kant, 2002, p. 222 [4:402]).[14] His fundamental worry about this formulation is that it does not seem to *explain* what is wrong with wrongful actions, such as failing to help others. As he says, the wrongness of slavery does not seem to be explained by pointing out that it is impossible for everyone to act on the maxim of the slave-owner. Kant's second formulation of the Categorical Imperative is the so-called formula of humanity: "Act in such a way that you treat humanity, whether in your own person or in any other person, always at the same time as an end, never merely as a means" (229–230 [4:429]). Alan Donagan (1977) has interpreted this formula as requiring respect for persons. Hill thinks that the idea of respecting persons is too vague to guide action. He suggests viewing Kant's formulations of the Categorical Imperative as different attempts to describe a point of view that can shape discussion and deliberation, rather than as attempts to state a precise criterion of right action or a precise decision procedure. On this basis, he proposes the idea of a Kantian legislative perspective, a perspective from which we can deliberate about proposed moral rules. In this, Hill is building on Kant's idea of a "kingdom of ends" (234 [4:433]).

One might view Thomas Scanlon's recent "contractualist" proposal as likewise proposing a perspective for moral deliberation rather than a precise criterion or decision procedure. Moral deliberation, says Scanlon, is fundamentally a matter of "thinking about what could be justified to others on grounds that they, if appropriately motivated, could not reasonably reject" (Scanlon, 1998, p. 5). An action is wrong, he says, if it "would be disallowed by any principle" that "could not reasonably be rejected, by people who were moved to find principles for the general regulation of behavior that others, similarly motivated, could not reasonably reject" (4). McNaughton and Rawling discuss Scanlon's approach in some detail.

Moral theory has been dominated by the debate about right action that I have been discussing, and many philosophers regret this. Virtue theory holds that the most fundamental matter of moral concern is the character of a virtuous person. The ethics of care holds that the most fundamental matter of moral concern is caring relationships. Both approaches aspire to turn normative theory away from a preoccupation with right action and toward an assessment of the broader issues of how to live and what kind of person to be. It is not that these approaches hold that issues about right action are unimportant. The idea is that they are secondary issues and that they cannot properly be understood until we have an adequate theory of moral virtue or of caring.

Any complete moral theory would have to make room for the idea of virtuous, caring agency. Nothing prevents an account of the virtues from being incorporated into a pluralistic moral theory alongside an account of moral duty. It can also be incorporated into a consequentialist framework.[15] But some philosophers, inspired in many cases by their reading of Aristotle's moral philosophy, believe that a theory that is adequate to the subtle experience of a mature moral agent must take moral character to be the basic moral concern. Virtue ethics, so understood, is widely seen to have great promise, and in recent years, a number of new approaches to virtue have appeared in the philosophical literature (see Copp and Sobel, 2004).

Julia Annas advocates an ambitious program of virtue ethics. In her chapter, she lays out the structure of virtue theory as it was developed in what she calls the classical version of the virtue ethics tradition. Such a theory was first articulated in a clear way by Aristotle, but Annas holds that the basic features of Aristotelian virtue ethics are common to all ancient ethical theory. Some contemporary versions of virtue ethics reject certain aspects of the classical theory and can best be understood by comparison with the classical version of virtue theory. Annas holds, however, that the classical version is the most attractive and defensible.

Theories in the classical tradition claim that moral virtue is necessary if one is to flourish. Annas insists that this does not mean that these theories ground virtue in self-interest, for in the classical view, flourishing is explained as consisting in part in being virtuous. A virtuous person must be fair, kind, generous, and so on, and his virtues lead him to be wholehearted in doing things for others. Virtue is a "disposition to do the right thing for the right reason in the appropriate way—honestly, courageously, and so on." It therefore involves acting both with an appropriate affect—with sympathy, for example—and with an appropriate understanding of the reasons for so acting.

In view of the latter point, one might think that virtue ethics cannot avoid problems in the theory of right action. Annas explains, however, that in the classical tradition, ethical understanding is viewed as involving the acquisition of something like a skill rather than learning a criterion of right action. A virtuous person has the skill to determine the right way to act. The rest of us may need to use principles and rules. But, as Annas explains it, virtue ethics denies that there is a *criterion* of right action. In virtue theory, it is true that, roughly, the right action is the action that a virtuous person would perform. But this is not intended to specify a *right-making property*. It is not meant to serve as a principle, or a criterion, or a decision rule.

The ethics of care sees a disposition to care appropriately for others as the chief characteristic of a morally desirable psychology. Such a disposition can be viewed as a virtue. In her chapter, however, Virginia Held rejects the idea that the ethics of care is a kind of virtue theory on the ground that its focus is on caring relations between people rather than on caring dispositions. The ethics of care clearly is not a virtue theory in the classical tradition discussed by Annas, for it rejects the idea that the proper exercise of practical reason is needed to enable one to determine how to act. It holds that the moral emotions, such as empathy and sensitivity, guide us to act properly. Beyond this, the ethics of care stresses the moral importance of meeting people's needs, especially the needs of people to whom we are related either intimately or in a relation that brings special responsibility, such as the relation to an infant. Society includes persons in various degrees of dependency. Caring is the glue that holds this together.

One could perhaps view the ethics of care as supplementing more traditional theories by stressing the importance of the moral emotions and situations of dependency. Yet it is intended as a new approach, on a par with deontology, consequentialism, and virtue theory. The ethics of care developed out of reflection on the implications of feminist insights for moral theory. Carol Gilligan's work in moral psychology was highly influential. Gilligan (1982) found that while boys tended to interpret certain stories as raising issues of justice, girls tended to interpret the stories as raising issues of care. Some philosophers found this suggestive of a new approach to ethics, and argued for the superiority of the perspective of care. Held cautions us, however, that issues of justice arise within caring relationships, so that a complete theory cannot ignore justice.

Both virtue theory and the ethics of care deny that moral understanding depends on a knowledge of principles of right action. These approaches to normative theory therefore tend to be sympathetic to particularism, which is discussed in the chapter by Lance and Little.

In order to evaluate the various theories I have been discussing, philosophers construct imaginary examples and then compare what the theories say about the examples with their "moral intuitions." I followed this strategy in objecting to some of the theories I have discussed. Philosophers pursue a similar strategy in evaluating metaethical theories, for a metaethical theory can be tested to see whether it conflicts with pretheoretical beliefs about morality. It might be objected that our moral intuitions may merely reflect our own parochial culture and that our pretheoretical intuitions may rest on naivete and inadequate thought. In his chapter, Michael DePaul examines in detail the methodology of seeking a "wide-reflective equilibrium" between theory and intuition. He argues that there is no sensible alternative, since the method basically consists in reflecting thoroughly and then trusting the conclusions we reach.

Moral philosophy can have an immediate significance for our lives that many other abstract areas of philosophy do not have. Normative theories have implications for how we are to live. And while metaethical theories may not have such implications, they can have implications for how we are to understand the implications of normative theory, so they can affect our understanding of claims about how we are to live. It is appropriate, therefore, to inquire into the relation between the theories we have examined and moral practice.

This is the topic of Gerald Dworkin's chapter. Dworkin argues that we need to make use of moral principles in order to satisfy a normative requirement on responsible moral inquiry and discourse—the requirement of "consistency," or systematic coherence. This is the requirement to conduct moral inquiry and discourse in such a way that our decisions about how to live are not "arbitrary" but are "principled," in a familiar intuitive sense. He therefore argues, by implication, that an adequate moral theory must articulate and defend moral principles.

This has been an introduction to moral theory wrapped around an introduction to the chapters in this book. The volume will have served us well if it helps to raise the level of debate in moral philosophy and to foster a heightened level of responsiveness and reasonableness in moral discourse.

NOTES

Several people provided helpful comments on earlier drafts of this essay, and I am grateful to all of them. I am especially grateful to Daniel Boisvert, Jamie Dreier, Tom Hurka, Kirk Ludwig, David McNaughton, Marina Oshana, Piers Rawling, Geoff Sayre-McCord, Jon Tresan, Anton Tupa, and Crystal Thorpe.

1. Quinn explains that a divine command view is compatible with a variety of positions on the relation between divine commands and ethical statuses such as rightness and wrongness. One view, for example, is that wrongness is identical to the property of being forbidden by God. Another is that wrongness is distinct from the property of being forbidden by God, but its instantiantion is brought about by the commands of God. Quinn takes the latter position. Both of these positions are versions of moral realism. I should note that, technically, a kind of divine command view could be offered as a normative theory rather than a metaethical theory. Such a view would hold that our most fundamental moral duty is to obey God's commands. This duty would not depend, however, on God's commanding that we obey him. It would be prior to God's commands. A view of this kind is compatible with a variety of metaethical positions including noncognitivism as well as moral realism. In what follows, I will explain what these positions come to as well as the distinction between a normative theory and a metaethical theory.

2. Theists often hold that it is a necessary truth that God exists. On this view, the conditional that if God does not exist, there are no obligations, has a necessarily false antecedent. There is controversy about the evaluation of conditionals with necessarily false antecedents, but a discussion of the controversy would be beyond the scope of this chapter. It seems to me that an adequate account would treat the foregoing conditional as following from the divine command theory, for its consequent follows from the conjunction of its antecedent with the theory. That is, there is a valid argument from the conjunction of the proposition that God does not exist and the divine command theory to the proposition that there are no obligations. (I am grateful to Kirk Ludwig for helpful discussion of this issue.) If one takes the first horn of the *Euthyphro* dilemma instead of the horn chosen by Quinn, one can avoid this difficulty. For on this view, God commands that one do one's duty, but our duties are obligatory independently of God's commands. Hence, God's non-existence does not, or would not, mean we have no obligations. But this view is incompatible with the divine command theory.

3. Moral realism is compatible with any theory about the nature of properties, including nominalism. See note 4. In what follows, I treat relations, such as the relation of being morally better than, as a kind of property. On some theories, rightness and wrongness themselves are best understood as relations. See Copp, 1995, pp. 218–223. See chapter 9 of this book, by James Dreier.

4. That is, the first realist doctrine is to be interpreted such that the term "property," as it occurs there, ascribes the same metaphysical status to moral properties, such as *wrongness*, as it ascribes to a non-moral property such as *redness* when it is predicated of such a property. A moral realist can be a nominalist, for although she says there are moral properties, she says they have the metaphysical status that any other

property has, *whatever* that is. Some philosophers would deny that there are any properties at all. But I take it that they do not mean to deny that red things have the "characteristic" of being red. They mean to reject the standard philosophical theories about
the nature of such characteristics. They would agree that sentences such as "There are
properties such as redness" can be used to express truths, but they reject standard philosophical theories of their truth conditions. If so, they may be in a position to accept
moral realism.

5. A moral claim is "basic" in the sense at issue just in case it is (or could be expressed in English by a sentence) of the form, 'A is M'—where 'M' is replaced by a
moral predicate and 'A' is replaced by a term that refers to or picks out a person, action
or action-type, character trait, social institution, or the like. A moral realist would say
that a basic moral claim ascribes a moral property. An example of a basic claim is the
claim that capital punishment is wrong. The proposition that nothing is morally wrong
is not basic.

6. For an example of a cognitivist functionalism that is roughly of this kind, see
Foot, 2001. For a critique, see FitzPatrick, 2000.

7. For the idea of a "response-dependent" property, see Wedgwood, 1998.

8. A similar view is proposed in Oshana, 1997. Various other conceptions of moral
responsibility are discussed by John Fischer in chapter 12 of this book.

9. My thinking about the two central disputes, and especially about the idea of a
basic matter of moral concern, has been influenced by Shelly Kagan's discussion of
foundational normative theories, and especially by his idea that consequentialist theories
can have different "evaluative focal points." See Kagan, 1998, pp. 202–204. I have benefited from the helpful comments of Daniel Boisvert, David McNaughton, Piers Rawling,
and Jon Tresan.

10. To be sure, Kantian theory takes rational agency to be valuable, and rights-
based theories take rights to be valuable. But they take judgments about *rational agency*,
or about *rights*, respectively, to be basic or fundamental, not judgments about value.
They do not qualify as consequentialist merely because they would agree that what, for
them, is the basic matter of moral concern is also valuable.

11. According to act consequentialism, as I formulated it, the right action is the
available action that would maximize the good. One might instead think that any alternative is permitted, provided it is above a threshold. Brink discusses a variety of possible views.

12. This is a crude presentation of an argument that first appeared in Nozick, 1974,
pp. 29–31, and was then elaborated in detail in Scheffler, 1982, ch. 4.

13. See Copp, 1995, pp. 201–209. The basic idea is that a moral code that is "justified" thereby has a truth-grounding status, a status such that relevantly corresponding
moral propositions are true. Hence, if a justified code includes a constraint against torture, then it is true that torture is wrong. Braybrooke (2003) argues that such a position
falls within the natural law tradition, broadly conceived. He says, "Natural law theory
founds moral judgments on what, given the nature of human beings and ever-present
circumstances, enables people to live together in thriving communities" (p. 125).

14. Numbers in brackets refer to the volume and page number in the standard
Prussian Academy edition.

15. This can be done in different ways, as illustrated in Hurka, 2000, and Driver,
2001.

REFERENCES

Bales, R. Eugene. 1971. "Act-Utilitarianism: Account of Right-Making Characteristics or Decision-Making Procedure?" *American Philosophical Quarterly* 8: 257–265.

Braybrooke, David. 2003. *Natural Law Modernized.* Toronto: University of Toronto Press.

Copp, David. 1995. *Morality, Normativity, and Society.* New York: Oxford University Press.

———. 2001. "Realist-Expressivism: A Neglected Option for Moral Realism." *Social Philosophy and Policy* 18: 1–43.

———. 2004. "Moral Naturalism and Three Grades of Normativity." In *Normativity and Naturalism,* ed. Peter Schaber, 7–45. Frankfurt: Ontos-Verlag.

Copp, David, and David Sobel. 2004. "Morality and Virtue: An Assessment of Some Recent Work in Virtue Ethics." *Ethics* 114: 514–554.

Darwall, Stephen. 1983. *Impartial Reason.* Ithaca, N.Y.: Cornell University Press.

Donagan, Alan. 1977. *The Theory of Morality.* Chicago: University of Chicago Press.

Driver, Julia. 2001. *Uneasy Virtue.* Cambridge: Cambridge University Press.

FitzPatrick, Willliam. 2000. *Teleology and the Norms of Nature.* New York: Garland.

Foot, Philippa. 2001. *Natural Goodness.* Oxford: Clarendon Press.

Frege, Gottlob. 1984. *Collected Papers on Mathematics, Logic, and Philosophy.* Ed. Brian McGuinness. Oxford: Blackwell.

Gauthier, David. 1986. *Morals by Agreement.* Oxford: Clarendon Press.

Gilligan, Carol. 1982. *In a Different Voice: Psychological Theory and Women's Development.* Cambridge, Mass.: Harvard University Press.

Hurka, Thomas. 2000. *Virtue, Vice, and Value.* Oxford: Oxford University Press.

Joyce, Richard. 2001. *The Myth of Morality.* Cambridge: Cambridge University Press.

Kagan, Shelly. 1998. *Normative Ethics.* Boulder, Colo.: Westview Press.

Kant, Immanuel. [1785]. 2002. *Grounding for the Metaphysics of Morals.* Trans. and ed. Thomas E. Hill, Jr., and Arnulf Zweig. Oxford: Oxford University Press.

Korsgaard, Christine. 1996. *The Sources of Normativity.* Cambridge: Cambridge University Press.

Mackie, J. L. 1977. *Ethics: Inventing Right and Wrong.* Harmondsworth, England: Penguin.

———. 1978. "Can There Be a Rights-Based Moral Theory?" *Midwest Studies in Philosophy* 3: 350–359.

McDowell, John. 1985. "Values and Secondary Qualities." In *Mind, Value, and Reality.* Cambridge, Mass.: Harvard University Press, 1998.

Nozick, Robert. 1974. *Anarchy, State, and Utopia.* New York: Basic Books.

Oshana, Marina. 1997. "Ascriptions of Responsibility." *American Philosophical Quarterly* 34: 71–83.

Parfit, Derek. 1984. *Reasons and Persons.* Oxford: Clarendon Press.

Rawls, John. 1980. "Kantian Constructivism in Moral Theory." *The Journal of Philosophy* 77: 515–572.

Ross, W. D. 1930. *The Right and the Good.* Oxford: Clarendon Press.

Scanlon, Thomas. 1998. *What We Owe to Each Other.* Cambridge, Mass.: Harvard University Press.

Scheffler, Samuel. 1982. *The Rejection of Consequentialism.* Oxford: Clarendon Press.

Slote, Michael. 2001. *Morals from Motives.* Oxford: Oxford University Press.

Smith, Michael. 1994. *The Moral Problem.* Oxford: Blackwell.

Wedgwood, Ralph. 1998. "The Essence of Response-Dependence." *European Review of Philosophy* 3: 31–54.

PART I

METAETHICS

CHAPTER 1

MORAL REALISM

GEOFFREY SAYRE-McCORD

PEOPLE come, early and easily, to think in moral terms: to see many things as good or bad, to view various options as right or wrong, to think of particular distributions as fair or unfair, to consider certain people virtuous and others vicious.[1] What they think, when they are thinking in these terms, often has a large impact on their decisions and actions, as well as on their responses to what others do. People forego attractive possibilities when they think pursuing them would be wrong, they push themselves to face death if they think it their duty, they go to trouble to raise their children to be virtuous, and they pursue things they take to be valuable. At the same time they admire those who are courageous and condemn people they judge to be unjust. Moral thinking is a familiar and vital aspect of our lives. Yet when people ask themselves honestly what it is they are thinking, in thinking some acts are right and others wrong, that some things are good, others bad, that some character traits are virtues, other vices, it turns out to be extremely difficult to say. This raises a puzzle that is at the center of our understanding of our selves and of our understanding of morality. Moral realism represents one way in which this puzzle might be addressed.

There is little doubt that the capacity to think in moral terms is tied in interesting and important ways to our emotions and feelings. Indeed, there's reason to suspect that in some cases people count as good whatever they like and reject as bad what they don't, that they register anything that is disadvantageous to themselves as unfair and find no such objection to what brings them benefit. But these suspicions travel with a criticism: that people who use the terms in these ways don't (yet) fully understand what they are claiming in saying that something is good or bad, fair or not.

The criticism reflects the fact that in thinking morally we seem not merely to be expressing or reporting our emotions and feelings. Rather, so it seems, we are expressing beliefs about the world, about how it is and should be. Moreover, the beliefs we express—again, so it seems—are either true or false (depending on how things really are and should be), and when they are true, it is not simply because we think they are. Thus, if things are as they appear, in thinking morally we are committed to there being moral facts. And in making moral judgments we are making claims about what those facts are, claims that will be true or false depending on whether we get the facts right. That things *seem* this way is pretty uncontroversial.

1. MORAL REALISM

With these appearances in mind, we are in a good position to characterize moral realism: it is the view that, in these respects, things are really as they seem. Moral realists hold that there are moral facts, that it is in light of these facts that peoples' moral judgments are true or false, and that the facts being what they are (and so the judgments being true, when they are) is not merely a reflection of our *thinking* the facts are one way or another. That is, moral facts are what they are even when we see them incorrectly or not at all.

Moral realists thus all share the view that there are moral facts in light of which our moral judgments prove to be true or false. Yet they needn't, and don't, all share any particular view about what those facts are, and they might well not be confident of any view at all. When it comes to moral matters, there is no less disagreement among realists than among people at large and no incompatibility between being a realist and thinking oneself not in a good position to know what the facts are.

Furthermore, being a realist is compatible with holding a truly radical view of the moral facts. As much as realism tries to conserve the appearances when it comes to accounting for the nature of moral thought and its commitment to moral facts, there is nothing morally conservative about its implications. One might well be a moral realist while holding that the vast majority of mankind has misunderstood the demands of justice or the nature of virtue. Indeed, according to moral realists, holding that justice or virtue have been misunderstood only makes sense if one thinks there is a fact of the matter about what justice and virtue are, a fact that others have failed to get right.

Finally, among realists there is serious disagreement even about what sort of thing a moral fact is. Thus some realists hold that moral facts are just a kind of natural fact, while others hold they are nonnatural or even supernatural. Some realists hold that moral facts are discoverable by empirical inquiry, while others see rational intuition or divine inspiration as essential to moral knowledge. Moreover, some realists believe that while there genuinely are moral facts, those facts are themselves dependent upon, and a reflection of, human nature or social practice. They thus combine a commitment to moral facts with a relativist or a contractarian or constructivist account of those facts.[2] Such views reject the idea that the moral facts exist independent of humans and their various capacities or practices. Yet, to the extent they are advanced as capturing accurately what the moral facts actually are, they are versions of moral realism. Needless to say, what one person might see as nicely accounting for the nature of moral facts, another might see as missing something essential or even as completely changing the subject.[3] Thus, what one person might embrace as a successful defense of moral realism, another might see as, at best, a view one would embrace once one had given up on the thought that there are genuine moral facts.

2. MORAL ANTIREALISM

Antirealists about morality reject the idea that there are moral facts and so reject the idea that, in the respects mentioned earlier, things really are as they seem. Some antirealists acknowledge that when we think in moral terms we are committed to there being moral facts. Moral thought and practice, they hold, presupposes and makes good sense only in light of there actually being moral facts. To this extent, they agree with moral realists. They go on to argue, however, that the presupposition is false, so our common moral practice is built on a mistake. Antirealists of this persuasion are often characterized as "error theorists." Their shared view is that moral thought and practice rests on an error and the error is to suppose that there are moral facts.[4]

Other antirealists, however, reject as mistaken the idea that moral thought and practice presupposes there actually being moral facts. They reject the idea that in making moral judgments we are expressing beliefs that might be true or false in light of (putative) moral facts. Indeed, they argue, a proper understanding of moral thought and practice shows that no appeal need be made to moral facts and that moral judgments should not be seen as being true or false in the way that nonmoral judgments concerning genuine matters of fact are either true or false. They of course acknowledge that people do sometimes speak of moral facts and of their own or other peoples' moral judgments being true or false. But such talk is misguided, they argue, if the appeal to moral facts and the truth of moral judgments is supposed to have any substantive implications when it comes to thinking about the real features of the world. Alternatively, it is trivial, they point out, if to say there are moral facts and that some moral judgments are true is simply another way of expressing one's moral commitments with no further commitments whatsoever. Either way, the fact that we sometimes speak of moral facts and the truth of moral judgments should not be taken as evidence that we are committed, as moral realists claim, to there being genuine moral facts and moral truths.

This kind of antirealism rests on drawing a contrast between, on the one hand, some areas of thought and talk (about, for instance, empirical matters concerning the external world) where facts are genuinely at issue and the judgments people make are literally, in light of those facts, either true or false and, on the other hand, moral thought and talk, where—the antirealists maintain—facts are not genuinely at issue and so the judgments people make are not literally, in light of such facts, either true or false. Antirealists of this persuasion are often called noncognitivists.[5] Their shared view is that moral thought and talk carries no "cognitive content" and so neither purports to report facts nor expresses a judgment that might be true because it gets the facts right.

While antirealists all reject the idea that there are moral facts in light of which some moral judgments are literally true, they need not, for that reason, be critics of moral thought. Noncognitivists, for instance, can perfectly consistently reject the idea that in thinking something good we are, in the way realists hold, committed to the existence of moral facts, and yet themselves think that moral thought and talk is itself good.[6] And error theorists too, despite their view that moral thought is cognitive and carries commitments we have reason to think are false, can be in favor of perpetuating the practice—they can think of it as a useful fiction and can even consistently believe (as long as they are not error theorists about all evaluative judgments) that it is good.

Of course, many antirealists are critics of moral thought. Some suggest that morality is nothing more than a myth introduced to keep people docile and easy to manage. Others see it as an extreme and dangerous version of our natural tendency to objectify our own tastes and force others to accommodate our wishes. And still others see moral thought as a vestige of outmoded and now indefensible ways of understanding our place in the world.

In any case, and by all accounts, moral realism is, at least initially, the default position. It fits most naturally with what we seem to be doing in making moral claims, and it makes good sense of how we think through, argue about, and take stands concerning moral issues.

Yet the burden can shift quickly. For while moral realists seem to have common practice on their side, they face a tremendous challenge: to make sense of what moral facts are, of how they relate to various other facts, of how we might learn about moral facts, and of why those facts matter to what we should do. If, as it seems, in making moral judgments we are claiming that things are a certain way, morally, what are we claiming? What makes it true that some act is wrong, another right, that one experience is genuinely valuable, another not? How does the nonmoral fact that some act was malicious (for instance) relate to it being morally wrong? Finally, why do the facts (supposing there are some) that make moral claims true set the standard for our behavior? A satisfying defense of moral realism seems to require answers to these questions.

Realists and antirealists alike grant that some acts are malicious, others kind, that some are pleasant, others painful, that some accord with prevailing cultural standards, others conflict with such standards. None of this is in dispute. But are there, in addition to facts of this sort, facts about what is morally right or wrong, virtuous or vicious, good or bad? That is the issue that divides realists from antirealists. And the job of defending realism requires giving a plausible account of the nature of moral facts. This, in turn, involves shouldering metaphysical, epistemic, and justificatory burdens. Specifically, moral realists need to offer an account of moral facts (1) that make sense of how those facts fit with other facts in the world, (2) that shows them to be facts to which we might have some access, such that we might have evidence for our beliefs concerning them, and finally (3) that reveals the facts as providing reasons to act or not act in various ways.

3. Reidentifying Moral Facts in Nonmoral Terms

Sensitive to the challenge, some moral realists have offered a range of different accounts that identify moral facts with facts that are taken to be less problematic. In *identifying* the moral facts with less problematic facts, they are holding not just that what is right or wrong depends in some way on these facts but that facts about what is right or wrong are those very facts.

Focusing just on the question of what it is for something to be good, for instance, some people have maintained that to be good is simply to be pleasant. Others have held that what is good is whatever satisfies a desire or perhaps a desire we desire to have. And still others have argued that for something to be good is for it to be such that a fully informed person would approve of it.

Switching from what is good to what is right, people have maintained that what makes an act morally right is that it maximizes happiness when all are taken into account, or that an act is morally right—for a person, in a particular culture—if and because it conforms to standards that are embraced by most people in that person's culture.

Each of these views (as well as many others that have been defended) offers an account of the moral facts that leaves those facts no more problematic than the relatively mundane empirical facts with which they are being identified, and in effect reduced, by these accounts. If one or another such account is correct, then moral facts are, when it comes to metaphysics, easy to accommodate. Indeed, a major attraction of these accounts is their ability to take the metaphysical mystery out of morality and offer a clear-headed account of the nature of moral facts. At the same time, if such an account is correct, there would be no special difficulty in thinking that we might get evidence as to whether something is good or right. And, finally, each of the proposals has some claim to having given an account of moral facts that reveals why such facts provide people with reasons to act, or refrain from acting, in various ways.

At the turn of the twentieth century, accounts of morality that identified moral properties with empirically discoverable natural features of the world were quickly gaining adherents. While there was serious disagreement as to which features in particular were the right ones, more and more people came to think that moral thoughts and claims must be about, and true in light of, the sort of natural properties that were open to empirical investigation.

The main alternative to such a view was that moral properties should be identified not with empirical features of the world, but with facts about God. Assuming, as most defenders of the latter view did, that God existed, identifying what was good with what pleased God, and what was right with what accorded with God's will worked to ensure that a commitment to moral facts did not introduce any new mystery. Moral facts are, on this account, plain matters of fact about God—even if often highly controversial and difficult to establish.[7]

Whichever view one embraced, whether one identified moral facts with natural facts or with religious facts about God, the idea was that moral thought and talk was committed to properties, and facts, and truths, that could just as well be expressed in nonmoral terms. Whether this worked to make moral realism more plausible depended, of course, on one's views of the properties, facts, and truths expressed in those nonmoral terms. Usually, though, the aim of those offering such accounts was both to clarify the nature of morality and to show that believing in moral facts did not require metaphysical or epistemological commitments beyond those one had already taken on board.

4. THE OPEN QUESTION ARGUMENT

Early in the twentieth century, all of these views, secular and nonsecular alike, faced a challenge that many have thought devastating and that has, in any case, largely structured the debate about moral realism since. This challenge came in the form of G. E. Moore's (1903) incredibly influential Open Question Argument. Moore's aim, in deploying the argument, was to show that all attempts to identify moral properties with properties that might be described in nonmoral terms fail. The argument goes as follows.

To the question "what is good?"—where we are not asking what things are good but rather what is the property goodness—there seem to be three and only three possible answers:

1. Goodness is a complex property that can be broken down by analysis into its parts, in which case one can offer an illuminating definition of the property that works by identifying the various parts that combine to constitute goodness (in the same way that, for instance, one might define the property of being a bachelor as being a male human over a certain age who is unmarried).
2. Goodness is a simple property that itself cannot be broken down by analysis into parts, in which case the only accurate definitions are those that trade in synonyms and so shed no real light on the nature of the property. (There must be at least some simple properties, Moore argued, since they are needed as the building blocks out of which all more complex properties would have to be built.)
3. Goodness is no property at all, and the word "good" is meaningless, in which case, of course, no definition can be offered.

Having set out these three possibilities, Moore first argued that goodness is not a complex and analyzable property, on the following grounds: Consider any proposed definition of "good," where the definition picks out some complex set of properties, x (satisfying a preference, say, or pleasing God, or whatever) and defines being good as being x, and so says, "x is good." (Here, the "is" is the 'is of identity' rather than the 'is of attribution'.) In each case, the proposal is purporting to offer an illuminating definition of goodness that explains its nature by identifying its constituent parts.

The test of any such definition, Moore maintained, was whether those who genuinely understood the terms in which the definition was offered recognized as clear—indeed as trivially obvious—that the property being defined and the complex of properties offered as defining it were one and the same. Consider, for instance, the question of whether some unmarried male human over age twenty-one is a bachelor. Anyone who understands the question, it seems, knows right

away what the answer is, without having to investigate the world or collect additional evidence. In contrast, Moore thought, for any definition of goodness that
identifies being good with some complex property of being x, there will remain
a substantive question of whether or not something is good even if it is clearly x.
And this fact shows, he held, that each such definition is inadequate. Take, for
example, the proposal that goodness should be identified with (the complex property of) satisfying a preference—so that, according to this definition, being good
and satisfying a preference are supposed to be one and the same thing. Were the
definition correct, anyone who understands the relevant terms should recognize
as trivially obvious that anything that satisfies a preference is (in virtue of that)
good. But, in fact, it is a substantive question whether satisfying a sadist's preference for the suffering of others is good at all.

That this is a substantive question—an "open" question—shows, Moore
maintained, that "satisfies a preference" and "good" differ in meaning (since
thinking something satisfies a preference is not identical to thinking it good) and
that they therefore refer to different properties. If they did have the same meaning
and referred to the same properties, then asking whether something that satisfies
a preference is good would not be an open question, in exactly the way asking
whether bachelors are married is not substantive. Substitute whatever definition
of "good" you please into the original proposition "x is good," and the question
will, Moore claimed, remain open.

If every proposed definition fails the test, Moore concluded, no definition
that identifies goodness with a complex property is adequate. Thus, when we claim
that something is good, we are claiming something different from what we are
claiming when we claim it satisfies a preference, or pleases God, or is approved
of by the majority, and so on.

Significantly, the very same considerations tell against various popular proposals that identify goodness with a simple natural property, such as pleasure. To
ask whether something pleasant is actually good (think here of the pleasure a
sadist might enjoy on hurting someone) is again to raise an open question—a
question the answer to which is not settled merely by knowing the meaning of
the terms in question. Other simple properties that might be expressed in nonmoral terms fare no better. Any attempt to define goodness in nonmoral terms—
either by identifying it with a complex property that might be analyzed into parts,
or even with the sort of simple properties some have proposed—will, Moore
concluded, fail.[8]

That leaves two possibilities. Either goodness is a simple, *sui generis* property,
which is distinct from all the properties various theories have privileged, or it is
no property at all. Against this last possibility—that goodness is not a property
and, therefore, "good" is meaningless—Moore pointed to the *intelligibility* of the
various open questions. That it makes sense to ask whether what satisfies a pref-

erence is good, or whether some pleasure is good, shows that all the terms involved are meaningful. Otherwise we would treat the question itself as nonsense. So that option is ruled out.

Goodness, therefore, must be a simple, *sui generis* property, which should not be thought identical to any of the properties, simple or complex, that we might describe in nonmoral terms. To identify it with some such property leads inevitably, Moore thought, to serious confusion and corrupt arguments.

Moore acknowledged that all things that are good might share some other property—they might all be pleasant, for instance, or all such that if we were informed we would approve of them, or all compatible with God's will. Whether things are this way or not, he argued, is something that can be settled only by investigating cases. But even if all good things do share both the property of being good and some other property, the properties would, for all that, still be different. "[G]ood is good, and that is the end of the matter. . . . [I]f I am asked 'How is good to be defined?' my answer is that it cannot be defined, and that is all I have to say about it" (Moore, 1903, p. 6).

Thinking that no illumination, and serious confusion, came from attempts to define, or even just give an account of, goodness, Moore turned his attention to trying to discover what things had the property of being good. He came to the conclusion that, while happiness is among those things that are good, so are truth, beauty, and knowledge. In fact, he argued that a great variety of things are good; just as a great variety of things are yellow. Although no one of them, nor all of them taken together, should be identified with goodness, each of them had the property of being good. He then went on, in the process of defending utilitarianism, to argue that "right," unlike "good," *could* be analyzed. His view was that for an action to be right is for it to be such that it produces the greatest possible amount of goodness. Where he differed from the old–style utilitarians, who embraced some version of naturalism, was in his view that goodness could not, in turn, be identified with any natural property.

Soon people applied the same line of reasoning to other moral concepts, arguing that rightness and courageousness, no less than goodness, were not definable. Rejecting Moore's view that in saying something is right we are saying that no alternative has better consequences, W. D. Ross (1930) pointed out that it was, apparently, an open question whether some option that admittedly had the best consequences (as, for instance, lying sometimes might) was nonetheless right. Considerations of this sort, marshaled against all attempts to define moral terms, led to the view that our moral theorizing needs to be carried on in its own terms, on its own terms, using introspection, intuition, and reflection.

5. NONCOGNITIVISM

The Open Question Argument convinced many people that moral properties should not be identified with natural properties. Yet many were troubled by the metaphysics of nonnatural properties put forward by Moore and Ross, as well as by the seemingly inevitable appeal to intuition as the basis of our knowledge of nonnatural properties. So people went back to Moore's original trilemma and argued that, despite appearances, moral terms are in fact (strictly speaking) meaningless. Moral thought and talk do have a purpose, and people do know how to use it. But its purpose, these noncognitivists argued, is to express (rather than report) attitudes and to influence behavior, not to express beliefs or to report (putative) facts. When people claim that something is good, we can explain what they are doing, in perfectly naturalistic terms, without any commitment to moral properties (and moral facts) at all, and with no need to identify moral properties with natural properties in the way the Open Question Argument showed must be mistaken.

The challenge facing noncognitivism is to explain why it *seems* as if moral sentences *are* meaningful, as if in judging something good or right, bad or wrong, we are not merely expressing our attitudes but are expressing beliefs that might be true or false (depending on the facts). Why does moral discourse exhibit so thoroughly the behavior of meaningful, factual discourse?

The simple answer—that it seems this way because it *is* meaningful, factual discourse—is not available to the noncognitivist. Less simple, but quite robust, answers are available, though. While the various answers differ in important ways, they mobilize a common strategy. That strategy is to appeal to some practical purpose moral thought and talk might have and argue that the purpose could be met, or met well, only if the practice of thinking through and expressing our attitudes had a structure that would make it look as if it were factual discourse that could be used to express beliefs and report (putative) facts.

Three features of moral discourse have stood out as especially needing some such explanation. One is that our moral views are commonly expressed by declarative sentences that appear to attribute properties to people and acts and situations and seem, as a result, to be genuinely evaluable as true or false. Another is that, in thinking morally, we seem to be constrained, appropriately, by the very same rules of inference that apply to factual discourse and seem to apply precisely because those rules are truth preserving. And the third is that our own views of our moral claims would have it that their claim on us, and their authority, is independent of our own attitudes.

Each of these three features of moral discourse is, at least initially, problematic for the noncognitivist, since the attitudes the noncognitivists see as expressed by our moral discourse (1) are not attitudes that involve ascribing moral properties to things and are not true or false, so (2) whatever rules of inference do apply to these expressions do not apply because they are truth-preserving, and (3) our moral attitudes appear to have no special authority and in any case are *not* independent of the attitudes of the person who holds them.

When it comes to these features of moral discourse, a cognitivist can rely on whatever explanations the noncognitivists are prepared to offer for the discourse they acknowledge to be uncontroversially factual. Exactly what these explanations are, it is worth noting, is itself controversial. But the cognitivists hold that, whatever they are, there is no special problem in accounting for moral thought and talk. Whatever the right explanations are, when it comes to the uncontroversial discourses, these explanations work too for moral discourse. The noncognitivists' distinctive position—that moral discourse differs, in the relevant way, from factual discourse—means they need not only to explain the relevant features of factual discourse but to explain as well, in a way that preserves the difference upon which they insist, why moral discourse appears to be, but is not, the same.[9]

This is no small task. Regularly noncognitivists have found themselves either (1) successfully explaining why moral discourse resembles the uncontroversially factual discourse, but losing the contrast that defines their view, or (2) successfully sustaining a contrast between moral discourse and uncontroversially factual discourse but being unable to explain why the two are so much alike. That things regularly turn out this way does not, of course, show that they will inevitably, but it raises a caution against thinking that noncognitivism has an easy way of maintaining its position while explaining the phenomena that all grant.

To take one example, people have recently suggested that talk of truth should be given a "minimalist" reading, according to which to say of some claim that it is true is just a way of re-making the claim. If this is right, then moral claims, no less than any others, will be counted as true by anyone willing to make the claims in question. And anyone willing to say that Hitler was evil should be prepared as well to say that it is true that Hitler was evil. According to minimalism about truth, talk of truth brings no further commitments. This makes available to the antirealists an easy explanation of why moral claims appear to be truth evaluable. But of course the antirealist, assuming she holds some moral views (for example, that Hitler was evil), cannot then characterize her distinctive view by saying that she denies that moral claims are true. She does not deny that (on this understanding of truth). A minimalist about truth who wants to reject realism about morality must then mark the contrast between her view, and a realist's view, in some other way. She might say that while moral claims are true, her antirealism comes with her rejection of moral properties and moral facts. Yet the same sort of considerations that have been offered in favor of minimalism about truth seem as well to speak in favor of minimalism about properties and facts. And minimalism about properties and facts makes it easier than it otherwise would be for an antirealist to explain why people talk of moral properties and moral facts. Yet each of these minimalisms brings in its wake the burden of finding some way, if not by appeal to notions of truth, or properties, or facts, to mark what it is that the antirealist is rejecting that the realist accepts.

6. REVISITING THE OPEN QUESTION ARGUMENT

For a long time, people assumed that the Open Question Argument showed that the only way to avoid the metaphysical and epistemological mysteries of nonnaturalism, without rejecting moral thought and practice as deeply misguided, was to embrace noncognitivism. And this provided the most powerful, though not the only, reason to find noncognitivism attractive.[10]

Yet the Open Question Argument, which appeared to force the choice, has relatively recently come under serious attack. Always, some have resisted the argument, maintaining that the apparent openness of the various questions was an illusion. According to them, thinking it was an open question whether, say, to be good is to be such as to satisfy a preference reflects a failure to understand fully the claims at issue. To insist otherwise, these people pointed out, is to beg the question.[11] In any case, appealing to the openness of various questions seemed less an argument than a reflection of a conclusion already reached. Suspicions were fueled too by dissatisfaction with noncognitivism and the sense that at its best it would leave moral discourse with none of the credibility it deserves.

But the most powerful grounds for rejecting the Open Question Argument came with the realization that two terms, say "water" and "H_2O," could refer to one and the same property, even though one would be asking a substantive question (that can be settled only by investigating the world) in asking whether H_2O is water. The realization that a proposed identity could both be true and yet fail the test of the Open Question Argument encouraged the hope that, after all, a naturalized metaphysics for moral properties could be defended. No longer did it seem that a successful defense was available only at the cost of embracing properties that were metaphysically and epistemically peculiar.

At the same time, even those tempted by the prospect of identifying moral properties with some (perhaps very complex) set of natural properties believe that the Open Question Argument reveals something crucial about the distinctive nature of our moral thinking. If, for instance, being good is a matter of having a certain natural property, there is little question that someone might think of something that it has that natural property, and not think at all that it is good in any way. So while the Open Question Argument moved too quickly from (1) noticing that thinking some thing has some natural property is different in some way from thinking it good to (2) the claim that the thoughts are therefore attributing distinct properties to the thing, the argument does properly highlight something distinctive about moral thinking. No defense of moral realism can be successful without giving an account of the distinctive nature of moral thought.

7. INTERNALISM

When it comes to accounting for what thinking of something as good might consist in, apart from merely thinking it has some natural property, people often appeal to the apparently intimate, and unique, connection between sincere moral judgment and action.

Many have thought that the distinctive feature of moral judgment is its link specifically to motivation. To honestly think, of something, that it is good, they maintain, is ipso facto to have some motivation to promote, preserve, or pursue that thing. Conversely, to discover of someone that he is actually completely indifferent to what he claims is good is to discover he does not really think it is good at all.[12]

The simplest and most plausible explanation of this connection between moral judgment and motivation (if there is such a connection) is that in making a genuine moral judgment we are expressing a motivational state. Assuming, as noncognitivists standardly do, that motivational states are distinct and different from beliefs, then in discovering that moral judgments express motivational states we are discovering that they express something other than beliefs. If they do not express beliefs, then they do not purport to report facts, and so cannot be true or false. In other words, motivational internalism (as this view is often called), when combined with the Humean view that motivational states (e.g. desire) and beliefs are distinct existences, implies noncognitivism and so antirealism.[13]

Moral realists have responded to motivational internalism in two different ways. One is by denying the Humean thesis that motivational states and beliefs are always distinct existences. Indeed, some realists argue, moral judgments themselves serve as counterexamples to the Humean thesis. Moral judgments, these realists maintain, express a distinctive subset of our beliefs: ones that do necessarily motivate. If so, then the motivational internalist's contention that sincere moral judgment necessarily carries some motivational implications is fully compatible with seeing those judgments as expressing beliefs that purport to report facts, and therefore are liable to being true or false.[14]

The other response realists offer to this argument is simply to deny motivational internalism, by arguing that sincere moral judgment does not always comes with motivation. Sometimes, these realists argue, a person can genuinely judge that something is, say, right, and yet—perhaps because she is evil, or suffers depression, or is weak-willed—be utterly unmotivated to take action. If this is possible, then motivational internalism is false: genuine moral judgment does not, after all, necessitate motivation. And this would mean the motivational internalist argument evaporates.

Rejecting motivational internalism is, of course, compatible with holding that there is a special connection between moral judgment and action. A common and plausible suggestion is that the crucial link between moral judgment and action is mediated not by motivation but by a conception of reason or rationality. After all, it seems that a person who fails to be motivated by what he judges to be good or right is thereby being irrational or (perhaps more weakly) is at least failing to respond to what he himself is committed to seeing as something he has reason to do.[15] Reason internalism (as it is sometimes called) retains the idea that there is an intimate link between moral thought and action but sees the link as forged by reason. This view has the resources to acknowledge that sometimes people fail to be motivated appropriately by their moral judgments while also being able to explain the distinctive connection between such judgments and actions.

The notions of rationality and reason in play here might well seem, in relevant respects, on a par with moral notions. If one doubts there are moral facts, in light of which our moral judgments might be true, one might well (on many of the same grounds) doubt that there are facts about reason, in light of which our judgments concerning reasons and rationality might be true. The Open Question Argument (whatever it might show) is, for instance, as applicable to proposed naturalistic definitions of reason and rationality as it is to proposed naturalistic definitions of value and rightness. So it is worth emphasizing that those who are defending reason internalism are not attempting to define moral judgments in natural terms (a project that would not be advanced by appeals to reason and rationality). Rather, assuming that the Open Question Argument leaves unsettled the issue of what sort of facts (natural or not) moral facts might be, it nonetheless appears to show that moral judgments differ in some important respect from many other (nonnormative) judgments. The challenge the Open Question Argument continues to pose, to anyone hoping to explain the nature of moral judgment, is to account for this difference. Realists and antirealists alike need to meet this challenge.

Motivational internalism offers one answer to the challenge: moral judgments (and perhaps other normative judgments, for instance those concerning rationality) are necessarily motivating, whereas the other judgments are not. Nonmoral judgments do, of course, often motivate, but their motivational impact depends on the presence of something else (a desire or preference or affective orientation) that is distinct and independent of the judgment.

Reason internalism offers another answer: moral judgments (and perhaps other normative judgments, for instance those concerning rationality) necessarily have implications concerning what people have reason to do, whereas other judgments do not. Nonmoral judgments do, of course, often have implications of this sort, but only in the company of moral (or other normative) judgments.[16] If reason claims are in the relevant respects on a par with moral judgments, then what follows is that judgments about rationality or reasons, no less than moral judgments, have implications concerning what people have reason to do or are committed to thinking they have reason to do.

8. COGNITIVISM

Whatever account one offers of the distinctive nature of moral (and perhaps other normative) judgments, another challenge awaits those who defend cognitivism: when one makes such judgments, what would or do constitute the relevant moral (or other normative) facts, in light of which the judgments are true or false? Noncognitivists do not face this question, of course. Their burden is to explain why the question faced by cognitivists seems so appropriate. Error theorists and realists, though, do need an answer.

Error theorists, even as they disagree among themselves as to what the right answer is, all think those answers reveal that moral claims could be true only under circumstances that, they believe, do not, and perhaps could not, obtain. Some realists agree with one or another of these accounts of what would be required, but reject the view that the relevant circumstances do not obtain. In these cases, their disagreement with the error theorists then lies not in the account of what moral claims require in order to be true but in their different views of what the world is like. Thus some error theorists and some realists might agree that the truth of moral claims would require objectively prescriptive facts, or categorical reasons, or nonnatural properties (to take three candidates) and then just disagree about whether such things exist. Alternatively, though, error theorists and realists might disagree on what moral claims presuppose, with (say) the error theorists maintaining they require objectively prescriptive facts, or categorical reasons, or nonnatural properties, and the realists disagreeing on each count even while agreeing that *if* moral claims did require such things, they would all be false. Thus some realists are realists precisely because they think that moral claims do not require the sort of facts that error theorists suppose they do.

Thus, if one is a cognitivist about moral claims, and so thinks that they purport to report facts and are, in light of whether the facts are as they purport, true or false, two considerations come into play in determining whether to be an error theorist or a realist. The first is: What would have to be the case for the claims to be true? The second is: Is there reason to think things are (at least sometimes) that way? Error theorists, in light of their answer to the first, give a negative answer to the second. Realists, who give a positive answer to the second, are committed to an answer to the first that makes that view defensible.

Predictably, a good deal of the debate about moral realism turns on whether realists have an account of morality that shows that the truth of moral claims would not have implications that are literally incredible. A realist who denies that there are objectively prescriptive facts, or categorical reasons, or nonnatural properties (or whatever) is then committed to saying that such things are not actually required in order for our moral judgments to be true. Another realist who grants that moral claims are true only in light of there being objectively prescriptive fact, or categorical reasons, or nonnatural properties (or whatever) is committed instead to defending the existence of such things. Either way, the burden of realism is to offer an account of moral judgments and the world in light of which it is reasonable to think that such judgments are sometimes actually true.

9. EXPLANATION AND JUSTIFICATION

Putting aside the putatively unpalatable metaphysical implications of our moral claims, moral realism faces an important challenge. As many would have it, we have positive reason to believe something only if supposing it true contributes in some way to explaining our experiences. If that is right, then we have positive reason to believe there are moral facts only if supposing there are makes such a contribution. Yet moral facts have seemed to many to contribute not at all to our best explanations of our experiences. We can, for instance, explain why people think stealing is wrong, why they approve of kindness, and why moral thinking takes hold in a society all without having to appeal to any facts to the effect that stealing really is wrong, that there is actually something good about kindness, or that morality is genuinely important. All of these phenomena are fully explicable, it seems, by appeal to social and psychological forces, all of which have their effects independent of what the moral facts might be, were there any. But if that is true across the board, so that we need not appeal to moral facts to explain our experiences, then we have no reason to think there are such facts.[17]

It may be, of course, that we can explain what is wrong with some action (as opposed to explaining why someone thinks it wrong) only by appeal to moral principles. And these moral principles, in turn, may be explicable by still other principles. Thus we may need to suppose there are moral facts in order to explain the truth of various moral claims (e.g., that some action is wrong). Yet this is just a matter of one part of the system explaining other parts. If no part of the system serves to explain anything about how or why we experience the world as we do, it seems reasonable to think that—even if there were moral facts—we would have no grounds whatsoever for thinking our moral beliefs were in any way sensitive to the facts being what they are. So we would, even supposing there are moral facts, never have grounds for thinking we got them right.

Against this line of argument, some moral realists have argued that moral facts do actually figure in our best explanations of our experience.[18] Just how moral facts do this, and why we should believe they do, has been controversial. Some defend the idea that moral facts explain our experience by, *contra* Moore, identifying such facts with certain natural facts that indisputably do play a role in explaining our experiences. Thus, for instance, if the best explanation of our use of the term "value" is that we are, in using it, picking out what would satisfy an informed preference (a preference the having of which does not depend on any sort of ignorance), and if what does or does not satisfy such preferences makes a difference to how satisfied we are with certain outcomes, then a full explanation of our thought and talk of value would, after all, appeal to what turn out to be facts about value. Assuming that our moral terms are correctly understood as referring to natural properties that clearly explain our experiences, the argument against realism fails. But of course, that assumes a lot, and many who are tempted by this argument are inclined to see all the proffered reductions of the moral to the natural as ultimately leaving the moral out of the picture altogether, protests to the contrary notwithstanding

One need not accept any particular reduction of moral properties to natural properties, though, to hold that moral facts might play an important role in explaining our experiences. And, if cognitivism is true, there is reason to think that those who hold a moral view at all are committed to thinking that moral facts explain their own beliefs, so that if the facts were different, they would think differently from the way they do. To hold otherwise, of one's own views, is to see them as insensitive to the truth they purport to capture. This commitment seems to come even if one has no view at all about whether the moral facts are natural facts or about how one's beliefs might be sensitive to the relevant moral facts.

At the same time, focusing on the role moral facts might play in explaining our experiences appears to misunderstand the primary role such facts are sup-posed to have—which is not to explain but to justify. The point of thinking about what is right or wrong, good or bad, just or unjust, is not, it seems, to figure out what happened or why, but to figure out what should happen and why. Thus if we discovered of some putative moral facts that they were irrelevant to what was justified and what not, we would have grounds for rejecting them as *moral* facts, even if they figured in some of our best explanations of our experiences. So whether or not moral facts figure in our best explanations, they had better figure in our best justifications.

If this is right, it puts an important constraint on any defense of moral realism: it must offer an account of moral facts in light of which the facts being one way rather than another makes a difference to what people are justified in doing. Put another way, a successful defense of moral realism requires showing that the fact that something is right or wrong, good or bad, makes a difference to what people have reason to do.[19]

10. REALISM'S PROJECT IN PROSPECT

Whether moral realists can give an account of moral facts that reveals them to be metaphysically palatable, epistemically accessible, and also relevant to what we have reason to do is of course wildly controversial.

At one extreme, some realists are so confident that there are moral facts, that no considerations to the contrary, no mysteries unsolved, no imaginable alternatives could convince them otherwise. For them, whatever the metaphysical implications, and epistemic requirements, might prove to be, their acceptability is in effect established by their necessity. This view seems at least implicit in the attitudes of many who hold that there are moral facts yet dismiss metaethical concerns as appropriately put aside or ignored.

At the other extreme, some antirealists are so confident that moral thought and talk is taste, preference, and desire made pretentious, that no considerations to the contrary, no mysteries unsolved, no imaginable alternatives could convince them otherwise. For them, the bankrupt nature of moral thought is so clear that no arguments to the contrary would seem anything other than testimony to the success of the fraud. This view seems at least implicit in the attitudes of many who disingenuously mobilize moral appeals with an eye solely to getting what they want.

In between these extremes falls a variety of views, some realist, some antirealist. Among the most promising are those that take seriously the challenge of explaining how it is that people have developed the ability to think in recognizably moral terms. That people have this ability is clearly a contingent matter. After all, some people evidently lack the ability altogether, and everyone, at some point in life, has not yet developed the ability. There ought to be a good explanation of how and why this ability emerged, an explanation that will, presumably, shed a fair amount of light on the nature of what we are doing in exercising the ability.

The most illuminating versions of this project, I think, take on the challenge of explaining normative thought in general and do not limit themselves to an account of morality. The aim, in this case, is not simply to explain our ability to think of things as right or wrong, virtuous or vicious, moral or immoral, but also our ability to think of people (ourselves included) as having reasons to do or think things, and as being justified in our actions or our beliefs. Much (although not all) of what is distinctive and problematic about moral thought and talk is true as well of normative thought in general. As a result, any account of moral thought that begins by supposing people already have the capacity to make normative judgments will probably be burying in that supposition aspects of our moral thought that are better brought out and explained.

This project of explaining the emergence of our capacity to think in normative (and more specifically moral) terms, is one that antirealists and realists alike can embrace.[20] Antirealists about morality are, of course, committed to holding either (if they are noncognitivists) that the resulting explanation will show that in thinking morally we are not deploying concepts and not forming beliefs but doing something else or (if they are error theorists) that the explanation will account for our capacity to deploy moral concepts and form moral beliefs, though we have no reason to think anything satisfies the concepts and so no reason to think the beliefs true.

The realist's ambition, in contrast, is to show that a full and adequate explanation of our capacity to think in normative terms, and more specifically in moral terms, underwrites the idea that we are deploying concepts and forming beliefs and that we have reason to think the concepts are sometimes satisfied and the beliefs sometimes true.[21]

The realists' most promising strategy for explaining our ability to think in normative (and more specifically moral) terms starts with the idea that people face the world, and each other, initially without normative concepts, indeed without concepts of any sort, even as they do possess a range of dispositions, abilities, reactions, and attitudes, as well as capacities for reflection and adjustment. In this way a realist can hope to show that the best general explanation of the emergence of concepts of whatever sort is an explanation that applies equally to the emergence of distinctively normative concepts. The main idea would be that the range of preconceptual dispositions, abilities, reactions, and attitudes people have will, taken together, both make possible and motivate the emergence of various conventions—conventions the presence of which work to constitute various concepts (concepts of size, of shape, of pleasure, of pain) by introducing practices in light of which judgments concerning these things can be seen as correct or not. These concepts—whichever ones the various conventions have worked to constitute—are then available for people to deploy in their thinking.

In principle, at least, conventions might emerge that make it possible for people to think that some things are pleasant, others blue, some round, still others heavy, all without their having the capacity to think of themselves as having reasons to think as they do, and all without their having the capacity to think of things as good or bad, right or wrong. In order to be credited with these various concepts, they need to have the dispositions that make it reasonable to see them as appropriately sensitive to evidence that the concepts in play are satisfied. But those dispositions need not include the capacity to form beliefs concerning evidence, nor the capacity to form beliefs to the effect that they have reasons to think one thing or another. One might be sensitive to things about which one has no beliefs.

Perhaps as the conventions necessary for the emergence of concepts develop, they simultaneously give rise to normative concepts (of reason or evidence or justification) and to nonnormative concepts (of size or shape or color or experience). Perhaps not. Either way, the realist's aim here will be to show that a general account of what is required for people to have concepts at all applies as well when it comes to explaining normative and specifically moral concepts. Needless to say, the various concepts will differ from one another in important ways; concepts of color differ from those of shape which differ from those of value and justification. Yet, whatever these differences, if the account we have to offer of our having any of these concepts applies as well to our having specifically normative concepts, the realist has grounds for rejecting noncognitivism.

Of course, to think that we deploy normative concepts and so can form normative beliefs is not necessarily to think the concepts have an application or the beliefs are ever true. After all, there is some explanation of people's concept of Santa Claus, and so of their ability to believe in Santa Claus, even though there is no Santa Claus. So the realist needs to go on and offer grounds for thinking that the normative concepts that have emerged are such that, given the evidence we have, they are sometimes satisfied. That such an explanation is available is not guaranteed, unfortunately. One might think that the concepts would not have emerged if they had no application. But that hopeful thought underestimates the extent to which the conventions that work to constitute concepts might be sensitive to pressures that would motivate the introduction of empty concepts.

Still, one of the striking and important features of our normative concepts is their liability to self-correction and adjustment. The concepts of reason, justification, and value that we deploy appear to be concepts that are appropriately adjusted and reconceived in light of the discovery that we have reason to think differently from the way we do. Shifts in our understanding of what is justified, or valuable, or just, regularly occur in light of the discovery that we are unable to justify our original views, and those shifts do not themselves represent abandoning the concepts. Certainly, appropriate corrections might not always be available—in which case the concepts would indeed emerge as having no application.

However, normative concepts are designed to shift specifically in light of what we have reason to think. And this provides grounds for thinking that at least some normative concepts might well survive as being such that we have reason both (1) to use them in our thinking and (2) to think of them that they are (sometimes) satisfied.

This is, of course, an optimism, and an inspecific optimism at that, since there is in it no antecedent commitment to just which normative concepts will prove sustainable in this way. Yet offering some reason to reject the optimism is, importantly, self-defeating, since it appeals itself to a normative concept that is, in this context, assumed to have application. One cannot intelligibly both think there is reason to reject a set of concepts and think that the (normative) concept of there being reason to do things has no application.

In any case, if we end up having reason to think that there are normative concepts and that at least some of them actually apply, various grounds for resisting moral realism disappear. In particular, a successful explanation of the emergence of normative concepts that works as well to reveal some of those concepts as actually satisfied means that some sense must have been made of the metaphysical, epistemic, and justificatory commitments that come with making distinctively normative judgments. So, to the extent that worries about moral concepts have to do with their normative nature, such worries must be misguided.

Thoughts that are specifically moral, though, may well introduce a range of particular commitments that go beyond what comes with normative thought in general. They may, for instance, travel with the idea that there are some ways of acting that all people have decisive reason to engage in, or refrain from, regardless of their interests and concerns.[22] If so, then an account of the normative notion of a reason that ties what people have reason to do to their interests or concerns will pose a substantial threat to the idea that moral claims are ever actually true (since it will undermine the idea that anyone ever has reason to do anything except in light of his interests or concerns). Normative realists who want also to be moral realists need to show either that moral commitments do not carry this distinctive commitment or that a proper understanding of what people might have reason to do is compatible with thinking there are some things people have reason to do, or refrain from doing, independent of their interests and concerns.

No part of the project I have described is easy. But, at the same time, I think there is no good argument, available ahead of time, for thinking it cannot succeed. In any case, some explanation of how and why we have acquired the ability to think in normative, and specifically in moral, terms must be possible and will, inevitably, be illuminating. Moral realism's ultimate success depends, then, on showing (*contra* noncognitivists) that these abilities involve deploying moral concepts and forming moral beliefs, and then on showing (*contra* error theorists) that we sometimes have evidence that these beliefs are true and that we have reason to be concerned about the things of which they are true.

NOTES

1. Throughout I will be focusing on *moral* terms, concepts, and thoughts; yet most of the issues that arise for these, and the various positions one might take concerning them, arise and are available with respect to other, normative yet nonmoral, terms, concepts, and thoughts (for instance, rational or justified terms, etc.).

2. How plausible relativism is, as a realist position, turns on how plausible it is to think it can play this vindicative role. Many people, though notably not most relativists, think that moral claims pretend to a kind of universality that is not compatible with relativism. Relativists, however, regularly (but not inevitably) see their view as accurately capturing the content of moral claims in a way that reveals them often to be true. See Harman 1975, Wong, 1984, and Sayre-McCord, 1991, for defenses of the idea that relativism is compatible with moral realism.

3. So, for instance, many theorists reject relativist proposals. They acknowledge that there are facts about, say, what acts are in accordance with norms that people in a community accept, but they argue that those are nonmoral facts about what people *think* is right or wrong and not—what is importantly different—moral facts about what *is* right or wrong.

4. Different error theorists offer different grounds for thinking there are no moral facts of the sort our moral thought presupposes. J. L. Mackie, 1977, for instance, maintains that there could be such facts only if there were "objectively prescriptive" features of the world that worked effectively to motivate all who recognized those features. Others maintain that there would have to be categorical reasons that apply to people independent of their interests and desires, still others that there would have to be a God who takes an interest in human activities. In each case, the argument starts by identifying something that would putatively have to be the case for there to be moral facts and then moves on to showing that whatever is supposed to be required is absent.

5. Noncognitivists differ among themselves as to what people are doing, if not expressing beliefs, when they are thinking morally. Emotivists hold that they are expressing emotion (Ayer, 1946, Stevenson, 1937); prescriptivists hold that they are offering universal prescriptions (Hare, 1952), and expressivists are inclined either to some other alternative noncognitive state or to some combination of these (Blackburn, 1993, Gibbard, 1990).

6. They can even endorse that part of the practice that involves talking of moral facts and moral claims being true or false. What they cannot consistently do is hold that talk of moral facts and of moral claims being true or false should be understood literally, in the way talk of empirical facts and of scientific claims being true or false, are to be understood. See Blackburn, 1993, and Gibbard, 1990, for defenses of this sort of view.

7. Those who rejected the existence of God and yet accepted this view of what moral facts would consist in (were there any) declared that because God is dead (as they often put it) all is permissible (Dostoyevsky, 1879). If good and bad and right and wrong depended upon God's pleasure or will and there was no God, they reasoned, there was no good and bad, right or wrong, either.

8. It should be no surprise that Moore began *Principia Ethica* quoting Butler's observation "Everything is what it is, and not another thing." Moore thought all attempts to define goodness involved thinking goodness was some other thing.

9. It is worth noting that the relevant way in which moral discourse differs need not be found in some difference in the explanation of these three features. It is open to a noncognitivist to hold that the three features, whether we are talking of moral discourse or factual discourse, are to be given the very same explanation across the board. For instance, a noncognitivist might hold that what explains the appropriateness of specific rules of inference, as they apply to factual discourse, is actually not that they preserve truth but that they have some other feature that they have when applied to moral discourse no less than factual discourse. Still, the noncognitivist is committed to saying there is an important difference and to doing so in a way that explains what appear to be telling ways in which they are the same. See Gibbard, 2003.

10. See Ayer, 1946.

11. See Frankena, 1939.

12. See Stevenson, 1937.

13. The *locus classicus* for this argument is David Hume's *Treatise of Human Nature*, 1739.

14. See McDowell, 1978, and Platts, 1979.

15. See Smith, 1994.

16. Hume's famous observation that no 'ought' can be derived (solely) from an 'is' reflects this point: nonnormative claims ('is' claims, as Hume thought of them) imply nothing normative (nothing about what ought to be) without relying, at least implicitly, upon normative premises.

17. See Harman, 1977, and Sayre-McCord, 1988.

18. See Sturgeon, 1985, and Boyd, 1988.

19. We are thus brought back to a version of reason internalism according to which moral facts are necessarily connected to what agents have reason to do.

20. David Hume's *Treatise*, 1739, is an early and especially systematic attempt to pursue this project. See also Gibbard, 1990, and Korsgaard, 1996.

21. There is, it should be said, plenty of room to end up a realist about reasons, or justifications, or something else that is recognizably normative, and an antirealist (most likely an error theorist) about morality. It is possible, but would be peculiar, for someone to be a realist about reasons and justification (and so embrace cognitivism about those judgments) yet embrace noncognitivism about moral thought. The arguments for noncognitivism seem to apply equally to moral and to all other normative judgments, while the considerations that tell in favor of cognitivism with respect to nonmoral, yet normative, judgments carry over, it seems, to moral thoughts as well.

22. This is, of course, Kant's proposal as to what is distinctive of, and peculiar to, moral judgments. See Immanuel Kant, 1785.

REFERENCES

Ayer, A. J. 1946. "A Critique of Ethics." In *Language, Truth and Logic*, 102–114. London: Gollanz.

Blackburn, Simon. 1993. *Essays in Quasi-Realism*. Oxford: Oxford University Press.

Boyd, Richard. 1988. "How to Be a Moral Realist." In *Essays on Moral Realism*, ed. G. Sayre-McCord, 181–228. Ithaca, N.Y.: Cornell University Press.

Brink, David. 1989. *Moral Realism and the Foundations of Ethics.* Cambridge: Cambridge University Press.

Dostoyevsky, Fyodor. 1879. *The Brothers Karamazov.* Translated by David McDuff. London: Penguin Classics, 2003.

Frankena, William. 1939. "The Naturalistic Fallacy." *Mind* 48: 464–477.

Gibbard, Allan. 1990. *Wise Choices, Apt Feelings: A Theory of Normative Judgment.* Cambridge, Mass.: Harvard University Press.

———. 2003. *Thinking How to Live.* Cambridge, Mass.: Harvard University Press.

Hare, R. M. 1952. *The Language of Morals.* Oxford: Oxford University Press.

Harman, Gilbert. 1975. "Moral Relativism Defended." *Philosophical Review* 84: 3–22.

———. 1977. *The Nature of Morality.* New York: Oxford University Press.

Hume, David. [1739]. 1888. *The Treatise Concerning Human Nature.* Ed. L. A. Selby-Bigge. Oxford: Oxford University Press.

Kant, Immanuel. [1785]. 1993. *Grounding for the Metaphysics of Morals.* Trans. James W. Ellington. Indianapolis: Hackett.

Korsgaard, Christine. 1996. *The Sources of Normativity.* New York: Cambridge University Press.

Mackie, J. L. 1977. *Ethics: Inventing Right and Wrong.* London: Penguin Books.

McDowell, John. 1978. "Are Moral Requirements Hypothetical Imperatives?" *Proceedings of the Aristotelian Society,* supplementary volume 52: 13–29.

Moore, G. E. 1903. *Principia Ethica.* Cambridge: Cambridge University Press.

Platts, Mark. 1979. "Moral Reality." In *Ways of Meaning,* 243–263. London: Routledge and Kegan Paul.

Railton, Peter. 1986. "Moral Realism." *Philosophical Review* 95: 163–207.

Ross, W. D. 1930. *The Right and the Good.* Oxford: Oxford University Press.

Sayre-McCord, Geoffrey. 1988. "Moral Theory and Explanatory Impotence." *Midwest Studies in Philosophy* 12: 433–457.

———. 1991. "Being a Realist about Relativism (in Ethics)." *Philosophical Studies* 61: 155–176.

Smith, Michael. 1994. *The Moral Problem.* Oxford: Blackwell.

Stevenson, Charles. 1937. "The Emotive Meaning of Ethical Terms." *Mind* 46: 14–31.

Sturgeon, Nicholas. 1985. "Moral Explanations." In *Morality, Reason, and Truth,* ed. David Copp and David Zimmerman, 49–78. Totowa, N.J.: Rowman and Allanheld.

Wong, David. 1984. *Moral Relativity.* Berkeley: University of California Press.

CHAPTER 2

THEOLOGICAL VOLUNTARISM

PHILIP L. QUINN

THEOLOGICAL voluntarism may be understood initially as a metaethical conception according to which ethics depends, at least in part, on something about God's will. Recent discussions of this conception have focused on the particular form it takes in divine command metaethics. According to a divine command conception, ethics depends, at least in part, on God's commands. It seems plausible to begin with the assumption, which is open to later refinement, that divine command theory is a species of theological voluntarism. If divine commands are expressions of some aspect of God's will, divine command theory is a specific kind of theological voluntarism. But if the possibility that ethics depends on God's will in some way not involving divine commands is not precluded, it remains an open question whether there are other species of theological voluntarism.

Most contemporary analytic philosophers do not accept divine command metaethics or any other kind of theological voluntarism. During the last three decades of the twentieth century, however, there was a revival of interest in divine command theory among analytic philosophers of religion. I think the upshot of this revival is support for the conclusion that a particular version of divine command metaethics is, from a philosophical point of view, a live option for theists of a certain sort. My aim in this essay is to argue for that conclusion.

The essay has seven sections. In the first, I rehearse some arguments internal to Christian theism that constitute a cumulative case for theological voluntarism. The second section presents the principles of a divine command theory of obligation and attempts to justify the theoretical decisions that lie behind my choice to formulate the theory in the way I do. In the third section, I set forth what I take to be the most powerful objection to this theory; it is a challenge adapted for application to my theory from a line of thought found in Plato's *Euthyphro*. The fourth section adds to the divine command theory of obligation a theistic account of ethical goodness according to which it depends on God but not on God's commands or will. In the fifth section, I defend the theory developed in the second and fourth sections against two objections that I find it easier to dispose of than the Euthyphro Objection but worth considering nevertheless because many people find them troublesome. The sixth section contains my defense of the theory against the Euthyphro Objection and against one further objection to which that defense gives rise. I note, however, that there is some tension between this defense and one of the strands in the cumulative case for theological voluntarism that is internal to Christian theism. So, in the seventh section, I try to resolve this tension by deliberating about a modernized version of the story of the *akedah*, the binding of Isaac, found in Genesis 22.

1. A CHRISTIAN CASE FOR THEOLOGICAL VOLUNTARISM

The argument for theological voluntarism from within Christian theism that I summarize in this section is a cumulative case argument with four parts. Cumulative case arguments are typically described in analogical terms. For example, the parts of a cumulative case support its conclusion in the way the legs of a chair support the weight of a seated person. No single leg can support all the weight, but the four legs together do the job. Similarly, all four parts of my cumulative case taken together lend considerable support to theological voluntarism, even though each of them on its own only gives it fairly weak support. The argument is internal to Christian theism in the sense that some of its premises are drawn from sources Christians do not share with nontheists or even with theists generally, and no attempt is made to support such premises with materials from sources shared by all theists or by theists and nontheists alike. I have discussed various parts of this case in greater detail in previous publications (see Quinn, 1990, 1992, 2000). Nevertheless, it seems to me important for two reasons to rehearse them, if only briefly, in this essay. First, they help to make it clear why theological voluntarism is, at least other things being equal, an attractive option for Christian theists. And, second, as I will show later on, there is some tension between parts of my case and views I shall endorse when I defend a divine command theory. I must resolve this tension if my defense is to be fully successful, and so I need to be explicit from the outset about how the tension is generated.

Before I provide a sketch of the cumulative case, let me issue four disclaimers. I do not claim that the four parts of my cumulative case exhaust the support for theological voluntarism to be found within Christianity. I leave open the question of whether further support for theological voluntarism can be derived from themes in Christian theory or practice other than those to which I appeal. Nor do I claim that the case for theological voluntarism is stronger than any case that might be made within Christianity for a rival conception of ethics such as natural law theory. I also leave open the question of how the case for theological voluntarism fares in comparison to any cases for competitors that might be constructed. I make no claims about whether similar cases for theological voluntarism can be built within Judaism or Islam. I leave open the question of whether theological voluntarism can be supported from within the traditions of either of the other two major monotheisms. And I make no claims about whether theological voluntarism can only be supported from within the perspective of a particular religion. I also leave open the question of whether the distinctively Christian assumptions of my case can themselves derive further justification from sources such as natural theology or religious experience that do not rest on theological presuppositions.

My cumulative case's first leg, so to speak, comes from Christian devotional practice. According to an old saying, the law of prayer is the law of belief (*lex orandi, lex credendi*). No doubt we should understand the principle expressed by the old saying to be governed by an implicit *ceteris paribus* clause, since popular devotion sometimes contains elements that are superstitious or even, as in the case of some cults, wicked. Yet, other things being equal, what is professed in Christian religious practice is a good guide to what ought to be affirmed by Christian theological theory. It is clear that Christian religious practice strongly emphasizes the theme of conforming one's own will to the will of God. Janine M. Idziak has collected numerous examples of this theme from Christian devotional sources such as hymns and prayer books (Idziak, 1997). Theological voluntarism reflects this theme at the level of metaethical theory. Moreover, there seems to be nothing superstitious or otherwise flawed about this aspect of Christian devotional practice. Hence it provides some support for theological voluntarism in accord with the principle of *lex orandi, lex credendi*.

The second leg of my cumulative case comes from the Christian New Testament. It is a striking feature of its ethics of love (*agape*) that love is the subject of a command. In Matthew's Gospel, Jesus of Nazareth states the command in response to a lawyer who asks which commandment is the greatest. Jesus replies: "You shall love the Lord your God with your whole heart, with your whole soul, and with all your mind. This is the greatest and the first commandment. The second is like it: You shall love your neighbor as yourself" (Matthew 22:37–39). Jesus endorses essentially the same command at Mark 12:29–31 and at Luke 10: 27–28. And in his last discourse to his followers, reported in John's Gospel, Jesus tells them that "the command I give you is this, that you love one another" (John 15:17). So the authors of these narratives of the life of Jesus agree that the Christian ethics of love for one another takes the form of a command. If Jesus is God the Son, as traditional Christians believe, this command has its source in and expresses the will of God. Thus the New Testament's agapeistic ethics provides some support for a specifically divine command version of theological voluntarism.

The case's third leg derives from a Christian tradition of interpreting stories in the Hebrew Bible that recount the incidents often described as the immoralities of the patriarchs. They are cases in which God commands something that appears to be wicked and, indeed, to violate a prohibition laid down by God in the Decalogue, which is the list of the Ten Commandments found at Exodus 20:1–17 and Deuteronomy 5:6–21. Three such cases come up over and over again in Christian biblical commentary. The first is the story of the *akedah*, which involves a divine command to Abraham, recorded at Genesis 22:1–2, to offer his son Isaac as a sacrifice. The second is the divine command reported at Exodus 11:2, which was taken to be a command that the Israelites plunder their oppressors on their way out of Egypt. And the third is the divine command to the prophet Hosea, stated first at Hosea 1:2 and then repeated at Hosea 3:1, to have sexual relations with a woman guilty of sexual sins. According to these stories, God has apparently commanded murder, theft, and adultery or fornication in particular cases. Moreover, the tradition of biblical exegesis with which I am concerned supposes that God actually did issue the commands reported in the stories. They therefore give rise to some tough ethical problems.

Thomas Aquinas confronts the problems posed by the three famous cases in the following passage:

> Consequently when the children of Israel, by God's command, took away the spoils of the Egyptians, this was not theft; since it was due to them by the sentence of God.—Likewise when Abraham consented to slay his son, he did not consent to murder, because his son was due to be slain by the command of God, Who is Lord of life and death; for He it is Who inflicts the punishment of death on all men, both godly and ungodly, on account of the sin of our first parent, and if a man be the executor of that sentence by Divine authority, he will be no murderer any more than God would be.—Again, Osee, by taking unto himself a wife of fornications, or an adulterous woman, was not guilty either of adultery or of fornication: because he took unto himself one who was his by command of God, Who is the author of the institution of marriage. (*Summa Theologiae* I–II, 100, 8)

In this passage, Aquinas reasons in the following way. Because God commanded the Israelites to plunder the Egyptians, what the Israelites took on their exit from

Egypt was due to them. Since theft involves taking what is not one's due, the plunder of the Egyptians was not theft and so was not wrong. Similarly, because God, who is lord of life and death, commanded Abraham to slay Isaac, Isaac was due to receive the punishment of death all humans deserve in consequence of Adam's original sin. Since murder involves slaying someone who is not due to be slain, Abraham's consent to the slaying of Isaac was not consent to murder and so was not wrong. And because God, who is the author of marriage, commanded Hosea to take the sinful woman as his wife, she was his wife, and so he was guilty of neither adultery nor fornication in having intercourse with her. In all three cases, the divine commands determined the ethical status of the actions in question; they transformed actions that otherwise would have been wrong into actions that were not wrong. And similar solutions to the problem posed by the (apparent) immoralities of the partriarchs are found in the work of Augustine, Bernard of Clairvaux, Andrew of Neufchateau, and other medievals. (For details, see Quinn, 1990.)

Of course it is open to Christians to reject the assumption that God actually issued all the commands reported in these biblical stories. But even Christians who treat one or more of these cases as merely possible, rather than actual, may concur with the tradition under consideration in thinking that divine commands would, if they were issued, make precisely the ethical difference the tradition says they actually did make. It seems to me there would be enough agreement among Christians about some possible or actual cases of this kind to warrant the claim that Christian moral intuitions yield confirming instances for a divine command ethics. Hence a venerable Christian tradition of biblical exegesis provides some support for a divine command version of theological voluntarism.

My cumulative case's fourth and final leg derives from more abstract theoretical considerations involving the doctrine of divine sovereignty. According to this doctrine, God is sovereign lord of the universe in the sense that things other than God depend on and are under the control of God. Two reasons why Christians would want to include a strong doctrine of divine sovereignty in theology pertain to creation and providence. Christian theology customarily insists on a sharp distinction between God and the created world. Traditional accounts of divine creation and conservation assert that each contingent being depends on God's power for its existence whenever it exists. God, by contrast, depends on nothing outside of God for existence. So God has complete sovereignty over the realm of contingent existence. Christians also typically hold that we can trust God's promises about the future and our salvation without any reservations. Even if God does not control the finest details of history because of a logically prior decision to create a world in which there is real indeterminism at the quantum level or libertarian free will, God has the power to ensure that the created universe will serve divine purposes for it and each of the rational creatures in it over the long haul. Hence God also has extensive providential sovereignty over the realm of contingent events. A Christian theology will have greater theoretical unity if it can extend divine sovereignty from the factual realm of contingent existence and events into the value domain of ethics. If this extension can be pushed far enough, the result will be a theology blessed with simplicity. Because unity and simplicity are important theoretical virtues, Christians will want them in their theological theory if they can be purchased at a reasonable cost. Adopting theological voluntarism would extend divine sovereignty into the ethical domain. It would therefore increase the unity and simplicity of Christian theological theory. Hence the desirability of theoretical unity and simplicity in Christian theology provides some support for theological voluntarism.

The strength of this cumulative case for theological voluntarism derives in part from the diversity of Christian sources to which it appeals. Considerations drawn from devotional practice, gospel ethics, scriptural hermeneutics, and theological theory converge in supporting, from within a Christian perspective, theological voluntarism or a divine command version of it. The case is clearly not conclusive. However, it suffices, in my opinion, to show that theological voluntarism is a prima facie attractive option for Christian theists. Whether it is an attractive option all things considered will, of course, depend on how well it stands up to philosophical criticism.

2. A DIVINE COMMAND THEORY OF MORAL DEONTOLOGY

A critical examination of theological voluntarism is best conducted in terms of a precisely formulated theory. In order to obtain such a theory, some choices among alternative possibilities need to be made and justified. The chief points of decision are represented in the following schema.

(1)   Ethical status E bears dependency relation D to divine feature F.

We thus need to answer three questions. What is it in ethics—what ethical status or statuses—that is dependent upon God? How do these elements of ethics depend on God, that is, what dependency relation do they bear to God? And what is it about God—what divine feature, broadly construed, is it—upon which these ethical elements depend? I shall take up these questions in reverse order.

Since divine commands are usually construed as expressions of God's will, it might be thought that a theory formulated in terms of states of God's will would get at deeper sources of ethical status than one formulated in terms of divine commands. But attempts to specify the sorts of divine volitions upon which ethical statuses depend must grapple with the difficulty that ethical transgression is not in every respect contrary to God's will. Wrongdoing that an omnipotent being could prevent occurs, and so God is willing to permit such wrongdoing. So ethical transgression is only contrary to what God wills in a particular way, and it is incumbent on a divine will theory to spell out the particular aspect of God's will on which ethical status depends. This task introduces theoretical complications for divine will formulations that do not bedevil divine command formulations. Hence it might also be thought that divine command formulations are to be preferred to divine will formulations on grounds of simplicity. These and other considerations that bear on the relative merits of formulations of the two kinds have been extensively debated in recent publications (see Adams, 1996, 1999, pp. 258–262; Murphy, 1998; Quinn, 2000).

For the sake of simplicity, I opt in this essay to bypass the issues raised in that debate and to work with a divine command formulation. I shall not try to elucidate the particular way in which ethical status depends on God's will. Since my chief aim is to respond to objections, this choice will not be a source of bias, provided it does not make the objections more or less difficult to answer than they otherwise would be. To help ensure that it does not, I shall assume that what God commands is necessarily coextensive with what God wills in the relevant way. I thus deprive myself, for example, of what some commentators have taken to be an attractive response to the *akedah*. I cannot consistently say that, though God did command Abraham to sacrifice Isaac, Abraham was nevertheless never required to do so because God never willed in the relevant way that Abraham sacrifice Isaac. I thus endorse the view that divine commands, when they are in effect, cannot fail to express what God wills in the relevant way.

There are several candidates worth considering for the relation between divine commands and ethical status. In a divine command theory of ethical wrongness, Robert M. Adams has proposed the relation of property identity. He says: "My new divine command theory of the nature of ethical wrongness, then, is that ethical wrongness *is* (i.e., is identical with) the property of being contrary to the commands of a loving God" (1987, p. 139). Though I know of no decisive argument against this proposal, I do not find it attractive because it is ruled out by fine-grained criteria of property identity of a sort I consider metaphysically plausible. An example is the criterion that property P is identical with property Q only if whoever conceives of P conceives of Q and vice versa. According to this criterion, being ethically wrong is not identical with being contrary to the commands of a loving God, since many people, especially nontheists, typically conceive of being ethically wrong without conceiving of being contrary to the commands of a loving God. Edward R. Wierenga makes use of a relation of agent causation in a principle of wrongness he advocates. His principle asserts:

> For every agent x, state of affairs S, and time t, (i) it is wrong that x bring
> about S at t if and only if God forbids that x bring about S at t, and (ii) if it is
> wrong that x bring about S at t, then by forbidding that x bring about S at t
> God brings it about that it is wrong that x bring about S at t. (1989, p. 217)

According to this principle, wrongness depends causally on divine commands in the sense that God brings it about that actions are wrong by prohibiting them. And, using one or another of the various definitions of supervenience proposed in the recent literature, a theory could be formulated in which wrongness supervenes on some property such as being forbidden by God or being contrary to the commands of God.

I know of no conclusive reason for preferring to explicate the dependency relation in question in terms of causality rather than supervenience or vice versa. Hence I wish to leave both these options open. Following the lead of those philosophers who speak of right-making or wrong-making characteristics, I shall think of divine commands making it the case that actions have ethical status, leaving open the question of whether the making at issue is the determination of causal production or the determination of supervenience. So I opt to understand the dependency relation that ethical status bears to divine commands in terms of divine commands being makers of ethical status. Thus actions might be made wrong either in virtue of the supervenience of wrongness on being divinely prohibited or in virtue of God causing them to be wrong by prohibiting them.

The theory I shall defend holds that the ethical statuses constitutive of deontology depend on divine commands. As it is usually understood, deontology works with three main concepts: rightness, wrongness, and obligation. Any two of these concepts can be defined in terms of the third. I take rightness to be my undefined, primitive concept. Right actions are permissible; they are actions that, ethically speaking, it is all right to perform. Using the concept of rightness, wrongness can be defined as follows. Actions are wrong if and only if they are not right. Wrong actions may be thought of as actions that are ethically forbidden or prohibited. Rightness and wrongness are collectively exhaustive and mutually exclusive; every action is right or wrong, and no action is both right and wrong. Employing the concept of wrongness thus defined, a definition of obligation is easy to formulate: Actions are obligatory if and only if not performing them is wrong. Obligatory actions may be thought of as actions that are demanded or required by ethics; they are actions whose performance is ethically necessary. I adopt the customary assumption that obligation is a proper subcategory of rightness: some actions are both right and obligatory, while others are right but not obligatory. Obligation and wrongness are matters of duty. Doing one's duty consists of performing obligatory actions and not performing wrong actions. In effect, therefore, deontology is a system of requirements, permissions, and prohibitions governing actions.

As I have described it, deontology is only a proper part of ethics. Ethics addresses the large question of how one should live one's life. Since people need certain character traits in order to live well, a complete ethics will contain an account of the virtues. Ethics also covers the axiological domain whose fundamental concepts are goodness and badness. Many things other than actions—for example, persons, habits, and motives—are correctly described as good or bad. Hence, the axiological domain does not coincide with the realm of deontology. What is more, even when we restrict our attention to actions, the fundamental axiological concepts mark different distinctions than do the main concepts of deontology, according to many conceptions of ethics. Such conceptions allow for supererogatory actions, understood to be actions that are good but not obligatory, as well as actions that are bad but not wrong, for instance, in cases in which, forced to choose between two bad courses of action, one's choice of the lesser of two evils is permissible. Ethics thus has the option of offering separate accounts of deontology and of axiology.

At this point, I shall regiment language a bit by stipulating that my divine command theory of the deontological realm is a theory of morality. I do not claim that this stipulation matches ordinary usage of the term "morality" and its cognates among philosophers. Many philosophers use the phrases "ethical theory" and "moral theory" interchangeably. However, I do think it comes close to the usage of those who, like Bernard Williams, regard morality as a peculiar institution we would be better off without. For when Williams explains the peculiarities of morality, his discussion focuses on the concept of obligation understood in a special way (see Williams, 1985, ch. 10). So it is natural enough to think of my divine command theory of obligation and the other two deontological statuses as a divine command account of morality.

A topic that deserves some comment is why a divine command theory should be, at least in the first instance, a theory of morality. It seems natural enough to suppose that, when God wills in the relevant way and so issues commands, such commands function legislatively to lay down moral law in a manner analogous to that in which the wills of human legislators, suitably expressed in votes, say, enact statutory law. And it also seems natural to think of doing one's duty by performing obligatory actions and not performing wrong actions as being obedient to moral law. G. E. M. Anscombe has exploited these natural connections of ideas in her influential attack on modern moral philosophy. As she sees it, there is something amiss in the realm of morality. Her recommendation is that

> the concepts of obligation and duty—*moral* obligation and *moral* duty, that is to say—and of what is *morally* right and wrong, and of the *moral* sense of 'ought', ought to be jettisoned if this is psychologically possible; because they are survivals, or derivatives from survivals, from an earlier conception of ethics which no longer generally survives, and are only harmful without it. (1981, p. 26)

The earlier conception is a divine law conception. In that conception, Anscombe argues,

> the ordinary (and quite indispensible) terms 'should', 'needs', 'ought', 'must'—acquired this special sense by being equated in the relevant contexts with 'is obliged', or 'is bound', or 'is required to', in the sense in which one can be obliged or bound by law, or something can be required by law. (1981, pp. 29–30)

It is not possible to have a conception of this sort, she thinks, unless one believes in God as a law-giver in the way many theists do.

Perhaps Anscombe's conclusion can be successfully resisted. A Kantian conception of moral law might be thought of as a secularized replacement for a divine law conception. On such a view, one's own practical reason is a faculty of self-legislation; it imposes obligations. So secular moral theorists could try to salvage morality by becoming Kantians of some sort. Anscombe treats the Kantian conception with scorn. She declares:

> Kant introduces the idea of 'legislating for oneself', which is as absurd as if in these days, when majority votes command great respect, one were to call each reflective decision a man made a *vote* resulting in a majority, which as a matter of proportion is overwhelming, for it is always 1–0. (1981, p. 27)

But she does not provide much by way of argumentative support for this declaration, and it could easily be contested. Nevertheless, Anscombe's positive point is well taken. There is a natural affinity between the concepts of morality and the concept of divine laws. Divine law conceptions of morality are not susceptible to criticism of the sort Anscombe sets forth. There is a similar affinity, which is analogically based, between the concepts of morality and the concept of divine commands. Divine command conceptions are also invulnerable to this kind of criticism. The latter affinity seems to me to provide sufficient justification for thinking that a divine command theory should be, at the very least, an account of the moral realm within ethics.

Having completed my explanation of why the principles I propose to defend have the particular shape they do, I am now in a position to state those principles. In doing so, I adapt the form used by Wierenga in the principle quoted earlier but omit some of the technicalities that complicate his principle. The three principles of my divine command theory of morality may be stated as follows.

(P1)   For all actions A, (i) A is morally right (permissible) if and only if God does not command that A not be performed; and (ii) if A is morally right (permissible), what makes A morally right (permissible) is it not being the case that God commands that A not be performed;

(P2)   For all actions A, (i) A is morally wrong if and only if God commands that A not be performed; and (ii) if A is morally wrong, what makes A morally wrong is God's commanding that A not be performed; and

(P3)   For all actions A, (i) A is morally obligatory if and only if God commands that A be performed; and (ii) if A is morally obligatory, what makes A morally obligatory is God's commanding that A be performed.

One might doubt the claim contained in (P1) that actions are made morally right by God's failure to command that they not be performed, on the grounds that a failure to act cannot make something the case. But, as Wierenga insists, in some instances, failures to act can do just this. He notes that "my failing to restrain my companion can make me an accomplice, or my failing to vote in two successive elections can make me ineligible to vote (without reregistering)" (1989, p. 217).

Let me conclude this section of the essay with four points of clarification. First, I assume that God can command both act-types; such as worshiping, which are repeatable, and act-tokens; such as George W. Bush worshiping at a particular time, which are not repeatable. So expressions that pick out act-types or expressions that pick out act-tokens may be substituted for the variable letter 'A' in (P1)–(P3). Second, I take (P1)–(P3) to have the modal status of metaphysical necessity. For reasons that will only become apparent in the sixth section of this essay, I want to ensure that certain counterfactual conditionals follow from these principles. Third, I follow traditional theism in assuming that God is a metaphysically necessary being. And, fourth, for reasons that will only become apparent in the final section, I assume that God never both commands that an action be performed and commands that it not be performed. If God commands that an action be performed, God does not also command that it not be performed.

3. THE EUTHYPHRO OBJECTION FORMULATED WITH HELP FROM CUDWORTH AND LEIBNIZ

The most powerful objection to divine command morality is sometimes thought to be rooted in classical antiquity. In the dialogue *Euthyphro*, Plato has Socrates ask Euthyphro to consider the following question: "Is what is pious loved by the gods because it is pious, or is it pious because it is loved?" (*Euthyphro* 10a) Commentators have suggested that the two parts of the question correspond to the horns of a dilemma. It has the following form. Either what is pious is loved by the gods because it is pious, or what is pious is pious because it is loved by the gods. Some of the discussion in the dialogue turns on special features of the polytheism of Greek popular religion. For example, Socrates suggests that the gods might disagree in their attitudes toward things usually regarded as pious, some of the gods loving them while others hate them. He persuades Euthyphro that in that case there would be things that are both pious and impious if things are pious because they are loved by the gods. This suggestion seems to be a real possibility for the quarrelsome gods portrayed in Homer's epic poetry, but it clearly is not a possibility for contemporary theists. So the question needs to be reformulated if it is to be addressed to contemporary divine command morality.

A question that should be asked by theists who believe that God issues commands is this: Are actions commanded by God because they are obligatory, or are they obligatory because they are commanded by God? And there is, of course, a similar question to be asked about wrongness and being prohibited or forbidden by God. The dilemma corresponding to the first question has the following form: either actions are commanded by God because they are obligatory, or actions are obligatory because they are commanded by God. It seems that both horns of the dilemma have consequences that are unacceptable to the divine command moralist (see Joyce, 2002, secs. 1–3).

The divine command theorist must reject the dilemma's first horn. If actions are commanded by God because they are obligatory, then such actions are obligatory prior to and independent of being divinely commanded. But divine command theorists cannot accept the view that actions are obligatory independent of being divinely commanded, because it is inconsistent with their position that divine commands make actions obligatory. Actions that are made obligatory by divine commands cannot also be obligatory independent of those commands. My divine command theory's principle of obligation, (P3), is thus inconsistent with the view that actions are obligatory independent of divine commands. In addition, this view undercuts one of the arguments in the cumulative case for a divine command conception of morality, since actions that are obligatory independent of God's commands are not actions over whose moral status God has sovereignty or voluntary control.

So the divine command theorist is stuck with the dilemma's second horn and must come to grips with two powerful objections.

The first is often described as the arbitrariness objection. If actions are obligatory because they are commanded by God, then it seems that obligation is completely arbitrary, because God could, just by commanding it, make any action whatsoever obligatory, and no matter how horrendous an action might be, it would be obligatory if God were to command it. As William P. Alston puts the arbitrariness objection, "[a]nything that God should decide to command would *thereby* be obligatory. If God should command us to inflict pain on each other gratuitously we would thereby be obliged to do so" (1990, p. 305). Wierenga calls this objection the "Anything Goes" objection. He finds it expressed in forceful and vivid language in Ralph Cudworth's *Treatise Concerning Eternal and Immutable Morality*. Cudworth writes:

> divers Modern Theologers do not only seriously, but zealously contend . . . *[t]hat there is nothing Absolutely, Intrinsically, and Naturally Good and Evil, Just and Unjust, antecedently to any positive Command of God; but that the Arbitrary Will and Pleasure of God,* (that is, an Omnipotent Being devoid of all Essential and Natural Justice) *by its Commands and Prohibitions, is the first and only Rule and Measure thereof.* Whence it follows unavoidably that nothing can be imagined so grossly wicked, or so foully unjust or dishonest, but if it were supposed to be commanded by this Omnipotent Deity, must needs upon that Hypothesis forthwith become Holy, Just and Righteous. (1976, pp. 9–10)

So consider some foul and depraved action, say, torturing an innocent child for one's own amusement. According to Cudworth, if actions are obligatory because they are commanded by God, then torturing an innocent child for one's own amusement would be obligatory if God were to command it.

The other objection to which the second horn of the dilemma gives rise is that it does not allow us to frame an adequate conception of God's goodness. Alston puts the objection in the following way'

> For since the standards of moral goodness are set by divine commands, to say that God is morally good is just to say that He obeys His own commands. And even if it makes sense to think of God as obeying commands that He has given Himself, that is not at all what we have in mind in thinking of God as morally good. We aren't just thinking that God practices what he preaches, whatever that may be. (1990, p. 305)

Wierenga calls his version of this objection the "Depriving God of Goodness" objection. If moral goodness consists in obedience to divine commands, then to say that God is morally good is just to say that God always obeys self-addressed commands. But since there is no moral value in always being obedient to self-addressed commands, the divine command theorist is unable to maintain that God is morally good. Wierenga finds a variant of this form of the objection set forth by Leibniz in his *Theodicy*. Leibniz argues as follows. "Those who believe that God establishes good and evil by an arbitrary decree . . . deprive God of the designation good," for "what cause would one have to praise . . . [God] for what he does, if in doing something quite different he would have done equally well?" (1952, para. 176) Of course, since I have stipulated that the word "morality" and its cognates are to apply exclusively to the deontological realm within ethics, I must not put this objection, as Alston and Wierenga do, in terms of moral goodness. I must instead take it to be the claim that the divine command theorist lacks the resources to frame an adequate conception of God's ethical goodness or deprives God of ethical goodness, where ethical goodness is the sort of goodness that falls within the axiological domain of ethics.

4. A BRIEF ACCOUNT OF GOD'S ETHICAL GOODNESS

It seems to me the strongest form of divine command theory is one according to which it is only a theory of morality and is not also a theory of the axiological domain. Alston suggests that the divine command theorist should "fence in the area the moral status of which is constituted by divine commands so that the divine nature and activity fall outside that area" (1990, p. 306). If this is done, the divine command theorist will be free to understand divine ethical goodness in some other way than obedience to self-addressed divine commands and to hold that divine goodness thus understood provides a constraint on what God can command, rooted in the divine nature. This suggestion seems to show promise of yielding a strategy for response to the two objections that derive from the second horn of our updated Euthyphro dilemma. But how are we then to understand God's ethical goodness?

Alston makes a radical proposal. It is that we think of the individual being God as the paradigm or supreme standard of ethical goodness. He develops the proposal in the following way.

> God plays the role in evaluation that is more usually assigned, by objectivists about value, to Platonic Ideas or principles. Lovingness is good (a good-making feature, that on which goodness supervenes) not because of the Platonic existence of a general principle, but because God, the supreme standard of goodness, is loving. Goodness supervenes on every feature of God, not because some general principles are true but just because they are features of God. (1990, p. 319)

Alston points out that thinking of the concept of goodness in this way would parallel our thinking about other concepts. According to cognitive scientists, some of our concepts are structured in terms of a prototypical individual and a system of relations of similarity to it. Or consider the concept of the meter of length, before it was redefined in terms of the wavelength of radiation of a certain sort. It was then the case that what makes a certain length a meter is its equality to a particular metal bar in Paris. Alston makes the analogy with goodness explicit in this fashion:

> What makes this table a meter in length is not its conformity to a Platonic essence but its conformity to a certain existing individual. Similarly, on the present view, what ultimately makes an act of love a good thing is not its conformity to some general principle but its conformity to, or approximation, to God, Who is both the ultimate source of the existence of things and the supreme standard by reference to which they are to be assessed. (1990, p. 320)

Of course, as Alston recognizes, the analogy is not perfect. While it is arbitrary which particular physical object was chosen to be the standard meter, Alston is not supposing that it is similarly arbitrary whether God or someone else serves as the standard of ethical goodness. A point in favor of Alston's proposal is that it does not undermine divine sovereignty. On his view, though goodness is independent of divine commands and so of what God wills in the way relevant to commanding, it is not independent of God or other aspects of God's nature and activities. However, if divine goodness thus understood is to constrain divine commands so that they are not arbitrary, the aspects of God's nature and activities on which it depends must not vary without restriction across possible worlds in such a way that anything goes with respect to what God can be or can do. Such limits are part of traditional theistic conceptions of God. It is usually assumed that the divine nature contains essential properties that God could not lack and that there are divine activities that God could not fail to engage in.

Alston's proposal has recently been developed into a comprehensive account of ethical goodness by Adams. On his view, which he describes as a kind of theistic Platonism, God is the Good Itself, the paradigm or standard of goodness. Creatures, their characters, their motives, and their deeds are good in virtue of bearing relations of resemblance to God. Recalling the story in Genesis 1 according to which humans were created in the image of God, theists might say that human goodness is a matter of standing in relations of imaging to God. Adams emphasizes that the Good Itself is infinite and transcendent and so is to some extent alien to us and beyond our cognitive grasp. As he puts it, in words he first applies to the Holy but then goes on to say are also true of the Good Itself, "[i]t screams with the hawk and laughs with the hyenas. We cannot comprehend it. It is fearful to us, and in some ways dangerous" (1999, p. 52). Though the Good Itself cannot, for Adams, be utterly opposed to the ideas of goodness we bring to theology from other spheres of life, it can be at odds with our ideas in some ways. To suppose that the Good Itself must conform to our ideas in every respect would be a form of idolatry; it would be set up our ideas rather than God as the ultimate focus of our devotion.

Adams constructs a divine command theory of obligation that is set within the context of, and is thus constrained by, this theistic axiology. Within this context, God's character or nature serves as a constraint on what God could command. The morality generated by divine commands cannot be utterly opposed to the beliefs about morality we bring to theology from ordinary life. As Adams insists, "we simply will not and should not accept a theological ethics that ascribes to God a set of commands that is *too much* at variance with the ethical outlook that we bring to our theological thinking" (1999, p. 256). Hence we should not believe that God could command just anything. Yet the framework Adams endorses allows us to ascribe to God a set of commands that is *somewhat* at odds with the ethical outlook we bring to theology because its standard of goodness, being transcendent, is to some extent beyond our cognitive grasp and is also fearful and in some ways dangerous to us. So we cannot rule out the possibility of there being at least a few genuine divine commands that shock us. And this possibility is enough to keep alive what Adams describes as "our darkest fear about God's commands—the fear that God may command something evil" (p. 277).

I concur with Alston and Adams in thinking that the strongest form of divine command theory is a divine command account of morality constrained by a theistic axiology rooted not in decrees of the divine will but in God's nature and character. I therefore hold that theological voluntarism should not be extended from deontology to axiology. I think restricting divine command theory in this way gives it its best shot at a successful response to the Euthyphro objection. But before I spell out that response, I shall make a brief detour in order to deal with a couple of other objections.

5. A Defense against Objections by Bentham and Frankena

There are, of course, many objections to divine command morality other than the Euthyphro objection. I have offered defenses against quite a few of them elsewhere (see Quinn, 1978, pp. 39–64, 1979, pp. 313–323). In this essay, I cannot, for lack of space, cover all of this territory again. However, I shall respond to two objections that, as I have learned from my teaching experience, students find troublesome.

The first is that divine command theory is of no practical use. A remark by Jeremy Bentham will serve to motivate the objection. He claims:

> We may be perfectly sure, indeed, that whatever is right is conformable to the will of God: but so far is that from answering the purpose of showing us what is right, that it is necessary to know first whether a thing is right, in order to know from thence whether it be conformable to the will of God. (1948, p. 22)

Bentham's remark suggests that a moral theory will be useless unless it answers to the purpose of showing us what is right, wrong, and obligatory. Obviously, many theists will not accept the assumption that, for example, we must first know whether an action is obligatory in order to conclude that it is commanded by God. Such theists will insist that scripture, tradition, and even, in some cases, personal religious experience are independent sources of knowledge of divine commands. But even they should be prepared to allow that these sources do not yield knowledge of divine commands governing the fine details of our obligations with respect to such urgent contemporary moral issues as euthanasia, physician-assisted suicide, human cloning, and stem cell research. So divine command moralists should grant that their theory does not provide us with a complete decision procedure for obligation—a way of deciding or determining, for every action, whether or not it is obligatory.

However, my divine command theory does not claim to provide a complete decision procedure for obligation. It only asserts that obligation stands in a certain sort of metaphysical dependency relation to divine commands, that God's commands make it the case that actions are obligatory. It makes no epistemological claims, and, in particular, it makes no claims at all about how we might come to know what God has commanded. It does not imply that we can come to know what is obligatory only by first coming to know what God commands. Hence the concession that it does not provide a complete decision procedure for obligation is not a refutation of it. And since similar points hold for rightness and wrongness, the concession that my divine command theory does not provide a complete decision procedure for morality fails to refute it.

Moreover, it does not seem that failure to provide a complete decision procedure is to be reckoned a flaw in a theory of the metaphysical foundations of morality. Presumably, it would be of theoretical interest to learn that what is obligatory depends on God's commands, even if this knowledge were by itself of no practical use. And it is worth noting that, if it were a flaw, this would serve as the basis for a *tu quoque* argument against the sort of act utilitarianism usually attributed to Bentham. According to act utilitarianism, an action is obligatory if and only if its consequences have greater utility than those of any other action available to the agent. Due to finite human computational capacities, we are not now and probably never will be in a position to calculate all the consequences of all the alternative actions open to the agent in many circumstances in which moral decisions must be made and then to rank-order their utilities. When this is pointed out to act utilitarians, some of them respond that it would be of theoretical interest to learn that their theory is true, even if applying it to get solutions to urgent moral problems is often not a practical possibility on account of human cognitive limitations. It would hardly be fair for act utilitarians who rely on this response in defending their theory to object to its use by divine command theorists in defense of theirs.

The second objection to divine command theory my students worry about is that it is bound to be socially divisive. William K. Frankena develops it this way:

> However deep and sincere one's own religious beliefs may be, if one reviews the religious scene, one cannot help but wonder if there is any rational or objective method of establishing any religious belief against the proponents of

other religions or of irreligion. But then one is impelled to wonder also if there is anything to be gained by insisting that all ethical principles are or must be logically grounded on religious beliefs. For to insist on this is to introduce into the foundation of any morality whatsoever all of the difficulties involved in the adjudication of religious controversies, and to do so is hardly to encourage hope that mankind can reach, by peaceful and rational means, some desirable kind of agreement on moral and political principles. (1973, p. 313)

Though Frankena is, in these remarks, discussing views in which the relation between religion and morality is supposed to be a matter of logic, he would presumably have similar concerns about my divine command theory in which the relation involves metaphysical dependency. And, of course, Frankena is quite correct in pointing out that religious disagreement has been and continues to be a source of serious conflict. Rivers of blood have been shed in the name of religion. Nevertheless, there are three things worth saying in response to his concern.

First, religious disagreement does not inevitably lead to disagreement at the level of moral principles. A divine command theorist can agree with a nontheistic Kantian moralist on the principle that torturing the innocent is always wrong. To be sure, they will disagree about why this is the case. The divine command theorist will hold that torture of the innocent is always wrong because God has prohibited it, while the secular Kantian may insist that it is wrong because it involves failure to treat the humanity in another person as an end in itself. But disagreement at the deepest level of the metaphysics of morals or at the highest level of metaethics is entirely consistent with considerable agreement on moral principles. Second, not all moral disagreement is dangerously divisive. A Christian may think that Mother Teresa was only doing her duty in accord with the gospel commandment to love the neighbor as oneself when she devoted herself to caring for wretched people in India. One of Mother Teresa's nonreligious admirers may believe that much of the good she did was supererogatory, consisting of deeds above and beyond the call of duty. But if they agree that she did a great deal of good for others, their disagreement about whether some her good works were obligatory or supererogatory is unlikely to provoke serious conflict between them.

Yet, third, even though disagreement about religion is likely to lead to less moral disagreement than one might at first have imagined, it seems quite unrealistic to expect agreement on all questions of moral and political principle as long as disagreement in moral theory persists. However, as Adams has pointed out, nothing in the history of modern secular moral theory gives us reason to expect that general agreement on a single comprehensive moral theory will ever be achieved or that, if achieved, it would long endure in conditions of freedom of inquiry. As anyone who has taken or taught a course in moral philosophy can testify, the subject abounds in strife among rival moral theories. The conclusion Adams draws, with which I agree, is that "the development and advocacy of a religious ethical theory, therefore, does not destroy a realistic possibility of agreement that would otherwise exist" (1993, p. 91). If those who accept a divine command theory advocate it, they will not make the situation of disagreement any worse than it already is in our pluralistic intellectual culture. Hence, even if it is granted, as I think it should be, that divine command theory is a somewhat divisive point of view, this concession does not yield a strong reason to refrain from advocating it.

6. A Reply to the Euthyphro Objection

Let us return now to Cudworth's contribution to our updated Euthyphro objection: Consider again the foul and depraved action of torturing an innocent child for one's own amusement. Cudworth's complaint is that divine command theory has as a consequence the following conditional.

(2)   If God were to command one to torture an innocent child just for the sake of amusement, it would be morally obligatory for one to torture an innocent child just for the sake of amusement.

Cudworth is correct about this point. Given that I am taking my divine command theory's three principles to be necessary truths, (2) is a straightforward consequence of (P3). However, a refutation of my divine command theory can be derived from this point only if it can be shown that (2) is false. How might this be done? Cudworth might insist that it is impossible for such a foul and depraved action to be obligatory. Thus he might say:

(3)   There is no possible world in which it is morally obligatory for someone to torture an innocent child just for the sake of amusement.

For the sake of argument, I shall grant that (3) is true. Cudworth might then go on to claim that the divine command theorist is committed to holding that God could command such a foul and depraved deed. In other words, he might claim that the divine command theorist has the following commitment.

(4)   There is a possible world in which God commands someone to torture an innocent child just for the sake of amusement.

If both (3) and (4) are true, then (2) is false and (P3) is also false. So a divine command theorist who accepts (3), as I have done, had better be prepared to reject (4) and to offer some reason for doing so.

I think a divine command theorist who shares the view I have adopted about how God's nature, character, and activities constrain divine commands is in a position to do precisely this. The following line of argument is available to such a theorist. By a necessity of the divine nature, God is essentially perfectly loving. A being who is essentially perfectly loving could not torture an innocent child just for the sake of amusement and could not command someone to do so. Hence (4) is false, and the antecedent of (2) is impossible. But according to the leading accounts of the semantics of counterfactual conditionals, a counterfactual with an impossible antecedent is true. Therefore, (2) is true. So (P3) is not refuted by having (2) as a consequence.

This line of argument, which is adapted from Wierenga, seems to me an adequate defense against Cudworth's objection (see Wierenga, 1989, pp. 220–221). Brad Hooker, however, has recently argued that it has unacceptable consequences. Hooker first argues that a divine command theory has the following consequence.

(5)   Before God made any commands, there were no moral requirements.

I will grant, for the sake of argument, that if there were times before God issued any commands, there were then no moral obligations. So I shall not challenge (5). Hooker next attributes to me the view that "even before God made any commands there were requirements of justice (inherent in God's nature) that constrained what God could command" (2001, p. 334). This leads him to propose the following premise.

(6)   Even before God made any commands, there were requirements of justice constraining God's commands.

And Hooker then draws from (5) and (6) the following conclusion.

(7)   Requirements of justice were not *moral* requirements.

He observes that requirements of justice *are* moral requirements and endorses the principle that if they *are* moral requirements, then they *were* moral requirements. From these assumptions, he infers that (7) seems false. I agree with Hooker in rejecting (7). Since I have also agreed not to challenge (5), I must reject (6). But, says Hooker, to reject (6) is "to abandon Quinn's defense of the Divine Command Theory against Cudworth's objection" (2001, p. 334).

Hooker is mistaken about this. On my view, before God issued any commands, if there were such times, there were no requirements or obligations bind-

ing anyone, and so there were no requirements or obligations of justice constraining God's commands. What constrained God at such times were not
requirements of morality but features of the divine nature or character that made
it impossible for God to do certain kinds of things or to issue commands of
certain sorts. Hooker's error is to attribute to me the view that, before God issued
any commands, there were requirements of justice inherent in God's nature. I am
prepared to say that the attribute of being essentially perfectly just is inherent in
God's nature. But it is not my view that this divine attribute must be explicated
in terms of God's perfect satisfaction of requirements of justice or fulfillment of
obligations of justice. As the account of goodness I have adopted, according to
which God is the paradigm of goodness, suggests, I take God's perfect justice to
be, like other divine ethical perfections, primarily an axiological matter of who
God is and what God does. If there is a secondary sense in which God is also
deontologically just in virtue of satisfying self-imposed requirements, God is just
in this sense only after having imposed such obligations on Godself by self-
addressed commands. Hence I can consistently reject (6) without abandoning the
defense of my divine command theory against Cudworth's objection. Hooker's
attempt to rehabilitate that objection is, therefore, a failure.

My response to the Leibnizian part of the Euthyphro objection should by this
point in the discussion be fairly obvious. The objection presupposes that, since
the standards of goodness are set by divine commands, to say that God is good
is to say that God always obeys self-addressed commands. On my view, however,
the standards of goodness are not set by divine commands. God's goodness is not
a matter of obedience to self-addressed commands; it is instead a matter of God's
having a nature that is loving, merciful, and so forth and acting in ways that flow
from having such a nature. Because the axiology I endorse rejects its presupposition, the objection does not apply to my view. Leibniz explicitly addresses his
variant of the objection to those who believe that God establishes good and evil
by an arbitrary decree. Since my metaethical account of goodness is not committed to the view that divine decrees determine good and bad, the Leibnizian
variant fails to get a grip on my position. Moreover, given the constraints that,
according to my axiology, the divine nature allows us to place on what God could
do, though it is true that whatever God were to do would be good, it remains
true that whatever God were to do would be praiseworthy. God could not and
so would not do anything for which God would not be praiseworthy.

The upshot is that a divine command theorist who accepts the axiology I
have taken over from Alston and Adams can accept the second horn of the
dilemma in the updated Euthyphro objection without being driven to the unpalatable conclusions advertised by Cudworth and Leibniz. It might be thought,
however, that I have purchased immunity from this objection at a price I cannot
really afford to pay. I made an appeal to theoretical unity and simplicity in the
leg of my cumulative case for theological voluntarism that rests on divine sov-

ereignty. Yet I have endorsed a disunified metaethics. Its divine command morality is coupled with an axiology in which goodness does not depend entirely on God's will. A simpler and more unified theory would make both deontology and axiology dependent on divine volitions; such a theory would be a comprehensive and thoroughgoing theological voluntarism in metaethics. My overall position is therefore objectionable, because its case for theological voluntarism is at odds with the shape I have given my theological ethics in order to make it defensible.

In response to this objection, I begin with the observation that my appeal to theoretical unity and simplicity only advocated purchasing them if they could be had at a reasonable cost. It did not argue that they should be obtained at all costs. An example will indicate why the difference is significant. According to a particularly simple and unified account of divine sovereignty, God is not only the cause of existence of all contingent things but is also the cause of God's own existence (*causa sui*). But the doctrine that God is *causa sui* is open to a serious objection. An entity must exist and have its causal powers prior to causing the existence of anything, and so even God cannot bootstrap Godself into existence. Assuming that this objection is compelling, we must conclude that God is not *causa sui*. Hence the unity and simplicity of the account under consideration are purchased at the price of incoherence, which is too high a price to pay. So theology must learn to live with the disunity of an account according to which divine causation explains the existence of all contingent things, and God's own existence is explained in some other way or is left unexplained. Similarly, the unity and simplicity of a thoroughgoing theological voluntarism are purchased at too high a price if a thoroughgoing theological voluntarism lacks a strong defense against the powerful Euthyphro objection. In that case, a theological ethics that contains a divine command theory of moral deontology must learn to live with an axiological theory of another sort.

Moreover, the disunity of my metaethics should not be exaggerated. Though my axiology does make goodness independent of divine commands, it does not render goodness independent of God. After all, if God did not exist, the Good itself, the paradigm of goodness, would not exist, and so nothing other than God would be good in virtue of standing in a relation of resemblance or imaging to God. My metaethics makes both deontogical and axiological statuses dependent upon God, though they depend on God in somewhat different ways. Hence my position does not compromise the doctrine of divine sovereignty. And my case for theological voluntarism is not in this respect at odds with my own metaethical position.

There is, however, another respect in which my overall position does suffer from internal tension that I have not yet resolved. My response to Cudworth's objection may seem to undercut my reliance on the possibility of there being cases like those of Abraham and Isaac, the Israelites and Egyptians, and Hosea and the sinful woman in my cumulative case for theological voluntarism. Given that I say it is impossible for God to command someone to torture an innocent child just for the sake of amusement, it may seem that I must also say that it is impossible for God to command Abraham to sacrifice Isaac, impossible for God to command the Israelites to plunder the Egyptians, and impossible for God to command Hosea to have sexual relations with the sinful woman. And if I must say such things, the leg of my cumulative case that involves the immoralities of the patriarchs collapses and will bear no weight.

Of course, logic alone does not force me to treat all these cases alike. And my intuitions about them do differ. Consider, for example, the Israelites and the Egyptians. The analogues of (2)–(4) for their case are the following claims.

(8)   If God were to command the Israelities to carry off the possessions of the Egyptians, it would be morally obligatory for the Israelites to carry off the possessions of the Egyptians,

(9)   There is no possible world in which it is morally obligatory for the Israelites to carry off the possessions of the Egyptians, and

(10) There is a possible world in which God commands the Israelities to carry off the possessions of the Egyptians.

In order to maintain my defense against Cudworth's objection, I must hold that (8) is true, and I must also hold that (10) is true if I am to use this case in my argument for theological voluntarism. I must therefore reject (9). But I do not think it is unreasonable for me to do so. My moral intuitions already tell me that it is morally permissible for a desperately poor person to take a loaf of bread from a grocery store without paying for it in order to keep from starving. So holding that there are possible worlds in which it is obligatory for the Israelites to carry off the possessions of the Egyptians subjects my combined modal and moral intuitions to very little strain. And I have a similar reaction to the case of Hosea. Thus I can maintain my defense against Cudworth's objection without paying the price of seeing the leg of my case for theological voluntarism that involves the immoralities of the patriarchs collapse.

The *akedah*, of course, is a different matter. What is commanded in that story is human sacrifice. My intuitions press me strongly in the direction of responding to Abraham's sacrificing Isaac in the same way I respond to someone's torturing an innocent child just for the sake of amusement. But if I do so, the leg of my cumulative case involving the immoralities of the patriarchs is weakened, even though it does not suffer complete collapse. What, then, do I make of the *akedah*? I address that extremely difficult question in the concluding section of this essay.

7. ABRAHAM'S QUANDARY

As I have pointed out, the *akedah* has been the focus of considerable attention in Christian traditions of biblical commentary. It has been much discussed by Jewish commentators (see Spiegel, 1993). The story is particularly disturbing because, as one recent study argues, there is "nothing in Genesis 22 to support the idea that God could not command the sacrifice of the son or that an animal is always to be substituted" (Levenson, 1993, p. 16). And it does not seem plausible to suppose, as many contemporary commentators do, that the point of Genesis 22 is to condemn child sacrifice, for "it is passing strange to condemn child sacrifice through a narrative in which a father is richly rewarded for his willingness to carry out that very practice" (p. 13). However, I am not competent to contribute to contemporary biblical scholarship. So I shall discuss a version of Abraham's predicament meant to highlight problems it raises for contemporary divine command theorists. Adams provides an elegant formulation of the quandary we may imagine a contemporary Abraham confronting. The Abraham he asks us to consider is someone who, though he recognizes their collective inconsistency, finds each of the following claims initially overwhelmingly plausible.

(11)   If God commands me to do something, it is not morally wrong for me to do it,

(12)   God commands me to kill my son, and

(13)   It is morally wrong for me to kill my son. (1999, p. 280)

Which of these three claims should divine command theorists deny if we place them in the situation of our contemporary Abraham?

It seems at first glance that divine command theorists must accept (11), but this is not the case. They could maintain that Abraham is in a moral dilemma. As Adams explains this possibility,

> if God commanded Abraham never, under any circumstances, to kill an innocent child, but also commanded him specifically to kill his (innocent) son Isaac, then, it might be argued, it would by wrong for Abraham to kill Isaac, because that would be contrary to God's general command, yet also wrong for him not to kill Isaac, because that would be contrary to God's specific command. (1999, p. 282)

And, indeed, according to my theory's principle of wrongness, (P2), it seems that in such a situation killing Isaac would be wrong, because it is an action such that God commands it not be performed by means of the general command never to kill an innocent child, yet not killing Isaac would also be wrong, because it is an action such that God commands it not be performed by means of the specific command to kill Isaac. But this way out of Abraham's quandary carries with it a very high price. It requires us to suppose that God, who is the paradigm of goodness, is unwilling to treat either killing Isaac or not killing Isaac as permissible in the circumstances, by not commanding that it not be performed, in accord with my theory's principle of rightness, (P1).

And, in any case, this way out is not available to me. For my theory's principle of obligation, (P3), seems, by the same token, to say that in such a situation, killing Isaac would be obligatory, because it is an action such that God commands it be performed by means of the specific command to kill Isaac, yet not killing Isaac would also be obligatory, because it is an action such that God commands it be performed by means of the general command never to kill an innocent child. Putting together the apparent implications of both (P2) and (P3) for such a situation thus yields results that violate two assumptions I have made. Given that the right and the wrong are mutually exclusive, I cannot say that killing Isaac would be both wrong and obligatory or that not killing Isaac would be both wrong and obligatory, because I have assumed that the obligatory is a proper subdomain of the right. And I cannot say that killing Isaac is an action such that God commands it be performed and commands it not be performed or that not killing Isaac is an action such that God commands it be performed and commands it not be performed, since I have also assumed that God never both commands that an action be performed and commands that it not be performed. So I must hold that Abraham is not in a moral dilemma. I shall therefore assume that divine command theorists should not deny (11). Accordingly, Abraham's choice boils down to denying (12) or denying (13). Faced with this choice, Abraham gets conflicting advice from two great modern philosophers, Kierkegaard and Kant.

Kierkegaard's advice is to affirm (12) and deny (13). In *Fear and Trembling*, Kierkegaard's pseudonym, Johannes de Silentio, concludes that "the story of Abraham contains therefore a teleological suspension of the ethical" (Kierkegaard, 1968, p. 77). It is a suspension of the ethical or, in the idiom of this essay, a suspension of the moral, because God, by commanding Abraham to kill Isaac, exempts Abraham from a moral principle that would otherwise be binding on him. In the circumstances, therefore, it is not morally wrong for Abraham to kill his son. The suspension is teleological because God suspends the moral in order to achieve a special goal (*telos*). According to Kierkegaard, God's goal in the story is to subject Abraham to a severe test of the depths of his faith, a test that Abraham passes by consenting to kill his son when commanded to do so. It is worth noting that the teleological suspension of the ethical plays the same role in Kierkegaard's thought about Abraham that the notion of being the executor of a death sentence by divine authority plays in the thought of Aquinas. In both cases, the general idea is that God can, in particular instances, create by fiat exemptions or dispensations from moral principles that would otherwise be in force.

Divine command theorists who follow Kierkegaard's advice will find that do-

ing so brings with it a benefit and a cost. The benefit is that their resolution of
Abraham's quandary allows them to use the story of Abraham and Isaac in a
cumulative case argument in support of their position. The cost is that they must,
in response to Cudworth's objection, treat the story of Abraham and Isaac in the
way I treated the case of the Israelities and the Egyptians, not in the way I treated
the case of torturing an innocent child just for the sake of amusement. In particular, they must hold that there are possible worlds in which human sacrifice is
not morally wrong. As I have already admitted, I find this counterintuitive. Other
divine command theorists who share my intuitions will, at this point, have to bite
the bullet and insist that it is true nevertheless. But biting this bullet does not
seem to be out of the question for someone who regards God's goodness as
transcendent and partly beyond the ken of humans, since it is open to such a
person to trust that God could see to it that obedience works out for the best,
even if no human is capable of seeing how this is possible.

Kant's advice is to affirm (13) and deny (12). In a famous passage in *The
Conflict of the Faculties*, Kant tells us precisely what Abraham ought to have done.
He writes:

> Abraham should have replied to this supposedly divine voice: "That I ought
> not to kill my good son is quite certain. But that you, this apparition, are God—
> of that I am not certain, and can never be, not even if this voice rings down to
> me from (visible) heaven." (1996, p. 283)

Abraham will affirm that it is wrong for him to kill his son because it is epistemically certain for him that he ought not to kill his son. According to Kant, he
will deny that God commands him to kill his son because it is not, and cannot
be, epistemically certain for him that the voice that rings down to him from the
sky is God's voice. But since Kant puts his point in epistemic terms, it is open to
a rather obvious objection. For traditional theists, God is, as Cudworth mentioned, omnipotent. It is within the power of an omnipotent being to give Abraham a sign that would make him epistemically certain that he has been commanded by that being to kill his son. Hence it is possible for God to give Abraham
a sign that would make him epistemically certain that he has been commanded
by God to kill his son. There is, however, a fairly direct response to this objection.
Even if it is within the power of an omnipotent being to torture an innocent
child just for the sake of amusement, it does not follow that it is possible for
God, who is both omnipotent and essentially loving, to torture an innocent child
just for the sake of amusement. Similarly, even granted that it is within the power
of an omnipotent being to give Abraham a sign of the kind in question, it does
not follow that it is possible for God, who is both omnipotent and essentially
loving, to give Abraham such a sign. So divine command theorists who take Kant's
advice can successfully resist the conclusion that it is possible for God to give

Abraham a sign that would make him epistemically certain that he has been commanded by God to kill his son.

Benefit and cost will be reversed if divine command theorists follow Kant rather than Kierkegaard. The benefit is that, in response to Cudworth's objection, they may treat the story of Abraham and Isaac in the way I treated the case of torturing an innocent child just for the sake of amusement and endorse the intuitively appealing view that there is no possible world in which human sacrifice is not morally wrong. The cost is that they may not use the story of Abraham and Isaac in a cumulative case argument for their view. They must acknowledge that the leg of the cumulative case that involves the immoralities of the patriarchs is weakened, even though it does not collapse, as a result.

Which guide should divine command theorists follow, Kierkegaard or Kant? My guess is that divine command theorists will, as a matter of fact, divide on this topic, some favoring Kierkegaard while others favor Kant. The issue seems to me to be one on which reasonable people may legitimately disagree. Abraham's quandary is a hard case; there are benefits and costs associated with both options; and there is room for reasonable disagreement about how to weigh them up. You pay your money, and you take your choice. I think a divine theorist could reasonably exercise either option. As I see it, the success of the defense of my divine command theory of morality that I have offered is independent of a divine command theorist's choice on that issue. So I conclude that my defense is, as far as it goes, successful both for divine command theorists who choose to be Kierkegaardians (or Thomists) about Abraham's quandary and for those who opt for the Kantian alternative on this point.

REFERENCES

Adams, Robert M. 1987. "Divine Command Metaethics Modified Again." In Robert M. Adams, *The Virtue of Faith and Other Essays in Philosophical Theology*, 128–143. New York and Oxford: Oxford University Press.

———. 1993. "Religious Ethics in a Pluralistic Society." In *Prospects for a Common Morality*, ed. Gene Outka and John P. Reeder, Jr., 93–113. Princeton, N.J.: Princeton University Press.

———. 1996. "The Concept of a Divine Command." In *Religion and Morality*, ed. D. Z. Phillips, 59–80. New York: St. Martin's Press.

———. 1999. *Finite and Infinite Goods: A Framework for Ethics*. Oxford: Oxford University Press.

Alston, William P. 1990. "Some Suggestions for Divine Command Theorists." In *Christian Theism and the Problems of Philosophy*, ed. Michael D. Beaty, 303–326. Notre Dame, Ind.: University of Notre Dame Press.

Anscombe, G. E. M. 1981. "Modern Moral Philosophy." In *Ethics, Religion and Politics: Collected Philosophical Papers,* 3:26–42. Minneapolis: University of Minnesota Press.

Bentham, Jeremy. [1789]. 1948. *An Introduction to the Principles of Morals and Legislation.* New York: Hafner.

Cudworth, Ralph. [1731]. 1976. *A Treatise Concerning Eternal and Immutable Morality.* New York: Garland.

Frankena, William K. 1973. "Is Morality Logically Dependent on Religion?" In *Religion and Morality,* ed. Gene Outka and John P. Reeder, Jr., 295–317. Garden City, N.J.: Doubleday.

Hooker, Brad. 2001. "Cudworth and Quinn." *Analysis* 61: 333–335.

Idziak, Janine M. 1997. "Divine Command Ethics." In *A Companion to Philosophy of Religion,* ed. Philip L. Quinn and Charles Taliaferro, 453–459. Oxford: Blackwell.

Joyce, Richard. 2002. "Theistic Ethics and the Euthyphro Dilemma." *Journal of Religious Ethics* 30: 49–75.

Kant, Immanuel. [1798]. 1996. *The Conflict of the Faculties.* In Immanuel Kant, *Religion and Rational Theology,* ed. Allen W. Wood and George di Giovanni, 233–327. Cambridge: Cambridge University Press.

Kierkegaard, Søren. [1843]. 1968. *Fear and Trembling.* In Søren Kierkegaard, *Fear and Trembling and The Sickness Unto Death.* Trans. Walter Lowrie. Princeton, N.J.: Princeton University Press.

Leibniz, Gottfried W. [1710]. 1952. *Theodicy.* Trans. E. M. Huggard. London: Routledge and Kegan Paul.

Levenson, Jon D. 1993. *The Death and Resurrection of the Beloved Son: The Transformation of Child Sacrifice in Judaism and Christianity.* New Haven, Conn.: Yale University Press.

Murphy, Mark. 1998. "Divine Command, Divine Will, and Moral Obligation." *Faith and Philosophy* 15: 3–27.

Quinn, Philip L. 1978. *Divine Commands and Moral Requirements.* Oxford: Clarendon Press.

———. 1979. "Divine Command Ethics: A Causal Theory." In *Divine Command Morality: Historical and Contemporary Readings,* ed. Janine M. Idziak, 305–325. New York: Edwin Mellen Press.

———. 1990. "The Recent Revival of Divine Command Ethics." *Philosophy and Phenomenological Research* 50, supp. (fall): 345–365.

———. 1992. "The Primacy of God's Will in Christian Ethics." In *Philosophical Perspectives,* vol. 6, *Ethics,* ed. James E. Tomberlin, 493–513. Atascadero, Calif.: Ridgeview.

———. 2000. "Divine Command Theory." In *The Blackwell Guide to Ethical Theory,* ed. Hugh LaFollette, 53–73. Oxford: Blackwell.

Spiegel, Shalom. 1993. *The Last Trial: On the Legends and Lore of the Command to Abraham to Offer Isaac as a Sacrifice: The Akedah.* Trans. Judah Goldin. Woodstock, Vt.: Jewish Lights.

Wierenga, Edward R. 1989. *The Nature of God: An Inquiry into Divine Attributes.* Ithaca, N.Y.: Cornell University Press.

Williams, Bernard. 1985. *Ethics and the Limits of Philosophy.* Cambridge, Mass.: Harvard University Press.

CHAPTER 3

ETHICAL NATURALISM

NICHOLAS L. STURGEON

THE term "ethical naturalism" has been used by philosophers as a name for a number of quite different views, only a few of which are the topic of this essay. Philosophers writing about ethics standardly draw a distinction between first-order and second-order questions. First-order questions are about which actions are right or wrong, which actions, character traits, and institutions good or bad, and the like. Second-order questions are about the status of the first-order questions: what their subject matter is, whether they have objective answers, what kind of evidence is relevant in addressing them. Most of the doctrines called "naturalism," including the ones on which I shall focus, fall in the second of these categories, though not all do. To begin with several that I shall identify only to put aside, the ancient sophists initiated a debate about whether morality exists by nature or by convention, and the term "naturalism" can of course be used for view that the correct answer is "by nature." Although this dispute is hard to pin down, it is presumably a second-order one. A related view—a first-order doctrine, and perhaps the one introductory students most often think of when introduced to the term—is that moral goodness or rightness consists in following nature, or in acting according to nature. This rather vague thesis, too, is one with a long philosophical pedigree. As Joseph Butler noted, it could mean, a bit more precisely, either that virtuous actions are ones that conform (in some sense to be explained) to the nature of things, or that they are the ones that conform more specifically to human nature. The Stoics held both versions of this view; Butler followed Aristotle in emphasizing a view of the latter sort (Butler, 1900, Preface and Sermons 1–3).

1. "Ethical Naturalism": The Standard Definition

For the last century of philosophical discussion, however, the term has most often been used to name a different doctrine, a second-order one, addressing a different issue. That issue is whether values and obligations, especially moral values and moral obligations, fit into a scientifically based, naturalistic view of the world. Ethical naturalism is understood as the view that they do. It holds, more specifically, (a) that such ethical properties as the goodness of persons, character traits, and other things, and such as the rightness or wrongness of actions, are natural properties of the same general sort as properties investigated by the sciences, and (b) that they are to be investigated in the same general way that we investigate those properties. It should be clear even from this preliminary statement of the doctrine that understanding it will depend heavily on understanding just what is to count as a naturalistic view of the world, or as a natural property, or as the appropriate way to investigate natural properties. It turns out, in fact, that in the debate about ethical naturalism these key notions have been understood in different ways. A naturalistic worldview, however, is virtually always understood to be one that at the very least rejects belief in the supernatural, so part of the issue under debate is what place there is for moral values and obligations in a world without a God or gods and without supernatural commands or sanctions. It of course continues to be a hotly debated issue in philosophy whether any such naturalistic metaphysical picture is correct. Whether ethical naturalism is a viable position can be of interest, however, even to someone who rejects a naturalistic metaphysical view. Theists, for example, sometimes object that an atheistic picture of the world leaves no place for morality and for moral knowledge; an ethical naturalist will reply that since moral facts are purely natural facts of the sort that can exist whether or not there is a God, and that can be known by unproblematic natural means, this objection is mistaken. So a theist who wants to assess this reply will have an interest in whether ethical naturalism is correct. It is probably true, however, that debates about ethical naturalism draw even more of their interest from the fact that many educated people, including many academic philosophers, do find a naturalistic metaphysics increasingly plausible in light of the impressive advances of the natural sciences in the last several centuries.

We can see why ethical naturalism, on this standard account of it, is different from the older doctrines I have mentioned. Some forms of ethical relativism hold that ethical right and wrong are fixed by nothing but social conventions; but since facts about social conventions are natural facts, these forms of relativism are usually considered naturalistic theories, in the standard sense of the term, even though they would fall on the "convention" side of the older convention-versus-nature debate. On the other hand, whether the view that morality exists "by nature" counts as a naturalistic view in this standard sense depends on the details. Some versions of the view that right actions are those that follow the nature of things, for example, construe the nature of things theologically, and so would not count. In addition, there are theories of ethics that do address the question of whether moral goods and obligations fit into a naturalistic worldview, and do so from a naturalistic perspective, but are not versions of what I am calling ethical naturalism. J. L. Mackie has argued that real ethical facts or properties—what he calls "objective values"—could not be natural, and has rejected them on that ground (1977, ch. 1). This is a view about ethics based on a naturalistic view in philosophy, but it is not ethical naturalism as the term is standardly defined. The same might be said about ethical noncognitivism, though the case is in one respect a bit trickier. Noncognitivism comes in a variety of versions; but in its original and standard formulation, it holds, with Mackie, that there are no moral facts— and a fortiori no natural moral facts—but adds that it was never the function of ethical discourse to attempt to state such facts in any case. The primary function of first-order ethical discourse, of arguments about better and worse, right and wrong, is instead said to consist in the expression of favorable and unfavorable attitudes toward things, or of prescriptions or of action-guides of some kind: in any case, not in the expression of beliefs assessable as true or false. For reasons I shall come to, some standard arguments for noncognitivism do not tie it to a naturalistic metaphysics: they present it, at least officially, as a view that should be equally plausible whether or not there is a God or a supernatural realm. I believe that it is safe to say, however, that virtually all of the philosophers who have defended this view have nevertheless been attracted to it largely because it promises plausibly to fit ethical discourse (though not, of course, ethical facts) into a naturalistic metaphysics. When it is held in this manner, then it is like Mackie's view in being held on the basis of a naturalistic worldview; but (whether it is held for that reason or any other) it is also like Mackie's view in not being a version of ethical naturalism.[1]

2. MOORE'S INFLUENCE

I have defined ethical naturalism primarily as a metaphysical doctrine (about what kind of facts moral facts are), though with an unsurprising epistemological corollary (that since moral facts are natural facts, we can know about them pretty much as we know about other natural facts). Many twentieth-century discussions of the doctrine, however, have taken it to include much more specific commitments in epistemology and in the semantics of moral terms. This is largely due to the influence of G. E. Moore, who in the first chapter of his *Principia Ethica* (1903) claimed to have refuted all forms of ethical naturalism, primarily by attacking what he took to be the doctrine's epistemological and semantic implications. Moore's argument is very dense and at some junctures difficult to interpret; it is also, by his own later admission and in the opinion of almost everyone who has written about it since the mid-twentieth century, confused in at least some respects.[2] But the argument has nevertheless been very influential, in ways that make it require attention from anyone interested in the debate about naturalism. Some of the influence has fallen outside academic philosophy. Moore introduced the expression "naturalistic fallacy" for the mistake—in his view, as the term suggests, an obvious mistake—that he supposed all proponents of ethical naturalism to have made; and although philosophers—by now realizing that the mistake, if there is one, is at least not so obvious as Moore supposed—have mostly stopped using this term, one still finds it in popular discussions of ethics.[3] But Moore also continues to influence philosophical discussion. For one thing, it was Moore who first defined the doctrine of ethical naturalism in the way that has become standard. And, more important, although no one now accepts Moore's arguments as they stand, a number of writers have maintained that Moore nevertheless accomplished something important, managing to point, however imperfectly, to difficulties of principle for naturalism that put it seriously on the defensive. So any assessment of naturalism needs to look at those arguments. As I shall make clear hereafter, there is certainly more to defending ethical naturalism than rebutting Moore, but that continues to be an instructive place to start.

Before I turn to Moore's argument, however, I need to note a peculiarity of his intended conclusion that has had a significant influence on subsequent discussions. This is that Moore took himself to be refuting far more than naturalism. He argued, to be sure, that ethical properties are not natural properties; but he thought that the very same pattern of argument that he used against naturalism also showed that ethical properties could not be "metaphysical" (that is, supersensible and supernatural) properties either. This means that Moore, famous as a critic of naturalism, was equally an opponent of supernaturalist views, such as theological theories of ethics. Goodness is not, to take one of his examples, the natural property of being what we desire to desire, but neither is it a metaphysical property such as conformity with God's will.[4] Moore even thought the mistake in these two kinds of view similar enough to call it by a single name, the "naturalistic fallacy," in both cases. And a few subsequent writers, taking this to be a key insight of Moore, have gone even further and called theological theories naturalistic.[5] In the face of this confusing terminological innovation—basically, extending the label "naturalistic" to any theory that was one of Moore's targets—I should emphasize that in this essay I shall continue to understand ethical naturalism to be the doctrine I have defined, that ethical facts and properties are, specifically, natural facts and properties, and that they are knowable in basically the same way that other natural facts and properties are known. I shall occasionally mention Moore's arguments against metaphysical ethics, however, when the comparison is helpful in throwing light on arguments for and against naturalism.

Even from this sketch of his conclusions, it should be clear why Moore's own view about ethics might strike a critic as rather peculiar: for he held that ethical properties are neither natural nor supernatural, and so have to fall in a category of their own. Since he then added to the sense of mystery in his account by saying that we could know of these properties only by a form of intuition about which little could be said, it is not surprising that one critical response to his arguments has been to accept the negative conclusions while rejecting his positive account. If goodness is provably neither a natural property nor a supernatural one, as Moore claimed to have shown, that might not be due to its being *sui generis,* as Moore concluded; it might instead be due to there being no such property at all. This line of thought has been crucial to some noncognitivists, who of course then supplement it with their own story about the attitude-expressing and action-guiding functions of moral discourse. This is one example of Moore's continuing influence even on critics of ethical naturalism who reject much of his own view. Since his own negative arguments are deliberately neutral on the question of whether a naturalistic worldview is correct, however, this means that this standard defense of noncognitivism is also officially neutral on that question. That is why I hesitated, earlier, to say that noncognitivism could be characterized as, officially, a philosophically naturalist view about ethics, while noting that its appeal has nevertheless been almost entirely to philosophical naturalists.

3. Moore's Argument

I can now turn to Moore's argument. Because of his commitment to consequentialism, a first-order ethical doctrine according to which the right thing to do is always to promote as much good as possible, Moore focused on the question of whether this central ethical property of goodness could be a natural property; but it has seemed clear to most readers that his arguments, if correct, could be generalized to show that no other ethical properties are natural, either. Moore took it as obvious that (1) if goodness is a natural property, then there must be some correct account of *which* natural property it is. To use his own examples, it might be that goodness is the same property as pleasure (or, strictly, as being pleasant) or that goodness is the same property as being what we desire to desire. In any case, on his view, naturalism will require that there be some correct property-identity statement of the form "Goodness = _____," where what goes in the blank is a term standing for a natural property. On the usual understanding of his argument, he then assumed (2) that any statement identifying properties in this way can be correct only if the two terms flanking the identity sign are synonyms for any competent speaker who understands them both; and he thought (3) that he had a reliable substitution test for synonymy. The test is that substitution of synonyms for one another should preserve the thought or proposition that a sentence, as used in a given context, expresses.

Armed with these assumptions, Moore argued that neither of his examples of proposed naturalistic identifications could be correct. The key to his argument was to apply the substitution test within a statement of the very naturalistic account being proposed. So, if "good" meant the same as "pleasant," the sentence "What is good is pleasant" would have to say the same thing, express the same thought, as the sentence "What is pleasant is pleasant"; and if "good" instead meant "what we desire to desire," then the sentence "What we desire to desire is good" would mean the same as "What we desire to desire is what we desire to desire." But Moore thought it obvious that these pairs of sentences do not express the same thought: that, in thinking that what is good is pleasant, or that what is good is what we desire to desire, we are not merely thinking that what is pleasant is pleasant, or that what we desire to desire is what we desire to desire. (He supported this by saying that it is an "open question" whether what is good is pleasant, in that we can at least understand what it would mean for someone to doubt it, but it is not in a similar way an open question whether what is pleasant is pleasant. So this is his famous "open question" argument against ethical naturalism.) From this he inferred that "good" is not a synonym of either of these expressions, and hence that goodness is not identical with either of the properties they represent. He claimed, moreover, that these examples are typical: that one will get the same result no matter what term for a natural property is tested for synonymy with "good." So goodness is not a natural property, and ethical naturalism is mistaken. (To get his parallel argument against metaphysical ethics, just consider terms for metaphysical properties instead of natural ones: Moore's claim again is that no such term will be synonymous with "good," and hence that goodness is not a metaphysical property.)

4. PROBLEMS FOR MOORE

How convincing should we find this? I shall mention three problems for the argument, of which the first two are commonly mentioned while the third is less often noted. (a) An initial problem is with Moore's assumption (3), that he has a reliable test for synonymy. For his test seems paradoxically stringent: if there are any synonyms, "brother" and "male sibling" must be such a pair, but in thinking that a brother is a male sibling we seem to be thinking more than just that a brother is a brother. So Moore's test seems to yield false negatives. There are ways of modifying the test so as to try to avoid this problem, but they make the test far less intuitive; they also invite the question whether, if the test is modified so as to pass this example, it might not pass some naturalistic definitions in ethics, too.[6]

(b) A difficulty that is more important (since most readers have agreed with Moore that none of the pairs of expressions in his examples are synonyms, whether or not he had a reliable test to prove this) is that his assumption (2), that property-identification statements can be true only if the terms flanking the identity sign are synonyms of one another, has in the last several decades been widely questioned. The most telling counterexamples are of apparent scientific discoveries, such as that heat is molecular motion or that pure water is H_2O (Putnam, 1981, pp. 205–211).[7] These look like reductive property identifications, and ones that are true by our best scientific account, but it is not plausible that the pairs of terms used in stating these identifications ever were or are synonyms of one another. So it seems open to an ethical naturalist who favors one of the reductive property identifications in ethics that Moore considers to say that her formula is like one of those, true but not true simply because the terms involved are synonyms of one another.

This reply provides a defense against Moore's objection to the metaphysical component in naturalism, the claim that ethical properties are natural. But it leaves a gap on the epistemological side.[8] Moore assumed that the naturalist would hold that we know the most basic ethical truths simply by seeing that the expressions in some proposed reductive definition for a key ethical term (such as "good" and "pleasant" or "good" and "what we desire to desire") are synonyms: that is how we might know that the good is just what is pleasant, or is just what we desire to desire. But since this second reply to Moore's argument defends ethical naturalism precisely by rejecting the thesis that any ethical term need be synonymous with a naturalistic, nonethical one, it leaves the naturalist in need of an alternative account of ethical knowledge. If we can't know the truth of any ethical principles just by knowing that certain terms used in stating them are synonyms, then how, exactly, are we supposed to have such knowledge? Moore himself believed, as I have mentioned, that our most basic ethical knowledge rests simply on intuition, but this is an answer unlikely to appeal to any ethical naturalist who relies on this second reply. It does not appear to be by intuition that we know that water is H_2O or that heat is molecular motion; these appear, rather, to be theoretical discoveries based ultimately on empirical evidence. So, if the ethical naturalist is to hold, as I have suggested a naturalist should, that our knowledge of ethical facts is obtained in much the same way as our knowledge of other natural facts, she will have to have to hold that knowledge of basic principles in ethics is also empirically based. I believe that this is correct, and I will say more later about what a naturalist can say about the role of empirical evidence in ethical thinking.

5. NONREDUCTIVE NATURALISM

(c) There is a further difficulty with Moore's argument that is less often noted. It is that his first assumption (1), about what an ethical naturalist must maintain, can also be challenged. Or, more precisely, it is ambiguous. Taken one way, it is unassailable; but taken as Moore appears to have taken it, and as many subsequent writers (including some defenders of naturalism) have taken it, it is more doubtful. What is quite certain is that an ethical naturalist, who holds about an ethical property such as goodness that it is a natural property, must also hold (to put the same point in a more roundabout way) that it is identical with a natural property, and so (to draw out a linguistic implication) that there is some true property-identity statement of the form "Goodness = _____," where the blank is filled with a term for a natural property. But from none of this does it follow, nor need an ethical naturalist believe, that we know of or will ever learn of *reductive* identities of the sort that Moore considered as examples. If goodness is a natural property, it is also identical with a natural property. That is because it is, unsurprisingly, identical with itself. In that case, too, there will also be at least one true property-identity statement featuring "goodness" on one side of the identity sign and a term for a natural property on the other: but, one should notice, if goodness *is* a natural property, then the identity statement "Goodness = goodness" fits that description. What Moore and many subsequent writers appear to have assumed is that naturalism must be committed to more than this: in particular, to the truth of some property-identity statement that has "goodness" (or some other transparently ethical term) paired with some clearly *nonethical* term (such as, in Moore's own examples, "pleasure" or "what we desire to desire"). They think that ethical naturalism must be, in this sense, *reductive*. But an ethical naturalist can deny that her view has this implication.

Her view *would* have this implication if we could make one additional assumption: namely, that we possess nonethical terms for all the natural properties there are. (For, in that case, if "good" stands for a natural property, as the naturalist claims, then there will also be a nonethical term that stands for the same property, and we can pair these two terms to get a true reductive property-identity statement.) But it seems extravagant to assume that we have nonethical terms for all natural properties. To take just one consideration, the paradigm examples of natural properties are those dealt with by the sciences (including, crucially, psychology: a reader will have noticed that Moore's two candidate definitions for "good" use psychological terminology). But a standard feature of scientific progress has been terminological innovation, in which new terms are introduced for properties not previously recognized, and there is no reason to think that this process is or ever will be at an end. So there is no assurance that, if "good" or some other transparently ethical term stands for a natural property, this must be a property that we can (or even: will be able to) also represent with nonethical terminology.[9]

This is one point at which it helps to remember that Moore thought that by this same pattern of argument he could prove not just that goodness isn't natural but also that it isn't metaphysical—that is, supernatural. For it is relatively easy to spot a difficulty with his argument against metaphysical ethics, a difficulty that the nonreductive naturalist will think arises for his attempted refutation of ethical naturalism as well. When metaphysicians or theologians talk about supernatural properties, they mention such properties as God's omnipotence, omniscience, and supreme goodness. Suppose, then, that we were to grant Moore that this kind of divine goodness was distinct from the metaphysical property of omnipotence and also from the metaphysical property of omniscience. Indeed, suppose that Moore could show it to be distinct from any metaphysical property that we could represent using only nonethical terminology. How would it follow from this that divine goodness was not a metaphysical property? That conclusion *would* follow if we assumed that nothing could count as a metaphysical property unless we had some nonethical terminology for representing it. But that seems an entirely unmotivated assumption. We would not think, about other properties, that they could not be metaphysical, simply because we found that we need some special terminology for representing them. It is plausible, for example, that we have no way of representing divine omnipotence without relying on some term from a cluster of interrelated "power" terms, but that would hardly show that omnipotence was not a metaphysical property. And, an ethical naturalist can ask, if there is no reason to think that we have nonethical terminology for all of the metaphysical properties there might be, why is there any more reason to assume that we have nonethical terms for representing all the natural properties?

6. ETHICAL CAUSATION

Like the second reply to Moore's argument, this third reply on behalf of ethical naturalism raises some epistemological questions. Just as someone might wonder what reason we could have to believe in some proposed reductive identification for goodness, if the reduction is not supposed to be analytic, so someone might wonder what reason we could have for thinking that ethical properties are natural if we lack the resources to say, in nonethical terms, exactly *which* natural properties they are. Here a good part of the answer, in both cases, can appeal to the apparent causal role of ethical properties in the natural order. Common sense agrees with a long tradition of philosophical thought in assigning ethical properties such a role.[10] Most of us can identify occasions on which we think we have benefited from someone else's goodness or been harmed by their moral faults. In Plato's *Republic*, Socrates is represented as arguing with Thrasymachus, and then with Glaucon and Adeimantus, about whether being a just person makes one's life better or worse: the characters disagree about the answer, but do not question that justice (of which they do not yet have an agreed account) is the sort of thing that might have one effect or the other. This matters in two ways.[11] First, if a naturalist really wants to use the identification of heat with molecular motion (for example) as a model for a reductive account of some ethical property, then it is worth noting that the grounds for the scientific identification lie largely in a matching of causal roles. There is a common-sense conception of heat that assigns it various causal powers (including what John Locke called "passive powers," dispositions to be affected in certain ways (Locke, 1975, 2.21.2, p. 237); and there is a physical account of a feature of matter that turns out, to a good approximation, to produce those same effects and to have the same causes. Because the approximation is not perfect, accepting the identification then requires some re-alignment of the common-sense conception. An ethical naturalist can argue that the same general pattern applies if we want to look for reductive accounts of ethical notions, with a similar intellectual pressure toward some refinement of our common-sense ethical conceptions for the sake of a better theoretical fit. She can also suggest that one reason the great historical works in ethics and political philosophy contain so much of what looks to contemporary readers like psychology and sociology is that the project of placing ethical facts in a causal and explanatory network requires some account of which places are available.

The same point about the apparent causal role of ethical properties can also help with the question of how ethical naturalism might be plausible in the absence of reductive property identities. For one thing, placing a property in a causal network is a way of saying something about which property it is, even if one lacks an explicit reduction for it. More important, a philosophical naturalist will believe that the mere fact that a property plays a causal role in the natural world provides a good reason for thinking that it is itself a natural property. I do not mean that we know a priori that only natural properties could have natural effects. For all we can know a priori, there might be gods or angels who produce natural effects in virtue of their specifically supernatural properties; and orthodox theists hold, in fact, that the entire natural world depends for its character and existence on a supernatural being—indeed, on the perfect goodness of such a being. Anyone who believed one of these views would have to take seriously the possibility that the causal influence of ethical properties, too, might be an example of the supernatural acting within the natural world. But philosophical naturalists do not believe in supernatural entities of these sorts and believe, indeed, that they have powerful philosophical arguments against the existence of any of them. And if, as they believe they can show, there are no *other* cases in which supernatural properties are efficacious in the natural order, it would seem anomalous to suppose that this was happening in the ethical case, absent the background metaphysical views that might explain how this could occur.[12] The apparent causal efficacy of ethical properties thus becomes a reason for taking them to be natural properties.

Since this argument relies on a naturalistic worldview,[13] it of course invites rebuttal from opponents prepared to challenge that overall metaphysical picture. It also needs to face objections, however, from opponents who may not want to take a stand on so large an issue, but who may think that they can identify some feature of ethical properties, so far overlooked in my discussion, that makes them unsuitable candidates for being natural properties. I will consider one objection of this latter sort later.

7. EXCEPTIONLESS PRINCIPLES?

If ethical naturalism is defended by the argument I have just considered, it can remain neutral on the question of whether we can ever find reductive naturalistic definitions for ethical terms. And that means that it has the advantage of also being able to remain neutral on another controversial question about ethics, concerning the role of general ethical principles. If we have a nonethical term standing for every property, that means that we will have a nonethical term for every property for which we have an ethical term. And in that case there will also be exceptionless generalizations linking ethical with nonethical terms. (For example, if "goodness" and "what we desire to desire" stand for the same property, then it is an exceptionless generalization that something is good if and only if it is something we desire to desire.) This is a noteworthy implication, because it has seemed to a number of philosophers that we are unable to formulate, and do not in our ethical thinking rely on, any generalizations about the good or the right that are entirely exceptionless. There is even debate about whether we should give weight to so-called *pro tanto* generalizations, such as that something tends to be good to the extent that it is pleasant, or that an action tends to be right insofar as it is the keeping of a promise.[14] Ethical naturalism as formulated by Moore, or even as formulated by more recent writers who add merely that the needed reductive definitions need not be analytic, is forced to take an extreme view on this issue, holding that there must, despite appearances, be exceptionless ethical generalizations corresponding to those reductive definitions. Nonreductive naturalism, by contrast, is not committed to one side or the other in this debate. This means, in particular, that it enjoys the advantage of not being threatened by our apparent inability to formulate plausible examples of such exceptionless generalizations.

8. Ethical Knowledge and the "Is-Ought Gap"

So far, I have offered several suggestions about the epistemology that an ethical naturalist might favor. For example, although it is doubtful that Moore has a reliable test for synonymy, neither is it very plausible that there are analytic reductive definitions for key ethical terms. So an ethical naturalist would be unwise to make the possession of ethical knowledge depend on such definitions. I have also suggested that any alternative epistemology for ethical naturalism should take advantage of the fact that ethical features appear to play a causal, explanatory role in the world, and in particular that they appear to play a role in causing (and thus can be cited in explaining) nonethical, paradigmatically natural facts. The mere fact that this is so is a premise in one argument for the second-order doctrine of ethical naturalism. Specific cases in which it is so, moreover, provide a way of inferring ethical conclusions on the basis of evidence, and so of coming to know them: it is not very controversial, to take just one example, that we draw first-order ethical conclusions about people's moral character on the basis of their behavior, and the ethical naturalist will hold that inferences like this can be a route to knowledge. (If this sort of knowledge develops in the right way, furthermore, it could underwrite reductive—though synthetic—naturalistic identifications for moral properties, and so provide a different sort of argument for ethical naturalism.) But I have not confronted what many readers of the standard twentieth-century literature will have come to think of as the central epistemological question naturalism faces. This is the question of how to infer values from facts or (in terms borrowed from David Hume) how to infer an *ought* from an *is*.[15] I have put off this question because I do not think that ethical naturalism requires a distinctive answer to it. But I should explain how the opposing view became so widespread among philosophers.

As I have defined ethical naturalism, all it requires, reasonably enough, is that since ethical properties are natural properties, knowledge of them should be obtainable in the same general way that we obtain knowledge of the other natural properties of things. What one takes this to imply about the details of moral epistemology will of course depend on how one thinks we obtain knowledge in other areas. A cluster of views that were highly influential among empiricist philosophers from the beginning through the middle of the twentieth century took a uniform stand on this question: namely, that the very meanings of our terms guarantee that certain inferences from our evidence to conclusions we take the evidence to support are in fact reasonable and warranted. Phenomenalism held that this was so for inferences from our subjective sensory states to facts about an external world; logical behaviorism held that it was so for inferences from observable behavior to conclusions about psychological states; and various forms of operationalism and instrumentalism made a similar claim about inferences from observable scientific evidence to conclusions apparently about unobservables.[16] Against this background, it is not surprising that ethical naturalism was commonly understood, by its defenders as well as its opponents, as having to hold that a similar thing is true in ethics: that the meanings of our ethical terms fix standards of evidence a priori, guaranteeing that certain common inferences from empirical, nonethical premises to ethical conclusions are reasonable or warranted.[17] (The epistemology already attributed to naturalists by Moore was clearly a special case of this one, moreover: if the terms "good" and "pleasant"—for example—are synonyms, then the meanings of our words certainly guarantee that there is a warranted inference from "This is pleasant" to "This is good.") Indeed, during the heyday of logical positivism and allied antimetaphysical views, a number of writers debating about ethical naturalism followed the fashion (or the pressure) of the times by putting metaphysical views about the nature of ethical properties entirely to one side and taking the doctrine to consist in nothing more than this thesis about the logical relation of ethical conclusions to empirical, nonethical premises. Ethical naturalism was thus understood at least to imply, and perhaps to consist in nothing more than, the thesis that there is no *is-ought* gap.[18]

It is important to emphasize, therefore, that a number of recent defenders of ethical naturalism have seen no reason to deny that there is an *is-ought* gap. The view that there is such a gap has continued for many to seem more plausible than the arguments sometimes proposed to establish its existence. One argument for a limited version of it, of course, is Moore's synonymy test, criticized earlier.

Another familiar argument is that ethical conclusions, because they are action-guiding, cannot be inferred from nonethical premises, which are not.[19] Besides relying on a challengeable claim about whether ethical conclusions are always action-guiding in a way that nonethical premises are not (about which more hereafter), this argument faces the problem that the conclusion of a valid inference may easily have a pragmatic property (such as being action-guiding) that is not possessed by any of the premises.[20] Arguably, the resilience of the doctrine has been due less to arguments such as these than to two other factors. First, the doctrine has always seemed plausible as applied to many examples. For example, although it is true, as I said earlier, that we commonly draw ethical conclusions about people's character from observation of their actions, it is fairly clear that in doing so we also rely on ethical background assumptions, about what sort of actions one would or would not expect from (say) a decent person. And, second, in a more recent climate of philosophical opinion in which doctrines like phenomenalism, logical behaviorism, operationalism, and instrumentalism have not only lost their status as orthodoxy but have been widely rejected, many have come to regard an *is-ought* gap as nothing special: they see similar gaps everywhere. For example, we draw psychological conclusions of all kinds (and not just ones about moral character) from what we observe of people's behavior, but it appears that we also rely in doing so on a background of substantive psychological assumptions.

It is still true that if we make one further familiar assumption, the existence of such a gap creates an interesting epistemological problem (though, for the reason I have just suggested, one that will be paralleled by a precisely similar problem in areas other than ethics). The additional assumption is the very traditional doctrine of foundationalism about propositional knowledge. This doctrine makes two claims: (1) that everything that we know is either (a) based by reasonable inference on other things we know, or else (b) known directly, without inference; and (2) that all of our knowledge of the sort (a), the sort based on inference, is ultimately founded entirely on knowledge of sort (b), direct knowledge. If we take the existence of an *is-ought* gap to mean that there are no reasonable inferences to ethical conclusions from entirely nonethical premises, then these two doctrines together imply that if we have any ethical knowledge at all, some of that knowledge must be direct or, to use another traditional term, intuitive. (For if we have any ethical knowledge by inference, that knowledge must, by foundationalism, be based by reasonable inference on things we know directly; and, by the *is-ought* doctrine, that will only be possible if some of that direct knowledge is already ethical.) Our options in ethical epistemology are thus reduced to ethical skepticism and ethical intuitionism. If assigning ethical knowledge to intuition is ruled out as too mysterious, as it was for most philosophical naturalists, the only nonskeptical option is to reject one of the assumptions that create the problem; and, so long as it was taken for granted that there were no comparable gaps in other naturalistic disciplines, the assumption that ethical naturalism was understood to reject was the existence of an *is-ought* gap. More recently, however, as it has come to be widely accepted that such gaps are everywhere, a number of philosophers, including a number of ethical naturalists, have thought that it is foundationalism that should be rejected instead. In their view, our reasoning in the sciences as well as in ethics involves the continuing accommodation of empirical information to a body of more theoretical views already tentatively in place, making mutual adjustments to achieve the best overall fit— a procedure that John Rawls called the search for a "reflective equilibrium" among our views of different levels of generality (though Rawls described the procedure only for ethics: Rawls, 1971, sect. 9). How, in either sort of case, does this give rise to knowledge? A variety of nonfoundationalist answers to this question are possible, but one leading suggestion is that knowledge is (roughly) true belief that is reliably produced and sustained. Proponents can point out that beliefs shaped by the kind of dialectical process just described will be reliably produced and regulated if enough of the beliefs involved are in relevant respects already approximately true, and that this will be true in ethics as much as in the sciences. This view also leaves it open for ethical views to be empirical—answerable to empirical evidence and in some cases supported by it—in the same way as are views in other naturalistic disciplines.

9. THE WRONG EPISTEMOLOGY?

Those inclined to skepticism about ethics may suspect this epistemological picture of being too permissive. To be sure, ethical reasoning can be shaped by empirical information if we also rely on ethical views we already hold and aim for the best overall reflective equilibrium in our views; but, by this standard, couldn't a believer in astrology or theology do a similar thing, thereby making those areas of thought into respectable empirical disciplines as well? (Of course, an advocate of astrology or theology might not see this question as embodying an objection. But I have suggested that the best argument for ethical naturalism depends on taking philosophical naturalism as a premise; and philosophical naturalists, impressed by the emerging scientific picture of the world, do in general regard astrology as fiction and are certainly committed to thinking of theology as a discipline without a subject matter. So they could not be happy with an epistemology that presented ethics as a respectable intellectual inquiry only at the cost of doing the same for astrology or theology.)

For a first answer, remember that, on the epistemology I have suggested, refining one's beliefs dialectically in the light of empirical evidence will produce knowledge only when the procedure is reliable, and it will be reliable in a given area only if enough of the background beliefs from which one begins are at least approximately true. So there is no implication that one can gain knowledge in just any area of thought by shaping one's views into an empirically informed reflective equilibrium. A subtler version of the question, however, might be this: won't it at least *look*, to any practitioner of this procedure, as if his starting assumptions were at least approximately true, and as if his own conclusions are correct, and his drawing them best explained by the very fact of their being correct?[21] Even if theological assumptions are as badly mistaken as philosophical naturalists claim, won't they look true to a committed theist, who may in turn think that it is the starting assumptions of the philosophical naturalist that are badly mistaken? Each can call the other's starting points mistaken, and can appear justified in so doing from within his own outlook. Is there no more neutral standpoint from which we can decide which side has the better case?

The answer to this important question largely depends, unsurprisingly, on what we mean by a neutral standpoint. When philosophers have often had in mind in looking for such a standpoint is an entirely a priori standard for evaluating, if not doctrines about the world, then at least research programs aimed at establishing such doctrines. Along with many philosophers who call themselves naturalists in, specifically, epistemology, I doubt the existence of a priori standards adequate for this task.[22] This certainly does not mean, however, that we have no broader picture of the world within which to address the question of whether theology, say, is as promising a discipline as the contemporary natural sciences. In particular, we can look at the history of these disciplines, including the history of their cultural roles—matters on which there is a lot of empirical evidence and also, at least at a sufficiently abstract level, considerable agreement among parties familiar with the evidence. It is on the basis of considerations such as these that philosophical naturalists think that the natural sciences, since the seventeenth century, appear to have become generally progressive disciplines, improving in their reliability at discovering surprising truths about the world, whereas theology has no such appearance; and they think that in making this case they are appealing, not just to standards internal to these sciences, but to ones that have been widely shared in other areas of thought. This is of course, as I acknowledged earlier, a controversial claim, and adequate defense of it would require a different essay from this one. Here I just note that philosophical naturalists do think such a defense is possible. Indeed, they are likely to point out that a familiar and characteristic result of beginning an investigation with an inheritance of partly theological assumptions, and thinking hard about how to accommodate a wide range of empirical information, is to move toward dropping the theology. (They will also of course need to say something about why this is not always the outcome.)

10. WHAT ABOUT DISAGREEMENT?

This reply quite naturally invites a further challenge, however: Just how successful, by these same naturalistic standards, does *ethical* thought look as a discipline? There are two quite different worries here. (1) First, there is a popular view according to which ethics (and more especially, morality) actually depends on such features of theistic religion as divine directives and divine sanctions. If this were so, then ethical thought would of course have to lack a subject matter if theology does. Even when recent academic philosophers have rejected ethical naturalism, however, this has rarely been their argument against the doctrine. In part this is because of the continuing influence of an argument derived from Plato's *Euthyphro* pointing out what is, at the very least, a deep internal difficulty in the view that the most basic ethical standards might depend simply on divine commands.[23] It is also, however, another mark of Moore's influence: for, recall, Moore thought that the same arguments by which he meant to refute ethical naturalism could be turned with equal effect against theological theories of ethics, thus showing that basic ethical truths could no more be theological facts than they could be natural ones. (It is of course open to theological ethicists, in reply, to adapt some of the points I have made earlier to parry Moore's objections to their view; but, in offering these replies, recent philosophical defenders of theological ethical views have not in general held that there could be no basis for ethics without a God.)[24] So I shall put that concern to one side here.

(2) Even if ethics is cut free from theology, however, there is still the question of how it looks on its own. For there is another familiar stereotype, this time one subscribed to by many philosophers critical of ethical naturalism, according to which ethical thought—meaning, here, the history of attempts to address first-order ethical issues—has been an obvious failure when compared with the paradigm naturalistic disciplines, the sciences. The problem is not just that there has been a lot of disagreement about ethics: it is rather, according to the objection, that in ethics the disagreement just continues, whereas in science disagreements get settled. This is an important objection. It deserves much more discussion than I can give it here. But I shall suggest some reasons why anyone, but in particular a philosophical naturalist, ought to be cautious about advancing so pessimistic an assessment.

A first point to keep in mind in thinking about this objection is that when issues get settled in the sciences (as, I agree, they often do), this does not mean that everyone with views on the issues comes to agree about them. Although there are contentious issues about human evolution, there are many that have been settled, including the question of whether humans originated through evolution by natural selection from another species. But there is hardly universal assent to this thesis; in the United States, opinion polls routinely show, in fact, that a large majority of adults disagree with it. What is meant, then, in saying that science has produced consensus on this topic? Plausibly, just that there has come to be agreement among well-trained, well-informed, competent inquirers. So, for a fair comparison, we should presumably ask what ethical debate has looked like when conducted by people who meet such minimum standards as being accurately informed, and well informed, about the nonethical facts, and such as being familiar with, and having given careful thought to, competing views and arguments. And one point that can be made on behalf of any view—not just ethical naturalism—according to which there are first-order ethical truths, and that can be made to philosophers whether or not they are philosophical naturalists, is that there has not been a long history of ethical debate meeting this description. Looking at the history of debate that plausibly comes close, and extrapolating to projections about what would happen if we tried this more often, moreover, can be reasonably encouraging. And there are some settled results, even in the face of popular disagreement: it is surely as certain as any finding in the sciences, to give one example, that there intrinsically nothing whatever morally wrong with a homosexual as opposed to a heterosexual orientation.

To philosophical naturalists, however—who are as I have suggested the prime candidates for being convinced of ethical naturalism—the defender of ethical naturalism can make an even more pointed argument, in two ways. First, a philosophical naturalist must think of the full and accurate nonethical information that we would want competent inquirers in ethics to have as including, crucially, the information that philosophical naturalism is true. For that is, according to philosophical naturalism, a most important fact about the world. And while agreement on this metaphysical position does not magically eliminate ethical disagreement, it does, I believe, pare down the reasonable alternatives in first-order ethics.[25] Second, and perhaps even more important in a quick argument such as the one I am offering here, anyone who thinks that a compelling overall case has been made for philosophical naturalism can, I believe, be forced into far greater caution than critics of ethical naturalism often display, about just what to take as evidence that ethics is (or is not) a progressive area of thought. For philosophical naturalists are, among other things, atheists. And this means that they are required to think, first, that (a) on an issue that is so emotional for many people that they find it impossible to consider changing their minds, and (b) on which views often seem so directly action-guiding that noncognitivist accounts of the language expressing them have been seriously defended in the philosophical literature,[26] and (c) on which the level of popular argument, on both sides, can be quite dreadful, there is nevertheless a fact of the matter. And they are also obliged to notice—a second point—that (d) on this heated issue the answer they regard as better supported is one that stands virtually no chance, under foreseeable conditions, of becoming more than a minority opinion in most contemporary human societies, and that (e) it is, furthermore, one on which they disagree, and expect to continue to disagree, with academic philosophical colleagues for whom they have both personal and intellectual respect. I list these points, of course, because it is so common to find philosophers taking one or more of them as a reason, even a decisive reason, for thinking some *ethical* issue unsettleable. I have agreed that the issue of how much of ethical disagreement can be settled is important, and that it is difficult. But I have also suggested that the history of ethical discussion, carefully viewed, affords some reasons for optimism. And, for the reasons I have just given, I think it quite certain that much of the pessimism about this question among philosophical naturalists, embodied in the stereotype mentioned earlier, is based on something less than a careful investigation of the question.

What counts as natural? This may be a useful point at which to return briefly to a question I mentioned early in this essay, of what is to count as a natural property. What I said initially is merely that natural properties are ones of the same general sort as those investigated by the sciences. But this is vague, and one might wonder whether we can do better. My suspicion is that at the level of general formulas we cannot—but the reasons why not are interesting. One common proposal has been that natural properties should be identified indirectly, as those represented by a specified vocabulary, such as that of the sciences, perhaps augmented by some common-sense terminology as well. But this is unlikely to be satisfactory. There are two problems. One that I emphasized earlier is that there is no reason to think that vocabulary of the sciences is or ever will be adequate to represent all the natural properties that there are. A different problem is that some of the vocabulary of the biological and human sciences—talk of health, for example—looks on the surface to be evaluative and so ethical in a broad sense. This will of course not look like a problem to the ethical naturalist, but it is likely to look like one to the opponent of naturalism, who will want a formulation of the issue that does not tip the scales toward naturalism quite so quickly.[27] And there is a problem of a similar structure about another common suggestion, that natural properties are just the ones that we can investigate empirically. So long as empirical investigation is understood as I have suggested, as involving a dialectical interplay with background theories already provisionally in place, this will look to most philosophical naturalists like an accurate characterization of natural properties, and an ethical naturalist will want to maintain that ethical properties are natural in this sense. The problem, however, is that this definition will look unsatisfactory to anyone who believes, as some philosophers have, that there can also be empirical evidence about the supernatural: evidence for the existence and goodness of a God, for example. It is not plausible that the success of this sort of natural theology would show that the divine attributes were really natural properties.[28] And someone might maintain, in the same vein, that even if ethical reasoning is empirical, it is nevertheless empirical reasoning about properties that are supernatural, not natural. I have explained earlier why a philosophical naturalist should doubt this, but my reasoning appealed to the overall case for philosophical naturalism, not to any quick or a priori definition of "natural property" that might settle such disputed cases. I suspect that the best we can do in such cases is to appeal to an overall picture in this way, and to analogies with other properties agreed to be natural (or not).

11. MOTIVES AND REASONS

It is worth keeping this problem in mind as I turn to the last problem I shall discuss for ethical naturalism, for it is one that reveals considerable disagreement about just which sorts of facts could fit into an entirely natural world. The objection is that naturalism is unable to accommodate the central practical role of ethics—and, more specifically, of morality—in motivating and providing reasons for action.[29] Mackie relies on an extreme version of this objection. He argues that our inherited, shared conception of morality requires that real moral facts (what he calls "objective values" or "objective prescriptions") would have to be guaranteed to provide any agent aware of them with an overriding reason for acting, a reason, moreover, that is in Immanuel Kant's terminology categorical rather than hypothetical in that it does not depend on the agent's contingent desires. And he argues that a naturalistic view of the world has no room for facts of this sort. A slightly different argument often pressed by noncognitivists focuses not on reasons for acting but simply on motivation, claiming that people's moral views have a necessary connection to motivation that beliefs about natural facts do not. As Hume, one inspiration for this view, puts it, "men are often govern'd by their duties, and are deter'd from some actions by the opinion of injustice, and impell'd to others by that of obligation" (1978, p. 457); beliefs about natural facts, by contrast, motivate only in conjunction with desires for various goals. Noncognitivists conclude from this that moral opinions are not essentially beliefs at all, but rather conative or desire-like states of some sort. Another option, of course, would be to conclude that they are beliefs, but not beliefs about *natural* facts.

In response, ethical naturalists typically accuse these views of exaggerating on the one hand the practical role reasonably to be expected of moral facts, and of understating on the other the practical role that natural facts can play. It is not plausible that moral opinions always motivate those who hold them. And if all that is true is that (as Hume says) they "often" do, then their motivational role begins to look suspiciously like that of more garden-variety beliefs: the "opinion of injustice" will deter those with a certain desire (to avoid injustice) but not others. There are several ways of weakening the thesis of a necessary connection between moral opinions and motivation to accommodate this and other objections, but the resulting doctrines do not always seem inimical to a naturalistic account of moral facts (nor are they always intended to be). It is also controversial whether moral facts need provide reasons for acting to any competent agent aware of them. Any claim that this is a plain a priori truth faces the difficulty that there is a history of skeptics who have denied it, seemingly without self-contradiction, and whose views find an echo in familiar currents of ordinary thought.[30] If there is a deep truth to be found in this area, it is likely more modest. On any plausible naturalistic account of morality, its role includes at a minimum promoting human goods about which people care a great deal; a central case will be resolving standard kinds of recurring conflict in mutually beneficial ways. It is, therefore, hard to imagine, on even the sparsest naturalistic account of reasons (i.e., that agents have reason to promote what they care about), that it would not turn out that typical humans would normally have reasons of considerable weight for promoting moral goods and honoring moral duties. I believe that, given a richer but still naturalistic account of reasons, and more details of human moral psychology, one can defend a less hedged version of this thesis; but even the hedged thesis is plausibly enough to satisfy any reasonable demand for a deep connection between morality and rational motivation.

It is also plausible, and recognized by most first-order ethical theories including naturalistic ones, that there is something special about moral motives. But it is far more controversial whether what is special about them must involve motivation by categorical reasons. In fact, it seems to me not beyond question for an ethical naturalist to recognize categorical reasons: for example, if one holds any naturalistic account of reasons, then it seems plausible that the natural fact *that one has a reason* to do a certain thing ought itself to count as a reason for doing it, and not just because one has a desire (if one does) to do whatever one has reason to do. In addition, it appears that the thought that one has a reason might motivate one even if one has forgotten what the reason was, and it is not obvious that this motivation should be ascribed to some desire (again, to do what one has reason to do) rather than just to the belief. It is often assumed that views such as these are not accessible to a philosophical naturalist, but when the case for this restriction is not just stipulative, it often appears to rest on one of the questionable arguments canvassed earlier: for example, that talk of such reasons does not appear to be analytically reducible to a value-free scientific vocabulary.[31] Still, most ethical naturalists have held that motivation, including moral motivation, depends on desires. They here understand desire broadly. It is not plausible that moral motivation could depend just on appetite or blind impulse. But desires here include reflective policies of action. They also include second-order desires, desires that are *about* the sort of desires one wishes to be moved by, and which can therefore embody a concern for one's own character and provide a perspective from which to endorse or resist other desires (including appetites and impulses) that present themselves. And they include not only altruistic desires but moral ones, desires to promote moral goods and respect moral requirements for their own sake: desires that can be seen as rational themselves, moreover, despite their noninstrumental character, to the extent that the *having* of them either conduces to, or is a component in, such valued ends as leading a fulfilling life. There seem to be ample resources here for recognizing moral motives as special without taking any reasons to be categorical.[32]

As I mentioned briefly earlier, some naturalistic ethical theories are relativistic, making one's obligations depend solely on one's society's rules, or one's own values, or one's own desires. Many readers see such views (often over the objections of their defenders) as deeply unsatisfactory, debunking accounts of morality. They are inclined to hold out for the existence of something supernatural (or, using Moore's special term, "nonnatural"), like the objective prescriptions that Mackie denies, because they fear that in their absence the only available accounts of ethics will be highly deflationary: if not Mackie's own official ethical skepticism,[33] then one of these relativisms. There is not space here to survey all the more optimistic naturalistic accounts of morality: especially if one keeps in mind that a naturalistic theory need not be reductive, their number is large. But I shall end by adapting a simple illustration from a surprising source. In a passage that not many philosophical readers seem to have noticed, Mackie concedes that all of the following could be true ("purely descriptively") in a purely natural world, entirely in the absence of anything objectively prescriptive. It could be that there is a single way of life that is appropriate for human beings, in that "it alone will develop rather than stunt their natural capacities and that in it, and only in it, can they find their fullest and deepest satisfaction." It could also be true, a fact "as hard as any in arithmetic or chemistry," that there are certain rules of conduct and dispositions of character that are similarly appropriate, in that they are needed to maintain this way of life. Mackie clearly has in mind, moreover, that the list of appropriate rules and dispositions would greatly resemble what most of us already thought were grounds for moral obligations and moral virtues. He is officially committed, of course, to saying that even in such circumstances there would be no real moral facts and no basis for distinctively moral motivation: it would still be false that there were any moral obligations or moral virtues. But a reader could be excused for finding his skeptical thesis, in this application, incredible. And, in fact, Mackie himself seems to agree, conceding that in this case that the purely natural fact that an action violates an appropriate rule could constitute a "piece" of its genuine moral wrongness, and by implication that a mere concern to avoid it for that reason could be a morally admirable motive.[34]

Mackie's stated objection to this naturalistic account of morality is that it assumes too uniform an account of human nature (1977, p. 232). One might argue in reply that an account recognizing different appropriate ways of life could easily be pluralist without being in any interesting sense relativist. More important, however, is that this objection to ethical naturalism is clearly an empirical one.

So Mackie's view seems not to be, after all, that a purely natural world could not, in principle, be a home to moral facts; it is rather that, in the natural world as we actually find it, the details are wrong. I suspect that many objections to ethical naturalism that are presented as difficulties of philosophical principle actually resolve into empirical disagreements in this way.[35] It is thus worth remembering that the empirical issues involved here are terribly complex, and that it is possible to defend more optimistic as well as more pessimistic assessments of human nature and the human condition. It is, in any case, a conclusion congenial to philosophical naturalism, that debates about whether and how ethical facts might fit into a naturalistic picture of the world often resolve into deep, difficult but obviously empirical questions.

NOTES

1. Another feature of the standard definition worth noting is that, although it makes clear why ethical naturalism is of interest mainly because of questions about how ethics could fit into a naturalistic worldview, it does not require that ethical naturalism be based on such a view. Ethical facts and properties might after all be natural facts and properties even if there were a God. If a theist views bond energies as natural properties, despite their ultimately depending in some way on God's creative will, then she could presumably view ethical facts in the same way, even if they are like other natural facts in depending ultimately on God's will. (This would not be a divine command theory: the dependence of moral facts would be on God's creative will, not what theologians call God's revealed will; see Adams, 1987a, pp. 128–143.) It is an interesting question whether this sort of position should be ascribed to any theistic philosophers in the history of philosophy. (Two very different but possible examples might be Hobbes and Butler.) Its claim to being a genuine version of ethical naturalism might be clearest in its epistemological implications. For, presumably, a theist of this sort who thought that we did not need to know theology in order to learn chemistry (despite God's being ultimately responsible for the bond energies) would also think that we did not need to know theology in order to know what is right and wrong (despite God's being ultimately responsible for that, too). And if someone holding this view came to doubt God's existence, this change in metaphysical view would presumably occasion no more doubt about right and wrong, at least in principle, than it would about bond energies.

2. Moore's argument is found in his *Principia Ethica*, 1903, pp. 1–17. Moore is quite critical of the details of this argument in a partially completed second preface that was not published until Thomas Baldwin included it in a revised edition of the same work (Moore, 1993, pp. 1–27).

3. In Wilson, 1975, the sociobiologist Edward O. Wilson declares that he is carefully avoiding the "naturalistic fallacy of ethics," which he describes as the mistake of concluding "that what is, should be."

4. The first of these examples is Moore's (1903, p. 15); the second is not, but it is one that clearly counts as "metaphysical" for Moore's purposes.

5. Thus C. D. Broad speaks of "theological naturalism" (1930, p. 259), as does A. N. Prior (1949, p. 100) (though with what appear to be "scare quotes"). R. M. Hare (1952, p. 82) says that it is best to confine the term "naturalism" "to those theories against which Moore's refutation (or a recognizable version of it) is valid"—and Hare takes Moore to have refuted supernaturalist theories. See also Pigden, 1991, p. 426.

6. C. H. Langford pressed this problem in Langford, 1968, pp. 322–323; Moore, 1968, p. 665, admitted that he did not know how to reply. R. M. Hare attempts to rescue the argument from this difficulty (1952, ch. 5).

7. Since Putnam and Saul Kripke (in Kripke, 1980) are prominent among the writers who have made this point about property identifications, a number of writers exploiting it have also explored the consequences of adopting the distinctive Putnam-Kripke line that such identifications, though a posteriori, are, if true, necessary: see, for example, Adams, 1987a. However, it is worth emphasizing that the key point, that terms can stand for the same property without being synonyms, is independently plausible and need not be tied to that framework. See, for one example, Harman, 1977, pp. 19–20.

8. This second reply will leave more than just a "gap" if naturalism is defined as it sometimes was by writers after Moore, as consisting *merely* of this thesis that Moore understood as its implication for semantics and moral epistemology, that there are reductive analytic definitions ethical terms. For, on that understanding of the doctrine, this second reply amounts to abandoning it entirely. I shall return later to this question of whether we can cross a supposed "fact-value" gap simply by appealing to the meanings of words. I should again emphasize, however, that in this essay I follow Moore in thinking of ethical naturalism as first of all a metaphysical thesis, about what kind of property ethical properties are.

9. Some philosophers attempt to get around this sort of difficulty by talking about the vocabulary not of, say, physics, but of "ideal physics" or "completed physics" (and so for other sciences). But they need to say more than they typically do about why we should think that any science could ever be "completed" in the way that they need. To mention just one problem, noted by Richard Boyd (Boyd, unpublished), there are on the usual understanding only countably many predicates in any language, but according to the best physics we now have, there are some continuous physical parameters. So there are (it appears) more physical properties than there are predicates in any language.

The idea that there may be natural properties for which we lack nonethical terminology is in fact a familiar one among philosophers discussing second-order questions about ethics. It was a common idea among noncognitivists such as Charles Stevenson and R. M. Hare that there are some ethical terms that combine the action-guiding role that noncognitivism takes as central with some descriptive, naturalistic content. It was also a common noncognitivist assumption that these terms for what Bernard Williams has called "thick" ethical concepts (such as being honorable or brutal or courageous) could be factored into the two elements, one describing a natural property in nonevaluative terms, the other performing a purely noncognitive function. But Williams agrees with John McDowell (McDowell, 1998b) that we may lack terminology subtle enough to carry out this factoring: he agrees, that is, that we may lack austerely nonevaluative terminology for representing the natural properties picked out by some ethical terms. This view has, moreover, been highly influential. See Williams, 1985, pp. 129, 140–142. My suggestion, of course, does not restrict this worry to the thick ethical terms.

10. There has been a debate about whether ethical properties really play the causal role that these patterns of thought assign to them. See, for example, Harman, 1977, ch. 1, 1986; Sturgeon, 1985, 1986a, 1998; and Thomson, 1996, pp. 73–91, 1998. The skeptics have now generally conceded that ethical properties at least *seem* to play a causal role, however, and that point is all I require here.

11. This point also aids the argument for ethical naturalism in another, more indirect way, by creating a problem for one of its prominent rivals, noncognitivism. Recall that noncognitivists agree with an ethical nihilist like Mackie that there are no ethical facts: what distinguishes noncognitivism is the thesis that it was never the function of ordinary ethical discourse to attempt to state such facts in the first place. It is an apparent problem for this thesis, that ethical discourse seems to include the cheerful attribution of causal powers to moral character traits in the ways these examples illustrate, and in this and other ways to treat putative ethical facts as explanatory. For, on the face of it, explanations involve the citation of allegedly explanatory facts. (This remains an objection to noncognitivism even if, as some of the writers mentioned in the preceding note maintain—and as Mackie, of course, would maintain—there turns out to be something wrong with all these ethical explanations. But an ethical naturalist will hold that they are not all mistaken.) For debate, see Blackburn, 1991, esp. pp. 41–42, 1993c; Sturgeon, 1986b, pp. 122–125, 1991, esp. pp. 27–30, 1995.

12. I have borrowed in this paragraph a few sentences from Sturgeon, 2003, pp. 537–538.

13. Thus although, as I pointed out in note 1, ethical naturalism as I define it does not require the truth of a naturalistic worldview, I do think that the best argument for the doctrine relies on philosophical naturalism.

The argument in the text was suggested to me by reflection on a standard argument for physicalism about the mental from the causal efficacy of the mental and the completeness of physics. (Indeed, if ethical properties are causally efficacious, there will be a similar argument to the conclusion that ethical properties must be not just natural but physical.) The most helpful discussion of this argument that I have seen is in Boyd, unpublished. There are good recent discussions in Papineau, 2001, and Loewer, 2001.

14. See the essays in Hooker and Little, 2000, for representative views.

15. Hume discusses the apparent difficulty of inferring an *ought* from an *is* in Hume, 1978, pp. 469–470. There is controversy about how well Hume's own distinction, and his thesis about it, map onto the twentieth-century discussion of whether ethical conclusions can be inferred from nonethical premises. (For one argument that Hume had a different distinction in mind, see Sturgeon, 2001b.) But convenience has entrenched the habit of referring to the alleged fact-value gap as an "is-ought gap," even among writers who doubt that this was Hume's own target.

16. These doctrines were held in a variety of forms. Hard-line versions of phenomenalism and logical behaviorism held that there were actually translations of conclusions about material bodies and other minds, respectively, into complex statements that were entirely about actual and possible evidence, but more moderate versions held only that there were connections of meaning sufficient to warrant reasonable (but perhaps not deductive) inferences to the conclusions. Instrumentalism is somewhat special because it involved an open concession to skepticism, admitting that belief in the truth of scientific theories, as opposed to their instrumental reliability, could not be justified on the evidence.

17. Here it is useful to look at Philippa Foot's account of the standard contrast, by the 1950s, between statements of fact and judgments of value: see Foot, 1978a, esp. pp. 110–111. Foot cites this accepted contrast in order to criticize it, but none of her criticism is directed at the essentially verificationist account of how statements of fact are related to the evidence for them. Hare explicitly affirms the contrast Foot is criticizing, including the account of how statements of fact are based on evidence, in Hare, 1963, ch. 1.

18. There are discussions of naturalism in this·vein in Ayer, 1946, ch. 6; in Hare, 1952, ch. 5; and, on the other side of the issue, in Foot, 1978a.

19. This is Hare's line in Hare, 1952.

20. A pragmatic property of a statement is one that depends, not simply on its meaning, but also on the beliefs and interests of the people using or hearing it. One example would be that of a statement's saying something surprising. Any course on philosophical paradoxes will provide examples of apparently valid arguments with individually unsurprising premises and surprising conclusions.

21. Judith Jarvis Thomson may be suggesting a version of this objection in Thomson, 1996, pp. 86–87.

22. Writers do not all agree about what naturalism in epistemology involves. In his seminal essay "Epistemology Naturalized" (1969a), W. V. O. Quine emphasized that epistemology needs to be continuous with empirical science, a "chapter of psychology" (p. 82) rather than of any a priori philosophy. He has also been widely understood, possibly correctly, as holding that epistemology could not therefore be normative or evaluative, dealing with such traditional questions as the justification of belief. I am sympathetic with the first of these claims, but no ethical naturalist is likely to accept the second. Ethical naturalism is after all the view that there can be natural facts, subject to empirical investigation, about which sorts of actions are justified; it is thus difficult to see why an ethical naturalist would doubt that there could also be natural, empirically ascertainable facts about the justification of belief. Quine—or at least his interpreters—seems simply to have assumed without argument that a naturalistic account of justification is impossible.

23. Philosophers who attach importance to this argument do not all agree on its formulation. One typical and accessible account is in Mackie, 1977, pp. 229–230; see note 34 hereafter.

24. Thus, Robert Adams, defending a divine command account of ethics that takes advantage of the possibility of synthetic property identities, remarks that if he came to believe that there was no God, he would not conclude that no actions were ethically wrong; rather, the term "ethical wrongness" would in that case turn out to represent some purely natural property instead (1987a, p. 141).

There are a few exceptions to the generalizations I have made in the text. Most notably, J. L. Mackie's view that real ethical facts would have to involve what he calls objective values, and that objective values could exist in a world with a God as traditionally conceived but not in a purely naturalistic world, appears to be a sophisticated version of the popular view that ethics depends, if not exactly on divine commands, then at least on a theistic metaphysics or something very similar. (See Mackie, 1977, ch. 1). I shall return to Mackie's views hereafter.

25. I of course do not mean that a secular moralist has nothing to learn from reli-

gious traditions of thought. As Philippa Foot remarks, St. Thomas Aquinas's ethical writings can be "as useful to the atheist as to the Catholic or other Christian believer" (1978d, p. 2). But a philosophical naturalist must also think that any ethical view that depends for its plausibility specifically on claims about the supernatural is on that account doubtful. To take one example, Peter Geach argues (1969, pp. 117–129) that a certain sort of extreme deontological position in first-order ethics makes sense only on the assumption that there is a God. Without agreeing with every detail of his argument, I think that his conclusion is correct; indeed, I think that a naturalistic view of humans tends to push first-order ethics in a consequentialist direction. Others, too, have suggested that one's stance on second-order questions in ethics might rationally influence the direction of one's first-order thoughts. Simon Blackburn, for example, writes that his own noncognitivist (or, as he would prefer, "projectivist" or "expressivist") position has, uniquely, an affinity for consequentialist moral theories, setting "a limit to the extent to which moral thought can oppose consequentialist, teleological reasoning" (1993a, p. 164). Interestingly, however, the feature of his view that he thinks points in this direction— seeing morality as a device enabling "things to go well among people with a natural inheritance of needs and desires that they must together fulfill"—is not specific to his noncognitivism, and is likely to appeal to any philosophical naturalist.

26. The appearance is not confined, as one might initially think, to the views of theists: one encounters students for whom it is virtually automatic to conclude that, if God does not exist, then all things are permitted and/or life is not worth living. And the noncognitivist accounts are not confined, as one might also have initially thought, to philosophers one would otherwise have thought of as atheists. I would count Braithwaite, 1953, as well as the "religion without propositions" approach of D. Z. Phillips in many writings, in this category, and neither is unsympathetic to religious views. Noncognitivist accounts of religious discourse face one problem in common with noncognitivist accounts of ethical discourse, namely a need to explain away the apparent use of the discourse in offering explanations: see note 11 earlier.

27. On the other hand, if the intuitive idea really is that natural properties are ones of the sort investigated by the sciences, the naturalist may ask why we must abandon that formula so quickly for more neutral ground once we notice that some sciences study how organs and faculties should function.

28. The problem does not just arise from theistic views. Philosophical naturalists are typically atheists who think that there is empirical evidence for their view. So they regard claims about the supernatural as answerable to evidence, and they think that evidence supports the view that supernatural properties are *not* instantiated. Perhaps we could nevertheless specify a way in which, on their view, it is only natural properties that are empirical, but this would take some work.

29. A number of recent writers try to find this concern behind Moore's open question argument (e.g., Darwall, Gibbard, and Railton, 1992, pp. 115–121), a reading that strikes me as quite strained if it is meant to comment on Moore's own intentions. (An earlier generation of critics complained that Moore, like other early twentieth-century ethical intuitionists, simply ignored the practical role of ethical thought: see Nowell-Smith, 1957, pp. 39–42, and Warnock, 1967, pp. 15–16). The clearer inspirations here are, as suggested in the text, from the eighteenth century: Hume and Kant.

30. Plato has Thrasymachus, and then Glaucon and Adeimantus, raise this chal-

lenge in the *Republic*. That it still resonates is illustrated by the usefulness of the *Republic* in teaching introductory ethics: as with that other famous skeptical challenge in Descartes's *Meditation* I, students are often more impressed by the challenge than they are by the author's attempt at a reply.

That resourceful skeptics deny a thesis is not a conclusive argument that it could not be a priori. Philosophical defenders of the a priori typically take mathematics to be a priori and allow, since there can be surprising results in mathematics, that there can be unobvious a priori truths. But philosophical naturalists (the prime candidates for becoming ethical naturalists) are typically among those least impressed with attempts at a priori rebuttals of skepticism.

31. There is a wide variety of views among philosophers about what sorts of reasons might be found in a purely natural world, often presented with little explicit defense. T. M. Scanlon suggests, in an aside, that *none* could be: he is, he says, "quite willing to accept that 'being a reason for' is an unanalyzable, normative, hence nonnatural relation" (1998, p. 11). On the other side, Philippa Foot has recently come to the view, which she earlier rejected, that the mere recognition of reasons for acting can motivate; but she does not see that as a departure from her career-long defense of what she calls naturalism in ethics. See Foot, 2001, pp. 18, 22–23; for her earlier views see Foot, 1978a, 1978b.

32. In this paragraph I have borrowed or adapted several sentences from Sturgeon, 2001a.

33. For reasons I explained earlier, Mackie's view is not commonly called a version of ethical naturalism. But his view is like some versions of ethical naturalism (especially as seen by their opponents) in embodying a highly pessimistic view of the prospects for ethics in an entirely natural world.

34. Mackie, 1977, pp. 230–231. In this brief aside on divine command theories of ethics—theories that see the distinction between moral right and wrong as created by God's commands—Mackie is suggesting a response to a standard objection to such views. The objection, adapted from Plato's *Euthyphro*, is that if moral right and wrong are simply created by God's commands, then those commands themselves must be morally arbitrary: they cannot themselves be *based* on moral considerations. Mackie's suggestion to the divine command theorist is to break the wrongness of an action into two pieces: one consisting entirely of the sort of natural inappropriateness I describe here, the other constituted by God's forbidding it (and thus creating an objective prescription against it) on the grounds of this inappropriateness. Note that for this defense to work, the natural inappropriateness must look a lot like real moral wrongness: for the fact that God bases his command on a concern to suppress it is precisely what is supposed to relieve God's command of the charge of moral arbitrariness. Note also that God's motivation, presumably morally admirable, is not itself a response to anything objectively prescriptive.

35. Compare Allan Gibbard's concession, on behalf of his noncognitivism, that his disagreement with ethical naturalists may in the end be an empirical one: Gibbard, 1990, p. 122n; compare p. 116. In general, the question, emphasized earlier, of whether ethical explanations can be illuminating enough to retain their place in a naturalistic explanatory repertoire is in large part empirical.

REFERENCES

Adams, Robert M. 1987a. "Divine Command Metaethics Modified Again." In Adams, 1987b, 128–143.

———. 1987b. *The Virtue of Faith.* New York: Oxford University Press.

Ayer, A. J. 1946. *Language, Truth and Logic.* London: Victor Gollancz.

Becker, Lawrence C., and Charlotte B. Becker, eds. 2001. *The Encyclopedia of Ethics.* 2nd ed. New York: Routledge.

Bernard, J. H., ed. 1900. *The Works of Bishop Butler.* 2 vols. London: Macmillan.

Blackburn, Simon. 1991. "Reply to Sturgeon." *Philosophical Studies* 61: 39–41.

———. 1993a. "Errors and the Phenomenology of Value." In Blackburn, 1993b, 149–165.

———. 1993b. *Essays in Quasi-Realism.* Oxford: Oxford University Press.

———. 1993c. "Just Causes." In Blackburn, 1993b, 198–209.

Boyd, Richard. Unpublished. "Materialism without Reductionism: Non-Humean Causation and the Evidence for Physicalism."

Braithewaite, R. B. 1953. *An Empiricist's View of the Nature of Religious Belief.* Cambridge: Cambridge University Press.

Broad, C. D. 1930. *Five Types of Ethical Theory.* London: Routledge and Kegan Paul.

Butler, Joseph. [1729] 1900. *Fifteen Sermons Preached at the Rolls Chapel.* In Bernard, 1900, vol. 1, 1–200.

Copp, David, and David Zimmerman, eds. 1985. *Morality, Reason and Truth.* Totowa, N. J.: Rowman and Allanheld.

Darwall, Stephen, Allan Gibbard, and Peter Railton. 1992. "Toward *Fin de Siècle* Ethics: Some Trends." *Philosophical Review* 101: 115–190.

Foot, Philippa. 1978a. "Moral Beliefs." In Foot, 1978c, 110–131.

———. 1978b. "Morality as a System of Hypothetical Imperatives." In Foot, 1978c, 157–173.

———. 1978c. *Virtues and Vices.* Berkeley: University of California Press.

———. 1978d. "Virtues and Vices." In Foot, 1978c, 1–18.

———. 2001. *Natural Goodness.* Oxford: Clarendon Press.

Geach, Peter. 1969. *God and the Soul.* New York: Schocken Books.

Gibbard, Allan. 1990. *Wise Choices, Apt Feelings: A Theory of Normative Judgment.* Cambridge, Mass.: Harvard University Press.

Gillett, Carl, and Barry Loewer, eds. 2001. *Physicalism and Its Discontents.* Cambridge: Cambridge University Press.

Hare, R. M. 1952. *The Language of Morals.* Oxford: Clarendon Press.

———. 1963. *Freedom and Reason.* Oxford: Clarendon Press.

Harman, Gilbert. 1977. *The Nature of Morality.* New York: Oxford University Press.

———. 1986. "Moral Explanations of Natural Facts—Can Moral Claims Be Tested against Moral Reality?" *Southern Journal of Philosophy* 24, supp.: 57–68.

Harman, Gilbert, and Judith Jarvis Thomson. 1996. *Moral Relativism and Moral Objectivity.* Oxford: Blackwell.

Hooker, Brad, and Margaret Little, eds. 2000. *Moral Particularism.* Oxford: Oxford University Press.

Hume, David. [1739–40]. 1978. *A Treatise of Human Nature.* Ed. L. A. Selby-Bigge. Rev. P. H. Nidditch. Oxford: Clarendon Press.

Kripke, Saul. 1980. *Naming and Necessity*. Cambridge, Mass.: Harvard University Press.

Langford, C. H. 1968. "The Notion of Analysis in Moore's Philosophy." In Schilpp, 1968, 321–342.

Locke, John. [1689]. 1975. *An Essay Concerning Human Understanding*. Ed. Peter Nidditch. Oxford: Clarendon Press.

Loewer, Barry. 2001. "From Physics to Physicalism." In Gillett and Loewer, 2001, 37–56.

Mackie, J. L. 1977. *Ethics*. Harmondsworth, England: Penguin.

McDowell, John. 1998a. *Mind, Value and Reality*. Cambridge, Mass.: Harvard University Press.

———. 1998b. "Virtue and Reason." In McDowell, 1998a, 50–73.

Moore, G. E. 1903. *Principia Ethica*. Cambridge: Cambridge University Press.

———. 1968. "A Reply to My Critics." In Schilpp, 1968, 535–677.

———. [1903]. 1993. *Principia Ethica*. Ed. Thomas Baldwin. Cambridge: Cambridge University Press.

Nielsen, Kai, and Jocelyn Couture. 1995. *On the Relevance of Metaethics*. Calgary: University of Calgary Press.

Nowell-Smith, P. H. 1957. *Ethics*. Harmondsworth, England: Penguin.

Papineau, David. 2001. "The Rise of Physicalism." In Gillett and Loewer, 2001, 3–36.

Pigden, Charles R. 1991. "Naturalism." In Singer, 1991, 421–431.

Prior, A. N. 1949. *Logic and the Basis of Ethics*. Oxford: Clarendon Press.

Putnam, Hilary. 1981. *Reason, Truth and History*. Cambridge: Cambridge University Press.

Quine, W. V. O. 1969a. "Epistemology Naturalized." In Quine, 1969b, 69–90.

———. 1969b. *Ontological Relativity and Other Essays*. New York: Columbia University Press.

Rawls, John. 1971. *A Theory of Justice*. Cambridge, Mass.: Belknap Press.

Scanlon, Thomas. 1998. *What We Owe to Each Other*. Cambridge, Mass.: Belknap Press.

Schilpp, Paul Arthur, ed. 1968. *The Philosophy of G. E. Moore*. 3rd ed. LaSalle, Ill.: Open Court.

Singer, Peter, ed. 1991. *A Companion to Ethics*. Oxford: Blackwell.

Sturgeon, Nicholas L. 1985. "Moral Explanations." In Copp and Zimmerman, 1985, 49–78.

———. 1986a. "Harman on Moral Explanations of Natural Facts." *Southern Journal of Philosophy* 24, supp.: 69–78.

———. 1986b. "What Difference Does It Make Whether Moral Realism Is True?" *Southern Journal of Philosophy* 24, supp.: 115–141.

———. 1991. "Contents and Causes." *Philosophical Studies* 61: 19–37.

———. 1995. "Evil and Explanation." In Nielsen and Couture, 1995, 155–185.

———. 1998. "Thomson against Moral Explanations." *Philosophy and Phenomenological Research* 43: 199–206.

———. 2001a. "Metaphysics and Epistemology." In Becker and Becker, 2001, 2:1087–1093.

———. 2001b. "Moral Skepticism and Moral Naturalism in Hume's Treatise." *Hume Studies* 27: 3–83.

———. 2003. "Moore on Ethical Naturalism." *Ethics* 113: 528–556.

Thomson, Judith Jarvis. 1996. "Moral Objectivity." In Harman and Thomson, 1996, 67–154.

————. 1998. "Reply to Critics." *Philosophy and Phenomenological Research* 43: 215–222.

Warnock, G. J. 1967. *Contemporary Moral Philosophy*. London: Macmillan.

Williams, Bernard. 1985. *Ethics and the Limits of Philosophy*. Cambridge, Mass.: Harvard University Press.

Wilson, Edward O. 1975. "Human Decency Is Animal." *New York Times Magazine*, October 12.

CHAPTER 4

....

NONNATURALISM

....

JONATHAN DANCY

1. SOME DISTINCTIONS

....

ETHICAL nonnaturalism is the claim that ethical properties, distinctions, and facts are different from any properties, distinctions, and facts that are worth calling natural. Ethical naturalism, as it is understood here, is the claim that all ethical properties (etc.) are also natural. The debate between these two camps is vitiated by the fact that there is no agreed account of what it is to be natural. This fact counts in favor of neither side, but it definitely counts against the sharpness of the debate; some would say that until we decide what it is to be natural, there is nothing to debate about.

Metaphysicians debate the rights and wrongs of a doctrine worth calling metaphysical naturalism: that the natural world is all there is. But one can be an ethical naturalist without being a metaphysical naturalist, and vice versa. For the debate between ethical naturalists and their nonnaturalist opponents is conducted among those who agree that there are ethical properties and facts, that is to say, among moral realists. A moral realist is someone who thinks that there are matters of ethical fact. A metaphysical naturalist who thinks that morality is not a matter of fact will neither assert or deny ethical naturalism; many noncognitivists are of this sort, and so they think that there is nothing for ethical naturalism to be about (Blackburn, 1998; Gibbard, 1990). However, most ethical naturalists are metaphysical naturalists. Indeed, as we will see, in most cases people adopt ethical naturalism as a result of some prior commitment to metaphysical naturalism.

There is another metaethical doctrine which calls itself naturalism; this is Aristotelian naturalism (Foot, 2001; Hursthouse, 1999), so called because it holds that moral distinctions are tightly grounded in considerations of human nature. But it takes no official stand on the debate between ethical naturalism and non-naturalism, as I have characterized it; Aristotelian naturalists could be ethical nonnaturalists. This chapter is therefore not concerned with Aristotelian naturalism.

In what follows, I first distinguish different varieties of ethical naturalism (which I will simply call naturalism from now on) and the arguments in favor of them. I then turn to the arguments on the other side. The most famous argument against naturalism appeals to the notion of normativity. I ask what normativity is and why it cannot be a natural feature or a feature of some natural thing. At the end I try to say why there is no form of naturalism that we should adopt.

2. VARIETIES OF NATURALISM

Naturalism comes in many forms. The most extreme naturalist I will consider here is Frank Jackson. Jackson (1998) offers two direct arguments for naturalism. The first of these is the simple claim that since we are natural creatures, any distinction we can grasp must be a natural distinction, one expressible (as he puts it) in descriptive terms. So if two actions are right, there must be a descriptively specifiable property that they both have; there must be a recurring descriptive pattern in the ways they are, despite any differences between those ways. This is not an argument that appeals to any special aspects of the moral, the ethical, or the evaluative. It is more like an argument in favor of a general metaphysical naturalism; not quite, because Jackson is arguing that *for us*, the natural world is all there is; so every moral property we can grasp must be natural like the others.

Jackson supports this very direct argument with another, which is much less simple and much less direct, and which appeals to special aspects of the evaluative. He argues that every evaluative predicate is necessarily equivalent to, and in fact has the same meaning as, some descriptive predicate, since for each evaluative predicate there is a descriptive predicate that it entails and that is entailed by it. He reaches this result by thinking about the relation between what he calls ethical nature (which I will call here evaluative nature, since the contrast between ethical and descriptive is peculiar)[1] and descriptive nature.

Start from a representative evaluative predicate E, perhaps "is a right action," together with an action that satisfies that predicate. There will be a complete description of that action and of the world in which it occurs, which is given by an enormous descriptive predicate D_1. D_1 will read "is an action of such and such a descriptive sort, done in a world of such and such a descriptive sort." Now D_1 entails E, by supervenience, for any action descriptively indistinguishable from the first one, and done in an indistinguishable world, must also be evaluatively similar, and so it is impossible for any other action to satisfy D_1 without satisfying E. But E does not entail D_1, for there may be other different actions that satisfy E, some done in the same world, others in different worlds. For each different action that satisfies E, there will, however, be a new action-in-world description D_2, D_3, D_4, D_5 . . . There may even be an infinite number of such descriptions, but any action that satisfies one of them will also satisfy E. Let us form, then, the disjunction of the descriptions of all such actions-in-worlds, Δ. What we find now is that E entails Δ, since if E is satisfied by an action in a world, that action must satisfy one of the action-in-world descriptions D_1–D_n and so satisfy the enormous disjunctive description Δ. But Δ also entails E, for if the enormous disjunctive description is satisfied, one of its disjuncts must be satisfied, and as I showed, each such disjunct entails E. So E both entails and is entailed by Δ. And since E was merely a representative evaluative predicate, we can conclude that for each such predicate, there is at least one descriptive predicate that both entails and is entailed by it, that is, is necessarily equivalent to it.[2]

We might think that this is all fairly innocuous, but Jackson then goes on to claim that necessarily equivalent predicates pick out the same property, hence that "ethical properties are possibly infinite disjunctive descriptive properties" (1998, p. 124). And he goes further still, claiming that when enough descriptive information is in, it is impossible for two people who share the same concept of right action to disagree about whether an action is right. He allows that we humans may still need the evaluative *predicate*, since our access to a possibly infinite disjunctive description is probably limited. Nonetheless, he claims, the *property* to which mastery of that predicate gives us access is a descriptive property, and there are two analytically equivalent ways of ascribing that property: the evaluative way and the descriptive way. In descriptive terms, this property is infinite, or at least potentially infinite, in two directions, outward and inward. It is infinite outward because there may be an infinite number of different descriptive ways that right actions-in-worlds may be. It is infinite inward because there is no limit to the number of things there are to be said in describing any one of those ways. But this double enormity gives Jackson no pause.

If everything so far is sound, Jackson has established that evaluative properties are some descriptive properties or other—possibly these doubly enormous ones. But it remains also possible that they are less enormous than this. If we want actually to isolate the descriptive property that a given evaluative property is, the method Jackson proposes is that of "Ramseyfication." Take all the things that mature folk morality would claim about (e.g.) rightness: remove the notion of "right" from them, and see which descriptive replacement for it would lead to the least disruption (i.e., keep the most such claims true). Then identify rightness with that descriptive property, whatever it is. It might, for instance, just be the simple property of being welfare-maximizing—though it probably won't be.

I said that Jackson's position is the most extreme form of naturalism. This is because of three aspects of his view. The first is the outlandish nature of the descriptive predicates[3] that Jackson claims to be analytically equivalent to evaluative predicates; most naturalists who offer necessary equivalents for "is right," say, offer much simpler ones such as that of "maximizes welfare." The second is his claim that the two ways of ascribing one and the same property are analytically equivalent. Most varieties of naturalism do not take this last step. Such "nonanalytic naturalisms" agree that evaluative properties are natural properties, so that there are two different ways of ascribing such a property; but they deny that the evaluative way of ascribing it has the same meaning, or invokes the same concepts, as any descriptive way of ascribing it. The third is Jackson's view that there *must* be a descriptive equivalent for every evaluative predicate; one can imagine a weaker view that holds merely that there *might* be a descriptive equivalent for some evaluative predicates, though there need not be for all; that is to say, this possibility cannot be ruled out, but there is nothing to show that things *must* be so in general.[4]

Though these weaker views are different from Jackson's view, they are similar enough to his to form a recognizable family, the members of which fall into two main groups: analytic naturalism and nonanalytic naturalism. But there is a type of naturalism that is utterly different from either of these. This is the ingenious position held by Richard Boyd (1988) and Nicholas Sturgeon (1988, 2003). I will focus here on Sturgeon. He starts by suggesting that goodness and other ethical properties appear to play a causal role in the world. All of us have at some time or other benefited from the goodness of others, and part of what led to the outcry against slavery in the United States was that the form of "chattel" slavery prevalent in the United States was much worse than the sorts of slavery found elsewhere. But Sturgeon does not move directly from this to the claim that goodness and wrongness are natural properties. To do that, he would have to claim (at least implicitly) that only the natural is capable of playing a causal role. Such a claim is dubious; it is often suggested that supernatural beings, such as God or the angels, are capable of playing a causal role, since they have the habit of occasionally interfering in the ordinary course of nature. This practice, it is suggested, does not make them any the less supernatural, or any the more natural. Sturgeon manages to avoid such difficulties. He claims merely that since moral properties are capable of playing a causal role, there is no reason to invent a special new metaphysical category, that of the "nonnatural," for them to come in. There is no reason to think of them as other than natural.

One can hardly say that there is a spectrum here, with Jackson's view at one end and Sturgeon's at the other. Sturgeon's view differs in style from nonanalytic naturalism and from Jackson's analytic naturalism; we could call Sturgeon's view "one-term naturalism" and the opposing views "two-term naturalism." For the latter views accept that each evaluative distinction must be capable of being captured in nonevaluative, "descriptive" terms. They deny that the evaluative way of capturing it might be the only way of doing so. For them, there are two vocabularies, evaluative and descriptive, and anything we can say or report in the evaluative vocabulary we must also be able to say or report in the descriptive one. Now this claim leads Jackson, at any rate, into difficulties. He has to characterize the difference between the two vocabularies, so that we know which terms come in which. This is not at all easy to do without begging some question. The way that Jackson hits on is to appeal to the distinction between "is" and "ought." He writes: "By the descriptive picture, I mean the picture tellable in the terms that belong to the 'is' side of the famous 'is-ought' debate" (1998, p. 113). Of course, in many cases it is controversial which side of the is-ought distinction a term will fall. Many concepts seem to have a bit of both about them, such as the concept of generosity or that of a turn (as in "it is not your turn"). Jackson deals with this by saying: "If it is unclear whether a term is or is not purely descriptive, then we can take it off the list of the purely descriptive" (p. 120). In my view, this leads to a problem. Take the whole spectrum of terms, from the most blatantly descriptive (or is-ish) to the most blatantly evaluative (or ought-ish). Jackson's initial argument, which appeals to supervenience, must allow that wherever on the spectrum we draw the line between the descriptive on the left and the evaluative on the right, what falls on the right will supervene on what falls on the left, and the distinctions drawable on the right must also be drawable on the left. But the more we reduce the scope of what is to count as descriptive, the fewer the distinctions that our descriptive vocabulary will be able to draw, but the greater the number of evaluative distinctions that need to be expressible descriptively. Eventually, one would suppose, the powers of the diminishing descriptive vocabulary will prove inadequate to its increasing task. This seems to me to cast doubt on Jackson's conciliatory definition of the descriptive-evaluative distinction. (See also Raz, 1999.)

Sturgeon faces none of these difficulties. He thinks that naturalism is not a doctrine about terms or about the relation between two vocabularies, and that there is no need to claim that there must be a way of expressing in one ("descriptive," or "natural") vocabulary what can be expressed in another ("evaluative" or "moral"). Sturgeon's view is that moral distinctions are *already* natural. We don't need to find a natural equivalent for them.

Here is a brief characterization of the main types of naturalism I have mentioned.

One-term naturalism (Sturgeon): Every normative fact is a natural fact, whether or not there is a descriptive way of capturing that fact in addition to the evaluative way.

Nonanalytic naturalism: For each evaluatively capturable fact, there must be a descriptive way of capturing that same fact, though the two ways of capturing it will never be analytically equivalent.

Analytic naturalism (Jackson): For each evaluatively capturable fact, there must be a descriptive way of capturing that same fact, and the two ways of capturing it will be synonymous, that is, analytically equivalent, that is, have the same meaning.

3. INITIAL COMMENTS ON THESE ARGUMENTS

Sturgeon's examples of moral properties or facts playing a causal role in the world are always going to be challengeable. Some will say that the cause of the antislavery movement in the United States was not that chattel slavery was worse than other sorts but the fact that people came to believe it worse. We might reply that they came to believe it worse because it was worse, or because it was so blatantly worse. With this reply we enter murky waters. As for the example of benefiting from the goodness of others, the response might be that what we benefit from are those features of others that make them good, for instance their concern for their fellows, or their willingness to put themselves second. It is the good-making features that are affecting the causal order, not the goodness that they make. So the examples are disputable. In a way, what is more interesting about Sturgeon's position is the combination of two claims: that there is no reason to think of moral properties as so different from (other) natural ones that we need to create a new category of the nonnatural for them, and that nonethical terms are not likely to be explanatorily equivalent to ethical ones. (See esp. Sturgeon, 2003.) Analytical naturalists will deny this last claim of Sturgeon. If evaluative distinctions are analytically equivalent to descriptive ones, for explanatory purposes it cannot matter which way one puts things. Even if all explanation is intensional, hence sensitive to one's choice of terms, it cannot be sensitive to the distinction between analytic equivalents.

Turning now to Jackson's first argument: this seems to me to be ineffective. I accept that for each learnable predicate there must be a repeatable pattern in the ways things can be, to which we can learn to respond, and it may be that each such pattern is a pattern of natural or "descriptive" features. But there is no reason why the pattern itself should be "descriptive." A pattern of natural features need not be a natural pattern. The point could not be made better than it is by John McDowell, who writes:

> [H]owever long a list we give of the items to which a supervening term applies, described in terms of the level supervened upon, there may be no way, expressible at the level supervened upon, of grouping just such items together. . . . Understanding why just those things belong together may essentially require understanding the supervening term. (1998, p. 202)

It is important here to notice that neither Jackson's point nor McDowell's reply is especially concerned with the relation between the evaluative and the descriptive. Both the point and the reply concern any predicate that applies, where it applies, in virtue of the application of other predicates. (Such predicates are called "resultant," "emergent," or "consequential.") Jackson's general idea is that the upper-level, resultant predicate can only be learnt by seeing the pattern it picks out at the lower level. But this claim seems to me to be falsified by the design structure of connectionist machines, if for no other reason. What I mean by this is that there is at least one model of rationality, the connectionist one, in which Jackson's claim is false. In fact, there is more than one; Roschian prototypes constitute another. I argue all these things in detail elsewhere (Dancy, 1999).

With Jackson's second argument, the crucial question is whether his supervenience-based argument succeeds in establishing that every evaluative fact can be reported in descriptive terms. For this it is required, not merely that for each evaluative sentence there is a necessarily equivalent descriptive one (this just means that where either is true, the other must be), but also that the two sentences express or pick out the same matter of fact (whether they have the same meaning or not). There are three steps in Jackson's argument, taken now about predicates rather than sentences. First, for each evaluative predicate, there is a necessarily equivalent descriptive one; second, those two predicates ascribe the same property. Third, they have the same meaning. If the second step can be resisted, the soundness of the third step becomes irrelevant. And if the second step fails, we lose a significant argument for nonanalytic naturalism.

Suppose that we don't accept Jackson's supervenience-based argument: are there any other arguments for nonanalytic naturalism? One possibility is to argue not from supervenience but from "resultance"; anything that has a normative property will have it in virtue of, or because of, other properties that it has got. (See Dancy, 1993, ch. 5.) Suppose that all the latter properties (the resultance base, as I call them) are natural; one could argue that any properties grounded in a natural base must themselves be natural. Beyond that, the situation seems to be that nonanalytic naturalism is normally held as a consequence of metaphysical naturalism, for which independent arguments may of course be given (meta-physical arguments, that is, not ones specifically concerned with ethics).[5] Such argumentation as is then provided consists largely in appeal to the model of scientific property identification, such as the identification of water as H_2O. But the role of that appeal, which I will be outlining shortly in discussing the Open Question Argument, is to show that there is a consistent form of naturalism that is not vulnerable to certain supposed nonnaturalist arguments. This is not an argument in favor of naturalism but defense against an argument against.[6]

Of course even if naturalist arguments don't succeed, this does nothing to establish the truth of nonnaturalism. If Sturgeon is right, there is just no need (so far as ethics is concerned, at any rate) even to introduce a potential category of the nonnatural. So let us see what the nonnaturalists have to say.

4. ARGUMENTS FOR NONNATURALISM: MOORE AND PARFIT

Nonnaturalists have traditionally been keen to refute all forms of naturalism at once, despite the differences I have been showing between those forms, by one big blockbuster argument. By far the most famous argument of this sort is G. E. Moore's Open Question Argument, which Moore took to refute all possible naturalist suggestions as to what natural property goodness might be (1903, ch. 1). Take any candidate natural property: the candidate that Moore actually considers is that goodness is "what I desire to desire." Moore suggests that there is a clear difference between the questions "Is what I desire to desire what I desire to desire?" and "Is what I desire to desire good?" And he takes it that the same difference would appear for every other candidate natural property. So if we take, for example, the suggestion that goodness is the property of welfare-maximizing, we see the same difference between "Is being a welfare-maximizer being a welfare-maximizer?" and "Is being a welfare-maximizer being good?" The suggestion is that the second question in these pairings is always substantial, while the first question is always trivial, and that this shows, in each case, that the claim that the property of goodness *is* the candidate natural property must be false.

This argument works by appeal to the idea that if a definition were sound, it would seem to be a sort of tautology to every competent speaker. Anything, then, that could seem surprising or informative to a competent speaker cannot be a correct definition. This idea can be, and has been, challenged by appeal to a distinction between obvious and unobvious analytic truths. Definitions are expressed in supposedly analytic truths, and if some of these are far from obvious, they may very well be surprising even to the most competent of speakers. Leaving that point aside, however, Moore's thought was that if being good is correctly definable as being a welfare-maximizer, the question "Is being a welfare-maximizer being a welfare-maximizer?" should seem no different from "Is being a welfare-maximizer being good?" But they do seem different, and so the definition is incorrect. Perhaps, indeed, Moore's argument will show that all such naturalistic definitions of ethical properties are wrong.

But now: couldn't there be two quite different terms, terms with different meanings, that pick out the same property? If there were, appeal to what the competent speaker knows would be incapable of telling us which pairs of terms in fact pick out the same property and which don't; *that* sort of fact is not what the competent speaker is supposed to know. What competent speakers know is the *meaning* of the terms in their language. But two terms could have different meanings and refer to the same property, and when that happens, it might not only be a considerable surprise to the competent speaker, but also very important to know, and not a trivial matter of definition at all. This is exactly what we see in the history of science. It was an important discovery that to be hot is to have a certain degree of molecular kinetic energy. If we had asked the competent speaker Moore's question—is there a difference between the question "Is having a certain degree of molecular kinetic energy having a certain degree of molecular kinetic energy?" and "Is having a certain degree of molecular kinetic energy being hot?"—the competent speaker would have said yes. But that would have done nothing whatever to show the scientific discovery to be wrong. What was discovered was not something about the meaning of words, and is not capable of being refuted by appeal to what the competent speaker knows. And the same, we might say, applies to the ethical "discovery" that being good is being a welfare-maximizer; nothing that Moore has to say can show otherwise. So as it stands, the Open Question Argument is at best a partial failure. Even if it succeeds in refuting all forms of analytical naturalism (and I suggested earlier a reason for thinking that it does not), it has nothing to say against nonanalytical naturalism.

Sturgeon (2003) points out a second defect with the Open Question Argument. This is that it assumes straight out that the term "good" does not itself pick out a natural property—the property of goodness. What Moore in effect argues is that whatever property "good" stands for, it does not *also* stand for any property picked out by some other term drawn from a nonethical vocabulary. But it remains possible, for all that, that the special property for which "good" stands is *already* natural—as Sturgeon himself holds it to be. The Open Question Argument simply does not address this possibility. Why didn't Moore see this? The only answer is that he took it as obvious that the term "good," and other such terms, such as "right," are quite different in style from any terms such as "causing more pleasure than pain." But we have yet to see what that difference in style might be, and to what extent nonnaturalists can appeal to it in argument with naturalists.[7] Moore made various attempts to pick out this vital difference in style. He suggested that the properties picked out by "good" and similar terms are special, in that they cannot be directly perceived, nor can their presence be inferred by any of the standard patterns of inference. He also suggested that those properties are not the business of the natural sciences or of psychology. But even if these things were true (which they probably are not) they are more like symptoms of the thing we are really after than ways of expressing its true nature.

The Open Question Argument probably cannot survive these objections. If there is to be a blockbuster argument against naturalism, we need to look elsewhere. Derek Parfit has recently been trying to do just this; he discusses two objections, which he takes from Sidgwick (1907, p. 26 n. 1) and which he calls the triviality objection and the normativity objection. I proceed here to lay out these objections in my own way. Parfit's work on this topic is still unpublished, and among the reasons for this is, as he says, "I know that my material on naturalism contains serious mistakes. And I make these mistakes in presenting the Triviality and Normativity Objections" (private communication, May 2002). Since both he and I think that any mistakes are reparable, here are the objections nonetheless.

The Triviality Objection. Take a standard version of analytic naturalism: the predicates "is right" and "minimizes suffering" have the same meaning. Now ask what, if so, could be meant by saying that this act of minimizing suffering is right. All that can be meant by this—since, according to the analytic naturalist, the predicates "minimizes suffering" and "is right" have the same meaning—is that this is an act of minimizing suffering, and that, as another way of saying the same thing, we could say that it is right. But this renders the second half of the utterance a merely trivial addition to the first; it is a comparatively insignificant fact that there is another way of saying that this action would minimize suffering. However, we all know perfectly well that the second half of the utterance is not a merely trivial restatement of what the first half said.

This argument will work equally well for any other version of analytic naturalism. All versions trivialize the utterance that, for them, plays the role played by "This act of minimizing suffering is right," in the example above. For each form of analytic naturalism, then, there is an evaluative utterance that it renders normatively trivial, though of course it will allow that all the others are normatively significant. (The one that loses its normative significance need not lose *all* significance, however; there may still be purposes for which it provides helpful information.) Note that the triviality objection does not show that *all* analytic naturalisms render *all* normative utterances normatively trivial; that is the business of the normativity objection.

One might think that this argument falls foul of the problem that faced Moore. Hasn't it merely shown that the two halves of the utterance have different meanings? Surely the strongest conclusion that can be drawn here is that natural

expressions and evaluative expressions never "say the same thing"—which seems
to amount to their not having the same meaning. This is all that Parfit initially
intends to show; his first target is analytical naturalism. But he then discusses a
way of adapting his argument so that it would apply to nonanalytic forms of
naturalism. Such naturalisms suppose that even if we do not just repeat ourselves
(i.e., say the same thing) when we say that an action with the relevant natural
property is right, we are nonetheless reporting the same fact twice in very different
language. So, again, what could be meant by saying that this act of minimizing
suffering is right? All that can be meant by this—since, according to the nonanalytic naturalist, the predicates "minimizes suffering" and "is right" ascribe the
same property—is that this is an act of minimizing suffering, and that, as another
way of reporting the same state of affairs, we could say that it is right. But this,
it may seem, renders the second half of the utterance "this act, which minimizes
suffering, is right" a merely trivial addition to the first, and so deprives such
utterances of their normative significance.[8]

Here then is an argument. At whom is it aimed? It gets no purchase on
Sturgeon at all, for it does nothing to show that "You ought to do A" does not
itself express a matter of natural fact. Parfit's question here is whether there is
any *other* expression that clearly states a matter of natural fact and states the same
fact as that stated by "You ought to do A"—to which his answer, like Sturgeon's,
is no. What Parfit's argument does is attack the other forms of naturalism. At
least, it attacks all forms that offer as candidate natural properties such properties
as minimizing suffering, the sort of property that we would happily invoke in
saying that an action is right *because it has such a property*. Parfit asks what could
be meant, within the constraints of naturalism, by saying that an action that has
that property is right. It seems true that no satisfactory answer appears. But at
best this casts doubt only on those forms of naturalism that offer fairly ordinary
candidate natural properties to be identical with rightness. If we take Jackson's
outlandish candidate, the vast disjunctive descriptive property, things are different.
There is no possible suggestion that a right action is right *because* it has that vast
descriptive property. So the suggestion that nothing significant is added to what
is reported by the description, when we continue "and it is right," is not so
troubling. The trouble came, it seems, from the suggestion that we are really
continuing "and it is right for that reason"—but Jackson's own view would not
suit that suggestion. In fact, on his view, no ordinary statement of the form "Acts
of such and such a nature are right" need be normatively trivial, even if true. So
I pass to Parfit's second objection.

The Normativity Objection. Moral and other evaluative facts have a feature
that no natural fact could have, namely, normativity. If we try to identify moral
facts, or facts about what we have most reason to do, with natural facts, their
normativity is lost.

With this objection, we reach the heart of the matter. But we can make no progress until we know what this normativity is. The nearest that I have got to this so far is to suggest that evaluative facts have a different "style" from that of nonevaluative facts, but this is not a lot of help. Let me therefore review some attempts to say what normativity is.

5. WHAT IS NORMATIVITY?

One suggestion is that normativity is a sort of prescriptive force, which some utterances have and other utterances do not. But though this idea might appeal to noncognitivists, it is not really available to realists. Realists think that moral utterances report how things are morally. If there is normativity around, it must belong to the thing thought and reported—to a fact. Facts, moral or otherwise, cannot have any sort of force. So realists have to think of normativity as a style that some matters of fact have and others do not. This is going to be difficult; it is what J. L. Mackie supposed to be impossible (1977, ch. 1).

It is true that the intuitionists allowed that moral utterances express attitudes of approval or disapproval (Ross, 1930, pp. 90–91, 1939, p. 255), and one might suppose that they are therefore in a position to say that such utterances have normative force. But, as realists, they took the expression of approval and disapproval to be secondary to the main business of moral utterance, which was to characterize correctly what it would be right or wrong, good or bad to do. It was because of the nature of what was said—as we would put it, because of its normativity—that the saying of it was capable of expressing the attitudes of which the emotivists made so much. So for the intuitionists, as for other realists, normativity is first and foremost a feature of the matters of fact expressed by moral utterances.

How are we to characterize that feature, then? One common approach appeals to motivational distinctions. We might say that someone who recognizes a normative matter of fact is necessarily motivated thereby—motivated either by what is recognized or by the recognition of it, according to one's position in the theory of motivation. So to be a normative fact is to be a fact that necessarily motivates anyone who recognizes it. But this claim seems too strong; there is general agreement that those suffering from extreme depression cease to be motivated by the moral reasons that they continue to recognize. We could weaken our claim and say that moral and other normative matters of fact are "intrinsically motivating," meaning by this that they are capable of motivating in their own right, but not that they always do so. But this seems to be as much true (if true at all) of some apparently nonnormative matters of fact, such as that this course of action promises a lot of pleasure. We might then try the idea that normative matters of fact necessarily motivate all who recognize them, on pain of practical irrationality (Smith, 1995). (Those suffering from extreme depression are to count as practically irrational for the while.) It is, of course, no objection to this characterization of normativity that it makes essential appeal to the probably normative notion of irrationality; for it is no part of my purpose here to characterize normativity in nonnormative terms. Whether that can be done remains to be seen; we should not suppose in advance that it either is or needs to be possible. But even so, this characterization seems likely to apply to some matters of fact that intuitively we will be supposing not to be normative; so even if it is necessary for normativity, it is not sufficient. For instance, a rational being who recognizes the fact that a certain action will make many people more comfortable without making anyone less comfortable might well be supposed necessarily to be thereby motivated, independently of how that fact is specified.[9] The conclusion that I draw from all this is that normativity cannot be explicated in terms of some relation to motivation, and that if it could, it is a feature that natural facts could have, and so would be of no help to the nonnaturalists. If we are to make the right sense of the debate between naturalism and nonnaturalism, we need to look further.

Where else can we look? A common approach has been to announce that "ought" is normative, and that anything else that is only explicable in terms of some relation to an ought is normative too. A fact will be normative, then, if it is a fact about an ought or is essentially related to such a fact. But there are considerable difficulties with this approach. The first is that it will probably exclude some notions that nonnaturalists have wanted to think of as normative. The particular notion I have in mind here is that of a reason. It is almost universally supposed that the notion of a reason is indeed explicable in terms of some relation to an ought. The standard form of explication is the one Ross used to explicate his notion of a prima facie duty: a feature is a reason for doing action A in one case if and only if in any case where that feature is present and there is no opposing reason, the presence of that feature makes it the case that one ought to do action A. This is rather clumsily expressed, but I hope that the general idea is clear; we are dealing here with a sort of isolation test for reasonhood. Unfortunately, it is easy to show that this test is misconceived. First, it assumes without argument that what is a reason in one case will be a reason in any case in which it appears. Second, that assumption could be avoided by adjusting the proposed account so that it reads "in any case where that feature is present as a reason and there is no opposing reason," but this would only have the effect of turning every feature into a reason for everything.[10] Third, it seems odd to try to characterize what it is to make the sort of contribution that a reason makes by appeal to a (probably rather rare) case in which it is the only reason. It is as if one were to try to explicate what it is to make a contribution to a conversation in terms of how things would have gone if there had only been one speaker. Finally, the account assumes that any reason is capable of standing alone as a reason: that there are no features that are reasons only if there are other reasons in play. This assumption is false. Consider a promise to do some action only if there is another reason to do it.[11] In the absence of a second reason, this promise fails to give us any reason at all. It is a situation in which we have either no reasons or two.

There are other ways of trying to show that the notion of a reason is necessarily explicable in terms of some relation to an ought. To mention just one more: a feature is a moral reason to do A if and only if, without that feature, doing A would have been less of a duty (or less pressing as a duty) than it is, or no duty at all. The definiens here is neither necessary nor sufficient for reasonhood. Suppose that "ought" implies "can." Then, on the proposed definition, the fact that one is able to do A turns into a reason for doing A, since without that feature we would have had no duty to do A. But this is ridiculous; so the definiens is not sufficient. But neither is it necessary. It is possible for a feature to be a reason for doing A in a case where, had that feature been absent, one would have had more, not less, reason to do A. This may sound surprising at first, because we have a great tendency to think of reasons in comparative terms, in the sort of way that the present definition appeals to. But there are many cases where if we were to remove a feature that counts in favor of what we propose to do, it will necessarily be replaced by a feature that counts even more strongly in the same direction. These are win-win situations, but none the worse for that. For example, suppose that there is an action that I am going to do, and I have to choose between doing it for a friend and doing it for a stranger. To do it for a friend would be good; friendship is a virtue, and acts done for friends get some of their value from that fact; but if I am not doing it for a friend, I will be doing it for a stranger, and this might create even more value.

One could continue on this line for some time. The point may, however, have been sufficiently made: even if the notion of an ought is normative, we cannot expect to be able to characterize normativity in terms of that notion alone.

We might still think that at least the following is true: If we have more reason to do A than to do B, we ought to do A rather than B. But even this is not so obvious. In my (perhaps idiosyncratic) view, there is room for what I call "enticing reasons," reasons that are to do with what is fun, amusing, enjoyable, pleasant, and so on. And these may differ from other sorts of reason precisely in failing to generate oughts. Why insist that you ought (other things equal) to take the most pleasant course? And even if one does insist on that, perhaps on the ground that there is an unbreachable connection between "ought" and "most reason," it is possible that the ought one ends up with is rather different from other oughts, since in the realm of enticers one has a sort of rational permission to please oneself, that is, to select the less enticing option rather than the more. But an ought that is compatible with a permission not to act is not as obviously normative as are the oughts with which I started, the moral oughts and their kin.

So even if we do start from oughts, we have to start from an obviously normative ought; and not all normative notions are very like those oughts. And when we have done this, what have we gained? We still haven't learned what normativity is. To say that "ought" is a normative notion was supposed to be informative, not merely to say that "ought" lies at the center of a group of notions that cluster around it. Effectively, we were trying to say what normativity is, and all we have achieved is to point to one central notion that has got it, or from whose presence in a fact the normativity of that fact is derived. There is a clear danger that our supposed explication of normativity will be little more than a list of the things that have got it.

What is more, a list of things that have normativity (even if in some sense correct)[12] will be of no help if we are trying to show that nothing natural is normative. Nonnaturalists surely have to try to say what normativity is, if they are hoping to show that it is a feature that nothing natural could ever have. And so far we have not made many strides in that direction.

The demand that we say something about what normativity is, which one might suppose to be in principle satisfiable, should be distinguished from the probably unsatisfiable demand that we say what normativity is in nonnormative terms. I agree with Derek Parfit's general point that it may be no more possible to do the latter than it is to say what the temporal is—what time is, as it were—in nontemporal terms. Our inability to give an "external" characterisation of the temporal in no way unsettles the conceptual health of the family of temporal notions, or shows that we don't know the difference between temporal notions and others. The situation may be, and probably is, the same with the family of normative notions. But this fact—if it is a fact—is of no help if we are trying to say why something natural cannot *also* be normative. For that purpose, we need more than an inexplicit sense that certain notions are similar to each other and different from other notions.

There remains a stubborn feeling that facts about what is right or wrong, what is good or bad, and what we have reason to do have something distinctive in common, and that this common feature is something that a natural fact could not have. But so far we have not been able to say anything very constructive about what this common feature is supposed to be, and as a result we are in no position to say why a natural fact cannot have it.

6. A Suggestion

The fact that one ought to do this rather than that, and the fact that one has reason to do this rather than that, bear their practical relevance on their face; they are explicit answers to the question what to do. Let us suppose that the central concepts in such facts, those of "ought" and of "reason," are therefore pivotal members of a special family of concepts: the N-family. The N-family is of course the family of normative *concepts*. We need not be sure yet which other concepts are members of this family. Any fact expressed in ways in which those concepts play no role may have practical relevance; some such facts are perhaps necessarily practically relevant. But that such facts are practically relevant is a further fact about them. As Parfit puts it, a fact that has normative significance need not for that reason be a normative fact. The difference here is between facts that might be mentioned in answers to the question what to do, and the facts that those facts are relevant to the question what to do. To give a *very* contentious example of this difference: the fact that this action would make many more comfortable and none less comfortable could well be mentioned in an answer to the question whether it is the thing to do, but is not the same fact as the fact that it is relevant to what to do. On this account, therefore, it is not a normative fact, though it is a fact of normative significance, one that makes a difference to what to do.

Some normative facts, then, are more complex than the simple fact that one ought to do this; they contain that fact, but they also contain what makes that simple fact the case. Such facts are of this form: that *p* makes it the case that one ought (or has reason) to act in way *w*. These metafacts are facts about some matter of fact and about its making a difference to how to act. They constitute direct answers not only to the practical question what to do, but also to the question why. It is these metafacts that I think of as the central normative facts, by reference to which the normativity of all others is to be understood. Each such fact is the fact that some other fact stands in a certain normative relation to an action (or a belief or a feeling or a desire ...); I have mentioned two such normative relations, that of "being a reason for" and that of "making it the case that one ought." Let us hope that these will prove to be enough.

Not all normative facts are exactly of this form. First there are those of the simpler form "X ought to A," which don't contain any answer to the question why one ought; such facts, I claim, are still explicitly normative, in virtue of their subject matter.[13] And there are further normative facts to take into account. Consider facts about value; are they normative facts? So far, it would seem not. That something (a violin or a piece of music, say) is good is not an explicit answer to any question what to do or what not to do. The sense in which value-facts are practically relevant is therefore not quite the same as the one I used in claiming practical relevance for facts about what one ought to do or has reason to do. The main difference is that the latter facts specify the action to be done. Though value-facts are about practical relevance, they do not themselves specify the actions concerned; they are silent about what stands on the right-hand side of the normative relation. Nonetheless, to say that something is of value is to say explicitly that its nature makes a difference to how to act, even though we are not told what difference it makes. Value-facts, then, are facts about practical relevance of a rather indeterminate sort (not merely facts *of* indeterminate practical relevance). As one might put it, if a violin is a good one it has reason-giving features, and we know on which side they fall (the pro rather than the con side, as it were)—but we don't yet know what those reasons are reasons to do, to believe, or to feel. In this sense, I want to say, value-facts are normative, and so the concepts centrally involved in them are in the N-family, but their normativity is less well focused.

This, then, is my initial account of what normativity is, an account written in explicitly normative terms (as predicted). It is a feature that a fact can have, and if a fact has it, it is because of that fact's subject matter. The account holds that the notions of reason and ought are the central normative notions.[14] Evaluative notions are normative, too, but they differ structurally from the deontic ones in terms of which normativity is characterized. What other notions have been called normative? One common claim is that the notion of belief is normative; Robert Brandom says that his account of belief is "normative all the way down" (1994, p. 638). Whether this is so or not, on my account, will depend on whether one thinks that believing has normative consequences, or that those "consequences" are better taken to be part of what it is to believe. Is it, that is, that the person who believes that *p* thereby puts herself in a position in which she ought either to abandon that belief or to believe that *q*, should she also believe that if *p*, then *q*? Or is it rather that to be in that position is part of what it is to believe that *p*? Either view is, of course, possible, but only on the latter would the notion of belief be normative; on the former, it is not normative itself, but it has normative significance—as do many other nonnormative notions.

It is worth pointing out that no appeal is here made to any necessary link between the recognition of a normative fact and being motivated by it. People can perfectly well know what they ought to do, and why, and be left cold by it. The same goes for knowledge of what is best, and of what one has reason (even most reason) to do. The appeal here is to the subject matter of the relevant facts, not to any role that recognition of those facts plays in motivation.

I have tried here to give some account of normativity without having more than half an eye on the issue that divides naturalists and nonnaturalists. The idea had been that once we had some understanding of what normativity is, we nonnaturalists would then be able to show that naturalism is a nonstarter. What is more, there was the hope that we would be able to show this all in one go, for any form of naturalism whatever. Certainly that is what Moore was trying to do with his Open Question Argument, and Parfit is essentially after the same prize. My own view, however, is that it is not going to be possible to extract any such blockbuster argument from the characterization of normativity that I have suggested in this section. The characterization will help significantly, of course. But to some extent the different varieties of naturalism each need their own treatment. This is the task to which I now turn.

7. NATURALISMS AND THEIR DEFECTS

Sturgeon's leading thought here is that there is no adequate reason to invent a special metaphysical category for normative facts, because they are all capable of contributing to the causal order. But this is a peculiar inference. The suggestion never was that these normative facts are incapable of contributing to the causal order, and that *therefore* they are special in a way that we dignify by calling them nonnatural. The point, as is now apparent, was rather that there is a difference in subject matter (as I originally put it, a difference in style) between the fact that another fact is of practical relevance and a fact that is of practical relevance. This difference would survive the discovery—if so it be—that facts of both styles can in their various ways affect the causal order. One might say the same about supernatural facts. These can, we suppose, also affect the causal order, since the exercise of supernatural power is supposedly the occasional cause of miraculous but natural events (unnatural perhaps, but not nonnatural). But we might still wish to work with a distinct metaphysical category of the supernatural. Returning then to the normative, normative facts have a distinctive subject matter, and this is what justifies our separating them from others, and placing them in a special category.

Sturgeon could accept the suggestion that normative facts are facts with a distinctive subject matter but could now say that if this is all that the difference between the normative and the nonnormative consists in, there is still no reason to suppose that normative facts cannot be natural. Why couldn't we think of facts about the practical relevance of other facts as natural—especially if they remain capable of contributing to the causal order? This is the point at which we can make no further progress without an acceptable characterization of the natural. For without such a characterization, the subject matter of normative facts is always going to make them look as if they are markedly distinct from the sort of facts that naturalists seem to feel comfortable with.[15] For instance, facts about which facts are of practical relevance to what do not look as if they form part of the subject matter of natural science, they seem to be neither observable nor inferable from what is observable in ways acceptable to such science, they do not form a recognizable part of what we call the natural world—and so on. The *only* characterisation of the natural that the normative does satisfy is the causal one—and that only *possibly*, the matter being very contentious.

All other forms of naturalism allow that there are two ways of capturing one and the same natural fact—the normative way and the nonnormative way. If asked whether the fact itself is normative or nonnormative, their best answer seems to be that the fact is natural and normative, however it is captured or expressed. For we have already decided that whether a fact is normative does not depend on the way it is expressed but on its subject matter. Now this seems to mean that the fact has, as it were, two subject matters. Or does it? I am pursuing the idea that the subject matter of a fact is not to be tied to the terms in which that fact is expressed. If so, we should not just assume that two forms of expression yield two subject matters, any more than that they yield two facts. So the naturalist idea has to be that the subject matter of the fact that this action would maximize welfare could be the same as that of the fact that that fact would make the action right.

Against this, the normativity argument maintains that if we identify moral facts with natural facts in this way, we abolish their normativity—that is, we change their subject matter. It is impossible to reply to this that we don't do that (identity is not reductive), because it just isn't true (and here is the response direct) that the fact that this action maximizes welfare (say) has the same subject matter as the fact that that fact would make the action right. The latter fact is a fact about the practical relevance of the former fact. Further, if we say there is only one fact, that fact will have to be the natural fact, and normative facts will have been abolished; that is, we will have lost the facts themselves, not just their normativity. So identity *is* reductive, in this case.

Then there is the triviality argument.[16] The charge here is that these naturalisms all start with some obviously right-making property, then reduce all others to that one, and then, by identifying rightness with that property, render normatively trivial the claim that actions with that property are right. In terms of reasons, we start from a feature that is an obvious reason for action, reduce all other potential reasons to this one, leaving us with only one sort of reason for action—and then at the last moment we identify that reason with overall rightness, thus rendering it impossible for us to say that it is a reason for action at all. Two things make it incapable of being a reason for action any more. The first is that since it is rightness, it cannot be what makes acts right (other than trivially, of course). The second is that rightness itself is not a reason for doing anything; the reason for doing something will be whatever feature makes it right, in a sense in which what makes an act right cannot be its rightness. (It is not "right because it is right.") In this way, naturalism seems to deprive us of a reason—and, what is more, of a reason that it needs if it is to get going in the first place. In depriving us of that reason, it renders its own central claim at best normatively trivial. The most the relevant remarks can now mean is not "This is a reason for that" but "This is the case, and as another way of reporting the same state of affairs, we could say that that is the case." But this last claim is normatively trivial, even if it might be important information in certain contexts.

8. REPLIES TO THESE ARGUMENTS

The question is whether we can or cannot argue directly from the normativity of such facts as that one ought to do A to their nonidentity with *any* fact capturable in ways that employ no normative concept.[17] The best suggestion I have come up with is that two such facts cannot be identical because they have different subject matters. But I have also suggested that naturalists do best to hold that the same matter of fact can be captured in ways that employ quite different concepts, so that identity of fact is detached from issues of how such facts can be captured. Am I now immediately rejecting this possibility, on the grounds that even if there can be more than one way of capturing one and the same fact (which there surely can), no fact can be expressed in more than one "family" of concepts? Hardly, it seems, because I will be asked what determines when we are dealing with different families rather than different groupings within a family, and no distinction such as the one I have drawn between normative and nonnormative could do other than beg this question. What differences between groupings of concepts are such that no fact could be equally well captured in terms of either grouping? To say that we are dealing with two "families" in the present instance is just to announce without argument that no fact characterizable in a way that employs concepts in the normative group is capturable in ways that don't. But what I had been hoping for is an argument.

Further: even if we allowed that normative facts have their own subject matter, why should we allow that to be enough to show that they cannot be natural? There are plenty of facts with their own distinctive style of subject matter—temporal facts, for instance, or mathematical ones—which we have no difficulty in thinking of as all broadly part of the natural picture. What is so special about the normative ones?

What is driving the nonnaturalists here is the thought that to say that a feature is practically relevant is to make a different sort of claim from any claim that does not explicitly mention practical relevance. The fact that something is of practical relevance is something over and above the something that is of practical relevance. We can talk till we are blue in the face about the way things are, but until we turn to the difference these things make to how to act, we have said nothing normative. There is a vital distinction between direct and indirect ways of answering the practical question what to do; one can answer that question without saying that what one has said is an answer to it. This is why identity of fact cannot be detached from issues of which family of concepts we are using; there just isn't a way of addressing in nonnormative terms the question whether a feature is or isn't of practical relevance.

To this the naturalist should say that the most we have yet learned is that normative facts are not identical with any first-order natural fact. But it is quite possible to have second-order natural facts; a causal fact is often thought of as the fact that one fact caused another fact. What is the basis of the argument that *these* particular second-order facts, the normative ones, cannot be natural? It appears to be their subject matter. If we do not use normative concepts, we cannot address the question what is practically relevant and what is not. Why is that question not a question of natural fact? At this point, again, we are thrown back upon whatever account of the natural the naturalists eventually agree upon. Our claim is that whatever they come up with, it will be impossible to identify these normative facts with any fact that they can allow to be natural. Take one final example of a natural metafact: that the fact that this action would cause pain is one that people want to take into account in deciding whether to do it. Is this a normative fact? Well, is it a fact about some fact's giving us a reason, or about some fact's making an action right? The nonnaturalists say no.

NOTES

In writing this essay, I have been enormously influenced by the work of Derek Parfit—work that is still in progress. Comments from him and from David Copp have much improved the end product, and I have also profited from discussion with Douglas Farland and Michael Ridge.

1. This contrast is peculiar because it seems to involve a cross-categorization. One can contrast the evaluative with the descriptive, and the natural with the ethical. The first contrast is a contrast between two sorts of utterance, or two sorts of predicate, or two sorts of speech act; it is to do with styles of thought and speech. The second one is a contrast between two types of property, say, or of fact. Since Jackson's argument, as I present it, concerns predicates, I express it in terms of the first contrast. (All this means that I find Jackson's concept of "descriptive nature" rather awkward.)

2. In his book, Jackson runs this argument for ethical sentences rather than ethical predicates; I have here tried to show how to run it in terms of predicates, to fit the focus of my discussion of naturalism (which concerns properties and facts rather than truths).

3. Of course the *properties* picked out by those predicates need not be so outlandish, since they can also be picked out by much less outlandish predicates, such as "good."

4. I will leave this "merely possible" naturalism out of account in what follows. The main reason for holding such a view would be the belief that nothing could show the categories of the normative and the natural to be mutually exclusive; they might overlap.

5. Jackson, by contrast, has at least one argument that makes no appeal at all to metaphysical naturalism: his argument from the supervenience of the ethical on the descriptive. This appeals to local facts about the ethical, not to general metaphysics.

6. I should mention here the sort of argument provided by moral functionalists, as exemplified by Michael Smith. Moral functionalists claim that the concept of rightness is the concept of whatever property plays a certain role. In *The Moral Problem* (1995) Michael Smith claims (pp. 177, 185) that the rightness of an act A in C is this feature: that we would desire that A be done if we were fully rational. And he moves from this to the claim that the rightness of an act A in C is that (natural, if you will) feature of A that we would desire acts to have in C if we were fully rational. It is hard to tell whether this is best viewed as an argument for analytic naturalism or for nonanalytic naturalism. But it is a fallacy anyway. It is one thing to say that being right is being what we would desire to do if we were fully rational; it is another to say that to be right is to have natural feature F, the feature that we would desire our acts to have if we were fully rational. Only the latter is a form of naturalism; and it cannot be established by appeal to the former.

7. I don't mean, by using the term "style," to suggest that the relevant difference will be a trivial or shallow one. One can think of the style of a fact in a way similar to the style of a building; there need be no suggestion that the same building could have been built in a different style.

8. Parfit is not happy with this argument as it stands, because of the relation between the following.

A: Heat is that property, whatever it is, that gives objects certain powers such as that of turning liquids into gases.
B: Molecular kinetic energy is the property that gives objects those powers.

Together these two entail that heat is molecular kinetic energy, which is an important discovery. Now on some criteria of fact-identity, A and B report the same fact. Suppose, however, that A is true in virtue of meaning alone. Can we avoid the conclusion that B is true in virtue of meaning alone?

9. In putting things in this way, I am to some extent loading the dice against naturalism. For a naturalist might well want to say that the fact that an action would make many more comfortable and nobody less comfortable is a normative fact. But what I am trying to do at this point is to develop a conception of normativity that can help to show what the nonnaturalists are driving at when they say that no natural fact could be a normative fact. (I am not trying [yet] to develop one that shows that the nonnaturalists are right about this.) The present conception of normativity, though a possible one, would be no help.

10. It would do this because every feature (even if it is not in fact a reason) is such that, if it were a reason and there were no other reason, it would decide the issue.

11. I owe this example to Michael Ridge.

12. Note that the naturalists have no reason at all to dispute this part of the story—quite the opposite. They are not trying to deny normativity or to maintain that there is no such notion, but to naturalize it.

13. This notion of the subject matter of a fact is not supposed to be tendentious. A good plumber knows pretty well everything there is to know about how to mend leaks. If what the plumber knows are facts, they have a subject matter, namely, how to mend leaks.

14. My own view is that the notion of ought can be explicated in terms of reasons

(in terms of the notion of "most reason," in fact); but I am not allowing that view to complicate the picture here.

15. Of course, Sturgeon could say that we are dealing with a spectrum here, and that normative facts stand at one end of it, with the spectrum shading gently away from them to the hard physical facts at the other end. But this is a picture that many nonnaturalists would be happy with. They would say it is not a form of natural*ism* at all.

16. As I said much earlier, this argument does not address the views of Jackson and Sturgeon.

17. It is worth noting that, as I have presented things, the naturalists are saying that *all* evaluative properties and facts *must* be identical with descriptive properties and facts, while the nonnaturalists are saying that none can be. Between these two views there is a large gap. Might it not be that some are and some are not? If things were to turn out that way, it would be a defeat for both sides. The naturalists' moral metaphysics would have to undergo serious readjustment. The nonnaturalists would be in a slightly better case; officially, they should be pleased by the discovery that there is irreducible normativity. But they would lose what is their main argument against the naturalists, which is that no normative property could be natural; and it is not clear what argument could be put in its place.

REFERENCES

Blackburn, Simon. 1998. *Ruling Passions.* Oxford: Clarendon Press.

Boyd, Richard. 1988. "How to Be a Moral Realist." In Sayre-McCord, 1988, 181–228.

Brandom, Robert. 1994. *Making It Explicit.* Cambridge, Mass.: Harvard University Press.

Dancy, Jonathan. 1993. *Moral Reasons.* Oxford: Blackwell.

———. 1999. "Can the Particularist Learn the Difference between Right and Wrong?" In *The Proceedings of the Twentieth World Congress of Philosophy,* vol. 1, *Ethics,* ed. K. Brinkmann, 59–72. Bowling Green, Ohio: Philosophy Documentation Center, Bowling Green State University.

Foot, Philippa. 2001. *Natural Goodness.* Oxford: Clarendon Press.

Gibbard, Allan. 1990. *Wise Choices, Apt Feelings.* Oxford: Clarendon Press.

Hooker, Brad, and Margaret Little, eds. 2000. *Moral Particularism.* Oxford: Clarendon Press.

Hursthouse, Rosalind. 1999. *On Virtue Ethics.* Oxford: Clarendon Press.

Jackson, Frank. 1998. *From Metaphysics to Ethics: A Defence of Conceptual Analysis.* Oxford: Oxford University Press.

McDowell, John. 1998. *Mind, Value, and Reality.* Cambridge, Mass.: Harvard University Press.

Mackie, John. 1977. *Ethics: Inventing Right and Wrong.* Harmondsworth, England: Penguin Books.

Moore, G. E. 1903. *Principia Ethica.* Cambridge: Cambridge University Press.

Parfit, Derek. Forthcoming. *Rediscovering Reasons.*

Raz, Joseph. 1999. "The Truth in Particularism." In *Engaging Reason,* 218–246. Oxford: Clarendon Press. Reprinted in Hooker and Little, 2000, 48–78.

Ross, Sir David. 1930. *The Right and the Good*. Oxford: Clarendon Press.
————. 1939. *Foundations of Ethics*. Oxford: Clarendon Press.
Sayre-McCord, Geoffrey, ed. 1988. *Essays on Moral Realism*. Ithaca, N.Y.: Cornell University Press.
Sidgwick, Henry. 1907. *Methods of Ethics*. London: Macmillan.
Smith, Michael. 1995. *The Moral Problem*. Oxford: Blackwell.
Sturgeon, Nicholas. 1988. "Moral Explanations." In Sayre-McCord, 1988, 229–255.
————. 2003. "Moore on Ethical Naturalism." *Ethics* 113: 528–556.

CHAPTER 5

ANTIREALIST EXPRESSIVISM AND QUASI-REALISM

SIMON BLACKBURN

1. SOME BACKGROUND

POSITIONS known as 'expressivist' in contemporary moral philosophy have an ancestry in the sentimentalists' opposition to rationalism in the eighteenth century, and particularly in the moral theory of David Hume (1888). In his *Treatise*, Hume undertakes to show that morality is "more properly felt than judged of," and firmly locates it as a delivery of our passions or sentiments. It is not the result of any kind of algebra or geometry of reason, and neither is it a matter of observation. Hume had many objections to these rival views, but most forcefully he argued that ethics is essentially a practical subject, and in order to control our practice it needs a motivational aspect that neither of these sources could supply. Moral commitments exist purely in order to determine preference and practice, whereas other commitments exist at the service of any desire that happens to come along and pick them up. This is not, of course, to say that we always do what we think we ought to do, for attitudes can have the most surprising expression, depending on what else is in the agent's psychological mix. It is at best to say that we do what we think we ought to do, or love what we admire, other things being equal. Other things are not always equal, and all that should be claimed is that when people knowingly succumb to temptation, or are attracted by what they know to be wrong, something is out of joint. The natural expressions of love are concern and kindness, but when things are out of joint, love leads people to kill that which they love.

Hume's view attracted few other philosophers, until in the twentieth century the objections to a rival, 'realist' theory, making ethics a matter of knowledge and truth, became sufficiently pressing to motivate philosophers to revisit the eighteenth-century tradition.

Shortly after the beginning of the twentieth century, G. E. Moore delivered what became known as the Open Question Argument against ethical naturalism. This argument purported to show that any adequate philosophy of ethics needed to put a distance between moral and ethical judgment, on the one hand, and judgment about empirical matters, or about the kind of things talked of in natural science, on the other hand. Moore's argument purported to separate strictly moral or ethical judgments, or what he called judgments of Goodness, from the whole field of empirical and scientific judgment. Judgments of Goodness give us the field of normative judgment, whereby we endorse some things and condemn others, or insist on some things and permit others. By Moore's argument, they are to be separated from judgments about how things stand, including how they stand psychologically. Judgments of health and happiness, what is actually desired or avoided, fall on the 'natural' side. Judgments of what ought to be the case, or what is good or desirable, fall on the normative side.

Of course, people will make normative judgments in the light of what they take the empirical and scientific facts to be. But the Open Question Argument asserts that people might take all the empirical and scientific facts as settled, but still have room to doubt whether a particular moral judgment, or judgment of Goodness, is the one to make in the light of those facts. In particular, people making a bizarre evaluation in the light of agreed facts might convict themselves of being unpleasant or idiosyncratic, but they do not disqualify themselves as not knowing the meaning of moral terms.

Similarly, those who look to rather different facts in the light of which to make judgments of Goodness do not thereby talk past each other. They are to be seen as disagreeing. But disagreement involves shared content of judgment, a content that one side judges true and the other side judges false. Hence, again, there is a space between the proposition or content judged and the underlying standards in virtue of which it is judged. Different standards may still result in the same verdict, and a dissident giving a different verdict can still be in the business of making valuations.

Moore himself took the argument to compel ethical intuitionism. This is the view that moral judgments have a distinct identity, and that these distinct, sui generis propositions are judged only by an equally distinct faculty of intuition, specially adapted to deliver them. Thinking of truth, the view would be that these propositions are made true or false by their own kinds of fact, facts about the normative order of things. It seems as though Plato was right, that there is a world of Forms, or Norms—a kind of cosmic determination of what is right or wrong, rational or unacceptable. Something above and beyond Nature, something nonnatural, includes haloes on some kinds of conduct, and razor wire forbidding others. These norms are, fortunately, accessible to human beings, but only through a strange, tailor-made faculty known as intuition.

It is easy to see that this yields no very satisfactory philosophy of value. Among other problems, it gives no account of why we should be interested in the propositions that, on the theory, form the subject matter of ethics. Just as colors seem to be entirely optional objects of concern, so norms, values, duties, rights, and indeed other things that float free of the natural world must surely be optional objects of interest. For those of us mired in practical matters, such as human pleasures and pains, desires and needs, the world of ethics would seem to be something of a distraction. If the normative nature of things is so distinct from their ordinary nature, it is not only difficult to see how it has to be an object of interest, but even difficult to see how it is possible for it to engage us. The 'magnetism' of Goodness seems quite inexplicable. Yet Moore's argument against naturalism seemed to block any return to saying that the subject matter of ethics is just underlying human pleasures and pains, desires and needs.

After Moore, philosophers fixing their gaze on judgments of Goodness eventually confronted the dilemma that either their content was equivalent to that of empirical or scientific propositions or it was not. If the former, the account conflates 'is' with 'ought' and falls to the Open Question Argument. If the latter, the account fails because of the nebulous subject matter with which it purports to deal. This impasse opened the way toward an entirely different approach. This did not stare at the judgment of Goodness, asking what was being judged true or false. Instead it asked what was being done by human beings when they go in for ethics. And there seemed to be an obvious answer: when people express themselves in the normative terms of ethics and morals, they are voicing practical attitudes and emotions. They may be doing other things as well: inviting or insisting on others sharing those attitudes or emotions, or prescribing ways to behave, or demanding conformity to ways of behaving. These practical functions seem to give ethics its identity. In that case, the function of normative sentences is not to represent either peculiar Moorean facts about the world or more mundane empirical facts about the world. It is to avow attitudes, to persuade others, to insist on conformities and prescribe behavior. So was born the 'emotivism' of A. J. Ayer and Charles Stevenson (Ayer, 1936; Stevenson, 1944). In Ayer's famous words:

> The presence of an ethical symbol in a proposition adds nothing to its factual content. Thus if I say to someone, "You acted wrongly in stealing that money," I am not stating anything more than if I had simply said, "You stole that money." In adding that this action is wrong I am not making any further

statement about it. I am simply evincing my moral disapproval of it. It is as if I had said "You stole that money" in a peculiar tone of horror, or written it with the addition of some special exclamation marks.

2. REFINING THE THEORY

This practical approach to the function of moral language and moral thought allows for a number of refinements. Although Ayer and Stevenson concentrated upon the practical function of expressing emotion, it was easy to see that in many cases, ethical thinking can be relatively unemotional. The eighteenth century worked in terms of sentiments and passions. A better term may be 'attitude' or 'stance'. R. M. Hare influentially put the issuing of prescriptions at the heart of his account (1952). In more modern writings, the approach is generically called 'expressivism', leaving some latitude in identifying exactly what is expressed. This latitude is not a weakness of the approach, but simply reflects the fact that our ethical reactions can be more or less emotional, more or less demanding, and more or less prescriptive. Different cultures may exhibit different ethical 'styles'. One may work in terms of sin, bringing in attitudes like disgust and fear of pollution. Another may work in terms of shame, with social sanctions expressed in terms of contempt and designed to arouse corresponding embarrassment or shame on the part of the wrongdoer. And a third may work in terms of guilt, with social sanctions expressed in terms of anger and resentment, and designed to arouse corresponding guilt on the part of the wrongdoer. In other words, the ethic of a culture can be 'variably realized' in the emotional tone that accompanies the practical pressures people put on themselves and others.

There is a need to give some further description of the territory, however. For if nothing more is said, expressivism would face the objection that the state of mind expressed may just be the state of mind of believing that something is Good, and no advance has been made. The most influential metaphor directing this part of the area has been that of Elizabeth Anscombe (1957). Anscombe contrasted two different ways of using a shopping list. In the first, the list directs the subject's purchases. It tells the subject what to do. In the second, the list records the subject's purchases. It records what the subject has bought. In the first use, the list is prescriptive or directive, whereas in the second, it is descriptive or representational. A philosopher like Moore conceives of normative propositions as representational, but then flounders on the question of what they represent. The expressivist approach conceives them as prescriptive or directive. In the best known way of explaining the metaphor, it is said that normative language has a different 'direction of fit' to the world. It exists in order to direct action and change the world. It does not exist in order to represent any natural part of it, and still less some occult part of it (Smith, 1988).

This makes it sound as though normative expressions are more like expressions of desire—which also have the different direction of fit with the world—than like expressions of representational states such as belief. So a direct approach to identifying the relevant attitudes would be to seek an outright reduction of moral attitude, for example, in terms of what we desire, or what we desire to desire. But such reductions are usually uncomfortable. Simple desire or liking scarcely gets us into the territory of ethics at all, not least since there need be no disagreement between two people, one of whom likes X and one of whom does not. At the least, ethics seems to concern desires that in some sense we insist upon, or which we demand from other people.

Desire to desire does not do either. For I may desire to desire X because I regret my feeble appetite for X and am aware that people who do desire X get more fun out of life. But that is different both from admiring X and admiring the desire for X. A better general description might locate the ethical in terms of those springs of action with which an agent is most identified, and this in turn would be manifested by things like reluctance to change or reluctance to tolerate variation. Ethics is about our practical insistences, including centrally those with which we set ourselves to comply, or hope ourselves to comply (Blackburn, 1998; Tiberius, 2000).

The obvious advantage of expressivism is that it has no difficulty accounting for the motivational nature of moral commitment. Moral commitment is described and identified in terms of its motivational function. Attitudes, for or against things, are unproblematically motivating. But then a difficulty opens up on the other side, falling into danger of making the connection too close, which means closing any space for the phenomena of weakness of will. We want to leave it open that an agent should judge, with certainty, that succumbing to some temptation is not the thing to do, but go ahead and do it anyhow. We do not always live up to our better selves. We may fail to do so when we are listless or peevish, or simply perverse or weak. The expressivist (like anybody else) should acknowledge such phenomena.

In order to accommodate them to an attitudinal account of ethical commitment, they should be diagnosed as cases of the house divided against itself. With weakness of will part of us pulls one way, but part of us pulls the other way, and on the particular occasion this is the part that wins. An attitude can be compared with a disposition, and dispositions do not always manifest themselves when you might expect them to do so. A fragile glass might unexpectedly bounce on being dropped instead of shattering. If it bounces too often, the view that it is fragile starts to lose ground. Similarly, if temptation wins too often, we begin to doubt the strength of the alleged moral commitment, and diagnoses of hypocrisy or mere lip-service to an ideal start to gain ground. But in honest-to-God weakness of will, the moral vector is still operating, and this can be shown by subsequent remorse, or embarrassment at being caught, or a variety of discomforts. Weakness of will is typically uncomfortable, just because our inclinations are out of line with what we would wish to insist on, from ourselves or others. If we consider an attitude such as disapproval of an action, the right thing for an expressivist to say is that such an attitude is (necessarily) such as to result in condemnation of the action or avoidance of the action, other things being equal. But this does not mean that in our actual psychologies, the attitude inevitably trumps whatever other desires or tendencies pull us toward the action. For other things are not always equal.

It is also plain that expressing an attitude should not be thought of simply in terms of letting other people know that you have the attitude. Rather, an attitude is put forward as something to be adopted. The action is one of attempting public coordination or sharing of the attitude. Similarly, the speaker's own state of mind is not the topic. Not only can one express attitudes one does not oneself hold, but one can sincerely express attitudes one falsely believes oneself to hold, and it can be one's subsequent behavior that informs someone of the mistake. This is no more than parallel to cases where in describing things one can say things one does not oneself believe, or which one sincerely but mistakenly supposes oneself to believe.

Expressivism thus distinguished itself from the position sometimes called naive or vulgar subjectivism, in which a speaker is interpreted as simply describing what he or she feels about an issue. For the naive subjectivist, ethical judgments are true or false according to whether the speaker is sincere. The truth-condition of a speaker's utterance "Hitler was abominable" is just that the speaker holds or feels that Hitler is abominable. This account is just wrong. It is not our practice to allow the truth of such a claim simply on the grounds that the speaker feels one way or another (the theory is also regressive, in that it still needs an account of what it is that the speaker feels, the content of the "that" clause). Expressivism avoids these problems by denying that the speaker is describing his own mind. He is voicing his mind, that is, putting forward an attitude or stance as the attitude or stance that is to be held.

An expressivist theory will also want to say something about strength of attitude. There is a difference, intuitively, between believing with not too much confidence that Saddam Hussein is very bad indeed and believing with a lot of confidence or certainty that he is at least rather bad. If expressivism is to cope with this kind of subtle difference, it will need a parallel difference in attitude. But since attitudes do not seem to be more or less probable, this may prove difficult to do. We might imagine an attitude of 'loathing', corresponding to the view that Saddam is very bad indeed, and an attitude of 'disliking', corresponding to the view that he is rather bad. This gives us one dimension of variation. Then the problem is that our moral beliefs seem to permit two dimensions: the very bad/rather bad dimension, and the probable/certain dimension. Here the solution will be to come up with a difference that plays the same function as the probable/certain dimension. We might suggest a difference in the 'robustness' with which an attitude is held, measured by the amount of evidence or persuasion it would take to shift it. Loathing of Saddam combined with a tincture of uncertainty about a lot of the evidence might succumb quite quickly to propaganda on his behalf, whereas dislike of him that is strongly founded would survive all but the most revisionary of stories about recent history.

At first sight, disagreement in attitude is easy to understand. If I am for something, and you are against it, then we disagree. If it is the time for our attitudes to issue in a choice, then, other things being equal, I will choose it and you will not, or I will require it and you will require its absence. But, as with confidence, there are subtleties here as well. I may admire something, but you simply have no opinion about it. Is this to count as disagreement? We might so count it: zealots reject anything other than precise conformity of attitude. This is the idea that if you are not with us you are against us, as when a true believer counts agnosticism as a heresy just as much as overt atheism. But in principle, having no attitude either way is to be distinguished from having thought about it and decided that there is equal merit on both sides. Again, the expressivist can point to the relative robustness of the different states. In probability theory, a gambler who has no opinion either way about whether a coin is biased may bet at the same rate as someone who has done exhaustive experiments and convinced herself that the coin is unbiased. The difference between them is that it would take more evidence to shift the betting rate of the second person than the first. Her betting rate is robust. Similarly, if someone has no attitude either way, they should be relatively quickly responsive to incoming evidence in favour of one side or the other. Whereas if someone has thought about it and arrived at the view that there are equal merits on each side, it will take more to persuade her of an asymmetry.

3. EXPRESSIVISM AND ERROR

Even if it provides a satisfactory account of the states of mind, the 'attitudes' associated with normativity, expressivism still faces problems. To many philosophers, it seems to take away too much. It seems to take away any notion of real normative truth. Indeed, that was one of its motivations, since it was difficulty with the nature of normative facts and our access to them that led to the flight from Moore. But then the fear arises that we are left with too little. The fear crystallizes around the idea that our language, thought, and practice are premised on the idea that there is a normative order, a way things ought to be. But expressivism tries to get by without saying this, and so in the eyes of critics it falls short of giving an adequate account of ethical language, thought, and practice. These are premised on allegiance to a moral 'reality'. But expressivism regards moral reality as a myth, and allegiance to it as self-deception.

This kind of unease can be expressed in many ways. When we moralize (using this is a catch-all term for any way of expressing evaluative or normative opinion), we think we are getting things right. We think some opinions are certain, and others less so. If we are of undogmatic temper, we may indeed worry whether our cherished moral opinion may, in fact, be mistaken. We certainly think others are often mistaken. We also go in for working out the implications of our views, sometimes getting ourselves into quite complex chains of moral reasonings. We do not automatically suppose that our first thoughts are our best thoughts. We go cautiously, acknowledge fallibility, and sometimes recognize that we were wrong. But sometimes we think we know the answer, and we think we know of methods for getting the answer. We prize our rationality, in this area as others, and our objectivity when we follow the argument wherever it leads. We also recognize that moral truth is often 'mind-independent'. Our thinking something is right or wrong does not make it so. Our responses have to answer to the moral truth. They do not create it.

All these thoughts and activities make up what we can call the realist surface of everyday moralizing. They seem to suggest that we take ourselves to be beholden to a moral reality, which we are attempting to represent correctly.

It can be held, and was held by John Mackie, that this realist surface of our moralizing shows that we are in the grip of a myth or error. Mackie thought that these features demonstrate our allegiance to the Moorean picture: a real normative order and mysterious access to it, and of course an equally mysterious interest in it (Mackie, 1977). But he also thought the Moorean picture was philosophically indefensible. As a result, our ordinary moralizing is predicated upon a false picture of the universe and what it contains. It is as erroneous as the picture of ethics as concerned with the commandments of God (if you believe in a particular God, substitute that it is as erroneous as the picture of ethics as concerned with the commandments of a different God). Since there is no God, or not that one, you cannot have that metaphysics, and since there is no Moorean reality, you cannot have that either. But that means rejecting the 'fictitious external authority' that is claimed for moral truth by ordinary moralizing.

Or at least, it seems to require doing that. But, perhaps wisely, Mackie faltered at drawing this consequence from his error theory. He recognized that some kind of practical discourse was going to take place. If it was not full-scale moralizing, it would have to be something without the realistic surface. It would be more overtly prescriptive and persuasive. So the idea becomes that expressivism is as good as it gets. It doesn't give us an account of our full-scale practice of moralizing. But it gives us a handy substitute, rejecting only those aspects of our practice and thought that are indefensible anyhow.

This in turn raises the question of how much escapes the wreck. If ordinary moralizing with its realist surface is indefensible, what does the defensible substitute look like, and how is it different? Perhaps it would look very different. For example, it might deal only in overt prescriptions like the Ten Commandments: thou shalt do this, thou shalt not do that. Or it might confine itself to overt expressions of being for something (Hooray!) or against it (Boo!). Such simple language would have no room for expressing thoughts of fallibility, or mistake, or improvement, or getting things right, nor any other thoughts that essentially involve some idea of moral truth or falsity.

But perhaps the defensible substitute would not look nearly as different as this, or even very different at all. This opens the door to the persona christened the "quasi-realist" (Blackburn, 1984, p. 171). Quasi-realism was explained as trying to earn, on an expressivist basis, the features that tempt people to realism. In other words, it suggests that the realistic surface of the discourse does not have to be jettisoned. It can be explained and defended even by expressivists. Perhaps surprisingly, thoughts about fallibility, objectivity, independence, knowledge, and rationality, as well as truth and falsity themselves, would be available even to people thinking of themselves as antirealists.

Quasi-realism is different from expressivism itself. As we have just seen, John Mackie was an expressivist but not a quasi-realist. And one might hold that the program of reconciling the realistic surface with the expressivist account is successful, but have other reasons for rejecting the expressivist account. But to the extent that quasi realism is successful, the doubts arising from the realistic surface of moralizing disappear. So quasi-realism is well seen as the attempt to save expressivism from error theory. It attempts to show that ordinary moral thought is not infected root and branch with philosophical myth.

Quasi-realism works to explain why things that steer philosophers toward realism need not do so. Suppose, for example, a realist trumpets the mind-independence of ethics. A person or a culture may think something right without that making it right. Denying women the vote is wrong, whatever your or I or anyone else thinks. Can an expressivist say as much? This is to be assessed in the standard way, of imagining scenarios or possible worlds in which you or I or others think that women should not have a vote, and passing a verdict on them. Naturally, these scenarios or possibilities excite condemnation, and so the answer is that denying women the vote is wrong, whatever you or I or anyone else thinks about it. In giving that answer one is, of course, standing *within* one's own moral view. One is assessing the scenario in the light of things one thinks and feels about such matters. But that is no objection, since there is no other mode of assessment possible. One cannot pass a verdict without using those parts of one's mind that enable one to pass a verdict.

Again, consider the idea that on some moral matter we may not know the truth. For example, imagine us wondering what to think about someone's conduct. Was he selfish and despicable, or prudently protecting himself in an unfortunate situation? Things are factored in; the matter is turned in different lights; things we do not know about may be suggested. Any verdict may be provisional and liable to reassessment in the light of further information, or a more imaginative understanding of information we already have. We may incline one way, but admit that we do not really know, just because we have a lively awareness of further evidence, further factors, possible improvements in our understanding of what happened or our reactions to what we know happened. Such things might dispose us to incline a different way. Again, the phenomenon seems entirely consistent with, and indeed explicable by, the expressivist.

For a final example, consider the idea that on any moral issue, there is just one right answer. Rather than seeing this as a metaphysical thesis, testifying to the completeness of Moore's world of Norms and Forms, the quasi-realist will encourage a pragmatic or practical construal. The doctrine can be seen as a strenuous piece of practical advice: when there are still two things to think, keep on worrying. Beaver away, and eventually, it is promised, one opinion will deserve to prevail. This is itself the expression of an attitude to practical reasoning (and by no means a compulsory one). Accepting such an attitude is not, however, the badge of realism, but simply the optimism that our best efforts can, in the end, close any issue, provided we keep at it long enough.

4. THE FREGE-GEACH ARGUMENT

In his essay "Assertion" (1965), Peter Geach picked up a problem from Frege and applied it to expressivism. The expressivist tells us what happens when a sentence is asserted. "Lying is wrong" expresses condemnation of lying. But what of the sentence "If lying is wrong, then getting your little brother to lie is wrong"? Here the sentence "lying is wrong" occurs, but no condemnation of lying is made.

This does not sound too daunting. It sounds at first blush as if there is simply a gap in expressivism, and a little further work to do. But Geach sharpened his point by considering elementary valid arguments such as the following.

(A)   Lying is wrong.
(B)   If lying is wrong, then getting your little brother to lie is wrong.
So: (C)   Getting your little brother to lie is wrong.

The expressivist says that (A) expresses an attitude to lying. But no attitude to lying is expressed by (B). So how can the two provide the premises for the valid deduction to (C)? The inference is clearly valid, yet the expressivist seems to say that there is a fallacy of equivocation.

Geach claimed that he had shown expressivism to be "hopeless," and in particular insisted that his argument refuted the prescriptive theory of R. M. Hare. But Hare (1970) pointed out that a parallel "equivocation" seems to affect most other semantic views. Consider an entirely nonevaluative instance of *modus ponens*:

(A')   The cat is on the mat.
(B')   If the cat is on the mat, the dog will shortly attack it.
So (C')   The dog will shortly attack it.

Here (A') is usually described as expressing a belief or an assertion. But the same sentence as it occurs in (B') expresses no belief or assertion. So equally there seems to be ground for the charge of equivocation. In classical or Fregean semantics, this is met by the distinguishing between the force with which a sentence is put forward and its sense. The sense is the thought it expresses, and thoughts can be put forward either assertively or not. So the force shifts, from (A') to (B'), but the identity of content remains, and is sufficient to ensure the validity of the argument. But then, in a parallel way, Hare pointed out that the attitude expressed in (A) remains "in the offing" in (B), and just as the classical notion of sense or 'thought' is postulated to provide something in common to occasions of assertion like (A) and others such as (B), so a notion of attitude or stance should be able to cover the same shift. Hare's point was later reinforced by Gibbard (1992a), who pointed out that any logically complex or indirect context marks an upgrade from simple signaling. Any sentence, considered as asserted, is something like an animal signal. But there is just the same problem of understanding the complexity that arrives when we move from simple signals to complex representations that are capable of negation, or of being elements of disjunctions or implications. This is a common problem for everyone, expressivist or not (Gibbard, 1992b).

In his *Spreading the Word* (1984), Blackburn started from Frege's own semantics, according to which in indirect contexts such as (B) or (B') the sense of a component sentence itself becomes the reference of the overall sentence. The proposition or thought that is ordinarily asserted by the component itself becomes the topic of the complex. So we should be able to view the conditional (B) as itself expressing something about the interplay of two first-order attitudes, in this case the disapproval of lying and the disapproval of getting your little brother to do it for you. In effect, the conditional voices a disapproval of any moral system, or sensibility, that contains the first but not the second. Coupled with premise (A), construed as voicing disapproval of lying, a sensibility must then contain the second, on pain of being so badly 'fractured' that one would not know what to make of the overall combination. The vice seemed sufficiently parallel to classical inconsistency to deliver a satisfactory expressivist theory of the inference, since logically valid inference and avoidance of logical inconsistency are generally regarded as coming to the same thing.

This idea of a fractured sensibility puzzled many critics, who argued that it would at worst deserve to be regarded as some kind of moral fault (Brighouse, 1990; Hale, 1986; Hurley, 1989; Schueler, 1988; Wright, 1988; Zangwill, 1992). In response to early critics, Blackburn (1988) modified the theory. Drawing on conceptual role semantics (Harman, 1974), he proposed to view the interplay between the two component attitudes in a different light. In conceptual role semantics, the conditional (B) is given its meaning simply by its role in forcing (A) to (C) (or not-C to not-A). Anyone voicing the conditional is announcing himself as 'tied to a tree', a situation in which if one side is closed off, the other must be adopted. This tie can be construed the same way whichever is the 'direction of fit' of the components. That is, it should not matter whether the limbs of the tree express attitudes or beliefs with truth conditions. The higher-order attitudes to attitudes of Blackburn (1984) remain in place only as motivations or justifications for conditionals, while it is their inferential role that gives their meaning. The proposal has continued to be controversial (Hale, 1993, 2002; Kölbel, 2002; Unwin, 2001; Wedgwood, 1997; responses include Blackburn, 1993, 2002).

Gibbard (1990) provided an elegant related semantical development of expressivism. In Gibbard's accounts, norms are treated rather like prescriptions. Accepting a normative directive is treated as basic and is assimilated to having a plan rather than having a belief. But only a limited number of statements express such acceptance directly. Others are explained by their inferential relations to this basic kind of state. The semantics proceeds by generalizing the classical view of inconsistency. What is especially wrong with an inconsistent set of statements is that it rules out all full possibilities. In the factual realm, this means ruling out all possible worlds. When we include plans as well as factual statements, inconsistency is generalized: what is wrong with an inconsistent set of statements-plus-norms is that it rules out every 'factual normative world'. Its special defect, in other words, is that it logically rules out every combination of plans with facts.

5. RIVALS

There are currently (2003) at least four influential approaches to the nature of ethics that dissent either from expressivism itself or from the combination of expressivism and quasi-realism. The first has derived from the work of writers such as Philippa Foot and pursues a generally Aristotelian tradition. The second derives from Thomas Nagel and John Rawls and pursues a Kantian, or Kantian-contractarian, tradition. The third is a resurgent 'naturalism', protected by various subtleties that might blunt the force of Moore's attack on what he saw as nineteenth-century ethical naturalism. The fourth, fictionalism, is a descendant of John Mackie's error theory and pursues the view that in moralizing we endorse certain kind of fiction.

Although the details differ, a common theme of the first three approaches is that the attitudes and stances highlighted by expressivists are themselves not 'mere' states of will or desire but are either motivated, or sustained, or confined and given their shape by some combination of reason and nature. But it has to be noticed at the outset that this is not itself a claim that expressivism needs to deny. Hume himself made no sweeping claims about the difference between his approach to ethics and that of Aristotle, and both he and subsequent expressivists are usually quite hospitable to the idea that what we can naturally admire or desire is heavily constrained by common elements of human nature, thereby making contact with large parts of Aristotle. Hume never suggests that we 'choose' our values in some kind of existentialist lunge, nor that we can just choose to cultivate whatever virtues we like. Hume's emphasis on a progress of the sentiments, as we mature and become experienced and imaginative in our reactions to things, is close to Aristotle's emphasis on the education and acculturation required of the person of practical wisdom.

Modern Aristotelian theories have further elements that are quite compatible with expressivism. For example, expressivists may adopt 'virtue ethics', in which the primary objects of evaluation are dispositions or traits of character that constitute virtues or vices, rather than acts or 'states of affairs'. Once more, Hume himself shows a lot of sympathy with this priority, although he also sympathizes with the view that there is an answer to the question of how any particular trait gets characterized as a virtue, namely that it is "useful or agreeable to ourselves or others." But the question of whether this is a necessary or useful measure of virtue is orthogonal to expressivism, for it hinges on one's attitude to this degree of utilitarianism, and an expressivist may go either way on that.

If there is an opposition from Aristotelianism, it may lie in the view that there is no 'disentangling' of fact from value. Taking a hint from Wittgenstein's rule-following considerations, John McDowell and others have supposed that 'thick' ethical terms, like "courageous" or "sympathetic" or "coarse" or "lewd," blend together fact and value in a seamless whole. To apply such terms is not first to get the facts and then to express an attitude to them, but to make an application, in one mental act, of a concept or rule that has been taught in some circumstances, and that, because of our common human natures, we are apt to go on and apply in the same new circumstances as each other.

The expressivist diagnoses the phenomenon differently. There is an attitude involved in the typical use of such terms, and the attitude conspires with judgment to drive the application. You do not call it courageous unless you approve of it for a certain reason, namely, that it involved some suppression of fear or capacity to overcome difficulty that would put others off. You do not call it lewd unless you want to express a rather complex reaction, or at least one of a possible range of complex reactions, to it as a display of sexual awareness. With a change in attitude would come a change in the application of the term, and with a sufficient change in attitude, the term may lose its identity altogether.

In practice, the Wittgensteinian approach and expressivism are not all that different. Each allows that morality requires a progress of the sentiments, that some are better at it than others, that there are mistakes and failures. Each, too, allows the motivating aspect of moral judgment. The expressivist does so directly, as I have shown, while the Wittgensteinian approach will assert that proper appreciation of someone's courage or lewdness both requires and engages potentially motivating sentiments of admiration or revulsion. Each approach allows talk of truth. The difference is not so much one of ethical theory, but one of an attitude to the possibilities of philosophy. The expressivist thinks that certain kinds of explanation of what we are doing are possible, for instance, in terms that contrast moral judgment with other kinds of representation of the way of the world. The Wittgensteinian is suspicious of the pretensions of philosophy and the possibility of theory. In Gareth Evans's phrase, the rule-following considerations act as a "metaphysical wet-blanket."

The rationalism of Kant is often opposed to expressivism, but once more the battlefield is confused. Kant is not concerned to deny that moral principles are expressions of resolutions or 'maxims' of the will. He is only concerned that some of them should be certified as binding by 'pure practical reason'. It is notoriously unclear what this means, but in principle it sounds like the consistent conjunction of expressivism with something akin to the injunction to avoid self-contradiction in theoretical reasonings. In other words, it is quite consistent to add to expressivism the thought that certain kinds of conduct, and especially conduct along the lines of 'making an exception of yourself' can be ruled out by reason alone. Indeed, Hume may be said to anticipate part of Kant by insisting that practical reasonings that deserve to be called ethical or moral need to be conducted from a "common point of view." This also makes him an ancestor of modern contractarian positions, even if these overtly owe their allegiance to Kant. R. M. Hare (1952) is an example of the view that ethics is a matter of issuing prescriptions—that nevertheless takes the form these prescriptions may take to be heavily constrained by Kantian considerations.

Naturalism is a broad church, and expressivism itself aspires to being a naturalistic story about human propensities to evaluate and forbid and require things. A rather different kind of naturalism works in terms of moral properties, which it then seeks to identify with 'natural' properties, meaning roughly those that could be the subject matter of a science: empirical or theoretical properties of people and things. A moral commitment, on this view, asserts the instancing of a property, just like an empirical or scientific commitment, whereas for the expressivist this is not so. However, expressivism's objection to an approach in terms of property identity does not rest with simple bald denial that as we evaluate or forbid we claim the instancing of properties, natural or otherwise. Rather, the expressivist will worry whether something has been left out. What seems absent from the property–identity theory is a description of what is different about people who accept the identity and people who do not. Thus if one person claims that goodness is happiness, and another, like Martin Luther, claims that goodness lies in suffering, the expressivist has a story about the difference between them. One approves of or admires happiness, and the other approves of or admires suffering. It is natural to say that their difference lies in their different *take* or perspective on the properties in question. But that difference in turn is just the difference in attitude that the expressivist highlights. The difference is not purely 'theoretical'. If we find against Luther, as we surely should do, we will find him horrifying or dangerous, not because he has made a theoretical mistake, akin to thinking that gold is a compound or that water is a carbohydrate, but because he is motivated to encourage or rejoice in suffering.

A final contested topic is the relationship between expressivism and quasi-realism on the one hand and doctrines known as deflationism or minimalism in the theory of truth on the other. On the one hand, a minimal theory of truth seems to bring aid and comfort to the quasi-realist. It means that there are no thoughts about truth that lie beyond his grasp. If a would-be realist announces that he believes that moral opinions can be true, or strictly and literally true, or really true, the expressivist can readily agree. He will have examples of moral opinions he holds—kicking blind beggars is bad; denying votes to women is wrong—and he can say that these are true because, for minimalism, this does no more than express the same attitude again. He can say that they are strictly and literally true, since for minimalism this goes no further. Minimalism denies that some true assertions 'literally' correspond with the world, while other true assertions only manage something less.

On the other hand, if minimalism takes everything, then there may be no vocabulary left in which to say what is distinctive about expressivism. Originally, as we saw, expressivism was a flight from supposing that ethics represents things as being one way or another, since the way it represents things as being would have to be thought of in terms of Moore's other world. But if 'represents' goes minimal, then there is no harm, no 'metaphysical inflation', in describing ethics as representational. "X is good" represents X as being good, just as "X is red" represents X as being red. To counter this threat, the expressivist has to deny that minimalism applies across the board. The line will have to be that whatever we say about truth, there are things to say about the use of predicates and sentences that are sufficient to make the direction-of-fit metaphor appropriate. And once that is appropriate, the expressivist can deploy it, as we have seen, to motivate the attempt to place ethics on the directive side rather than the representational side.

REFERENCES

Anscombe, Elizabeth. 1957. *Intention.* Oxford: Blackwell.

Ayer, A. J. 1936. *Language, Truth and Logic.* London: Victor Gollancz.

Blackburn, Simon. 1984. *Spreading the Word.* Oxford: Oxford University Press.

———. 1988. "Attitudes and Contents." *Ethics* 98: 501–517.

———. 1993. "Gibbard on Normative Logic." In *Philosophical Issues 4: Naturalism and Normativity,* ed. Enrique Villanueva, 60–66. Atascadero, Calif.: Ridgeview.

———. 1998. "Trust, Cooperation, and Human Psychology." In *Trust and Governance,* ed. Margaret Levi and Valerie Braithwaite, 28–45. New York: Russell Sage Foundation.

———. 2002. "Replies." *Philosophy and Phenomenological Research* 65: 164–176.

Brighouse, M. H. 1990. "Blackburn's Projectivism—An Objection." *Philosophical Studies* 12: 225.

Geach, Peter. 1965. "Assertion." *Philosophical Review* 74: 449–465.

Gibbard, Allan. 1990. *Wise Choices, Apt Feelings: A Theory of Normative Judgment.* Cambridge, Mass.: Harvard University Press.

———. 1992a. "Moral Concepts: Substance and Sentiment." In *Philosophical Perspectives,* vol. 6, *Ethics,* ed. James E. Tomberlin, 199–221. Atascadero, Calif.: Ridgeview.

———. 1992b. "Thick Concepts and Warrant for Feelings." *Proceedings of the Aristotelian Society,* supp., 66: 267–283.

Hale, Bob. 1986. "The Compleat Projectivist." *Philosophical Quarterly* 36: 65–84.

———. 1993. "Can There Be a Logic of Attitudes?" In *Reality, Representation, and Projection,* ed. John Haldane and Crispin Wright, 337–363. Oxford: Oxford University Press.

———. 2002. "Can Arboreal Knotwork help Blackburn out of Frege's Abyss?" *Philosophy and Phenomenological Research* 65: 144–149.

Hare, R. M. 1952. *The Language of Morals.* Oxford: Oxford University Press.

———. 1970. "Meaning and Speech Acts." *Philosophical Review* 79: 3–24.

Harman, Gilbert. 1974. "Meaning and Semantics." In *Semantics and Philosophy,* ed. Milton K. Munitz and Peter K. Unger, 1–16. New York: New York University Press.

Hume, David. [1739]. 1888. *Treatise of Human Nature.* Ed. L. A. Selby-Bigge. Oxford: Oxford University Press.

Hurley, Susan. 1989. *Natural Reasons: Personality and Polity.* New York: Oxford University Press.

Kölbel, Max. 2002. *Truth without Objectivity.* London: Routledge.

Mackie, J. L. 1977. *Ethics: Inventing Right and Wrong.* Harmondsworth, England: Penguin Books.

Schueler, G. F. 1988. "Modus Ponens and Moral Realism." *Ethics* 98: 492–500.

Smith, Michael. 1988. "Reason and Desire." *Proceedings of the Aristotelian Society* 88: 243–258.

Stevenson, Charles. 1944. *Ethics and Language.* New Haven, Conn.: Yale University Press.

Tiberius, Valerie. 2000. "Humean Heroism: Value Commitments and the Source of Normativity." *Pacific Philosophical Quarterly* 81: 426–446.

Unwin, Nicholas. 2001. "Norms and Negation: A Problem for Gibbard's Logic." *Philosophical Quarterly* 51: 60–75.

Wedgwood, Ralph. 1997. "Non-Cognitivism, Truth and Logic." *Philosophical Studies* 86: 73–91.

Wright, Crispin. 1988. "Realism, Antirealism, Irrealism, Quasi-Realism." *Midwest Studies in Philosophy* 12: 25–49.

Zangwill, Nicholas. 1992. "Moral Modus Ponens." *Ratio,* 5: 177–193.

CHAPTER 6

BIOLOGY AND ETHICS

PHILIP KITCHER

1. THREE PROGRAMS

SINCE the late nineteenth century, the relation between biology and ethics has been an alluring swamp in which any number of scholars have floundered. In what follows, I'll attempt to lay some duckboards across treacherous terrain. It is eminently possible, however, that this essay will extend the list of failed explorations.

Some uses of biology within moral theory are surely uncontroversial. Discoveries about hitherto unknown sensitivity to pain, whether in human beings or in other animals, would generate new consequences for any position committed to the avoidance of pain. Evidently biological findings can combine with moral premises to yield new moral conclusions. What has been much more tantalizing is the thought that advances in our knowledge of the living world, specifically of ourselves, could lend support to *basic* moral principles and perhaps even lead us to appreciate *novel* basic principles.

As every beginning student learns, Hume gave us a talisman for resisting that thought. In its rough version, it cautions against deriving statements containing "ought" from statements bereft of any such normative language. Counterexamples to the rough version are well known (see Prior, 1949). One class, not widely represented in the literature, focuses on the relaxation of obligations: if it's part of the logic of "ought" that "X ought to A" implies "X can A," then the factual discovery that A is beyond X's powers implies that it is not the case that X ought to *A*. Defenders of Hume will respond, quite reasonably, that this (like the other famous counterexamples) misses the point. For Hume was concerned with *positive action-guiding* principles, and nobody has shown how to derive one of *these* from factual claims—or even how to offer a cogent nondeductive argument that will lead from factual premises to positive action-guiding principles.

In the wake of Darwin's great biological achievement, many enthusiasts have supposed that they could parlay evolutionary understanding into ethical innovation. When naysayers greet their proposals by citing Hume, would-be Darwinian moralists reply that the "naturalistic fallacy isn't as much of a fallacy as it's cracked up to be" (Wilson, 1979, 68). To settle the issue, one needs to go beyond these blunt charges and countercharges. A more appropriate use of Hume's insight is to follow the Darwinian moralizing with the careful attention to the forms of sentences that excited Hume's recorded puzzlement.[1] Consider recent suggestions that our knowledge of the molecular basis of heredity supplies us with a fundamental ethical imperative (to ensure the continued reproduction of human DNA) or that the history of selection against mating with close relatives supports a moral ban on incest.[2] It's surely pertinent to ask how the factual premises are supposed to be linked to the normative conclusions. The weakness of the connections can be exposed by considering possible situations in which any continued human reproduction would involve unacceptable coercion (imagine a tiny population in the wake of a nuclear holocaust) or in which the only possibilities for expressing sexual love required breaches of the incest ban and in which there were neither dangers of severely afflicted offspring nor the exploitation that is typical of actual incest (imagine an idealized development of the first act of *Die Walküre*).[3]

If all ventures in relating biology to ethics were either as trivial as my example of applying new knowledge to existing moral principles or as crude as the projects just considered, there would be little more to say. But there are three other programs that are significantly more interesting and sophisticated. Instead of trying to use biology to generate substantive moral principles, these ventures endeavor to *explain the meaning* of central moral terms by drawing on biological insights. All of them try to connect our contemporary biological understanding to major themes in the history of moral philosophy, although they celebrate different heroes.

One project aims to revive central notions from Aristotelian ethics. Thomas Hurka, for example, has suggested that we can view moral imperatives as directing us to develop our nature and that this is to be elaborated by unfolding the human essence (1993). Philippa Foot asks: "Why . . . does it seem so monstrous a suggestion that the evaluation of the human will should be determined by facts about the nature of human beings and the life of our own species?"[4] She tries to dispel the illusion that this is "monstrous" by delineating an account of 'good' as a functional term, and arguing that moral principles articulate the kinds of human goodness. Both of these accounts, while often original and insightful, founder, I believe, because of the failure to take the details of current biological understanding sufficiently seriously. Hurka doesn't appreciate the extent to which contemporary evolutionary biology undermines his appeal to essences, while Foot explicitly adopts a pre-Darwinian conception of function that either offers no way of connecting her moral conclusions to biological facts or else does so only because the conception already tacitly presupposes certain moral ends and values.[5] Later in this essay, I'll try to demonstrate how some ideas from the neo-Aristotelian program can be developed in terms of a more thorough engagement with biology.

The second and third programs both try to rearticulate the ideas of more recent thinkers. It's a striking fact about modern moral and political philosophy that it so often appeals to speculative stories about the origins of human social behavior. Indeed, one way to sympathize with the simple sociobiological approaches I glanced at earlier is to imagine a biologically informed person reading Hobbes, or Hume, or Rousseau: our imagined reader thinks "This is all ungrounded conjecture—but now we *know* something about human origins, so we can redo the project in light of our knowledge." If the reader doesn't have a clear understanding of what "the project" is, then the likely outcome will be the simple substitution of evolutionary stories (not always very well grounded ones, at that) for historical moral speculation, and the upshot will be sociobiological disaster. That doesn't mean, however, that more careful readers can't do better.

For most such readers, Hume is particularly relevant. His emphasis on our natural fellow-feeling resonates with a prominent strain in contemporary evolutionary theorizing, the attempts to explain the origin and maintenance of dispositions to cooperation. Ironically, the same philosopher who is wheeled out to guard the moral highway against intrusions from marauding Darwinians also serves as a source of inspiration to those who want to take a less direct route.

The second and third programs I have differentiated are distinguished by the places where they begin. One starts from considerations in contemporary moral philosophy and invokes parts of biology to elaborate those considerations. Thus Simon Blackburn updates many of Hume's central themes by using ideas from studies of the evolution of cooperation.[6] Allan Gibbard (1990) takes noncognitivism as his point of departure, appealing to studies in behavioral biology to provide an intricate account of the origins and development of our reactive emotions and attitudes. In both instances, it seems to me that the moral philosophy comes first, and the biological materials enter as they are taken to be relevant.

By contrast, the third program begins from a more systematic survey of those biological findings that might be brought to bear on the kinds of issues raised by Hume (among others). Thus Elliott Sober (in collaboration with the biologist David Sloan Wilson) is concerned to understand the evolution of altruism, and to evaluate the Humean suggestion that we have propensities to fellow-feeling (Sober and Wilson, 1998). Brian Skyrms (1996) considers a wider variety of attitudes and behavior, using the perspective of evolutionary game theory to illuminate forms of human cooperation.[7] Although themes from the history of moral philosophy are used to focus the investigation, there's a clear sense in both these works that the biological details should come first and that the moral chips will fall where they may.

It's worth asking just what work the appeals to biology are doing in these latter two programs. An unkind response to the Blackburn-Gibbard approach would be to suppose that bits and pieces of biology are serving as window dressing for ventures in moral philosophy that could be carried on without them. Similarly, one might commend Sober and Skyrms for offering us evolutionary explanations of the origin and maintenance of aspects of human behavior and society, without supposing that their conclusions had any relevance to moral philosophy.[8] In the next two sections, I will offer my own version of the third program as a prelude to making as clear as possible the implications of the biological findings. I'll then return to the philosophical work I've briefly considered here, and to the nagging worry that, in this area, the price of avoiding fallacies is philosophical irrelevance.[9]

2. BIOLOGICAL AND PSYCHOLOGICAL ALTRUISM

In the past decades, evolutionary theorists have solved a longstanding problem, the problem of *biological altruism*. As the behavioral biologist defines the term, an organism A acts altruistically toward another organism B just in case A's action increases B's reproductive success while diminishing A's own reproductive success. It's important to emphasize that biological altruism is quite different from our ordinary conception (the one that is pertinent to morality). For biological altruism has nothing whatsoever to do with the intentions of the agent, and organisms incapable of having intentions (plants, for example) can be altruistic in the biological sense. The concept is important precisely because the existence of biological altruism is, from a Darwinian perspective, profoundly puzzling. Organisms that raise the reproductive success of others at reproductive cost to themselves would appear to be doomed in the struggle for existence. Yet the natural world offers abundant instances of organisms who appear to behave in a biologically altruistic way—birds who give alarm calls in the presence of predators, primates who form alliances with others in situations that place them in danger, to cite just two celebrated examples. Thus there arises the general question: How is biological altruism possible?

The standard answer to the question divides the cases into two main types. Consider first examples in which the beneficiary is a close relative of the altruist. If we suppose that the altruistic disposition has a genetic basis, then the first Darwinian thought is that the underlying alleles (the forms of the pertinent genes) are likely to decrease in frequency in the population because the altruist has a smaller expected number of offspring. But, as W. D. Hamilton saw clearly, the lost representation through progeny might be made up for by a considerably increased number of allele copies in the offspring of the beneficiary—close relatives are likely to share copies of the alleles in question.[10] If you decrease your own reproductive success by one child, while increasing your sibling's reproductive success by four, then, since your sibling has a chance of 0.5 of carrying the 'altruistic allele', the expected representation of that allele in the next generation goes up.[11]

What about cases in which the beneficiary isn't a close relative? Here the favored strategy has been to appeal to *reciprocal altruism*. Imagine that organisms interact with one another on a repeated basis. If one acts today to incur a small reproductive loss that provides a large reproductive gain for the beneficiary, and if the favor is returned tomorrow, then both gain. Although the idea was originally introduced by Robert Trivers (1971), the contemporary version develops ideas of Robert Axelrod and William Hamilton (1981; see Axelrod, 1984).

We start from the idea of a standard prisoner's dilemma. In this game, two players interact. If both cooperate, then they both receive the same relatively good outcome. If one cooperates and the other defects, then the cooperator gets the worst outcome and the defector receives an outcome that is slightly better than the reward for mutual cooperation. If both defect, then both receive an outcome that is a bit better than the worst outcome but considerably worse than the outcomes received for mutual cooperation. If the game is just played once, it's not hard to see that defecting is a dominant strategy—you do better to defect no matter what the other player does. Axelrod and Hamilton consider a scenario in which organisms from a population are paired at random and then interact, receiving the payoffs for a standard prisoner's dilemma. The interactions between the pair are repeated an indefinite number of times (in other words, there's a very high probability that each time you play the game, you will then go on to play it with the same player again; sooner or later, though, the sequence will terminate).[12] Then the organisms return to the original population, and new pairings are drawn; the sequence of interactions is repeated. The process continues through many rounds. At the end, we look to see which strategies for playing the repeated prisoner's dilemma have received the largest payoffs (construed as measured in units of reproductive success—to a first approximation, the number of offspring an organism leaves). On the basis of computer simulations and mathematical analyses, Axelrod and Hamilton concluded that a particular cooperative strategy— tit for tat (TFT)—would be favored in this selective regime. In their terminology,

TFT is nice (it starts by cooperating), provokable (it responds to defection by defecting on the next round), and forgiving (it returns to cooperating once the partner has again once cooperated). So we have an explanation of how biological altruism toward nonrelatives (specifically following the strategy TFT) can be *maintained* under natural selection (accounting for the *origination* of TFT under natural selection is rather more tricky).

The theoretical results I've outlined solve the puzzle I began with, for recall that that puzzle was to explain the *possibility* of biological altruism in a Darwinian world.[13] But there's another interesting question I might have asked: How is *human* altruism evolutionarily possible? One way of seeing that this issue hasn't yet been resolved is to recognize that accounts of *biological* altruism don't bear on the evolution of *psychological* altruism, the concept with which we're normally concerned. But there's a more subtle point. We may not even have accounted for the evolution of biological altruism in the past history of our own species. Any how-possibly explanation proceeds by supposing that certain conditions obtain, and if we have reasons to think that those conditions are highly unlikely, then the puzzle at which the explanation was directed stands. Consider, from this perspective, altruistic behavior toward nonrelatives, which we might take to have emerged in our hominid or primate past. If we're to apply the standard Trivers-Axelrod-Hamilton account to understand this form of behavior, then we have to assume that there was some pairing device that operated on populations of our ancestors, forcing them to play indefinitely repeated prisoner's dilemma in the way envisaged. That assumption looks highly implausible. But if the conditions of the how-possibly explanation don't obtain, then we have no explanation at all.

There are ways of trying to do better. For example, one can suppose that our ancestors formed a loose population in which there were frequent opportunities for cooperating with one another on important tasks or for tackling the tasks alone. Given superficially plausible assumptions, one can show that this regime allows for the evolution of biologically altruistic behavior.[14] Unfortunately, it doesn't probe the conditions for primate sociality deeply enough. When one turns to the details of social interactions among our evolutionary relatives, it's very hard to envisage that the selection pressures were sufficiently strong to shape altruistic dispositions toward nonrelatives. (The benefits from cooperative hunting, for example, don't seem to be large enough; nor do the gains from social grooming appear to be anywhere near large enough to justify the amount of time invested in it.) It also becomes apparent that the actual forms of behavior found among higher primates don't match the strategies recommended by the theory. (We find nothing like tit for tat or discrimination against organisms who don't cooperate.) Finally, there's a more straightforward difficulty. The scenario envisages some group of our ancestors forming a loose population—that is, being sufficiently able to tolerate one another's presence to be in the same geographical region at the same time. Noninterference with others, especially under conditions of scarcity, represents a more primitive form of altruism toward nonrelatives, one whose presence must be explained by a deeper analysis.

We can gain clues to the needed analysis by considering the diversity of social relations among our close evolutionary relatives. Gibbons form small family units, each defending a territory; orangutans are relatively solitary, the largest stable groups typically consisting of a female and one or two young; gorillas assort into small groups, usually with a single mature male and a few females and juveniles; only among chimpanzees and bonobos do we regularly find societies that contain adults of both sexes. The available evidence indicates that our hominid ancestors lived in something like the chimp-bonobo pattern. The biological puzzle, then, is to understand why this particular mode of altruism and competition emerged.

The primatologist Richard Wrangham has proposed (1979) that the differences in social structures can be seen as the result of different female foraging strategies that impose constraints on male behavior. I generalize Wrangham's account by considering an abstract problem, the *coalition game*. Suppose we have a population of organisms of various degrees of strength, competing for scarce resources; under these conditions, weak organisms with a disposition to form coalitions can survive; if all organisms in the population pass through a stage in which they are relatively weak, the propensity to coalition-formation is likely to become prevalent. More exactly, one can show, under a wide variety of mathematical developments of the scenario, that coalitions will form, that the coalition-forming progress will escalate, that as larger coalitions form, rewards will be determined by subcoalitional structure, and that the process of escalation will eventually terminate.[15] In short, the coalition game reveals the patterns of associative behavior we find in chimpanzees and bonobos. I suggest that it forms the basis for richer cooperative ventures, and that such ventures should be understood against the background of the requirements of maintaining one's place within coalitions and subcoalitions.[16] To a first approximation, altruistic behavior emerged in our ancestral lineage as a result of the selection for coalition-forming propensities that gave rise to opportunities for optional games, both stages mediated, of course, by considerations of relatedness and kin selection.

None of this would be of any particular relevance to moral philosophy unless it took us beyond the bare notion of biological altruism. I claim that it helps us to understand the existence, and limits, of a richer kind of altruism. *Psychological* altruism, I suggest, consists in a tendency to adjust one's desires, plans, and intentions in light of one's assessment of the desires, plans, and intentions of others, the adjustment consisting in bringing one's own attitudes closer to those attributed to the others (closer in the sense that the altruist comes to have wants, plans, and intentions with a content that is favorable to the other's achieving or fulfilling his wants, plans, and intentions);[17] the adjustment must be explained by the perception of the others' attitudes, and that explanation must not involve any expectation that the adjusted attitudes will prove instrumentally effective in realizing one's *un*adjusted goals.[18] Skepticism about altruism thrives, of course, in supposing that such expectations are lurking in the background, whether or not people are conscious of them. Hence the tendency to suppose that ascriptions of altruism represent a kind of softheaded sentimentality.

Careful observation of nonhuman primates supplies a number of instances in which the animals seem to be adjusting their actions (and their intentions) to their perceptions of the needs of others, and where there's no serious chance of obtaining a future benefit. The clearest cases are those in which an animal goes out of its way to aid another, even though the other is weak and incapable of any reciprocation and even though the action is unobserved by conspecifics (see De Waal, 1996; Goodall, 1986). Faced with such examples, the skeptic can only insist that there must be an underlying calculation of self-interest, because natural selection would have favored dispositions always to calculate one's own payoffs, even if the calculation has gone mysteriously awry on the present occasion. But that rejoinder evaporates once we have a clear view of the evolutionary origins of sociality (the preconditions for adjustment of behavior to others). One of the important features of the coalition game is that attempts to calculate good strategies for playing it are hopeless. A blind disposition to empathize with others would do just as well as (maybe better than) a process of estimating future benefits.[19] Skeptics offer highly implausible accounts of examples of apparent altruism because they suppose that evolution "must have" produced different proximate mechanisms—but their evolutionary expectations are ill founded. They think, for example, the natural selection would have placed a premium on an ability to perform Machiavellian calculations, and to manipulate others to one's own selfish ends.

We thus arrive at a Humean conclusion. Human beings, like chimpanzees and bonobos, have dispositions to respond to the perceived needs and wants of others, capacities for fellow-feeling, and it's possible that these dispositions/capacities are the psychological basis of the form of association that our hominid ancestors shared with our evolutionary cousins. So far this is only a small step along the path from biology to ethics. I'll now try to show how we can go further.

3. AN EVOLVED CAPACITY FOR NORMATIVE GUIDANCE

Hume claimed that our capacity for fellow-feeling was limited. Primatology provides a basis for endorsing his conclusion. Let's start with a dramatic example.

During the 1970s and 1980s, researchers spent the daylight hours observing the behavior of a colony of chimpanzees in Arnhem, Holland. They duly recorded patterns of association, alliances that enabled animals to obtain outcomes they wanted. For some years, two males had supported one another in this way until the two, in concert, dethroned the male who had previously been dominant. At that point, one of the males forsook his old coalition-partner (friend?), pursuing a strategy apparently aimed at monopolizing the females of the colony. This action precipitated a series of intense conflicts, with swiftly changing alliances and profound social instability. In the end, the male who forsook his old alliance was savagely attacked by the former dominant male and the forsaken friend, and the attack proved fatal (De Waal, 1984).

This dramatic incident may seem to revive the skeptic's case, inspiring the judgment that the male who broke with his ally with the aim of gaining a reproductive monopoly had been calculating all along, using his erstwhile friend as a means in social negotiation. The verdict seems unwarranted. To say that a primate calculates on one occasion, when the benefits of a particular action are large and obvious, is not to say that calculation always goes on. The argument of the previous section led to the conclusion that a disposition to empathize with others and to adjust actions to their needs seems to underlie some observed behavior, and there's no good evolutionary reason to hypothesize a psychological calculation that has misfired in the cases at hand. It's quite compatible with that to suppose that the disposition is incompletely pervasive, that there are contexts in which it is overridden by powerful self-directed desires. One way to articulate Hume's point is to contend that this is the ancestral hominid condition: we have capacities for fellow-feeling that enable us to assort in chimp-bonobo-hominid mixed-adult groups, but those capacities are always vulnerable in situations where social defection would bring an evident reward.

Observers of chimpanzee society know very well that the situation is often tense. Although smaller coalitions (dyads) are frequently quite stable, social bonds between allies are ruptured, and after the breach, significant time has to be invested in making peace. Mutual grooming (as well as other gestures of reassurance) is omnipresent in chimpanzee social life, far beyond the extent to which it is needed for hygienic purposes (removing parasites from the fur), because of the constant need to repair the social fabric. There seems to be a delicate interplay of opposing forces—the altruistic dispositions drawing animals to act together and the selfish disruptions threatening to decompose the social group—and this interplay is mediated by enormously time-consuming activities of peacemaking. If, as seems likely, this was our ancestral condition, then neither Hobbes nor Hume was completely right about the state of nature, although we can concede to the former the idea of a constant threat of overt conflict and to the latter that this comes about because of the limitations of our fellow-feeling.[20]

That is not the way we live now. From the time of recorded history to the present, human beings have lived in enormously bigger groups.[21] Contemporary people are able to deal with large numbers of individuals with whom they don't interact on a daily basis. We don't spend hours each day grooming one another, but we do engage in an extraordinary spectrum of cooperative activities. How have we managed to do these things?

I offer a conjecture: we evolved a capacity for normative guidance. Our ability to transcend the limited size and extreme fragility of early hominid social life rests on a capacity for articulating rules and using those rules to shape our wishes, plans, and intentions, so that the frequency with which the altruistic tendencies that underlie cooperation are overridden is diminished. If we envisage the psychological lives of chimpanzees (and early hominids) as a melee in which the urgings of altruism are countered with the shouts (or whispers?) of selfish desires, then our ancestors acquired a psychological modification that enabled them to add a further, possibly a controlling, voice to the hubbub, one whose evolutionary function was to reinforce those pressures that would preserve the social fabric. Here I commit myself to a claim about adaptive advantage: hominids with the tendency to act on the altruistic dispositions would have fared better than those without. Here I can only gesture at the basis for the advantage; within the framework of a coalitional structure, loyal partners earn a reputation as good coalition-mates, and this secures them access to advantageous coalitions (and to the sub-coalitions that influence the distribution of resources).[22]

The question I have posed concerns how a particular transition in hominid social life could have happened, and the last paragraph tries to sketch a *possibility*. The principal reason for taking the possibility seriously lies in the difficulty of thinking of serious rivals. But I should note an interesting feature of my conjecture. It's a familiar fact that societies we tend to think of as living closer to the conditions of our ancestors' life have elaborate systems of division into groups— "elementary structures of kinship"—and that these systems are expressed in rules enjoining loyalty and revenge. If we suppose that a capacity for normative guidance served the evolutionary function of promoting social cohesion, then we might expect that the rules shaping individual attitudes would have specified the conditions under which one is to act with one's allies, that they would have corresponded to the sorts of imperatives anthropologists have discerned. If normative guidance is to serve as a preemptive surrogate for grooming (and other retroactive peacemaking activities), then it will be important to specify the clan structure, to announce when you should act with the clan, and to identify the conditions under which a clan, or subclan, should take revenge on a group within the broader community.

My conjecture provides a way of linking biology with ethics. Our evolutionary history made of our early hominid ancestors partially altruistic animals who were able to engage in a limited kind of society. Some of their descendants—also our ancestors—acquired the capacity for normative guidance, and were able to shape their attitudes by socially shared rules. They invented *proto-morality*, perhaps little more than some judgments about who belonged with whom and a few crude injunctions about loyalty and revenge. Hominid groups could then have transmitted their framework of rules across the generations, sometimes with modifications and extensions. As groups split, there would have been occasions for divergent cultural evolution; later, as different societies encountered one another—sometimes, perhaps, merging—there would have been eclectic mixtures. Across thousands of years, in distinct cultural lineages, our ancestors may have conducted a wide variety of "experiments in living."[23] The cultural lineages currently terminate in the systems of morality found in our world. One of them is ours.

We can trace the latter stages of this process of cultural evolution by looking at the history of religious, legal, and moral ideas from the dawn of written history to the present. More important, we can use the earliest documents we have to try to reconstruct what might have occurred in that enormous period for which no written evidence is available. Early Mesopotamian law codes, versions of myths (the Gilgamesh epic is a prominent example), and the Egyptian *Book of the Dead* contain a scatter of moral precepts and ideals. Reading them, it's evident that a primary function of the rules they contain is to bring peace in situations of potential social conflict—kings, lawgivers, and heroes are praised for creating harmony within their communities. To a modern eye, the piecemeal character of the rules is quite striking; the fragments of the law codes offer directives about very specific social situations (the causing of miscarriages to the daughters of others, the failure to use an orchard one has rented, the joint maintenance of irrigation systems). But what we have, of course, is a tiny sample of the tablets that once existed, and even those that are most complete (for example those recording the code of Hammurabi) are plainly intended to offer extensions and amendments to an existing system of social rules. The picture we obtain shows how societies that have achieved unprecedentedly high concentrations of population are encountering novel sources of social conflict and how they are modifying their traditional norms to cope with them.[24]

Another striking feature of the fragmentary texts that have been preserved is the presence of moral themes we might have taken to be inventions of later generations. Nietzsche famously argued that the injunction to forgive your enemies was a Judeo-Christian subversion of an older "heroic" morality, but the idea is already present in Mesopotamian and Egyptian texts.[25] So, of course, is the *lex talionis*, often in forms that exact strict reciprocity (for example, someone who kills the daughter of another Babylonian "seigneur" is punished through the death of one of his own daughters). Further in these texts, as in many unrelated traditions, the rules for proper conduct are backed by a sanction that goes beyond human punishment. Parts of the moral system are absorbed into a frame-

work of socially administered law, but deviations are inevitably witnessed by unseen beings who can inflict punishment either in this life or the hereafter
(Westermarck, 1912).

The invention of writing comes at least five millennia after the condensa-
tion of human populations into agricultural settlements in the Middle East, and
the evidence of trading suggests that our ancestors had had to formulate rules
for interacting with relative strangers for at least another ten thousand years.
So, at a conservative estimate, the cultural evolution that led from the simple
proto-morality of loyalty and revenge rules to the earliest legal and moral documents took fifteen thousand years. Given the pace of cultural evolution, it's
not surprising that even a minute sample of texts should reveal a large proportion of the themes that have dominated moral discussion through recorded history. I extend my conjecture. During at least fifteen thousand years, different
lineages of our Paleolithic and Neolithic ancestors explored virtually all the systems of rules and ideals for regulating conduct that have figured in the everyday conduct of most people (including most contemporary people). Many of
those systems did badly in the cultural competition: the groups that adopted
them were not very good at transmitting their ideas to contemporaries and descendants.[26] The systems that survived were absorbed in later moral practices
and figured in the codes that emerge in the Mesopotamian and Egyptian texts.[27]
Cultural evolution continued as the central themes are transmitted to the He-
brews and the Greeks. Like the Judeo-Christian tradition, Plato was a footnote
to the history of morality.

There is, of course, an interesting history that leads from the ancient world
to us. That history involves the systematization of specific rules that seem to be
introduced case by case in the ancient traditions. Perhaps most important, it involves an eradication of divisions that we take to be artificial, and the extension
of protections to individuals who are (by our lights) not viewed as fully human—to barbarians as well as citizens, slaves as well as freemen, the poor as
well as the wealthy, women as well as men. Quite evidently, the precepts that
commend themselves to Enlightenment thinkers and their intellectual heirs are
not those that figure in the code of Hammurabi. The interesting philosophical
question concerns whether their metaphysical and epistemological status can be
understood without recognizing the process from which they have emerged.
There is a pronounced philosophical tendency to believe that we can understand major parts of our practices and views of the world—mathematics, science, religion, and morality, for example—simply by analyzing closely the contemporary versions. As I'll suggest hereafter, I think this tendency should be
resisted.

4. A New Perspective in Metaethics

I have told an admittedly speculative story about the genealogy of morality, one that sees its roots in the evolution of psychological capacities that made social life possible for us, that claims that a decisive extension of our social possibilities occurred with the acquisition of an ability to prescribe norms, that sees a long process of cultural exploration of the norms with which that ability could be filled out. If telling this story has any philosophical relevance, it will be because it offers a new perspective in metaethics. Let's inquire, then, whether central questions look different in light of my historical perspective.

Can we make sense of moral knowledge? It's no accident, I think, that philosophers most attuned to the biological roots of our moral capacities should have been drawn toward noncognitivism—to think that the surface forms of moral judgments deceive us, that we aren't really uttering straightforward declarative sentences but expressing emotive reactions (or, if we are uttering declarative sentences, that what we say is, strictly speaking, false).[28] If one thinks, for example, that moral precepts serve the function of coordinating human social behavior, then neither their introduction nor their refinement will look much like an episode in which somebody acquires a new piece of knowledge: the kinds of positions adopted by Blackburn and Gibbard are thus eminently comprehensible. I'll try to show how my genealogical story sharpens the noncognitivist challenge.

Why do we accept the moral judgments we do? The genealogical story supplies an explanation. Each of us inherits a moral framework from those who socialize us, and, through our lives, we try to refine and extend that framework, rooting out inconsistencies and coming to judgments on the basis of psychological capacities that were initially shaped by our early training. What are the possibilities for finding moral knowledge here?

One is that most of us are incapable of obtaining moral knowledge by ourselves. To the extent that we know, it's because we've been taught by others, and knowledge is ultimately traceable to a few people—religious leaders? great philosophers?—who enjoyed special faculties that the herd don't possess. But where, when, and how did their exceptional enlightenment occur? On Mount Sinai? In Kant's study? Or in Moore's rooms in Trinity? For each of the cases, it's easy to envisage how to extend the psychosocial explanation to the supposedly grounding episode. Rather than suppose, for example, that Moore's judgment that the only things with intrinsic value are personal relationships and beautiful things was based on some special intuitive apprehension unavailable to the rest of us, we can see it as the end result of a complex personal journey that began with his late Victorian socialization and led through his everyday conversations and experiences to his emotional rejection of some aspects of his culture and his emotional identification with others (Moore, 1993, sec. 113). In ethics, as in mathematics, the appeal to intuition is an epistemology of desperation.

Perhaps we do better to imagine that moral knowledge is generated by some ability that we all share. When we see children setting light to a cat, do we *perceive* the wrongness of what they are doing? Is it necessary to invoke the "fact that it is wrong" to explain the judgment?[29] Apparently not. Our society has trained us to produce that kind of response to that kind of incident, and it's plain that societies sometimes vary in the moral judgments induced by perception.[30] But that shouldn't be the end of the matter. Aspiring cognitivists should note that social training is also important to scientific judgments—as when a technician judges that an electron has passed through a cloud chamber or when a biologist perceives that some of the bacteria have incorporated extra DNA. Can't we say that, given that training, technician and biologist would have made the judgments they do, whether or not an electron or transgenic bacteria were present? For these individuals make the judgments they do on these occasions because they have been trained to respond to particular sorts of visual stimulations in particular ways. In the scientific case, however, even if the nonsocial facts have no role to play in the *immediate* judgment, there's a deeper explanatory question to which they are relevant. Why are these kinds of training given to the pertinent observers? Here we must turn to the history of the cultural practice, and that history involves the adoption of procedures on the basis of evidence that they serve as reliable ways of detecting facts about the world. If we pose the analogous question for the history of the moral practices into which we have been socialized, my conjectural genealogy offers no analogous consolation. At the initial stage, protomorality is introduced as a system of primitive rules for transcending the fraught sociality of early hominids: there's no issue here of perceiving moral truths. Nor at any further stage is there a need to suppose that moral truths play a role in constraining the normative systems adopted. The criterion of success isn't accurate representation but the improvement of social cohesion in ways that promote the transmission of the system itself.

I've offered only the skeleton of a line of reasoning, and it would be quite premature to claim that cognitivism must surrender at this stage. My point, however, is that confrontation of the question of moral knowledge with the genealogical perspective exacerbates the noncognitivist challenge, enabling us to deal with the epistemological questions in a sharper way.

Can we account for moral objectivity? Starting with the question of moral knowledge can make noncognitivism look quite attractive, but it's a familiar point that the pressures toward making sense of moral knowledge arise from concerns with the objectivity of morality. If moral judgments express our reactions, if those reactions are socially shaped, and if the criteria for successful social shaping ultimately trace to strategies that promoted cultural transmission (in a highly contingent historical process, to boot), then we seem to lose any conception of moral objectivity. Again, it's no accident, I think, that the philosophers most interested in the biological basis of morality struggle with issues about objectivity (Blackburn, 2000, ch. 9; Gibbard, 1990, chs. 8–13).

An obvious source of the craving for objectivity stems from the activity of comparing moral practices. If we look at another moral lineage and find differences in its moral verdicts, we don't want to suppose that the differences cannot be assessed. Even more obviously, I think, when we make comparisons with earlier stages of our own lineage, we don't think of what we find as *mere* differences— we used to think that slavery was tolerable and now we don't, and that's all there is to it. In both cases, what we are after is a conception of moral *progress*. Our comparison of earlier and later stages of our cultural lineage aims at the view that we have made moral progress; by the same token, the cross-lineage comparison concerns the question of whether we'd make moral progress by incorporating some parts of their moral practice into ours. So we can reduce the problem: Can we make sense of moral progress?

You might think not. For you might suppose that progress in any practice involving judgment requires the judgments made at later stages to be closer to the truth than those made at earlier stages. Hence, if you abandon moral truth (and the cumulative acquisition of moral truth in the genealogy of morals), you can't have a concept of progress. The supposition seems mistaken. Progress as convergence on the truth is too simple a view even for the paradigm case, that of the sciences.[31] Nor is there any reason to believe that ethical practice must admit the same reconstruction as scientific practice. So there's no knockdown objection to the possibility of progress. It's an open question: Can we make sense of moral progress?

Here, perhaps, the neo-Aristotelian ideas of Foot and Hurka can help us. Both Foot and Hurka think of moral precepts as capturing what is important to human functioning, and I complained earlier (without much argument) that their proposals foundered because of their pre-Darwinian approaches to function and essence. The notion of attending to the function of moral rules (ideals, concepts, systems, or whatever) allows an obvious way of generating a notion of moral progress. Just as we can think of progress in technology as consisting in the proliferation of devices that are better able to fulfill their functions, so too, perhaps, in morality.

On the face of it, there seems to be a serious problem in applying this to the account I've given (or to those of Blackburn and Gibbard, both of whom link moral norms to human cooperation). To say that people have made moral progress when the practices of later stages of moral lineages do better at fostering social cohesion invites the charge that there are plenty of morally repulsive ways of eliminating social conflict (several of them prominent in the twentieth century). Further, if this conception of moral progress even accommodates the most salient examples—the recognition of people not previously included as having moral standing—it appears to do so for the wrong reasons: even if the abolition of slavery made life go more smoothly, decreased social friction is hardly *constitutive* of the moral progress we sense here.

My story did indeed suppose that morality entered, and was refined, as a device for going beyond chimp-bonobo-hominid social rupture and repair, but it also assumed that the advance occurred in a very special way. The more immediate function of normative guidance (and the rules of proto-morality) was to reinforce the psychological capacities that made sociality possible for us in the first place. Those psychological capacities involved an ability to empathize with the needs and interests of *some* others to *some* extent, and they were reinforced by directives to take greater account of other people's plans and projects, even when there is, at least initially, no empathetic response.[32] We can say, then, that the primary function of morality is to extend and amplify those primitive altruistic dispositions through which we became social animals in the first place, and that this has the secondary effect of promoting social cohesion. On the account of functions I prefer, the function can be ascribed to the impact on our altruism, even though the processes of selection (natural and cultural) may attend to differences in social harmony.[33] We might say that the function of morality is the enhancement of social cohesion *via* the amplification of our psychological altruistic dispositions.

Two further aspects of moral progress deserve at least brief mention. First, there appears to be a kind of moral progress that consists in the proliferation of options that people can pursue. To adapt a Millian phrase, we are all "greater gainers" when each of us has the opportunity to frame his or her life by selecting from a larger menu of alternatives. I see this as a less direct consequence of the refinement of moral systems. As our ancestors were able to engage in a richer repertoire of cooperative ventures, they created roles that had not previously been available, and as these roles became more widely available, people made moral progress.

Second, as I've noted in my conjectural genealogy, moral systems have often obtained a purchase on individual decisions, especially on decisions whose effects are hard for fellow group members to monitor, by invoking the idea of (an) unseen observer(s). The overwhelming majority of the world's moral practices are intertwined with religious views. One of the ways of making moral progress consists in freeing ourselves of the need for this system of enforcement, in rejecting the false religious presuppositions, and in disentangling and dismissing the special injunctions that the religious framework has introduced. In part, this is simply a matter of replacing superstition with true belief (or with the absence of judgment)—and notions of truth and falsity apply directly here because the religious claims purport to describe the decisions and volitions of person-like entities. It's also a matter, however, both of reinforcing our altruistic dispositions, preventing irrelevant moral commands from interfering with the plans and interests of our fellows, and of expanding the range of options available to people. We should think of our moral system as a spare and streamlined device for developing the dispositions that first made social beings of us, unfortunately overlain with excrescences that were once useful in ensuring conformity, but that can now be scraped away to beneficial effect.

I have not offered anything like a complete account of moral progress. Plainly, an enormous amount needs to be done both to work out the details of the responses I've sketched, and to consider the phenomena of moral progress more systematically. My goal has been only to indicate how the genealogical perspective might provide new ways of thinking about moral objectivity.

Can we make sense of moral authority? My third and last question takes up the obvious thought that efforts to situate morality in human cultural and biological history inevitably end up debunking morality. Or, if they do not, it's because some version of the naturalistic fallacy lurks in the background. One way to dramatize the challenge is to imagine how someone—the *nihilist*, to give the person a name—might draw on the story I've sketched to resist the claims of morality.

When the nihilist looks back on the history of morality, he sees a succession of practices that are more or less successful in fostering social cohesion, and that prevail insofar as they have those features that promote cultural transmission. But, now that this history is clearly understood, he asks why he should commit himself to the latest version of the practice, or indeed to any other such version. The history of other human cultural practices may leave us free to reject the most recent variants, or even to walk away from them entirely—the nihilist invites us to think of fertility rites, taboos, and religious worship. Why should morality be any different?

An obvious response would invoke the idea of moral progress. Yet, even if we suppose that something like the conception I've sketched can be worked out, the nihilist may see the characterization of some lineages as making progress as simply tagging certain trends with an honorific label. What bearing does the "progressiveness" of the moral tradition that stands behind the practices of his community have on his actions and his life? Once again, he may compare morality with other aspects of human culture, claiming that, with respect to religion (say) we can baptize some trends as "progressive," even though to do so would provide no rationale for continuing a tradition that counted as "progressive." Why, then, is morality different?

Here's a fuzzy, but suggestive, answer. To identify with a moral tradition that is progressive in the sense briefly sketched earlier is to extend the path our ancestors traversed in becoming fully human. If the nihilist steps outside moral traditions altogether, or even if he makes a regressive shift from the practice that has been bequeathed to him, he is failing to realize his full human potential. If this answer is to prove satisfactory, then it will have to give serious content to the idea of "full humanity," and to do so in a way that forestalls the obvious complaint that the nihilist doesn't care at all about becoming "fully human." He belongs to the species. Why should he care about the attitudes of other members, past or present, or the evolutionary pressures that shaped them?

My outline of the emergence of normative guidance helps here. Our incompletely pervasive, fragile dispositions to psychological altruism enabled our remote ancestors to attain a particular form of sociality, the tense mode of social life we find among contemporary chimpanzees. The capacity for normative guidance enabled us to reinforce our primitive pro-social dispositions, thereby developing part of ourselves. The line of development thus marked out can be viewed as a way of extending that aspect of our nature—our psychological altruism—that made genuine human life (the social life that transcended the interactions of chimpanzees) possible. To repudiate the authority of norms is thus to abandon one's human identity, to prefer to it a nonhuman mode of psychological life. It's to declare, in effect, that one doesn't see anything valuable in the transition that took us beyond the social world of chimpanzees. In a milder fashion, to make a regressive shift from the moral practice passed on in social training is to take a step back toward that nonhuman mode.

From the perspective I've sketched, nihilism begins to look like a psychopathology, a deliberate rejection of part of ourselves. It's as if the nihilist had decided to abandon the use of some faculty—the ears or the memory—in some exercise of self-mutilation. But, of course, a *spirited* nihilist will resist this way of putting things. She will suggest that it isn't a matter of *going backward* but of *going beyond*, that, just as my genealogy sees the acquisition of normative guidance as a decisive step in the evolution of humanity, so too the abrogation of normative guidance that she recommends is a further shift (the arrival of the *Übermensch?*). There's no doubt that this is a *possible* rejoinder, one that substitutes for the subtraction (or mutilation) perspective the idea of an addition (or completion) of ourselves. But if this is the nihilist's preferred tack, then we need more than the bare claim that what she envisages is progressive—enough detail about the advance must be provided to show why this develops who we really are. In effect, the spirited nihilist plays by the rules of the game that links moral progressiveness to authority over human action, seeing the abandonment of normative guidance as a further progressive shift, but this idea leaves the nihilist hostage to questions about what this shift really is and whether it can rightly be viewed as progressive.

If nihilism is to be a coherent attitude, one that someone could sustain, then it's crucial to remain unfazed by any connection between development of some of our psychological capacities and any authority over human action. In effect, the nihilist must insist that she doesn't care whether a particular capacity (the capacity for normative guidance) reinforced the tendencies that made sociality possible, and indeed made specifically *human* sociality possible; she still wants to suspend the operation of that capacity. There's no doubt that members of our species could have that wish. What's at issue is whether they can avoid the characterization of it as an exercise in self-mutilation, an interference with normal human functioning. Nor is this a small excision—something equivalent to the removal of one's tonsils or a vasectomy—but the deletion of a capacity central to human lives. (Of course, the notion of centrality invoked here needs further explication and defense.)

If this embryonic account of the authority of morality can be articulated further, then we seem to have some commitment to normative governance. The question that next confronts us is how the capacity for normative governance is to be filled out. Here, I suggest, my genealogical story portrays us, like our predecessors, as building from the cultural lore we inherit, modifying the rules handed down to us where they appear to promote further moral progress. We have no basis for thinking that the normative systems we're likely to achieve will be final and complete, or that the elements of the systems that figure in different lineages can always be combined. The story is compatible with an irreducible pluralism of values. Nonetheless, each of us tries to move forward from where we start, attempting to develop our humanity—the form of sociality that took us beyond the chimpanzees—as fully as possible.

5. Conclusion

I began by recognizing that ventures in connecting biology and ethics are philosophically perilous. The view I've outlined in this essay should make it clear why that is so. Even if much of the detail I've offered is mistaken, the connections between biological facts and questions about the status of morality are extremely complicated. To work out a convincing story about how current moral practices might have emerged would require a vast amount of information from diverse fields: evolutionary theory, primatology, psychology, anthropology, and history (and maybe more). The quick survey of three metaethical questions undertaken in section 4 reveals that there are significant philosophical possibilities that need to be explored in light of a careful genealogy. To the best of my knowledge, none of the many attempts to relate biology and ethics succeeds in acknowledging all these complexities. I hope, as I said, to have laid some duckboards across a swamp, but I fear that it's all too likely that I have joined my predecessors in the murky depths.

NOTES

Many thanks to David Copp for his patience, his encouragement, and his excellent suggestions.

1. "In every system of morality I have hitherto met with, I have always remarked that the author proceeds for some time in the ordinary way of reasoning, and establishes the being of a god, or makes observations concerning human affairs; when of a sudden I am surprised to find that instead of the usual copulation of propositions *is* and *is not*, I meet with no proposition that is not connected with an *ought* or an *ought not*. This change is imperceptible, but is, however, of the last consequence. For as this *ought* or *ought not* expresses some new relation or affirmation, it is necessary that it should be observed and explained; and at the same time that a reason should be given for what seems altogether inconceivable, how this new relation can be a deduction from others which are entirely different from it." Hume, 2000, III-i-1.

2. Ruse and Wilson, 1986. Of course, it would be hard to claim the incest prohibition as a fundamental new moral principle, but I'll let this pass.

3. Insofar as the prohibition of incest amounts to a correct moral principle, it's noteworthy that the biological emphasis on avoiding the combination of dangerous recessive alleles covers only one aspect of the situation—as the actual literature on incest makes clear, incestuous relations are typically coercive and exploitative. Wagner's depiction of Siegmund and Sieglinde succeeds because he inverts the normal contrast: the incest is the one example of free mutual love in a brutal world.

4. Foot, 2001, 24. Rosalind Hursthouse and Michael Thompson have taken similar approaches; their writings have both influenced and been influenced by Foot's.

5. I've detailed the problems for Hurka's approach in Kitcher, 1999. Foot's views are subject to parallel difficulties; I won't, however, try to argue for this here.

6. Blackburn, 2000. The connection with Hume permeates the book, but is especially evident in chs. 6 and 7.

7. I should note that Skyrms is rather more skeptical than Sober about the project of moral theory.

8. I'm not sure that either Sober or Skyrms would be much worried by the criticism. They would probably be more bothered by the charge (often leveled against evolutionary accounts of this kind) that their proposed explanations were speculative stories—although they could defend against that charge by claiming only that they intended to show how apparently problematic phenomena are evolutionarily possible.

9. In effect, I'll be attempting a project that spans the three programs I've distinguished. A similar venture is undertaken in the last chapter of Nozick, 2001. For reasons of space, I don't undertake a detailed comparison here.

10. This is a very quick sketch of the important idea of inclusive fitness (and of kin selection). Hamilton's original essays are in Hamilton, 1996, parts I and II. For a simpler exposition, see Kitcher, 1985, ch. 3.

11. Effectively, your sibling can be expected to have two extra offspring with the altruistic genotype, providing a net gain of one. Although I hope the example makes the point clear, it is *vastly* oversimplified.

12. The important point here is that neither player knows how long the sequence will last.

13. I should note that, although I've given the orthodox solutions here, Sober and Wilson have argued for a perspective that offers a unified treatment of the cases. In Sober and Wilson, 1998, they propose a revival of the much-debated notion of group selection. My own judgment is that the envisaged reformulation offers a few interesting special cases but that it doesn't give a perspicuous account of the two central approaches I've reviewed here.

14. For the optional games framework introduced here, see Kitcher, 1993a, and Batali and Kitcher, 1995. I should note that this framework also solves some technical difficulties in the Axelrod-Hamilton approach.

15. The coalition game is mathematically complex, and doesn't lend itself to the simple techniques one can use for games like prisoner's dilemma. It is possible, however, to prove some general results, and these results have been confirmed by computer simulation (here I am greatly indebted to Herbert Roseman). As with many of the claims in this section and the next, detailed elaboration and defense will be given in a book on which I'm currently working.

16. Hence, an interaction that appears to be a prisoner's dilemma (or other simple game) may actually have a different structure because of the consequences for coalition membership.

17. By contrast, *spite* consists in modifying one's attitudes to oppose the aims ascribed to others. The notions I introduce here can be made precise. For a preliminary attempt to do so, see Kitcher, 1993a; more refined treatment will appear in the book mentioned in note 15.

18. So, for example, in a reciprocal interaction with someone else, you shouldn't want to promote a cooperatively beneficial outcome because you have calculated that forming that desire will be useful in achieving your own independent aims.

19. This is because good strategies are exceptionally dependent on the precise conditions of the setup; if our ancestors had computed their best possibilities, they would have had to have extraordinary mathematical talents and amazingly full information!

20. Hobbes makes his point about the state of war by a comparison to British weather: "For as the nature of Foule weather, lyeth not in a showre or two of rain, but an inclination thereto of many dayes together: So the nature of War, consisteth not in actuall fighting; but in the known disposition thereto, during all the time there is no assurance to the contrary" (Hobbes, 1651, I-13). Hume insists on the existence of some dispositions to respond to the concerns and needs of others: "Let us suppose a person ever so selfish, let private interest have engrossed ever so much his attention, yet in instances where that is not concerned he must unavoidably feel *some* propensity to the good of mankind and make it an object of choice, if everything else be equal" (Hume, 1998, V-2).

21. Chimp and bonobo troop sizes range from around 30 to 140. For much of human prehistory, hominid bands were in this range. Quite early in the Neolithic, however, there were much larger settlements (Jericho, Çatal Hüyük), and the distribution of tools and the natural resources used in making them strongly suggests that there were at least temporary associations of much larger groups of *Homo sapiens* considerably earlier (possibly even 20,000 years before the present).

22. In the work cited in note 15, I provide much more detail about this, and explore the connection with systems of punishment.

23. The phrase is John Stuart Mill's. See Mill, 1974. For a twentieth century attempt to work out the theme, see MacBeath, 1950.

24. See the Hammurabi code. Reprinted Pritchard, 1969.

25. Nietzsche, 1887; there are similar formulations in Pritchard, 1969.

26. Note that they have been quite good at having *biological* descendants. But the important measure in cultural evolution is to transmit one's cultural items, perhaps by "infecting" other groups, perhaps by founding a lot of descendant groups in which those items are adopted. I develop the theory of cultural evolution presupposed here in Kitcher, 2001a, and in the work cited in note 15.

27. And, of course, there were other important cultural lineages that gave rise to the contemporary systems that prevail in other parts of the world.

28. Or possibly toward an "error theory." See Mackie, 1977.

29. The example was originally introduced by Harman (1977, pp. 4–8). The case precipitated an interesting dialogue between Harman and Nicholas Sturgeon. (See Sturgeon, 1985.)

30. As in the example of the response of many German people to Nazi brutality. Sturgeon would claim, I think, that these are cases in which social training interferes with a normal perceptual capacity.

31. I try to explain why in Kitcher, 2001b. Roughly, the idea is that, although the sciences aim at truth, the idea that they aim at the complete truth is a chimera, and the ways in which the *selection* of scientifically significant truths proceeds is a function of our evolving interests.

32. Of course, acquisition of the rules may issue in amplified emotional reactions. For my purposes, it doesn't matter whether we become more full of Humean benevolence or remain like Kant's "not the worst product of creation."

33. See the analysis in Kitcher, 1993b.

REFERENCES

Axelrod, Robert. 1984. *The Evolution of Cooperation.* New York: Basic Books.
Axelrod, Robert, and William Hamilton. 1981. "The Evolution of Cooperation." *Science* 211: 1390–1396.
Batali, John, and Philip Kitcher. 1995. "Evolution of Altruism in Optional and Compulsory Games." *Journal of Theoretical Biology* 175: 161–171.
Blackburn, Simon. 2000. *Ruling Passions.* New York: Oxford University Press.
De Waal, Frans. 1984. *Chimpanzee Politics.* Baltimore: Johns Hopkins University Press.
———. 1996. *Good Natured.* Cambridge, Mass.: Harvard University Press.
Foot, Philippa. 2001. *Natural Goodness.* Oxford: Oxford University Press.
Gibbard, Allan. 1990. *Wise Choices, Apt Feelings: A Theory of Normative Judgment.* Cambridge, Mass.: Harvard University Press.
Goodall, Jane. 1986. *The Chimpanzees of Gombe.* Cambridge, Mass.: Harvard University Press.

Hamilton, W. D. 1996. "The Genetical Evolution of Social Behavior." 2 parts. In *Narrow Roads of Gene Land*. San Francisco: Freeman.

Harman, Gilbert. 1977. *The Nature of Morality*. New York: Oxford University Press.

Hobbes, Thomas. [1651]. 1996. *Leviathan*. Ed. J.C.A. Gaskin. Oxford: Oxford University Press.

Hume, David. [1751]. 1998. *An Enquiry Concerning the Principles of Morals*. Ed. Thomas L. Beauchamp. Oxford: Oxford University Press.

———. [1739]. 2000. *A Treatise of Human Nature*. Ed. David Fate Norton and Mary J. Norton. Oxford: Oxford University Press.

Hurka, Thomas. 1993. *Perfectionism*. New York: Oxford University Press.

Kitcher, Philip. 1985. *Vaulting Ambition*. Cambridge, Mass.: MIT Press.

———. 1993a. "The Evolution of Human Altruism." *Journal of Philosophy* 90: 497–519.

———. 1993b. "Function and Design." *Midwest Studies in Philosophy* 18: 379–397.

———. 1999. "Ethics and Perfection." *Ethics* 110: 59–83.

———. 2001a. "Infectious Ideas." *Monist* 84: 368–391.

———. 2001b. *Science, Truth, and Democracy*. New York: Oxford University Press.

MacBeath, Alexander George. 1950. *Experiments in Living*. London: Macmillan.

Mackie, J. L. 1977. *Ethics*. Harmondsworth, England: Penguin.

Mill, John Stuart. [1859]. 1974. *On Liberty*. Ed. Gertrude Himmelfarb. Harmondsworth, England: Penguin.

Moore, G. E. [1903]. 1993. *Principia Ethica*. Ed. Thomas Baldwin. Cambridge: Cambridge University Press.

Nietzsche, Friedrich. [1887]. 1996. On the Genealogy of Morals. Trans. Douglas Smith. Oxford: Oxford University Press.

Nozick, Robert. 2001. *Invariances*. Cambridge, Mass.: Harvard University Press.

Prior, A. N. 1949. *Logic and the Basis of Ethics*. Oxford: Clarendon Press.

Pritchard, James, ed. 1969. *Ancient Near Eastern Texts Relating to the Old Testament*. Princeton, N.J.: Princeton University Press.

Ruse, Michael, and E. O. Wilson. 1986. "Moral Philosophy as Applied Science." *Philosophy* 61: 173–192.

Skyrms, Brian. 1996. *Evolution of the Social Contract*. Cambridge: Cambridge University Press.

Sober, Elliot, and David Sloan Wilson. 1998. *Unto Others: The Evolution and Psychology of Unselfish Behavior*. Cambridge, Mass.: Harvard University Press.

Sturgeon, Nicholas, L. 1985. "Moral Explanations." In *Morality, Reason, and Truth*, ed. David Copp and David Zimmerman, 49–78. Totowa, N.J.: Rowman and Allanheld.

Trivers, Robert. 1971. "The Evolution of Reciprocal Altruism." *Quarterly Review of Biology* 46: 35–57.

Westermarck, Edward. 1912. *The Origin and Development of the Moral Ideas*. London: Macmillan.

Wilson, E. O. 1979. "Comparative Social Theory." In *The Tanner Lectures on Human Values*. Salt Lake City: University of Utah Press.

Wrangham, R. W. 1979. "On the Evolution of Ape Social Systems." *Social Science Information* 18: 335–368.

CHAPTER 7

....

SENSIBILITY THEORY AND PROJECTIVISM

....

JUSTIN D'ARMS

DANIEL JACOBSON

1. PERCEPTIONS OF VALUE

....

DAVID Hume was skeptical about the idea that we *perceive* values or, more specifically, virtue and vice. "Take any action allowed to be vicious," he wrote,

> [e]xamine it in all lights and see if you can find that matter of fact . . . which you call vice. . . . The vice entirely escapes you, as long as you consider the object. You can never find it until you turn your reflection into your own breast, and find a sentiment of disapprobation, which arises in you, toward that action. (Hume, 1978, pp. 468–469)

Hume explained the alleged impossibility of observing moral qualities in the act itself through an analogy with beauty, which he also claimed to arise from our sentiments rather than directly from our senses:

> Euclid has fully explained all the qualities of the circle; but has not in any proposition said a word of its beauty. The reason is evident. The beauty is not a quality of the circle. . . . It is only the effect, which that figure produces upon the mind, whose peculiar fabric or structure renders it susceptible of such sentiments. In vain would you look for it in the circle, or seek it, either by your

own senses or by mathematical reasonings, in all the properties of that figure. (Hume, 1975, pp. 291–292)

These claims strike some philosophers as obviously false. "Hume's confident assertions about the unobservability of beauty are breathtakingly counter-intuitive," David McNaughton writes. "We see the beauty of a sunset; we hear the melodiousness of a tune; we taste and smell the delicate nuances of a vintage wine. Hume's denial that we can detect beauty by the senses flies in the face of common experience" (1988, p. 55). Understood as a phenomenological claim, this seems obviously correct—so obviously that one should doubt whether Hume meant to be denying it. Surely, when we find something beautiful, delicious, or even virtuous, we experience this as a matter of sensitivity to the observed object: the sunset, the wine, the person. But what kind of sensitivity is this? McNaughton intends to make a theoretical as well as a phenomenological objection to Hume; he claims that there is no difference in kind between the perception of value and other, more straightforward forms of perception.

Of course we use our senses to detect value, but do we literally see the beauty of a face, taste the deliciousness of food, and so forth? Here is a reason to doubt it. Tell me truthfully that the wine is delicious, and you haven't yet described the character of its flavor; tell me that my blind date is beautiful, and I have no idea what she looks like.[1] The primary likeness among the diverse objects we classify as beautiful, delicious, virtuous, and so forth, Hume asserts, lies not in how they look or taste but in how they make us feel. Even if I am acquainted with delicious and beautiful things, the only sense in which I can confidently anticipate the experience of something on the basis of a purely evaluative characterization of it—for instance as delicious or beautiful—concerns how I can expect to feel toward it. I will be *pleased* by the taste of the wine, the look of the face, the sound of the tune.

Surely there is something to this thought. Indeed, McNaughton seems to accept it, notwithstanding his criticism of Hume. Against the suggestion that values cannot be perceived because evaluative experience is primarily a matter of feeling, he replies: "The crucial mistake . . . is to fail to realize that a way of seeing a situation may itself be a way of caring or feeling" (1988, p. 113). If values can be perceived, then it seems that the perceptions of vice, beauty, and so forth must be located in our sentiments. This is already a difference in kind from perception, since ordinarily one can see things without feeling any particular way about them. Moreover, the substantially greater variability in sentimental response, as compared to visual and aural responses, helps explain the much greater disagreement found in evaluation. These considerations suggest that talk of the perception of value should be taken metaphorically.

Despite their differences, McNaughton and Hume seem to converge on *sen-timentalism*: roughly, the thesis that evaluation is to be understood by way of human emotional response. Emotions might figure in evaluative thought in several different ways, however. A tension still exists between Hume's (seemingly skeptical) suggestion that beauty is not a quality of the circle but only the sentimental effect it has on our minds and McNaughton's (avowedly realist) claim that such sentimental effects constitute perceptions of the beauty that is indeed a quality of the circle. Yet it is surprisingly difficult to say what ultimately hangs on this dramatic-sounding dispute over whether values exist in the world or are only in our minds. What is really at issue here? It will help to compare three different accounts of how the sentiments might be involved in evaluation—objectivism, perceptivism, and projectivism—each of which can be illustrated by considering an analogous theory about colors and their appearance.

According to the *objectivist* view, commonly called physicalism, colors are microphysical properties of surfaces.[2] They are fully objective properties of material objects, possessed irrespective of any relation to our color experience. Of course, green objects tend to look a certain familiar way to normal humans under suitable conditions. Color experience plays a crucial epistemic role as our basic form of sensitivity to colors. Nonetheless, the property to which our term "green" refers is this response-independent microphysical property. Thus an alien physicist with no visual system could potentially be in a better epistemic position with respect to colors than are we, with our deficiencies of night vision and the like.

Similarly, the objectivist about value holds that evaluative properties are fully objective properties of valuable things, possessed irrespective of any relation to our subjective sentimental responses. As with color appearances, human sentiments might have a legitimate epistemic role as sensitivities to value. But the objectivist must explain why our sentiments happen to track values more or less reliably, and it is far from obvious how to make this plausible within the theory's framework. Those classical forms of objectivism that rely crucially on claims of moral perception, which we will loosely refer to as intuitionism, have simply posited a faculty of moral sense or rational intuition with which we perceive and are moved by values.[3] It is easy to agree with John McDowell that this "primary-quality model turns the epistemology of value into mere mystification" (1985, p. 132).

Objectivism contrasts with the *projectivism* suggested by Hume's claim that beauty, virtue, and the like are not qualities of external objects. Rather, they are mere "projections" of our sentiments, which we unwittingly spread upon the world. Like perception, projection too is being used metaphorically in this context. It is helpful to think of slide projectors, which cast a photographic image onto what is really a blank screen. Were this technology able to fool the eye, it would be important to guard against deception by reminding ourselves that the image is not a property of the screen itself. Consider projectivism about color, which holds that colors are not actually properties of the objects to which we ascribe them.[4] Since the green appearance of grass is a feature of our visual field that is projected onto the colorless external world, our color judgments are systematically mistaken in the manner Hume suggests: We erroneously suppose an object (the grass) to have a property (greenness) that is really only in our minds (as a green appearance). Similarly, the projectivist holds that evaluative judgments issue from our "gilding or staining . . . natural objects with colors, borrowed from internal sentiment," as Hume describes it (1975, p. 294). Contemporary projectivist theories of value include error theory and noncognitivism, a distinction we will discuss later.

The middle ground between objectivism and projectivism is occupied by what we will call *perceptivism:* the view that colors and values are real—in a sense to be explained—despite essentially involving subjective responses. The perceptivist theory of color is known as dispositionalism. What it is for an object to be green, on this view, is for it to be disposed to present a green appearance to normal humans under suitable conditions. Like physicalism, dispositionalism holds that colors are real properties of the objects to which we ordinarily ascribe them. Moreover, color appearances are epistemically useful, since green appearances often indicate the presence of greenness. Even if some microphysical property causally responsible for these appearances were identified, however, the dispositionalist would deny that this property is greenness. Dispositionalists take colors to depend essentially on color appearances; hence they consider colors to be "response-dependent" properties.[5] Perceptivism can also be construed as a theory of value with two main variants. The most straightforward version is similarly dispositionalist: it identifies values as dispositions to produce Humean "passions"—sentiments and desires—in properly situated observers.[6] We will ultimately concentrate on another form of perceptivism, known as sensibility theory, which also focuses on sentimental responses while insisting that values do not merely *dispose* us to respond with feelings but *merit* those responses.

Sentimentalist forms of perceptivism render the epistemic role of the sentiments in perceptions of value less mysterious than does objectivism, because these theories implicate the sentiments in the metaphysics of value. What it is for something to be valuable or virtuous, on this view, is for it to elicit (or merit) certain sentiments. Perceptivism enjoys some prima facie advantages over its rivals, again helpfully illustrated by considering colors. Since projectivism implies that all color judgments are false, it conflicts with the compelling thought that some color appearances are veridical and others misleading. It also seems peculiar to claim, with the objectivist, that green is a purely physical property, like that of being spherical, which is only contingently connected to any manner of appearance. Of course, both the projectivist and the physicalist have responses to these objections. Nevertheless, perceptivism's ability to hold both that some things really are green, and that greenness is essentially a matter of how things appear visually, surely counts in its favor. And the same goes for value—or so perceptivists suggest.

In one respect, perceptive and objective views of color and value are united against projectivism. Both theories assert that colors and values are real properties of the objects to which we ascribe them, a claim that projectivism seems committed to denying. Yet there is a subtler respect in which perceptivism and projectivism are natural allies. Despite their disagreement about the metaphysics of value, perceptivists and projectivists agree that evaluative *concepts* depend essentially upon human propensities to have certain sorts of subjective experience. In what follows, we shall explore perceptivism and projectivism as rival developments of Humean sentimentalism.[7] We earlier characterized that doctrine somewhat vaguely, as the suggestion that evaluation is to be understood by way of human emotional response. That characterization was deliberately ambiguous between a proposal about evaluative concepts and one about value itself—that is, between claims about the constituents of evaluative thought and its purported object. We can now be more precise. Sentimentalism, as we shall understand it, is the thesis that evaluative concepts are *response-invoking:* they cannot be analyzed or elucidated without appeal to subjective responses—in particular, to the sentiments.[8]

Our taxonomy is unfortunately complex, partly because we have to integrate preexisting terminology with some of our own. In particular, we have sought to draw attention to the respect in which some mutually antagonistic forms of perceptivism and projectivism can be seen as united in their embrace of sentimentalism. The following table offers a rough-and-ready guide to the debate (sentimentalist theories are shown in italics).[9]

	Color	Value
Objectivism	Physicalism	Intuitionism Robust naturalist realism
Perceptivism	Dispositionalism	Dispositionalism Desire-based *Emotion-based* *Sensibility theory*
Projectivism	Projectivism	Projectivism *Noncognitivism* Error theory

Since we have introduced projectivism and perceptivism as rival theories about properties, we should say a bit more about the relation of their metaphysical claims to the sentimentalist account of concepts. For the perceptivist, the response-dependence of properties is in a sense derivative from the response-dependence of concepts.[10] Color and value properties are identified by appeal to a way in which they must be conceived. As McDowell puts it, they are "qualities not adequately conceivable except in terms of certain subjective states" (1985,

p. 136). The nature of these features of the world is supposed to depend upon how they must be conceived. This explains the perceptivist's insistence that a microphysical property of surfaces could not be the property green, since any such property could in principle be conceived of by appeal to a purely physical concept. Projectivists, by contrast, hold that there are no color or value properties in the external world. Yet they grant that we are intractably committed to thinking and speaking of things as colored and valuable; hence, they aspire to give a philosophical account of the content of such thought and discourse that makes sense of it. Value and color concepts must exist, because our commonplace judgments presuppose them, even if there are no properties for which they stand. Both the projectivist and the perceptivist thus hold that evaluative concepts are fundamentally about emotional responses—or, at any rate, about some essentially practical response.[11]

This practical aspect of evaluation makes problems for dispositionalism specifically as an account of value, which do not apply to the case of color and other secondary qualities. Values seem to be irreducibly normative: they can only be understood in terms of how we *should* respond, as opposed to how people actually *do* respond in any given circumstance. The alternative form of perceptivism about value, which has been dubbed *sensibility theory,* seeks to capture the intuitively compelling aspects of dispositionalism while accommodating this disanalogy between value and color.[12] The most difficult of these positions to characterize directly, this approach is exemplified by the work of John McDowell, David Wiggins, and David McNaughton; it is also embraced in some respects by Bernard Williams (1985, 1996) and Jonathan Dancy (1996), although each rejects other parts of the program (see also Helm, 2001; Mulligan, 1998). In this essay we shall elaborate and appraise what we take to be the core tenets of the view, without worrying about whether any given author holds all of them.

Sensibility theory aspires to vindicate the phenomenology of valuing as a matter of sensitivity to features of the world, while acknowledging that values are founded on human sentimental responses. This makes values subjective in one sense but objective in another: they are really there to be experienced, not merely figments of the subjective states that purport to be experiences of them. Although values are essentially tied up with patterns of affective concern, nothing about this admitted subjectivity of values requires that we regard evaluative thought as a matter of projecting onto reality something that isn't really there. Rather, as Wiggins puts it, values are "primitive, *sui generis,* incurably anthropocentric, and as unmysterious as any properties will ever be to us" (1987b, p. 195).

All sentimentalists urge that an important advantage of their view is that it makes sense of *internalism:* the claim that there is a necessary connection between value judgment and motivation or the will. Such theories seem well positioned to explain this connection because of the role they accord to the emotions, which are fundamentally motivational states, in evaluation. This advantage is evident by comparison with the intuitionism of G. E. Moore, H. A. Prichard, and other early twentieth–century moral realists. According to Moorean intuitionism, values are metaphysically independent but intrinsically motivating "nonnatural" properties; while Prichard claimed that to apprehend one's duty is at once to recognize an absolute moral truth and to be moved to act by it. Intuitionism thus secures internalism at the cost of positing mysterious nonnatural properties apprehended by intuition. It therefore proved vulnerable to a more metaphysically circumspect, naturalistic alternative offered by noncognitivist projectivism.

Noncognitivism eschews talk of the apprehension of value, focusing instead on the mental states involved in evaluative judgment. On this view, to judge something good requires somehow being moved favorably by it—perhaps to choose or get it, or at least to approve of it. While differing in the details, sensibility theory, too, holds that a necessary condition of judging something to be valuable is that one be properly motivated by it.[13] Noncognitivism makes this connection straightforward by identifying evaluative judgment with some motivational state, thus implying that moral convictions are not beliefs but attitudes—albeit perhaps complex ones. This focus on the psychology of evaluation seemed to many philosophers preferable to intuitionism's stipulation of intrinsically motivating nonnatural properties.

Sensibility theory defines itself in opposition to both these alternatives. Though its leading proponents decline to call their view either cognitivist or realist, they are willing to describe it as "antinoncognitivist" and "antiantirealist." Despite granting a role to the sentiments in the perception of value, they deny the projectivist suggestion that evaluative judgments are merely sentimental attitudes or more complex noncognitive states. Rather, value judgment involves sensitivity to evaluative properties that are (sometimes) possessed by their objects. Nevertheless, McDowell and Wiggins also expressly distance themselves from the objectivist tradition exemplified by intuitionism. They think it untenable to treat values as being "simply *there*, independently of human sensibility" yet nevertheless intrinsically "such as to elicit some 'attitude' or state of will from someone who becomes aware of [them]" (McDowell, 1985, p. 132). Sensibility theory thus claims both metaphysical and epistemological advantages over intuitionism. First, it aspires to give an account that explains how values could be essentially related to human concerns, thereby avoiding the mystery of nonnatural properties. Second, it seeks to develop an epistemology that explains how we can obtain evaluative knowledge by means of ordinary human sentiments and attitudes.

Sensibility theory aspires to vindicate perceptions of value by appealing to the sentiments, thereby earning the talk of evaluative truth and knowledge that is simply appropriated by intuitionism. It does so by offering an account of how we possess evaluative concepts that echoes the story dispositionalism tells about color concepts. Just as we grasp the sense of "green" by having perceptual faculties that acquaint us with what green looks like, Wiggins suggests, "we grasp the sense of a [value-predicate] by acquiring *a sensibility all parties to which respond in a particular way to certain particular features* in what they notice in any given act, person, or situation" (1990, p. 74; emphasis added). Values require a sensibility to be perceived because "our subjective responses to objects or events will often impose groupings upon them that have no purely naturalistic rationale" (Wiggins, 1987b, p. 193). Were there any such rationale, we might use it to formulate objectivist evaluative principles. We could say that what makes something funny, for instance, is its incongruity; and what makes something fearsome is its dangerousness—where incongruity and danger are understood as empirical, observer-independent properties. However, our patterns of response and criticism are too unruly for any such treatment to be tenable and substantive. If our responses are uncodifiable, and if values depend on those responses, then values, too, cannot be codified in rules.

Both projectivist and intuitionist accounts are claimed to neglect the role of a sensibility, acquired through one's ethical upbringing via a process of habituation. McDowell thus claims: "In moral upbringing what one learns is not to behave in conformity with rules of conduct, but to see situations in a special light, as constituting reasons for acting" (1978, p. 85). The special way of seeing characteristic of the virtuous person more closely resembles a skill than a set of beliefs. To have this skill—the sensibility that is characteristic of virtue—is at once to have the ability to see what to do and the motivation to do it. Hence, proponents of sensibility theory contend that philosophers who have recoiled from intuitionism to projectivism have thereby passed over what McDowell calls a "fully satisfying intermediate position" (1981, p. 215), on which moral and other values are genuinely there in the world and give us reason to act—albeit reasons that can be appreciated only if one has been inculcated into the proper sensibility.

There is a dual burden on sensibility theory. It must actually develop such an account of moral perception and knowledge, so that its claims about the apprehension of values and reasons amount to more than the intuitionist's "bogus epistemology" (McDowell, 1987, p. 162). Moreover, its advocates need to explain why their theory cannot be co-opted by a sophisticated form of projectivism. In the rest of this essay, we will treat projectivism mainly as a foil for sensibility theory. (A more detailed defense of the projectivist program can be found in Blackburn, chapter 5 in this volume.) That is, our primary concern is whether sensibility theory succeeds in distinguishing itself from projectivism, as promised.

2. SENTIMENTALISM

As we've seen, both contemporary projectivism and sensibility theory embrace the sentimentalist claim that evaluative concepts are response-invoking—they are essentially bound up with subjective human feelings.[14] Before turning to the dispute between the two theories, we need to examine this claim and its motivations in more detail. Sentimentalism characteristically pairs each evaluative concept with a distinct sentimental response. The judgment that a person is virtuous is explicated by appeal to a feeling of specifically moral approval of him, which Hume called "approbation"; and the judgment that something is funny is associated with feelings of amusement at it.[15]

One common objection to this approach is that there don't seem to be enough distinct emotions to differentiate the variety of broadly positive and negative evaluations. What is approbation, one might wonder, other than an approving judgment of an agent's character, perhaps accompanied by some sort of positive affect? Yet surely we can approve of people for other reasons, for instance, as being novel and interesting, without thinking them virtuous. If Humean approbation is simply approval, then it cannot be used to distinguish evaluations of virtue from these other appraisals. If instead approbation is stipulated to be approval felt toward a person specifically for her virtue, then a sentimentalist characterization of virtue by appeal to approbation seems to presuppose the very notion it was introduced to explain. Finally, if approbation is held to be some other kind of sentiment altogether, then it will be necessary to explain the difference between it and other species of approval. To forestall such worries, we shall focus primarily on the most promising cases for sentimentalism, where there are identifiable emotions ready to hand. (We will briefly discuss more problematic cases in section 5.)

Consider those evaluative concepts with seemingly overt sentimental affiliations, such as *funny, shameful, disgusting,* and *fearsome.* It is hard to deny that these concepts are somehow about the emotional reactions that commonly accompany judgments deploying them: amusement, shame, disgust, and fear, respectively. One reason *funny* begs to be understood as a response-invoking concept is that it is so difficult to give an account of the content of comic judgments without invoking amusement. The failure of every effort to construct a philosophical theory of humor, which would provide objective criteria of the funny, should make one skeptical of the prospects for any response-independent account. These theories do not fail entirely—each has its kernel of truth—but none comes close to being adequate. Perhaps the most famous account holds that incongruity is the essence of the comic. But the incongruity theory of humor is ultimately undone by the need to expand its central notion so as to accommodate more of what people find funny. Roger Scruton makes this point incisively: "To know what is meant by 'incongruous' you would have to consult, not some independent conception, but the range of objects at which we laugh" (1987, p. 162). This is not merely a defect of one particular account but a flaw common to every attempt to develop a theory of humor. These theories are inevitably vulnerable to counterexamples from which they can be rescued only by letting our sense of humor enter through the back door, illicitly determining when the putatively objective criterion is met.

Part of the difficulty with giving an objectivist (as opposed to sentimentalist) elucidation of *funny* is that people have such disparate senses of humor. Its application, like that of many evaluative concepts, seems to be *essentially contestable:* disputes over their application are endemic and cannot be settled by philosophical analysis or scientific discovery. Consider the core moral concept, *wrong.* Some deontologists hold that certain types of action, such as torture, are intrinsically wrong under any circumstances; moreover, their certainty about such judgments is impervious to theoretical argument. Yet some consequentialists will insist that there are circumstances under which any action—even torture—is morally required. Indeed, such a consequentialist can be expected to embrace the conclusion that it is obligatory to torture the terrorist in the clichéd ticking-bomb scenario. He will urge that the refusal to do so, may the heavens fall, amounts to moral squeamishness.

However one comes down on this issue, it is hard to claim that one's opponent is less than a fully competent user of moral concepts, though of course both sides cannot be correct about their application. It is equally difficult to see how any empirical discovery could break the stalemate, since no facts about the hypothetical scenario are in doubt. Considerations like these have led many philosophers to conclude that the concept *wrong* is essentially contestable. Yet this raises a puzzle. When parties to a moral dispute can disagree over the standards of wrongness as systematically as do our deontologist and consequentialist, one must wonder if they share the same moral concept—whether they mean the same thing by "wrong."[16] The alternative seems even more extreme, since if there is no univocal meaning of moral terms, then disputants are simply talking past each other. As we shall see, sentimentalism promises to help solve the puzzle over essential contestability and univocity.

While such fundamental moral concepts as *good* and *wrong* are the main subject of metaethics, they are not our paradigm cases for a sentimentalist treatment. Concepts like *funny* and *shameful* may be less important than those, but an analogy seems to hold. Their predication is subject to fundamental dispute, for which reasons can be given and taken, but agreement between fully informed and rational agents cannot be ensured. Hence similar worries about univocity might be expected to arise in all such cases. But response-invoking concepts have the signal advantage of promising to make sense of normative dispute by securing a common subject matter without foreclosing substantive debate. Thus, according to Wiggins,

> [W]e can fix on a response . . . and then argue about what the marks are of the property that the response itself is made for. And without serious detriment to the univocity of the predicate, it can now become essentially contestable what a thing has to be like for there to be any reason to accord that particular appellation to it, and correspondingly contestable what the extension is of the predicate. (1987b, p. 198; cf. Gibbard, 1992a)

Roughly speaking, claims about what is funny, shameful, and fearsome are claims about what to be amused by, to be ashamed of, and to fear. A primary motivation for sentimentalism is its promise to secure a shared subject matter for evaluative dispute (for instance, over what is wrong or funny) among people with different outlooks (ethical perspectives or senses of humor). This agreement in meaning is a prerequisite for genuine disagreement. People can disagree about whether some joke is funny because they share the sentiment of amusement, which gives them something for their dispute to be about—roughly, whether or not to be amused by the joke.

But it turns out to be surprisingly difficult to offer a plausible sentimentalist proposal. Consider this straightforward suggestion. Something is funny just in case one is amused when attending to it; similarly, the shameful is anything one feels ashamed of (in oneself) or contempt for (in others) when one thinks that feature obtains. There are various superficial difficulties with this proposal, which might be fixed piecemeal; but a deeper problem infects the basic approach. Common sense tells us that particular emotional episodes are unreliable guides to value. Surely, you can fail to be afraid of things you should—things that are truly fearsome and threatening—even if you are aware of them. And you can be ashamed of things that, on reflection, you do not deem shameful. In short, there is a *critical gap* between sentiment and value, analogous to the difference between something looking red and being red. For sentimentalism to get off the ground, it must accommodate the critical gap: it must allow us to criticize specific emotional episodes as misperceptions of value.

Projectivism might seem to help circumvent the problem. Since the projective metaphor suggests that sentiments are evaluative appearances projected onto a value-free reality, it implies that there are no facts for appearances to track. If nothing really is shameful, funny, or wrong, then all sentimental appearances are equally misleading; hence, there is no point in critical reflection upon the *correctness* of our emotional responses. A projective sentimentalism thus seems to solve the critical gap problem on the cheap by denying the possibility that appearances can come apart from reality, since in reality evaluation is merely the projection of our sentiments onto the world. In the following section, we shall consider whether projectivism succeeds in bridging the critical gap in a way that can support a sentimentalist theory of value.

3. CONTEMPORARY PROJECTIVISM AND THE CONFLATION PROBLEM

According to the projectivist theory of color, color experience is a mere figment of our mental states: appearances projected onto the world, corresponding to nothing factual. Similarly, according to an *error theory* of value, all our sentiments are misleading because all value judgments are false.[17] A similar problem arises for both theories, since, whatever our philosophical theory, we will continue to see colors and to care about values. Hence, the very idea that our evaluative practices might be systematically in error, much less that we should try to avoid the mistake of moralizing, can seem absurd. Another form of projectivism therefore reinterprets evaluative judgment in a more ontologically modest fashion, so as to avoid convicting it of pervasive error (Blackburn, 1985). *Noncognitivism* takes evaluation to be fundamentally prescriptive or expressive rather than assertoric. Value judgments are not false, because they are not even apt for truth— they are more like commands or exhortations than statements of fact. The simplest proposal, made by emotivism, claims that they are expressions of emotion made for persuasive purposes. Noncognitivism thus seems able to avoid the conclusion that all evaluations are false, without positing evaluative facts to which they must answer.

Whereas error theory charges ordinary moral thought with mistake, the noncognitivists view it as innocent, considered in itself. There is nothing wrong with moralizing per se; the error lies in philosophical theories that treat moralizing as a matter of discovering and reporting on moral facts. Noncognitivism thus aims to understand moral thought and discourse rather than to reform it. Yet emotivism fails on these terms because it cannot save enough of the phenomena. There is an obvious and uncontroversial difference between being in an emotional state and making an evaluative judgment—between being amused, ashamed, or angry and thinking something genuinely funny, shameful, or wrong. Emotivism assimilates these states, however, by identifying the thought that something is funny with the state of being amused at it, and so forth.[18] Although noncognitivism denies the theoretical claim that there are evaluative facts to which our judgments must answer, it cannot deny that our judgments come apart from our actual emotional responses. That critical gap—between judgment and response—is not

a theoretical claim but a fact about ordinary practice, which is among the phenomena to be explained.[19]

This objection and others have led recent philosophers in the noncognitivist
tradition to develop more sophisticated theories. Allan Gibbard's norm expressivism and Simon Blackburn's quasi-realism understand evaluations not as mere
sentiments but as more complex, higher-order attitudes. Whereas emotivism identifies thinking that someone has done wrong with being angry with her, norm
expressivism identifies it with acceptance of a norm calling for such anger. The
posited mental state of norm acceptance is still a kind of attitude, an endorsement
of the emotional response as appropriate, but such attitudes can diverge from
one's sentiments. You can find yourself getting angry at the bearer of bad news,
for example, despite thinking that you shouldn't "blame the messenger." Thus
sophisticated projectivism has developed the ability to recognize a respect in which
particular emotional responses may be defective and others apt, while denying
that there are any evaluative facts against which to measure them. The account
thereby acknowledges and explains the critical gap by understanding it as being
a gap between sentiment and evaluative judgment—between having some emotional response and endorsing it as appropriate.

This focus on evaluative judgment rather than value itself invites the objection
that projectivism makes morality into a merely psychological phenomenon. Even
the most sophisticated forms of noncognitivism seem to locate the wrongness of
cruelty in some complex mental attitude that is not apt for truth. Does this imply,
implausibly, that the only thing wrong with cruelty is that we don't like it (or
endorse disapproval of it)? However the theory is embellished, it ultimately seems
to rest on nothing but attitudes—indeed, contingent attitudes we merely happen
to have, since, notoriously, not all humans have scorned cruelty. Yet this must be
false. Surely cruelty would be wrong even if we didn't think so, and regardless of
anyone's responses or attitudes.

The contemporary projectivist response is to insist upon a distinction between
two stances we can adopt toward questions about value, one internal to the practice of moralizing and another external to it. When we take the internal stance
of a participant in moral practice, we use evaluative terms to defend and dispute
our commitments; whereas when we take the external stance, we are giving a
philosophical theory of moral practices. The projectivist can deny that the wrongness of cruelty has anything to do with people's attitudes toward it, by giving that
claim an internal reading that expresses his unconditional acceptance of a norm
condemning cruelty. The norm is unconditional, in that it is accepted regardless
of his own attitudes, and endorsed even for the hypothetical circumstance in
which he changes his mind. He can express the unconditional nature of this norm
by saying "It's true that cruelty is wrong" or even "Cruelty would be wrong
whether or not I disapprove of it"; but he must admit, from the theorist's perspective, that these locutions do not add anything to the claim that cruelty is

wrong. This is a problematic maneuver, since it can easily seem like something is being given with one hand (the participant's) and taken away with the other (the theorist's). But we do not see this as a decisive problem for projectivism; in fact, we will ultimately suggest that sensibility theory requires an analogous argument and similar finesse.

However that may be, there is a problem with contemporary projectivism's attempt to account for the critical gap by identifying evaluative judgment with higher-order states of endorsement. In order to save appearances, the projectivist needs to allow for critical reflection on the *correctness* of our sentimental responses. He needs to make sense of the fact that we can be ashamed of things we do not think shameful. Sophisticated projectivists appeal to higher-order attitudes to explain this phenomenon: in such cases we are feeling shame we do not endorse, because it conflicts with our norms for what to be ashamed of. But not all these higher-order attitudes are suitable to the task at hand. Consider Blackburn's account of how we can improve our evaluative views through critical reflection upon them. He writes:

> My attitudes ought to be formed from qualities I admire—the proper use of knowledge, real capacity for sympathy, and so on. If they are not, and if the use of those capacities and the avoidance of the inferior determinants of opinion would lead me to change, then the resulting attitudes would be not only different, but better. (1980, p. 79)

These are all fine normative considerations, but theoretical reflection shows that not all good criticism of our evaluative attitudes is relevant to their correctness. The feelings one endorses as admirable or desirable may come apart from the evaluative judgments one accepts. Projectivism faces a *conflation problem:* it is ill equipped to differentiate between various kinds of endorsement of our sentiments, so as to fix on those that constitute evaluative judgment.[20]

There are various reasons for criticizing (or endorsing) an emotional response, only some of which are relevant to whether or not the sentiment gets evaluative matters right. Having done some reading in positive psychology, a person might come to the conclusion that she would be both happier and more virtuous were she to become more optimistic. She might decide that the attitude of the optimist, whose somewhat less accurate view of the world leads her to have fewer regrets than the pessimist, is "not only different, but better." Nevertheless, this criticism of regret has nothing to do with any judgment about what is genuinely regrettable. Similarly, moral reasons not to feel a sentiment are surely relevant to whether one endorses it, but they may be irrelevant to whether it is appropriate in the sense bearing on ascription of the associated evaluative property. Someone who finds himself envious of a good friend's promotion might think this reaction speaks ill of him—envy being one of the deadly sins. His higher-order attitudes condemn his feelings on moral grounds, as inferior. Yet this does not commit

him to denying that the promotion is enviable. In short, the trouble for projectivism is that the question of what sentiments or attitudes one endorses feeling
about something is a different question than whether it is truly funny, enviable,
regretable, and so forth.

Projectivists need to find a way of differentiating among the panoply of
higher-order attitudes, so as to distinguish those that constitute an agent's evaluative judgments. But the theory seems barred by its antirealist commitments
from using the most natural idioms for doing so. We need to fix on the attitude
associated with thinking that an emotion gets it right: that the amusing joke really
is funny, the regretted decision truly regrettable, and so on. Call this the judgment
that amusement is a *fitting* response to its object. A tenable sentimentalism requires an account of fittingness. And the challenge for projectivism is to demonstrate that judgments about the fittingness of emotions, as distinct from generic
endorsements of them, are best understood as noncognitive attitudes. It remains
to be seen whether a projective sentimentalism can develop the resources needed
to solve this conflation problem.

4. DISPOSITIONALISM AND SENSIBILITY THEORY

Contemporary noncognitivism tries to account for the critical gap not as a difference between sentimental appearance and evaluative reality, but as a difference
between sentiment and judgment. Since the theory is committed to denying that
evaluative thought is a matter of forming evaluative beliefs that can be true or
false, though, it has some difficulty saying just what constitutes an evaluative
judgment. As we've seen, attempts to understand them as higher-order attitudes
toward sentimental responses run into trouble differentiating distinct questions.
Perhaps the critical gap must be approached head-on, as a gap between sentimental appearance and reality. Evaluative judgments could then be understood as
beliefs about that reality.

This approach is suggested by the central perceptivist analogy between values
and secondary qualities. Recall the dispositional analysis of color, on which it is
a priori that "X is red if and only if X is such as to look red to normal human
observers under standard conditions." While this account is circular, in that it
uses *red* on both sides of the biconditional, it is nevertheless commonly granted
to give a substantive characterization of redness, because it specifies the extension
of this property by appealing to a particular sort of qualitative state (that of seeing

red). With an account of the property in hand, the dispositionalist can then treat judgments of redness like ordinary predications: to judge something red is simply to ascribe that property to it.

Dispositionalism makes room for the possibility of ignorance and error about colors, which is one of the traditional hallmarks of realism. The mere fact that something looks red (to someone on some occasion) does not ensure that is red, because the conditions might be nonstandard. Redness thus maintains a measure of independence from our beliefs about it, which is a prerequisite for the claim that redness is a real feature of objects and not a mere figment of our experience.[21] Nevertheless, dispositionalism inevitably forecloses the possibility of ignorance and error under those privileged conditions. Colors are not entirely independent of us; they are not primary qualities. Dispositionalism must specify the privileged conditions for color vision substantially. Were they identified simply as whatever conditions ensure that appearances are not deceiving, the biconditional would become trivially true and uninformative.[22] Thus 'standard conditions' must be shorthand for some specific set of conditions, presumably having to do with daylight on earth, under which we are prepared to say that color appearances are guaranteed to coincide with color reality.

Similarly, sentimentalist dispositionalism about value holds that what it is for something to possess a specific value is for it to be disposed to produce the associated sentiment from a specified class of responders under certain conditions. Evaluative reality is, again, partly independent of human beliefs and reactions, since our actual sentiments might differ from those we would have under the privileged conditions. This proposal might even promise to vindicate talk of sentiments as perceptions of value, since our sentiments signal the presence of evaluative properties that produce them in us. But there are significant differences between colors and values, which make the analogy difficult to sustain in crucial respects. In particular, the task of specifying standard conditions and observers for evaluative judgment is fraught with difficulty.

The basic problem is that our emotional propensities differ far more than does our color vision. Moreover, where we do find variation in color perception, as with colorblindness, we find both a supermajority (to supply a standard of correct color vision) and an identifiable anatomical deficit (to justify the claim that colorblind vision is not just different but worse). Recall that the main challenge for dispositionalism was to identify privileged conditions under which we are prepared to foreclose the possibility of ignorance and error. This challenge might be met satisfactorily in the case of color, but it seems hopeless in the case of value. Even if we could develop the notion of normal emotional response, such responses would not give a plausible standard of value. It might be normal to be afraid of spiders, for instance, but that does not suffice to show that they are fearsome. Whatever standard conditions are chosen, we should not be inclined to grant that people under those conditions cannot be mistaken about values—

unless the observers and circumstances are described simply as ideal, of course, in which case the characterization becomes trivial.

The proponents of sensibility theory doubt that there is any way to fill out the relevant clauses so as to make dispositionalism a substantive and plausible account of value. Thus, although McDowell explicitly appeals to the analogy between values and secondary qualities, he also insists upon a crucial difference between them: "The disanalogy . . . is that a virtue (say) is conceived to be not merely such as to elicit the appropriate 'attitude' (as a colour is merely such as to cause the appropriate experiences), but rather such as to *merit* it" (1985, p. 143). By invoking the overtly normative notion of merit, this proposal eschews any attempt to characterize values in purely descriptive terms, and avoids the need to identify circumstances under which sentimental responses are immune from error. It therefore comports better with the suggestion that values are essentially contestable. The focus on merited responses also promises to explain what is at issue in the many seemingly cogent evaluative disputes that cannot settled by empirical investigation: these are disagreements over what response is merited. Disputants can criticize as unmerited even very common patterns of response—such as survivor guilt, fear of spiders, and regret over the bad outcomes of good decisions—and they can back up these claims with reasons that will sometimes be persuasive.

Dispositionalism promised an account of how secondary qualities might depend in essential ways on human subjective experience, yet maintain enough independence to confer a form of objectivity on the properties. Sensibility theory invites us to retain this lesson for values while abandoning the dispositional model that was introduced to teach it. But the dispositional model lent credence to talk of perception and objectivity by offering a specific account of what color properties are and how we come to interact with them. If colors are dispositions to produce certain sensations in perceivers, then they may be said to impinge themselves upon us by causing us to have the visual experiences we do.[23] Once the dispositional model is set aside in favor of the merit schema, though, it is much less clear what kind of explanatory role is played by the values that sensibility theory claims are really there to be experienced. How does the fact that some sentiment is merited impinge itself upon observers, or otherwise explain features of our experience?

Although he grants that values will not figure in causal explanations of our experience, McDowell thinks this no concession about their reality. The right question, he suggests, is not whether values pull their weight in causal explanations, but whether they can consistently be explained away. When we justify our fear by appealing to the fearfulness of our circumstances, we are engaged in an attempt to make sense of our affective responses to the world. And this endeavor "will simply not cohere with the claim that reality contains nothing in the way of fearfulness" (1985, p. 144). An example will help elucidate this argument. The current proposal models a sensibility on some specific emotional capacity, understood as a sensitivity to a particular realm of value, like a sense of humor. The merit schema applies, because to judge something funny is not merely to think it causes amusement, even regularly, but to think the thing merits amusement. But what can that mean—what merits amusement?

In some ways, the comic is an especially hard case for sensibility theory, since people often allow for "blameless" disagreement rather than insisting on the correctness of their opinions. Even here, though, we have practices of criticism and notions of improvement, which seem to presuppose that the sentiment is fittingly directed toward some objects and not others. Some things are genuinely funny (such as early Woody Allen movies) and others are not (the later ones). Moreover, it is a commonplace that comic sensibilities can to some extent be refined and improved through training. We expect that as a person matures, her sense of humor will become more sophisticated, especially if she is exposed to the right objects: wit, satire, and the darker, less facile forms of comedy. There is even a small critical vocabulary with which we evaluate senses of humor—for instance as crude, juvenile, or tasteless. It thus seems possible not merely to alter but to improve a person's sense of humor. Some such criticism purports to do so in the relevant way: by making its possessor more sensitive to the funny. As we move from amusement to reactions we take more seriously—such as fear, anger, and shame—the practices of criticism and justification are grounded in much richer sets of reasons. Furthermore, it is difficult to see how we could give up these practices without treating our emotional lives as a welter of irrational affect by abandoning intuitively compelling distinctions between justified and unjustified fear, anger, amusement, and the like.

McDowell seems to think that these practices commit us to the reality of values. Others will find it doubtful that such truisms about evaluative thought and discourse could suffice to establish the reality of the properties that serve as their subject matter.[24] In any case, if there is nothing more to the sensibility theorist's claim of evaluative reality than an endorsement of the practices of reason-giving with which we criticize and justify our responses, the projectivist need not disagree. He will simply insist that these practices are themselves expressions of ever more complicated noncognitive attitudes. This cannot be simply asserted, of course—it must be shown. And the conflation problem looms as an obstacle to any such demonstration.

While the move from dispositionalism to the merit schema seems to us a necessary step toward a plausible sentimentalism, it invites a question that obscures the difference between theories still further. How does thinking of a sentiment as merited differ from adopting a second-order attitude of the sort suggested by Gibbard and Blackburn? Sensibility theory, too, must solve the conflation problem—it requires an account of how to distinguish, among the many reasons one might have for thinking a response merited, the ones that are legitimately taken as relevant to judgments attributing the paired property. The question is which reasons for and against feeling shame are relevant to the issue of whether shame is fitting. It is no help to say "only those that speak to whether a characteristic is really shameful," unless we have some purchase on what it is for something to be shameful other than for it to merit shame.

We suggested earlier that noncognitivism is barred by its antirealist commitments from using the most natural idioms for solving the problem. But it is not at all clear that sensibility theory's appropriation of those idioms makes any advance against the conflation problem. Indeed, as projective and perceptive sentimentalism grow more sophisticated, it becomes increasingly difficult to see what is at stake in their heated dispute over the reality of values. Both sides want to maintain that some things are, and others are not, shameful, funny, and wrong; and they both hold that, in order to explain such thought, one must advert to higher-order criticism and endorsement of our sentiments.

5. Varieties of Sentiment and Value

We have suggested that the metaphysical dispute between sensibility theory and projectivism, manifested in their antithetical metaphors of perception and projection, amounts to less than first appears. When the two theories are considered as alternative forms of sentimentalism, however, another issue becomes evident that may prove more significant. Because projective sentimentalism aspires to give a reductive analysis of evaluative concepts in terms of specific emotions and higher-order attitudes toward them, it requires these emotions to be independently identifiable. For example, in order to analyze the funny by way of amusement, we must be able to grasp that sentiment without appealing to the concept *funny*. Proponents of sensibility theory deny this possibility, insisting that these emotional responses contain the very content projectivists invoke them to explain. Thus, Wiggins claims,

> there will often be no saying exactly what reaction a thing with the associated property will provoke without direct or indirect allusion to the property itself. Amusement for instance is a reaction we have to characterize by reference to its proper object, via something perceived as funny (or incongruous or comical or whatever). There is no object-independent and property-independent, "purely phenomenological" or "purely introspective" account of amusement. (1987b, p. 195)

This is a significant challenge. We think sensibility theorists are right to press this point, as projectivists have not yet established that the mental states to which they appeal really are prior to the concepts they purport to explain.[25] Wiggins proposes that there is no priority between sentimental responses (such as amusement, shame, and moral indignation) and their associated concepts (*funny*, *shameful*, and *wrong*). He suggests instead that these concepts and responses arise together, in pairs, through a coevolution in which the character of the response and the extension of the predicate influence one another. Hence, no noncircular account of either concept or response is possible, because each depends essentially upon the other.[26] While we acknowledge the significance of this objection, we think it can be answered in this case and certain others. We doubt that the only way to home in on amusement is with the concept *funny*—partly because we are more sanguine about the availability of a distinctive phenomenology for amusement than is Wiggins, and partly because there seem to be other resources for discriminating between sentiments than the introspective methods he considers. As Blackburn notes, one can also identify amusement by its primary behavioral expression: laughter.

McDowell responds to Blackburn by focusing the challenge less narrowly on phenomenology. He asks:

> But what exactly is it that we are to conceive as projected on to the world so as to give rise to our idea that things are funny? "An inclination to laugh" is not a satisfactory answer; projecting an inclination to laugh would not necessarily yield an apparent instance of the comic, since laughter can signal, for instance, embarrassment just as well as amusement. Perhaps the right response cannot be identified except as amusement; and perhaps amusement cannot be understood except as finding something comic. (1987, p. 158)

Granted, amusement is not simply the disposition to laugh. Yet this is precisely where phenomenology seems most helpful, as there are evident differences between nervous, embarrassed, or hysterical laughter and the sort characteristic of amusement. Most obviously, only the last is pleasant. Phenomenology (as well as facial expression, behavior, and physiology) can help to pick out amusement— even if no "purely introspective" account is available—without appeal to the concept *funny*. We suspect that a number of emotions can be similarly identified via their motivational roles, typical eliciting conditions, and characteristic expressions (such as blushing, trembling, laughter, or tears)—as well as by how they feel.

In fact, a lively program of psychological research aims at providing characterizations of emotions that do not appeal to the evaluative concepts sentimentalists invoke them to explain (e.g. Ekman, 1994; Lazarus, 1994; Rozin, Haidt, and McCauley, 2000; Tooby and Cosmides, 1990). It would be a mistake for sentimentalists to bet against this program across the board. Indeed, even McDowell grants that it is plausible to suppose that disgust, at least, is a "self-contained psychological [item], conceptualizable without any need to appeal to any projected [property] of disgustingness" (1987, p. 157). McDowell thinks this can be safely granted, in part because he thinks that the disgusting is not an evaluative but a dispositional property. He does not seem to consider that the merit schema applies even to so humble a response as disgust, in virtue of the critical gap between sentiment and value. Not everything that nauseates, even regularly, is judged disgusting. Ever since an ugly food poisoning incident years ago, I cannot eat whitefish salad; but though it reliably disgusts me, I still consider it a delicacy—albeit one I can no longer enjoy. More generally, people often dispute such judgments, arguing about whether some edgy comic is funny or an exotic food disgusting, rather than simply relativizing their claims.[27] It thus seems that with disgust, as well as amusement, sensibility theory must be prepared to concede the priority of emotional response to evaluative property. The question then becomes how many such independently identifiable sentiments exist.

Although we find ample evidence of a class of natural emotions with cross-cultural homologues, despite their variable eliciting conditions, we will not argue for this claim here.[28] Instead, let us focus on the sentiments McDowell and Wiggins consider in detail: amusement, disgust, and fear. These are good examples for sentimentalism, because it is plausible that, no matter how different our dispositions to respond may be, these sentiments provide a shared subject matter for discussion about what is funny, disgusting, and fearsome. But it is no coincidence that they are also cases where the priority claim seems most plausible. These emotions are syndromes of cognitive, affective, motivational, and behavioral changes, which arise in patterns displaying some degree of consistency across times and cultures—perhaps because of our shared evolutionary history. Such natural emotions are amenable to study as distinctive psychological syndromes, just as projectivism requires.

Yet, however substantial the list of natural emotions turns out to be, it will surely capture only a limited range of evaluative concepts. Perhaps the most important question, and certainly the most disputed, is whether that range will include the fundamental moral concepts *right* and *wrong*. One recent attempt at a projective sentimentalist moral theory is Gibbard's (1990) proposal to explicate such judgments as expressions of norms for guilt and anger—where these are held to be natural emotions in our sense.[29] While this proposal has much to recommend it, it also faces some serious obstacles. Even were Gibbard's moral theory vindicated, though, sentimentalism would have to go much further in order to cover the entire evaluative domain. It must adduce sentiments corresponding to other moral concepts (such as *justice* and *desert*), as well as concepts of virtue and vice, and various other more specific values. These include what Bernard Williams (1985, esp. p. 129) terms "thick concepts," such as *treachery, promise, brutality,* and *courage*, which have more determinate descriptive content than the fundamental moral concepts. We think it implausible to suppose that a sufficient number of distinct natural emotions can be found to characterize all these concepts. While two competing strategies for handling this problem have been suggested by the leading projectivists (Blackburn, 1992; Gibbard, 1992b), neither is wholly satisfactory, and we are skeptical about the prospects for any unified sentimentalist treatment.[30]

The great promise of Wiggins's "no priority" approach is that it provides a general account with which perceptivist sentimentalism might hope to characterize evaluative concepts. Since Wiggins uses the concepts themselves to make fine-grained distinctions among responses, he can tailor each response to fit its associated concept. This allows him to adduce distinct forms of disapprobation corresponding to wrongness, injustice, cowardice, and so on. Each pair of evaluative concept and sentimental response results from the sort of process described earlier, on which they arise and are refined together. The responses thereby partially determine the content of the concepts, while the concepts partially fix the character of the responses. This makes the relation between concept and response circular; but Wiggins claims that this is not a vicious circularity, because it is true and informative in virtue of its sentimentalism. As he puts it, "one would not . . . have sufficiently elucidated what value is without this detour" through the sentiments (1987b, p. 189). Wiggins's speculative genealogy of evaluative concepts seems plausible in some cases, but his account is too sweeping, and it conflicts with a primary motivation for sentimentalism.

Even if one grants that circular elucidations are sometimes informative, Wiggins's strategy seems unable to secure univocity alongside essential contestability.[31] Sometimes apparent disagreement in evaluation is specious, because the disputants do not share the same evaluative concept. This possibility must be taken seriously when the following conditions obtain. Parties to an evaluative dispute have very different views about a concept's extension, and they differ about what other features make the concept applicable in a given case; there are no established traditions of deference to mutually recognizable experts; the dispute cannot be settled by conceptual analysis or empirical inquiry; and it cannot be understood simply as a question of what to do. Our example of the deontologist and the consequentialist suggested that this is how things stand with *wrong*.

Wiggins would say that what makes it possible for them to be talking to, rather than past, each other is a shared sentiment of moral disapprobation whose appropriateness is at issue. He thus requires an account of moral disapprobation that ensures both disputants have this specific sentiment in their emotional repertoire, or at any rate understand it well enough to debate its appropriateness. Yet his account of the sentiments seems to make this requirement impossible to meet. If moral disapprobation must be individuated by appeal to the concept *wrong*, then the sentiment will inherit the ambiguity of that concept. Hence, the claim that our antagonists are disputing the fittingness of the same sentiment can be no more secure than was the claim that they are deploying the same concept. We therefore think sentimentalism can make headway on the problem of univocity only if the sentiments it invokes can be identified independently of the evaluative concepts they are supposed to explicate.[32]

If so, then Wiggins's account cannot secure univocity. Moreover, the inclusiveness of his account of evaluative concepts is no virtue unless the various sentiments are properly understood as playing a similar role in evaluation, even as we move away from our paradigm: the regulative concepts associated with the fittingness of some natural emotion. But we are impressed by the heterogeneity of evaluative concepts, and we doubt that they all bear the same sort of relation to sentimental response. The examples on which we have focused most attention here (*funny*, *shameful*, *disgusting*, and so forth) are the most plausible candidates for a straightforward response-invoking account as regulative concepts. Other evaluative concepts are more difficult to characterize and some seem uncongenial to sentimentalism. This is not to deny that many thick concepts have deep intimacies with emotional responses and may be amenable to a sentimentalist elucidation; rather, it is to insist that they not be shoehorned into the model of regulative concepts. We think that the most promising approach for the sentimentalist is to pursue different patterns of elucidation for different evaluative concepts, while remaining open to the possibility that some such concepts have no essential connection to the sentiments at all.

6. CONCLUSION: VALUES AND REASONS

Thus far, we have considered several ways of developing a sentimentalist theory of value, on which (certain) evaluative concepts are to be understood by appeal to affective responses. Yet sensibility theory has greater ambitions. Its advocates aspire to give an account not merely of the content of value judgments but also of the acquisition of evaluative and even ethical knowledge.[33] That is, they aim to explain how we can know what we have most reason to do. This aspiration demands more from the notion of a sensibility than the models we have yet considered can provide. In order to be the source of such knowledge, a sensibility must be something more substantial than the basic conceptual competence that an emotional capacity can supply. Since a bad sense of humor is a sense of humor nonetheless, it takes more than mere susceptibility to the relevant emotion in order to know what is genuinely funny, shameful, or fitting of pride. McDowell has done the most to develop such an account, and in what follows we will focus on his view.

McDowell suggests that a sensibility is an integrated set of emotional, cognitive, and motivational tendencies, inculcated through training and habituation until it becomes "second nature." A properly developed sensibility is like a skill—a form of knowhow rather than knowledge of a set of rules—with which the virtuous person sees what to do. "Occasion by occasion," he writes, "one knows what to do, if one does, not by applying universal principles but by being a certain kind of person: one who sees situations in a certain distinctive way" (1979, p. 73). The success of this program depends crucially on its ability actually to adduce a sensibility-based moral epistemology that can vindicate the claim that the virtuous person sees what to do, notwithstanding his admission that "the perceptual model is no more than a model" (1985, p. 133). Even if the phenomenology of moral judgment is as peremptory and noninferential as the perceptual metaphor suggests, it will not suffice simply to declare that the virtuous can see, and thereby know, what to do. In order to earn, rather than simply appropriate, talk of moral truth and knowledge, McDowell must confront his admission that talk of the perception of value is metaphorical. To his credit, acknowledges this burden forthrightly:

> Earning truth is a matter of supplying something that really does what is
> merely pretended by the bogus epistemology of intuitionism. Instead of a
> vague attempt to borrow the epistemological credentials of the idea of percep-
> tion, the position I am describing aims, quite differently, at an epistemology
> that centers on the notion of susceptibility to reasons. (McDowell, 1987, p. 162)

But this talk of susceptibility to reasons does not in itself improve matters, since the notion of a metaphorically perceptible "space of reasons" hardly palliates the obscurity of intuitionism. Rather, whatever epistemological credentials sensibility theory earns issue from an account of moral psychology borrowed from Aristotle, on which there is a special kind of skill characteristic of the virtuous person: a form of knowhow sometimes referred to as practical wisdom. The virtuous person has a reliable ability to do the right thing in the situations confronting her, even though she may be unable to articulate how—or even what—it is she knows. Several familiar features of McDowell's Aristotelian moral psychology, which might be termed its "single–mindedness," cannot be explored here.[34] Instead, we will focus on how the theory can harness this *skill model* of virtue to utilize the perceptual metaphor innocuously, without misappropriating the epistemic credentials of perception.[35]

Most philosophers grant that not all knowledge is propositional, and that many skills deserve to be considered forms of knowledge despite primarily involving abilities rather than beliefs. In general, possession of a skill cannot be well understood in terms of rules and principles, even when there are good principles to be had.[36] Thus the chess master can be said to "see" that the positional advantage gained by sacrificing a pawn exceeds its cost, even if he cannot frame this knowledge in a principle applicable by someone lacking the master's expertise. His claim to see what move to make is vindicated by his tendency to win games. Perceptual locutions can be understood simply as reflecting this commonplace about skills: one can know how to do something without being able to

articulate what one knows. As McDowell puts the point, "if one cannot formulate what someone has come to know when he cottons on to a practice, say one
of concept-application, it is natural to say that he has seen something" (1979,
pp. 72–73).

In addition to offering a plausible way to develop the perceptual metaphor,
the skill model provides the best prospects for vindicating the leading thought of
sensibility theory: that possession of a sensibility at once allows you to see what
to do and motivates you to do it. The process of habituation by which virtues
are inculcated develops more than the knowledge of what a virtuous person would
do in various circumstances. It ultimately requires one to act as the virtuous
person does, with proper feeling and for the right reasons. The point of this
doctrine is not just that there is something especially admirable about a person
whose feelings are in harmony with his acts. Furthermore, only the person whose
emotional responses are appropriately attuned to the demands of a situation can
be relied upon to act in the right way.[37] A kind person's sentiments motivate the
actions he performs—often unreflectively, in circumstances where choices must
be made without hesitation or doubt. And since the kind person must be able to
handle gracefully a variety of situations, many of which cannot be anticipated
beforehand, the crucial forms of recognition and reaction must be relatively automatic yet sensitive to context, in a manner that resists formulation in general
principles. It seems plausible, then, to think that his affective dispositions—such
as the tendency to feel pity and sympathetic embarrassment for others—both
allow him to see the kind thing to do and motivate him to do it.[38]

Even if we grant these claims for the sake of argument, however, McDowell's
neo-Aristotelian moral epistemology nevertheless faces a serious skeptical challenge. The fact that the kind person has a reliable knack for seeing the kind thing
to do does not entail that he knows there is reason to act as kindness dictates.
His cultivated sensibility may play a crucial role in allowing him to recognize the
demands of kindness, and it may also move him toward kind action. Perhaps it
is even true that sentiment-laden sensibility he possesses gets him to see *by* moving
him to act. But the fact that a trained motivational state is implicated in the
ability to apply some evaluative predicate cannot ensure that there is reason to
act as the predicate dictates and the motive urges.[39] It is one thing to know how
to apply a concept that purports to be reason-giving, and quite another to know
what one actually has reason to do. Indeed, some authentically Aristotelian virtues
strike modern readers, including McDowell himself, as dubious.[40]

The problem is that the skill model fits what might be called "faux virtues,"
traits inculcated through the same developmental process of imitation and emotional feedback, as well as it does the genuine article. Hence, only some sensibilities—or perhaps only one—supply what the moral epistemology requires: a susceptibility to genuine reasons. Whether or not he has an adequate answer,
McDowell confronts this problem directly. He writes:

Any second nature of the relevant kind, not just virtue, will seem to its possessor to open his eyes to reasons for acting. What is distinctive about virtue, in
the Aristotelian view, is that the reasons a virtuous person takes himself to discern really are reasons; a virtuous person gets this kind of thing right. (1996,
p. 189)

At first glance, this looks like just the sort of table-thumping to which the
intuitionist must resort in cases of fundamental moral disagreement. Were this
all McDowell had to say—that what distinguishes real from faux virtue is simply
that only one *really is* a susceptibility to reasons—then he would have failed to
improve upon the "bogus epistemology" of intuitionism.

However, McDowell is better understood as denying the need for the sort of
external grounding that the intuitionist was vainly claiming to supply. He grants
frankly that the claim that one sensibility and not another constitutes a sensitivity
to genuine reasons begs the question against those who possess conflicting sensibilities. Although we must critically scrutinize our ethical concepts, "the necessary scrutiny does not involve stepping outside the point of view constituted by
an ethical sensibility"; rather, the excellence of the reasons to act revealed by our
sensibility is "vindicated from within the relevant way of thinking" (1987, pp. 162–
163). The trouble is that projectivists, too, when speaking from the participant's
perspective, can offer such limited justifications. McDowell's stance mirrors the
projectivist's claim that he can continue to participate in moral discourse, in good
conscience and without loss of morale, despite his antirealist metaethical theory.

Consider, for instance, Blackburn's dual insistence that "[w]hat makes cruelty
abhorrent is not that it offends us, but all those hideous things that make it do
so" (1988, p. 172); and that "[our] [projectivist] explanation of what we are doing
when we say such things in no way impugns our right to hold them, nor the
passion with which we should do so" (1985, p. 157). These claims seem comparable
to McDowell's praise of Aristotle's "enviable immunity" to the task of seeking
justifications that do not presuppose the excellence of some particular sensibility.
According to McDowell, "what has happened to modernity is rather that it has
fallen into a temptation, which we can escape, to wish for a foundation for ethics
of a sort that it never occurred to Aristotle to supply it with" (1996, p. 195). We
are not convinced that this justificatory demand is the symptom of some sort of
modern malaise, or that McDowell's terse appeal to coherentism suffices to put
it to rest. But however that may be, the same conclusion seems to emerge, ironically, from the development of both sensibility theory and projectivism. Although
one view claims to vindicate ethical knowledge and the other officially abjures it,
they agree that our ordinary moral practices do not require the epistemological
support intuitionism merely pretends to provide.

Even if sensibility theory cannot establish itself as a satisfying intermediate
position between intuitionism and projectivism, it nevertheless contributes importantly to our understanding of value by drawing further attention to the com-

plex role of the sentiments in evaluation. This is a significant result, which we think projectivists have not adequately acknowledged. Suppose it can be established that kindness and the like—including both real and faux virtues—are best modeled as skills guided by an emotionally laden sensibility. It will then take practice and habituation to become expert in recognizing the demands of kindness, though a novice or a dispassionate observer may be able to identify obvious instances of kind behavior. Moreover, an expert will typically be moved accordingly, because what allows her to "see" the kind thing to do is an intrinsically motivating sentimental response.[41]

These considerations give substance to McNaughton's suggestion that certain aspects of the world can be *seen by feeling*, in the innocuous sense that they are made salient by the sentimental response manifest in a particular sensibility. Although McNaughton posed this thought as a challenge to Hume, a projectivist can grant that the kind person's cultivated sensibility enables him to see what is the kind thing to do. The emotions will then play an important role in securing certain types of knowledge—which is perhaps a surprising admission for the projectivist to make.[42] (After all, Hume famously distinguished between reason, whose task is the discovery of truths, and the passions, which serve only to move the agent to action.) This point can be conceded without capitulation, however, because the projectivist still has grounds for denying that the knowledge manifest in a sensibility counts as knowing what to do—that is, as ethical knowledge. Hence, McDowell's claim that only those purported reasons that the virtuous person descries really are reasons is acceptable only from the participant's standpoint, where it is also superfluous; it is unsupported from the theoretical standpoint.

Recall the clashing metaphors with which we began: that of projection (of sentiments or attitudes) and perception (of values or reasons). There is something insightful and something misleading about each. The perceptual metaphor makes better sense of the compelling thought that evaluative responses can be correct or mistaken, but it exaggerates the similarity between the sentiments with which we "perceive" values and ordinary faculties of perception. It thereby suggests a model of value as ontologically independent of valuers, and of evaluative experience as passive receptivity to the impingement of values, which even sensibility theorists acknowledge to be unsustainable. The projective metaphor avoids these difficulties, but it can seem insufficiently respectful of our evaluative commitments. By encouraging an understanding of values as figments of our feelings, it threatens to undermine the practice of moralizing. While contemporary projectivists urge that there is no reason to lose morale, it is unclear what kind of mistake they can attribute to those who do—unless it is the charge of taking metaphysics too seriously. Ultimately, the choice of metaphors dividing these theories seems less significant than the sentimentalism they both embrace, and the modest, anthropocentric conception of value it encourages.

NOTES

We thank Talbot Brewer, Janice Dowell, Luc Faucher, Bennett Helm, Don Hubin, Mark LeBar, David Sobel, Sigrun Svavarsdottir, Christine Tappolet, and especially David Copp for their comments on earlier drafts of this essay. We are also grateful for funding provided by the Franklin and Marshall Workshop in Moral Psychology and by a faculty leave grant from Ohio State University.

1. The obvious retort for McNaughton here is: "Of course I've told you something about the wine's flavor: it's delicious." The trouble with this response is that a delicious port tastes more like one fit only for cooking than like an equally delicious Montrachet. Admittedly, something similar is true of relational properties such as large and small: a small elephant is more like a large elephant, in size, than like a small dog. What counts as large depends upon the kind of object in question. Nevertheless, a large dog is to a small dog, visually, as a large building is to a small one; whereas nothing similar holds for beauty.

2. Variants of this thesis are differentiated and criticized in Boghossian and Velleman, 1991.

3. Intuitionism has recently enjoyed a philosophical rehabilitation, in part because it has given up on the notion of a faculty dedicated to the perception of nonnatural evaluative properties. Although McNaughton and others claim that intuitionism can credit our ability to perceive values to reason alone, this response does not satisfy McDowell. The vague assimilation of such a cognitive faculty to the senses, he writes, "gives this intuitionistic position the superficial appearance of offering an epistemology of our access to evaluative truth, but there is no substance behind this appearance" (1987, p. 154). We will not consider these developments here; for more detail, see Stratton-Lake, 2003. Nor will we discuss naturalistic forms of objectivism (referred to as "robust naturalist realism" in the table hereafter), which do not rely on the perceptual metaphor for their epistemology of value.

4. This was the view of Galileo and Locke, more recently defended by Paul Boghossian and David Velleman, 1989.

5. Most of the literature on response-dependence focuses on concepts rather than properties. For a helpful recent discussion of response-dependence about properties, see Wedgwood, 1998.

6. For a desire-based dispositional theory of value, see Lewis, 1989.

7. While sentimentalism in our sense is clearly nascent in Hume's ethical writings, it is controversial whether he favored a perceptive or projective sentimentalism. See Sainsbury, 1998.

8. Although we would prefer not to proliferate terminology, the term 'response-dependent' has come to be associated too closely with dispositionalism for our purposes. Response-dependent concepts, which make essential reference to our actual dispositions, are just one variety of response-invoking concept.

9. We use "robust naturalist realism" in the table as a capacious term for those theories that are not nonnaturalist, like intuitionism, but are more "robustly" realist than is perceptivism (whose advocates are not agreed about whether to call their view

realist). We will not be discussing these theories or the nonsentimentalist forms of dispositionalism, and this chart is not meant to be exhaustive.

10. Philip Pettit, 1991, defends a hybrid view according to which these properties are objective but the concepts of them are response-dependent. Even so, his position more closely resembles perceptivism than objectivism, because he holds that what fixes the referent of color and value terms are subjective propensities. For Pettit, too, then, the nature of such properties derives from human responses.

11. There are also nonsentimentalist forms of noncognitivism, including R. M. Hare's prescriptivism. However, we will avoid further subdivision here and consider only sentimentalist noncognitivism (also known as expressivism).

12. This name for the approach was coined by Stephen Darwall, Allan Gibbard, and Peter Railton, 1993. We follow this nascent terminological convention because we need a name for the view under discussion, which its proponents have not provided; but we do so with some hesitation. We must grant at the outset that at least some of its advocates would balk at the terms with which we describe the view, starting no doubt with the word 'theory'.

13. For discussion of some differences between the kinds of internalism adopted by projectivism and sensibility theory, see Darwall (1997).

14. Although we will sometimes refer to being in a given sentimental state as "feeling" it, and to such states as feelings, we do not mean to suggest that sentiments or emotions are simply feelings, or that what differentiates them is primarily phenomenological.

15. We will alternate between talking about the content of concepts and of judgments applying those concepts, as is convenient. By 'judgment' we mean the mental state of reaching an evaluative verdict—whether that state is understood as a belief or some noncognitive attitude, and whether or not it is publicly expressed. Concepts are essential constituents of such verdicts.

16. One obvious proposal is that they both mean "not to be done" by "wrong"; that is, perhaps they both used "wrong" to express an overall verdict regarding how a person is to act. But someone might think it an open question whether or not to perform certain wrong actions, perhaps because nonmoral considerations sometimes outweigh moral ones. A more promising proposal is that they mean "not to be done from the moral point of view"; but that suggestion merely relocates the problem, since the disputants may not agree on what counts as the moral point of view.

17. Mackie, 1977, is the *locus classicus* of this position.

18. According to emotivism, to claim that something is funny is to express, not to report, this state of mind; but this is still to identify the judgment (as opposed to the avowal) with that mental state.

19. See Greenspan, 1988, for discussion of such cases.

20. We develop the conflation problem in more detail in D'Arms and Jacobson, 2000b.

21. See Pettit's discussion of the cosmocentric thesis, 1991, pp. 590–595.

22. Furthermore, the availability of such a priori truths would not differentiate secondary qualities from primary ones. (Compare "X is square if and only if it would look square to a normal observers under those conditions—whatever they may be—which ensure that things that look square are square.") For a discussion of this substantiality requirement, see Wright, 1992, p. 112.

23. This is controversial. McDowell urges that dispositions themselves cannot explain our experiences, as "[t]he weight of the explanation would fall through the disposition to its structural ground" (1985, p. 142). Others, however, allow that dispositions can be causes, e.g., Crane, 1998; Cuneo, 2001.

24. Crispin Wright, 1992, for instance, distinguishes between the question of whether a given discourse contains the resources necessary to support a notion of (minimal) truth for its sentences, which he thinks comic discourse does, and the question of realism with respect to the discourse, where he is inclined toward antirealism about the comic.

25. Blackburn questions the force of this objection, on the grounds that if projectivism is true, "our best vocabulary for identifying the reaction should be the familiar one using the [evaluative] predicates we apply to the world we have spread" (1980, p. 79). This seems true but inadequate, since the projectivist account demands that there be something we can "spread" before these predicates are in place. Indeed, McDowell agrees that "once we have done the spreading, the resulting way of talking will no doubt seem more natural to us than any other. But that is not the same as saying that there is no alternative way of identifying the response. And if there is no alternative way, then . . . it is obscure why we should allow *that* to be consistent with projectivism" (1987, pp. 158–159 n. 15). We agree.

26. Actually, Wiggins expresses the no-priority and coevolution claims as views about *properties* (rather than concepts) and responses. We have changed the terminology because we think the claims are more easily understood in terms of concepts. Both Wiggins and McDowell certainly accept the conceptual version of the no-priority thesis; indeed, that is the version their arguments seem to support. And we think the relevant dispute between sensibility theory and projectivism is more helpfully couched in terms of the relation between sentiments and evaluative concepts.

27. Sometimes one does retreat to an overtly relativized descriptive claim, such as "It's funny to me" or "I find it disgusting." But these locutions show that ordinary, nonqualified judgments of the funny and the disgusting have broader purport; they are not merely personal reports.

28. We consider this question, and argue for the priority of natural emotions to their associated evaluative concepts, in D'Arms and Jacobson, 2003.

29. We explore some difficulties with Gibbard's proposal in D'Arms and Jacobson, 1994.

30. For reasons to doubt the prospects for a unified account of thick concepts, see Scheffler, 1987.

31. This objection is developed further in D'Arms, forthcoming.

32. Wiggins addresses this objection (but does not, one may feel, answer it) in a long footnote. He writes: "my answer to the question about univocity is simply that you do not need complete agreement about the marks of the property, or total coincidence in your conceptions of it, in order to mean the same thing by the predicate that stands for the property, or to be concerned with same attitude directed towards it. (Do you need complete agreement about magnetic compasses—do we all have to have identical conceptions of a magnetic compass—in order to mean the same by 'magnetic compass'? Surely not)" (1987b, p. 212). The trouble with this response is that *magnetic compass* is not an essentially contested concept. Paradigm cases are not in serious dispute, and such limited disagreement as we may find over the extension of this predicate can be settled by appeal to the authority of experts, and ultimately, if necessary, by stipulation. Hence,

there is no special problem about univocity with respect to this concept—no positive reason for supposing that its users may be talking past one another. The sentimentalists' (correct) insistence that this is not how things stand with values is what gives rise to a distinctive problem of univocity.

33. At any rate, McDowell clearly has such aspirations. Wiggins (1976, pp. 95–96), in contrast, distinguishes between what he calls evaluative and practical (or "directive") judgments, and he suggests that his account is only of the former. In fact, Wiggins seems to leave open the possibility that directive judgments—about what to do—might be amenable to some sort of noncognitivist treatment. Elsewhere, however, he too seems to harbor grander ambitions for the theory.

34. McDowell's single-minded moral psychology includes his commitment to the silencing of lesser reasons, a particularly strong version of the unity of the virtues thesis, and the claim that it is impossible for anyone who is not fully virtuous to share the virtuous person's conception of the facts.

35. For further discussion of the skill model, and of its costs and benefits for virtue ethics, see Jacobson, forthcoming.

36. Support for this model of skill acquisition and possession can be found in a series of articles by Hubert L. Dreyfus and Stuart E. Dreyfus. See esp. Dreyfus and Dreyfus, 1990.

37. And since his acting in the right way is what leads us to say that he knows what do, emotional responses play a critical epistemic role in this Aristotelian sensibility theory—they help the virtuous person know what to do. Note, however, that the claim that a virtuous person's responses are appropriate is ambiguous in just the way that emerged earlier in our discussion of the conflation problem. The notion of appropriateness that characterizes the virtuous person's responses would seem not to be that of fittingness but an ethical appraisal, tied more tightly to right action. We consider this issue and its consequences for virtue theory in D'Arms and Jacobson, 2000a.

38. It is worth noting that this suggestion is considerably more modest than McDowell's claim that the kind person's conception of the facts cannot be shared by anyone who isn't kind himself.

39. Our point is not to deny that there are reasons to be kind—we agree that there are. But this is a further claim, not established simply by demonstrating that those who are expert at kindness have a special ability to recognize its demands.

40. "I am unabashed about abstracting from Aristotle's substantive ethical views," he writes, since "it seems obvious that if anything in Aristotle's ethics can still live for us, it is his moral psychology, as a potential frame for a more congenial list of virtues" (McDowell, 1996, p. 195 n.).

41. We say "typically" because of the possibility of disaffection or simulation, either of which might produce some simulacrum of a sentimental responses in someone properly trained but unmoved on a particular occasion. Also note that this is a frankly anthropocentric moral epistemology, which is not intended to rule out the possibility of an alien with another form of epistemic access.

42. Indeed, these points could perhaps be granted by a certain kind of robust realist as well, in which case the Aristotelian moral epistemology would be neutral between a variety of theories. The challenge for a realist attracted to this epistemology is to explain *why* it should be that emotional responses are crucial to knowing what to do, if facts about what to do are wholly independent of subjective responses.

REFERENCES

Blackburn, Simon, 1980. "Opinions and Chances." In Blackburn, 1993, 75–93.

———. 1985. "Errors and the Phenomenology of Value." In Blackburn, 1993, 149–165.

———. 1988. "How to Be an Ethical Antirealist." In Blackburn, 1993, 166–181.

———. 1992. "Morality and Thick Concepts—II: Through Thick and Thin." *Proceedings of the Aristotelian Society*, supp., 66: 285–299.

———. 1993. *Essays in Quasi-Realism.* New York: Oxford University Press.

Boghossian, Paul, and David Velleman. 1991. "Physicalist Theories of Color." *Philosophical Review* 100: 67–106.

Boghossian, Paul, and David Velleman. 1989. "Colour as a Secondary Quality." *Mind* 98: 81–103.

Crane, Timothy. 1998. "The Efficacy of Content: A Functionalist Theory." In *Human Action, Deliberation, and Causation*, ed. J. Bransen and S. E. Cuypers, 199–225. Dordrecht: Kluwer.

Cuneo, Terence. 2001. "Are Moral Qualities Response Dependent?" *Nous* 35: 569–591.

Dancy, Jonathan. 1996. "In Defense of Thick Concepts." *Midwest Studies in Philosophy* 20: 263–279.

D'Arms, Justin. Forthcoming. "Two Arguments for Sentimentalism." *Philosophical Issues* 15.

D'Arms, Justin, and Daniel Jacobson. 1994. "Expressivism, Morality, and the Emotions." *Ethics* 104: 739–763.

———. 2000a. "The Moralistic Fallacy: On the 'Appropriateness' of Emotions." *Philosophy and Phenomenological Research* 61: 65–88.

———. 2000b. "Sentiment and Value." *Ethics* 110: 722–748.

———. 2003. "The Significance of Recalcitrant Emotion (or, Anti-Quasijudgmentalism)." In *Philosophy and the Emotions*, ed. A. Hatzimoysis, 127–146. Cambridge: Cambridge University Press.

Darwall, Stephen. 1997. "Reasons, Motives, and the Demands of Morality." In Darwall, Gibbard, and Railton, 1997, 305–312.

Darwall, Stephen, Allan Gibbard, and Peter Railton. 1993. "Toward *Fin de Siècle* Ethics: Some Trends." In Darwall, Gibbard, and Railton, 1997, 3–50.

———, eds. 1997. *Moral Discourse and Practice: Some Philosophical Approaches.* New York: Oxford University Press.

Dreyfus, Hubert, and Stuart Dreyfus. 1990. "What Is Morality? A Phenomenological Account of the Development of Ethical Expertise." In *Universalism versus Communitarianism: Contemporary Debates in Ethics*, ed. David Rasmussen, 237–264. Cambridge: MIT Press.

Ekman, Paul. 1994. "All Emotions Are Basic." In Ekman and Davidson, 1994, 15–19.

Ekman, Paul, and R. J. Davidson, eds. 1994. *The Nature of Emotion: Fundamental Questions* New York: Oxford University Press.

Gibbard, Allan. 1990. *Wise Choices, Apt Feelings: A Theory of Normative Judgment.* Cambridge, Mass.: Harvard University Press.

———. 1992a. "Moral Concepts: Substance and Sentiment." *Philosophical Perspectives* 6: 199–221.

———. 1992b. "Morality and Thick Concepts—I: Thick Concepts and Warrant for Feelings." *Proceedings of the Aristotelian Society*, supp., 66: 267–283.

Greenspan, Patricia. 1988. *Emotions and Reasons: An Enquiry into Emotional Justification.* London: Routledge.

Helm, Bennett. 2001. *Emotional Reason.* Cambridge: Cambridge University Press.

Hume, David. 1975. *Enquiries Concerning Human Understanding and Concerning the Principles of Morals.* Ed. P. Nidditch. Oxford: Clarendon Press.

———. 1978. *A Treatise of Human Nature.* Ed. P. Nidditch. Oxford: Clarendon Press.

Jacobson, Daniel. Forthcoming. "Seeing by Feeling: Virtues, Skills, and Moral Perception." *Ethical Theory and Moral Practice.*

Lazarus, Richard. 1994. "Appraisals: The Long and the Short of It." In Ekman and Davidson, 1994, 208–215.

Lewis, David. 1989. "Dispositional Theories of Value." *Proceedings of the Aristotelian Society,* supp., 63: 113–137.

Mackie, J. L. 1977. *Ethics: Inventing Right and Wrong.* New York: Penguin Books.

McDowell, John. 1978. "Are Moral Requirements Hypothetical Imperatives?" Reprinted in McDowell, 1998, 77–94.

———. 1979. "Virtue and Reason." In McDowell, 1998, 50–73.

———. 1981. "Non-Cognitivism and Rule-Following." In McDowell, 1998, 198–218.

———. 1985. "Values and Secondary Qualities." In McDowell, 1998, 131–150.

———. 1987. "Projection and Truth in Ethics." In McDowell, 1998, 151–166.

———. 1996. "Two Sorts of Naturalism." In McDowell, 1998, 167–197.

———. 1998. *Mind, Value, and Reality.* Cambridge, Mass.: Harvard University Press.

McNaughton, David. 1988. *Moral Vision: An Introduction to Ethics.* Oxford: Blackwell.

Mulligan, Kevin. 1998. "From Appropriate Emotions to Values." *Monist* 81: 161–188.

Pettit, Philip. 1991. "Realism and Response-Dependence." *Mind* 100: 587–626.

Rozin, Paul, J. Haidt, and C. McCauley. 2000. "Disgust." In *Handbook of Emotions,* ed. M. Lewis and J. Haviland-Jones, 637–653. New York: Guilford Press.

Sainsbury, R. M. 1998. "Projections and Relations." *Monist* 81: 133–160.

Scheffler, Samuel. 1987. "Morality through Thick and Thin: A Critical Notice of Ethics and the Limits of Philosophy." *Philosophical Review* 96: 411–434.

Scruton, Roger. 1987. "Laughter." In *The Philosophy of Laughter and Humor,* ed. John Morreall, 150–172. Albany: State University of New York Press.

Stratton-Lake, Philip, ed. 2003. *Ethical Intuitionism.* Oxford: Oxford University Press,

Tooby, J., and L. Cosmides. 1990. "The Past Explains the Present: Emotional Adaptations and the Structure of Ancestral Environment." *Ethology and Sociobiology* 11: 375–424.

Wedgwood, Ralph. 1998. "The Essence of Response-Dependence." *European Review of Philosophy* 3: 31–54.

Wiggins, David. 1976. "Truth, Invention, and the Meaning of Life." In Wiggins, 1987a, 87–137.

———. 1987a. *Needs, Values, Truth.* Oxford: Blackwell.

———. 1987b. "A Sensible Subjectivism?" In Wiggins, 1987a, 185–214

———. 1990. "Moral Cognitivism, Moral Relativism and Motivating Moral Beliefs." *Proceedings of the Aristotelian Society* 91: 61–85.

Williams, Bernard. 1985. *Ethics and the Limits of Philosophy.* Cambridge, Mass.: Harvard University Press.

———. 1996. "Truth in Ethics." In *Truth in Ethics,* ed. Brad Hooker, 19–34. Oxford: Blackwell.

Wright, Crispin. 1992. *Truth and Objectivity.* Cambridge, Mass.: Harvard University Press.

CHAPTER 8

....

MORAL SENTIMENTALISM AND MORAL PSYCHOLOGY

....

MICHAEL SLOTE

The eighteenth-century British moral sentimentalists attempted to deal systematically with both normative and metaethical questions. This essay will discuss the history of sentimentalism, but will do so, in substantial part, as a means to demonstrating the contemporary viability of an overall sentimentalist approach to ethics. I shall first explore some of the prospects of a contemporary normative (and virtue-ethical) sentimentalism, and then complete the picture with a sentimentalist account of the nature of moral judgment. Along the way, I shall borrow from certain recently discussed moral-psychological examples, in order to show some of the advantages of sentimentalism over ethical rationalism.

The original proponents of "moral sentimentalism" were (the third Earl of) Shaftesbury, Francis Hutcheson, David Hume, Adam Smith, and (somewhat ambiguously) (Bishop) Joseph Butler. (The expression "moral sense theory" applies somewhat more narrowly to those sentimentalists—like Hutcheson and, sometimes, Hume—who spoke of the sentiment of moral approval as derived from a special or distinctive sense conceived as analogous to the five senses.) The sentimentalists were united in their rejection of Hobbesian egoism and their belief in certain naturally developing unselfish sentiments like benevolence and family affection. But the sentimentalists also largely opposed the rationalist idea that reason, rather than feeling, is the source of moral judgment and of (nonselfish) moral behavior. (There will be no time to discuss sentimentalist views about extramoral practical reason.)

Moral sentimentalism has had an important influence on philosophical theories of ethics down to the present day, and although current ethical theory may be dominated by (Kantian, but also other forms of) rationalism, there are nowadays some important sentimentalist trends as well. On the side of normative ethics, these include, most prominently, the recently developed ethics of caring. In metaethics, they include views—like emotivism, projectivism, and ideal observer theory—that treat feeling as the fulcrum of moral utterances or judgments. Moral sentimentalism has always treated moral psychology as central to understanding ethical phenomena, and I want to begin substantive discussion of the issues surrounding sentimentalism with two moral-psychological examples—one from Michael Stocker, the other from Bernard Williams—that help the sentimentalist make a case against ethical/moral rationalism.

Stocker asks us to imagine someone visiting a sick friend in the hospital who insists, to his friend and to himself, that his visit is motivated by a sense of duty rather than any feeling or concern for his friend. Stocker points out that most of us find such a person morally unattractive, but Kantian and other forms of rationalism have a difficult time accommodating that intuition because of their typical insistence on the moral merit of acting from a sense of duty (conscientiously) and on the relative or absolute lack of moral merit in actions done from (mere) feelings like benevolence and love. Similarly, Bernard Williams describes a hypothetical case where a man who sees that both his wife and some stranger are in danger of drowning has to decide whom to save. If, in order to justify saving his wife, the man first checks or thinks he has to check to see whether morality accords him and others a permission to favor one's wife over strangers, then, according to Williams, he "has one thought too many." Once again, we would morally approve of him more if, without consulting moral principles, he saved his wife out of a feeling of *concern for her*.

These examples have led philosophers to worry about the Kantian moral-psychological emphasis on being guided by moral principles and a sense of conscience, and they have led many in the direction of forms of virtue ethics that place particular relationships at the center of the moral life. What has not so widely been recognized, however, is that cases like those mentioned by Williams and Stocker also favor sentimentalism over rationalism. Though they (threaten to) move us away from Kantianism and toward virtue ethics, they favor a sentimentalist virtue ethics based on feelings like love and concern for others (benevolence) more than rationalist virtue-ethical approaches like those of Aristotle and the Stoics. For the latter, too, emphasize the role of specifically and explicitly ethical thinking within the moral life, but sentimentalism primarily appeals to "natural virtues" that involve no thought of the moral, and this is very much in keeping with the Stocker-Williams examples. I shall begin my discussion of moral sentimentalism, however, with a selective overview of some themes from Hutcheson and Hume. The larger significance (as I take it) of the two mentioned examples will then emerge from my discussion of moral sentimentalism as an overall approach to ethical theory.

1. HUTCHESON, HUME, AND AFTER

Although the movement known as moral sentimentalism is commonly regarded as having begun with Shaftesbury, Hutcheson and Hume are probably its most clear-cut and typical representatives. Hutcheson, in particular, acknowledged the strong influence of the Christian ideal of agapic love on his view that universal benevolence is the morally best of human motives and that all of morality can be understood by reference to that motive. To that extent, the agapic side of Christian moral doctrine (and some of its Jewish antecedents) can be said to anticipate and exemplify a form of moral sentimentalism that contrasts rather starkly with the rationalism of ancient Greek (virtue) ethics, which saw all ethically valid choice as guided by reason and had little or no room for virtues like compassion, self-sacrifice, and (even) kindness.

However, in *On the Original of Our Ideas of Beauty and Virtue*, Hutcheson translates the idea that we should love all other people as God loves us (his children) into the more secular or more impartialistic assumption that universal benevolent concern for others determines the content of morality. The goodness of such benevolence Hutcheson takes to be intrinsic, that is, independent of its consequences; and he rates other motives in terms of how intrinsically far they are from universal benevolence, so that more extensive forms of benevolence, like love of one's compatriots, stand higher than narrower motives, like family feeling. Acts are said to be morally better or worse depending on how well they further the goals of universal benevolence, and this led Hutcheson to enunciate and defend the first known version (at least in English) of the principle of utility. But because the idea that acts are better or worse depending on the extent that they tend toward the greatest happiness is derived (in part) from universal benevolence seen as an intrinsically praiseworthy motive, Hutcheson is commonly regarded as a virtue ethicist, not as a consequentialist—even though his views and Hume's certainly, in actual historical fact, led *toward* utilitarianism.

In *Illustrations on the Moral Sense*, Hutcheson holds that moral approval/disapproval and moral judgment are effected through what he called a (divinely implanted) *moral sense,* analogous to the familiar five human senses but directed to the moral qualities of actions understood by reference to universal benevolence.

This was one of the most controversial and seemingly obscure aspects of Hutcheson's sentimentalism, and subsequent sentimentalists like Hume and Smith rejected the literal idea of a moral sense (though Hume allowed himself sometimes and loosely to use such language). Another highly controversial aspect of Hutcheson's views lay in his (proto-utilitarian) assumption that all morality could be subsumed under universal benevolence. Joseph Butler, in a form of criticism that would later be frequently directed at utilitarianism, argued that morality has an important aspect of *justice* that characteristically runs counter to the dictates or motive of benevolence: as, to use Hume's examples, when we are morally obligated to repay a loan to a rich bigot or profligate, but could have done more good by giving the money to some poor family.

Hume incorporated both these major criticisms into his *Treatise of Human Nature* and (more briefly) his *Enquiry into the Principles of Morals*, and he also developed a more pluralistic view of the nature and sources of human virtue than we find in Hutcheson. Hume thought certain motives or character traits are valued for their "utility" to the agent or to people generally, but other traits are "immediately agreeable" in various ways and as such also count as virtuous. Hume is a virtue ethicist who regards the moral qualities of actions as derivative from that of the motives that lie behind them, but he also divided the virtues into natural and artificial ones, and this division puts some pressure on the virtue ethics.

Natural virtues like benevolence and gratitude can exist independently of human artifice, that is, of the social conventions that make advanced society possible, and one can possess and exemplify such virtues in one's actions without thinking about the moral character of what one is doing. A benevolent person may just want to help someone she sees to be in trouble, and the thought that such action is morally obligatory or virtuous on some given occasion may not play any role in getting her to act helpfully. By contrast, artificial virtues like justice (by which Hume means respect for property) and fidelity to promises seem to be unthinkable in the absence of certain social conventions and involve an explicit sense of right and obligation. We keep promises, for example, because we think it obligatory to do so, not because some nonmoral, natural motive like benevolence impels us to do so. The proof of this, as Hume learned from Butler, is the fact that we feel obligated to keep promises even on occasions where benevolence would lead us *not* to do so (e. g., the case of returning money borrowed from a rich bigot or profligate rather than doing something more humanly useful with the money). Justice and fidelity are governed by a strict sense of right and wrong whose *general* beneficialness and efficacy in us can (Hume thinks) be explained in empiricist/sentimentalist terms; but this idea puts pressure on Hume's belief in virtue ethics. If the rightness or wrongness of actions depends on their motive, how can the underlying motive in cases of justice and promise-keeping be a concern to *do what is right*? Hume says that this involves arguing in a circle, and many subsequent critics have seen the point as showing a weakness in the overall Humean approach to justice, and so on. But Hume (like Butler) at least saw that justice sometimes seems to take moral precedence over natural motives like benevolence, something Hutcheson explicitly denied.

Hume's views also differ from Hutcheson's on the nature of moral approval and judgment. Hume denies the literal existence of an (unanalyzable) moral sense and sought to account for moral approval of virtue via the same basic psychological mechanisms that operate within a virtuous individual. According to Hume, we have a psychological tendency to be affected by the pleasures and pains of others, and the (lesser) pain we feel sympathetically at the pain of others ties in with our wanting, virtuously and benevolently, to relieve their suffering. (Hume's sentimentalism partly rests on the assumption that psychological mechanisms/feelings like sympathy play a role in our moral activity in a way that reason or the knowledge of eternal moral truths cannot.)

But Hume holds that mechanisms of sympathy also underlie our moral approval/disapproval and judgments. We disapprove the malice or indifference that leads someone to harm another person, and that disapproval is (or is closely related to) the pain that we sympathetically feel at the pain that has been inflicted on that other person. But for purposes of unambiguous public communication, we have to correct for personal biases that would lead most of us, for example, to feel more pain at harm caused to our friends than at harm caused to strangers or historical personages. Genuine moral disapproval thus requires us to subordinate our sympathetic reactions to a general point of view that abstracts from our particular relations to those involved and simply (i.e., impartially) considers how badly people are (or are likely to be) affected by certain actions due to certain motives.

Moral approval and disapproval are, for Hume, (corrected) feelings, but it is not clear how he understands the connection between such feelings and claims about virtue, right, and wrong. Hume suggests a number of different and mutually incompatible theories about this. Sometimes, he seems to assume an emotive view of moral utterances according to which they merely express positive or negative feeling. Elsewhere, he suggests what has come to be called projectivism, the view that the moral characteristics we seem to see in various traits are just a projection of our own feelings onto the world—he says that we "spread" our own feelings onto the world. Finally, Hume sometimes seems to be suggesting that we understand moral judgments as being about the (hypothetical) approval and disapproval reactions of an informed "judicious spectator." Unlike emotivism and projectivism, such an "ideal observer" theory treats moral utterances as true and false, but as about human reactive tendencies rather than about objective moral facts or attributes that would be independent of such reactions.

It will be interesting to consider how Hutcheson's and Hume's ethical and metaethical views might be borrowed, altered, and winnowed in an attempt to develop a contemporary form of moral sentimentalism, but before I do that, it is important to say some things about historical developments subsequent to Hutcheson and Hume. Eighteenth-century moral sentimentalism both yielded and yielded *to* nineteenth-century utilitarianism, and the transition is in fact rather distinctly marked. In *A Fragment on Government*, Jeremy Bentham famously describes how reading Hume's account of the artificial virtues led him to act utilitarianism and, in particular, to denying (Hume's belief in) the wrongness of optimific (or benevolently motivated) violations of the useful social/moral rules governing property and promises. If, as he reasoned, benevolence and utility motivate and justify the rules, then, *pace* Hume, they can also justify occasional violations of the rules, and this yields act utilitarianism and goes against the strict observance of moral obligations of fidelity and justice that Hume was intent on justifying.

So act utilitarianism emerged out of a critical disagreement with Hume, but at the same time much of its character as an approach to morality can be traced to ideas in Hume and Hutcheson. Both saw human good in terms of pleasure and saw moral obligation and virtue as (at least partly) defined by reference to the attainment of, or the benevolent desire to produce, good consequences for human (or sentient) beings, and these themes emerge as central in utilitarianism. However, utilitarianism decisively discards the virtue-ethical element in Hutcheson and Hume, placing its foundational emphasis on what counts as good for us rather than on the motives that underlie our actions. To be sure, moral sentimentalism limped alongside utilitarianism in the late nineteenth century: for example, in the form of James Martineau's sentiment-based virtue ethics. But (for reasons it would be very difficult to trace) a genuine revival of moral sentimentalism didn't begin to occur till the late twentieth century. For although "emotivism" represents a sentimentalist kind of metaethics and was around through most of the twentieth century, the idea of a normative (virtue) ethics based in sentiment was pretty much in the shade until the so-called feminine ethics of caring emerged during the 1980s.

Carol Gilligan's book *In a Different Voice: Psychological Theory and Women's Development* appeared in 1982 and Nel Noddings's *Caring: A Feminine Approach to Ethics and Moral Education* in 1984, and in their somewhat different ways, both pick up the frayed or broken threads of historical sentimentalism. Gilligan argued that men and women tend to conceive morality in different ways: men in terms of autonomy, rights, and justice; women in terms of connection with and caring for other people. Noddings then went on, in her book, to articulate and defend in its own right a "feminine" morality centered specifically on the ideal of caring: whether we act rightly or wrongly depends primarily on whether we act from caring concern for others.

Noddings showed more explicit awareness than Gilligan (initially) did of the connection of their ideas to historical moral sentimentalism (especially Hume).

But the idea of a morality of caring is in any event rather similar to Hutchesonian and Humean (normative) virtue ethics: benevolence and caring are both sentiments in the eighteenth-century sense, and an ethics of caring sees morality as based in feeling, or in motives that involve feeling, *rather than* in reason or rational principles. It also offers a justification for deemphasizing moral rules or principles (and explicit moral thinking more generally) that takes us somewhat beyond views expressed by Hutcheson and Hume.

Hutcheson had claimed that universal and other forms of approvable benevolence aim at the good/welfare of others rather than aiming to do what is right or virtuous, and he argued in particular that conscientious (principled) concern for rightness and virtue shows a self-centered concern for one's own moral status that detracts from the moral goodness of one's motives. Hume, less extremely, held that the moral goodness of at least certain (natural) motives is independent of any concern to conform to the dictates of valid moral rules or morality. But those who favor an ethics of caring often criticize the use of supposedly rational moral rules or principles on the somewhat different grounds that this interferes with the immediacy of one's concern for others and thus leaves us *less connected with others than is desirable*. Caring ethics criticizes traditional "masculine" approaches like Kantian ethics and social contract theory because they see human beings as primarily or originally separate from others or autonomous and see our obligations to others as derivative from and secondary to that original status. For the caring ethicist, moral connection to others is primary and "not up to us": for example, the moral obligation to act caringly toward family members or those who need our immediate help is not a matter of what we have chosen or would choose under certain idealized conditions but rather is simply *given*.

But, according to the ethics of caring, traditional moral theories (other than utilitarianism, which is a special case, given its connection with sentimentalism) compound their problem of disconnection by insisting that the ideal moral agent should make use of moral rules and be conscientious rather than motivated by natural, feelingful motives. Kantian and Rawlsian rationalism derive their normative principles concerning our relations with others from assumptions about human beings conceived as autonomous. But they compound the normative emphasis on or presupposition of separateness with a moral psychology that, by urging us to be morally explicit and principled, again (or in this further way) disconnects us from others. By contrast, the ethics of caring sees normative ethics as based in assumptions of foundational moral connection with others and, by placing a premium on immediate concern with the welfare of others, shows its preference for connection *over* separateness in this further, moral-psychological way.

However, the argument for sentimentalism over rationalism here doesn't just depend on assuming that moral connection is simply more attractive than moral autonomy or separateness. For the aforementioned Stocker and Williams examples can help to put flesh on such an argument. There is, intuitively, something morally unattractive about the husband who has to consult morality (moral principles) and also about the hospital visitor who acts conscientiously rather than from friendly feeling (or love). This has force against the rationalist assumptions that there is no (or lesser) merit in acting from feeling and that it is never morally inappropriate to regulate one's actions by moral principles or considerations of conscience. The earlier examples thus *support* sentimentalism over and against traditional forms of rationalism (though not necessarily against utilitarianism, which doesn't see the principle of utility as always ideally action-guiding and which is at least as much allied with sentimentalism as with rationalism).

But I now need to expand my discussion. What I have shown of the earlier and recent history of sentimentalism and my treatment of the Stocker/Williams examples give us reason to think that sentimentalism has certain desirable features lacking in rationalism. The question, then, is whether sentimentalism can in contemporary terms be viewed as, or made to be, a viable systematic alternative to rationalism. This depends in great part on whether normative sentimentalism can handle questions that rationalism prides itself on being able to deal with: in particular, issues of deontology that utilitarianism, for example, seems to give us a less than adequate picture of. It also depends on whether we can *combine* normative sentimentalism with a supporting (or at least compatible) form of meta-ethics, something that Hutcheson and Hume sought to do, but that has not, as far as I am aware, been attempted in recent discussions of sentimentalism.

2. Empathy and Normative Sentimentalism

In order to see how a contemporary sentimentalism might at this point be further developed, I would like to pick up on a feature of Noddings's account of caring that I have not previously mentioned. Noddings speaks of the "engrossment" of the caring person in the one cared for and emphasizes the way in which such engrossment involves seeing and feeling things as the other does. This is fairly close to the idea of empathy, and clearly empathy is or should be an element in the description of the moral psychology of caring. But empathy can do more than that for sentimentalism. It can help us see and justify certain *normative distinctions*, and, as a result, it has normative or substantive implications that caring considered merely as such doesn't have.

Thus consider our relations with (lower) animals. There is nothing in the idea of caring taken on its own that dictates or recommends that human beings care more, be more concerned, about fellow humans than about animals, but intuitively we are permitted and it is even morally better for us to have such differential concern (within limits). However, such differential concern *can* be understood and perhaps even justified by reference to empathy or, more accurately, to an ideal of empathic caring, of caring *as anchored* in fully developed human empathy. We have greater empathy, on the whole or typically, for fellow humans than we have for animals (and even, I think it could be argued, for our pets); but before I say anything more about this specific issue, I need to get a bit clearer on the term "empathy." This is a word that only entered our language at the beginning of the twentieth century, and Hume's talk of sympathy, for example, relates to both (what we would today call) empathy and (what we would today call) sympathy.

Now how empathy is related to, yet different from, sympathy is a very complex question I cannot fully discuss here. But we can somewhat clarify this issue if we notice that what we ordinarily call empathy is a (Clintonesque) matter of feeling, for example, someone else's pain, whereas sympathy involves feeling *for* the pain of another. Clearly, too, I can feel for someone else's embarrassment, feel sympathy for it, without feeling anything like embarrassment myself, and thus without *empathizing* with the other's embarrassment, so the concepts are definitely different.

Recent psychology has placed empathy, rather than sympathy, at the root of "prosocial behavior" and of genuine altruistic or caring motivation. Thus two important books—C. D. Batson's *The Altruism Question: Toward a Social-Psychological Answer* and Martin Hoffman's *Empathy and Moral Development: Implications for Caring and Justice*—summarize recent experimental studies of empathy and argue that the development of empathy plays a crucial role in the development of (long-term) genuinely altruistic, caring motivation. Batson thinks the evidence for genuine altruism is less clear-cut than Hoffman believes it is, but both hold that the capacity for empathy increases as a child becomes cognitively more sophisticated about other people. Hoffman in particular also stresses the educative value of getting children or others to recognize the effects of their actions, for better or worse, on other people. Such "inductive discipline" helps turn our basic capacity for empathy into a practical concern for others that (for example) anticipates the harm we may do them by performing certain acts and thereby gets us to refrain from doing such acts.

Now Hoffman and (to a lesser extent) Batson also emphasize certain "biases" that are built into human empathy. One of these, for example, is a certain bias in favor of (dealing with) nearby and visible danger as opposed to distant and unseen danger that I shall be saying more about later. But to get back—finally—to the issue of our moral duties or obligations to humans versus (lower) animals, we also seem to have an empathic bias in favor of fellow humans. Although this is something that Batson and Hoffman don't specifically discuss, it is fairly clear, given what they say about empathy and empathic bias, that it is easier for us to empathize with the frustrations, the pains, the opportunities, the satisfactions of humans than with those of animals. (Similar points apply to the distinction between born children and fetuses, but there is no space to discuss that here.) Now if there is a bias in favor of the human built into human empathy, then this is something that is not going to go away; but rather than call it a bias, implying something unfair and unjustifiable, the moral sentimentalist can argue that the bias—better: the preference—in favor of our own species is in fact morally justifiable. If the best account of morality we can give regards fully developed human empathic caring as the morally highest form of motivation, then if such motivation has a preference for humans built into it, the sentimentalist can hold that such a preference actually is morally justified. (And this will be all the clearer, if it turns out, as I shall argue hereafter, that developed empathy is the grounding basis *for moral judgment*.)

Similarly—and this is another familiar "bias" or "preference" or "partiality"— we favor our own children over other people's children, and it seems easier, more inevitable, that we should deeply empathize with the tribulations and successes of people who are near and dear to us than with those of strangers. But speaking common-sensically, or intuitively, it would seem that, given a choice between helping strangers and helping (say) one's own child, it is (other things being equal) morally better and even obligatory to help one's own child, and, once again, sentimentalism can make use of an ideal of fully developed human empathy to account for and to that extent justify this common-sense intuition.

Nor does it make sense at this point to object to such an argument on the grounds that sentimentalism is thereby illicitly moving from facts about human psychology to value judgments about certain motives and actions. For the facts of human psychology don't tell us which actual or potential motives are moral better than which others. More particularly, the sentimentalist (normative) virtue–ethical theory I am sketching says that the rightness and wrongness of actions depends on underlying motive and then makes the specific further claim that fully empathic caring/concern for others is the morally best of human motives. But none of this follows or is supposed to follow from anything established by pure or scientific psychology or, for that matter, from facts about how human beings typically are, given how *lacking* in empathy many people seem to be. A virtue ethics of empathic caring has to be tested, rather, as all basic moral views are tested, namely, in terms of its intuitive plausibility and in terms of the plausibility of the claims about particular cases that follow from it (together with other assumptions one is making). One such claim is the view, asserted earlier, that it is better to care more about and prefer one's own children. Another, also asserted earlier, is that we should care more about and prefer humans to animals. And the fact that such intuitively or antecedently plausible conclusions follow stands in favor of a moral sentimentalism that rests, not merely on caring, but on caring as grounded in the human capacity for empathy.

So a present-day sentimentalism is capable of justifying certain important intuitive moral distinctions. But at this point the rationalist may well object that there are other distinctions which sentimentalism is far less capable of justifying. Deontology, for example, is (very roughly) the view that there is an important moral distinction between doing and allowing and, to speak of a particular instance, between killing and letting die. But it is difficult to see how ideals of caring or developed empathy can support such distinctions. Hutcheson seems to have rejected deontology, and utilitarianism is notorious for its inability to fully justify our deontological intuitions. But, on the other hand, Hume's sentimentalist attempt to ground the deontology of promise-keeping and respect for other people's property appears to argue in a circle. (It has other problems as well, and in fact Hume never even *attempts* to justify the distinction between doing and allowing.) By contrast, rationalism at least has an ongoing program of attempting to vindicate deontology, so if the prospects for present-day sentimentalism to justify deontology really are hopeless, then sentimentalism may simply be less promising than rationalism (and that might help explain why there are more contemporary rationalists than sentimentalists). But, in fact, I think the situation for sentimentalism is far from hopeless, and let me try briefly to explain why.

However, in order to do so, it will help if I first discuss our bias, briefly mentioned earlier, in favor of seen and near suffering/danger over unseen and distant suffering/danger. Given what has now been said, it can be held that that bias is explainable via the fact that it is easier for us to empathize with (the plight of) those we see and that such a difference holds for those whose empathy is fully developed. Given our sentimentalistic moral ideal, this then leads us to the conclusion that it is right and appropriate to be more concerned about those we see. But if that is correct, then moral sentimentalism can offer an answer to Peter Singer's famous argument, in "Famine, Affluence, and Morality," regarding our stringent and practically unlimited obligations to provide monetary and other help to distant starving or sick people. According to Singer, sheer distance cannot make a difference to the help we owe (are obligated to give) to someone, so if we are obligated to save a child who is drowning right before our eyes, even at some substantial personal cost (perhaps it will make us late to an important appointment), then it would seem that we are similarly obligated to save a single child's life by making a contribution, say, to Oxfam. But the same point iterates with regard to other children we can similarly save, and, according to Singer, we end up with a (cumulative or aggregate) obligation to give away most of our money in order to help those who are and remain more needy than we are.

Many philosophers have objected to Singer's rather iconoclastic conclusion (after all, most of us don't initially think that we *are* obligated to practically beggar ourselves for the sake of the more needy), and one argument has been that distance intuitively *does* make a difference to our obligations. What hasn't been seen, however, is that Singer's arguments can also be blocked by an appeal to considerations of empathy, and I think this sort of objection is more effective than an appeal merely to spatial distance, both on intrinsic intuitive grounds and because of all the other areas or topics where empathy appears to make an intuitive moral difference. We have/develop more empathy for someone whose plight (whose body) is visible to us: that is part of "here-and-now bias" that Hoffman thinks has been shown to be built into reactive human nature; and this can then lead the sentimentalist to the conclusion that it is morally all right and even preferable to be more concerned about and practically (i.e., in our actions) engaged with trouble or suffering that we see (and, perhaps, more generally, perceive).

However, talk of a "here-and-now bias" also suggests that we are biased in favor of present danger and suffering, *even if we don't immediately perceive it*, and indeed, Hoffman and others believe that various studies indicate such a further empathic preference or partiality. If, to choose an example famous among ethicists, miners are trapped underground because of a cave-in, the public will typically respond with or at least advocate costly rescue efforts. And if anyone were to suggest (as Charles Fried does in *An Anatomy of Values*) that we should use the available money to install safety equipment in the mine that will later save a greater number of lives, rather than save (the smaller number of) those who are now in danger because of the cave-in, most of us would recoil with a certain horror or disbelief. The explanation, once again, has to do with our tendency to feel greater empathy for those who are in "clear and present danger," and this bias toward the now operates independently of perception—the public doesn't have to know the miners personally or see (pictures of) them in order to prefer rescuing them to (within limits) saving a greater number of future miners through the installation of safety devices.

But now it is time to generalize these examples and move toward a sentimentalist account of the empathic roots of deontology. The suffering or danger of those we see or perceive has, we might say, a certain *perceptual immediacy* for us because of our empathic tendencies. Similarly, suffering or danger that is current or present-tense has what we might call a *temporal immediacy* for us. Quite apart from any explicitly moral thoughts or considerations, our empathic tendencies move us to be more concerned about what is thus either perceptually or temporally immediate for us, and I believe that an analogous kind of immediacy lies behind the appeal of deontology.

At its most basic (at least on one basic construal of what is at stake in deontology), deontology distinguishes between doing (or causing) and allowing and, more specifically for a given instance, between killing and letting die. But the difference between causing harm (like death or pain) and merely allowing it is a difference in the closeness (or strength) of one's causal connection to the harm or pain, and this difference in what we can call *causal immediacy* makes a difference to normal human reactions. Just as we are, other things being equal, more empathically involved in and responsive to pain or danger that we perceive or that is "clear and present," so too do we react in empathic terms more strongly to the possibility of causing harm or pain than we do to the possibility of merely allowing such. The latter is less immediate for us, and in fact we react viscerally to, *flinch from*, our own (potential) causing of harm and pain much more than we do with regard to harm and pain that our actions or inactions may merely *allow*.

To be sure, one *might* argue at this point that these "deontological reactions" are in fact not analogous to what happens with what we perceive and what is temporally present. These latter are facts in the world, not moral assumptions, so there is, in the Humean sense, a natural tendency to prefer the perceived and the present that allows us to ground relevant moral distinctions in clearly sentimentalist terms. But, someone might object, what makes us prefer to allow harm rather than cause it is not some fact about causal immediacy, about our potential causal relation or connection, in the world, to the harm in question, but rather simply the fact that we have all been taught that harming/killing is morally wrong and worse than allowing harm/death.

Now this difference or disanalogy is certainly possible, but the naturalness of the original analogy does lend some support to the idea that deontology can be based in natural tendencies of human empathy, that it is (other things being equal) morally worse to kill, say, than to allow death because human empathy tends to make us "flinch" or "recoil" more from the former than from the latter. And perhaps the following further consideration can help consolidate the case for a sentimentalist account of (at least the rudiments of) deontology.

Imagine someone who orders or pays for a "hit" rather than himself killing some person he wants dead. What would his motive be for preferring not to do the killing himself? Possibly he may think that the other person will be a more reliable or efficient or untraceable killer, but even when such factors *aren't* present, a person might still prefer to have someone else do the killing. But surely it is implausible to suppose that someone willing to order a hit prefers that to killing someone himself because it is morally worse to kill than to order or arrange a killing. Surely, *such* a person is morally too "far gone" to make such an explanation of his unwillingness or reluctance to kill at all plausible. What remains as a plausible explanation, though, is that such a morally corrupt person might still find the act of killing distasteful, might still psychologically recoil from killing, and my view is that the causal immediacy of this relation to death (rather than any moral belief or judgment) is an important part of what moves such a person to order or commission a hit.

But if we can be sensitive to the smaller causal difference, in a situation, between killing and ordering a killing, that makes it all the more likely that we can be empathically sensitive and reactive to the greater causal/situational difference between killing and allowing to die, and it would seem, therefore, that moral sentimentalism can offer normative backing for the core idea of deontology. Kantian and other rationalist efforts to defend deontology are notoriously controversial, but even if it makes sense for rationalists to continue looking for new ways (or bolstering previous ways) of defending deontology, a sentimentalism that relies explicitly on human empathy has strings to its bow and cannot be regarded as hopeless or a nonstarter in this area.

Of course, I have not here said anything about respect for property and promises. These, too, are deontological issues, and although there is no space to do so here, the sentimentalist approach I prefer would treat them, not (as Hume, seemingly hopelessly, attempts to do) as involving artificial virtue, but in relation to nonartificial, or natural, empathic caring. Notice, then, too, how all such sentimentally defended deontology differs from rationalist versions or accounts of deontology. The rationalist typically holds that we conform to deontological standards by paying attention to and being guided by moral principles or (as with Aristotelian particularism) by certain situation-specific moral beliefs. But, in line with what I said earlier about its preference for connection with others, the present sentimentalist account and defense of deontology sees deontology as requiring no explicit adverting to moral principles or assumptions. It is the forms and varieties of human empathic connection with others that underlie deontological moral standards (as well as the standards that, *pace* Singer, make it morally preferable to favor those we see or who are near and dear to us), and it is normal and natural too, therefore, to conform to or comply with those standards without having them in mind as principles or rules for guiding one's own or others' actions. (A great deal more needs to be said about how this is possible, but in any event, the sentimentalist can also agree with Martin Hoffman's view that when moral rules/principles are psychologically grounded in developing human empathy, they can frequently play a useful action-guiding role.)

In fact, then, moral sentimentalism is *actually in favor* of what Michael Stocker calls moral "schizophrenia," by which he means a split between the principles and claims that morally justify actions and the considerations that actually motivate moral agents when they perform justified actions. But since *such* schizophrenia actually facilitates or is presupposed by what sentimentalism (at least in recent times) has regarded as a morally desirable or praiseworthy degree of connection with others, there is no reason to be afraid of it. And since the *absence* of moral schizophrenia involves the agent in a conscientious dutifulness that in some measure separates her (psychologically) from the other and that we might, therefore, want to call morally to some extent *autistic*, we can even say that schizophrenia is a desirable feature of sentimentalism and tends to favor it over rationalism. In any event, we have been come quite a distance from Williams's and Stocker's examples and what they say about their significance. (Although Stocker argues that there is something wrong with any view that entails schizophrenia, he at one point says that the use of principles or moral assumptions can undesirably interfere with our personal connection with others, and indeed his own hospital example tends to make schizophrenia seem more rather than less acceptable.)

3. MORAL APPROVAL AND DISAPPROVAL

I have said enough now (for this limited space) about normative (virtue-ethical) moral sentimentalism, and I need at this point to take up some central issues in metaethics. It would good to be able to account for or explicate moral utterances or concepts in sentimentalist terms, and sentimentalism, at least historically, has sought to base moral claims or utterances in the approval or disapproval of those who make the claims or give vent to the utterances. But this creates problems for sentimentalism, because (as Thomas Reid was perhaps the first to note [1764]) it threatens sentimentalist metaethics with circularity. The sentimentalist seeks to analyze moral utterances or judgments in terms of feelings like approval and disapproval, but what if, in fact, approval and disapproval aren't mere feelings (even "corrected" ones) *but themselves contain or involve, respectively, the belief or judgment that something is right and the belief or judgment that something is wrong*? The threat of such a circle and the sheer plausibility of the idea that approval and disapproval have conceptual/cognitive content has made many ethicists very wary of sentimentalist accounts of moral judgment, and they are right to be wary.

What I would like to propose here, however, is that sentimentalism is in fact in a position to make good on its essential assumption that approval and disapproval are (nonjudgmental) feelings and can on that basis then offer an account of what moral judgments or moral utterances are. To that end, it will be useful, I think, to say a bit more about eighteenth-century sentimentalist theories of approval/disapproval. Some of their shortcomings may help point the way to some more promising contemporary possibilities.

I mentioned earlier that Hutcheson sees moral approval and disapproval as operating via a distinct moral sense, whereas Hume bases these moral feelings in mechanisms of sympathy. I assume that postulating a psychological mechanism is preferable to postulating an unanalyzable new form of perception or sensing, but there is a problem with Hume's specification of the mechanisms of approval because of its emphasis on the effects or consequences of what we approve or disapprove of. For Hume (and leaving aside the issue of correcting), we approve traits or motives that (tend to) have beneficial effects and disapprove those that (tend to) have harmful effects because of our sympathy with those very effects.

Adam Smith criticized Hume's theory here for its inability to explain why we don't morally approve and disapprove of inanimate objects for *their* effects on human happiness and unhappiness, and although Hume tries to answer this objection in the *Enquiry*, what he says is neither clear nor convincing. In my view, the problem with Hume's approach to approval is that it involves the approver/ disapprover in sentimental identification or sympathy with those affected by actions *rather than* with those one is actually approving or disapproving of, that is, with moral agents. And (not surprisingly) Adam Smith in his work *The Theory of Moral Sentiments* offers an account of approval/disapproval in terms relating more to agents. Smith says that we approve someone's motives if, when we put ourselves in his position, we find that we would have the same sort of motivation. Now this involves or comes close to involving what we would today call empathy, but I think Smith's agent-focused account of approval and disapproval won't quite do, because of certain possibilities of moral self-criticism. After all, I may be more vengeful, say, than I think I ought to be, but does that mean I will or do disapprove of someone who is less vengeful than myself and who has quite different motives/feelings in certain situations where I recognize that I would be vengeful? (There are similar problems about those whose feelings/motives are supererogatorily good and also better than those of the approver/disapprover.)

What I suggest, then, is that we retain Smith's (un-Humean) idea that approval/disapproval most basically involves a feeling of (something like) empathy vis-à-vis agents, but make the adjustments necessary to avoid the just-mentioned implausible consequences of Smith's specific theory. Approval and disapproval of actions and their agents, I want to say, involve (the sentiment and mechanism of) empathy, but, to put the matter somewhat too baldly, the empathy involved here is empathy *for the agent's empathy or lack of it*. Ever since Shaftesbury, sentimentalists have noted the warm and tender quality of felt (empathic) concern for others—and the absence of that quality in those who exhibit a lack of concern for or hostility toward the welfare of others. But this is warmth/tenderness or its opposite in *agents*, and the view I want to suggest argues that an empathic moral judge or observer will pick up on those qualities of agents and register them in herself as, respectively, approval and disapproval. When I, as judge or nonagent observer, empathically feel the warmth of an agent as displayed in a given action, then the derivative or reflecting warmth I feel *is* a (morally nonjudgmental) feeling of approval toward the action or its agent qua doer of that action; and, similarly, when the agent's actions display an absence of warmth/tenderness, my observer empathy will register or reflect the contrast with agential warmth as a cold feeling or (as we say) "chill" of disapproval. (Such a theory is not supposed to account for the nonmoral and even contramoral *admiration* that, as Susan Wolf and I have pointed out, people feel, e.g., toward Groucho Marx's sarcastic wit or Gauguin's single-minded dedication to his art.)

This theory has its own distinctive way of accounting for the corrections that Hume thought essential to true moral approval and judgment—it can say, for one thing, that the warmth a mother feels toward her son on death row is *not* approval of his murdering ways because it is not (causally speaking) an empathic reflection in the mother of any warmth the son displays as an agent. Rather, it involves the mother's (agential) concern for the son as a nonagent, as someone potentially affected for better or worse by the actions of other agents. If we make such causal distinctions as to source of empathic feelings of warmth, we can accomplish what Hume sought to achieve via the idea of correcting, but this must for the present remain a promissory note. For the moment my most pressing question is how to incorporate such a sentimentalist theory of approval/disapproval into an account of the meaning of explicit moral utterances or claims.

4. MORAL JUDGMENTS AND MORAL RELATIVITY

There are a variety of possible sentimentalist views about how (morally nonjudgmental) feelings play a role in moral utterances or claims, and most of them can be found in Hume. Hume's ideas about the nature of moral utterances are difficult to interpret, and that is because at various points he suggests different theories all of which are mutually inconsistent. For example, Hume at one point in the *Treatise* says that morality is more properly felt than judged of, and this certain suggests (and anticipates) the emotivist idea that moral utterances or sentences express (positive or negative) feelings (of approval or disapproval) rather than making claims/judgments or expressing beliefs about the world.

However, in other famous passages Hume seems to espouse the kind of projectivism that Simon Blackburn has in recent years defended (in neo-Humean terms). For Hume speaks of the mind's propensity to "spread itself" on external objects and of our tendency to "gild" or "stain" all material objects with "colours borrowed from internal sentiment," and this suggests (in contrast with emotivism) that moral claims really are claims, but that they involve systematically mistaking our internal sentimental states of approval/disapproval for something outside or independent of those states. But this sort of approach will leave many moral philosophers unsatisfied and skeptical, because it is so uncharitable to our human tendency to think we are saying something that can be true (though it may be false) when we make moral claims. A sentimentalist view that is more in line with what we ordinarily and intuitively think about the nature of the moral judgments we make will to that extent (at least) be preferable to both projectivism and emotivism, and, interestingly enough, Hume himself expresses and discusses such a view in various places.

What has come to be known as the "ideal observer theory" (and in more recent contexts and with somewhat altered emphasis, the "response-dependent view") of moral judgments treats moral claims concerning any given entity as claims about how calm, disinterested, and relevantly informed "judicious spectators" or "ideal observers" would tend to react to the entity. On such a view, the moral claim, for example, that a given trait is morally bad asserts that human beings have the disposition or tendency to react with (a sentiment of) disapproval to that trait under certain ideal or idealized conditions, and, as I indicated, Hume in a number of places seems to favor such a view of moral utterances. Certainly, given the methodology briefly introduced earlier, this approach has at least something in its favor: the fact that it makes moral judgments susceptible to both truth and falsity and to both (epistemic) reasonableness and unreasonableness—as most of us, independently of philosophy, tend to think they are. But, independently of philosophy, most of us think that moral judgments are true about something other than and independent of *our own moral reactions*. Surely, claims about the wrongness of some act or trait seem to be primarily about the act or trait rather than primarily about our reactions or tendencies to react to them, and ideal observer theory doesn't do justice to this aspect of our "manifest image" of moral judgments.

What would be more in line with common opinion would be some form of (what is known as) *moral realism*, a view that would treat the goodness or wrongness of acts, traits, and motives as properties at least somewhat independent of our dispositions to react to such things. But this might seem a tall order for a sentimentalist theory of morality—with its emphasis, precisely, on internal states of feeling—to accomplish, and I believe Hume himself nowhere suggests such a view. However, the possibility of what might be called "sentimentalist realism" has been suggested, or at least hinted at, by a number of philosophers, including David Wiggins, Nicholas Sturgeon, and Stephen Darwall (the latter two argue that Hutcheson, though not Hume, may be interpretable as such a realist).

A fully developed sentimental realism would make use of an analogy between the sensory (e.g., colors) and the moral that projectivism and ideal-observer/response-dependent theories also rely on. But it would understand that analogy by reference to Saul Kripke's ideas about "reference fixing." On Kripke's view, a phrase like "what explains (or underlies) the sensation of red I am having" fixes the reference, though it doesn't give the meaning, of our term "red." Accordingly, that term picks out a property in objects that is possibly identical with some surface feature of those objects (in relation to surrounding objects) and that is "rigidly" the same in all possible worlds (even those where different external properties normally cause us to have sensations of red).

Applying such a theory to moral properties, we can say that (statements about) moral approval and disapproval fix the reference of moral properties/claims, but that, like color properties, moral properties are external to or independent of these moral reactions. Moral claims would not, then, be *about* our reactive sentimental dispositions, but their (objective) reference would be fixed by facts about those dispositions, and such a view clearly deserves to be called a form of (sentimentalist) moral realism. Since (as far as I can tell) this way of proceeding sits better with our antecedent opinions about what moral utterances/ claims *are* than any other known form of sentimentalist metaethics, I think there is reason for the modern-day sentimentalist to examine and develop it further. In addition, since this approach treats our capacity for empathy as fundamental to moral judgment, it lends metaethical support to the earlier-defended normative view that moral distinctions can be due to differences in deep-seated human empathic tendencies. However, by way of bringing this essay to a close, I would like to say something about how such an approach stands in relation to issues of relativism or relativity, and then go on to consider some important further issues about the relativity, or lack of it, that characterizes sentimentalism and rationalism.

An ideal observer theory treats moral judgments as about human dispositions to respond to things, and one of the implications of (at least the cruder forms of) such a theory is that if human beings had different dispositions, things would have different moral properties from those they have in the actual world. But if that means that under different conditions, torturing people and malice would be morally good, we may have reason to worry that ideal observer theory treats moral judgments as unsatisfyingly relative or relativistic, something that moral rationalism deliberately seeks to avoid. The Kripkean approach avoids this conclusion by holding that, although our actual reactions serve to fix the reference of moral terms/concepts, the (basic) truths that can be stated using such concepts (e.g., that red is such-and-such physical reflectance property or that moral goodness consists in empathic concern for others) are *necessary truths*. This allows sentimentalism to be less relative and is more in line with what the rationalist aspires to, but the issue of precisely *how much* relativity it is realistic to ascribe to moral judgments is a very delicate issue I don't have space to discuss here. (For example, sentimentalism and rationalism might both want to consider the extent of our obligations to, and the obligations of, beings incapable of empathy.)

A more pressing issue for sentimentalism, however, arises from the way it makes moral distinctions follow distinctions in human empathy. As we saw earlier, this allows us to draw and justify certain important and intuitive moral distinctions, but may it not also lead us to draw certain invidious and unintuitive moral distinctions? If, for example, white people tend to empathize more easily with other whites than they do with blacks, will this not permit and recommend morally repugnant forms of *discrimination*? Interestingly, however, studies of such cross-racial differences in empathy seem not to indicate any very marked or *basic* human tendency toward preference on the basis of (similar) skin color (though it is not entirely clear whether the fact that sentimentalism leaves certain moral issues in this way open to empirical investigation favors sentimentalism or whether it threatens it—as some, but not all, rationalists will hold). In addition, Jorge Garcia and others have argued that a slight preference for those similar to one (physically or in terms of shared history/roots) may be morally acceptable and even desirable, if it doesn't go as far as callous indifference or hatred or (what we would call) prejudice toward those who are different.

Finally, I should mention a potentially more worrisome objection of relativism concerning differences of empathy between men and women. Following the psychoanalyst Nancy Chodorow, Carol Gilligan argued that men have to learn to separate themselves from their mothers in a way that women don't and that this makes men stress and embody autonomy more than women and leaves women with a greater overall tendency toward empathic connection with others. But if, as I have suggested here, morality is to be measured in terms of empathy and women tend to develop greater empathy than men, doesn't this treat men, invidiously and unfairly, as second-class moral citizens? However, it isn't just sentimentalism that faces this problem. If (as Kant held) morality requires us to emphasize our own autonomy and separateness from others, then women will be at a moral disadvantage vis-à-vis men if their tendency to stay (more) tied to their mothers leaves them less able to treat people as fully separate and autonomous. Given factual differences of this kind, both rationalism and sentimentalism may be in difficulty.

However, recent discussions of this issue have noted that in certain ways, and given their strong tendency toward connection with the mother, women may have a more difficult time empathizing with others than men do. Empathy doesn't involve obliterating the distinction between self and other, and if men may end up having some problems connecting with others, women may, if they don't sufficiently separate from their mothers, have the opposite problem of losing a sense of the boundaries between themselves and others. This, too, interferes with empathy, and the point is well illustrated in what is known as "substitute success syndrome," a problem that seems to beset women more than men and that involves living through one's spouse or children and an unwillingness to see the latter as having their own independently valid sources of aspiration and interest.

In that case, a sentimentalism focused on empathic caring may not so much see women as morally better than men as see men and women as subject to equally real but different vices that interfere with ideal empathic caring from opposite directions. Moreover, if the vice of too much connection threatens women much more than men and the vice of too little threatens men more than women, then we can invoke Aristotle (toward a rather un-Aristotelian end) and say that morally good empathy lies in a mean between a vice typical of men and a vice typical of women. This means that a moral sentimentalism that regards men and women as morally *different* needn't, in the end, have the invidious implication that either sex is morally superior to the other.

REFERENCES

Batson, C. D. 1991. *The Altruism Question: Toward a Social-Psychological Answer.* Hillsdale, N.J.: Erlbaum.

Blackburn, Simon. 1984. *Spreading the Word.* Oxford: Oxford University Press.

Blum, L., M. Homiak, J. Housman, and N. Scheman. 1973. "Altruism and Women's Oppression." *Philosophical Forum* 73: 222–247.

Darwall, Stephen. 1995. *The British Moralists and the Internal 'Ought': 1640–1740.* New York: Cambridge University Press.

Firth, Roderick. 1952. "Ethical Absolutism and the Ideal Observer." *Philosophy and Phenomenological Research* 12: 317–345.

Fried, Charles. 1970. *An Anatomy of Values.* Cambridge, Mass.: Harvard University Press.

Garcia, Jorge. 1996. "The Heart of Racism." *Journal of Social Philosophy* 27: 5–45.

Gilligan, Carol. 1982. *In a Difference Voice: Psychological Theory and Women's Development.* Cambridge, Mass.: Harvard University Press.

Hoffman, Martin. 2000. *Empathy and Moral Development.* New York: Cambridge University Press.

Hume, David. 1739. *A Treatise of Human Nature.*

———. 1751. *An Enquiry Concerning the Principles of Morals.*

Hutcheson, Francis. 1738. *On the Original of Our Ideas of Beauty and Virtue.* 4th ed.

———. 1742. *An Essay on the Nature and Conduct of the Passions and Affections. With Illustrations on the Moral Sense.* 3rd ed.

Johnston, Mark. 1993. "Objectivity Refigured: Pragmatism without Verificationism." In *Reality, Representation and Projection,* ed. J. Haldane and C. Wright, 85–130. Oxford: Oxford University Press.

Kripke, Saul. 1980. *Naming and Necessity,* Oxford: Blackwell.

Noddings, Nel. 1984. *Caring: A Feminine Approach to Ethics and Moral Education.* Berkeley: University of California Press.

Reid, Thomas. 1764. *Inquiry into the Human Mind on the Principles of Common Sense.*

Singer, Peter. 1972. "Famine, Affluence, and Morality." *Philosophy and Public Affairs* 1: 229–243.

Slote, Michael. 1983. *Goods and Virtues.* Oxford: Oxford University Press.

Smith, Adam. [1759]. 1790. *The Theory of Moral Sentiments.*

Stocker, Michael. 1976. "The Schizophrenia of Modern Ethical Theories." *Journal of Philosophy* 73: 453–466.

Wiggins, David. 1987. "A Sensible Subjectivism?" In *Needs, Values, Truth,* 185–214. Oxford: Blackwell.

Williams, Bernard. 1981. "Persons, Character, and Morality." In *Moral Luck.* New York: Cambridge University Press.

Wolf, Susan. 1982. "Moral Saints." *Journal of Philosophy* 79: 419–439.

CHAPTER 9

MORAL RELATIVISM AND MORAL NIHILISM

JAMES DREIER

1. WHAT ARE NIHILISM AND RELATIVISM?

MORAL nihilism and moral relativism are metaethical theories, theories of the nature of morality. Nihilism is the view that there are no moral facts. It says that nothing is right or wrong, or morally good or bad. Nihilists believe that moral language is infected by a massive false presupposition, much as atheists understand religious talk. While nihilism is sometimes associated with the 'anything goes' outlook that Nietzsche seems to be propounding in some of his writings, nihilists nowadays typically deny that their doctrine is a moral position. John Mackie, who called his own nihilism an "error theory," was careful to insist that his was not a theory of what to do.

Relativism is the view that moral statements are true or false only relative to some standard or other, that things are right or wrong relative to Catholic morality, say, and different things are right or wrong relative to Confucian morality, but nothing is right or wrong *simpliciter*. Just as Einstein's theory of relativity says that various physical attributes like mass, length, and duration have definite quantitative measures only relative to a frame of reference, so moral relativism says that determinate answers to questions about what we morally ought to do can only be had once a frame is specified, either explicitly or tacitly. There are a number of versions of relativism, because there are various candidates for sources of frames.

Relativism and nihilism share ontology. Both doctrines are skeptical about freestanding moral facts, of some principles of action having a special authority that picks them out of the hodgepodge of conventions. Instead, relativists and nihilists see just us people with our moral feelings and social rules, valuing some things in a special way, perhaps, and then projecting these values into the world. Relativism can then be seen as a tactical retreat made by common sense in the face of the nihilist threat. Persuaded that absolute morality is a pipe dream, a relativist suggests that we might still salvage much of moral practice, moral thought, and moral talk by relativizing. Relative morality may be less than common sense could hope for, but it is better than nihilism's nothing. For their part, nihilists don't reject the relativized judgments of relativist theory, but (like many absolutists) they don't believe that the relativized practice, thought, and talk are *moral* practice, thought, and talk.

It might be thought that relativists and nihilists do differ on a crucial point of ontology. Relativists do believe that there are such things as moral properties, only they are relative properties (as Einsteinians believe that there is such a thing as duration, only it is duration relative to an inertial frame), while nihilists do not. But this is a misleading way to think of the situation. Nihilists do agree that there is such a thing as an act's being wrong-relative-to-utilitarianism, or good-relative-to-Aristotelian-virtue-theory. They count these relative properties among the constituents of the universe. They differ from relativists in doubting that these relative properties are 'the moral properties'. This difference is a difference over language, though, not a difference over ontology.

Nihilism especially is a radical thesis, violently contrary to common sense; relativism is less radical but still revisionary of common sense. At least, in one way nihilism is more radical: it says that every positive moral judgment (to the effect that something or other is wrong, or right, or morally good or bad) is false, whereas relativists think that most common sense moral judgments are likely to be true. There is another sense, to be explained in section 7, in which relativism is more radical, because it is more revisionary.[1] This sense is a semantic sense. In any case, each metaethical theory is at odds with common-sense moral thinking. But their common skepticism can also seem to be forced on us by serious, hard-nosed reflection. Moral absolutist philosophers often portray relativism as an exotic skeptical doctrine delivered by some special philosophical theory, and they see (and portray) themselves as defenders of common sense against the bizarre, much as traditional epistemologists think of themselves as defending our ordinary claims to knowledge against radical skeptical challenges. I doubt, though, that relativism and nihilism about morality really do have a relation to common sense that is similar to the one that epistemological skepticism has. Few people, even sophisticated and reflective people, ever take seriously the idea that nobody knows anything at all, or anything about the external world. Many nonphilosophers do take seriously the idea that there is no absolute morality, however, and not always or only because they have been influenced by moral philosophers.

Why does the rejection of Absolutism seem so plausible to many people?

2. WHY REJECT ABSOLUTISM?

It is easy to see how something could be good *relative to a standard*, but difficult to see how something could be good, not merely according to this or that standard, but simply. The idea of something's being good, not according to some standard but just by possessing a property of goodness, does not even make much sense. If some standard were special, were the *right* one, then something could be good absolutely by being good relative to that standard. In some contexts, there does seem to be a standard that is built in conceptually, and in these contexts we are comfortable with attributions of goodness. Even here, though, we are not apt to resist the suggestion that good and bad are relative to the standard in question.

We can start with some straightforward attributions of goodness and badness, attributions that have no problematic feel. Once we make clear and explicit what is going on in these straightforward cases, we can better understand what does seem problematic in the problematic cases.

We know that a good clock is one that (among other things) tells the time accurately. That clocks that lose a minute each hour are not good clocks is not controversial. Suppose someone personally preferred analog clocks whose hands do not move at all. He might have reasons, or he might just prefer stopped clocks on a whim. If he expressed his preference by saying that stopped clocks are good, though, he would simply be mistaken. Similarly for a computer operating system: even if someone prefers an operating system that crashes frequently, she cannot correctly say that stability in an operating system is bad. In general, the standards for artifacts seem to be built in to the concepts we use to pick out the artifactual kinds. We might put it this way: to understand the concept of a clock is already to know what makes a clock a good one. And someone whose standards for can openers are very different from the ordinary one has thereby lost contact with the concept of a can opener.

Next, consider what makes a good astronomer, or a good shepherd. These questions could be a bit controversial at the edges. For example, it may be controversial among astronomers whether doing lots of observation is more important than working out mathematical theories. Still, there cannot be controversy about whether an astronomer who knows physics is better than one who doesn't, and it is not a possible view that shepherds are better when they feed their sheep to wolves. Like artifact concepts, many concepts of jobs or roles come with standards built into them.

What about kinds that are not defined by their function? We do not expect anyone to ask which in a pile of stones is the best stone, or which element in the periodic table is the best element. Which is the best artificial fiber? Well, some fibers are better for making sleeping bags, others are better for making socks. When no standard comes automatically with a concept, we have no idea what to think about which such things are good and better until we bring in a standard. In cases when a number of different standards could be in play, we are happy to disambiguate and answer relative to one standard, then relative to another, but it is hard even to understand a question about which standard is the right one. This maple would make a better spot for a tree house, and that cherry is better for producing food, and the spruce will make a better Christmas tree, but which is really the better tree?

The question about good trees is distinct from a question about what is good for a tree. We do seem to have some conception, perhaps inchoate and vague, of what counts as good *for* an organism.[2]

So much for good (and bad); what about right and wrong? Wittgenstein pointed out that we understand the question of which road is the right road once a destination is specified (though really we would probably also need to know whether the traveler wanted a scenic route or a fast one), but only relative to the destination (1965, pp. 3–12). Questions of right action show up in games, and in law. The right move in chess is relative to the rules of chess, including the specified goal of checkmating the opponent. A legal wrong is relative to a system of laws: something that is legally wrong in Pittsburgh may not be legally wrong in Calcutta, and vice versa. Rules forbid and permit, and right and wrong need a specification of rules before they get a determinate content.

How, then, can things be morally good and bad, and morally right and wrong? If the concept of morality came with a definite set of rules and standards, moral goodness would be no more controversial than clock goodness, and moral wrongness would seem no more mysterious than the wrong move in chess. Doesn't the concept of morality come with at least some built–in rules? A restriction against harming innocent people, a requirement that we tell the truth, a low evaluation of refusing to help those in need? Some have thought that the concepts of the virtues can fill the role filled by functions in attributions of goodness to artifacts or professions. But although we may have more or less firm views about what is morally permissible and which traits of character are virtuous, these views are not matters of linguistic or conceptual competence in matters of ethics as they are in discussions of artifacts and jobs and games. Someone who thinks that rooks are permitted to move diagonally simply doesn't know chess. Someone who thinks that killing the innocent is permissible when it increases gross domestic product may be morally defective, but his deficit is not semantic.

Good and bad are relative to standards; right and wrong are relative to rules. When standards or rules are built into a concept, questions of bad and wrong can be answered 'absolutely' because they can be answered relative to the standards that everyone accepts by virtue of their conceptual or semantic competence. In questions of morality, no such standards seem to be available. If no set of rules is built into the concept of morality, where might we find some? One possibility is that there are many sets of moral rules, and that we can decide which things are wrong only relative to one or another of them, much as we can decide which fibers are better only relative to a purpose. If this possibility is the most plausible, then relativism will also be a plausible account of moral rightness and goodness. Another possibility is that although there is no particular set of rules whose acceptance is constitutive of competence with the vocabulary or concepts of morality, there are nevertheless considerations that will or would force all rational beings in the end to accept the same rules. The situation might be something like the situation of mathematicians debating Goldbach's conjecture. Nobody thinks a number theorist who doubts the conjecture is thereby shown to be incompetent in the language of arithmetic, even supposing that there is an undiscovered proof of the conjecture. If there is such a proof, it is unobvious (in the extreme!), deriving its conclusion from axioms of number theory in an enormously complicated way. Suppose, as some rationalists believe, there is some sort of derivation of a certain system of moral rules from the basic precepts of rationality. Morality might then be said to be 'relative' to that system of rules, but still in some sense absolute. For taxonomic purposes, we can count this kind of rationalist view as relativist, since it does say that all moral facts are relative to a system. Admittedly, it is what you might call a 'degenerate' version, as if there turned out to be a single *correct* physical frame of reference (the ether, say) to which all judgments of duration, length, speed were to be relativized in the ideal physical account of the world. Some people would not call this possibility 'relativism'. I will not fight over the word.

These considerations are not decisive. They are merely suggestive. I think they are responsible for the intuitive plausibility of relativism. Some people think that moral judgments are intrinsically, conceptually, by their very nature nonrelative. They think that if relative judgments of right and wrong are all that are available, then rather than showing morality to be relative, this will show that there is no moral rightness.

3. Arguments for Nihilism

The most influential and best known arguments for moral nihilism are from John Mackie's *Ethics: Inventing Right and Wrong*. As Mackie presented them, his argument from queerness and argument from relativity are independent arguments to the same conclusion, namely, that there are no objective moral values. As I understand them, the two arguments are not really independent, and, furthermore, they are both closely related to Gilbert Harman's argument for nihilism. I will set out the three arguments, and then explain how they are related.

3.1. Mackie's Queerness Argument

Mackie wrote:

> If there were objective values, then they would be entities of qualities or relations of a very strange sort, utterly different from anything else in the universe. Correspondingly, if we were aware of them, it would have to be by some special faculty of moral perception or intuition, utterly different from our ordinary ways of knowing anything else. . . . This queerness does not consist simply in the fact that ethical statements are 'unverifiable'. (1977, pp. 38–39)

What *is* so 'queer' about objective values? And does this queerness cast doubt on their existence? Mackie seems to have had two queer features in mind. First, although it is not merely being 'unverifiable' that he thought queer, Mackie did think that the apparently complete separation of objective value from ordinary perception and observation was very suspicious. The 'faculty of moral perception' he thought a 'very lame answer' to the question of how we might find out about objective right and wrong. Gilbert Harman's observation argument follows up this complaint. Second, Mackie argued that the role that objective values would have to play in motivation is completely unlike the role that ordinary properties play.

> Plato's Forms give a dramatic picture of what objective values would have to be. The Form of the Good is such that knowledge of it provides the knower with both a direction and an overriding motive; something's being good both tells the person who knows this to pursue it and makes him pursue it. . . . Similarly, if there were objective principles of right and wrong, any wrong (possible) course of action would have not-to-be-doneness somehow built into it. (1977, pp. 38–39)

I will develop Mackie's line of thought in the subsection hereafter entitled "Mackie's Internalist Argument."

3.2. Mackie's Argument from Relativity

Mackie starts the relativity argument by pointing out that moral codes have varied from society to society and time to time. "Such variation is in itself merely a truth of descriptive morality," he says, "a fact of anthropology which entails neither first order nor second order views." Still, he argues, "radical differences between first order moral judgments make it difficult to treat those judgments as apprehensions of objective truths" (1977, p. 36).

Mackie's argument seems to be misnamed. An argument *from* relativity ought to proceed from a relativistic premise. Mackie's does not so proceed, nor could it, since it would be question-begging to assume that moral values are relative when arguing against the existence of absolute moral values. The starting point of Mackie's argument is not the relativity of moral value, in any case, but rather the *diversity* of moral values, across cultures and throughout history. Here, by "moral values" I mean not the moral facts of the matter (if there are any) but the values *held* or *subscribed to* by one or another group of people. So the diversity premise is empirical, and though no detailed evidence for it is presented, it does seem to be fairly secure. But how, precisely, does the argument go? On the face of it, the argument is as follows.

Moral values have differed from time to time and place to place.
Therefore, there are no objective moral facts.

Now, this argument is obviously missing a premise. What is the missing premise? To make the argument valid, the missing premise must be (or entail) the following.

If moral values differ from time to time and place to place, then there are no objective moral facts.

What reason is there to believe this conditional premise? Is it just obvious? It is certainly not obvious to everyone. To see why it looks problematic, compare this argument:

Theories of the nature of stars have differed from time to time and place to place.
If theories of the nature of stars differ from time to time and place to place, then there are no objective stellar facts.
Therefore, there are no objective stellar facts.

It is possible that there really are no objective facts about stars, but this argument is unlikely to convince anyone that there aren't. The first premise is true, but the second, conditional premise is very dubious. The mere existence of difference of opinion does not, obviously, show that there is no truth of the matter.[3]

Both of Mackie's arguments get a little help from an argument for nihilism from Gilbert Harman, to which I now turn.

3.3. Harman's Observation Argument

Harman's observation argument begins from the fact that

> [o]bservation plays a role in science that it does not seem to play in ethics. The difference is that you need to make assumptions about certain physical facts to explain the occurrence of the observations that support a scientific theory, but you do not seem to need to make assumptions about any moral facts to explain the occurrence of . . . so-called moral observations (Harman, 1977, p. 6)

Suppose you see some boys pouring gasoline on a cat and setting the cat on fire. Your 'moral observation' is that these boys are very bad (or at least, that they are doing something very bad). Now suppose that a physicist sees a vapor trail in a cloud chamber. Her observation: "There goes a proton." Now in each case, the 'observation' depends on some background theory that the observer holds. Your moral observation depends on your holding certain moral views, otherwise you would not see what the boys were doing as 'bad'. But similarly, the physicist would not see the vapor trail as a proton if she did not hold a certain background theory of atomic particles. Observations are *theory laden*. Yet there is an important difference. When we try to explain the physicist's observation, we have no choice but to mention the proton itself. At first, we might just cite the existence of a vapor trail plus the physicist's background beliefs. But what explains the vapor trail? The presence of a proton. Perhaps not; perhaps there is an alternative explanation. If there is a *better* explanation available, then the observation does not, in fact, support the conclusion that there is a proton present. If *no* observations require that we suppose that protons are present for their explanation, then we do not have any real reason to believe in protons. And that, according to Harman, is our actual situation with respect to moral properties. The moral badness of the boys' actions does not enter into our best explanation of the 'moral observation'. Rather, we fully explain the observations by referring to the plain, nonmoral features of the boys and the cat, and also the moral feelings and upbringing of the observer (you). "The fact that you made a particular moral observation when you did does not seem to be evidence about moral facts, only evidence about you and your moral sensibility" (Harman, 1977, p. 6).

3.4. The Best Explanation

Harman's argument is explicitly about explanation. The best explanation of the phenomena of moral experience, he claims, involves no mention of moral facts or properties. This claim has been disputed (Sturgeon, 1985). But if it is true that moral properties and facts do not explain anything, that is a compelling reason to doubt their existence. It's not so much that there could not be facts and properties that don't explain anything. Maybe there can be. The point is rather that we have no good reason to believe in purported properties and facts if it turns out they play no role in our explanations (of observations, Harman says). Could there be some subatomic particles, *eudaemons*, that, unlike photons, electrons, neutrinos, have no effect on observed phenomena? Nothing rules out the possibility. But we have no reason to believe in eudaemons. If for some reason someone did believe in eudaemons, we would expect to raise doubts in his mind if we could show him that nothing they do ever explains anything we observe.

Both of Mackie's arguments are also about explanation, although not explicitly. First, Mackie could not have overlooked the glaring problem with the diversity argument as I presented it. Could he have intended some other version? Here is some evidence:

> [T]he argument from relativity has some force simply because the actual variations in the moral codes are more readily explained by the hypothesis that they reflect ways of life than by the hypothesis that they express perceptions, most of them seriously inadequate and badly distorted, of objective values. (Mackie, 1977, p. 37)

Mackie's point is that the *best explanation* for the diversity of moral views is a nihilist explanation. Compare the unconvincing argument about stellar facts. The diversity of astronomical theories seems to be best explained by defects in the observational capacity or theoretic understanding of ancient astronomers; without telescopes and radio observations, they could not hope to understand the nature of stars. When we try to explain why early observers thought that the stars were tiny pinpricks of light, our best explanation involves the facts as we know them about the stars themselves (their distance, their actual luminosity, complicated facts of relativity physics). If Mackie is right, then our best explanation of why other cultures at other times and places disagreed with our own moral views involves our different customs, psychology, and interests, but never the moral facts themselves. So the argument from relativity, which might better be called the argument from diversity, is really an argument to the best explanation.

Again, why exactly is the queerness of moral properties supposed to impugn their status? What exactly is so queer about them? In part, the answer is that moral properties do not seem to enter into causal relations with the world we know. The epistemology of moral facts is queer because we are not in causal contact with the moral realm; our basic moral values do not depend counterfactually on the moral properties themselves. In the ordinary course of discovering that a rock is radioactive, we test by means of a device that registers the presence of radioactivity. Our belief that the rock is radioactive then depends counterfactually on the radioactivity itself: if the rock *were not radioactive*, the Geiger counter *would not have beeped*, and then we *would not have believed* that the rock was radioactive. But our moral values do not seem to depend counterfactually on the presence of moral properties.

The point is not merely that we have available some other explanation for moral judgment that does not mention any moral properties explicitly. After all, when you judge that I am in a good mood, there is presumably some explanation for your judgment that does not explicitly mention my mood. That explanation might instead mention the expression on my face, and my expression might in turn be explained by the state of my brain. Where are the moods? Well, presumably, my mood just is (a function of) the state of my brain. There are no special mood properties of me, above and beyond the states of my brain. It is rather that some families of brain states hang together in 'mood' categories. Similar points might be made about biological properties (say, being alive) and even chemical properties (whose role in explanation might be replaced by the properties recognized by physics). Might moral properties *reduce* to physical ones, in the way that chemical or biological or mood properties reduce to some more basic properties? Some philosophers have thought so.[4] If they do, then the nihilistic explanation argument is rendered harmless. I explain in section 6 why it is doubtful that moral properties could reduce to any descriptive ones.

The metaphysics of moral properties is queer because they are causally isolated. Of course, there may be other sorts of explanation than causal explanation. Mackie himself recognizes that mathematics may seem as queer as ethics, since numbers, like wrongness, are not to be found in time and space. But mathematical facts enter into scientific explanations all the time, so our reasons for believing in mathematical facts are reasonably secure.[5]

As I mentioned, there is another queer feature of moral properties, what Mackie calls their intrinsic action-guidingness or "to-be-doneness." I will explain later how that feature figures in arguments for relativism and nihilism. For now, I will sum up the arguments about explanation.

We value things, some of them in a specially moral way, and we commonly and unreflectively think and say that laws are wrong, that people are no good, that rights are being violated. However, our best explanation of the facts of our valuing, and of the courses of events surrounding bad laws and men, is itself couched in nonmoral terms: the history of our community and our own upbringing explains why we value what we value, and the ordinary, nonmoral features of laws and men explains their causes and effects. If moral properties do not explain anything, then we have no reason to believe in them, and we do have reason to doubt their existence.

3.5. Relative Moral Facts Explain

Notice, though, that the explanation arguments apply to *absolute* moral facts and properties. A relativist need not fear them. First I shall show that this is true, and then explain why. When the Patriots beat the Steelers in fall 2002, that was because the Patriots were a better team. Their being a better team does explain the victory. Longtime chess champion Gary Kasparov is enjoying the moment because he just made the right move; its being the right move explains Gary's mood. Evaluative and normative facts can comfortably fit into naturalistic explanations when they are relative to definite standards. The standards for football teams have as their whole point to approve of teams with stable tendencies to win games, so one team's being better than another *according to those standards* quite naturally explains a victory.[6] Moves of chess are right or wrong relative to the rules of chess (including the objective), with the right ones being those that give their maker the best chance of winning. According to moral relativists, moral rightness and wrongness and moral goodness and badness are also relative to standards; they are, therefore, fit to play the same sort of role in explanations that football team goodness and chess move rightness can play.

What explains this difference? Why are relativized evaluative facts fit to explain phenomena while absolute ones are not? We might put it this way. The fact that A is better than B *according to standard S* is itself a natural fact. There is nothing more to the fact that the Patriots are a better football team than the Steelers (according to the standard for evaluating football teams—but this relativization literally goes without saying) than the fact that their members have physical and mental abilities that give them the stable disposition to win a game against the Steelers under ordinary circumstances. There is nothing more to the fact that Kasparov's move was the right one than the fact that it increases his chance of winning. Once relativized, the evaluative and normative claims *reduce* to natural or empirical ones, in the sense that there are natural or empirical facts that, once they are mentioned, complete the explanation; mentioning the relativized evaluative facts doesn't add anything. Reduction here is a metaphysical relation. A chair is nothing more than the clump of molecules that compose it, and the fact that Kasparov's move was the right one (according to chess standards) is nothing more than the fact that among the available legal moves, it was the one that maximized his chance of winning. Likewise, the fact that giving lots of money to famine relief is *good-according-to-utilitarianism* can explain why some people do it, and perhaps why someone who does it is likely to perform other acts that reduce suffering.

Could absolute moral facts also reduce to natural facts? Rightness and wrongness of chess moves, after all, are, in a sense, absolute: they are relative to *the correct* rules and objective of chess. Maybe there is such a thing as absolute moral wrongness, namely, wrongness according to *the correct* moral rules. For instance, if utilitarianism is the correct moral theory, then moral rightness just is the tendency to increase the net sum of happiness over unhappiness. That tendency can certainly figure in perfectly good explanations of natural facts. But it is very doubtful that moral facts could reduce to natural ones in this way, at least if they are absolute moral facts. The obstacle to reduction is the essential practical aspect of moral judgment, the second queer feature that Mackie discusses. I will postpone my discussion of this feature to section 6.

4. Relativism

Here is one version of moral relativism.[7]

Evaluative and normative expressions need a standard to give them a determinate content. The essence of relativism is that moral expressions are no different from other evaluative and normative expressions. They are incomplete; they need a standard to complete them. The semantic value of a moral expression, then, is a function that takes standards as its argument and returns determinate contents as its values. Compare the semantic values of *indexicals*, expressions like 'me', 'yesterday', and 'here'. According to the standard semantics for these terms, their meaning is a function from *contexts* (of utterance, inscription, or thought) to *contents* (Kaplan, 1989). For example, the semantic value of 'here' is the function that takes any context to the place in that context, so that 'here' refers directly to the place in which it is uttered or written, 'yesterday' refers directly to the day before the context of utterance or thought, and 'me' refers directly to the speaker. The point of including 'directly' in each case is that once fixed by the context, the terms carry their reference no matter how they are embedded into a complex sentence. Thus, if I say, "Mom told you to come here," I do not report that Mom told you to come to *her* location but to mine (the location of the context of utterance, not the embedded context), and if you tell me on April 1, "Last Christmas I promised you that I would send you the paper yesterday," you aren't reminding me that you'd promised to send me the paper on Christmas Eve but rather on March 31, the day before the day of *utterance*.

To be a bit vague, we might say that the predicate 'morally good' always picks out some property, but different properties in different contexts. To be a little more specific, we could say that it always picks out the property of meeting the relevant standards in the context, to a high degree. And similarly for 'wrong': it picks out the property of violating a rule of the relevant system of rules in the context, and likewise for other moral predicates. But this still leaves things rather vague. What *are* the relevant standards and systems? What makes some standard the relevant one in a context? To a first approximation, a relativist can say that the relevant standards are those of the speaker (or writer, or thinker; but hereafter I will restrict attention to spoken sentences). Presumably, when you say that abortion is morally wrong, you are adverting to *your* moral system of rules. As a first approximation of an explication of relativism, this specification is not too bad, but it does seem a little too simplistic. When I report Peter Singer as believing that eating meat is morally wrong, I am not saying that he believes eating meat violates a rule of *my* moral system. A more plausible version of relativism will say that a number of factors go into determining which system or standard is relevant; the speaker's own moral outlook is one, but other factors, especially considerations of conversational salience, may override. Notice that even those expressions that are uncontroversially indexical are more complicated than the simplest semantic model makes them out to be. When I remind you on Halloween, "I've been saying all month that you shouldn't put off till tomorrow what you can do today," I am not reminding you that all October I've been telling you not to put off until All Saints' Day what you can do on Halloween. When a mountain climber points to his map and worries, "I thought we were here but apparently we aren't," he isn't announcing that he is not after all in his location. So even if it turns out that moral terms cannot plausibly get their content always from the moral system and standards of the speaker, even if it turns out that it is very difficult to specify clearly in advance exactly which system is going to be the relevant one, that needn't be an objection to the theory. It is a feature of indexicals in natural language that the specification of their semantic value is messy.

This indexical account of moral judgment has several advantages. I will mention two. First, it explains the connection between, say, calling something wrong and the natural features of something that make it wrong. Calling something wrong does attribute a property to it, but the property it attributes isn't a special *sui generis* property; rather, it is just some natural property, the 'wrong-making' property. Similarly, saying that something occurred yesterday is, obviously, saying that it occurred on some actual day, even though 'yesterday' is not a name of a special day, apart from Halloween, October 27, January 3, and the other days of the year. It is no mystery that for any pair of events you name, *if* they both occurred on the same day of the year, then *either* they both occurred yesterday *or* neither of them did. That this conditional should be true is a consequence of the proper understanding of indexicals. Similarly, the fact that any two actions that are alike in their natural properties must either both be wrong or both not be wrong is a consequence of the indexical understanding of moral judgment.

Second, and related, the indexical account of moral judgment explains why moral judgment does not reduce to nonmoral judgment. Famously, we cannot deduce indexical judgments from nonindexical ones. For example, unless we already know which day is *today* (more naturally, unless we know *what day it is*, an indexical kind of knowledge), we cannot deduce from the date of an event whether it occurred yesterday. Similarly, the moral properties of an event do not follow analytically from its natural properties. The moral judgment is always another judgment, above and beyond naturalistic description. The indexical account says that this gap is, in fact, the gap between nonindexical and indexical statements. So the 'autonomy of the moral', as it is sometimes called, is an instance of the well–understood autonomy of the indexical.

There are other versions of relativism. The indexical version is just an example.

5. SHOULD WE BE *AGAINST* RELATIVISM?

In many circles, including some professional philosophical ones, moral relativism is something of a bogeyman. That a certain position "leads to moral relativism" is supposed to be a serious objection to it.[8] In American politics, moral relativism is decried as a symptom and cause of cultural decay. Is moral relativism something to fear, something to stand against?

In the first place, awful social consequences of the spread of moral relativism, if there are any, in no way count against the truth of the theory. Suppose we decided that belief in moral relativism leads to a meaningless life with no hope. That would obviously not show that the theory is false. Compare a common view about determinism: some people (incompatibilists, philosophers call them) think that if laws of nature determine the behavior of human beings, then nobody is ever responsible for anything he does. It would probably be a bad thing if most people believed that they are not responsible for anything they ever do. But that is not an argument against incompatibilism or determinism.

Second, it has been claimed that moral relativists are not consistent. For instance, Bernard Williams attributes the following argument to (unnamed) anthropologists:

'Right' means (can only be coherently understood as meaning) 'right for a given society'.

'Right for a given society' is to be understood in a functionalist sense. Therefore, it is wrong for people in one society to condemn, interfere with, etc., the values of another society.

"This is *relativism*," says Williams, "the anthropologists' heresy, possibly the most absurd view to have been advanced even in moral philosophy" (1972, p. 20). The absurdity, it turns out, is that the conclusion is inconsistent with the premises, since "wrong" is intended there absolutely, and not in the relative sense allowed by the premises; so Williams says, at any rate, and since the anthropologist is a character in Williams's discussion rather than a real scholar, Williams's characterization is definitive.[9] In any case, the point is that having denied the meaningfulness of absolute attributions of rightness and wrongness, the heretical anthropologists find themselves with moral beliefs that can only be expressed in absolutist language. Similarly, philosophy professors sometimes report that their students (and colleagues) hold both relativistic metaethical views and also absolutist particular moral views (for instance, Pojman, 1989, esp. p. 25).

These are anecdotes, and Williams's is not even an anecdote about a real person. But suppose that it does turn out that many moral relativists end up making absolutist judgments. What would that show? Is it an argument against relativism? It looks like an *ad hominem* argument. That adherents of a theory contradict themselves may count against *them*, but it doesn't per se count against the theory. Imagine that many seventeenth–century physicists accepted Newton's mechanics but frequently found themselves describing the world around them, in everyday conversation, with Aristotelian concepts. Their backsliding wouldn't count against Newtonian mechanics, so why should backsliding by anthropologist or undergraduate relativists count against relativism?

The real objection might be a little different. Suppose the reason anthropologist and undergraduate relativists backslide is that relativism has implications that we do not or even cannot accept. Then the objection could be cast as a *modus tollens* argument: if moral relativism is true, then so are these consequences; but the consequences are false, so moral relativism is false. If moral relativism has unbelievable or highly counterintuitive *logical* consequences, then we have an important philosophical objection. What might these consequences be?

Bernard Williams thought it a fallacy to infer a principle of tolerance from relativistic premises, and the form of argument he presented certainly is fallacious.[10] Yet moral relativism is commonly associated with tolerance, indeed with an extreme, paralyzing tolerance. Relativism is thought to destroy grounds for moral criticism, leaving us with only the thought "Well, they have their way and we have ours." What can we make of this thought?

On the face of it, Williams was right to think of this inference as a fallacy, indeed a non sequitur. Consider this argument:

Moral rightness and wrongness are always relative to some standard.

Therefore, we cannot (or ought not) judge other cultures (or people).

Plainly the conclusion does not follow, and the argument looks so bad that we ought to try to find a better one in the neighborhood. We might try adjusting the conclusion, or else add a plausible premise, or both. Now the conclusion might be adjusted by adding "according to our own standards." If some other culture does not subscribe to a morality that affords individuals protections, in the form of rights, against the will of the majority, relativism might imply that we cannot or ought not to evaluate their laws and other state actions according to how well they protect those rights.[11] Why should *they* abide by *our* standards, if there is no sense in which ours are correct? Compare systems of etiquette. In some cultures it is a compliment to the chef to slurp your soup at the table. In ours, it is rude. But if someone from our culture considered diners in the other rude because they slurped their soup, that would display a misunderstanding. Once we understand what etiquette is, we realize that behavior at a given time and place is rude only when it violates the etiquette standards for (accepted in) that time and place. Why should *they* follow *our* standards?

Even if morality is relative, it is not relative in the way that etiquette is relative. If it is relative, it is so more in the way that judgments of beauty and taste are relative. A thirteenth–century Cherokee might find Debra Winger very ugly. By her own culture's standards, she is beautiful, but that needn't sway the Cherokee. He judges beauty from his own perspective, by his own standards. Of course! I personally find Vegemite disgusting. Australians eat a lot of it, produce a lot of it, and apparently find its taste pleasing. Nevertheless, I stand by my own judgment. Vegemite tastes terrible. Australians eat something with a terrible taste, and apparently they like it. If pressed, I will say that it tastes good to them, and bad to me, and that's all there is to it; there is no further question of whose taste is correct. A moral relativist must say the same about the protection of individual rights: it is morally important according to our moral outlook, unimportant according to others, and no further question of which standards are correct. Still, when we actually make moral judgments, we can quite properly make them from our own perspective. Riding roughshod over the interests of the minority is wrong, even over there, and Vegemite is still foul-tasting stuff.

The analogy with taste and aesthetics might suggest a way of improving the tolerance argument. When I despise Vegemite and you adore it, we can each shrug off the difference: to each his own. We can each recognize that our different tastes mean that we should eat different things. You go ahead and eat Vegemite, and I'll eat artichokes. Though our tastes differ, we can each see that the other is acting sensibly and appropriately. The to-each-his-own judgment we end up with doesn't clash with the first–order judgment of taste. Things are different with morals. Our moral standards count it wrong to disenfranchise a political minority for the sake of social stability, while the majoritarians' standards count it right. If morals are relative in the way that taste is, shouldn't we conclude that it is sensible and appropriate for us to protect minority voting rights over here and for them to eliminate them over there? If so, the tolerance argument has been fixed. The missing plausible premise would be something like: when evaluations are relative, let each follow her own.

There is a mistake in this line of reasoning, however. The relativity of morals and taste may be the same, but their subject matter is different. Morality is about what to do. Taste is not. Taste can, of course, be relevant to the question of what to do, but it is not directly relevant in the way that morality is. To judge that something is morally wrong is to judge that people ought not to do it. To judge that something tastes bad is not to judge that people ought not to eat it. When we are trying to make up our minds about what is morally right and wrong, we are trying to decide what people ought to do. We have no choice but to use some standards or other. And, naturally enough, we use our own. They are our standards! We accept them. We find them compelling. So when, upon reflection, we judge that it is morally wrong for the majoritarians to disenfranchise their political minority, we are already committed to the judgment that they ought not to do it. In this way, moral judgment is unlike the judgment that artichokes taste good, which does not commit me to the judgment that you ought to eat them.

When we make political judgments, especially judgments about other people's political systems, there are special complications that I ignored in my spare and simplistic example (of the majoritarians). For one thing, external judgments to the effect that another system is unjust always hint at the possibility or even advisability of intervention. Intervention, by force or economic or political pressure, might be ill advised, even to prevent injustice, for any number of reasons. It may have unintended but foreseeable consequences that we ought to avoid; it may set a precedent we ought not to set; or, more interesting, it may itself violate the rights of the unjust society (and its members). To take an intranational example, the Augusta country club has no women members, allegedly because of a traditional but unwritten policy. I think this policy is morally wrong. I also think Augusta should be permitted to follow it. The members and the board of the club have a right, I say, to engage in their repugnant behavior. That right is against the state; it means that the club shouldn't suffer legal sanctions as a result of their practice. International examples are trickier, partly because the association of citizens in a nation is not voluntary as the association of members in a club is. Still, we might think that although the oppressive practices of the majoritarians are unjust, their nation has a right of autonomy that forbids us from interfering. But that's not because of moral relativism. The idea of national autonomy is as much at home in absolutist conceptions of the nature of morality.

In sum, moral relativism as I have been understanding it does not seem to have any particularly unpalatable normative moral consequences. Indeed, it seems unlikely that moral relativism itself has normative moral consequences, any more than the metaaesthetic view that beauty is in the eye of the beholder has any particular implications about what is beautiful, or the view that taste is relative to the taster has any particular implications about what tastes good.[12]

6. The Internalist Argument to Nihilism or Relativism

The 'queerness' of moral facts, mentioned in Mackie's argument, has to do with what Mackie calls their intrinsic action-guidingness, their 'to-be-doneness', or what Stevenson (1937, pp. 14–31) called their 'magnetism'. Roughly put, the idea is that moral goodness seems to have a queer kind of force built in, so that the mere apprehension of it by rational agents compels them toward it. Put in a more sober, less extravagant-sounding way, the internalist thesis is that it is part of our concept of a moral judgment that a person does not count as sincerely accepting it unless she recognizes it as having *some* reason-giving force. Motivation, or at least reason-giving force, is *internal* to moral judgment, according to Internalism (Darwall, 1997, pp. 305–312; Falk, 1948, pp. 111–138; Smith, 1994).

It is important to the plausibility of internalism that we not overstate it. It is commonplace, almost trite to observe that people, even good people, can recognize the right thing to do and fail to do it. But here is a thought experiment to give support to the weaker internalism that says that *some* motivating reason must be internal to genuine, sincere moral judgment.

Imagine that we were to uncover a long-lost culture of isolated speakers of English. The dialect they speak is almost like ours, but they do not use any of our moral language. Linguistic anthropologists tell us that these speakers have a handful of extra lexical items, and they want some advice about how to interpret them. The items can be separated into two classes. One class is centered on the terms 'Gog' and 'Bab', and it seems to match in extension our moral terms. The words don't find much use in the community, though. People aren't sure what the point of them is, although they have no trouble agreeing that, for instance, lying is Bab and giving special attention to friends and family is Gog. The other class of words center around the terms 'Noog' and 'Nad'. These words have the extension of the utilitarian notions of good and bad: things are Noog insofar as they contribute impartially to the general happiness, and Nad insofar as they detract therefrom. This second class of words figures centrally in the lives of the long-lost culture. People are motivated, in a dutiful, serious way, to do and pro-mote what they judge to be Noog, and they are ashamed when they do things they judge to be Nad. You and I, I will suppose, are not utilitarians. Our common-sense moral view is much less tidy, but it departs from utilitarianism in significant ways. What shall we tell the anthropologists? It is undeniable, I think, that there is at least a very strong reason to say that the second class of words are the moral words. Surely these people are utilitarians; surely they have utilitarian beliefs. There may be some intuition pulling us in the other direction, too: couldn't we say that the long-lost culture still does know and correctly judge right and wrong, but that they no longer care about it? We are torn, I think, because the extension of our moral judgments is semantically important, and not just its role in our practical deliberation. The point of the thought experiment is that the functional role of moral judgment is also tied to it conceptually, and not just as an interesting coincidence to be explained by empirical psychology (as, for example, the concept of being high above the ground might be tied psychologically to fear). Deciding what is morally right is, in part, deciding what to do, or what to favor.

We can rebuild Mackie's argument (for nihilism) so that its internalist premise is explicit.

Mackie's Internalist Argument

Moral goodness would have to be such that sincere judgment about *it* is intrinsically motivational.

But, there is no property such that sincere judgment about it is intrinsically motivational.

So, there is no such thing as moral goodness.

The first premise is the internalist one. The story of the long-lost culture supports something like this premise. Ethical internalists sometimes insist on a very strong version of the principle. They say that on each occasion of use, each competent speaker who says that something is morally good must thereby be motivated to pursue, or bring about, or aim at, the thing she is calling good. The story I told does not support such a strong claim, nor, frankly, does the very strong claim seem to be true. What does seem (to me) to be true, and what the story does support, is that *on the whole*, or *for the most part*, it must turn out that *most* people who judge something good *generally* are thereby motivated. If that weaker claim were not true, then there would be no temptation in our story to translate 'Noog' as 'good.' It would seem obvious that 'Gog' meant 'good,' even though the members of the culture *by and large* and *for the most part* used the concept of 'Noog' in their practical deliberations in the same way that we use 'good'. Mackie seems to have subscribed to the stronger version of internalism. But the argument seems to work if we substitute the weaker. Making the substitution completely explicit will make the ensuing discussion very cumbersome, so I will stick with the terse version, and hope it will not be misleading.

The second premise expresses a Humean conception of motivation, and it is not uncontroversial. How do we know that there aren't any properties the mere cognition of which carries with it some motivational, reason-giving force? After all, *moral* properties do seem to be like that! Why should this count against them? I cannot hope to settle this question with any finality here. But let us be clear, at least, about what is at stake. There certainly may be some properties that do, as a matter of fact, always give you and me some reason to act when we become aware of them. There may be lots of things that we simply find attractive. And there may even be some things, some properties, that all human beings find attractive, and even more, there may be deep psychological and evolutionary explanations for why we do. The Humean premise of Mackie's internalist argument need not deny any of this. The connection between properties and motivational reasons that the second premise denies is a very strong, logical connection. For the premise to be false, there would have to be a property whose apprehension would move any rational being as such. The apprehension itself would have already to be a motivational state. It is this internal connection that Humeans deny. They say: Representation of the world as being this way or that is one thing, and motivation is another. For a representation of the way the world is to make a difference in our deciding what to do, it must first be joined with some sort of desire, or valuing, or aim of ours. What seems so 'queer' about moral judgment is that it purports to be a representation of how things are, while at the same time embodying an aim. But these are two quite different functions of a state of mind, and although they may, of course, be joined in a complex state (as, for instance, when I believe and hope at once that I remembered to turn off the stove before I left home this morning), they will always be conceptually separable.

So much for (the internalist version of) Mackie's argument. Internalism can instead be employed in an argument for relativism.

Internalist Argument for Relativism

Moral goodness is such that sincere judgment about *it* intrinsically motivates.

But, which properties motivate depends on the psychology of the judging agent.

So, which properties are the moral ones depends on the psychology of the agent.

The mystery of intrinsic motivation is eliminated, the relativist points out, if only we will understand that each person judges morally according to *her own* moral standards. And having moral standards is, at least in part, caring about things in a certain way. Thus, the long-lost culture of our thought experiment judges Nood and Nad according to the standards of utilitarianism, which its members accept; that is just to say that they care, in a serious and moral sort of way, about the happiness and suffering of all people. We make sense of their judgment by supposing that human happiness and suffering is what it is *about.* By contrast, people who judge from a more Kantian, or a more rights-based, moral perspective can be best understood as making judgments *about* what maxims could be endorsed as universal laws of nature, or about how to treat people as ends in themselves rather than solely as means to the ends of others.

Each of the two arguments takes internalism seriously. And, as I said, nihilism and relativism share an ontology. We might say that if internalism is true, then morality is either relative or unreal.[13] Suppose we are convinced by this argument to a disjunctive conclusion. How might we choose between the disjuncts?

7. Nihilism or Relativism?

Nihilism is a radical thesis, more radical, as I said, than relativism. On the other hand, the nihilist position that I have examined has a claim to be truer to common sense moral concepts than relativism is. Nihilism recognizes that common-sense moral concepts are absolutist concepts: our moral thoughts are 'as of' a single, independently existing moral order. When we judge that the actions of a terrorist cell are *wrong*, we are not, it seems, judging that those actions are wrong-relative-to-our-standards. If terrorists have different moral standards from ours, then they have incorrect, abhorrent moral standards! So much the nihilist grants ordinary moral thinking. But he then regrets to inform ordinary thought that it is based on a mistake. There is nothing in the world that answers to the ordinary language of morals.

This point, that nihilism may be truer to common-sense moral concepts than relativism, can be made sharper by means of the *disagreement argument.*[14] Suppose we have a report of the statements of a horrible terrorist, among which is this:

(A)   The intentional slaughter of millions of innocent noncombatants is morally justified as a means to promote my ends.

We may suppose that according to the horrible terrorist's own moral outlook, the slaughter of millions *is* in fact justified. Leaders of the allied antiterrorist forces issue a joint statement, including the following.

(B)   The intentional slaughter of millions of innocent noncombatants cannot
be morally justified under any circumstances.

Here are two related, fairly obvious semantic and conceptual points about (A)
and (B). First, (B) *disagrees* with (A); by issuing (B), the allied leaders are expressing their disagreement with (A). Second, (B) might be prefaced, without
significant change in meaning, by the sentence "(A) is not true." These are rather
obvious points about ordinary language; they are not the product of any theory.
It is therefore a bit of an embarrassment to a relativist that he has to deny both
of these rather obvious points.

In the first place, the relativist thinks of (A) and (B) as containing an implicit
relativization to the speaker's moral outlook, much as statements about what is
or is not law are implicitly relativized (when they are not explicitly so) to a legal
system. If I am on the telephone to my uncle in Las Vegas, he might declare:
"Prostitution is legally permitted." Suppose my son overhears the conversation
(my uncle speaks very loudly on the telephone) and asks, "Is prostitution really
legally permitted?" My wife, shocked, tells him, "No, prostitution is not legally
permitted." My wife has not disagreed with my uncle. The implicit relativization
removes whatever appearance of disagreement inheres in the surface structure of
the statements. Furthermore, once she understood the situation, my wife would
certainly not preface her own statement by the verdict "What your uncle says is
not true." Both statements, my wife's and my uncle's, can be true, and so my wife
and my uncle are not disagreeing. So much is plain and common-sensical for
statements of law, but moral judgments appear to be quite different. It just seems
wrong to say that (A) and (B) don't really disagree. And this suggests that the
linguistic intentions of speakers is, often at least, absolutist rather than relativist.

Relativists may agree, to some extent. For pre-theoretic moral ideas to be all
they aspire to be, a relativist might say, there would have to absolute standards
for moral concepts to latch onto. But since there aren't any, relativism suggests,
why not make do with the relative standards that we actually do have? There is
no need to abandon moral judgment altogether, so long as we are willing to tone
down its aspirations.

Compare common-sense judgments of mass, or length, or duration. For all
but the more sophisticated folk of the last century or so, all such judgments have
been absolute on their face. A policeman on the witness stand testifies that while
staking out the apartment, he saw the defendant enter and then leave one hour
later. The defense cross-examines: When you say it was one hour later, can you
provide an inertial frame? "A duration of one hour must, officer, be relative to
one inertial frame or another, you know." The policeman denies that he meant
any such thing. "Just one hour, is all I meant, not relative to any of your fancy
frames." In a very straightforward sense, the policeman's *intention* was to name
an absolute duration, of the sort that is simply not recognized in relativistic phys-

ics. Is the policeman's testimony thereby impeached? Has he said something false? We would not ordinarily say so. To put it briefly: the policeman's judgment had a false presupposition behind it. His own conception of the world, adequate and accurate enough for his own purposes, is not really correct. But the false presupposition, the incorrect *theory* that the policeman himself would give if carefully questioned, does not seem to infect the integrity or veracity of his ordinary, first-order judgments. What the policeman said, we believe, is true; only his background absolutist theory of it is mistaken. So it is with ordinary moral judgment, a relativist may say. Most often it doesn't even occur to us to inquire into the metaphysics behind our ordinary moral judgments. Perhaps if we did, many of us would find a latent absolutism hidden there as a kind of presupposition. But that metatheory, even if it is incorrect, needn't infect first-order moral judgments. So long as the ordinary judgments are understood relative to whatever standards make most sense in the context, they can be perfectly correct, just as the policeman's judgments are perfectly correct if understood relative to the inertial frame of the courtroom. Nihilism is no more called for in ethics than it is in commonsense physics.

NOTES

I thank the participants in my 2001 graduate seminar at Brown University, as well as those at the January 2003 Ethics Discussion Group meeting at the Australian National University, where some of these ideas were discussed. And I thank most especially David Copp for comprehensive comments, to which I was not able to respond as comprehensively as I would have liked.

1. I thank Laura Schroeter for making me see this point.
2. Philippa Foot thinks so. See Foot, 2001, esp. chap. 2. The idea, as I understand it, is that we have some conception of a species that includes what counts as a healthy, or normal, organism of that species, and this conception will include standards for how the organism is doing.
3. Indeed, proper difference of opinion is often taken to 5show that we are presupposing that there *is* a truth of the matter. "And differing judgments serve but to declare / that truth lies somewhere, if we knew but where." (William Cowper, "Hope.")
4. See Sturgeon, 1985, for discussion of the complexities of reduction.
5. Whether we really have reason to believe in numbers is, of course, a question much trickier and more difficult than I can even begin to discuss. For one thing, reference to numbers may be eliminable in mathematical reasoning, as in Field, 1980. Mackie himself says that he believes the queerness of mathematics can be removed by some kind of naturalistic reduction, but also that if he is wrong then we should be error theorists about numbers, too. See, Mackie, 1977, p. 39:

Indeed, the best move for the moral objectivist is not to evade this issue, but to look for companions in guilt ... [f]or example ... our knowledge and even our ideas of essence, number, identity.... This is an important answer to the argument from queerness. The only adequate replay would be to show how, on empiricist foundations, we can construct an account of the ideas and beliefs and knowledge that we have of these matters. I cannot even begin to do that here, though I have undertaken some parts of the task elsewhere. I can only state my belief that satisfactory accounts of most of these can be given in empirical terms. If some supposed metaphysical necessities or essences resist such treatment, then they too should be included, along with objective values, among the targets of the argument from queerness.

6. Nor is the explanation utterly trivial. Sometimes the better team doesn't win, as Kordell Stewart noted after his team lost to the Patriots in the 2001–2 playoffs; luck is also involved.

7. I have defended a similar version in Dreier, 1990, 1992.

8. For example, Terry Horgan and Mark Timmons, 1996, argue against New Wave moral realism by *reductio ad relativism*.

9. Ruth Benedict and Melville Herskovitz are commonly cited as anthropologists guilty of the worst relativist fallacies. Since anthropologists do not write like philosophers, and are generally interested in somewhat different issues, it is difficult to say exactly what philosophical view real anthropologists of the mid–twentieth century held. My understanding is that their philosophical view was close to Edward Westermarck's. See Westermarck, 1932.

10. Williams later finds some coherent forms of moral relativism. See Williams, 1975, and 1985, esp. chap. 8.

11. Some of Michael Walzer's early work suggests this sort of relativism. See especially his *Spheres of Justice* for a version that tries to build plausible limits to toleration while respecting cultural autonomy. Walzer's book is probably best understood as an argument for valuing political autonomy, and not as resting on any particular conception of the nature of morality.

12. Whether moral relativism has *any* normative moral implications is a sticky question, largely because it is much murkier than it may appear exactly what it is for a theory to have normative moral implications. For one attempt to spell it out, and some suggestions about other metaethical views that may carry over to moral relativism, see Dreier, 2002.

13. There are other possibilities. One, which I will not explore in this essay, is that the Humean premise is wrong. That way lies Kantian rationalism. It says that although moral judgment is intrinsically motivational, motivation is not relative to contingent psychology but is built into rational agency. If Kantian rationalism is correct, then morality may be real, intrinsically action-guiding, and still absolute. The second possibility is expressivism, which I do not have the space to discuss in this essay.

14. Many philosophers have discussed one or another version of the disagreement argument. One version is in Moore, 1912, pp. 42–43.

REFERENCES

Brink, David. 1986. "Externalist Moral Realism." *Southern Journal of Philosophy,* supp. 24: 23–42.

Darwall, Stephen. 1997. "Reasons, Motives, and the Demands of Morality: An Introduction." In *Moral Discourse and Practice,* ed. Stephen Darwall, Allan Gibbard, and Peter Railton, 305–312. New York: Oxford University Press.

Dreier, James. 1990. "Internalism and Speaker Relativism." *Ethics* 101: 6–26.

———. 1992. "The Supervenience Argument against Moral Realism." *Southern Journal of Philosophy* 30: 13–38.

———. 2002. "Meta-Ethics and Normative Commitment." *Philosophical Issues* 12: 241–263.

Falk, W. D. 1948. " 'Ought' and Motivation." *Proceedings of the Aristotelian Society* n.s. 48 (1947–48): 111–138.

Field, Hartry. 1980. *Science without Numbers.* Oxford: Blackwell.

Foot, Philippa. 2001. *Natural Goodness.* New York: Oxford University Press.

Harman, Gilbert. 1977. *The Nature of Morality.* New York: Oxford University Press.

Horgan, Terry, and Mark Timmons. 1996. "From Moral Realism to Moral Relativism in One Easy Step." *Critica* 28: 3–39.

Kaplan, David. 1989. "Demonstratives." In *Themes from Kaplan,* ed. Joseph Almog, John Perry, and Howard Wettstein, 481–614. New York: Oxford University Press.

Mackie, J. L. 1977. *Ethics: Inventing Right and Wrong.* London: Penguin.

Moore, G. E. 1912. *Ethics.* New York: Holt.

Pojman, Louis. 1989. "A Critique of Ethical Relativism." In *Ethical Theory,*ed. Louis Pojman, 25–32. Belmont, Calif.: Wadsworth.

Smith, Michael. 1994. *The Moral Problem.* Oxford: Blackwell.

Stevenson, Charles. 1937. "The Emotive Meaning of Ethical Terms." *Mind* 46: 14–31.

Sturgeon, Nicholas. 1985. "Moral Explanations."In *Morality, Reason and Truth,* ed. David Copp and David Zimmerman, 49–78. Totowa, N.J.: Rowman and Allanheld.

Svavarsdóttir, Sigrun. 1999. "Moral Cognitivism and Motivation." *Philosophical Review,* 108: 161–219.

Westermarck, Edward. 1932. *Ethical Relativity.* London: Kegan Paul.

Williams, Bernard. 1972. *Morality: An Introduction to Ethics.* New York: Harper and Row.

———. 1975. "The Truth in Relativism." *Proceedings of the Aristotelian Society* 75: 215–228.

———. 1985. *Ethics and the Limits of Philosophy.* Cambridge, Mass.: Harvard University Press.

Wittgenstein, Ludwig. 1965. "A Lecture on Ethics." *Philosophical Review* 74: 3–12.

CHAPTER 10

HUMEAN THEORY OF PRACTICAL RATIONALITY

PETER RAILTON

THE Humean theory of practical rationality has exerted a far-reaching influence on debates in moral theory, the philosophy of mind, and the human sciences generally. It has served as the basis for critiques of *moral rationalism* (roughly, the view that moral requirements are requirements of practical reason itself) and *moral cognitivism* (the view that moral judgments can be, strictly speaking, true or false), and as part of the foundation for modern rational choice theory. Often contrasted with Aristotelian or Kantian theories of practical rationality, as in effect their main philosophical rival, the Humean theory is sometimes seen as advocating an essentially *instrumental* or *hypothetical* conception of practical reasons, the core of which is the thought that the one practical principle required of rational agents is a form of means/end rationality, and that no ends as such are rationally required, favored, or prohibited.

It is a genuine question whether modern Humean theories of practical reason are wholly faithful to the views of David Hume himself. Some interpreters claim that Hume was a thoroughgoing skeptic about practical reason, even of an instrumental kind. Others claim that Hume clearly endorsed means/end reasoning as a form of practical rationality, while others make the yet stronger claim that Hume accepted and used a substantive distinction between "reasonable" and "unreasonable" conduct—his criticisms were meant to show only that human reason, as a strictly inferential faculty, was incapable on its own of capturing this distinction, since sentiments and passions play an ineliminable role in being reasonable. I shall call the Hume-inspired instrumentalist theories that now occupy center stage in most philosophical and social-scientific discussions *neo-Humean theories of practical rationality*. They share certain remarkably clear and compelling basic principles, which I will consider before entering into vexed questions about interpreting the historical Hume. A theory of practical reason typically involves a theory of *action* and a coordinate conception of the possible role of *reason* or *reasons* in action.

1. NEO-HUMEAN THEORIES OF ACTION

According to the neo-Humean theory of action, actions are behaviors suitably caused by an intention, which is understood to involve, at a minimum, a belief-desire pair (see Davidson, 1963). For example, Anne wants to send a fax and believes that she can do it at her office. She goes to her office *intentionally*, because the trip is undertaken under this organizing idea. This idea therefore supplies her with what can be said to be a hallmark of intention, namely, a ready answer to the question "What are you doing?" (Anscombe, 1957). Since her idea of what she is doing reflects her beliefs and desires, it points to a causal-psychological *explanation* of her act. At the same time, because this explanation reveals the positive light in which she saw the action, it permits us to grasp her *rationale* in doing it. Thus the causal and normative senses of acting for a reason go hand in hand, even if one is not reducible to the other.

To be sure, the rationale thus identified need not be a good one, or one endorsed by us, in order for us to see the sense in which she is acting intentionally, or for a reason. The fax might not be worth sending, or it might have slipped Anne's mind that her office is closed today for repairs. Good and bad rationales share a distinctive form. Not every way beliefs and desires can cause an act will afford a "rationalizing explanation" of it (Davidson, 1963). Suppose that I am anxious about a meeting's outcome, and these disturbing beliefs and desires unsettle me, causing me to talk excessively and repetitively without realizing it. This excess jabber is the causal upshot of my beliefs and desires, but not therefore intentional—indeed, I have no rationale for it. (By contrast, an actor playing the role of someone in an unsettled state might intentionally improvise repetitive chatter; if questioned about his departure from the script, the actor could supply the rationale that he was attempting to represent more vividly the character's internal disturbance.) Spelling out the conditions of rationalizing causal explanation to exclude such "deviant" causal pathways between beliefs and desires on the one hand and action on the other proves difficult. Yet the link to causal explanation is an essential anchor for the theory and a source of much of its appeal in philosophy and the social sciences. By constraining the attribution of an agent's reasons for an act to causally efficacious factors figuring in an appropriate way in explanations of a certain form, it can introduce real empirical content into intentional explanation. Moreover, the causal connection plays an essential role in neo-Humean, compatibilist accounts of freedom of the will, which identify free action, roughly, as action in which one is doing what one wants to do *because* one wants to do it, without interference.

What of the normative side? What might justify calling causal factors "reasons" for an act at all, much less "good reasons," rather than mere causes? Perhaps normativity enters the scene because once an action is seen as being done under an idea, we can introduce a relevant notion of *correctness* in action. Thus, when Anne departs for the office with the idea of sending a fax, but forgetting that her office is closed for the day, this act will not succeed in realizing this governing idea, owing to a failure of fit between her conception of what she's doing and what she can and will actually do. We might thus say that her act was a *mistake*, and certainly she is likely to do so as well. But in what sense?

The neo-Humean will note that her act was based in part upon a belief that was mistaken, and that, by extension, the act itself was a mistake on her part. But this extended sense of "mistake" is not equivalent to the sense in which the belief itself is incorrect. Beliefs are false whenever the representation they contain is false. But actions are a form of organized activity that does not possess orthodox truth conditions as such. Similarly, according to the neo-Humean, Anne's *desire* to go to her office today might involve or depend upon various beliefs, but desires as such are not strictly true or false. Notions of "incorrectness" are applied only derivatively to desires, goals, and actions. Thus, a "mistaken desire" is understood by the neo-Humean to be a desire based upon ignorance, false beliefs, or erroneous inference. The corresponding idea of "correctness" or "rationality" in desire might be something like: what one would want (or want oneself to do or seek) if one were well informed and reasoning validly (Brandt, 1971).

The neo-Humean account draws upon a plausible division of mental states. Beliefs are *cognitive* states, representational in their primary function. With this "mind-to-world direction of fit," they straightforwardly inherit the truth conditions of the representations they take as their objects. Their relation, if any, to will or motivation is psychological and subject-dependent rather than logical or necessary. Desires, by contrast, are *conative* states, functioning primarily to supply motivation to bring the world into accord with their constituent representation. For example, my desire to be drinking a glass of water is not made false by the fact that I am not, in fact, drinking water. On the contrary, this fact, plus my thirst, might make that desire eminently appropriate. Thus desires are said to have a "world-to-mind direction of fit"—they move us to bring the world into accord with their constituent representation (Humberstone, 1992; Smith, 1994).

2. NEO-HUMEAN THEORIES OF PRACTICAL REASON

This "belief/desire asymmetry" helps explain not only their complementary roles in causing and explaining action, it also fits with a compact and compelling explanation of the *is/ought* distinction and related fact/value distinction. Beliefs concern what *is* the case according to the agent; their satisfaction conditions are met when agents get the facts right. Belief "aims at truth," and thus notions of truth and objectivity, and norms of evidence and propositional logic, apply to belief and to reasoning concerning belief, *theoretical reason*, by its very nature. Desires and values, by contrast, concern what *is to be* or *ought to be* the case according to agent; they "aim the agent toward an end," namely, the desired object or valued state. They have action-guiding force on behalf of what they represent, not simple credence in it. They therefore lack straightforward truth conditions, and one cannot straightforwardly apply the same notions of objectivity, or norms of logic and evidence, to desire and to reasoning that concludes in action, *practical reason*. No wonder questions about "What to do?" cannot be answered by the same scientific methods as "What to believe?" This corresponds to the common-sense view that beliefs and factual judgments are "objective" and subject to authoritative expertise or methods, while desires and value judgments are "subjective" and liable to unresolved ultimate conflict, a point that has been used to support noncognitivism about value judgments (see Ayer, 1936).

Theoretical reasoning does have a role in practical reason. For example, it permits the agent to reach conclusions about cause-and-effect relations that could reveal certain acts to be effective means to the agent's ends, or reveal empirical features of possible ends. But a further form of reasoning, instrumental or means/ends reasoning, is needed in order to put theoretical conclusions into practice: an agent who has a desire to E and believes that A-ing will help bring about E is therefore said to have a reason to A, other things equal. Since the end E is supplied by the agent's desire rather than by reason itself, this is also often called a *hypothetical* conception of practical reasoning, in contrast to the *categorical* conceptions found among rationalists, according to which some acts or ends are required independently of any antecedent motivation.

This way of contrasting of hypothetical and categorical conceptions of rationality is, however, misleading. According to an instrumentalist, agents are rational (roughly) to the extent that they take the means appropriate to their ends, relative to what they believe. *This* claim is categorical rather than hypothetical—it does not depend upon the agent possessing any antecedent higher-order desire "to take the means appropriate to ends." Indeed, if this sort of desire were required, a regress would arise: after all, one would need an antecedent desire to act upon one's higher-order desire in turn, and so on (see Dreier, 1997; Railton, 1997). Thus the issue is not whether instrumentalists can accommodate categorical rational requirements but rather what is, on their view, categorically required for practical rationality (Korsgaard, 1986).

Practical reasoning can be judged in terms of norms of *efficiency*: Does the agent arrive at an intention to act in a way that tends to realize her ends as much, or more, than available alternatives? A practically rational agent looks to balance or prioritize the strengths of her desires or ends, to consider outcomes in terms of their probability, and to choose causally effective means. The beliefs and estimates of relative strength of desire or probability of outcomes upon which the agent draws can be criticized as mistaken or irrational, as can her use of logical or instrumental reasoning, but her intrinsic desires or ultimate ends and their relative strengths are simply taken as they might be, or would be with more information.

A great advantage of this neo-Humean picture of practical reason is that fits so well into modern *rational choice theory* and *rational decision theory* in their orthodox forms. These theories afford our most systematic and well-developed account of how considerations bear on decisions. They permit the balancing of diverse ends and multiple sources of information, envisaging an agent facing a choice to be equipped with a set of desires or values (*utilities* or *preferences* concerning possible outcomes) and a set of beliefs (*subjective probabilities* or *expectancies*) concerning the facts. In the orthodox version, the rational choice for the agent—whether the agent is an individual or an organized group—is the one that *maximizes expected utility* (the product of utility and probability) or *moves the agent to a point in her preference ordering at least as high as any alternative* (see Kaplan, 1996; Luce and Raiffa, 1957).

These are "rational" choices in the sense that alternatives would in a relatively clear sense be less promising, by the agent's own lights, to promote the constellation of ends she seeks, and so seem needlessly costly or self-defeating according to a rationale she herself could understand. Note that there is nothing essentially egoistic or hedonistic about this conception of utility, preference, and choice. An agent can most prefer impersonal or self-denying goals. The notion of 'self-defeat' at work here has to do with failure to meet one's own goals, whatever their content.

This "Hume-Ramsey" theory of rational choice can also be used in empirical inquiry. An assumption of rationality in something like the Hume-Ramsey sense enables us to infer an agent's beliefs and desires from his choices and actions. Such choices are said to "reveal" preferences and subjective credences, a technique often used in so-called benefit-cost analysis or risk assessment. Although it has many complexities and many forms, and raises issues about how well human conduct actually approximates the theory or which standards of choice are most appropriate, the Hume-Ramsey theory is the backbone of a great deal of reasoning in economics, cognitive psychology, and public policy, both theoretical and experimental.

The neo-Humean theory is sometimes called *internalist* with regard to reasons for action, because it treats some sort of motivation on the part of the agent, such as desire, as a necessary component of intentional action, while also treating desire as a genuinely motivational psychological state. Thus, in order to say that an agent *has a reason* to perform act *A*, we must show that some or other motivation for doing *A* could be found or mobilized *within* the agent's actual or potential motivational repertoire by a suitable means—information, instrumental deliberation, experience, and so on (Williams, 1981). This affords a relatively transparent way of explaining how this reason could support a *practical* 'ought', or reasoning that can conclude in action.

At the same time, the neo-Humean theory is typically said to be *externalist* with regard to morality, and this has long been a source of criticism. An agent will have a practical reason to be moral, according to the neo-Humean, only if some suitable motivation, such as desire, is available to support it. To say that neo-Humean agents by their nature have a reason to be moral, then, would require showing that anyone meeting even the minimum conditions of this account of practical rationality—however his actual motivational repertoire might vary, and so long as his beliefs and ends are subject to relatively minimal norms and conditions of coherence—must have some intrinsic desire-based motive to be moral (see Smith, 1994). Otherwise, it would be from the standpoint of rationality a contingent matter whether a given agent has a reason to be moral, and there could in principle exist fully rational agents to whom morality could not be practically justified without supplying some incentive external to it. Clearly, we can threaten a person with punishment or sanction were she not to behave according to moral norms, but this would merely be instrumental motivation, based on the agent's intrinsic aversion to pain rather than to immorality as such. Since it is difficult to show that anyone capable of instrumental efficiency in action would *necessarily* possess a motivational repertoire capable of morally appropriate motivation, the neo-Humean often claims—or is criticized for being committed to—a kind of *skepticism* with respect to the "rational authority" of morality. It would be a serious liability of neo-Humeanism if it required outright skepticism about morality, for example, if the standing of morality presupposed a notion of "rational authority" incompatible with neo-Humean views about motivation. However, a neo-Humean can argue that motivational externalism is compatible with the existence of good reasons to be moral. As in epistemology, logic, and aesthetics, one can say that good, justifying reasons exist for judgments or actions that mere rationality does not suffice to make us responsive to—other capacities are required.

3. SOME CRITICISMS

Though admirably clear, several difficulties confront the neo-Humean approach. First, while many find it obvious that no goals are inherently irrational, others find this deeply bizarre. Some desires strike us as pointless or crazy (Gibbard, 1990; Parfit, 1984). A person who vows at age fifteen in a fit of anger about being teased by friends "never to speak to anyone ever again," and who then spends the balance of his long life holding himself to this vow out of an unrelenting desire to hold to his vow to spite his friends—such a person strikes most of us as irrational, however amazingly efficient he is at realizing this goal. While very few would dispute that a capacity for means/end reasoning and goal-realization are part of practical rationality, the distinctive neo-Humean claim has been that this capacity is the very essence of it.

A second class of problems for the neo-Humean theory concerns questions of rational action in situations where coordination among agents is possible, and that place certain goals within the reach of agents only if they can act in coordinated or cooperative ways that they cannot individually bring about. After all, many of the most important goals and projects of life involve acting effectively with others—even such basic tasks as learning language and using it communicatively. Yet individually optimal expected-value calculations can lead to failures to initiate or sustain cooperation even among nonmalicious agents (e.g., in the problems in the form of prisoners' dilemmas; see Regan, 1980, for discussion). This can lead to an individual's own goals being less well realized in the end than they could otherwise be, by placing outcomes that depend upon cooperation or coordination out of her reach. There appears, then, to be a *global* instrumentalist argument for being disposed to cooperate and to limit one's case-by-case instrumentalist reasoning. The difficulty is that this therefore cannot be the upshot of case-by-case instrumentalist reasoning alone.

A special instance of the problem of coordination arises within the agent over time. If intentions to act are, or involve, belief-desire pairs playing a certain causal role, then they will change as beliefs and desires change in their content or force—whatever the origin of this alteration. How then can a neo-Humean agent make a commitment to himself or to others to act in a certain way or hold to a certain agreement? If we say that commitment is just one more desire, then as that desire changes, commitment will come and go. This makes neo-Humeans look unreliable as partners, and incapable even of effective long-term planning for their own purposes. But many of the most important goals and relationships we have depend upon a capacity to make such commitments, and to hold ourselves to them even when we'd prefer not to. The "bare bones" belief-desire account may have to be supplemented to include something that can play the role of commitment or resolve if certain important goods are to remain within the effective range of practical reason (Bratman, 1999).

The problem of self-coordination over time, like the problem of interpersonal coordination among agents, could furnish grounds for a wider conception of what instrumental rationality really involves. After all, if the key idea of instrumentalism is that rationality is a general-purpose ability to identify and follow appropriate means to ends, then full instrumental rationality would itself involve the capacities needed to coordinate and cooperate, to form and follow plans, and so on. The fault might lie less with the idea that rationality is instrumental than with the overly simple ways in which the "instrumental principle" has usually been conceived.

Such an enrichment of instrumental rationality need not be antithetical to neo-Humeanism. I have already shown that the neo-Humean cannot defend his position as "purely hypothetical," and therefore innocent of any categorical notion of practical reasons. An agent who has desire D and who believes that the only way to realize D is to perform act A is said to have a hypothetical reason to A, other things equal. But what if the agent recognizes this, and finds himself with no motivation to A, or even a strong intrinsic aversion to A-ing (say, to accept a horribly painful shot to prevent rabies)? Having a motivation is a psychological matter, and nothing about desiring an end seems to guarantee psychologically that one will also desire the means that turn out to be necessary to it. A defender of the hypothetical conception might reply: "But no one can be said to have a desire D unless he is, or is disposed to be, motivated to take the means necessary to it." But then the view will have been saved at the expense of making it impossible to violate. Norms require the possibility of violation as well as adherence. To be true to his theory, an instrumentalist must reply: "This person is simply irrational. Rational people are motivated to take necessary means to their ends, independently of whatever else they might contingently desire." But this categorical principle seems to many philosophers simply false: merely having an end (a psychological state) cannot suffice—analytically or metaphysically—to give an agent a reason to act, or to make the act in any sense normatively correct. A person who wants to create mass panic might reason (accurately, let us suppose) that the best available means to this end is to release poison gas in an urban subway system; but it might sensibly be questioned whether she (or anyone) has any good reason at all to do this, or that his act will count as well aimed or well done if it succeeds (Hare, 1971). Similarly, if this person chooses an inappropriate means to his end, we can say that this is an error in the execution of his aim, but such a judgment has "narrow scope" for normative purposes. In contrast to the case of belief, where we credit someone with "wide scope" correctness in belief—having "gotten it right"—even if he who arrives at the truth on the basis of evidence we cannot see as offering a good epistemic reasons (say, the interpretation of Tarot cards), we need not credit someone with "wide scope" correctness in action who successfully executes an act that we cannot see as based on good practical reasons. We may see the well-executed act as a mistake.

The neo-Humean can argue in response to such criticisms that the very possibility of practical rationality requires that individuals be able to attribute some degree of *default* authority to the ends they happen have. Suppose it were otherwise, and one could not take any goal as a reason for action without first certifying that it is genuinely desirable. We cannot desire at will, and we can assess claims on behalf of desirability only from where we now are. How might one arrive at judgments of desirability, or reflect critically on a claim that a certain end is intrinsically desirable, if one cannot make any use of one's existing desires and motivational repertoire as starting points? *Ought* implies *can*, and it must be allowed that any process or desire formation, criticism, and revision will involve a role for bare facts about "what matters" to us as we actually are.

Third, though beliefs and desires are plainly different in many respects, can the neo-Humean version of the belief-desire asymmetry—and associated fact/value distinction—be defended? Many of the arguments neo-Humeans offer on behalf of the idea that desire cannot be based upon reason could be applied with equal force to belief. Beliefs are not bare propositions but attitudes that play an elaborate functional role in the human system of expectation and action. They are not "bare" or "inert" representations, and their functional nature involves faculties other than the merely cognitive. Nor are they merely "aimed at truth"— the most effective way to assure truth in one's beliefs would presumably be to restrict oneself to tautologies. Believers need to have multidimensional norms permitting tradeoffs between content and evidence, explanatoriness and reliability, particularity and generality, relevance and alternatives. No one set of such norms seems rationally required. It is unclear in epistemology, as well as ethics, how to resolve fundamental differences between individuals concerning which claims or rules of inference are "self-evident" or basic. Attempts to defend such a position would seem to need principles of evidence and logical validity, thus begging the question. Thus, neither belief nor desire seems to be based on the faculty of reason alone.

Much more can be said on behalf of the neo-Humean account of practical reason. But any such defense must provide justification not only for attributing some default and defeasible normative force to instrumental reasons, which seems very plausible, but also that the instrumental principle suffices for practical rationality, which is much more questionable.

4. HUME'S THEORY OF ACTION

The position set forth by the young Hume in the *Treatise of Human Nature* was re-presented more eloquently but perhaps less sharply—or perhaps, according to another view, significantly modified—in later works. What we might call his theory of human action (though it appears to apply to a wider domain of human and even animal behavior than contemporary theories of "action for a reason") presents itself as based upon an analysis of psychological faculties: reasoning, imagination, sensation, memory, motivation, and passion. These faculties are linked together causally, via functional and structural relations, some of which are "initial," others acquired through association and habit. Belief gives to an *idea*—a mental representation or "copy"—the same force upon feeling and action that sensation gives to the impressions of experience. It is a "firm conception" of a representation that gives rise to corresponding expectations (projects or "spreads" the mind), something "*felt* by the mind" that gives ideas "more force and influence; infixes them in the mind; and renders them the governing principles of all our actions" (*Treatise*, app.). This "infixed" disposition to rely upon an idea in thought and action can be strengthened noninferentially by "vivid impressions" (current experience), "custom" (frequency of past conjunctions in experience), and "association" (e.g., by resemblance among ideas) (for a recent defense of a dispositional account of belief in Hume, see Loeb, 2002; see also Owen, 1999). Deductive and causal reasoning (inferences among ideas) are based upon these immediate thought transitions, rather than the other way around. This is a "bottom up" conception, according to which we account for the possibility of inference by steps not themselves requiring the mediation of further judgment involving an inferential principle (*Treatise*, I.iii.7).

Desires involve affect ("immediate agreeableness" and "disagreeableness") and motive, though they are not necessarily egoistic or hedonistic. The vengeful person likes the idea of hurting another and wants to do this, even to his own loss; the loving parent likes the idea of helping his children without requiring reference to his own well-being; and all of us can experience some measure of "sympathy" for others, which makes us experience their feelings immediately in ourselves, by a kind of emotional resonance, and be moved to respond accordingly (*Treatise*, II.1.11). Thus, "the minds of men are mirrors to one another" (*Treatise*, II.ii.5), and problems of coordination and cooperation with others, and with oneself over time, depend for their resolution on such sympathy—humans are "fitted for" society, and "can form no wish, which has not a reference to society" (*Treatise*, II.ii.5).

The link between belief, desire, and action, then, is a natural consequence of the functional tendencies already present in belief and desire, as situated in a human psyche. Here, too, we find a "bottom up" picture. A great deal of intentional action involves no act of deliberate judgment. As I write sentences, speak with a friend, or walk through familiar buildings or streets, my activity is constantly intentional but seldom involves a distinctive judgment or reflection. Activity can be guided by an idea or representation without further judgment when belief and desire—both, for Hume, action-guiding states of mind—share an object, so that action can result from a state of "understanding and passion" without the intermediation of a distinctive faculty of self-willing. Hume's theory of action is thus of a piece with his overall account of mind and the self, which sought systematically to avoid positing a "self-within-the-self."

By contrast, an account of action that requires an "act of the will" on the part of the agent in order to forge together the components of action into an intention seems to posit an inner self acting intentionally as a precondition for intentional action. For either the process of forming of a will is itself an action, or it is a "merely natural sequence" that results causally from the agent's current thoughts, aims, and expectations. If it is the former, then a regress is launched; if it is the latter, then the theory already concedes that intentional action can arise "naturally," without a prior act of will to set it in motion. Hume in effect offered an account of intentional action that shows how behavior can be guided "under an idea," but that avoids displacing the problem of action onto an inner agent. Agency can belong to the active states of belief and desire, and decision and deliberation can be the result of processes that are not themselves decisions or deliberations. "Unless nature had given some original qualities to the mind, it cou'd never have any secondary ones; because it wou'd have no foundation for any action, nor cou'd it ever begin to exert itself," Hume argued (*Treatise*, II.i.3). What, then, does this theory say about the nature of practical reason?

5. HUME'S THEORY OF PRACTICAL REASON

The *Treatise* ringingly concludes that since evaluative attitudes are "original existences" rather than "copies" or representations that could be strictly speaking true or false, and since reason is concerned with matters of truth or falsity, it follows that morality cannot be based on reason alone. Hume writes, infamously, that " '[t]is not contrary to reason to prefer the destruction of the whole world to scratching of my finger" (*Treatise*, II.iii.3). Indeed, even prudence cannot be based on reason alone: " 'Tis as little contrary to reason to prefer even my own acknowledged lesser good to my greater" (*Treatise*, II.iii.3). And in a perfectly general way, Hume argues that the transition from the descriptive language of *is*—the domain of truth and falsity, strictly speaking—to the normative language of *ought* is not an inference that could issue from reason alone (*Treatise*, III.i.1).

This is not, however, because belief belongs to the cognitive side of our faculties, while desire belongs on the side of feelings. For in part I of the *Treatise*, Hume has concluded that *"belief is more properly an act of the sensitive, than of the cogitative part of our natures"* (*Treatise*, I.iv.1). This is so even in the case of beliefs of the kind found in mathematics or empirical, causal science. Thus *"belief is nothing but a peculiar feeling, different from the simple conception"* (*Treatise*, app.). The historical Hume thus seems not to accept the form of belief-desire asymmetry central to neo-Humeanism. For reasons touched on earlier (namely, that a state of belief is not a mere idea but a "manner of conceiving" an idea, an attitude toward a representation, which gives it a certain role in the individual's thought and action), this might be a point in his favor. Moreover, it places his view closer to the contemporary psychology of belief than the neo-Humean position. Even the much-aligned "association of ideas" that underlies Hume's account of inference and reasoning, and of the *"apropos* of discourse," has come in for new life in contemporary neuroscience, as connectionist or network models of the brain have gained strength against more classically computational models. Moreover, cognitive psychology, evolutionary psychology, and neuroscience are giving increasing emphasis to the role of feeling in cognition (Damasio, 1994). Prominent in these accounts are the roles of default trust and empathy, akin to Humean ideas of belief and sympathy (see Axelrod, 1984; Baron-Cohen, 1995).

For philosophers, however, Hume's thoroughgoing recourse to feeling and association to explain the nature and operation of belief and desire immediately raise the question whether the upshot is skepticism about theoretical and practical reason alike. Some would say so, that Hume has replaced normative principles with mere psychological regularities (Korsgaard, 1997). However, Hume could say on his behalf that even the most elevated rationalist theories must, if they are to be relevant to human thought and action, show how actual states of the human mind could realize the a priori psychology they presuppose. Positing inner states that lead to regress or that could not in principle be realized by "mere causal processes" would only be to exclude any actual human psyche from ever attaining them. Hume's account, by contrast, could, if successful, permit a belief-desire psychology to explain how our actual states of mind could deserve the name of reasons or reasoning. Hume's theory (and the brief description offered here is but one possible interpretation of complex and difficult body of work) is designed precisely to provide a psychological infrastructure that could support human de-liberative and rational capacities without presupposing the operation of these ca-pacities as preconditions for its own existence. Even the hard-core rationalist might find a use for Hume's account, since philosophers almost universally hold it to be an a priori principle that normative attribution supervenes upon non-normative facts, and Hume's account would afford a way of seeing how this could be so.

The *Treatise* itself appears to conclude that our substantive ways of forming belief and acting are in fact largely "reasonable." In any event, Hume takes them to be nonoptional. "I may, nay I must yield to the current of nature, in submitting to my senses and understanding" (*Treatise*, I.iv.7). Human belief and action, even human reasoning and judgment themselves, presuppose substantive, initial psy-chological dispositions to trust one's perceptions, memories, motives, and asso-ciations of ideas. These dispositions, he argues, could never be arrived at or jus-tified by reasoning or understanding alone, since any such process of thought must use them itself. A thoroughgoing rationalism would simply be its own un-doing, either via circularity or regress (*Treatise*, I.iv.7).

However, a thoroughgoing skepticism would be equally self-betraying in a different way. If the skeptic claims that we are unreasonable not to accept her skeptical conclusions, because she has made an argument to which we have no adequate counterargument, she unwittingly shows her own unskeptical acceptance of logic and reason. The skeptic faces an awkward choice: either acknowledge logical principles as normative for thought, and thereby abandon thoroughgoing skepticism, or deny logical principles this status, but be unable to offer any reason or argument on behalf of this sweeping claim.

The result for Hume is neither pure skepticism nor its refutation, but a "scep-tical solution" that is a mixture of an initial, default trust or nonskepticism toward ordinary experience and belief-formation, while recognizing that one can offer no self-standing reason for this. This mixed view is the only stable position of the mind in the world. He recommends: "In all the incidents of life we ought still to preserve our scepticism," though "[w]here reason is lively, and mixes itself with some propensity, it ought to be assented to" (*Treatise*, I.iv.7). As I noted earlier in discussing instumentalism, a similar doctrine applies in the case of desires—attributing to desires a default normative authority is to be mixed with a recog-nition that this is no proof of their aptness, only an acknowledgement of their indispensability if apt action is ever to be undertaken at all.

Hume thus seems to have had as his primary target not the very idea of giving a normative theory of how to conduct ourselves in thought and action, but rationalist versions of such theories and the disingenuous forms of skepticism they feed into. In general, when Hume uses the term 'reason' for a human faculty, he has in mind something much narrower than our overall ability to be responsive to reasons. He means to pick out *reasoning*—"demonstrative and probable reasonings" (*Treatise*, I.iii.9). We find an echo of Hume's view in the modern Bayesian position that all reasoning, deductive as well as inductive, calls for "priors"—degrees of subjective credence in principles and hypotheses that one relies upon initially without question, and that cannot, without circularity or regress, be justified by argument *ab initio*. The question of rationality in belief and action is not "How to start from scratch?" but "Where to go from here?" And where to begin the dynamic process of belief revision, other than with what we now find credible? Or the dynamic process of desire revision, other than with what we now find desirable?

6. SOME CRITICISMS

Hume's theory thus allows substantive elements of "reasonableness" and substantive capacities to be responsive to reasons into his account of belief and action without requiring an a priori justification. Such elements can continue to earn our allegiance in the long run by vindicating (though not *validating*) themselves over the course of experience, stabilizing themselves in our mental economy rather than destabilizing or undermining themselves. In this, Hume's theory may come closer to fitting common-sense notions of what is rational or reasonable. This process resembles a kind of dynamic reflective equilibrium, and allows for a good deal of revision as experience grows. But it provides no a priori guarantee that the revisions are *improvements*, or that the end result is correct and free of arbitrary contingencies. We could be caught in a self-reinforcing circle of mutually compensating error.

Hume must concede to the skeptic that we cannot close the question whether *any* of our currently accepted beliefs, desires, or principles is truly valid. Even principles of logic cannot be defended in a purely a priori manner. Moreover, Hume's reliance upon a posteriori stability runs its own risk of being circular, and without normative force. Lacking recourse to a priori justification, and without awareness of Darwinian theory or the possibilities of evolutionary epistemology that have been explored in recent philosophy, Hume is left in the first *Enquiry* to marvel at what remains for him a "kind of pre-established harmony between the course of nature and the succession of our ideas" (*Enquiry Concerning Human Understanding*, V.ii). Many find this position manifestly inadequate, even *faut de mieux*.

A second broad area of dissatisfaction with Hume's view is that the "reasonableness" of morality becomes a contingent *practical* question rather than a question that can be settled a priori. Since reason alone cannot either require or explain moral motivation, humans can be expected to be moral only to the extent that they reliably possess and act on certain desires. For Hume, we are equipped by nature with natural sentiments of self-concern over time, generosity toward those close to us, and sympathy, which can be extended to anyone. Overall, he thinks the balance in us as individuals often favors other-oriented feeling over self-oriented feeling. These natural sentiments can be mobilized as well on behalf of acquiring new motives for rules or conventions that can regulate public life in accord with principles of justice and "artificial" virtue, the benefits of which for general well-being we can recognize and will tend to approve. These natural and acquired mechanisms are by and large reliable enough to make sociability, co-operativeness, civility, and morality widespread human phenomena, and part of a happy human life. The immoral or amoral individual suffers less from a defect of reason as such than from alienation from normal human sociability or relat-edness, which can infect him from within even if he is socially successful in other ways. We do not envy the "sensible knave" his life (*Enquiry Concerning the Principles of Morals*, IX.ii).

Hume saw this account of the role of sentiments and passions as components of moral conduct and public justice as having an important explanatory advantage over rationalist and more narrowly "moral sense" theories. Feelings, motives, and beliefs that are not inherently moral can be redeployed on behalf of morality, accounting for its capacity to appeal and motivate, on the one hand, and, on the other, for the possibility that moral or just conduct can compete with other genuine advantages or appeals in ways that correctness in reasoning alone cannot resolve. Hume's account thus dispenses with special-purpose motivational or cog-nitive faculties, and helps us see how morality could be attainable by those with normal human psychologies.

However, since the force of morality, according to Hume, depends upon sentiment and desire, and not on reason alone, it looks as if lack of moral mo-tivation would not be a *rational* defect. What then becomes of ideas of obligation or duty, which are supposed to bind agents *categorically* even in the absence of favorable motivation or feeling? To some extent, Hume could respond by pointing out that even Kant required that we posit in human empirical psychology certain desires not themselves derivable from reasoning alone, the so-called moral feeling, without which humans would experience no subjective force of duty (*Metaphysics of Morals*, 6.399–400). The idea, shared by Hume and Kant, that human moral conduct depends empirically upon the presence of appropriate desires, is not equivalent to the idea that the moral principles to which the agent conforms are hypothetical or conditional in form. A principle that makes no reference to our personal motives or ends can engage us, on Hume's and Kant's accounts, since non-self-interested motivation, such as that based subjectively upon generalized or direct sympathy or the "moral feeling," respectively, permits empirical moti-vation of an impartial sort.

Still, for Hume, facts about what motivating reasons we have will always depend upon contingent facts about what we, our world, and our relation to it, happen to be like. No particular set of desires is a condition on rationality. Perhaps that is as it should be—we should never have expected otherwise. But all this comes as a disappointment to some of the loftiest aspirations of philosophy.

NOTE

I thank the editor for his insightful comments and patience. Thanks, too, to my colleague Louis Loeb for discussions of belief in Hume.

REFERENCES

Anscombe, G.E.M. 1957. *Intention.* Oxford: Blackwell.

Axelrod, Robert. 1984. *The Evolution of Cooperation.* New York: Basic Books.

Ayer, A. J. 1936. *Language, Truth, and Logic.* London: Gollancz.

Baron-Cohen, Simon. 1995. *Mindblindness: An Essay on Autism and the Theory of Mind.* Cambridge, Mass.: MIT Press.

Brandt, Richard. 1971. *A Theory of the Good and the Right.* Oxford: Oxford University Press.

Bratman, Michael. 1999. *Faces of Intention.* Cambridge: Cambridge University Press.

Cullity, Garrett, and Gaut, Berys, eds. 1997. *Ethics and Practical Reason.* Oxford: Oxford University Press.

Damasio, Antonio R. 1994. *Descartes' Error: Emotion, Reason, and the Human Brain.* New York: Putnam.

Davidson, Donald. 1963. "Actions, Reasons, and Causes." In *Essays on Actions and Events.* Oxford: Oxford University Press.

Dreier, Jamie. 1997. "Humean Doubts about the Practical Justification of Morality." In Cullity and Gaut, 1997, 81–99.

Gibbard, Allan. 1990. *Wise Choices, Apt Feelings: A Theory of Normative Judgment.* Cambridge, Mass.: Harvard University Press.

Hare, R. M. 1971. "Wanting: Some Pitfalls." In *Agent, Action, and Reason*, ed. Robert Binkley, Richard Bronaugh, and Ausonio Marras, 81–127. Toronto: University of Toronto Press.

Humberstone, Lloyd. 1992. "Direction of Fit." *Mind* 101: 59–83.

Hume, David. 1888. *Treatise of Human Nature.* Ed. L. A. Selby-Bigge. Oxford: Oxford University Press.

———. 1975. *Enquiries Concerning Human Understanding and Concerning thePrinciples of Morals.* Ed. P. H. Nidditch. Oxford: Clarendon.

Kant, Immanuel. 1996. *The Metaphysics of Morals.* Trans. Mary Gregor. Cambridge: Cambridge University Press.

Kaplan, Mark. 1996. *Decision Theory as Philosophy.* Cambridge: Cambridge University Press.

Korsgaard, Christine M. 1986. "Skepticism about Practical Reason." *Journal of Philosophy* 83: 5–25.

———. 1997. "The Normativity of Instrumental Reason." In Cullity and Gaut, 1997, 215–254.

Loeb, Louis E. 2002. *Stability and Justification in Hume's "Treatise."* Oxford: Oxford University Press.

Luce, Duncan R., and Raiffa, Howard. 1957. *Games and Decisions: Introduction and Critical Survey.* New York: Wiley.

Owen, David. 1999. *Hume's Reason.* Oxford: Oxford University Press.

Parfit, Derek. 1984. *Reasons and Persons.* Oxford: Oxford University Press.

Railton, Peter. 1997. "On the Hypothetical and Non-Hypothetical in Reasoning about Thought and Action." In Cullity and Gaut, 1997, 53–79.

Regan, Donald. 1980. *Utilitarianism and Cooperation.* Oxford: Oxford University Press.

Smith, Michael. 1994. *The Moral Problem.* Oxford: Blackwell.

Williams, Bernard. 1981. "Internal and External Reasons." In *Moral Luck,* 101–113. Cambridge: Cambridge University Press.

CHAPTER 11

MORALITY AND PRACTICAL REASON: A KANTIAN APPROACH

STEPHEN DARWALL

A central claim of the Kantian approach to ethics is Kant's famous thesis that moral obligations or oughts are "categorical imperatives." This *Kantian thesis* has four aspects: *normativity, universality, supremacy,* and *necessity. Normativity* says that if an act is morally wrong, then there is some genuinely normative reason not to do it. *Universality* stresses that this holds universally, for every agent and every situation. *Supremacy* says further that the reasons against wrongdoing are invariably conclusive, that they always override or defeat any reasons to the contrary. And *necessity* asserts that these three aspects all hold, not thanks to some contingent feature that moral agents might have or lack, but necessarily.

To be sure, it must be a necessary truth that, if an act violates norms we identify as moral, then there will be conclusive "moral reasons" against so acting, that is, *reasons from the perspective of these norms.* But this trivial proposition is not itself normative. It is possible to accept it but to deny (as Nietzsche did) that deliberation need take any account of "moral reasons" at all. The Kantian thesis, by contrast, is a normative thesis of considerable strength. It claims that there are always genuine normative reasons not to violate moral obligations, that these are invariably supreme, and that this all holds necessarily.

Kant himself made much of the fact that these ideas have a firm foothold in moral common sense and experience. Only rarely do people take a purely external perspective on morality, violating what they acknowledge to be moral obligations with equanimity (Kant, 1996a, p. 424). More usually, we fashion some self-justifying or self-excusing narrative for ourselves ("everybody does it") or find ourselves subject to feelings, such as guilt, that take a form of the Kantian thesis, self-addressed: "I really shouldn't have done that."

Nevertheless, even if we were all to agree that moral oughts are categorical imperatives in each of these four aspects, it wouldn't follow that they really are, not even in any aspect. Moral common sense is not self-vindicating. Though we accept moral norms, we can still ask whether we should accept them.

Whether moral imperatives are categorical or not is one of the most fundamental questions of moral philosophy. But there are actually two different issues here: one conceptual or analytical, and the other genuinely normative. The conceptual question is whether moral imperatives *purport* to be categorical in any or all of the aspects I have mentioned. We can ask, for example, whether moral oughts purport to be genuinely normative, such that, if it turns out that there is in fact no valid normative reason not to do what is morally wrong (just because it is wrong), the claim that there are things one morally ought not do will be false, invalid, or unsupported (normativity). And we can ask similarly whether moral oughts purport to be normative for all agents in all cases (universality), whether they purport invariably to provide conclusive reasons (supremacy), and whether they purport to give such reasons necessarily, or just thanks to contingent features of human agents and their normal context (necessity).[1]

Suppose, however, that the answer to all these conceptual questions is yes. Suppose, that is, that as a conceptual matter, moral oughts purport to be categorical in all four aspects. From this it would not follow that there actually exist any categorical moral oughts in any aspect. Even if genuine moral oughts would provide, even necessarily, valid normative reasons that are conclusive for all agents in all situations, it might be that no putative moral ought actually provides these reasons ever, for anyone in any situation. Or maybe they provide them, but only for some individuals in some situations. Or perhaps for all, but without being invariably conclusive. Or perhaps they are always conclusive, say, for human agents, but only thanks to some contingent human characteristic, such as the capacity for human sympathy, that a moral agent might conceivably lack. All that would follow from answering yes to all these analytical, conceptual questions is that there are oughts with these four aspects *if there are any valid moral oughts at all*. A skeptic who denies that we have conclusive, or even any, reason to do what people identify as morally wrong, could accept these conceptual claims of categorical purport and deny that there are any valid moral oughts, that is, that what anyone says (or could say) is morally wrong, is really wrong. He could, of course, admit that there are things that are "wrong," that is, from the perspective of "moral" norms. But he would deny that these norms really bind us as they purport to.

Kant argued both that moral oughts purport to be categorical imperatives in all four aspects and that they actually are. He thought that it is part of the very idea of moral duty that it purports to provide conclusive reason for acting necessarily to any agent. And he thought there actually are moral duties that invariably and necessarily provide such conclusive reasons. At the same time, Kant recognized that the latter normative thesis does not follow from the former conceptual one. Indeed, the very structure of his *Groundwork of the Metaphysics of Morals* is informed by this recognition. Kant tells us that the *Groundwork's* first two chapters "proceed analytically," "explicating the generally received concept of morality" to show that the "Categorical Imperative" (CI) and "autonomy of the will . . . li[e] at its [morality's] basis" (Kant, 1996a, pp. 392, 445).[2] Kant formulates the CI variously, most famously in terms of not acting on a principle we could not will all to act on and respecting human dignity, or, as he also says, treating "humanity" or "rational nature" always as an "end" and never as a "means only." And "autonomy," for Kant, is "the property of the will by which it is a law to itself independently of any property of the objects of volition" (5.4, p. 440). Thus in *Groundwork* I and II, Kant argues that the very idea of moral duty entails that the will is bound by a law, the CI, which is at once the fundamental principle of morality (and so the source of all moral duties) and *the will's own law*. It follows that moral duties purport to bind a will *as such*, independently of any contingent features. So moral oughts purport to bind all wills necessarily.

Kant concludes at the end of chapter II, therefore, that "whoever holds morality to be something and not a chimerical idea without any truth must also admit the principle of morality brought forward [the CI]" (Kant, 1996a, p. 445). Nevertheless, he notes that for all that conceptual analysis can reveal, morality might be a mere "phantom of the brain"[3] (p. 425). The most that reflection on morality and its central ideas can establish is that moral oughts *purport* to be categorical imperatives deriving from the CI. It cannot support the Kantian Thesis as a normative claim in *any* aspect, much less, in all. To establish that, Kant says, we need a "critique" of "pure practical reason" (1996b, p. 445), which Kant undertakes, first, in *Groundwork* III and later in *The Critique of Practical Reason*.

In what follows, I shall present what I take to be the strongest case for the Kantian thesis: the analytical or conceptual interpretation in section 1, and the normative interpretation in section 2. Many of the materials for this case are provided by Kant's own arguments. Nonetheless, I believe that these can, and must, be supplemented to be maximally convincing. The key to doing so, I shall suggest, is a proper understanding of what I shall call the "second-personal" aspect of morality. Moral obligations, I shall argue, are tied conceptually to moral *responsibility*, and therefore, to reasons we can *address* as *demands* to one another as free and equal moral persons. An appreciation of the second-personal character of moral accountability, I shall claim, must enter both into an adequate under-standing of the concept of moral obligation, in section 1, and as the source of our awareness of the distinctive kind of freedom, autonomy, that a Kantian must hold is necessary to vindicating the categoricality of moral reasons, in section 2.

1. ANALYZING MORALITY

In this section, I shall seek to make clear the Kantian case for the conceptual thesis that moral oughts purport to be categorical imperatives.[4] First, however, we need to understand this claim better in its various aspects.

1.1. Aspects of Categorical Imperatives

1.1.1. *Normativity*

Consider the judgment that it is wrong intentionally to mislead potential investors by hiding losses. Normativity says that if this is wrong, then there is a genuinely normative reason for corporate officers not to engage in this deception. But what is meant by such a "normative reason"?

"Reason for acting" can mean three different things. A *normative reason* for acting is something that counts in favor of or *justifies* an action in deliberation about what to do (Darwall, 1983, pp. 28–32). This contrasts with an explanatory sense in which 'reason for action' refers to anything that might *explain* an action. Many things can be reasons for an action in this latter sense that are not normative reasons. My forgetting about a meeting yesterday might explain why I missed it, and so be a reason I missed it in that sense. But obviously it wasn't a (normative) reason for me *to* have missed it.

An especially important kind of explanatory reasons are *an agent's reasons* for acting (sometimes also called "motivating reasons").[5] These are considerations the agent herself counts or counted in favor of her action and on the basis of which she acts or acted. My forgetting was obviously not *my* reason for missing the meeting either. Since I forgot about it, I didn't even have a reason for missing it; it wasn't something I intentionally did.

Although agents' reasons differ from normative reasons, there are important connections between these. In order for a consideration to be someone's reason, it must be something the person himself takes as a normative reason. And there may be an important relation in the opposite direction as well. *Existence internalism* is the view that a necessary condition of something's being a normative reason for an agent is that it be a consideration on the basis of which he *can* act, in some suitable sense. It must be possible for it to be *his* reason—to motivate him under some suitable conditions.[6]

The putative normativity of moral oughts, then, is their giving agents normative reasons for acting. We need not worry at this point whether the reasons derive from the fact that the action is wrong, from considerations that make it wrong, or from both.

1.1.2. *Universality*

Universality asserts that Normativity holds universally. In *any* situation where an agent morally ought to do something, there will be some normative reasons for her to do so. (Universality just makes explicit what was already implicit in normativity.) Now, as I shall show, it is an important contention of Kant's that moral oughts are always backed by universal *principles*. But that needn't be true for universality to hold. All that universality requires is that it be everywhere true that an agent who morally ought to do A has some normative reason to do A, whether this reason derives from some universal principle or not.[7]

1.1.3. *Supremacy*

Normativity does not, however, entail that moral oughts provide *conclusive* reasons, all things considered. So far, all we have is that when an agent morally ought to do something, there is *some* genuinely normative reason to do it. *Supremacy* adds that there is always conclusive reason, all things considered, for agents to act as they morally ought.

It is important to note that supremacy only claims that moral reasons are always conclusive when they derive from (or support) a moral *obligation*. It does not claim that moral reasons always outweigh other reasons. It only says that there can never be sufficient reason to do what is *wrong*. (I am assuming that 'wrong' and 'morally obligatory' are contradictories.) For example, it seems that there is always a moral reason to give to *any* worthy charity, but failing to do so is not always wrong. It is wrong, of course, not to engage in charitable giving at all or to fail to do so sufficiently. So supremacy says that there is conclusive normative reason for everyone to give to the morally required extent. It does not say, however, that the moral reasons supporting donation to any particular charity invariably outweigh the reasons for not giving, if failing to give to that charity would not be wrong. (Of course, it doesn't say that they don't outweigh these latter reasons either.)

Reasons provided by moral oughts might be invariably supreme because they are guaranteed to *override* other normative reasons, because they invariably *defeat* (that is, reduce or undermine the force of) other reasons, or through some combination of these. Can moral reasons actually reduce or eliminate the weight of a countervailing reason? It surely seems that they can. Consider, for example, the pleasure a torturer might take in seeing her victim squirm. In such a case, the wrongness of torture or of taking pleasure in others' pain seems not only to outweigh any reason provided by the pleasure; it seems to "silence" it.

1.1.4. *Necessity*

We can bring out the necessity aspect of the Kantian thesis by comparing a Hobbesian view of morality's normativity. Hobbes by and large agrees with Kant that moral obligations are invariably supremely binding in the sense that no one ever has adequate reason to violate them. Even in the state of nature, Hobbes thinks, covenants bind when they are not voided by a reasonable suspicion that they will not be honored by others (Hobbes, 1994, pp. 82–94). When I reasonably believe that the person with whom I have covenanted will do his part, Hobbes believes that I have, on balance, conclusive reason to do mine also. Even so, Hobbes thinks that what makes this true are contingent features of the human situation: the violence and insecurity of the state of nature, the need for confederates in self-defense, and the role of covenants and the reputation for keeping them in confederacy and in establishing a sovereign. If facts such as these didn't make it invariably in one's interest to be perceived as someone who can be trusted to keep covenants, there wouldn't be reason for one to keep them.

So although Hobbes affirms supremacy, he denies necessity, since he holds that supremacy depends upon contingent features of the human situation. The Kantian thesis, by contrast, is meant to hold for all possible situations—not just situations human beings can be expected actually to face, given our psychology and circumstances, but situations any moral agent, that is, any agent subject to a moral ought, might conceivably face. Hobbes denies necessity because he believes that the ultimate source of the normativity of moral reasons, self-interest, is *external* to what grounds the moral ought.[8] For Kant, however, the source of the moral ought's normativity is *internal* to morality itself. For any possible moral agent, regardless of contingent differences, therefore, there will always be conclusive moral reason not to do what is wrong.

1.2. The Conceptual Claim

The analytical or conceptual interpretation of the Kantian thesis is that moral oughts purport to be categorical imperatives in all four aspects. This is not, again, the normative claim that there actually are valid moral oughts in these aspects. It is the conceptual thesis that moral oughts are staked, as we might put it, on this normative claim. Only if the normative claim is true are there any true or valid moral oughts.

Why should we accept this conceptual claim? Kant himself offers a number of different arguments, and I believe there is another powerful argument that rests on the idea of moral accountability. First, however, I shall consider Kant's reasons.

Kant sounds a major theme in the *Groundwork*'s preface. A "pure moral philosophy," he says, must be "cleansed of everything that may be only empirical and that belongs to anthropology" (1996b, p. 389). Kant's idea is not, as some have understood him, that human contingencies are nowhere relevant to moral duties. After all, Kant's own derivations of specific duties from the CI appeal to human contingency.[9] His point is rather that even when contingencies are relevant to the content and scope of specific human moral duties, this relevance is always itself a consequence of some deeper norm or principle that applies to us, not as human but as one free and rational agent among others.

"Everyone must grant," Kant writes, "that a law, if it is to hold morally, that is, as a ground of an obligation, must carry with it absolute necessity" (1996b, p. 389). Partly, Kant means that moral obligations are moral necessities; they (purport to) say what we *must* do. But that is not his main point here. He goes on: "[T]he command 'thou shalt not lie' does not hold only for human beings, as if other rational beings did not have to heed it, and so with all other moral laws properly so called" (p. 389). Ultimately, Kant claims, every human moral duty derives from a "law" that applies necessarily to all rational beings.

Kant is here arguing analytically, asking us to reflect on our own concepts of morality and moral duty. But we may want to reject his example.[10] Why *should* the moral duty not to lie apply to every rational being?[11] Consider for a moment, however, how we would have to support a counterexample. Must we not imagine rational beings who are somehow invulnerable to deception or who never or rarely rely on others for information, or something similar? And if so, wouldn't we end up proving rather than disproving Kant's point? In effect, would we not implicitly appeal to some principle that *does* apply to all rational beings, namely, that it is wrong for any rational being to lie in any circumstance in which she is interacting with beings who have the kind of vulnerability and need for information that we do?[12]

Now Kant believes that the CI, in its various formulations, underlies every moral duty and that this explains what contingencies are relevant to specific duties (see Buchanan, 1977). But at this point in his argument, Kant is relying on no such premise. He is simply trying to convince us that the very idea of moral duty presupposes *some* principle that applies to all rational agents. Suppose that we were to believe, like Sidgwick, that all duties derive from the principle of universal benevolence (Sidgwick, 1967). To whom would we then think the fundamental duty to promote maximal pleasure applies? To *human* beings only? What is the magic of biological species membership? Surely there are aspects of being human, such as requiring a functioning kidney, that have no intrinsic relevance to our being subject to moral oughts. So the question must then be: What are the features that human beings have that makes them subject to moral obligation (when they are)? Kant's answer is very persuasive: It is our being free and rational agents.[13]

Kant concludes that the very idea of moral duty entails that its ultimate scope is free and rational beings as such. So, whether *Star Trek*'s Vulcans actually exist or not, it is nevertheless true that *were* they to exist, they would be just as much bound by moral obligations as we are. The specific content of their moral duties might be different, since their situation might differ in morally relevant ways. But there would nonetheless have to be some deeper principle that applies equally to them and to us (and from which whatever differences in the specific contents of our respective obligations would derive).[14]

Kant concludes that the most fundamental moral principles must therefore apply to any *possible* (free and) rational agent. So they apply to rational agents *necessarily*, and they must, consequently, be knowable a priori.

A second important Kantian theme is that the characteristics that make us subject to moral oughts, free and rational agency, are also sufficient for us to comply with them. This idea arises in various contexts in Kant's thought. One is the "fact of reason": Kant's claim in the *Critique of Practical Reason* that we are conscious of our freedom through an awareness of being bound by the moral law (Kant, 1996a, p. 30). Kant there asks us to suppose that a person is demanded by his prince, on pain of immediate execution, to give false testimony against "an honorable man" (p. 30). And he points out that although the person might himself be unable to say whether he would in fact refuse this demand, "he must admit without hesitation that it would be possible for him" to do so, since he sees that he ought to. "He judges, therefore, that he can do something because he is aware that he ought to do it and cognizes freedom within him, which, without the moral law, would have remained unknown to him" (p. 30).

This seems right. However, to the extent it does, it must be because the person himself is already thinking of moral norms as (purporting to be) supremely binding. And moral norms *do* seem to differ fundamentally from others in the kind of authority they represent themselves as having. Although accepting norms of etiquette, for example, commits one to regarding them as having *some* normative weight, it does not seem to require one to think that etiquette's norms bind unconditionally, or that oughts of etiquette are invariably supreme. Acknowledging only a conditional and restricted normativity for etiquette seems in no tension whatsoever with accepting etiquette wholeheartedly. But this is apparently not the case with morality. Anyone who accepted *moral* obligations only under certain conditions, for certain purposes, or so long as it didn't conflict with certain other considerations, could hardly be said to have fully accepted moral norms.

Kant's explanation of this phenomenon is that, unlike more local and restricted norms, moral oughts purport to bind us as one free and rational being among others. So long as this condition is satisfied (and as there are forms of interaction sufficient for moral questions to arise), we are perforce subject to an ought (the moral ought) that presents itself as both unconditional and supreme. So we must, therefore, regard ourselves as able to comply simply by exercising the capacities by virtue of which we are subject to them.

1.3. Morality as Reciprocal Accountability

In addition to these considerations, there is another strong source of support for the conceptual interpretation of the Kantian thesis, one I will also draw on at the end of section 2 to support the thesis's normative interpretation. This is the idea that moral obligation essentially involves moral responsibility or accountability.

To begin, note that the aspects of the Kantian thesis I have considered thus far can sometimes characterize normative demands other than moral ones. The laws of logic, for example, seem just as binding on all rational beings as any moral demands might be. If I am considering whether to believe that q, and I know that p and that if p, then q, then the normative reasons I have to believe q would seem no less inescapably conclusive than any reason for acting that might derive from a moral obligation. But there is a significant difference between the two cases, nonetheless. Despite an obvious sense in which the logical rule of *modus ponens* is nonoptional, there is another in which whether I violate it can be "my own affair." There are contexts in which being illogical or not is my own business.[15] But it is never in this sense "up to me" whether or not to violate moral obligations.[16] If I am morally required to do something, then I am accountable or answerable for doing it in a way that I am not accountable, automatically anyway, for logical inferences. The apparatus of "reactive attitudes" such as indignation and resentment, and of charge, excuse, culpability, and so on, is part and parcel of morality in a way that it isn't of logic.[17]

"We do not call anything wrong," Mill says, "unless we mean to imply that a person ought to be punished in some way or other for doing it; if not by law, by the opinion of his fellow creatures; if not by opinion, by the reproaches of his own conscience."[18] To judge an action wrong is to see the agent as rightly subject, lacking adequate excuse, to some sanction or other form of other- or self-directed, second-personal reactive attitude like blame or guilt, that might constitute holding her morally responsible.

It is a conceptual truth that conduct that is morally wrong is blameworthy if the agent lacks an adequate excuse. What generates the "problem of free will," indeed, is the special sense of responsibility we attribute to agents when we judge their conduct to be morally reprehensible. The attribution of wrongdoing is a *charge*, and the worry determinism poses is that charges of moral responsibility might be universally deflected if determinism were true. Of course, there is a sense in which logical reasoning must be free also, namely, it must be independent of irrelevant external influence. But no one worries that our practices of logical criticism might lack support if determinism were true. It is the connection between imputing wrongdoing and moral responsibility or accountability that raises the worry.[19]

Any way of developing this idea must invoke a conception of a moral community to whom agents are accountable (if only to God).[20] Utilitarian conceptions, like Mill's, understand practices of moral accountability in instrumental and functional terms and reckon membership in the moral community in whatever way seems likeliest to advance overall happiness.[21] For Kantians, however, the moral community is a "realm of ends," that is, of all moral agents whose rational nature makes them ends in themselves (Kant, 1996b, pp. 428–440). The very qualities that make one subject to morality—the capacity for free and rational agency—also give one *standing in the community to whom all agents are accountable*. This means that morality is fundamentally a matter of mutual or *reciprocal* accountability and respect. Every free and rational agent, every *person*, is equally accountable to every other as members of the moral community.[22] And whereas the function of holding people accountable is always entirely instrumental for a utilitarian like Mill, for Kantians it is itself part of valuing moral agents intrinsically, of respecting their dignity as free and equal persons.

On a Kantian approach, therefore, morality concerns mutual *respect* in two different senses. First, the *content* of moral norms is understood to require respect for others as free and equal persons in various dimensions of our common life. But second, and equally important, the *application* of moral norms through practices of mutual accountability also involves agents expressing mutual respect. It is a reflection of the latter point that the forms of moral accountability are *second-personal*. They are addressed person-to-person, with a common presupposition of equal standing. Imputations of wrongdoing are *addressed* to those of whom they are made in a way that, for example, artistic criticism need not be.[23] Artists are not answerable to their critics as moral agents are to the moral community. And holding moral agents thus answerable is itself a way of respecting them as equal members.

The distinctively moral emotions reflect this second-personal character. Compare guilt and shame, for example. There is nothing essentially moral about shame. One can be as ashamed of things one cannot help, of parentage or pimples, as about anything one freely did. And the phenomenal presentation of shame need involve no imagined address or second-personal response. To feel shame (of one familiar kind, at least) is to feel as if one is rightly regarded or seen in a certain way *third*-personally, for example, appropriately disdained for one's parents or pimples.[24] Neither is shame's natural expression any form of address. To the contrary, it is a desire to disengage and disappear. Guilt, on the other hand, has a second-personal feel to it, as though it were a response to a charge or to blame.[25] And its characteristic expression is second-personal also, a desire to make amends to someone wronged and to own responsibility to those to whom one is accountable.

Appreciating moral obligation's essential tie to moral responsibility brings to light a powerful reason why moral demands must purport to be categorical in the aspects I have distinguished. Blaming someone commits one to thinking there was a good reason for the person not to have done what he did (normativity). It would simply be incoherent to judge someone blameworthy while acknowledging there really was no reason whatsoever for him not to have acted as he did.[26] It seems incoherent, indeed, to blame while allowing that the wrong action, although recommended against by some reasons, was nonetheless the sensible thing to do, all things considered (supremacy). Part of what one does in blaming is simply to say that the person shouldn't have done what he did, other reasons to the contrary notwithstanding.[27] After all, if someone can show that he had good and sufficient reasons for acting as he did, it would seem that he *has* accounted for himself and defeated any claim that he is to blame for anything. Accepting blame involves an acknowledgment of this proposition also. To feel guilt is, in part, to feel that one shouldn't have done what one did.

It follows that moral demands can play the role they purport to have in practices of accountability only if they purport to be normative and supreme. What guarantees the other two elements of categorical purport, universality and necessity, on a Kantian theory, is the way moral accountability itself involves reciprocal recognition of the dignity of free and equal persons. In addressing one another as mutually accountable, agents reciprocally recognize their equal dignity and presuppose that they are bound in common by norms they have the capacity to follow just by virtue of this recognition. This means that when we hold one another accountable for complying with moral obligations, we are presupposing *autonomy*; we are assuming that we are bound by moral norms that apply to us simply as free and rational wills *and* that we can comply with these by exercising these capacities.

This is also, I believe, the deepest idea underlying Kant's claim that the idea of moral duty commits us to a *formal* principle of the will, the CI, that all moral agents must be assumed capable of following in their moral *reasoning*. We could hardly be responsible for complying with moral imperatives if what makes us subject to them (moral agency) did not itself include capacities the exercise of which enables us to comply with them. If compliance with the moral law required special knowledge or special motivation, it would be unintelligible to think that we are appropriately held accountable for it.

2. VINDICATING MORALITY

It is one thing to show that moral demands purport to be categorical imperatives, however, and another to show that such categorical demands actually exist. So far we have seen why Kantians think that moral obligations present themselves to moral agents as supremely authoritative demands that each is accountable for following as one free and rational agent among others. But what might vindicate this presentation? What can show that there really *are* any such demands? Why should we think we really are accountable to one another as free and rational for anything?

According to Kant, any such vindication requires a "critique" of "pure practical reason." Kant's basic strategy is to show that commitment to moral demands is presupposed from the deliberative perspective of a free rational agent. To act at all, Kantians argue, an agent must take herself to have normative reasons. For behavior to so much count as action, there must be something that is the agent's reason for so acting. And for something to be an agent's reason, she must regard it as a normative reason for her to act.[28] Moreover, Kantians claim that to be a normative reason for acting, a consideration must be appropriately anchored in some norm to which all rational agents are subject. If, for example, the fact that something is in my interest is a reason for me to do it, it must be because rational agents should act in their own interest. It follows that the deliberative standpoint commits one to the existence of some such norms (Kant, 1996b, p. 412). So far, however, there is nothing that a non-Kantian need disagree with (although particularists might balk at the move to universal norms). The question, nonetheless, remains: Why suppose that moral norms are among these rational norms?

2.1. Non-Kantian Alternatives

Much discussion of "Why should I be moral?" has taken it for granted that there exists a default core of rational norms and practical reasons that do not include moral demands, and that morality can be vindicated only by building out somehow from these. Kantians are bound to object to this approach, and it is useful to see how they can.

2.1.1. *Instrumentalism*

There is a form of the *instrumental principle*, that one should take the necessary means to one's ends, that is an uncontroversial norm of practical reason. *Instrumentalists* hold that it is the sole rational norm and, consequently, that any normative reason must derive from an agent's ends or desires. If this were so, it would follow that an agent has reason to do as he morally ought only if that accords with his desires. Against this, Kantians argue that appreciating what is uncontroversial in the instrumental principle shows why instrumentalism cannot be correct.[29]

It is agreed by Kantians and non-Kantians alike that it is irrational to have the following *combination* of attitudes: having a given end, believing that some means is necessary to achieve that end, and failing to intend to take those means, or, worse, intending not to do so. Instrumentalism concludes from this uncontroversial point that the fact that one has a given end or desire is a reason for one to take the means necessary to realize it. And they conclude from their contention that the instrumental principle is the only rational norm, that such end- or desire-based considerations are the only reasons for acting. However, these further propositions are not uncontroversial; neither do they follow from any uncontroversial rational norm. This is because the instrumental principle is a norm of rational consistency with "wide scope."[30] It concerns the rational incoherence of simultaneously having A as end, believing B is necessary to achieve A, and intending not to do B. This combination of attitudes is rationally impermissible. But it doesn't follow from this that if one does have A as end, and believes B necessary to A, that one should intend B. Neither does it follow that these facts would be reasons for one to intend B. Perhaps one should give up end A.

The situation is exactly analogous with theoretical reasoning. There is an analogous "wide scope" consistency requirement. It is similarly contrary to reason simultaneously to believe p, believe if p, then q, and believe not-q. And similarly, it does not follow from this that if one believes p, and believes if p, then q, then one should, or has reason to, believe q (or should not believe not-q). Perhaps one should believe not-p.

It is a familiar saying that instrumental reasoning issues in "hypothetical" rather than categorical imperatives. But care is required in interpreting this commonplace. The imperatives or prescriptions that follow from the instrumental principle tell the agent either to take the means or to give up the end or the belief that the means in question is the only one. They do *not* tell the agent, if A is your end and B the only means, then you should do B. There is a sense in which they do recommend B *hypothetically*, but that is: conditionally on a "hypothesis" the agent is committed to assuming *in having A as his end*, namely, that there is some reason for A to be done. They do not recommend doing B simply on the condition that the agent desires A or has A as end. In this way, they are just like hypothetical theoretical reasoning: *assuming* that p, and if p, then q, then q.[31]

It follows that instrumentalism cannot be true. Since the instrumental principle is a consistency norm, it cannot possibly be the only norm of practical reason. Or rather, if it is, then there are no reasons for acting at all, since these would have to be anchored in some other norm of practical reason. But we can deliberate as agents at all only if we take some things as normative reasons for acting. So we must reject instrumentalism.

2.1.2. *Default Egoism*

A second strategy that is sometimes employed against the Kantian thesis is to hold that there is, indeed, an undeniable source of nonmoral normative reasons, namely, the agent's own good or welfare, but that the same cannot be said for moral reasons. No agent can sensibly deny that his own good gives him reasons, but there is no incoherence in denying that moral obligations do.

But in what sense is it true that no one can sensibly deny that one's good gives one reasons? No doubt, very few people would deny this. But it is also true that very few people would deny that moral obligations are reason-giving. To many, if not most, the latter seems no less evident than the former. Moreover, defenders of "default egoism" cannot simply assert that their view is more obviously *true*, since that just begs the question. Their claim would have to be that it is in some way self-contradictory or incoherent to deny that one's good is reason-giving, although it isn't to deny that moral obligations are. But is that really so?

Suppose I hate myself or think I am of no value and unworthy of anyone's concern. In so regarding myself, I might think that the fact that an action would promote *my* welfare, that it would be good for *me*, gives me no reason whatsoever to do it. I might even think that the fact that an action would benefit me is a reason for me not to do it. After all, I might think, I am dirt, or a being just not worth caring about. Would I be making some kind of conceptual error? Would I fail to understand either the concept of my own good or that of a reason for acting? It seems obvious that I would not. No doubt I would be mistaken or confused about my own value. If I appreciated my value better, I would see my own good as reason-giving. But if so, it is not obvious how I could do that without also appreciating why it is such as to give reasons to anyone. After all, what led to my skepticism about the reason-giving power of my good for me is that I am unworthy of concern *period*. It wasn't my thinking I had low value *to me*. Why would that thought amount to anything for someone who hates or is indifferent to herself?

Denying that one's own welfare is reason-giving thus seems to involve no conceptual incoherence. If the concept of a person's good or welfare is (essentially) normative, therefore, its normativity cannot be agent-relative. It cannot consist in entailing reasons distinctively for the agent whose good it is. Rather, what the reflections in the last paragraph suggest is that welfare is normative for *care*.[32] What is for someone's good is what one should want for her insofar as one cares for her. And reasons to promote someone's good derive from the fact, if it be a fact, that she is worthy of concern, as it will seem to the agent she is when he cares for her. But if that is so, then default egoism cannot possibly be correct. It cannot possibly be the case that the agent's own good is reason-giving for her but for no one else.

Of course, that doesn't prove that any beings do have a value that makes them worthy of concern. Indeed, the coherence of my denying that my good is a source of reasons itself depends on the coherence of my denying that I am worthy of concern. The point, first, is that someone can coherently deny that her own good is reason-giving, just as it is possible coherently to deny that moral obligations are reason-giving. So the case for the validity of moral reasons is no worse than that for prudential ones on that score. And second, the agent's own good will be reason-giving for her only if she has a value that makes it reason-giving for anyone.

2.1.3. *Humean Internalism and Internal Reasons*

In subsection 1.1.1, I noted a line of thought according to which anything that can be a normative reason for acting must be a consideration that the agent can, in a suitable sense, be motivated by and act on herself as *her* reason. This general line is called *existence internalism,* because it states a condition for the existence of normative reasons in what can be the agent's motives (reasons).[33] Since Humean theories of motivation deny that pure reason can motivate, Humean existence internalists assert that normative reasons are constrained by an agent's "subjective motivational set."[34] Following Bernard Williams, they call these "internal reasons." Humean internalists deny that there are any "external reasons," that is, reasons that are independent of the agent's subjective motivational capacities.

Kantians are also existence internalists, for reasons that will emerge hereafter. But since they believe that pure reason can be practical, they deny that all reasons must be internal reasons in Williams's Humean sense. (Alternatively, they argue that an agent's motivational set includes certain norm-guided capacities that are part of practical reason.) Moreover, they maintain that Humeans cannot plausibly claim that an agent has reason to do only what he desires (to the extent that he desires). In the relevant sense, an agent's actions can't fail to reflect his strongest desires. So if normative reasons were to vary with strength of desire, it would be impossible for an agent ever to do otherwise than what he had the weightiest normative reasons for doing. This would deprive "normative" reasons of any guiding or normative force.

Worse, it is not obvious why Humeans are entitled to assume that an agent's desires are even *a* source of practical reasons. This is a consequence of what has been called the "backgrounding of desire" (Darwall, 1983; Pettit and Smith, 1990). To an agent who desires that p, it is not as if *her desiring* p somehow makes it true that there is reason for her to bring about p. For example, to a person with a normal survival instinct who wants to escape a burning building, it is not as if she must find a way out because this is what *she wants*. The fact that in getting out alive she will satisfy a desire of hers is apt to strike her as beside the point or, at best, as a trivial bonus. It is more like she must escape because she must live. Her reasons derive from the *object*, rather than from the fact, of her desire. And her desire seems less a source than a response to reasons that are there anyway (Scanlon, 1998, pp. 33–55). So Humeans need some argument to show that an agent's subjective motivational set is even so much as *a* source of practical reasons.

Kantian internalists agree with Humeans in holding what Christine Korsgaard calls the "internalism requirement": p can be a reason for S to do A, only if S would be motivated by p to do A *insofar as she is rational* (Korsgaard, 1986, p. 11). For Humeans, however, all rationality is either instrumental or theoretical. Kantians deny that this can exhaust practical reason. We have already seen why they hold that practical reason must include more than instrumental rationality. But the instrumental principle is really the only principle of *practical* reason to which Humean internalists are entitled. Consistently with their position, Humeans may indict various forms of irrationality in belief, but as Hume himself pointed out, when a desire is caused by a false or unsupported belief, what Humeans *should* say is that, strictly speaking, it is the *belief* that is irrational, not the desire (Hume, 1978, p. 415). To say otherwise, they must embrace substantive principles of *practical* reason that go beyond any of theoretical rationality and the instrumental principle.

Of course, they may do this. They may put forward substantive principles of practical reason that relate rational desire somehow to theoretical rationality. But such principles must now be defended *as normative principles of practical reason*. It isn't enough just to point to uncontroversial principles of *theoretical reason*, since what is in question is *practical* irrationality. And if a desire is the result of a mistaken or unsupported belief, that just seems a consequence of theoretical irrationality, not irrationality of a distinctively practical kind.

Kantians can argue, therefore, that none of these non-Kantian strategies can establish a default nonmoral core of practical reasons. So even if Kantians cannot simply assume that moral obligations create normative reasons, that just means that they are in the same dialectical position as their critics. Anyone thinking seriously in this area at all must start from the assumption that there are *some* normative reasons for acting, since that is a necessary presupposition of the deliberative standpoint. And no principle of normative reasons is self-authenticating and immune to criticism.

2.2. Kantian Strategies in the Field

Despite their disagreements otherwise, Kantians and Humean internalists share an important area of agreement. Both reject the rational intuitionist doctrine, as represented, say by G. E. Moore or W. D. Ross, that substantive normative facts exist independently of our capacities to recognize and be motivated by them (Moore, 1993; Ross, 1963).[35] Now there is a sense in which all parties, including rational intuitionists, can agree with Korsgaard's "internalism requirement" that "practical reasons ... must be capable of motivating *rational* persons," since even intuitionists will think that those who are not moved to do as they ought are less than fully rational (Korsgaard, 1986, p. 11, emphasis added). But intuitionists are not really existence internalists in any important sense, since they hold that whether a deliberative process (or agent) *counts* as fully rational depends on its (or the agent's) responsiveness to independent facts about normative reasons. On their view, figuring in motivating reasoning is no part of what makes something a reason. According to both Humeans and Kantians, by contrast, motivation is not just an appropriate response to substantive normative facts that reason somehow discovers; it is internal to a *reasoning* that is essentially *practical* and involves the will.

As against Kantians, however, Humeans believe that motivation comes entirely from an agent's subjective motivational set and not from reasoning. But it seems possible for someone to desire an end and to accept that it can be accomplished only if certain means are taken but refuse to take the means. Christine Korsgaard's Tex, for example, believes he will live only if his leg is amputated, wants to live even at that cost, but will not bring himself to intend the amputation (Korsgaard, 1997, p. 238). According to the instrumental principle, Tex should either decide to amputate his leg or give up his end of staying alive. Were he to deliberate properly, therefore, he would be moved either to give up this end or to undertake the amputation. So Kantians claim that if Humeans accept the instrumental principle as a normative principle of practical reason, they are committed to accepting that (instrumental) reasoning can be practical.

Were they to accept this, Humeans would then agree with Kantians that reason can be practical in virtue of its *form*, that is, through formal or procedural aspects of practical reasoning that neither track independently established, substantive reasons nor can motivate only through some further desire. Since, however, the instrumental principle cannot be a source of reasons itself, Kantians add that practical reasoning must also include formal *reason-grounding* norms, specifically, the CI. The CI tells us to act only on principles that we can, and *would* from a standpoint impartial between agents, *will* that all agents act on. Since the CI involves the will in its very reasoning, it does not require a special desire to motivate. In willing that everyone act on a certain principle, I already have some motivation to do so myself.

That there must be formal reason-grounding norms to which we are subject as free and rational wills is what Kant means by "autonomy of the will": "the property of the will by which it is a law to itself independently of any property of the objects of volition" (1996b, 440). It is their allegiance to autonomy that leads Kantians to reject a purely definitional form of internalism, such as even intuitionists can accept. In their view, as in that of Humean internalists, something's standing as a normative reason ultimately depends on its being motivating (treated as a reason) in fully rational deliberation, where the latter is determined by internal, formal features of the deliberative process, not by its responsiveness to independently establishable normative reasons.

But what, exactly, supports the doctrine of autonomy of the will and rules out intuitionism? Kantians cannot simply assume autonomy. They must show that it is somehow anchored within the deliberative standpoint. This is another version of the problem that Kant faces at the end of *Groundwork* II. Maybe the idea that the will is not simply subject to laws, but a "law to itself," is just a "phantom of the brain."

2.2.1. *The Regress and "Practical Identity" Arguments*

One attempt to argue for autonomy and its Kantian equivalents (the CI in its various formulations) is Korsgaard's "regress argument," which she advances as an interpretation of the derivation of Kant's Humanity or End-in-Itself Formulation of the CI (FH): "So act that you use humanity, whether in your own person or in the person of any other, always at the same time as an end, never merely as a means" (Kant, 1996b, p. 430; Korsgaard, 1996a, pp. 259–262).[36] Whenever rational agents act for the sake of some end, they necessarily take their end to have value. But ends can have value either conditionally, or unconditionally, and conditionally valuable ends can give agents reasons only if their conditions are met. So an agent must take the conditions of her end's value to be realized. Normative reasons for acting really do exist, as a rational agent must assume, therefore, only if the conditions of some ends' value are actually satisfied. From here, Korsgaard reasons that something can serve as a sufficient condition of an end's value only if it is itself "unconditionally good" (p. 260). So an agent must take it that there is something that is unconditionally good. She concludes with the familiar Kantian doctrine of the dignity of the rational will. Nothing else is unconditionally valuable, so, by process of elimination, the necessarily existing unconditional value must be humanity or the rational will itself. The will is thus a law to itself in this sense.

This argument is vulnerable to a simple objection. It is not logically necessary that the condition of a thing's value be valuable itself, either conditionally or unconditionally (Kerstein, 2001; Rabinowicz and Rønnow-Rasmussen, 2000). If, as Korsgaard's Kant holds, the rational will is the source of value in the sense that rationally willing something makes it good, then presumably it is also the source of disvalue; rationally rejecting something must likewise make it bad. But by parity of reasoning, we should conclude that the rational will is also unconditionally bad (Kerstein, 2001). So even if an agent must take some ends to be good, and even if, consequently, she must take the conditions for that to be satisfied, this can give her no reason for thinking that rational agency or the good will or anything else is unconditionally good. Any justification for these claims must come from some other source.

More recently, Korsgaard has put forward a different argument for the Formula of Humanity (FH) that is rooted in the self-reflective character of a free agent's deliberative standpoint (Korsgaard, 1996b). Assume that agency requires some degree of self-reflection, that the agent must see himself as "something over and above all [his] desires" who "*chooses* which desire to act on" (p. 100). This commits the agent to a "practical identity," some normative conception of himself, which he draws on in deliberation. Now almost any practical identity we may have is optional, but there is one, Korsgaard argues, that I cannot question as a deliberating rational agent, namely, my identity as a deliberating rational agent.

It follows, Korsgaard concludes, that I must treat my own humanity or rational agency as a source of normative reasons for me. For the Kantian thesis to follow, however, we need further that I must treat the rational nature of others as such a source also. Here Korsgaard draws on Wittgensteinian themes about the impossibility of a private language (Korsgaard, 1996b, pp. 131–136). The basic idea, as I understand it, is that the claim that the agent's rational nature is a source of reasons distinctively to *him* treats these reasons as an essentially private phenomenon of the kind that Wittgenstein showed to be incoherent. The moral of the private language argument for practical philosophy, Korsgaard argues, is that all reasons must be "public and shareable" (p. 136). Consequently, whatever reasons an agent's normative identity as rational gives him must be public and shareable too. Therefore, the rational nature of others is no less normative for him than is his own.

It will help in evaluating this argument to have before us a running comparison with *theoretical reasoning*, that is, with reasoning about what *to believe*. I shall argue that philosophical considerations, like Wittgenstein's private language argument, that aim to support general demands for publicity, authority, and (a kind of) freedom common to theoretical and practical reason are impotent to ground the distinctive kind of *practical* freedom (autonomy) that is required by the Kantian thesis.

The standpoint of theoretical reason is no less self-reflective in the sense Korsgaard mentions than is that of practical reason. A rational believer, like a rational agent, must be able to see herself as "something over and above" her inclinations to belief as these are given in experience. She must be able to step back, say, from an inclination to believe that an apparently bent stick in water is bent and ask whether she should believe that it really is. And she must also see her reasoning as free in an important sense. She must presuppose that her thinking about what to believe can be normatively guided and that it is sufficiently independent of "alien causes" or distorting factors, that it is broadly responsive to evidence in the right way and not merely the causal upshot of factors that have no relation to the truth of what she believes. Finally, a rational believer must give her own theoretical reasoning some authority. She must be prepared to take the fact that she herself is convinced by the case for some proposition as giving her some reason to believe it (or, at least, some reason to think that the case-based considerations she takes to be reasons are reasons indeed). So in this sense, at least, she must see her identity as a theoretical reasoner as normative for her; she must have some trust in her own ability to gather evidence, make inferences, and so on. And this trust cannot be *essentially* private; she must presuppose that she has rational belief-forming capacities that others can have also.

Even so, the freedom and authority that a theoretical reasoner must presuppose is nothing like *autonomy*. Autonomy, for Kant, is the will's being subject to no external standard drawn from the nature of its objects, but "a law to itself." By contrast, someone working out what to believe must see his reasoning as ultimately responsible to an independent order of fact (his belief's appropriate objects) that determines the correctness of his beliefs. Kant himself notes the difference. Although theoretical reasoning is "determined by the constitution of the object," Kant says that practical reasoning "has to do with the subject" (1996a, p. 20). The reason, in Kant's view, is that practical reasoning presupposes autonomy, a kind of freedom that has no analogue in theoretical reasoning.

I will pursue the comparison between theoretical and practical reason further hereafter. It should already be clear, however, that nothing within the standpoint of theoretical reason authorizes a self-reflective rational believer to treat her identity, as such, as an *independent* source of reasons in the way that autonomy requires and that, according to Korsgaard, a self-reflective practical reasoner must regard her practical identity as a rational agent. It follows that neither the contrast between an active reasoning self and a passive locus of inclinations on the one hand nor the freedom and authority necessary for reasoning in general on the other can warrant an assumption that (the agent's) rational nature is itself a source of practical reasons. Both of the former hold in the theoretical sphere, but a self-reflective, free theoretical reasoner has no warrant to take her own rational nature as an independent source of reasons for belief. She must take her reasons for belief to be ultimately anchored in objects that her beliefs aim accurately to represent.

Now Korsgaard is of course right that the Kantian strategy is committed to the idea that an agent's rational nature is an independent source of *practical* reasons. This is required by autonomy, the idea that the will is a "law to itself" independently of any features of its objects. The issue, however, is what supports this idea. What in a critique of practical reason, that is, within presuppositions we are committed to from the deliberative standpoint, should convince us that Kant, rather than the rational intuitionists, is right?

2.2.2. *The Argument of* Groundwork *III*

A similar problem infects Kant's argument for the CI in chapter III of the *Groundwork*. Kant begins with an account of the will as including "negative" freedom: "*Will* is a kind of causality of living beings insofar as they are rational, and *freedom* would be that property of such causality that it can be efficient independently of alien causes *determining* it" (1996b, p. 446). To this negative freedom, he adds a further, "positive concept of freedom" as also a defining aspect of the will: "a causality in accordance with immutable laws but of a special kind" (p. 446). The relevant laws are "practical laws" rather than "laws of nature." To deliberate at all, Kant is saying, a rational will must assume that she can follow norms of rational conduct independently of "alien causes." The point is not that anyone must *believe* that she can make rational decisions. One may believe, even correctly, that one can't. The point is that when one deliberates, one is presupposing that one can. Intelligible deliberation must proceed on that assumption.

Directly following this general definition, however, Kant adds: "what, then, can freedom of the will be other than autonomy, that is, the will's property of being a law to itself" (1996b, p. 447). But why does this follow? Compare, again, theoretical reason. Someone trying to figure out what to believe must also see her reasoning as guided by rational norms and not simply the upshot of "alien causes." But that doesn't mean that she must see her belief-forming capacity as a "law to itself," in the sense of being an ultimate source of normative reasons for belief. Ultimately, the trustworthiness of reasoning as a guide to belief depends on its relation to what is the case, to the objects that her beliefs aim accurately to represent. Autonomy of the will, on the other hand, is the idea that reasons for action can have their source in the will itself, irrespectively of any such independent standard.

So the question persists, what in the standpoint of practical reason commits a deliberating agent to autonomy of the will? In the *Groundwork*, Kant claims that it is impossible for an agent to act at all except under the idea of freedom. Deliberation is guided by normative reasons, and "one cannot possibly think of a reason that would consciously receive direction from any other quarter with respect to its judgments" (Kant, 1996b, p. 448). But freedom of this kind is, as we have seen, a presupposition of freedom of both practical and theoretical reason, and it doesn't amount to autonomy. So what is it about the practical standpoint *in particular* that rules out intuitionism and should lead an agent to accept autonomy and thus Kantian internalism in the practical sphere?

By the time he wrote *The Critique of Practical Reason*, Kant had given up on this line of thought. Correctly, he sees that the distinctively practical freedom represented in autonomy of the will is related to the recognition of a distinctive *kind* of practical reason, one embodied in the moral law, in accepting which one must conclude one can act contrary to any desire, however strong.[37] As I shall explain better in the next two subsections, freedom of this kind is profoundly different from any involved in theoretical reasoning.

2.3. Transition: Modeling Practical on Theoretical Reasoning

To develop this last point further, and to prepare the way for an alternative grounding of autonomy that might secure the Kantian thesis, I want in this section to consider what an intuitionist picture that models practical reason on theoretical reason might look like. The intuitionist view that works best for my purposes is Moore's in *Principia Ethica*, according to which there is a single basic ethical concept: intrinsic value or the idea of a possible state of the world's being intrinsically good or such as "ought to exist for its own sake" (Moore, 1993, p. 31).[38] This makes deliberation a matter of working out what outcomes or possible states ought to obtain (to what degree) and what the agent can do to bring them about (p. 77).

On Moore's picture, normative reasons for acting all derive from the intrinsic value and disvalue of possible outcomes or states of affairs. For any possible outcome that an agent can produce, the weight of any reason for her to do it is proportional to the value of that state taken together with the costs of bringing it about.

Compare now the way a Moorean agent would view his deliberative situation with the outlook of a theoretical reasoner. Belief aims to represent an objective world in a believer-neutral way and so is regulated by the facts of this world, so far as we can discern them. Of course, what reasons people have to believe things depend in many ways on where they stand in relation to the world. But ultimately their reasons must be grounded in something that is independent of their stance, namely, what is the case believer-neutrally. The Moorean conception of practical reasons as rooted in intrinsic value is a practical analogue of this picture. Moorean intrinsic value is roughly the world as it *should be*—the 'normative world'. And action, for a Moorean agent, is purely instrumental. What action is *for*, we might say, is to bring about the normative world, to produce agent-neutrally valuable outcomes and prevent disvaluable ones.[39] That doesn't mean that the agent is himself an instrument. He can see himself and his deliberations as self-reflective and free in the same way a rational believer can. He will take his judgments of value and instrumental reasoning to be normatively guided and independent of alien causes, no less than any reasoner must. And he will see himself not simply as the sum of his actual inclinations or evaluative 'intuitions' but as a being who can make world-guided empirical judgments and normative-world-guided evaluative judgments in order to work out which action has the property that "more good or less evil will exist in the world, if it be adopted than if anything else be done instead" (Moore, 1993, p. 77).

It is important to see that this picture actually fits pretty well the way things seem from the naive first-person perspective of an agent with desires. Desires have possible states as objects, and to an agent with the desire for some state, it will seem as if the world should contain that state.[40] If I want the world to be without hunger, then it will be to me as if the world should be without hunger. Or if I just want not to be hungry myself, it will be to me as if *my* not being hungry would be good, that is, that the world should be such that the person in it identical to me is not hungry.[41] It wouldn't be far wrong to say that our desires seem to give us the world as it should be, the normative world, seen from their point of view. This, again, is a consequence of the "backgrounding of desire," discussed in subsection 1.1.3. What's more, to an agent viewing the world simply from his desires' perspective, it will seem that the question of what to do is identical to the question of which acts would produce the best states.

From the naive first-person perspective of an agent with desires, then, the default theory would seem to be some form of intuitionist consequentialist realism. The agent's desires, and the rational choices she makes on their basis, will seem to be normatively guided insofar as they are guided by the normative world.[42] And, analogously to the theoretical case, her best evidence will apparently be provided by desires she has when best informed about and most accurately perceiving their objects.

2.4. A Second-Personal Kantian Strategy

If this is right, it is far from being the case that autonomy is something we must presuppose to reason practically at all. To the contrary, the default assumption of a *naive* practical standpoint seems to *exclude* autonomy. In calling this perspective "naive," however, I have meant to signal that it involves illusions that, according to Kantians, a philosophically more sophisticated picture will unmask. Note again that both Humean and Kantian forms of existence internalism agree on this.[43] Both affirm that what makes something a normative reason is that it would be taken as such by agents and motivate in rational deliberation, where what makes deliberation "rational" are formal features of the deliberative process that are independent of whatever material normative reasons it might recognize.

We have already seen (in subsections 2.1.1 and 2.1.3) why Kantians think that

Humean versions of internalism must be rejected. But I have yet to show an adequate Kantian rationale for internalism itself, and thus, for rejecting the default realism of the naive first-person practical standpoint. In this subsection I shall argue that this is to be found in the way we presuppose autonomy, along with the dignity of persons and its CI equivalents, when we recognize a distinctive kind of reason for acting—*second-personal* reasons—a kind that lacks any structural analogue in reasons for belief.[44] Second-personal reasons are reasons that, to exist at all, must be able to be *addressed* second-personally ("I" or "we" to "you") by free and rational agents to other agents.[45] Examples are reasons that derive from orders, demands, requests, and claims. All second-personal reasons have a structure that differs from that I have just noted of reasons for belief and the reasons for action apparently given through desire. On a Kantian picture, moreover, the moral law embodies *purely* second-personal reasons. Moral claims and demands are not only addressable in the way that orders are; we address them simply *as persons* to others simply *as persons*.

Kant says that a person "possesses a *dignity* . . . by which he exacts *respect* for himself from all other rational beings in the world" (1996c, pp. 434–435). This point deserves a more fundamental role in Kant's thought than he actually gives it. It means that the dignity of persons is a source of *demands* (as Kant also says), that is, second-personal reasons we have the standing to *address* to one another as equal, free, and rational agents. We demand respect for our common dignity when, as I discussed in subsection 1.3, we enter into the second-personal relations involved in holding one another accountable for living up to the moral obligations that our dignity gives us standing to demand of each other.

Second-personal reasons are addressed to their addressees as rational persons, although not always as simply so, and they presuppose their acceptability to addressees as such persons. The point is not just that addressing second-personal reasons presupposes their validity. That is true when we attempt to give someone a reason of any kind, second-personal or not. Rather, since the address of second-personal reasons invariably presupposes that the addressee is *accountable* (to someone) for complying with them, it must presuppose as well that the addressee can be expected to accept the reasons and the authority relations in which they are grounded and be motivated by this acceptance. We can hardly hold people accountable on terms that they cannot be expected rationally to accept. Moral obligations, therefore, presuppose that the addressee can hold *herself* accountable as a person for compliance by taking a second-personal standpoint on herself and being motivated by a form of reasoning she must be assumed capable of in being subject to moral demands at all. In Kant's view, the required form of reasoning is the CI.

Since, as I shall show, second-personal reasons of whatever kind can neither derive from nor reduce to the value of outcomes, addressing them presupposes agents' freedom to act on reasons that find no footing in the first-person perspective of a desiring agent, and this dispels the naivete of that standpoint. What's more, addressing second-personal reasons necessarily presupposes a distinction between the justifiability of making a demand (with sanctions for noncompliance) that is itself part of holding the addressee accountable and so respecting her standing as a free and rational agent, on the one hand, and the mere threat of those very same sanctions without the requisite second-personal authority, which would constitute coercion and so violate this standing, on the other. It follows that second-personal address invariably presupposes that addresser and addressee share a common authority or dignity as persons (and the CI equivalents of this idea). It is second-personal engagement, therefore, that supplants the naive standpoint of a desiring agent and commits us to autonomy of the will and the moral law.[46]

To begin to appreciate the distinctive character of second-personal reasons, consider, first, how rational believers can give each other reasons for belief. If someone tells you that p, this can give you a reason to believe p only if what she says or her saying it is evidence of p.[47] Even when another person just tells you "p," her testimony must give you evidence that p is the case in order to give you a reason to believe it. If you have no reason to treat what she says or her saying it as evidence of the truth of what she says, she can give you no reasons for belief.

Likewise with advice. An advisor can give an advisee reasons for acting either by citing considerations that are reasons independently ("Eating fat is bad for your heart") or by simply advising someone to do something without mentioning more specific reasons. But even in the latter case, any authority an advisee accords an advisor depends on the advisor's relation to reasons for acting that are there anyway, quite independently of his authority to give them through advice. Advice is a kind of conduit to these reasons or a promissory note that they exist.

There is, however, a kind of practical case where we recognize authority of a different kind, namely, to make demands or claims directly on another's *actions*, and where the relevant authority is a standing to address reasons to another that would not have existed independently of this authority. This is the point of Hobbes's famous contrast between "counsel" and "command."[48] In this kind of case, one person gives another a reason for acting, not by expressing his belief (even his beliefs about practical reasons, as in advice) but by expressing his desire or will. Here the reason seems to depend entirely on the *relationship* of addresser to addressee, specifically, on the addressee's *authority* to address the reason and *expect* uptake or compliance.

Take orders, for example. When a sergeant tells her platoon to fall in, her charges take it that the reason she gives them derives from the nature of their relationship, on her having the authority to demand that her platoon act in this way, rather than from any independent value she reveals to them in her order. Something similar holds for decrees, legislative acts, requests, demands, reproaches, and claims more generally. When a legislature expresses its legislative will, it is understood to give citizens a reason to comply that derives, not from the independent value of some state that is its will's object, but from the authority legislative bodies have with respect to citizens. Of course, various conditions must be satisfied for this authority to exist in the first place, and neither a sergeant nor a legislature can require, or even request, that a person do just anything.

In cases like these, it seems clear enough that the relevant reasons simply would not exist but for the authority to address them second-personally in the requisite ways. But what can this have to do with morality? We don't think that moral obligations require anything like an actual order to exist. So what can moral obligations have to do with second-personal reasons?

Consider, however, two different ways in which you might try to give someone a reason to stop causing you pain, say, to remove his foot from on top of yours. One would be vividly to describe your pain so that the other might come to see it as a bad feature of the world, something the world should be without. If, for example, you could make the other feel sympathy for you and your plight and induce in him a desire that you be free of pain, then you would successfully give him a reason to move his foot. This would not be a second-personal reason, however. Its cogency would be independent of being addressable in any way. The other person would appropriately regard what you say or do simply as evidence of how the world should independently be. And the reason would be agent-neutral rather than agent-relative; it would seem to exist equally for anyone to do whatever might bring about that desirable feature of the world.

Alternatively, you could ask or insist that the other move his foot as a way of advancing a valid demand, from one equal member of the moral community to another, that he stop *causing* you pain.[49] This would address a second-personal reason that presumes on your equal authority as members of the moral community to demand that people not step on one another's feet. Here the reason would be agent-relative, addressed distinctively to the person causing another pain rather than implicitly to anyone who might be in a position to relieve it. It would appeal to a norm of an implied community of mutually accountable equals rather than to a normative world that might hold independently of the possibility of mutual address. The reason would purport, therefore, to be independent of the agent-neutral value of outcomes, hence of anything that could be the object of a desire from a naive first-person standpoint.

When we hold each other responsible for complying with moral obligations, for example, not to step on one another's feet, we presuppose the authority to demand this of one another. If the argument of subsection 1.3 is correct, the very concept of moral obligation entails that what is wrong is what we hold persons responsible for and demand they not do. When we appeal to the obligation not to step on others' feet, therefore, and hold someone accountable for this, we presuppose a valid demand that we address to him. Unlike an order, however, one doesn't have to actually make such a demand individually for it to be in force. Rather, one presupposes that this is something that we all implicitly demand of one another as members of an implied moral community.

What this means on a Kantian view is that not stepping on one another's feet is something we *will* (that is, demand) of one another (and will that we hold one another responsible for) from a perspective that we share as free and equal rational agents, from, that is, the perspective of the moral community or "realm of ends." It is part, if you like, of the moral community's "general will."[50] This makes a version of the CI (in its "realm of ends" formulation [Kant, 1996b, p. 433]) implicit in our reasoning when we address one another as mutually accountable persons with equal dignity.[51] When we hold one another responsible, we presuppose that we can each regulate our conduct by taking this second-personal perspective on ourselves through CI reasoning.

To make demands either explicitly or implicitly, however, we must presuppose the *authority* to do so. This is what makes the reasons that derive from moral obligation second-personal. Even if each of us accepted a norm requiring us not to step on one anothers' feet, it would not follow from what we accept that there is a moral obligation not to do so or that doing so would be wrong. No authority to require, demand, or hold others responsible for compliance follows from the fact that agents' have conclusive reason to comply with what we could demand if we had the authority. But this second-personal authority *is* involved in claims of moral obligation, and, consequently, in what you would be appealing to were you to put forward a moral demand that another person take his foot off of yours in a case like this. The reasons you would be addressing simply wouldn't have existed but for the authority to address them second-personally in this way.

Addressing any second-personal reason presupposes the authority to address it. And since second-personal reasons invariably imply accountability, the addresser must also presuppose that the addressee can be expected to *accept* the addressed reasons and the authority relations in which they are grounded, and that she can *act* on the reasons just by virtue of accepting these. Since second-personal reasons do not derive from the (agent-neutral) value of outcomes, hence from anything that can be the object of a desire, this already commits addresser and addressee to presupposing a kind of freedom that is beyond any that is assumed in the naive first-personal practical standpoint.

Kant's follower, Johann Gottlieb Fichte, argued that it is possible for agents to acquire a practical awareness of their distinctive freedom as agents only by entertaining a second-personal claim or "summons" (*Aufforderung*) that is addressed to them by another agent (Fichte, 2000, pp. 4–81). A Fichtean summons is not just an imperative designed to influence or modify behavior; it is an addressed second-personal *reason*—a consideration by which it is supposed an agent can freely determine herself by accepting its validity. To take up a summons, therefore, just *is* to relate to another agent relating to one and, so, to deliberate on the assumption that both are free agents. And even to consider a second-personal reason is already to recognize an implicit claim for consideration and, therefore, to respect the other as, as Rawls puts it, "a self-originating source" of valid claims (1980, pp. 543, 546).

Obviously, not all second-personal reasons are addressed to individuals *simply* as rational agents. More specific authority relations are frequently presupposed: sergeant to private, king to subject, and so on. But even such specific summonses are tied to a presupposition of the addressees' capacity, as free and rational, to act on a free acceptance of the reasons they address and the authority on which they depend. For example, theological voluntarists like Pufendorf held that moral reasons are created in this fashion by God's authoritative will as expressed to God's human subjects (Pufendorf, 1934, I.i.§2–6, pp. 4–7; I.vi,§4, p. 89).[52] But Pufendorf also thought, correctly in my view, that it is possible for God to create moral reasons in this fashion only if he and we both presuppose that we can be moved by a free acceptance of his authority, so that ultimately we can hold ourselves accountable second-personally by making the same demands of ourselves that he makes of us.[53] This meant, as his critics pointed out, that Pufendorf needed to assume a source of authority and normative reasons beyond God's command that any rational agent could be expected to accept.[54]

Pufendorf makes a crucial distinction between motivation by fear of God's power, on the one hand, and by respect for his authority, on the other. In Pufendorf's view, it is part of the very idea of moral obligation that any agent subject to it be able to determine himself not just by fear of a sanction but by accepting that the sanction "falls upon him justly" (Pufendorf, 1934, p. 91). Pufendorf's thought has two important aspects. One is that the address of any second-personal reason presupposes that the addressee is accountable to the addresser for compliance, which requires addresser and addressee alike to presuppose a distinction between justly applying, or putting the addresser on notice of, a sanction for free noncompliance, which fully recognizes the addressee's standing as free and rational, on the one hand, and, on the other, *simply* threatening the sanctions without the relevant authority, which would constitute coercion and so be a violation of this authority. Any form of second-personal address at all is thus committed to some form of the idea that free and rational agents, that is, agents who are capable of second-personal, reciprocally recognizing interaction, have a common authority or dignity as such. The second aspect of Pufendorf's thought is an internal reflection of the first, from the point of view of the addressee. To act on an acceptance of the addresser's authority and the reasons she addresses, the addressee must be able to internalize and be motivated by the same second-personal accountability-seeking demands and reactive attitudes that the addresser must believe will be warranted should the addressee fail to comply. The addressee must consequently be able to hold himself accountable by making the very same second-personal demands of himself, for example, through a sense of guilt (an imagined second-personal acknowledgment of warranted blame).

But what authority is a free and rational agent bound to accept and recognize? Only, it would seem, whatever authority one is committed to in making and considering second-personal claims and demands in the first place. Making and entertaining demands and claims second-personally at all is *already* to be in a relation in which each reciprocally recognizes the other and gives him an authority as a free and rational person.[55] Even to consider seriously another's claim is to reflect back to the addresser recognition of his authority to submit claims for consideration (which is itself a kind of claim). And making a demand or claim is putting it forward as something the other can accept and be held to consistently with his authority as free and rational. Addresser and addressee are thus committed in common to the idea that there are valid second-personal reasons that derive from the authority that free and rational persons have to make demands of one another; they are committed, that is, to the equal dignity of persons.

It follows further that the address of second-persons presupposes autonomy, that the will is a law to itself independently of any properties of the objects of desire. I showed earlier that, since second-personal reasons cannot be reduced to outcome value, the address of any second-personal reason assumes the freedom to act on a kind of reason that finds no reflection in the naive first-person standpoint. And now it is apparent that, even when they presuppose more specific or hierarchical authorities, second-personal reasons are nonetheless addressed to free and rational agents, albeit, in these cases, agents who can be expected to accept more specific authority relations in which they happen to stand. Addressing second-personal reasons of any kind therefore assumes that there are laws that free and rational wills stand under as such, independently of the value of any outcome that might be the object of a desire, even in the case where their specific requirements are conditional on more specific authority relations.

What demands can one free and rational will make on another and reasonably expect acceptance? The very logic of the question suggests the reasoning of the CI: whatever demands a free and rational agent would will that each be able to make on all in a mutually accountable, reciprocally respecting community of equals, that is, a kingdom of ends. Thus second-personal reasoning presupposes both autonomy of the will *and* the CI.

To make these points more vivid, consider the example that Kant invokes in his "fact of reason" (1996a, p. 30). Kant's point, recall, is that if a prince were to threaten death if one did not betray an honest person, one would have to think it *possible* to refuse because one would think one *should* do so. Now this already commits one to a kind of freedom beyond any involved in the naive first-person standpoint. The moral demand not to betray others is an agent-relative 'deontological constraint'. It is not simply the idea that betrayals are bad things to occur—something the world should be without. If that were so, then if, by some causal process, one's betraying someone would lead another person not to go through with an exactly similar betrayal as he otherwise would have, then it would be a matter of indifference in this case whether or not one betrayed another person *oneself*. It seems clear enough, however, that such a betrayal would be wrong and, therefore, that there is an agent-relative injunction not to betray others that cannot be reduced to the agent-neutral badness of any outcomes that such a betrayal might bring about, *including* whatever intrinsic disvalue a betrayal might add to the world itself.

Nevertheless, this freedom is not yet autonomy. For all I have yet said, there might simply exist, as rational intuitionist deontologists like Ross and Richard Price believed, valid agent-relative principles, such as the principle not to betray others, that embody material normative reasons for acting, where this has nothing to do with formal features of the will or practical reasoning, with the will's being a "law to itself." So far, it looks as though all the "fact of reason" involves is that *if* one recognizes such reasons, then one must admit that one can act on them.

I have been arguing, however, that, when we recognize that it would be *wrong* to betray someone, that one has a moral obligation not to do so, we must accept as well that we are *responsible* for not doing so, that such a betrayal would be *culpable* lacking adequate excuse. And I have noted that we can hold someone accountable for doing something only if we think she can hold herself accountable by taking a second-personal standpoint on herself and being motivated by a form of reasoning in which she makes the relevant demands of herself, which reasoning we can assume her capable of in being subject to moral demands at all. It follows that if we think ourselves subject to moral demands by virtue of being free and rational agents, we should conclude further that these are demands we are able to make of ourselves within our own practical reasoning, that is, that the will is a "law to itself." If this is right, it is the connection of moral obligation to responsibility that underlies autonomy of the will and the relevant form of reasoning (the CI).

2.5. Freedom, Desire, Morality, and Practical Reason

When I considered Kant's argument for the CI in *Groundwork* III earlier, I showed that he mistakenly assumed that autonomy is presupposed in practical reasoning of any kind. To the contrary, I noted, a naive first-person standpoint presupposes a species of freedom that is structurally analogous to that of theoretical reason. When an agent deliberates from such a perspective, he takes the reasons his desires present him to be grounded, not in his own will, but in desirable features of his desires' objects, as he views them under his desires' influence. It is only when an agent is addressed in a way that makes him aware, simultaneously, of a potential source of reasons in the will of another rational and free agent *and* in his own rational will, that the naivete of his prior standpoint is revealed and he becomes aware of and committed to reasons anchored in the rational authority of *a free rational agent*, himself or another.

Imagine that A and B desire the same apple. Desire here is backgrounded, with A and B individually seeing their desires or wills, not as a source of reasons, but as responses to reasons that are there anyway. Suppose that A attempts to give B a reason to let him, A, have the apple, by *expressing* his desire, saying that his (A's) having the apple is a valuable state (and noting that, so far as he can tell, B's having it is not). This cannot succeed, since from B's perspective, nothing is to be said for A's having the apple and everything is to be said for B's. B has no reason to trust A's judgment that A should have the apple, since, from B's perspective, A's judgment is illusory, a mere expression of A's desire. Any such attempt of A to give B a reason would not differ structurally from theoretical reason-giving. It could succeed only to the extent that B has reason to think there exists some reliable relation between A's judgment and the normative world it purports to represent. It would not yet be an instance of second-personal claim-making. Indeed, even if A and B could agree that A's *or* B's having the apple would be equally valuable, this would give them no basis for awarding or dividing it, since it would not amount yet to the idea that they have an equal *claim.*

Suppose now that A attempts to give B a second-personal reason. "I would have the apple," A says. "So you, B, should let me have it." For the first time, B feels the force of A's will as purporting to be reason-giving for her. And, for the first time, in response, she feels the force also of *her own rational will* as no less a reasonable basis for such a claim and therefore a source of reasons. "I, too, would have the apple," she might respond, and continue: "Neither of us can assume any antecedent authority with respect to the other, so it would be unreasonable for you to expect me just to let you have the apple. Neither can I reasonably expect this of you. Even so, we are already implicitly reciprocally recognizing each other's authority to make claims of one another at all by addressing these claims and considerations to each other as free and rational. So we are already reciprocally recognizing one another as (in Rawls's terms) 'self-originating sources of valid claims' " (Rawls, 1980, pp. 543, 546).

A and B are thus already committed to equal dignity and autonomy of the will, that is, to the idea that there are reasons for acting that do not derive from the value of any outcome or state, but just from their being free and rational wills relating to one another. Their interactions now presuppose that persons have, as such, an equal authority to make demands of each other as persons, as well as the capacity to accept such demands and act on them just by virtue of their practical reason. But this could be true, again, only if what they need in order to accept and act on such claims is simply the capacity to be part of a community of reciprocally recognizing, mutually accountable equal persons—a realm of ends. And that is simply the capacity to guide their conduct by the CI, not to will or claim for themselves what they would not will for all to be able to demand in a community of reciprocally respecting equals.

For the Kantian, then, the ultimate justification for thinking that what makes something a normative reason is its suitability to be taken as a reason and motivate in (formally) rational deliberation—is autonomy of the will. Simply by engaging each other in practical reasoning second-personally, rational agents presuppose autonomy and, simultaneously, the form of reasoning represented by the CI. That free and rational agents would thus necessarily take moral demands—demands free and rational persons can make of each other—to be universally supremely normative makes it the case that they actually are.

Of course, there is nothing in the naive standpoint of a desiring agent that logically forces second-personal engagement, with its consequent commitments to autonomy and morality. But the Kantian can plausibly argue that in this, as in other areas, social engagement increases sophistication. Once an agent's deliberative field has been decentered by second-personal engagement, the naive realist outlook of desire seems, on reflection, to be quite incredible.

NOTES

1. I should note that it is consistent with the claim that moral oughts necessarily provide conclusive reasons for acting to all moral agents that specific moral obligations can themselves depend on contingent features. For example, it might be that, given the laws and conventions in the United States, it is wrong to drive on the left side of the road. Had our laws and conventions been different, like those in Britain, say, the situation would have been reversed; it would have been wrong to drive on the right rather than the left. When contingency is thus involved in specific moral obligations, what matters is whether this is so by virtue of something further, say, some universal principle, that binds us necessarily.

2. The Universal Law Formulation (FUL) of the CI is "Act only in accordance with that maxim through which you can at the same time will that it become a universal law" (Kant, 1996b, p. 421), and the Humanity or End-in-Itself Formulation (FH) is "So act that you use humanity, whether in your own person or in the person of any other, always at the same time as an end, never merely as a means" (p. 429). Kant maintains that the various formulations of the CI are equivalent (p. 436).

3. This translation is H. J. Paton's. See Kant, 1970, p. 112.

4. I assume that "morally ought" is equivalent to "morally obligated to" and that S morally ought to do A if, and only if, it would be wrong for S not to do A.

5. Sometimes 'motivating reason' is used to refer the mental state of taking something as a normative reason or being disposed to act on it as such a reason. See, e.g., Smith, 1994, pp. 92–93, 131–133.

6. An especially influential version of this idea can be found in Williams, 1981. For

a discussion of the distinction between existence internalism and judgment internalism, see Darwall, 1983, pp. 54–55, 1992, 1996. Other important discussions are Falk, 1947–48; Frankena, 1958; and Korsgaard, 1986.

7. "Particularism" is the position that moral obligations and normative reasons do not require universal principles. See, e.g., Dancy, 1993; Hooker and Little, 2000.

8. For an analysis of Hobbes's views along these lines, see Darwall, 1995, pp. 53–79.

9. Thus the impossibility of willing, or even conceiving, a world in which everyone makes false promises when it is to his advantage is that this would cause a general undermining of trust making it impossible to promise (Kant, 1996b, p. 422). In addition, its being impossible sensibly to will that everyone refuse to aid others when it is disadvantageous depends upon its being the case that "many cases could occur in which one would need" the good will of others (p. 423).

10. Specifically, *moral particularists*, who deny that claims of moral right and wrong presuppose or entail universal principles, might reject Kant's example on these grounds.

11. At this point, we need not be concerned with the question of whether there is an absolute prohibition on human beings lying in any situation. Kant notoriously thought this. The question here is what makes a being subject to the prohibition on lying, to the extent that is prohibited.

12. I am not saying that Kant would accept that this is what underlies the wrongness of lying, just that if someone were to think that our lying is wrong for this reason, he would be committed to some such principle.

13. I shall explore what free and rational agency involves in section 2.

14. I believe that this can be made consistent with the phenomena that particularists frequently draw upon, namely, that a reason need not hold "everywhere," as Jonathan Dancy puts it, so long as we understand rational norms as involving "ceteris paribus" defeasibility clauses in ways that are similar to the role such clauses play in physical laws. On this point, see Pietroski, 1993.

15. Of course, if I am reasoning with others, it may not be.

16. The root of this idea is in John Stuart Mill's remark that "we do not call anything wrong, unless we mean to imply that a person ought to be punished in some way or other for doing it; if not by law, by the opinion of his fellow creatures; if not by opinion, by the reproaches of his own conscience" (1979, pp. 47–48). On the conceptual tie between the idea of wrong and blame and guilt, see also Adams, 1999, esp. p. 238; Baier, 1966; Brandt, 1979, pp. 163–176; Gibbard, 1990, p. 42; Skorupski, 1999, p. 142.

17. The term comes from Strawson, 1968. More precisely, Strawson calls these "participant reactive attitudes" ("natural human reactions to the good or ill will or indifference of others towards us," p. 80). These attitudes are "second-personal," in the sense both that they are felt in response to something second-personal (an attitude *directed* towards one) and that their natural expression is also directed toward their object. For example, both anger and fear have intentional objects, but anger is directed towards its object in a way that fear is not.

18. See note 16. This puts it too strongly, since we may think what someone did wrong, but that she shouldn't be punished, even by her own conscience, because of excusing conditions.

19. The key to answering the worry, I believe, is to appreciate, as Scanlon points out, that since the worry arises within our practices of accountability, an adequate response can be worked out within those very practices (Scanlon, 1988).

20. Even if it is a community of one, as in early modern versions of theological voluntarism, according to which moral accountability is only to God. On this point, see Darwall, 2004.

21. Thus Mill says of the concept of a right, which he relates to that of justice and more generally to wrong (wronging someone): "To have a right, then, is I conceive, to have something which society ought to defend me in the possession of. If the objector goes on to ask why it ought, I can give no other reason than general utility" (1979, p. 52). This makes rules determining right and wrong "practice rules," in Rawls's sense (Rawls, 1955). Although this is the form that, it would seem, a utilitarian approach to responsibility must take, I believe it is vulnerable to the Strawson's argument in "Freedom and Resentment" (1968) that it provides a justification of "the wrong kind" for practices of responsibility as we understand them.

22. Compare Locke: " 'Person' is a Forensick Term appropriating Actions and their Merit; and so belongs only to intelligent Agents capable of a Law" (1975, p. 346). For an excellent discussion of this element of Kant's view, see Korsgaard, 1996a, pp. 188–221.

23. The point is not just that holding people morally responsible and demanding mutual respect attempts to communicate something to their "objects"; artistic criticism can be addressed to artists in this sense. The idea is rather that it presupposes and attempts to establish a second-personal accountability relation in which the other is called to respond second-personally, to "account for" himself.

24. Thus, although Strawson claims otherwise, I would say that shame is not a reactive attitude in Strawson's sense.

25. This is true, I think, even when the relevant conduct is self-regarding, for example, failing to follow an exercise regimen one has set for oneself. Here the second-personal relation is internalized; one blames oneself.

26. John Skorupski makes a similar point (1999, pp. 42–43), as does Williams (1995, pp. 40–44).

27. Someone might reject this, arguing that there are cases where we judge it sensible for someone to do something, say, to go along with a criminal gang when it would be too risky to resist, where we nonetheless hold the person morally responsible and think she acted wrongly. If, however, the risks were too great to reasonably *expect* the person to resist, then this would seem to defeat the claim that the person acted wrongly. (An alternative would be to continue to maintain that the person acted wrongly but say she is not to blame because the personal risks excuse her wrongdoing. One problem with this alternative is that we typically distinguish between conditions that excuse and those that justify.) And if the personal risks are not too great to expect resistance, then I think there is at least a significant tension between blaming someone and acknowledging that there was sufficient reason for her not to resist. I am indebted to David Copp for pressing these questions and for discussion of them.

28. Various issues arise here, for example, about cases of *akrasia,* or "weakness of will," in which a person apparently acts against what she believes she has the best reasons to do. Still, the Kantian will argue, even an akratic agent must take herself as having *some* reason to do what she is doing.

29. In what follows, I draw on Darwall, 2002.

30. For this way of putting the point, see Broome, 1999. For different formulations, see Dancy, 2000, p. 43; Darwall, 1983, pp. 15–17, 43–50; Greenspan, 1975; Hare, 1971.

31. An analogous line of thought applies to formal theories of decision, which as-

sume some ranking of preferences (utilities) and subjective probabilities. Here, too, the uncontroversial kernel of such theories can be seen in terms of hypothetical reasoning and the demand for practical consistency, extended now to the more complex case in which agents must deal with potentially conflicting ends and preferences. The rational force of the principle of maximizing expected utility (preference-satisfaction), like that of instrumental reasoning, is that of a consistency demand requiring that an agent *either* choose the utility-maximizing act or change her preferences or probability estimates. In particular, the formal theory of decision does *not* entail that an agent's preferences give her reasons for acting. As with instrumental reasoning, it says which action is most highly recommended, conditionally or hypothetically—conditionally, however, not on the agent's having the preferences and beliefs she does, but on what she assumes in having those preferences and beliefs. (For further discussion of this point, see Darwall, 1983, ch. 6.)

32. I argue for this in Darwall, 2002, ch. 1.

33. See the references in note 6.

34. The term comes from Williams, 1981.

35. More classical intuitionists would include eighteenth-century thinkers such as Samuel Clarke and Richard Price. For more contemporary versions, see Parfit, 1997, and Stratton-Lake, 2002.

36. A somewhat similar line is pursued by Wood, 1998, pp. 127–134. Wood's argument is more complex. I cannot fully respond to it here, but I believe the considerations in this and the next subsection provide the basis for such a response.

37. Kant thinks that reasons for acting grounded in the moral law are formal, since they do not derive from properties of the objects of desire (the value of outcomes or states of affairs). So his thinking that autonomy is related to the recognition of reasons grounded in the moral law is no movement away from his doctrine that practical reason is practical in virtue of its form. I am indebted to David Copp for pressing me to clarify this point.

38. Moore speaks of things rather than states as being intrinsically good, but this doesn't matter for my purposes. A thing ought to exist if, and only if, the state of its existing ought to obtain. In what follows, I draw from Darwall, 2003, pp. 468–489.

39. It is consistent with this that actions have Moorean intrinsic value, but this is still value as an existent, state, or outcome not, as an action—its being a good thing that the action be taken or "exist." What makes something a *good action* is its instrumental capacity to produce good outcomes (including the outcome of that very action's being taken or existing).

40. I draw here from Darwall, 2001.

41. From this naive perspective, the reason will seem to be agent-neutral, as if there is a reason for anyone to relieve my hunger. Here I agree with Thomas Nagel's similar claim (1986, pp. 156–162) that pain presents itself not as bad *for me* but as bad period.

42. Here see Stampe, 1987.

43. See subsection 2.1.3 and the introduction to subsection 2.2.

44. On the various formulations of the CI, see note 2.

45. There are a number of passages in Korsgaard's writings that suggest this line, but they are insufficiently distinguished, I believe, from the Wittgensteinian considerations mentioned above. See, for example, Korsgaard, 1996b, pp. 139–143.

46. I can only sketch the arguments for these claims here. For a fuller version, see my book *The Second-Person Standpoint*, forthcoming.

47. On the epistemology of testimony, see Burge, 1993; Coady, 1992; Foley, 1994. I have been much helped by discussion with Edward S. Hinchman, and by Hinchman, 2000.

48. See, for example, Hobbes: "We must fetch the distinction between *counsel* and *law,* from the difference between *counsel* and *command.* Now *COUNSEL* is a *precept,* in which the reason of my obeying it is taken from *the thing itself* which is advised; but *COMMAND* is a *precept,* in which the cause of my obedience depends on *the will of the commander*" (1651, chapter XIV, paragraph 1).

49. Others might do so also, of course.

50. Kant said that it was Rousseau who impressed the dignity of persons on him. I believe that the Rousseauean notion of "general will" is also implicit in his thought.

51. As I am interpreting it, the "realm of ends" formulation of the CI requires us to act according to principles that we would will, from the standpoint of equal member of the realm of ends, that all comply with and be held accountable for complying with.

52. I discuss this aspect of Pufendorf's views in Darwall, 2004.

53. This claim is implicit in Pufendorf's distinction between coercion and being under an obligation. Many things can "influence the will to turn to one side" or the other, but other evils "bear down the will as by some natural weight, and on their removal [the will] returns of itself to its former indifference." Obligation, however, "affects the will morally," so that it "is forced of itself to weigh its own actions, and to judge itself worthy of some censure, unless it conforms to a prescribed rule." In effect, Pufendorf here invokes a notion of *internal* blame or censure, that is, accepting blame as justified (blaming oneself in authorizing the view of the other who blames one; 1934, I.vi,§5, p. 91).

54. This criticism was made, for example, by Cudworth, 1996, pp. 18–19. Pufendorf believes that we should accept God's superior authority as deriving from a debt of gratitude to our creator and sustainer (Pufendorf, 1934, p. 106).

55. There may seem to be many obvious counterexamples to this claim. Most vividly, what about orders to children or to slaves? It is important to distinguish, again, the pure claim from any attempt simply to cause a certain action or response and from mixed cases. As I am understanding them here, claims are issued with the aim of getting a certain response *in virtue of a recognition that the validity of the claim creates a reason so to respond.* Thus, a pure order is issued to gain a response by virtue of a recognition that the validity of the order (one's authority to issue such an order) gives a reason. By their very nature, then, claims are issued to beings who are implicitly regarded as competent to recognize their valid, reason-giving character and to freely act on them. Of course, one can do this even if one doesn't *believe* that the addressee is thus competent. The point is that one regards or treats him as though he were. And frequently, of course, for example, with children, this is done to insinuate proleptically the very recognition on the addressee's part that is necessary for the claim to "come off."

REFERENCES

Adams, Robert. 1999. *Finite and Infinite Goods.* New York: Oxford University Press.

Baier, Kurt. 1966. "Moral Obligation." *American Philosophical Quarterly* 3: 210–226.

Brandt, Richard. 1979. *A Theory of the Good and the Right.* Oxford: Oxford University Press.

Broome, John. 1999. "Normative Requirements." *Ratio* 12: 398–419.

Buchanan, Allen. 1977. "Categorical Imperatives and Moral Principles." *Philosophical Studies* 31: 249–260.

Burge, Tyler. 1993. "Content Preservation." *Philosophical Review* 102: 457–488.

Coady, C.A.J. 1992. *Testimony: A Philosophical Study.* Oxford: Oxford University Press.

Cudworth, Ralph. 1996. *A Treatise of Eternal and Immutable Morality.* Ed. Sarah Hutton. Cambridge: Cambridge University Press.

Dancy, Jonathan. 1993. *Moral Reasons.* Oxford: Blackwell.

———. 2000. *Practical Reality.* Oxford: Oxford University Press.

Darwall, Stephen. 1983. *Impartial Reason.* Ithaca, N.Y.: Cornell University Press.

———. 1992. "Internalism and Agency." *Philosophical Perspectives* 6: 155–174.

———. 1995. *The British Moralists and the Internal 'Ought': 1640–1740.* Cambridge: Cambridge University Press.

———. 1996. "Reasons, Motives, and the Demands of Morality: An Introduction." In *Moral Discourse and Practice,* ed. Stephen Darwall, Allan Gibbard, and Peter Railton, 305–312. New York: Oxford University Press.

———. 2001. "Because I Want It." *Social Philosophy and Policy* 18: 129–153. Also in *Moral Knowledge,* ed. Ellen F. Paul, 129–153. Cambridge: Cambridge University Press.

———. 2002. *Welfare and Rational Care.* Princeton, N.J.: Princeton University Press.

———. 2003. "Moore, Normativity, and Intrinsic Value." *Ethics* 113: 468–489.

———. 2004. "Autonomy in Modern Natural Law." In *New Essays in the History of Autonomy,* ed. Natalie Brender and Larry Krasnoff, 110–131. Cambridge: Cambridge University Press.

———. Forthcoming. *The Second-Person Standpoint.*

Falk, W. D. 1947–48. "Ought and Motivation." *Proceedings of the Aristotelian Society* 48: 492–510.

Fichte, Johann Gottlieb. 2000. *Foundations of Natural Right.* Ed. Frederick Neuhouser. Trans. Michael Bauer. Cambridge: Cambridge University Press.

Foley, Richard. 1994. "Egoism in Epistemology." In *Socializing Epistemology: The Social Dimensions of Knowledge,* ed. Frederick F. Schmitt, 53–73. Lanham, Md.: Rowman and Littlefield.

Frankena, William. 1958. "Obligation and Motivation in Recent Moral Philosophy." In *Essays in Moral Philosophy,* ed. A. I. Melden, 40–81. Seattle: University of Washington Press.

Gibbard, Allan. 1990. *Wise Choices, Apt Feelings: A Theory of Normative Judgment.* Cambridge, Mass.: Harvard University Press.

Greenspan, P. S. 1975. "Conditional Oughts and Hypothetical Imperatives." *Journal of Philosophy* 72: 259–276.

Hare, R. M. 1971. "Wanting: Some Pitfalls." In *Agent, Action, and Reason,* ed. Robert

Binkley, Richard Bronaugh, and Ausonio Marras, 81–127. Toronto: Toronto University Press.

Hinchman, Edward. 2000. "Trust and Reason." Ph.D. diss., University of Michigan.

Hobbes, Thomas. 1651. *Philosophical Rudiments Concerning Government and Society.* London: R. Royston.

———. 1994. *Leviathan.* Ed. Edwin Curley. Indianapolis: Hackett.

Hooker, Brad, and Margaret Olivia Little, eds. 2000. *Moral Particularism.* Oxford: Oxford University Press.

Hume, David. 1978. *A Treatise of Human Nature.* Ed. L. A. Selby-Bigge. 2nd ed., with text revised and variant readings by P. H. Nidditch. Oxford: Clarendon Press.

Kant, Immanuel. 1970. *Groundwork of the Metaphysics of Morals.* Trans. H. J. Paton. New York: Harper Row.

———. 1996a. *Critique of Practical Reason.* In *Practical Philosophy,* trans. and ed. Mary J. Gregor, with a general introduction by Allen Wood. Cambridge: Cambridge University Press. References are to page numbers of the canonical *Preussische Akademie* edition.

———. 1996b. *Groundwork of the Metaphysics of Morals.* In *Practical Philosophy,* trans. and ed. Mary J. Gregor, with a general introduction by Allen Wood, 43–108. Cambridge: Cambridge University Press. References are to page numbers of the canonical *Preussische Akademie* edition.

———. 1996c. *Metaphysics of Morals.* In *Practical Philosophy,* trans. and ed. by Mary J. Gregor, with a general introduction by Allen Wood. Cambridge: Cambridge University Press. References are to page numbers of the canonical *Preussische Akademie* edition.

Kerstein, Samuel. 2001. "Korsgaard's Kantian Arguments for the Value of Humanity." *Canadian Journal of Philosophy* 31: 23–52.

Korsgaard, Christine. 1986. "Skepticism about Practical Reason." *Journal of Philosophy* 83: 5–25.

———. 1996a. *Creating the Kingdom of Ends.* Cambridge: Cambridge University Press.

———. 1996b. *The Sources of Normativity.* Cambridge: Cambridge University Press.

———. 1997. "The Normativity of Instrumental Reason." In *Ethics and Practical Reason,* ed. Garrett Cullity and Berys Gaut, 215–254. Oxford: Clarendon Press.

Locke, John. 1975. *An Essay Concerning Human Understanding.* Ed. Peter H. Nidditch. Oxford: Oxford University Press.

Mill, John Stuart. 1979. *Utilitarianism.* Ed. George Sher. Indianapolis: Hackett.

Moore, G. E. 1993. *Principia Ethica.* Rev. ed., with the preface to the (projected) second edition and other papers, ed. with an introduction by Thomas Baldwin. Cambridge: Cambridge University Press.

Nagel, Thomas. 1986. *The View from Nowhere.* New York: Oxford University Press.

Parfit, Derek. 1997. "Reasons and Motivation." *Proceedings of the Aristotelian Society,* supp., 71: 99–130.

Pettit, Philip, and Michael Smith. 1990. "Backgrounding Desire." *Philosophical Review* 99: 565–592.

Pietroski, Paul. 1993. "Prima Facie Obligations: Ceteris Paribus Laws in Moral Theory." *Ethics* 103: 489–515.

Pufendorf, Samuel. 1934. *On the Law of Nature and Nations.* Trans. C. H. Oldfather and W. A. Oldfather. Oxford: Clarendon Press.

Rabinowicz, Wlodek, and Toni Rønnow-Rasmussen. 2000. "A Distinction in Value: Intrinsic and for Its Own Sake." *Proceedings of the Aristotelian Society* 100: 33–51.

Rawls, John. 1955. "Two Concepts of Rules." *Philosophical Review* 64: 3–32.

———. 1980. "Kantian Constructivism in Moral Theory." *Journal of Philosophy* 77: 543, 546.

Ross, W. D. 1963. *The Right and the Good.* Oxford: Clarendon Press.

Scanlon, T. M. 1988. "The Significance of Choice." In *The Tanner Lectures on Human Values,* ed. Sterling McMurrin, 8:149–216. Salt Lake City: University of Utah Press.

———. 1998. *What We Owe to Each Other.* Cambridge, Mass.: Harvard University Press.

Sidgwick, Henry. 1967. *The Methods of Ethics.* 7th ed. London: Macmillan.

Skorupski, John. 1999. *Ethical Explorations.* Oxford: Oxford University Press.

Smith, Michael. 1994. *The Moral Problem.* Oxford: Blackwell.

Stampe, Dennis. 1987. "The Authority of Desire." *Philosophical Review* 96: 335–381.

Stratton-Lake, Philip, ed. 2002. *Ethical Intuitionism: Reevaluations.* Oxford: Clarendon Press.

Strawson, P. F. 1968. "Freedom and Resentment." In *Studies in the Philosophy of Thought and Action,* pp. 71–96. Oxford: Oxford University Press.

Williams, Bernard. 1981. "Internal and External Reasons." In *Moral Luck,* 101–113. Cambridge: Cambridge University Press.

———. 1995. "Internal Reasons and the Obscurity of Blame." In *Making Sense of Humanity,* 35–45. Cambridge: Cambridge University Press.

Wood, Allen. 1998. *Kant's Ethical Thought.* Cambridge: Cambridge University Press.

CHAPTER 12

FREE WILL AND MORAL RESPONSIBILITY

JOHN MARTIN FISCHER

MUCH has been written recently about free will and moral responsibility. I will focus on the relationship between free will, on the one hand, and various notions that fall under the rubric of "morality," broadly construed, on the other: deliberation and practical reasoning, moral responsibility, and ethical notions such as "ought," "right," "wrong," "good," and "bad." I shall begin by laying out a natural understanding of freedom of the will. Next I develop some challenges to the common-sense view that we have this sort of freedom. I will go on to explore the implications of this challenge for deliberation, moral responsibility, and the central ethical notions.

1. FREE WILL AND THE CHALLENGE FROM CAUSAL DETERMINISM

We naturally think of ourselves—"normal" adult human beings—as "free." That is, we take it that we have a certain distinctive sort of control. I shall use "free will" (or "freedom of the will") as an umbrella term to refer to the sort of freedom or control we presuppose that we human beings possess, and that is connected in important ways to ascriptions of moral responsibility. As I shall be employing the term, "free will" need not entail that we have a special faculty of the will, but only that we have a certain kind of freedom or control. But what is this freedom?

It is extremely natural and plausible to think that the typical adult human being has freedom in the sense that we often (although perhaps not always) have the freedom to choose or refrain from choosing a particular course of action (where "course of action" can refer to an omission as well as an action, narrowly construed) and to undertake or refrain from undertaking this course of action. That is, we take it that we often (although perhaps not invariably) have 'alternative possibilities': although we actually choose and undertake a particular course of action, we had it in our power (or "could have") chosen and undertaken a different course of action. Of course, we recognize that sometimes we are "coerced" or "compelled" to choose or act as we do; and some individuals never have control over their choices and actions (because of significant mental illness, brain damage, and so forth). But we assume that the typical adult human being, at least sometimes, has more than one available path. That is, we assume, in Borges's phrase, that the future is a garden of forking paths.

But there are various skeptical worries or challenges to the intuitive notion that we have free will in the sense that involves alternative possibilities. One of the most important such challenges comes from the doctrine of causal determinism. Causal determinism is the thesis that every event (and thus every choice and bit of behavior) is deterministically caused by some event in the past; thus, every choice and bit of behavior is the result of a casual chain, each link in which is deterministically caused by some prior link (until one gets to the beginning, if there is a beginning). More specifically, one can say that causal determinism is the doctrine that a complete statement of the laws of nature and a complete description of the temporally nonrelational or 'genuine' facts about the world at some time T *entail* every truth about the world after T. That is, if causal determinism is true, then the past and the natural laws *entail* a unique present and future path for the world. Note further that if someone had available to her the description of the past and the statement of the laws, she could with certainty say what happens in the present and what will happen in the future. But it does not follow from the truth of the metaphysical doctrine of causal determinism that anyone actually has access to the relevant truths about the universe or its laws.

I contend that no human being currently knows whether or not the doctrine of causal determinism obtains. Certain physicists believe that the study of physical phenomena at the micro level renders it very plausible that causal determinism is false (and thus that 'indeterminism' is true). Note, again, that indeterminism is a metaphysical rather than an epistemic doctrine; that is, causal indeterminism posits indeterminacies in nature, not just incompleteness in our understanding of nature. But other physicists (and philosophers) cling to the view that causal determinism is true, and that what appear currently to be genuine metaphysical indeterminacies reflect mere inadequacies in our knowledge of the world (Honderich, 1988).

Since we cannot be certain at this point that causal determinism is false, it is perhaps worthwhile to think about what would follow, if it turned out that causal determinism is true. It is troubling that there is a very potent argument, employing ingredients from common sense, which appears to show that if causal determinism indeed turned out to be true, then no human being would have free will in the sense that involves alternative possibilities. The argument appears to show that the future is not a garden of forking paths, on the assumption of causal determinism. The following is an informal and intuitive presentation of the argument (Fischer, 1994, 1999, p. 100; Ginet, 1990; van Inwagen, 1983).

Suppose I make some ordinary choice C at time $T2$. If causal determinism is true, then the total state of the universe at $T1$ together with the laws of nature entail that I make C at $T2$. Thus, it was a necessary condition of my making a different choice at $T2$ that either the state of the universe at $T1$ have been different from what it actually was or some proposition that expressed a natural law would not have expressed a natural law. But, intuitively, I cannot—do not have it in my power—at any time so to behave that the past would have been different from the way it actually was. And, similarly, I cannot at any time determine which propositions express the natural laws. Intuitively, the past and the natural laws are "fixed" and not "up to me." It seems to follow from the foregoing ingredients that I could not have chosen otherwise than C at $T2$, if causal determinism turned out to be true.

Here is a slightly different way of presenting basically the same argument (Fischer, 1994, pp. 88–94). As I suggested earlier, intuitively the past and the laws of nature are fixed and out of my control. The future is a garden of forking paths: the paths into the future extend from a given past, holding the laws of nature fixed. So, one might say that my freedom is the freedom to extend the actual (or given) past, holding fixed the laws of nature. Assume, again, the truth of causal determinism, and that I make choice C at $T2$. It follows from the assumption of causal determinism that the state of the world at $T1$ together with the laws of nature entail that I make choice C at $T2$. So in all possible worlds with the same laws as the actual world in which the past is just as it actually is, I make choice C at $T2$, Thus, it is logically impossible that my making some other choice C^* at $T2$ be an extension of the given past, holding fixed the natural laws. It is evident, then, that if causal determinism is true, I cannot make any other choice than the one I actually make.

The foregoing argument, suitably regimented and refined, appears to be generalizable to show that if it turns out that causal determinism is true, then no human being has the sort of free will that involves alternative possibilities—freedom to choose or do otherwise, or the power to select one path the world will take, from among various paths that are "genuinely" or "really" open. This argument for 'incompatibilism'—the incompatibility of causal determinism and (in this instance) the sort of free will that involves alternative possibilities—has been the focal point of much discussion. Although the argument is controversial, here I shall not explore the ways in which it can be resisted (see Fischer, 1994). Rather, I shall assume that the argument is sound and explore the implications of this assumption. As I proceed in this essay, I shall focus on the question of what would follow, in terms of "morality," broadly construed, if we in fact lack the sort of free will that involves alternative possibilities. I shall also consider whether there are features of causal determinism that would threaten morality, apart from its ruling out free will (in the sense that involves alternative possibilities).

2. DELIBERATION AND PRACTICAL REASONING

2.1. Taylor and van Inwagen

One of the most central aspects of human "persons" is that we can engage in significant deliberation and practical reasoning. In deliberating, we consider and weigh reasons for (and against) various courses of action. We seek to "figure out what is best to do" and to act in accordance with this sort of judgment about what is best, all things considered. We are fallible in our judgments, of course, and certainly we sometimes fail to act in accordance with our judgment about what is best to do, all things considered. But in any case, the process of deliberation (or practical reasoning) involves identifying and weighing reasons with an eye to figuring out what we have sufficient reason to do.

Some philosophers have argued that it is a conceptual truth that I cannot engage in deliberation if I do not believe that I have free will, in the sense that involves alternative possibilities. After pointing out that I can deliberate only about my own behavior (and not the behavior of another), that I can deliberate only about future things (rather than present or past things), and that I cannot deliberate about what I already know that I am going to do, Richard Taylor adds: "And, finally, I cannot deliberate about what to do, even though I may not know what I am going to do, unless I believe that it is up to me what I am going to do" (1983, pp. 38–39). He goes on to argue that the relevant notion of "up to me" is incompatible with causal determinism; on this notion, an act's being "up to me" implies that it is up to me whether or not I do it.

I am not convinced by Taylor that I would not or could not engage in deliberation, if I believed that causal determinism were true and thus that I have it in my power only to choose to do (and to do) what I actually choose to do (and do). As long as I do not know what I will in fact choose, it seems that there is a perfectly reasonable point to deliberation; after all, I still need to figure out what I have sufficient reason to do and to seek to act in accordance with this judgment. This purpose of deliberation would not disappear, in a world in which I knew that it is not "up to me" (in the sense that involves alternative possibilities in which the actual past and natural laws are held fixed) what I will choose. Note that it may still be true, even in a causally deterministic world, that in a particular context I would choose a course of action if and only if I were to judge it best. Further, it does not follow simply from causal determinism that there is some special sort of obstacle to my choosing a particular course of action; causal determinism does not entail that I have some kind of phobia or compulsion that would rule out my choosing a certain sort of action. And if one insists that it is a *conceptual truth* that my process of weighing reasons would not count as "deliberation," then so be it: call it "deliberation*" or simply "figuring out what it would be best to do," and there can be a clear point to such activities even in a world in which I know that I have only one path that is genuinely available into the future.

Peter van Inwagen holds a view that is similar to, but slightly different from, Taylor's. On van Inwagen's account, an agent who believes that he does not have free will (in the sense of alternative possibilities) can deliberate, but in so doing he would be contradicting himself. Van Inwagen says: "In my view, if someone deliberates about whether to do A or to do B, it follows that his behavior manifests a belief that it is *possible* for him to do A—that he *can* do A, that he has it within his power to do A—and that it is possible for him to do B" (1983, p. 155). Thus, an individual who sincerely believes that he lacks free will (understood as earlier) would be contradicting himself in deliberating—he would be holding an inconsistent set of beliefs. Whereas this is not impossible, it is certainly undesirable; for example, holding inconsistent beliefs guarantees that at least one of one's beliefs is false (van Inwagen, 1983, p. 158).

But I am not convinced that van Inwagen is correct to say that deliberation manifests the belief in free will (understood as earlier). He says:

> Anyone who doubts that this is indeed the case may find it instructive to imagine that he is in a room with two doors and that he believes one of the doors to be unlocked and the other to be locked and impassable, though he has no idea which is which; let him then attempt to imagine himself deliberating about which door to leave by. (1983, p. 154)

I agree that it would be odd to think that I could deliberate about which door actually (or "successfully") to open. But surely in such a case I could deliberate about which door to *choose* to open. That is, I could weigh reasons and come to a judgment about which door it would be best to seek to open, and I could form an intention—choose—to act in accordance with my judgment. There is not the same intuitive oddness about saying that I could deliberate about which door to choose to push against that there is to saying that I could deliberate about which door "to leave by." It is important to note that van Inwagen does not purport to be offering an *argument* for the contention that anyone who deliberates must believe that he has alternative possibilities, apart from his invocation of the example of the alleged oddness of deliberating about which door to leave by.

But van Inwagen may reply that the apparent lack of oddness in supposing that I could deliberate about which door (say) to choose to open stems precisely from the fact that I can suppose that I am able either to choose to open door *A* or choose to open door *B*. I am not so sure, however, that this is the explanation of the asymmetry in our intuitions between deliberating about which door *to open* and deliberating about which door *to choose to open*. Suppose I do in fact choose to open door *A*. Now if causal determinism is true and the argument for the incompatibility of causal determinism and free will (understood as involving alternative possibilities) is sound, then it turns out that, unbeknownst to me, just prior to my choice I did not have it in my power to choose to open door *B*. Further, it seems to me that I could know that causal determinism is true and that the incompatibilist's argument is sound, and thus that whichever choice I make is the only one I actually can make. This knowledge does not eliminate the point of deliberation (the need to figure out which door it would be best to choose to open); and I do not have any hesitation in supposing that, even with the knowledge that whatever door I choose will be the *only* door I in fact can choose to open, I can deliberate about which door to choose to open. Thus I do not believe that the asymmetry in our intuitions between deliberating about which door to open and deliberating about which door to choose to open stems from an asymmetry in our beliefs about alternative possibilities.

In a causally deterministic world (and given the incompatibilistic argument), *every* choice and action would be such that, if I make it (or perform it), I could not have made another choice (or performed another action). But it seems to me that there could still be a perfectly reasonable point to deliberation, and that I need not contradict myself in accepting the truth of causal determinism, the soundness of the argument for incompatibilism, but nevertheless deliberating. All that is required is that I have an interest in figuring out what I have sufficient reason to choose, and that I do not know which course of action I will in fact choose to take (and take; Bok, 1998, pp. 109–114). Further, van Inwagen has not produced an example in which it is obvious that *this* yields an odd result.

2.2. Searle

John Searle has argued for a point related to the claims of Taylor and van Inwagen, but it is slightly different. Searle's contention is that there would be *no point* to practical reasoning or deliberation, if I knew that causal determinism were true. Searle says:

> The gap can be given two equivalent descriptions, one forward-looking, one backward. Forward: the gap is that feature of our conscious decision making and acting where we sense alternative future decisions and actions as causally open to us. Backward: the gap is that feature of conscious decision making and acting whereby the reasons preceding the decisions and the actions are not experienced by the agent as setting causally sufficient conditions for the decisions and actions. As far as our conscious experiences are concerned, the gap occurs when the beliefs, desires, and other reasons are not experienced as causally sufficient conditions for a decision (the formation of a prior intention . . .). (2001, p. 62)

Searle goes on to say:

> I am advancing three theses here.
>
> 1. We have experiences of the gap of the sort I have described.
> 2. We have to presuppose the gap. We have to presuppose that the psychological antecedents of many of our decisions and actions do not set causally sufficient conditions for those decisions and actions.
> 3. In normal conscious life one cannot avoid choosing and deciding.
>
> Here is the argument for 2 and 3: If I really thought that the beliefs and desires were sufficient to cause the action then I could just sit back and watch the action unfold in the same way as I do when I sit back and watch the action unfold on a movie screen. But I cannot do that when I am engaging in rational decision making and acting. I have to presuppose that the antecedent set of psychological conditions was not causally sufficient. Furthermore, here is an additional argument for point 3: even if I became convinced of the falsity of the thesis of the gap, all the same I would still have to engage in actions and thus exercise my own freedom no matter what. . . .
>
> For example, there is a kind of practical inconsistency in maintaining the following two theses:
>
> 1. I am now trying to make up my mind whom to vote for in the next election.
> 2. I take the existing psychological causes operating on me right now to be causally sufficient to determine whom I am going to vote for.

The inconsistency comes out in the fact that if I really believe 2, then there seems no point in making the effort involved in 1. The situation would be like taking a pill that I am sure will cure my headache by itself, and then trying to add some further psychological effort to the effects of the pill. If I really believe the pill is enough, then the rational thing to do is to sit back and let it take effect. (2001, pp. 71–72)

In discussing Searle's view, I would first point out that when Searle first introduces the notion of a "gap," it is a point about our *experiences*. Recall that he says, for instance, "the gap is that feature of our conscious decision making and acting where we sense alternative future decisions and actions as causally open to us." But he goes on to say: "We have to presuppose the gap. We have to presuppose that the psychological antecedents of many of our decisions and actions do not set causally sufficient conditions for those decisions and actions." If the second sentence of the latter quotation is intended as exegetical, then "the gap" is now thought to be not so much a feature of our phenomenology as of the objective relationship between our mental states.[1] This is somewhat confusing. From now on, I will take "the gap thesis" to be the claim that both our experience and the objective reality of the relationship between our mental states is indeterministic.

I believe that Searle's view is incorrect. Note that Leibniz describes what is essentially this view as the "Lazy Sophism":

This . . . demolishes . . . what the ancients [the Stoics, perhaps following Cicero] called the "Lazy Sophism," which ended in a decision to do nothing: for (people would say) if what I ask is to happen it will happen even though I should do nothing; and if it is not to happen it will never happen, no matter what trouble I take to achieve it . . . But the answer is quite ready: the effect being certain, the cause that shall produce it is certain also; and if the effect comes about it will be by virtue of a proportionate cause. Thus your laziness perchance will bring it about that you will obtain naught of what you desire, and that you will fall into those misfortunes which you would by acting with care have avoided. We see, therefore, that the connexion of causes with effects, far from causing an unendurable fatality, provides rather a means of obviating it. (1985, I, sec. 55, p. 153)[2]

It seems to me that Searle's view about deliberation falls prey to the same objections as the views of Taylor and van Inwagen. I believe that there would be a clear point to deliberation and practical reasoning, even if I were to reject the gap: I would still have an interest in—and deeply care about—figuring out what I have reason to do, and seeking to act accordingly. Even if the gap thesis is false, and antecedent psychological states are causally sufficient for my decision, and I know this, *it does not follow that I know what decision I will make and what action I will perform.* Hence, insofar as I care about acting in accordance with what I have, all things considered, reason to do, there is a clear point to engaging in deliberation.

Recall that Searle says that there is a practical inconsistency in maintaining the following.

1. I am now trying to make up my mind whom to vote for in the next election.

2. I take the existing psychological causes operating on me right now to be causally sufficient to determine whom I am going to vote for.

He says holding these two theses would be like "taking a pill that I am sure will cure my headache by itself, and then trying to add some further psychological effort to the effects of the pill." But in Searle's analogy, you *know* that the pill will cure your headache; in contrast, I am *not* assumed to know whom I will vote for in the next election. If I *did* know whom I would vote for, I agree that the point of making up my mind would appear to vanish.[3]

Suppose I know that my decision about the next election is causally determined by my current configuration of mental states (desires, beliefs, and so forth). Still, I can also know that my decision will *depend* on my practical reasoning in the following sense: if I were to judge it best, all things considered, to vote for candidate A, I would vote for candidate A; but if were to judge it best, all things considered, to vote for candidate B, I would vote for candidate B. Further, I can know that nothing distorts or impairs my practical reasoning—my ability to recognize the reasons there are, and to weigh them with an eye to making an all things considered judgment as to what is best. That is, nothing in the doctrine of causal determinism entails that the counterfactuals (that specify the relevant sort of dependency) are false, and nothing in this doctrine entails that I have any special sort of impairment of my capacity to engage in practical reasoning— certain phobias, compulsions, mental illnesses, and so forth. And, finally, nothing in the doctrine of causal determinism entails that I do not care about choosing and acting in accordance with my judgment about what is best to do. So there is a clear point to deliberation, even if I believe that antecedent mental states are causally sufficient for my decision.

Imagine, to make the point dramatically, that there are two doors in front of you, and you must choose which door to open. You know that behind door 1 is a million dollars, and behind door 2 is a den of rattlesnakes. Imagine, further, that you know that causal determinism is true, that causal determinism rules out alternative possibilities, and that causal determinism in itself does not entail that one has any physical paralysis or impairment of the human capacity for practical reasoning (no intense phobias, compulsions, paranoid schizophrenia, and so forth). Would Searle really not deliberate? What would he do—flip a coin, act arbitrarily, or what? Would he simply "sit back and watch the action unfold"? It would seem perfectly reasonable (at the very least) to take into consideration what is behind the doors, and to choose and act accordingly. Having collected the million dollars, you might pause to reflect that it turns out that that was the *only* thing you could have done (as long as this thought would not unduly delay the celebration!).

Searle admits that it is conceivable that our experience of indeterminism does not map onto the reality of the brain (and that the neurobiological events are causally deterministic); but he argues against this as follows.

> This result, however, is intellectually very unsatisfying, because, in a word, it is a modified form of epiphenomenalism. It says that the psychological processes of rational decision making do not really matter. The entire system is deterministic at the bottom level, and the idea that the top level has an element of freedom is simply a systematic illusion. . . . The thesis is epiphenomenalistic in this respect: there is a feature of our conscious lives, rational decision making and trying to carry out the decision, where we experience the gap and we experience the processes as making a causal difference to our behavior, but they do not in fact make any difference. The bodily movements were going to be exactly the same regardless of how these processes occurred.
>
> Maybe that is how it will turn out, but if so, the hypothesis seems to me to run against everything we know about evolution. It would have the consequence that the incredibly elaborate, complex, sensitive, and—above all—biologically expensive system of human and animal conscious rational decision making would actually make no difference whatever to the life and survival of the organisms. Epiphenomenalism is a possible thesis, but it is absolutely incredible, and if we seriously accepted it, it would make a change in our worldview, that is, in our conception of our relations to the world, more radical than any previous change, including the Copernican Revolution, Einsteinian relativity theory, and quantum mechanics.
>
> Why would [the hypothesis under consideration] render consciousness any more epiphenomenal than any other higher-level feature of a physical system? After all, the solidity of the piston in the car engine is entirely explained by the behavior of the molecules but that does not render solidity epiphenomenal. The difference is this: the essential characteristics of solidity matter to the performance of the engine, but the essential characteristic of conscious decision making, the experience of the gap, would not matter in the least to the performance of the agent. The bodily movements would have been the same, regardless of the experiences of the gap. (2001, pp. 285–286)

I have argued earlier that we do not need to presuppose a "gap" of the sort to which Searle is referring in order to engage in practical reasoning. I have suggested that practical reasoning may require an "epistemic gap"—it may be necessary that we not know exactly what we will choose and do, in order for there to be a point to practical reasoning (and deliberation). Searle's gap then is not an "essential characteristic of conscious decision making." And the epistemic gap clearly *would* make a difference: if it didn't exist, it might well not be reasonable to deliberate, and so my bodily movements might be quite different.

Note that, on the view of practical reasoning I am suggesting, psychological processes of rational decision-making *do* matter in a straightforward sense: if my deliberations had gone differently (and had thus issued in a different judgment as to what is best, all things considered), then my decisions and bodily movements would have been different. It is *not* the case that the bodily movements are going to be exactly the same, regardless of how my deliberations go. This, surely, is the important point about the causal efficacy of practical reasoning. So "the incredibly elaborate, complex, sensitive, and—above all—biologically expensive system of human and animal conscious rational decision making" *does* make a difference to the life and survival of organisms. Surely what is evolutionarily important in our capacities for practical reasoning is a certain capacity to recognize and respond to reasons; it seems bizarre to suppose that what is crucial to our survival—and the crowning glory of evolution—is the experience of the causal insufficiency of our mental states! If there is a gap here at all, it is in Searle's argument.

2.3. Kantian Approaches

I further contend that I can at the same time (or from the same "perspective") acknowledge both that my choice is causally determined (and thus that I have but one path genuinely available to me) and deliberate about which choice to make. That is, when I am engaged in practical reasoning and deliberation, I can continue to believe, and to acknowledge, that I am causally determined and thus not free. This follows both from the fact that the theses I acknowledge are metaphysical contentions, the truth of which can leave an epistemic gap, and from the distinctive purpose of practical reasoning. I can thus accept that the characteristic purposes of theoretical and practical reasoning diverge, while maintaining that an agent engaged in practical reasoning can in fact continue to hold such deliverances of theoretical reasoning as that he is causally determined and thus not free (in the sense of possessing alternative possibilities, construed incompatibilistically).

My view here is in stark contrast with the "neo-Kantian" two-perspective approach developed by such philosophers as Hilary Bok (1998) and Christine Korsgaard (1996b). For example, Hilary Bok says:

> If, when we engage in practical reasoning, we must regard ourselves as standing in the order of reasons rather than the order of causes, and if those orders are distinguished from one another by the relations of necessity to which they appeal, when we engage in practical reasoning we will not regard ourselves as subject to the same sort of necessity appealed to by theoretical reason. Theoretical necessity is causal: one object acts on another, thereby rendering some change in the latter necessary. To see oneself as necessitated in this way is to see oneself as passive: acted on rather than acting. (p. 160)

Further, she says:

> Because we regard ourselves as subject not to causal but to rational necessity, when we engage in practical reasoning we regard ourselves not as the passive object of external forces but as determining our own conduct; not as acted on

by things outside us but as choosing for reasons that we are free to accept or reject. And we regard these choices not as events that might simply befall us and with which we might or might not identify but as necessarily our own. For these reasons, as Christine Korsgaard writes, "[a]t the moment of decision, you must regard yourself as the author of your action." (p. 161; quoting Korsgaard, 1996a, p. 319)

But whereas I agree that at the moment of decision, one must in some suitable sense see oneself as the author of one's decision, I do not think that it follows that one must at that moment believe (either occurrently or dispositionally) that one is not causally determined. I certainly do not think that it should be accepted as uncontroversial that it follows from my choice's being causally determined that I am not the author of it or that I am merely passive with respect to it—these claims require argumentation, as there are ways of seeking to explain authorship and the difference between activity and passivity that are consistent with causal determinism.

In addition, the quotations from Korsgaard and Bok raise the vexing issue of the relationship between their notion of "regarding" and the more ordinary notion of "believing." With respect to this issue, consider the following passage from Bok.

> Insofar as regarding our choices as caused involves regarding them as determined by antecedent events, we cannot regard ourselves as caused to choose as we do when we engage in practical reasoning. [Here Bok inserts a footnote pointing us to Kant, *Grounding for the Metaphysics of Morals*, Ak. 448, and Korsgaard, 1996a, 162–163.] This is not because we believe we are not caused to choose as we do, but because when we engage in practical reasoning, we are concerned with another form of determination. (1998, p. 161)

Bok, however, faces the following dilemma. When we engage in practical reasoning, either we do in fact believe that we are not causally determined or we do not so believe. If we do, then it is obvious that a belief we have from the practical perspective can come into direct conflict with a belief we could have from the theoretical perspective. But it is a central feature of Bok's approach that the two perspectives cannot conflict in this way; the claim that the two perspectives cannot conflict is essential for Bok's project of showing freedom to be compatible with causal determinism.

Thus it seems as if Bok must say that, when we engage in practical reasoning, we do not believe (even dispositionally) that we are not causally determined. (I suppose the picture here is that, when one takes up the practical perspective, one does not believe in either causal determinism or its denial—one fails to form either of these beliefs.) But this leaves the notion of "regarding" somewhat mysterious; it seems as if, from the practical perspective, we *regard* ourselves as not subject to causal necessity but we do not *believe* we are not subject to causal necessity.

But if regarding is prized apart from believing in this way, what exactly is it to regard ourselves as not subject to causal necessity?[4] Further, I find it unattractive to suppose that from the practical perspective I cannot have (even dispositionally) a belief such as that causal determinism is false. Of course, the mere fact that, when engaged in practical reasoning, I am "concerned with" another form of necessitation does not entail that I do not—perhaps dispositionally—believe that I am in fact subject to causal necessitation. After all, when I am "concerned with" the leaking plumbing in my house, it does not follow that I do not believe (perhaps dispositionally) that the house is painted white (or that George Washington was the first president of the United States). If I do in fact have the belief that causal determinism is false, then why should I be precluded from having access (even dispositionally) to this belief when I take up the practical perspective? On this picture, the practical perspective is epistemically partitioned off from the rest of the agent in a puzzling way. The resulting compartmentalization is very unattractive, and, as I have suggested earlier, unnecessary.[5]

3. MORAL RESPONSIBILITY

3.1. The Concept of Moral Responsibility

Some philosophers have argued that if we lacked free will (in the sense that involves alternative possibilities), then we could not legitimately be considered morally responsible agents. There are, of course, different accounts of the concept of moral responsibility, as well as its conditions of application. I will simply sketch three views about the concept (or "nature") of moral responsibility; an elaboration of these accounts is beyond the scope of this essay. There are more extended discussions in Fischer and Ravizza (1998) and Fischer (1999).

On the first view about the nature of moral responsibility, an agent's moral responsibility consists in her being an appropriate candidate for ascriptions of certain ethical predicates, such as "good," "bad," "courageous," "charitable," "dastardly," "cruel," and so forth. The view is often put in terms of a metaphor; on this approach, an agent is morally responsible insofar as she has a "moral ledger." The ascription of moral predicates corresponds to making marks on the ledger (Zimmerman, 1988, p. 38).

A second view contends that when an agent is morally responsible for some behavior, it would not be inappropriate to expect the agent to provide an explanation of the behavior in question. On this view, when the agent is morally responsible in this sense, it *follows* that he has a moral ledger; but it is the expectation that the agent can provide a certain sort of explanation that is the *essence* of moral responsibility (Oshana, 1997).

A third sort of account of the nature of moral responsibility follows Peter Strawson (1962). Followers of Strawson include Paul Russell (1995) and R. Jay Wallace (1994). On this view, roughly speaking, an individual is morally responsible for some behavior in virtue of being an apt target for one of the "reactive attitudes" on the basis of the behavior. According to Strawson, the reactive attitudes include gratitude, indignation, resentment, love, respect, and forgiveness, and they manifest our involvement with other human beings in distinctively interpersonal relationships. There are various versions of the "Strawsonian" approach to the concept of moral responsibility.

In what follows I shall not take a stand on the correct account of the concept of moral responsibility. I shall simply speak of moral responsibility and let the reader fill in her favorite account of its nature. No matter what particular account of the concept of moral responsibility one accepts, it is clear that if it turned out that human beings lacked free will, there would be a deep and disturbing challenge to the idea that we are in fact morally responsible.

3.2. The Principle of Alternative Possibilities (PAP) and the Frankfurt-Type Examples

As I suggested earlier, we naturally think that the future is a garden of forking paths—that we at least at some important points in our lives have more than one path branching into the future. If this intuitive picture turned out to be false, then it would seem that we could not legitimately be held morally responsible for our behavior. After all, if I don't have free will in a sense that involves alternative possibilities, then I *have* to choose (and do) what I actually choose (and do). And if I have to choose what I do in fact choose, then presumably I am *compelled* so to choose, and cannot fairly be considered morally responsible for my choice. It is very plausible, then, to accept something like the "principle of alternative possibilities" (PAP), according to which an agent is morally responsible for (say) an action only if she could have done otherwise (Frankfurt, 1969). If PAP is true, then moral responsibility requires free will (in the sense that involves alternative possibilities); and if causal determinism rules out such alternative possibilities, it would thereby rule out moral responsibility.

Peter van Inwagen gives a particularly pointed defense of PAP:

> If we do not have free will, then there is no such thing as moral responsibility. This proposition, one might think, certainly deserves to be a commonplace. If someone charges you with, say, lying, and if you can convince him that it was

simply not within your power *not* to lie, then it would seem that you have done all that is necessary to absolve yourself of responsibility for lying. . . .

[W]ithout free will there is no moral responsibility: if moral responsibility exists, then someone is morally responsible for something he has done or for something he has left undone; to be morally responsible for some act or failure to act is at least to be able to have acted otherwise, whatever else it may involve; to be able to have acted otherwise is to have free will. Therefore, if moral responsibility exists, someone has free will. Therefore, if no one has free will, moral responsibility does not exist. (1983, pp. 161–162)

Van Inwagen goes on to say: "It would be hard to find a more powerful and persuasive argument than this little argument" (1983, p. 162). But whereas PAP might appear to be an obvious truth, it has been questioned by some philosophers. These philosophers contend (in one way or another) that what matters for moral responsibility is how the relevant choice or action is brought about, not whether the agent has alternative possibilities available to him. In contemporary philosophy, Harry Frankfurt has helped to focus the case against PAP with a set of examples with a characteristic structure (1969). These examples contain fail-safe mechanisms that (allegedly) both make it the case that the agent has no (relevant) alternative possibilities and also play no role in the agent's actual choice and action. Frankfurt says that if something plays no role in the agent's choice and action, then it cannot be relevant to his moral responsibility; thus, it would follow that the mechanisms in question both make it the case that the agent has no alternative possibilities and do not thereby threaten the agent's moral responsibility.

Here is a version of my favorite 'Frankfurt-type case'. Jones is in a voting booth deliberating about whether to vote for the Democrat or the Republican. After weighing reasons and deliberating in the "normal" way, he chooses to vote for the Democrat. Unbeknownst to him, Black, a neurosurgeon with Democratic sympathies, has implanted a device in Jones's brain that monitors Jones's brain activities. If he is about to choose to vote Democratic, the device does not intervene. If, however, Jones were about to choose to vote Republican, the device would trigger an intervention that would involve electronic stimulation of the brain sufficient to produce a choice to vote for the Democrat and an actual vote for the Democrat.

Now one might ask how the device can tell whether Jones is about to choose to vote Republican or Democratic. Frankfurt himself did not say much about this difficult problem, except that "Black is an excellent judge of such things." We can, however, add a "prior sign" to the case, as follows (Blumenfeld, 1971). If Jones is about to choose at $T2$ to vote for the Democrat at $T3$, he shows some involuntary sign—say a blush, a furrowed brow, or a neurological pattern in his brain readable by some sort of "neuroscope"—at $T1$. If it detects this, Black's device does not intervene. But if Jones is about to choose at $T2$ to vote Republican at $T3$, he shows a different involuntary sign at *T1*. This would trigger Black's device to intervene and cause Jones to choose at *T2* to vote for the Democrat and actually to vote for the Democrat at *T3*.

It seems that Black's device is precisely the kind of fail-safe device described earlier: it plays no role in Jones's deliberations, choice, or action, and yet its presence renders it true that Jones could not have done otherwise than choose and vote Democratic. Indeed, it seems that in this case Jones freely chooses to vote Democratic, freely does so, and can be considered morally responsible for his choice and action, even though he does not have alternative possibilities (given the presence of Black's device). This suggests that there is a kind of freedom or control—corresponding to choosing and acting freely—that does not require alternative possibilities, and that *this* sort of control (and not the alternative-possibilities control) is the freedom-relevant condition necessary for moral responsibility. There seem to be two kinds of freedom or control, and the Frankfurt-type examples help us to prize them apart.[6] It appears, then, that we have a counterexample to PAP.

3.3. A Dilemma for the Frankfurt-Type Examples

The suggestion (emerging from the Frankfurt-type examples) that moral responsibility does not require free will in the sense that involves alternative possibilities has not been entirely irresistible. In fact, a huge literature has developed surrounding these examples (e.g., Fischer, 1999; Widerker and McKenna, 2003). Consider the following dilemma in response to the Frankfurt-type examples (Ginet, 1996; Kane, 1985, 1996, pp. 142–150; Widerker, 1995a, 1995b; Wyma, 1997). Notice that in the typical presentation of the examples (as earlier) it is not made *explicit* whether causal determinism obtains. So suppose first that causal determinism obtains in the example. Now it would seem question-begging to conclude straight-forwardly from the example that Jones is morally responsible for voting for the Democrat; after all, the issue of whether causal determinism is compatible with moral responsibility is in dispute. But if it is assumed that causal determinism is false, and specifically that there is no deterministic relationship between the prior sign at *T1* and Jones's subsequent choice at *T2*, then Jones would appear to have free will at (or just prior to) *T2*: he can at least begin to choose to vote for the Republican. After all, given the prior sign and the laws of nature, it does *not* follow that Jones will choose at *T2* to vote for the Democrat (on the current assumption of causal indeterminism). So, the proponent of the dilemma says that either Jones is not morally responsible or there are alternative possibilities for Jones: one does not have a single context in which it is *both* true that Jones has no alternative possibilities and is morally responsible for his choice and action.

This is indeed a worrisome challenge to the conclusion that I (and others) draw from the Frankfurt-type examples—that PAP is false. Elsewhere I have presented a strategy of response to the dilemma (Fischer, 1999, 2002). Here I wish briefly to sketch this response, and then to consider an important objection to it.

3.4. A Response to the Dilemma

First consider the possibility that causal determinism is false (in the relevant way). Various philosophers have proposed that one can construct versions of the Frankfurt-type cases in which the agent is morally responsible and yet there are no alternatives at all, or at least no *robust* alternatives (Fischer, 1999; Widerker and McKenna, 2003). I think it is promising that such an example can be constructed, although I shall not attempt to defend this possibility here.

Suppose that causal determinism is true. That is, suppose that there is indeed a causally deterministic relationship between the sign exhibited at T_1 and Jones's choice to vote for the Democrat at T_2. Now it follows, given the argument for the incompatibility of causal determinism and the sort of control that involves alternative possibilities, that Jones does not have the power at T_2 to refrain from choosing to vote Democratic at T_2. It is not my strategy, however, simply to claim that Jones is obviously morally responsible for his choice; I agree that this would not be dialectically kosher.

Rather, I begin by suggesting that the fact that Black's device would intervene and ensure that Jones would choose to vote for the Democrat (and indeed vote for the Democrat), if Jones had shown a different sign at T_1, does not in itself show that Jones is not morally responsible for his actual choice (if he is in fact not morally responsible). That is, I am not supposing at this point that Jones is morally responsible for his actual choice at T_2 to vote for the Democrat. Rather, I am saying that the fact that he cannot do otherwise does not in itself (and apart from indicating or pointing to some *other* fact) make it the case that Jones is not morally responsible for his choice at T_2.

It seems evident to me that the fact that Black's device would intervene in the counterfactual scenario and ensure that Jones choose to vote for the Democrat is *irrelevant* to the "grounding" of Jones's actual moral responsibility for choosing to vote for the Democrat (and actually doing so). Something grounds moral responsibility, in the sense in question, insofar as it explains (or helps to explain) why the agent is morally responsible, *apart from simply being an indicator of something else that in fact explains the agent's moral responsibility*. Black's counterfactual intervention does not make any difference as to Jones's moral responsibility; if Black's device were "subtracted" from the example (to use Frankfurt's phrase), this would not change my assessment of Jones's moral responsibility in any way. Thus, I think that the example renders it plausible (although it does not decisively establish) that Jones's lack of alternative possibilities is *irrelevant* to the *grounding* of Jones's moral responsibility.

It is important to be a bit more careful here. I have claimed that consideration of the example of Jones (a typical Frankfurt-type case) should first elicit the intuition that the fact that there is a fail–safe device present that would intervene in the counterfactual scenario is *irrelevant* to the grounding of Jones's moral responsibility. My contention is that this then *suggests* that even if Jones had *no* alternative possibilities at all, this would be irrelevant to the grounding of his moral responsibility. It would then follow that in a causally deterministic world, in which it is assumed that Jones has no alternative possibilities at all, his lack of alternative possibilities would be irrelevant to the grounding of his moral responsibility. That is, his lack of alternative possibilities cannot in itself and apart from indicating something else explain why Jones is not morally responsible, if Jones is in fact not morally responsible.

In my view, this then is the moral of the Frankfurt-type cases. They suggest that alternative possibilities are irrelevant to the grounding of moral responsibility. Thus they are an important step along the way toward arguing that causal determinism is compatible with moral responsibility. Of course, someone might say that alternative possibilities are a necessary condition for moral responsibility because their presence indicates *some other factor* (perhaps causal indeterminism in the actual sequence), which must be present for there to be moral responsibility (Della Rocca, 1998; Ekstrom, 1998, 2000, esp. pp. 181–214). This is a perfectly reasonable position, which can then be addressed; I shall briefly discuss this maneuver hereafter. But it does not diminish the importance of the moral of the Frankfurt-type cases; in my view, once one establishes that alternative possibilities are irrelevant to the *grounding* of moral responsibility, it is considerably *easier* to argue that causal determinism (and the lack of alternative possibilities) is compatible with moral responsibility.

3.5. A Recent Objection and a Further Reply

Before I address the contention that alternative possibilities indicate some other factor that grounds moral responsibility, I wish to consider a recent objection to my strategy for dealing with the "deterministic" horn of the dilemmatic attack on the Frankfurt-type examples. My contention is that Black's presence and counterfactual intervention is irrelevant to the grounding of moral responsibility. But someone might grant this, while insisting that it is not pertinent, since it is not Black's counterfactual intervention but the condition of the world at T_1 (including the sign Jones exhibits) that makes it true that Jones does not have it in his power at T_2 to choose to vote for the Republican. If it is the condition of the world at T_1 that makes it true that Jones cannot at T_2 choose to vote for the Republican, then it is not so obvious that what makes it the case that Jones cannot at T_2 choose otherwise is irrelevant to the grounding of Jones's moral responsibility. This line of attack has been developed by Stewart Goetz (forthcoming).

Goetz says:

> [The Frankfurt-style example] creates the appearance that it is Black's device, which is in the alternative sequence of events, that makes it the case that Jones is not free to choose otherwise. This appearance is *illusory* because without the obtaining of causal determinism in the actual sequence of events, the device cannot prevent Jones from making an alternative choice, and with causal determinism in the actual sequence of events it is not the device that prevents Jones from making an alternative choice. In short, if Jones is not free to choose otherwise, it is because of the occurrence of causal determinism in the actual sequence of events and not because of Black's device in the alternative sequence.

Goetz goes on to say:

> [Fischer's strategy] requires the truth of causal determinism in order to create the *illusion* that it is the presence of something in the alternative sequence of events (e.g., Black's device) that makes it the case that Jones is not free to choose otherwise. It is only through this illusion that one is tempted to endorse the conclusion of the first step of Fischer's argument, which is that the lack of alternative possibilities is not sufficient for the lack of moral responsibility, and, thereby, Jones might be morally responsible even though he is not free to choose otherwise. Once this illusion is exposed, one's initial conviction that the lack of an alternative choice is sufficient for the lack of moral responsibility is vindicated.

Goetz's point could be put as follows. What really makes it the case that Jones cannot choose otherwise at T_2 is the prior state of the world together with the laws of nature. In other words, what makes it the case that Jones lacks an alternative possibility at T_2 is causal determination in the actual sequence. So it is quite beside the point that Black's counterfactual intervention is irrelevant to the grounding of Jones's moral responsibility; after all, it is *not* Black's counterfactual intervention that makes it the case that Jones cannot choose otherwise at T_2. Thus we do not have a case in which the fact that the agent could not have chosen (or done) otherwise is irrelevant to the grounding of his moral responsibility.

Frankfurt-type scenarios are cases in which an action is 'causally overdetermined'. The overdetermination is considered 'preemptive' rather than 'simultaneous'. In simultaneous overdetermination, two causal sequences both operate and actually issue in the overdetermined action (or event). In preemptive overdetermination, some event is actually caused in a certain way, and would have been caused in a different way, had the actual causal sequence not taken place.

So, in the Frankfurt-type scenario presented earlier, Black's device is part of what makes it the case that Jones's choice at T2 is preemptively overdetermined.

What is also of note is that in these scenarios, Jones's *inability to choose (or do) otherwise* is *also* overdetermined. (I would describe the overdetermination here as simultaneous rather than preemptive; but the proper way to describe it is a delicate matter, as the thing in question is a fact—a modal fact—rather than a concrete action or event.) It is not only the act that is overdetermined; it is also the agent's lack of alternative possibilities. So my response to Goetz is as follows.

In the Frankfurt-type scenario, *two* causes make it the case that Jones is unable to choose otherwise at T2: the prior condition of the world (together with the laws of nature) and Black's counterfactual intervention. What the examples show is that *the mere fact* that Jones is unable to choose otherwise does not *in itself* establish that Jones is not morally responsible for his choice. This is because Black's counterfactual intervention is one of the factors that make it the case that Jones is unable to choose otherwise at T2, and yet it is irrelevant to the grounding of Jones's moral responsibility. Considering this factor (the counterfactual intervention), and bracketing any other factor that might make it the case that Jones is unable to choose otherwise at T2, it seems to me that Jones may well be morally responsible for his action. The mere fact that he lacks alternative possibilities, then, cannot in itself be the reason Jones is not morally responsible, if indeed he is not morally responsible.

Now, of course, it is *also* true that the prior condition of the world, together with the natural laws, makes it the case that Jones lacks alternative possibilities. But, given that the mere fact of lacking alternative possibilities does not in itself rule out moral responsibility, why should *this way* of lacking alternative possibilities rule out moral responsibility? Why exactly should the significance of causal determination be that it rules out alternative possibilities? This is exactly what the Frankfurt-type examples call into question.

In an interesting passage, Goetz (forthcoming) says:

> The proponent of PAP thinks that the lack of the freedom to choose otherwise does not by itself explain the absence of moral responsibility. This is because he believes that when this lack obtains, its obtaining is itself explained by, and can only be explained by, the occurrence of causal determinism in the actual sequence of events. What the advocate of PAP believes, then, is that when an agent is not morally responsible because he is not free to choose otherwise, he lacks moral responsibility *not* simply because he is not free to choose otherwise but because he is not free to choose otherwise *because of causal determinism.*

Precisely this move is made by Derk Pereboom (2001, p. 3). But why exactly does it *matter* that causal determination rules out alternative possibilities? If the mere fact of the lack of alternative possibilities does not in itself rule out moral responsibility, why would a particular *way* of expunging alternative possibilities rule out moral responsibility? Granted that causal determination is a certain way of taking away alternative possibilities, why should it be thought that causal determination threatens moral responsibility in virtue of constituting *a way of ruling out alternative possibilities*? The Frankfurt-type examples, then, suggest that one needs to look in a different direction if one seeks to argue that causal determination rules out moral responsibility.

The dialectic could be put somewhat differently. There can be two different ways in which some factor renders an agent unable to choose or do otherwise (or eliminates alternative possibilities). In one way, the factor does not play a role in the actual sequence; it does not flow through the actual course of events. In another way, the factor does flow through the actual sequence. The Frankfurt-type scenarios are all cases in which there exists some ability-undermining factor that does *not* play a role in the actual sequence leading to the relevant choice and action. So it seems unfair to extrapolate from this sort of factor in the Frankfurt-type cases; that is, even if we are initially inclined to say that the agent is morally responsible in the Frankfurt-type cases (based on prescinding from other factors and focusing on the counterfactual intervener setup), it would not follow that the agent is morally responsible in a causally deterministic world.

To reply, I grant that the Frankfurt-type examples are not *decisive*. That is, they do not provide examples that would absolutely and uncontroversially decide the issue about the relationship between causal determinism and moral responsibility. But I certainly do not believe that it is reasonable to expect such examples here—or in any contentious area of philosophy! And, as I argued earlier, the Frankfurt-type examples suggest that if causal determination is indeed problematic, it is not so in virtue of flowing through the actual sequence *and thereby ruling out alternative possibilities*.

3.6. Source Incompatibilism

So far I have been primarily concerned with the issue of whether alternative possibilities are relevant to the *grounding* of moral responsibility. As I pointed out earlier, even if they are irrelevant to the grounding of responsibility, they may nevertheless be relevant to responsibility as a *sign* of something else that in fact grounds moral responsibility. Many years ago, I emphasized that the mere fact that the Frankfurt-type examples show that alternative possibilities are not required for moral responsibility does *not* in itself show that *causal determinism* is compatible with moral responsibility (Fischer, 1982). I pointed out that causal determinism is a thesis about the "actual sequence" and thus that it does not follow from the falsity of PAP that causal determinism is compatible with moral responsibility.[7] As I put it:

> Both the compatibilist and the incompatibilist alike can unite in conceding that enough information is encoded in the actual sequence to ground our responsibility attributions; as philosophers we need to decode this information and see whether it is consistent with deterministic causation. (Fischer, 1982, p. 40)

In my subsequent work, I have explored various ways in which it might be thought that causal determination in the actual sequence rules out moral responsibility (Fischer, 1994, esp. pp. 147–54, 2002). I have in the end concluded that causal determination in the actual sequence does not rule out moral responsibility.

Other philosophers have disagreed, contending that causal determination in the actual sequence rules out moral responsibility "directly" (and not in virtue of expunging alternative possibilities). Robert Kane (1996) has argued that in order to be morally responsible, we have to meet a condition of "ultimacy," according to which the "causal buck must stop here"; that is, we cannot be mere intermediate links in a causally deterministic sequence that begins prior to our births. Similarly, Laura Ekstrom (2000) argues that the past and laws "push" us into our choices and actions, if causal determinism is true. She thus argues that causal determination in the actual sequence is incompatible with moral responsibility. In addition, although Derk Pereboom believes that versions of the Frankfurt-type examples successfully show that PAP is false, he nevertheless defends the following principle.

> An action is free in the sense required for moral responsibility only if it is not produced by a deterministic process that traces back to causal factors beyond the agent's control. (2001, p. 3)

I believe that none of the arguments purporting to show that causal determination in the actual sequence rules out moral responsibility is particularly strong, although this of course is a highly contentious matter. One of the difficulties is to see how to *argue* for the incompatibility claim; after all, Pereboom's principle seems to be a simple *restatement* of incompatibilism about causal determinism and moral responsibility, not an argument for it. In any case, I would contend that the Frankfurt-type cases at least help us to make progress toward defending the compatibility of causal determinism and moral responsibility, insofar as they help us to take a very important *first step*: they render it plausible (although they do not decisively establish) that the sort of free will that involves alternative possibilities does not ground attributions of moral responsibility, that is, it does not in itself and apart from indicating some other factor explain why we are morally responsible, if we are in fact morally responsible.

4. Ethical Judgments

4.1. Judgments of Deontic Morality

Earlier I pointed out that there are various accounts of the concept of moral responsibility. On the "ledger view," if an agent is morally responsible, then she has a moral ledger—the marks correspond to various sorts of moral judgments. Some philosophers hold that these judgments include claims about what the agent ought and ought not to do, and what is right or wrong for the individual to do. These philosophers thus connect moral responsibility tightly to the appropriateness of judgments about ought, ought not, right, and wrong. Peter van Inwagen appears to make this sort of connection in the continuation of a passage quoted earlier:

> If someone charges you with, say, lying, and if you can convince him that it was simply not within your power *not* to lie, then it would seem that you have done all that is necessary to absolve yourself of responsibility for lying. Your accuser cannot say, "I concede it was not within your power not to lie; none the less you ought not to have lied." (1983, p. 161)

On this sort of approach to moral responsibility, if (contrary to van Inwagen) one has successfully defended the compatibility of causal determinism (and the lack of the sort of free will that involves alternative possibilities) with moral responsibility, one has thereby defended the compatibility of causal determinism (and the lack of free will) with judgments employing "ought," "ought not," "right," and "wrong." But one might accept an alternative account of the concept of moral responsibility, or even a ledger view according to which the relevant "marks" correspond to (say) "goodness" and "badness" but not "ought," "ought not," and so forth. If one accepted (say) a Strawsonian account of moral responsibility (or the sort of ledger view just sketched), it might be that causal determinism is compatible with moral responsibility but *not* with judgments employing "ought," "ought not," "right," and "wrong." This is precisely the view held by Ishtiyaque Haji. Haji (1998, 2002) accepts the conclusion of the Frankfurt-type cases that moral responsibility does not require alternative possibilities and further that it is compatible with causal determinism; but he rejects the contention that causal determinism is compatible with judgments employing "obligation," "ought," "ought not," "right," and "wrong." (Following Haji, I shall call the latter "judgments of deontic morality.") On this sort of view, the Strawsonian "reactive attitudes" are prized apart from the judgments of deontic morality, and whereas the former are compatible with causal determinism, the latter are not. (Note that Haji distinguishes judgments pertaining to notions such "goodness" and "badness" from the judgments of deontic morality; he is willing to concede that the former sorts of judgments are entirely compatible with causal determinism.)

Why might one think that the judgments of deontic morality are incompatible with causal determinism? I will treat "ought not" and "wrong" as interchangeable, and "ought" and "obligatory" as interchangeable. I shall lay out the argument with respect to "wrong." It will be easy to see how to construct parallel arguments for the other judgments of deontic morality. Here is a simple version of the argument:

1. Suppose some individual, John, does something morally wrong.
2. If John's Xing was wrong, then he ought to have done something else instead.
3. If John ought to have done something else instead, then he could have done something else instead.
4. So John could have done something else instead.
5. But if causal determinism is true, then John could not have done anything other than he actually did.
6. So, if causal determinism is true, it cannot be the case that John's Xing was wrong. (Copp, 1997; Haji, 2002; Pereboom, 2001; Widerker, 1991)

This is a potent and disturbing argument. I have sought to argue that causal determinism is compatible with moral responsibility. This result would be considerably less interesting if causal determinism were nevertheless incompatible with the central judgments of deontic morality. There are however various ways of seeking to block the conclusion of the argument. I have discussed the rejection of premise 2 elsewhere (Fischer, 2003; a reply to Yaffe, 1999). Here, however, I shall focus on the rejection of premise 3 (and thus the rejection of the ought-implies-can maxim (henceforth "the Maxim").

4.2. Copp's Defense of the Maxim

I believe that there are Frankfurt-type omissions cases that are relevantly similar to Frankfurt-type cases with respect to actions. That is, there are cases in which an agent is morally responsible for not Xing, although she cannot in fact X. I argue for this position in Fischer and Ravizza (1998, 123–150). Some of these are cases in which an agent is blameworthy for not Xing and yet she cannot X. In fact, I believe that anyone who accepts the Frankfurt-type action cases must accept that there are such omissions-cases (Fischer and Ravizza, 1998, pp. 123–150; Frankfurt, 1994). Further, the basic intuitions elicited by the Frankfurt-type cases conflict with the Maxim and cast doubt on its intuitive plausibility. Although this certainly does not decisively refute the maxim, it does suggest that it is not ad hoc for anyone who accepts that the Frankfurt-type cases show that moral responsibility does not require alternative possibilities to reject the Maxim. (Ishtiyaque Haji has presented a useful critical discussion of my argument [2002, pp. 43–47].)

But rejection of the Maxim comes at a steep price. In the most detailed, sustained, and penetrating discussion of the motivation for the Maxim of which I am aware, David Copp (2003) contends that it is preferable to preserve the Maxim than to reject PAP on the basis of the Frankfurt-type cases (or on any other basis). Copp presents two primary arguments on behalf of the Maxim, and it will be useful to discuss each of them.

Copp contends that there is a conflict between the interpretation of the Frankfurt-type cases according to which they show that moral responsibility does not require alternative possibilities and the Maxim. According to Copp, "[this] is not a conflict between intuition and a recherché theoretical proposition. It is a conflict among intuitions" (2003, p. 271). Copp says:

> The most basic motivation for the Maxim, it seems to me, begins with the thought that it would be unfair to expect a person to do something, or to demand or require that she do it, if she lacked the ability to do it. This thought is about what we might call 'agent-requirements,' which arise in cases in which an authoritative agent requires someone under her authority or jurisdiction to do something. An example might be a situation in which a boss requires an employee to do something that the employee lacks the ability to do. A supervisor at the post office might demand that a mail carrier cook a soufflé for everyone in the post office in the next five minutes when the mail carrier does not even know what a soufflé is. We can imagine many similar cases, including cases in which a parent expects a child to do something she cannot do, or a teacher requires a student to do something she cannot do, or a sergeant requires a recruit to do something she cannot do. The intuition is that agent-requirements of this kind are morally unfair when the person of whom the demand is made lacks the ability to comply. (p. 271)

Copp goes on to claim that although the intuition elicited earlier is about "agent-requirements" rather than "moral requirements," he contends that a similar point applies to moral requirements. As Copp puts it, "if there would be unfairness in the latter case [the mere agent-requirement case], then there is surely a kind of unfairness in the moral requirement in the former case even if there is no agent who is being unfair" (2003, p. 272). So the first argument in favor of the Maxim is the intuition that it would be *unfair* to morally require someone to do something, if he cannot do the thing in question.

Copp's second argument in favor of the Maxim is based on metaethical considerations about the "point" of moral requirements. Copp says:

> The heart of the argument is roughly as follows: any moral theory must somehow account for, or make room for, the intuition that there is a *point* to re-

quiring an action, namely, crudely, to get it done. Clearly, moreover, an action will not be done if the prospective actor cannot perform it. . . .

The argument can be summarized as follows. If an agent is morally required to do A in a particular situation, then all other options she faces are morally ruled out. If the agent cannot do A, then doing A is not among her options. Hence, if an agent is morally required to do A but cannot do A, then *all* of her options are morally ruled out. But information that an agent is morally required to do something provides her with guidance among her options by distinguishing between options that are morally ruled out and options that are not morally ruled out. If all of an agent's options are morally ruled out by a moral requirement, then information about the requirement cannot provide her with such guidance. Given then that moral requirements have a characteristic relevance to our decisions, by distinguishing between options that are morally ruled out and options that are not morally ruled out, it follows that if a person cannot do A, it is not the case that she is morally required to do A. That is, the Maxim follows from the intuition about the relevance of moral requirements to decision-making. (2003, pp. 272, 274)

Copp thus offers two strategies for motivating the Maxim: the fairness argument and the argument from the relevance of moral requirements to decision-making. He thus points out that if one favors one's intuition that the Frankfurt-type examples show (albeit not decisively) that PAP is to be rejected, then one must give up strong intuitions about fairness and the relationship between morality and practical reasoning. Copp thinks that giving up these latter intuitions would be too steep a price to pay. In accepting PAP, however, Copp admits that his view might be open to incompatibilist worries; if causal determinism turned out to be true along with PAP, then there emerges the danger that no one could legitimately be accountable (blameworthy) for what she does. In the end, Copp concludes that "any adequate analysis of the ability to act must be compatibilist. It must be such that the ability to do something other than what one actually does is compatible with determinism" (2003, p. 295).

I shall first consider Copp's argument from fairness. More specifically, the contention is that it would be unfair to hold someone blameworthy for failing to do X, if he could not do X. In order to bolster this judgment, Copp invokes an example in which it does seem unfair to require a mail carrier to cook a soufflé for everyone in the post office in five minutes. But I would reply that it is crucial to distinguish two importantly different sorts of omissions: "simple" and "complex" omissions. If one focuses solely on complex omissions, it does indeed seem as if it would be unfair to hold an individual blameworthy for failing to do X, if he is unable to do X. But my intuitions about *simple* omissions are quite different. Mark Ravizza and I distinguish between simple and complex omissions and develop accounts of moral responsibility for both types of omissions (1998, pp. 123–150).

Consider an example offered by Harry Frankfurt:

Imagine that a person—call him "Stanley"—deliberately keeps himself very still. He refrains, for some reason, from moving his body at all. . . . [S]uppose that here is someone with a powerful interest in having Stanley refrain from making any deliberate movements, who arranges things in such a way that Stanley will be stricken with general paralysis if he shows any inclination to move. Nonetheless, Stanley may keep himself still quite on his own altogether independently of this person's schemes. Why should Stanley not be morally responsible for keeping still, in that case, just as much as if there had been nothing to prevent him from moving had he chosen to do so? (1994, pp. 620–621)

I agree with Frankfurt here. And surely Stanley could be considered blameworthy, should something morally important hang on his moving his body rather than keeping still.

Stanley's not moving his body, or refraining from moving, is a "simple omission": the omission is entirely constituted by his failure to move his body. There are many more such omissions, and in these cases it is plausible that the agents are indeed morally responsible—and potentially morally blameworthy—although they could not have refrained from keeping still (Clarke, 1994, pp. 195–208; Fischer and Ravizza, 1998, pp. 123–150; Glannon, 1995, pp. 261–274; McIntyre, 1994, pp. 453–488).

I do not have any "proof" of my contention that in simple omissions, an agent can be blameworthy for failing to do X, even though she could not have done X. It seems to me, however, that this is a completely reasonable intuition, shared by many philosophers and supported by a range of examples. I agree, however, that it seems upon initial consideration that in cases of complex omissions, an agent cannot be blameworthy for failing to do X, unless she can in fact do X.

My purpose here is simply to suggest that *there are* cases in which an agent can legitimately be considered blameworthy for failing to do X, although she could not have done X. I would contend that Copp fails to see this because he focuses entirely on a proper subset of cases—the complex omissions. If I am correct, then the argument from fairness is vitiated—there are cases in which it would not be unfair to blame someone for failing to do something she could not do (and never could do).

Now I suppose someone could say that because it is obviously unfair to blame someone for his failure in the complex omissions cases, we should conclude that it would *also* be unfair to blame the agent in the simple omissions cases. But I think that this gets the dialectic wrong: we are supposed to be generating general principles by reference to intuitions about *all* of the relevant cases. It would seem inappropriate to generate such a principle on the basis of a proper subset of the cases, and then apply it to *all* of the cases, even when it does not seem to yield the correct results in all of the cases.

What would be ideal is a theory that explains exactly why the agents are indeed morally responsible in the simple omissions cases and not morally responsible in the complex omissions cases (discussed earlier). Such an explanation would obviously not invoke the notion of inability to do otherwise, lest it lead to implausible results in the simple omissions cases. Mark Ravizza and I have offered just such a theory of moral responsibility for omissions; on this approach, moral responsibility is associated with freedom (or control) but not the sort of freedom (or control) that involves alternative possibilities (1998, pp. 123–150).[8] Quite apart from whether this theory is adequate, my point here is that Copp has not really motivated the central claim of the argument for fairness: he has relied on only a proper subset of the relevant data.

Copp's second argument in favor of the Maxim pertains to the role of moral requirements in guiding action. I agree that moral requirements play a distinctive and important role in guiding our practical reasoning (and, thus, our behavior). But, as earlier, in my discussion of practical reasoning and deliberation, it is crucial to distinguish between genuine metaphysical possibilities and 'epistemic possibilities', or possibilities that obtain for all the agent knows. An epistemic possibility is not ruled out by the agent's knowledge. Indispensable to the proper analysis of deliberation and also the Frankfurt-type examples is the fact that one's metaphysical possibilities (the paths that are genuinely available to one) may diverge from one's epistemic possibilities (that paths that are, for all one knows, available to one). I would contend that moral requirements rule out certain of the courses of action that are, for all we know, open to us—certain epistemic possibilities.

Recall Copp's argument, which begins as follows.

> If an agent is morally required to do A in a particular situation, then all other options she faces are morally ruled out. If the agent cannot do A, then doing A is not among her options. Hence, if an agent is morally required to do A but cannot do A, then *all* of her options are morally ruled out. But information that an agent is morally required to do something provides her with guidance among her options by distinguishing between options that are morally ruled out and options that are not morally ruled out. (2003, p. 274)

Given the distinction between the two different kinds of possibilities, the argument becomes, in my words:

> Given an agent is morally required to do A in a particular situation, then all other epistemic options she faces are morally ruled out. If the agent cannot do A, then doing A is not among her metaphysical options. Hence, if an agent is morally required to do A but cannot do A, then *all* of her options are morally ruled out. But information that an agent is morally required to do something provides her with guidance among her options by distinguishing between options that are morally ruled out and options that are not morally ruled out.

It is evident where the problems lie. The conclusion that if an agent is morally required to do *A* but cannot do *A*, then *all* of her options are morally ruled out, infelicitously elides the distinction between epistemic and metaphysical options. From the mere fact that an agent lacks a certain metaphysical option it does *not* follow that she lacks the corresponding epistemic option. So, from the mere fact that an agent in fact *cannot* do *A,* it does not follow that she knows that she cannot do *A.* Thus, all that follows from the moral requirement and the metaphysical fact is that all of the agent's epistemic alternatives are ruled out, *except A.* But there is nothing problematic about this; and now the moral requirement can have its distinctive role in guiding deliberation and action. Moral requirements insert themselves into the space of epistemic possibilities, not directly into the space of metaphysical possibilities.

I conclude that despite his noteworthy efforts, David Copp has not successfully presented a compelling motivation for the Maxim. If we reject the Maxim, we can reject PAP. And we are thus not pushed toward a compatibilist account of freedom; as I explained earlier, a compatibilist must say that we are free either to "change" the past or the natural laws. That is, the compatibilist must *deny* that our freedom is the freedom to extend the given past, holding the laws of nature fixed. But this is quite implausible.

5. CONCLUSION

Causal determinism threatens our intuitive and natural view of ourselves as having free will in the sense that involves genuinely available alternative possibilities. It threatens the common-sense view that the future is a garden of forking paths. For all we know, causal determinism might turn out to be true. In this essay, I have explored the question of what would be lost in a world without free will of this sort. Would there still be a point to deliberation and practical reasoning? Could there be moral responsibility and ethical judgments?

The discovery that causal determinism is true would significantly alter our picture of ourselves: in my view, giving up the view that the future is a garden of forking paths is a major change, with important resonances in the way we understand and couch our deliberation, moral responsibility, and ethical judgments. But I do not believe that we would need entirely to jettison any of these aspects of our moral lives. I believe that deliberation, moral responsibility, and judgments of deontic morality are compatible with causal determinism and the lack of free will (in the sense involving alternative possibilities, understood as earlier).

Other philosophers are not so sanguine, and there is a bewildering distribution of views on these issues. As I have shown, Peter van Inwagen is a philosopher who believes that causal determinism and the lack of free will would rule out both moral responsibility and judgments of deontic morality, as well as rendering us inconsistent every time we deliberate. Thus, van Inwagen and I represent, as it were, "corner positions." There are various "in-between" views. Ishiyaque Haji contends that causal determinism and the lack of alternative possibilities are completely compatible with robust moral responsibility but *not* with judgments of deontic morality. In contrast, Derk Pereboom is willing to concede that robust moral responsibility (involving, say, reactive attitudes such as indignation and resentment) does not require free will in the sense that involves alternative possibilities, but he insists that causal determinism indeed rules out such moral responsibility.[9] Nevertheless, he believes that causal determinism is compatible with judgments of deontic morality. Similarly, Saul Smilansky holds that causal determinism rules out robust moral responsibility, but not the judgments of deontic morality. Both Pereboom and Smilansky argue that although causal determinism would rule out robust moral responsibility, it still leaves room for something akin to moral responsibility—something that is significant and valuable. It also leaves room for various ethical judgments. So whereas Haji thinks that the more significant threat from causal determinism is to the judgments of deontic morality, Pereboom and Smilansky argue quite the opposite. In contrast, both van Inwagen and I view the threats from causal determinism as equal in strength (although we come to opposite conclusions).

A recurrent theme has been the difference between an agent's epistemic possibilities and metaphysical possibilities, given the truth of causal determinism. This disparity is crucial to understanding practical reasoning and deliberation in a causally deterministic world. It is also an indispensable ingredient in the description of the Frankfurt-type examples. In addition, the nonidentity of these two sets of possibilities explains how moral requirements can play their signature role of guiding action, even in a causally deterministic world. On my view, the collapse of these two sets into one—the set of metaphysical possibilities—would be a dramatic as the collapse of the wave pocket in quantum mechanics. My view is the opposite of the famous biblical contention that the truth shall make us free. But this is really not surprising: If I genuinely knew all my future choices and behavior, then it would seem to me that I *could* just sit back and let the future unroll.

John Searle writes:

> Suppose you go into a restaurant, and the waiter brings you the menu. You have a choice between, let's say, veal chops and spaghetti; you cannot say: "Look, I am a determinist, che sara, sara. I will just wait and see what I order! I will wait to see what my beliefs and desires cause." (2001, p. 14)

Given the fact that the sets of metaphysical and epistemic possibilities are not identical, no determinist need reason in the indicated way. But if we collapse the sets into one, "che sara sara" would not be inappropriate, or out of tune.[10]

NOTES

I am grateful to David Copp for his extremely careful and helpful comments, as well as for his patience and support. I am also thankful for scholarly and philosophical help from Gideon Yaffe.

1. I am indebted to David Copp for this point.

2. I am grateful to Gideon Yaffe for providing this reference.

3. As David Copp has pointed out in a personal communication, July 2004, even if I knew whom I would vote for, I might care to know why I would vote for this person and whether I have good reasons. This might give me a reason to make up my mind even if I know whom I will vote for.

4. Various philosophers wish to distinguish some sort of "proto-belief" state, such as "taking," or "accepting," that falls short of being a genuine belief; but if this is what regarding consists in, it is still unclear why it cannot conflict with the deliverances of theoretical reason.

5. For further discussion, see Fischer, 2001; Wallace, 2000. In addition, David Copp has pointed out that in deciding what to do, surely we need to bring our empirical beliefs to bear, including beliefs about cause and effect. To put it mildly, Bok's approach seems very puzzling.

6. Frankfurt distinguishes between freedom of choice and freedom of action, on the one hand, and choosing freely and acting freely, on the other. The former notions imply alternative possibilities (freedom to choose otherwise and freedom to do otherwise), whereas the latter do not. Mark Ravizza and I, 1998, distinguish between "regulative control," which implies alternative possibilities, and "guidance control," which does not. We seek to give detailed accounts of guidance control of actions, omissions, and consequences.

7. Subsequently, such philosophers as Robert Kane, 1996, and Derk Pereboom, 2001, have emphasized this point.

8. Fischer and Ravizza, 1998, 123–150. The theory offers a systematic approach to responsibility for actions, omissions, and consequences; it employs he notion of "guidance control" rather than "regulative control." (The latter sort of control requires alternative possibilities, whereas the former does not.) The theory is systematic in the sense that the accounts of guidance control of consequences and omissions build on and extend the account of guidance control of actions.

9. A similar view is defended by Eleonore Stump, 1988, 1990, 1999, as well as David Hunt, 2000.

10. There may be cases in which an agent knows in advance what he or she will choose (and do), because choosing otherwise would be "unthinkable." Various authors,

including Frankfurt, 1988a, and Wolf, 1990, believe that such "volitional necessity" is compatible with moral responsibility. Gary Watson, 2002, helpfully discusses this sort of necessity. If such volitional necessity exists, and if it makes literally true that one can know what one will choose in the future, and if it is indeed true that the relevant agents are morally responsible for their choices (and *not* in virtue of past choices, of which it was true that it was epistemically possible for the agent to choose otherwise), then perhaps there is an asymmetry between moral responsibility and deliberation, as regards the collapse of epistemic and metaphysical possibilities. The collapse would not entail the lack of moral responsibility, even if it entailed there being no point to deliberation. (But see note 3 in regard to this last point, about deliberation.)

REFERENCES

Beaty, Michael D., ed. 1990. *Christian Theism and the Problems of Philosophy*. Notre Dame, Ind.: University of Notre Dame Press.

Blumenfeld, David. 1971. "The Principle of Alternate Possibilities." *Journal of Philosophy* 67: 339–344.

Bok, Hilary. 1998. *Freedom and Responsibility*. Princeton, N.J.: Princeton University Press.

Buss, Sarah, and Lee Overton, eds. 2002. *Contours of Agency: Essays on Themes from Harry Frankfurt*. Cambridge, Mass.: MIT Press.

Clarke, Randolph. 1994. "Ability and Responsibility for Omissions." *Philosophical Studies* 73: 195–208.

Copp, David. 1997. "Defending the Principle of Alternate Possibilities: Blameworthiness and Moral Responsibility." *Nous* 31: 441–456.

———. 2003. " 'Ought Implies 'Can', Blameworthiness, and the Principle of Alternative Possibilities." In Widerker and McKenna, 2003, 265–300.

Della Rocca, Michael. 1998. "Frankfurt, Fischer and Flickers." *Nous* 32: 99–105.

Ekstrom, Laura. 1998. "Protecting Incompatibilist Freedom." *American Philosophical Quarterly* 35: 281–291.

———. 2000. *Free Will: A Philosophical Study*. Boulder, Colo.: Westview Press.

Fischer, John Martin. 1982. "Responsibility and Control." *Journal of Philosophy* 89: 24–40.

———. 1994. *The Metaphysics of Free Will: An Essay on Control*. Oxford: Blackwell.

———. 1999. "Recent Work on Moral Responsibility." *Ethics* 110: 93–139.

———. 2001. "Book Review of Hilary Bok, *Freedom and Responsibility*." *Mind* 110: 432–438.

———. 2002. "Frankfurt-Style Compatibilism." In Buss and Overton, 2002, 1–26.

———. 2003. " 'Ought-Implies-Can', Causal Determinism, and Moral Responsibility." *Analysis* 63: 244–250.

Fischer, John Martin, and Mark Ravizza. 1998. *Responsibility and Control: A Theory of Moral Responsibility*. Cambridge: Cambridge University Press.

Frankfurt, Harry G. 1969. "Alternate Possibilities and Moral Responsibility." *Journal of Philosophy* 66: 829–839.

————. 1988a. "Rationality and the Unthinkable." In Frankfurt, 1988b, 177–190.

————. 1988b. *The Importance of What We Care About.* Cambridge: Cambridge University Press.

————. 1994. "An Alleged Asymmetry between Actions and Omissions." *Ethics* 104: 620–623.

Ginet, Carl. 1990. *On Action.* Cambridge: Cambridge University Press.

————. 1996. "In Defense of the Principle of Alternative Possibilities: Why I Don't Find Frankfurt's Argument Convincing." *Philosophical Perspectives* 10: 403–417.

Glannon, Walter. 1995. "Responsibility and the Principle of Possible Action." *Journal of Philosophy* 92: 261–274.

Goetz, Stewart. Forthcoming. "Frankfurt-Style Counterexamples and Begging the Question." *Midwest Studies in Philosophy* 29.

Haji, Ishtiyaque. 1998. *Moral Appraisability.* New York: Oxford University Press.

————. 2002. *Deontic Morality and Control.* New York: Cambridge University Press.

Honderich, Ted. 1988. *A Theory of Determinism.* 2 vols. Oxford: Oxford University Press.

Hunt, David. 2000. "Moral Responsibility and Avoidable Action." *Philosophical Studies* 97: 195–227.

Kane, Robert. 1985. *Free Will and Values.* Albany: State University of New York Press.

————. 1996. *The Significance of Free Will.* New York: Oxford University Press.

Kant, Immanuel. [1785]. 2002. *Grounding for the Metaphysics of Morals.* Trans. and ed. Thomas E. Hill, Jr., and Arnulf Zweig. Oxford: Oxford University Press.

Korsgaard, Christine. 1996a. "Morality as Freedom." In Korsgaard, 1996b, 159–187.

————. 1996b. *Creating the Kingdom of Ends.* Cambridge: Cambridge University Press.

Leibniz, Gottfried. 1985. *Theodicy.* Trans. E. M. Huggard and C. J. Gerhardt. La Salle, Ill.: Open Court.

McIntyre, Alison. 1994. "Compatibilists Could Have Done Otherwise: Responsibility and Negative Agency." *Philosophical Review* 103: 453–488.

Oshana, Marina. 1997. "Ascriptions of Responsibility." *American Philosophical Quarterly* 34: 71–83.

Pereboom, Derk. 2001. *Living without Free Will.* Cambridge: Cambridge University Press.

Russell, Paul. 1995. *Freedom and Moral Sentiment: Hume's Way of Naturalizing Responsibility.* New York: Oxford University Press.

Searle, John R. 2001. *Rationality in Action.* Cambridge, Mass.: MIT Press.

Strawson, Peter. 1962. "Freedom and Resentment." *Proceedings of the British Academy* 48: 187–211.

Stump, Eleonore. 1988. "Sanctification, Hardness of the Heart, and Frankfurt's Concept of Free Will." *Journal of Philosophy* 85: 395–412.

————. 1990. "Intellect, Will, and the Principle of Alternate Possibilities." In Beaty, 1990, 354–385.

————. 1999. "Alternative Possibilities and Moral Responsibility: The Flicker of Freedom." *Journal of Ethics* 3: 299–324.

Taylor, Richard. 1983. *Metaphysics.* 3rd ed. Englewood Cliffs, N.J.: Prentice Hall.

van Inwagen, Peter. 1983. *An Essay on Free Will.* Oxford: Clarendon Press.

Wallace, R. Jay. 1994. *Responsibility and the Moral Sentiments.* Cambridge, Mass.: Harvard University Press.

————. 2000. "Book Review of Hilary Bok, *Freedom and Responsibillity.*" *Philosophical Review* 109: 592–595.

Watson, Gary. 2002. "Volitional Necessities." In Buss and Overton, 2002, 129–159.–

Widerker, David. 1991. "Frankfurt on 'Ought Implies Can' and Alternative Possibilities." *Analysis* 51: 222–224.

———. 1995a. "Libertarian Freedom and the Avoidabiliity of Decisions." *Faith and Philosophy* 12: 113–118.

———. 1995b. "Libertarianism and Frankfurt's Attack on the Principle of Alternative Possibilities." *Philosophical Review* 104: 247–261.

Widerker, David, and Michael McKenna. 2003. *Moral Responsibility and Alternative Possibilities.* Aldershot, England: Ashgate.

Wolf, Susan. 1990. *Freedom within Reason.* Oxford: Oxford University Press.

Wyma, Keith. 1997. "Moral Responsibility and Leeway for Action." *American Philosophical Quarterly* 34: 57–70.

Yaffe, Gideon. 1999. " 'Ought-Implies-Can' and the Principle of Alternative Possibilities." *Analysis* 59: 218–222.

Zimmerman, Michael J. 1988. *An Essay on Moral Responsibility.* Totowa, N.J.: Rowman and Littlefield.

PART II

NORMATIVE ETHICAL THEORY

CHAPTER 13

....

VALUE THEORY

....

THOMAS HURKA

THE theory of value or of the good is one of the two main branches of ethical theory, alongside the theory of the right. Whereas the theory of the right specifies which actions are right and which are wrong, the theory of value says which states of affairs are intrinsically good and which intrinsically evil. The theory of the right may say that keeping promises is right and lying wrong; the theory of value can say that pleasure is good and pain evil, or that knowledge and virtue are good and vice evil. Since these states are not actions, they cannot be right or wrong, but they can have positive or negative value.

The theory of value is important, first, because it gives content to some important claims about the right. Consequentialists about the right hold that one ought always to do what will result in the best outcome; to know what this implies, we must know in particular what makes outcomes good. Even nonconsequentialists usually recognize some moral duty to produce good outcomes, and that duty, too, needs content (see Ross, 1930, ch. 2). There is no point telling people to promote the good without telling them what the good is. Second, on some nonconsequentialist views, the duties that compete with promoting the good likewise presuppose claims about the good. These duties can make it wrong to do what will have the best overall outcome, for example, wrong intentionally to kill one innocent person even if this will save five innocent people's lives. But some say this is because, given an initial intrinsic value of life, there is not only a duty to promote and preserve it but also a separate and stronger duty not to destroy it; there can also be separate and stronger duties not to destroy other goods, such as knowledge and virtue (Finnis, 1980, ch. 5). On this view, even the duties that constrain pursuit of the good concern the good, though as something to be respected rather than simply brought about. Finally, the theory of value is important in itself. Often things happen that do not result from anyone's choice and could not have been prevented by choice. They therefore cannot be right or wrong, but they can be intrinsically good or evil. Thus, it can be evil if someone suffers pain as a result of an entirely unforeseeable accident or good if she enjoys serendipitous pleasure; it can likewise be good if she stumbles onto valuable knowledge or is born with a virtuous character. Whereas the theory of the right judges only actions people voluntarily control, the theory of value can range over all the states of affairs the world contains.

Consistent with this point, there are several competing views about what value is. One holds that goodness is an unanalyzable property that can be had by states of affairs regardless of their connection to choice (Moore, 1903, ch. 1; Ross, 1930, ch. 4); others analyze the good as that the love of which is correct or as that which people have moral reason to desire and if possible pursue (Brentano, 1969, p. 18; Sidgwick, 1907, p. 112). But these views are less different than they seem. Those who treat goodness as unanalyzable usually agree that the good is what it is correct to love and what people have reason to desire; their only dispute with the other views concerns whether these latter claims are self-standing or derive from one that is more fundamental. There are also competing accounts of what it is for goodness to be intrinsic. A strict view says a state's intrinsic goodness can depend only on its intrinsic properties, those that do not involve relations to other states; it therefore tests for intrinsic value by asking whether a universe containing only a given state and no other would be good (Moore, 1922, 1903, pp. 93, 95, 187). A less strict view equates a state's intrinsic goodness with that portion of the overall goodness of the world that is located in or attributable to it, whatever properties that goodness depends on. Both these views distinguish intrinsic from instrumental goodness, or goodness as a means to something else that is good. But they differ about what can be called conditional goodness. Consider the claim that pleasure is good only when it is the pleasure of a morally virtuous person (Kant, 1997, p. 7). On the strict view, the goodness this claim ascribes is not intrinsic, since it depends on a relation between the pleasure that has it and virtue; on the looser view, it is intrinsic. As we will see, however, this difference has no substantive implications, since any claim that can be made using the one definition of "intrinsic" can also be made using the other. This chapter will therefore adopt the looser view and allow that a state's intrinsic goodness can in principle depend on its relations.

Assuming these conceptual issues settled, philosophers have defended very different views about which states are intrinsically good and evil. In the last part of the twentieth century, there was a tendency to prefer theories of value that are simple and austere, with only a few goods and only ones seen as making modest claims. But there is no persuasive rationale for these preferences. It is true that a theory should try other things equal to unify its values, and the more it can do so the greater its appeal. But the unification cannot be at the expense of intuitive credibility, and in particular cannot justify ignoring values that seem intuitively compelling. Nor is there any reason why the facts about value must fit some preconceived ideal of austerity. The more credible view is that there is an immense variety of at least initially plausible intrinsic values and of ways of combining them. Some of these values can be unified to some degree, and showing how is one task of theory. But it is hard to see them all being reduced to a single fundamental value; in addition, while some make relatively modest claims, others are more extravagant. The realm of value, in other words, is rich in possibilities and in subjects for debate. This chapter will survey a series of candidate intrinsic values, in rough sequence from the less to the more controversial.

1. HEDONISM

The simplest theory of value is hedonism, which holds that only pleasure is intrinsically good and only pain intrinsically evil. Hedonism was defended in the ancient world by Epicurus and criticized by Plato and Aristotle; it was also defended by the classical utilitarians, notably Jeremy Bentham and Henry Sidgwick, and retains adherents today (Bentham, 1970, ch. 1; Sidgwick, 1907, bk. 3, ch. 14). It is a simple theory because it restricts good and evil to the one dimension of felt pleasure and pain, so there is only the one intrinsic good and one intrinsic evil.

Despite its simplicity, hedonism can be formulated in different ways, depending, first, on how the concept of pleasure is understood. One view identifies pleasures as sensations with an introspectible quality of pleasantness and pains as ones with the contrary quality of painfulness; this leads to a version of hedonism in which the only values are feelings with these introspectible qualities. Against this view it is sometimes objected that there are no such qualities; there is no feeling in common between, say, the pleasure of drinking beer and that of solving a crossword puzzle. But the view's defenders can reply that the quality of pleasantness is never experienced alone. Pleasurable sensations always have other introspectible qualities that make them as wholes very different, but they share the quality of pleasantness and can be ranked in pleasantness, just as we can rank the loudness of sounds that differ radically in pitch and timbre (Kagan, 1992, pp. 172–173). A rival view identifies pleasures as those sensations people want to have and to continue having just for their qualities as sensations. It is not clear, however, that this view successfully picks out only pleasures; can someone not want the sensation of redness just as that sensation? In addition, the view seems to point beyond hedonism to the more general theory that the good is whatever people desire, regardless of whether it is a sensation (Griffin, 1986, pp. 7–10). Nonetheless, a second version of hedonism identifies its good as a sensation people want just for its qualities as a sensation.

However it understands pleasure, hedonism normally values both of what can be called simple and intentional pleasures. Simple pleasures are unstructured sensations with whatever feature makes them pleasures; they include, most notably, bodily pleasures such as those of taste and touch. Intentional pleasures, by contrast, are directed at an intentional object; one is pleased by something or that something is the case, for example, that one's friend got a promotion. Intentional pleasures are more complex than simple ones and raise more complex moral issues; I will discuss some of these hereafter. But both types are pleasures and can be compared for their degrees of pleasantness.

To yield determinate value-judgments, hedonism must be able to measure quantities of pleasure and pain. There are several dimensions to this measurement. If pleasures are discrete sensations, it is better to have more than fewer of them and also better to have ones that last for a longer time. In addition, it is better to have pleasures that are more intense, just as it is worse to have more intense pains (Bentham, 1970, ch. 4). But there are different views about how the intensities of these two states compare. The most common view, held for example by Bentham and Sidgwick, treats pleasure and pain symmetrically, so a pain of a given intensity is always exactly as evil as a pleasure of the same intensity is good. But a different view holds that pain is a greater evil than pleasure is a good. Its most extreme version holds that pleasure is not good at all, but this implies that a life with many intense pleasures and only a few mild pains is on balance not worth living. A more moderate version holds, more plausibly, only that pain of a given intensity is worse than pleasure of the same intensity is good, so it is more important to prevent the pain than to provide the pleasure. (This gives pain some priority over pleasure, but not infinite priority.) And this view can be extended to give disproportionate weight to more intense pains, so that given an intense pain for one person and two pains of just over half the intensity for two other people, it is more important to relieve the one intense pain. Within the general framework of hedonism, this view attaches the greatest ethical significance to very intense pains (Mayerfeld, 1999, ch. 6).

A final issue concerns the related concepts of happiness and suffering. Though happiness is a more inclusive concept than pleasure—to call someone happy is to say more than that he is experiencing some pleasurable sensation now—some philosophers define it in terms of pleasure, so a happy life is one with a clear preponderance of pleasures over pains. But others treat happiness as a distinct state, one involving a feeling of satisfaction with one's life as a whole, in at least most aspects and including the past and future as well as the present (Nozick,

1989, ch. 10; Sumner, 1996, ch. 6); an analogous view equates suffering or despair with dissatisfaction with one's life as a whole. Some who take this view treat happiness as the central hedonic value, so what is to be promoted is not individual pleasurable feelings but this more general state of life-satisfaction. But within a framework that values sensations, it is hard to see the rationale for this view. If happiness is good feeling about one's life as a whole, why should it count more than similar feelings with other intentional objects or with no objects at all? Happiness may be more stable than other good feelings, but that does not make it intrinsically more important. And the same is certainly true of bad feelings. Though despair about one's life as a whole is certainly an evil, no one would on that basis deny that intense bodily pain is comparably evil.

Hedonism is persuasive when it says that pleasure is a good and pain an evil, but its stronger claim that these are the only intrinsic values has met with many objections. One is that hedonism can count as morally ideal a life containing only mindless pleasures and none of the higher achievements in art, science, and personal relations that are the distinctive prerogative of human beings. This objection has been raised in fiction, from the lotus-eaters of Homer's *Odyssey* to Aldous Huxley's *Brave New World*; it is also expressed in Robert Nozick's fantasy of an "experience machine" that, by electrically stimulating the brain, can give one the illusion and therefore the pleasure of any activity even though one is not actually engaged in it (Nozick, 1974, pp. 42–45). While hedonism implies that a life spent entirely on the experience machine would be ideal, Nozick and others find it deeply impoverished. A second objection is that hedonism gives positive value to pleasures that are morally vicious. If a torturer takes sadistic pleasure in his victim's pain, hedonism says this makes the overall situation better than if the torturer were indifferent to the pain or, worse, pained by it. But surely it is compassion that is good and sadism that is bad (Brandt, 1959, pp. 315–318; Broad, 1930, pp. 234–235). Those who are persuaded by these objections may adopt a rival "perfectionist" theory that values human excellences or perfections such as knowledge, difficult achievements, and moral virtue instead of or as well as pleasure. But before I examine perfectionism, I should consider a second theory that shares important features with hedonism.

2. DESIRE THEORIES

Hedonism can be called democratic about the value of activities, since it holds that how good they are for a given person depends on how much he in particular enjoys them. As Bentham put it, if the pleasure they give is the same, pushpin (a game similar to tiddly-winks) is as good as poetry. But hedonism is not completely democratic, since it requires people to prefer pleasure and the avoidance of pain to everything else. Not everyone does this. At the end of his life, Freud refused painkillers in order to keep his mind clear for thinking, and this type of preference for a perfectionist good over pleasure is in fact quite common. Many people at least sometimes prefer knowing the truth or pursuing a difficult goal to an alternative that would be more pleasant. According to hedonism, when they do this they are wrong.

Some who cannot accept this claim may move to a more fully democratic theory, one that equates the good in a person's life with his getting whatever he desires (Griffin, 1986, chs. 1, 2; Parfit, 1984, pp. 494–499; Rawls, 1971, pp. 395–433). If he wants pleasure, then pleasure is good for him, but if he prefers clear thinking, then that is better. Because people often do want pleasure, this theory's implications often coincide with those of hedonism; in addition, the known satisfaction of a desire, even for something other than pleasure, usually brings some pleasure. But the theories diverge whenever the pleasure a person will get from satisfying a desire for something other than pleasure is less than the alternative pleasure he forgoes, and they can also diverge in another type of case. Imagine that a person wants to be respected by her coworkers, believes she is respected, and derives pleasure from her belief, whereas in fact her co-workers ridicule her behind her back. Hedonism says their ridicule is not bad for her, since it does not affect her feelings, but a desire theory can say it makes her life worse, by frustrating an important desire.

Like hedonism, a desire theory can be formulated in different ways. One version says that what is good is the state of affairs in which a desire exists and is satisfied. But, assuming that the satisfaction of more intense desires is better, this implies that people should form intense desires that are guaranteed to be satisfied, such as that grass be green and that two plus two equal four. Apart from its counterintuitiveness, this is not what desire theorists typically say. Most of them hold that when a person desires some state of affairs, that state is what is good; the desire is a condition of value in something else rather than a part of what has value. This second version of the theory can tell people to form some desires if that will help them satisfy other, more fundamental desires, but it says nothing about what their fundamental desires should be. Rather than using values to guide desire, this theory waits for desires to create value, treating them as items outside the realm of good and evil that give value to items within it.

There is another point where versions of the desire theory can differ. Many philosophers present the theory as defining what is good *for* a person or constitutes her well-being, and some desires seem irrelevant to this issue. If I want some person I once met but have not heard of since to flourish and she does so, how does this make *my* life better? Or how does it increase my well-being if, unbeknownst to me, my desire that there be life on Mars is satisfied? One response to this difficulty is to count as good only the desire-satisfaction a person knows about and feels satisfaction in, but this brings the theory close to hedonism and prevents it from saying that being ridiculed behind one's back can make one's life worse. The more common response, therefore, is to place a content restriction on the desires relevant to a person's good: only desires about *his* life contribute to his good, whereas desires about distant people or planets do not (Parfit, 1984, p. 494). Deciding exactly which desires concern his life is difficult, but desires for internal states of himself obviously count, as do some desires for relations between himself and others, such as his desire that he not be ridiculed. But however the relevant boundary is drawn, only the satisfaction of desires about his life counts toward his good.

A further possible modification responds to the fact that people sometimes desire what is not good for them, so getting it does not benefit them. In many cases, they desire one thing only as a means to a second, secure the first, and find that it does not produce the second; for example, they desire money only because they think it will make them happy, get the money, and find they are not happy. These cases pose no special problem if the desire theory values the satisfaction only of desires for things as ends rather than just as means, which it is independently plausible for it to do. But there may be cases where a person's desire rests on a false belief that is not about means, and some theorists respond to them by equating a person's good with the satisfaction not of her actual desires but of those desires she would have if she were fully informed and rational (Brandt, 1979, ch. 6; Griffin, 1986, chs. 1, 2). They identify her good not by looking at what she actually wants but at what she would want in some idealized circumstances. A sophisticated version of this theory equates a person's good with what her fully informed self would want for her uninformed self, taking the latter's uninformedness into account (Railton, 1986, p. 16). These informed-desire theories are still democratic, since what different people would want if informed may be different. But they define the good in terms of hypothetical, idealized desires rather than actual ones.

Desire theories are popular, especially among economists but also among philosophers, and for several reasons. They seem to simplify the metaphysics of value, making it not a mysterious addition to the universe but the product of human desires. They are democratic and also make value comparatively easy to identify and measure. If we want to know what is good, we find out what people desire; if we want to know its degree of goodness, we find out how intensely they desire it, or how many other things they would risk to get it. Desire theories also partially answer objections to hedonism like those about the experience machine, since they say that if people do not want to plug in, as most of us do not, plugging in is not best for us. But they do not completely answer the objection, since they also say that for people who do want to plug in, doing so *is* best. Many philosophers reject this claim, holding that some features of life that are excluded by the machine, such as real knowledge, achievement, and attachments to other people, are good in themselves and regardless of whether they are desired. Like hedonists, these philosophers deny that value is created by desire; on the contrary, they think value should guide desire, so good desires are those directed at what is independently good. But now the independent good is not just pleasure but, on what I have called a perfectionist view, includes other intrinsic excellences.

3. PERFECTIONISM

Perfectionism has been prominent in the history of philosophy, defended in the ancient world by Plato and Aristotle and later by St. Thomas Aquinas, Georg Wilhelm Friedrich Hegel, Karl Marx, Friedrich Nietzsche, and others. Like hedonism and the desire theory, it comes in different versions, depending on which particular states of humans are deemed good. Some perfectionists give the highest value to knowledge, especially philosophical or religious knowledge; others prefer active goods such as political achievement and the creation of art; yet others emphasize moral virtue. While agreeing that the good is not just pleasure or desire-satisfaction, they place it in different human excellences. Some perfectionist theories are ineliminably pluralistic, recognizing a number of different goods with no unifying explanation of why they are goods. But the perfectionist tradition has also tried to unify its various values under some more abstract heads.

This unification is possible to some extent between the theoretical good of knowledge and the practical good of achievement. Both these goods involve, first, a matching relation between a mind and the outside world. To count as knowledge a belief must be true, whereas achievement involves making the world match a goal one has formed. The direction of match in the two cases is different, with one's mind having to match the world in knowledge and the world coming to match one's mind in achievement. But both goods involve some matching and therefore capture a central part of what is missing on the experience machine: people who plug into the machine are disconnected from reality, having mostly false beliefs about their situation and never actually achieving any goals. Second, there are further similarities in the factors determining degrees of these values. Many writers on knowledge say its most valuable instances have contents that both stretch across space, times, and objects and also explain many other items of knowledge, which are therefore subordinate to it in an explanatory hierarchy of knowledge. This happens, for example, when a scientist knows an abstract physical law and uses it to explain many particular physical phenomena. Similarly, writers on achievement often value goals that stretch across times and persons and require many other subordinate goals to be achieved as means to them. This gives special value to political achievements and the carrying out of a plan for one's life as a whole, as well as to particular activities that are complex, intricate, and challenging. In their different domains, then, knowledge and achievement again instantiate a common formal structure (Hurka, 1993, chs. 8–10).

Perfectionism can also unify the moral virtues. Instead of just adding benevolence, courage, and the like to its list of goods, it can say they are all higher level intrinsic goods that involve morally appropriate attitudes to other goods and evils. If knowledge and the pleasure of others are good, then caring positively about them, or desiring, pursuing, and taking pleasure in them for their own sakes, is also good and constitutes virtue; by contrast, caring negatively about them, for example, by trying to destroy them, is evil and vicious. The first of these claims makes benevolence a virtue; the second makes malicious envy a vice. This account of the virtues, which was popular with early twentieth-century perfectionists such as Hastings Rashdall, G. E. Moore, and W. D. Ross, does not unify the virtues with other goods; on the contrary, it emphasizes their distinctness from goods that are not in the same way higher level. But it does give the virtues and vices a common explanatory ground (Hurka, 2001; Moore, 1903, pp. 204, 208–209, 211, 217; Rashdall, 1907, 1: 59, 2: 41–42; Ross, 1930, pp. 134, 160).

A theory can also see some intrinsic values as instantiating other, more fundamental values to a high degree. For example, it is plausible that an important element in a good human life is deep and loving relationships with a spouse, children, or friends. And though some have treated these as constituting a distinct good, they can also be seen as involving, alongside intense enjoyment, thorough knowledge of another's character, the pursuit of goals that extend beyond the self and over time form a complex hierarchy, and moral virtue, as one cares about others' happiness, success, and good character for their own sakes. Loving relationships may be a very great good, but they may just instantiate other goods to a very high degree (Hurka, 2001, pp. 35–36; Ross, 1930, p. 141).

Some more ambitious approaches try to unify all the perfectionist goods. One appeals to the concept of human nature, which in different formulations it takes to consist in those properties essential to humans, distinctive of them, or essential and distinctive (Hurka, 1993, ch. 2). Its central idea is that the good in a human's life consists in the full development of whatever is fundamental to human nature; it is often generalized to hold that the good of any natural thing consists in developing its nature. This view can generate different particular values, depending on which properties it takes to constitute human nature. Aristotle, the first and best known proponent of this approach, believed that it is fundamental to humans to be rational and that the best life therefore is most rational (1984, bk. 1, ch. 7). Marx (1977) held, rather differently, that it is essential to humans to engage in productive, cooperative labor, while Nietzsche held that humans fundamentally exercise a will to power (1966, secs. 36, 186, 259, 1968, secs. 55, 693). But all these philosophers grounded their specific values in the same abstract ideal of developing human nature. The second approach, adopted by Idealists such as Hegel and F. H. Bradley, tries to unify the different perfections under the heading of "organic unity," or unity-in-difference. On this view, intrinsic value is created whenever initially diverse elements are brought into an organized unity, or when a whole contains tightly related but also strongly differentiated parts. The degree of this whole's value depends both on the degree of its parts' differentiation and on the degree of their final unity, and all other values somehow instantiate this basic value of organic unity (Bradley, 1927, pp. 74–81, 247–249; 1897, chs. 24, 25; Nozick, 1981, pp. 415–450).

To be successful, these unifying approaches must have an intuitively plausible abstract principle, which each, to some extent, has. They must also yield an attractive list of concrete goods, and here, too, each has some success. It is plausible that humans are essentially rational, given the central role rationality plays in explaining human behavior, and rationality is also realized to a high degree in the forms of knowledge and achievement described earlier. These forms likewise involve organic unity, both in the matching they require between a mind and the world and in the hierarchical structuring of beliefs and goals that gives them their greatest worth. But the approaches have a harder time accommodating moral virtue. They have certainly tried to: Aristotle held that developing the rationality that constitutes human nature entails being virtuous, while Bradley argued that a unified self is necessarily a virtuous self. But each of these claims is disputable. If we include rationality in human nature because it explains human behavior, can it not be as present in vice as in virtue? Is a person who carries out a complex plan aimed at hurting many people not exercising rationality as much as if he benefited them?[1] To say that rationality involves knowing about and pursuing the good is to give up the ambition to ground all goods in human nature; on the contrary, it is to assume there are goods independent of this nature and constraining its content. And can a self not be as unified around evil ends as around good ones? Though a perfectionist theory can unite some of its goods under more abstract heads, it is not clear that it can successfully unite them all.

It may be, then, that the most plausible perfectionist theories are pluralistic, and there is another factor that pushes in the same direction. Most value theorists grant that pleasure is to some degree good and, even more commonly, that pain is evil, and it is hard to see how these values can be unified with perfectionist ones. Can a person who suffers pain not still develop his human nature and still instantiate organic unity? (Pain often signals disruptions in unified human functioning and can cause further disruptions, but the question is whether it is contrary to such functioning in itself.) If he can, the resulting theory will be pluralistic in another respect, combining perfectionist values with hedonic or desire-based ones that are independent of them.

The simplest such theory treats the two types of good as independent, simply adding them to determine the overall value in a person's life at a time. But a more complex view says they only have significant value in combination: pleasure on its own has little worth, as do perfectionist activities on their own, and significant goodness results only when a person engages in a perfectionist activity that she also wants and takes pleasure in for its own sake. John Stuart Mill's theory of "higher pleasures" has this form. By holding that all goods are pleasures, Mill agreed with Bentham that a perfectionist activity such as reading poetry has no value if it is not accompanied by pleasure. But he denied that when it is accompanied by pleasure, its value is determined entirely by the intensity or quantity of that pleasure. There are considerations of quality that make a pleasurable reading of poetry better than an equally pleasurable playing of pushpin, and in fact Mill held that the resulting higher pleasure is much better than lower pleasures such as those of the body. For him, both pleasure and perfectionist activities have little value on their own; what is significantly good is only the combination of the two (1979, pp. 7–11; see also Frankena, 1973, pp. 89–92; Parfit, 1984, pp. 501–502).

4. COMPARISON AND AGGREGATION

The values I have identified so far are instantiated in states of individual persons at individual times. A person can feel a pleasure at a given time, or know one or more truths, or be pursuing a goal that he will eventually achieve. But a complete theory of value must be able to combine these values into measures of the goodness or evil of larger states of affairs and, ultimately, of the whole universe. This process has two parts. First, the theory must be able to compare different values to determine the overall value in each person's life at each time. Then it must be able to aggregate these measures across times and persons to arrive at measures of the total value in each person's life through time and then in a whole population. I shall consider these tasks in turn.

The topic of comparison raises the question of whether some values are higher or greater than others. The strongest claim here is that one good is infinitely or lexically greater than another, so even the smallest quantity of the former outweighs any amount of the latter. This type of claim is sometimes made about virtue, which is said to have infinite value compared to pleasure and even to all nonmoral goods (Ross, 1930, pp. 150, 152). High-minded though it sounds, this claim is hard to accept intuitively. It implies that if a virtuous person suffers unremitting and agonizing pain, then, despite that pain, his life is overwhelmingly good with only a tiny admixture of evil; it also implies that if this person were slightly less virtuous but enjoyed ecstasy, his life would be worse. And lexical claims are in general dubious. Whatever considerations make a state such as pleasure good to some degree seem also to suggest that it is good enough to at least sometimes outweigh instances of other goods and evils.

This leaves nonlexical comparative claims, which say that one good is only finitely greater than one or more others. This type of claim has again been made about virtue in comparison with nonmoral goods, about knowledge in comparison with practical achievement, and about numerous other values. But it cannot always be formulated strictly. Imagine that we have measured each of two goods on its own cardinal scale and, given those scales, have decided that one unit of the first good equals two units of the second. This seems to make the first good finitely greater than the second, but its doing so depends on our choice of units on the scales, which is arbitrary. If we had measured the first good using units that are four times larger, the 2: 1 ratio would have run in the opposite direction. So we cannot say strictly that one of these goods is greater than the other, but we can say this in a less formal way. If the result of our comparative judgments is that most people should spend most of their time pursuing the first good rather than the second, or should usually prefer its instances in conflicts with the second's, then for practical purposes, the first good is finitely greater.

Some claims of this sort are intuitively attractive, for example, the claim that pain is a greater evil than pleasure is a good. But others are harder to accept. Thus, the claim of Aristotle, Aquinas, and others that knowledge is a greater good than practical achievement is hard to reconcile with the many parallels between the two. If both these goods involve a matching relation between a mind and the world, as well as hierarchically ordered mental states, should their values not also be roughly similar? As for virtue, the most plausible view is that it is a lesser good in the following sense: that its instances always have less value than their particular intentional objects. Although compassion for another's pain is good, for example, it cannot be as good as the pain is evil; it cannot be better for there to be pain and a feeling of compassion for it than no pain and no compassion. Similarly, it cannot be better for a person to have a vicious impulse and feel shame about it than to have no such impulse and no shame. This is not to say that virtue can never outweigh nonmoral goods. If an attitude can have as much as one half of its object's value, then virtuously pursuing another person's ten units of pleasure can have more value than one unit of pleasure for oneself, so preferring the other person's ten units makes one's own life better. But virtue remains a lesser good in the sense that it always has less value than its specific intentional object (Hurka, 2001, ch. 5).

There is another, different issue about comparison. It concerns not how the individual values weigh against each other but what pattern an ideal combination of them has. Imagine that a number of goods are of roughly equal value, so it is in that respect a matter of indifference how a person chooses among them. We may nonetheless have views about what mixture of them he should seek in his life. One view says he should aim at a well-rounded achievement of all the goods, so his life embodies a variety of values rather than specializing narrowly on any one (Hurka, 1993, ch. 7). A contrary view says he should choose one good—it does not matter which—and concentrate on it, so his greatest achievement of a value is as great as possible. The practical implications of these views depend on how pursuing a variety of goods affects one's achievement of them individually. If seeking variety hampers this achievement, resulting in a mediocre dilettantism, even the first view favors some specialization; if it enhances one's achievement of the individual goods, say by cross-fertilization, even the second view favors some well-roundedness. But any position on this issue presupposes an abstract view about which pattern of goods in itself makes a life best, and here the two contrary views just described are at least initially plausible. Parallel views are possible about other topics. Thus, one can hold that a group of people such as a society do best when they achieve excellence in a wide variety of domains; perhaps this is part of what is admirable about ancient Greece. Or one can say that, although certain animal species are intrinsically of equal value, the world is better when it contains a broad diversity of species rather than only a few.

Having arrived at a measure of each person's overall achievement of all values at each time, a theory must aggregate these measures across times and persons. It must decide how a person's values at different times combine to determine the value in her life as a whole, and how the values in different people's lives combine to make up the value in a population or in all humanity. These are parallel issues, and they are also difficult. About each several different views are possible, but none is entirely free of difficulties.

The simplest aggregative view involves addition, so the value in a life equals the sum of the values at its individual moments, and the value in a population equals the sum of the values in its members. This view was taken by the classical utilitarians, especially Bentham and Mill, and also by some perfectionists. But it has several troubling implications. Across persons, it implies that we would make the world much better if we created a large number of new human beings, even if their lives had much less of what gives life value than those of existing people. Against this, some philosophers deny that adding new people does anything to make the world better (Narveson, 1967); others hold that population additions can make the world only a little better. But both groups deny the strong duty to procreate that follows from an additive view. Relatedly, this view implies what have been called certain "repugnant" conclusions. Try to imagine an ideal life, one that lasts a long time and scores very highly on whatever dimensions make life good—it is intensely happy, involves deep understanding and important achievements, and is thoroughly virtuous. On an additive view, there is another, longer life that would be better even though its value at any particular time is negligible. If this second life is long enough, the sum of its values across times will be greater than in the supposedly ideal life. Or try to imagine an ideal population, one in which a large number of people all enjoy wonderfully valuable lives. On an additive view, there is another, larger population that is better, even though its members all lead lives that are barely worth living (McTaggart, 1921, 1: 452–453; Parfit, 1984, pp. 387–390).

These implications are avoided by a different approach, which equates the aggregate value in a collection of states with the average value per member. It denies that a very large population of people with lives barely worth living has great value; on the contrary, it holds that because of its low average, this population has minimal value, and it makes a similar claim about a long life with a low average value per time. But this averaging view makes other problematic claims. It holds that, no matter how high the current average well-being per person, adding extra people even slightly below that average makes the population worse, so there is a duty not to procreate, and it holds this even if the additions will have no effects on existing people. It likewise holds that if additional years in a life will be below the average for a person's life to now, those years should not be lived—it would be better if the person died (Parfit, 1984, p. 420). Claims like these are at least intelligible, given perfectionist values; many believe that a career in, say, sports or art is better if it ends near its peak rather than continuing through a long period of decline. But the claims are hard to accept when applied to other values such as pain—we would not say that adding pain of less than the current average intensity makes things better—or to all values taken together. And in some versions, the averaging view has even more horrific implications, for example, that it is best to kill off any below-average members of a population.

Some other aggregative views echo the two pattern-views about comparison, those valuing, respectively, well-roundedness and specialization. One such view values equality in the distribution of other goods, holding that a society in which, say, happiness is equally distributed can be better than an unequal society, even though the sum of happiness in the second society is greater (Parfit, 1995; Temkin, 1993). A contrary view, defended by Nietzsche, holds that the value of a society depends primarily or solely on the achievements of its few most excellent members, so everyone else should dedicate themselves to improving the lives of those few (Nietzsche, 1966, secs. 126, 199, 257, 258, 260, 265, 1968, sec. 246, 252, 373, 660, 681, 766, 877, 881, 987, 997); a parallel view about times says the value of a life depends primarily on its achievements at its few best moments. These aggregative views do not address the issues about collection size that distinguish the additive and averaging views; those must be settled some other way. But taking a collection's size as given, they are like the parallel views about comparison in preferring certain patterns of distribution within it.

There can also be issues about where a view aggregates first: across times or across persons. Consider a view that values equality in people's happiness but aggregates across times by adding. If it first adds across times and then equalizes across persons, it will end up caring about equality in the total happiness in people's lives as wholes, or in their total life-happiness. This means that if a person who is a little better off than another person now was much worse off in the past, the view will not mind the present inequality and may even want it increased, to further reduce the inequality between their lives as wholes. It will also not object to practices that treat people of different ages differently, such as mandatory retirement, so long as these practices treat them all the same way through time. But the view has very different implications if it first equalizes across the states of different persons at each time and then adds across times. In this formulation, it does object to mandatory retirement, for treating the old at a time worse than the young at that time, and cares about equalizing only in the present and the future. If someone who is a little better off now was much worse off in the past, the view still says the present inequality is evil and should be removed (McKerlie, 1989).

Claims about aggregation, especially when they concern whole populations or the entire universe, can seem remote from everyday moral thinking. How are such grand issues relevant to the ordinary moral agent? But when interacting with another person, we do not want to give him a short-term benefit that will make his life as a whole worse, and whether that happens depends crucially on how his life's overall value is determined. Similarly, we do not want to benefit some people in a way that makes our society as a whole worse, which presupposes a view about social aggregation. Unfortunately, we often do not know the other facts needed to determine these aggregate values and therefore cannot judge our actions decisively. But, for two reasons, this need not be a debilitating disadvantage. First, sometimes our current action will have no effect on those other facts. If it will increase the aggregate in a large collection, it will do so only by changing some local facts, so we need attend only to those facts. Second, even when it may affect remote facts, it can often do so in either of two contrary ways that are equally probable; here we can let these probabilities cancel each other out and again attend only to local facts. Even in these cases, however, if an action is right because of its effects, it is so ultimately because of its effects on value as completely aggregated across times and persons.

5. The Principle of Organic Unities

Though most of the values I have examined so far have involved discrete states of individual persons at individual times, some views make the value these states contribute to the world depend on their relations to other states. These views presuppose an important principle that Moore called the principle of organic unities.

Stated generically, this principle says that the value of a whole need not equal the sum of the values its parts would have on their own; if two or more states enter into the relations that constitute a given whole, the resulting value may be either more or less than those states had when apart (Moore, 1903, pp. 27–36, 92–96, 183–225). This principle is illustrated, first, by views that value organic unity itself. If two organic unities are combined into a single, larger unity, the result is more unity and therefore more value than existed before. But the principle is also implicit in Mill's theory of higher pleasures, which holds that a perfectionist activity, such as reading poetry, adds value to a life only when it is accompanied by pleasure in it for itself, as well as in views that value knowledge and achievement, well-roundedness, and distributive equality.

There are, however, two different ways the principle can be interpreted, with the choice between them depending in part on what we think it is for value to be intrinsic (Hurka, 1998). Assume first the strict view, on which a state's intrinsic goodness can depend only on its intrinsic properties. Given this view, it cannot be that when parts enter a whole, the parts' values themselves change; the parts must be exactly as good or evil inside the whole as outside it. Instead, any additional value that results from their combination must be located in the whole as a whole, or in the whole considered as a separate entity comprising those parts in those relations, with this value of the whole as a whole to be added to the values in its parts to determine its value overall. But the looser view that allows intrinsic value to depend on relations involves no such condition. When parts enter a whole, their own values can change, so if the whole is better or worse, it can be because those parts are better or worse.

The difference between these interpretations does not affect the overall values of states of affairs, which can always come out exactly the same. Whatever final value the first or holistic interpretation arrives at by finding additional value in a whole as a whole, the second or variability interpretation can arrive at that final value by changing the values in its parts. And sometimes the difference seems not to matter at all. This is true, for example, of Mill's theory of higher pleasures. The holistic interpretation says that when a person who reads poetry takes pleasure in doing so, his reading still has zero value, but there is additional value in the reading-plus-pleasure-in-reading, while the variability interpretation says the reading itself now has value. There seems nothing significant to choose between these claims. The same is true of claims about well-roundedness, which can either value variety as a holistic property of collections or say the value of increases in a given good becomes greater the less that good has been achieved compared to other goods.

In other cases, however, one interpretation seems to fit a given view better than the other. Thus, the variability interpretation seems best for claims about the value of knowledge and achievement, which are usually seen as states of an individual. If someone's long-time pursuit of an important goal turns out successful, that is normally seen as making her life and activities better rather than creating new value in a whole combining those activities, their external result, and the relation between them. But the rival holistic view seems best for claims about equality. If two people enjoy equal happiness, that does not make either person's happiness itself better; instead, the additional egalitarian value is located in the relation between their levels of happiness as a relation.

Other values raise more complex issues. One I have not yet discussed is desert, which makes it good if people get what they deserve and evil if they get the opposite (Feinberg, 1970; Kagan, 1999; Sher, 1987). People can be said to deserve different things on different bases: medals for acting bravely, punishments for committing a crime, or income for making economic contributions. But a prominent view holds that people deserve happiness if they are virtuous and suffering if they are vicious. In terms of organic unities, this means the combination of virtue and happiness in the same life has positive value over and above the values the virtue and happiness would have alone, whereas the combination of virtue and suffering has negative value. But there are different ways in which these additional values can be analyzed.

Some of these values clearly call for a holistic treatment. Consider the retributive claim that a vicious person deserves pain, so it is good if he is punished. A variability interpretation will say that, when combined with his vice, his pain is transformed in value from purely evil to purely good (Feldman, 1997). But this implies that our emotional response to his pain should be pure and simple pleasure, which is counterintuitive. The morally best response to deserved punishment is sombre, mixing pleasure that justice is being done with pain at the infliction of pain. And this can only be so if the pain, while good as deserved, remains evil as pain. But the contrary case of undeserved pleasure may demand a different treatment. Some theorists hold that when a vicious person enjoys pleasure, his pleasure is not good as pleasure and therefore is not good in any respect. Its being combined with vice destroys the pleasure's value—a variability claim. Other theorists reject this claim, holding that undeserved pleasure is still good as pleasure, though less good than it is evil as undeserved and therefore evil on balance. This view allows a consistent holistic treatment of desert-values, but the competing view that undeserved pleasure is not good as pleasure requires mixing a variability treatment of one such value with a purely holistic treatment of the others.

Similar issues arise for some intentional pleasures and pains, those involving virtue and vice. (This is why these hedonic states raise more complex issues than simple ones.) Consider compassionate pain, or pain at another's pain. It is not, strictly speaking, an organic unity, since instead of combining two separate states by a relation it is a single state with two aspects. But it is like deserved pain in that these two aspects retain when together the same value they would have if apart, so, while good as compassionate, it is also evil as pain. This is why we sometimes do not share our bad news with friends, to spare them the pain of sympathizing with us. But some take a contrary view of sadistic pleasure, holding that, like undeserved pleasure, it has no value as pleasure. For them, the presence of vice destroys the goodness of the pleasure, leaving the sadism purely and simply evil. Their view again requires combining a variability treatment of one value in a family with a nonvariability treatment of the others.

Other variability claims emerge if a theory treats some values as agent-relative, so they are greater from some people's point of view than from others'. So far I have tacitly assumed that all values are agent-neutral, so they all make the same claim on all agents. If one person's pleasure is good, it is equally good from all persons' points of view and gives them all equal reason to pursue it. But this view has implications that some find counterintuitive. Imagine that a father's child is in pain, but he knows that at the same time some other child in a distant country is experiencing equal pain. If pain is agent-neutrally evil, then each child's pain is, from his point of view, equally evil and he should be equally moved by each. If he cares more about his child's pain, feeling more upset about it and trying harder to relieve it, his combination of attitudes is out of proportion to its objects' values; in a theory of virtue, this means his attitudes involve at least a failing in virtue and maybe a vice (Stocker, 1996, p. 319). Many reject this claim, saying that a father should care more about his child's pain and is seriously failing in virtue if he does not prefer it to a stranger's. A value theory can capture their view if it makes the agent-relative claim that from a parent's point of view, his child's pain is a greater evil than a stranger's. Perhaps all pain has some agent-neutral value, so everyone has some reason to relieve it, but a child's pain makes greater demands on her parent.

Whether a theory can make this claim, however, depends on how it understands the properties of goodness and evil. If these are simple, unanalyzable properties, it is hard to see how a state of affairs can have one of them "from one point of view" but not "from" another. Surely it must either have the property or not. But there is no such difficulty if the good is analyzed as that which it is correct to love or which people have reason to desire and pursue, since it can be correct for a person to care more about his child's pain or he can have stronger reason to relieve it. In fact, given either of these analyses, many agent-relativities about value are possible. From each person's point of view, the goods of people who stand in many relations to her, including those of spouse, friend, and fellow citizen, can be greater than the otherwise similar goods of people who do not. Of course, the strength of the agent-relativities generated by these different relations may be different; thus, the degree of preference one should show a fellow citizen may be less than for one's child. But they will all make some goods count more from a given person's point of view than others. And although this is not a standard case of organic unities, it does involve a variability claim. If the value for me of a given person's pain depends on that person's relation to me, then the pain's value does not depend just on its intrinsic properties but can vary as its relations do.

The principle of organic unities complicates the theory of value, allowing the goodness or evil contributed by a state of affairs to be affected by its relations to other states or by the relations between its parts. But it also enriches the theory, since those relations often do have intuitive moral significance.

6. ENVIRONMENTAL VALUES

There remains a final possible extension of the realm of value—to nonhuman animals and even nonanimal parts of the environment. Some philosophers reject these extensions, saying that intrinsic values are restricted to humans or, more plausibly, to beings with conscious minds, so there can be nothing good or evil in a world without such minds. But if this is true, it can only be so substantively rather than as following from the nature or definition of value; there is nothing self-contradictory about ascribing value to nonmental states. And if it is substantive, the claim can also be denied, as it is denied by views that posit distinctively environmental values.

The least contentious such values are the pleasures and pains of animals that can feel them or the satisfaction of their impulses or desires. These values have been recognized by classical hedonists; thus, Bentham said the important question about animals is not "Can they reason?" but "Can they suffer?" (1970, pp. 282–283 n.; see also Singer, 1975). Animals may not be capable of as varied or as intense pleasures as humans, but when their pleasures and especially pains are similarly intense, they should have similar value. Perhaps there is some agent-relativity here, so from a human's point of view the pain of other humans counts somewhat more, but the pains of other species are still to some significant degree evil, and their prevention can justify the sacrifice of some human good.

There can also be perfectionist values in animals and even in plants. If there are human excellences such as knowledge and achievement, there can be animal excellences such as speed, robust health, and skill in hunting prey. More generally, if it is good for humans to develop their nature, understood as involving the properties essential to and/or distinctive of humans, it should likewise be good for other species to develop their natures (Attfield, 1987, ch. 3). This has again been recognized, with many classical perfectionists situating their claims about human nature within a broader scheme in which the good of all living things consists in developing their natures. This scheme raises the question of how the perfections of different species compare with each other, and here different views are possible. A radical species-egalitarianism says the development of each species's nature is exactly as good as the development of any other's, so any preference among species is immoral (Taylor, 1996, ch. 6). But the more traditional view, expressed in the idea of a "great chain of being," is that some species' development is greater or higher than others'. If their natures involve more complex or sophisticated capacities, their perfections have more value (Attfield, 1987, ch. 5; Lovejoy, 1936). This view again implies that human goods count more than nonhuman ones, but it still grants some value to the latter. A world in which even lower animal and plant species flourish is better than one in which they do not, and the achievement of this good can justify some sacrifices by humans.

There can also be value in the variety of nonhuman species. Many environmentalists hold that a world with many different animal and plant species is better than one that is biologically less diverse, so the preservation of diversity is an important goal. This value can be seen to arise in the aggregation of species-values, so the preservation of a species counts for more the fewer similar species exist, but it is a further addition to the list of nonhuman goods.

This last value of variety shades into more holistic ones. Some environmentalists find a prime intrinsic value not in individual plants or animals but in integrated ecosystems such as the tropical rain forest. Here the symbiotic relationships between living things, or the ways their different activities support each other and the life of the whole, are the prime ground of value, and individual organisms are only means to this larger good. The classic expression of this holistic view is Aldo Leopold's claim that something is right if it tends to preserve "the integrity, stability, and beauty of the biotic community" (1949, p. 224–225; see also Callicott, 1989). This environmental holism is often regarded as an extravagant view, since it locates value far from individual states of individual minds. But if the good is just what we ought to desire and pursue, there is no reason in principle why it cannot attach to environmental wholes. In fact, the value of these wholes can be seen as just another instance of the organic unity or unity-in-difference that has been valued within states of mind such as knowledge and achievement. Of course, a view that values ecological wholes must weigh their goods against the goods, assuming it recognizes them, of individual nonhuman organisms and of humans and their mental lives. But though this cannot be done precisely, it surely can be done in some cases. Thus, preserving an ecosystem can sometimes justify culling a particular species whose population growth threatens the ecological balance, and can also justify the human efforts this culling requires.

The importance of nonhuman values can be illustrated by two thought-experiments. Imagine that you are the last human, the last member of the species before it goes extinct, and can either detonate a bomb that will destroy all life forever or refrain and leave behind you the existing rich variety of plants and animals. If all values were located in human minds, there would be no reason to prefer one of these choices to the other. Yet many will hold, as the more radical environmental views do, that there is a strong moral duty not to detonate the bomb (Routley, 1973, p. 207). Or imagine that humans can, at no cost to their own well-being, implant life on a previously barren planet such as Mars and then let it develop by its own process of natural selection. On the narrower view, there is no reason to do this; on the broader environmentalism, anything that increases the life, variety, and vibrancy in the universe makes the universe better (McKay and Haynes, 1990, p. 144).

7. CONCLUSION

The theory of value is important for several reasons. It gives content to our duty to promote good and prevent evil and perhaps also to stronger duties not to destroy good directly. It also matters in itself, determining, apart from any issues about duty, which states of affairs are intrinsically desirable or make the world better. But the topic of value is also one where many different views are at least initially attractive. Some of these views value competing states of human minds, such as pleasure, knowledge, and virtue; others value patterns of distribution across these states, such as equality or the proportioning of happiness to virtue; yet others compare or aggregate goods differently, while a final group values states of the nonhuman environment. The debate between these views is not easily resolved, but its sharpness, and the way the competing positions all make plausible claims, only underscores the importance and fascination of issues about intrinsic value.

NOTE

1. To say that rationality involves knowing about and pursuing the good is to give up the ambition to ground all goods in human nature; on the contrary, it is to assume there are goods independent of this nature and constraining its content.

REFERENCES

Aristotle. 1984. *Nicomachean Ethics.* In *The Complete Works of Aristotle,* ed. Jonathan Barnes, trans. W. D. Ross and J. O. Urmson. Princeton, N.J.: Princeton University Press.

Attfield, Robin. 1987. *A Theory of Value and Obligation.* London: Croom Helm.

Bentham, Jeremy. 1970. *Introduction to the Principles of Morals and Legislation.* Ed. J. H. Burns and H.L.A. Hart. London: Methuen.

Bradley, F. H. 1897. *Appearance and Reality.* 2nd ed. Oxford: Clarendon Press.

———. 1927. *Ethical Studies.* 2nd ed. Oxford: Clarendon Press.

Brandt, Richard B. 1959. *Ethical Theory.* Englewood Cliffs, N.J: Prentice-Hall.

———. 1979. *A Theory of the Good and the Right.* Oxford: Clarendon Press.

Brentano, Franz. 1969. *The Origin of Our Knowledge of Right and Wrong.* Trans. Roderick M. Chisholm and Elizabeth Schneewind. London: Routledge and Kegan Paul.

Broad, C. D. 1930. *Five Types of Ethical Theory.* London: Routledge and Kegan Paul.

Callicott, J. Baird. 1989. *In Defense of the Land Ethic: Essays in Environmental Philosophy.* Albany: State University of New York Press.

Feinberg, Joel. 1970. "Justice and Personal Desert." In *Doing and Deserving,* 55–94. Princeton, N.J.: Princeton University Press.

Feldman, Fred. 1997. "Adjusting Utility for Justice: A Consequentialist Reply to the Objection from Justice." In *Utilitarianism, Hedonism, and Desert,* 151–174. Cambridge: Cambridge University Press.

Finnis, John. 1980. *Natural Law and Natural Rights.* Oxford: Clarendon Press.

Frankena, William K. 1973. *Ethics.* 2nd ed. Englewood Cliffs, N.J.: Prentice-Hall.

Griffin, James. 1986. *Well-Being: Its Meaning, Measurement, and Moral Importance.* Oxford: Clarendon Press.

Hurka, Thomas. 1993. *Perfectionism.* New York: Oxford University Press.

———. 1998. "Two Kinds of Organic Unity." *Journal of Ethics* 2: 299–320.

———. 2001. *Virtue, Vice, and Value.* New York: Oxford University Press.

Kagan, Shelly. 1992. "The Limits of Well-Being." *Social Philosophy and Policy* 9: 169–182.

———. 1999. "Equality and Desert." In *What Do We Deserve? Readings on Justice and Desert,* ed. Louis P. Pojman and Owen McLeod, 298–314. New York: Oxford University Press

Kant, Immanuel. 1997. *Groundwork of the Metaphysics of Morals.* Trans. Mary Gregor. Cambridge: Cambridge University Press.

Leopold, Aldo. 1949. *A Sand County Almanac.* London: Oxford University Press.

Lovejoy, Arthur O. 1936. *The Great Chain of Being: A Study of the History of the Idea.* Cambridge, Mass.: Harvard University Press.

Marx, Karl. 1977. *Economic and Philosophical Manuscripts* (excerpt). In *Karl Marx: Selected Writings,* ed. David McLellan. Oxford: Oxford University Press.

Mayerfeld, Jamie. 1999. *Suffering and Moral Responsibility.* New York: Oxford University Press.

McKay, Christopher P., and Robert H. Haynes. 1990. "Should We Implant Life on Mars?" *Scientific American* 263(6): 144.

McKerlie, Dennis. 1989. "Equality and Time." *Ethics* 99: 475–491.

McTaggart, J.M.E. 1921. *The Nature of Existence.* 2 vols. Cambridge: Cambridge University Press.

Mill, John Stuart. 1979. *Utilitarianism.* Ed. George Sher. Indianapolis: Hackett.

Moore, G. E. 1903. *Principia Ethica.* Cambridge: Cambridge University Press.

———. 1922. "The Conception of Intrinsic Value." In *Philosophical Studies,* 253–275. London: Routledge and Kegan Paul.

Narveson, Jan. 1967. "Utilitarianism and New Generations." *Mind* 76: 62–72.

Nietzsche, Friedrich. 1966. *Beyond Good and Evil.* Trans. Walter Kaufmann. New York: Vintage.

———. 1968. *The Will to Power.* Trans. Walter Kaufmann and R. J. Hollingdale. New York: Vintage.

Nozick, Robert. 1974. *Anarchy, State, and Utopia.* New York: Basic Books.

———. 1981. *Philosophical Explanations.* Cambridge, Mass.: Harvard University Press.

———. 1989. *The Examined Life: Philosophical Meditations.* New York: Simon and Schuster.

Parfit, Derek. 1984. *Reasons and Persons.* Oxford: Clarendon Press.

———. 1995. "Equality or Priority?" The Lindley Lecture. Lawrence: Department of Philosophy, University of Kansas.

Railton, Peter, 1986. "Facts and Values." *Philosophical Topics* 14: 5–31.

Rashdall, Hastings. 1907. *The Theory of Good and Evil.* 2 vols. London: Oxford University Press.

Rawls, John. 1971. *A Theory of Justice.* Cambridge, Mass.: Harvard University Press.

Ross, W. D. 1930. *The Right and the Good.* Oxford: Clarendon Press.

Routley, Richard. 1973. "Is There a Need for a New, an Environmental Ethic?" In *Proceedings of the Fifteenth World Congress of Philosophy 1,* ed. Bulgarian Organizing Committee, 205–210. Sofia, Bulgaria: Sophia-Press.

Sher, George. 1987. *Desert.* Princeton, N.J.: Princeton University Press.

Sidgwick, Henry. 1907. *The Methods of Ethics.* 7th ed. London: Macmillan.

Singer, Peter. 1975. *Animal Liberation.* New York: New York Review of Books.

Stocker, Michael. 1996. *Valuing Emotions.* Cambridge: Cambridge University Press.

Sumner, L. W. 1996. *Welfare, Happiness, and Ethics.* Oxford: Clarendon Press.

Taylor, Paul. 1986. *Respect for Nature: A Theory of Environmental Ethics.* Princeton, N.J.: Princeton University Press.

Temkin, Larry S. 1993. *Inequality.* New York: Oxford University Press.

CHAPTER 14

SOME FORMS AND LIMITS OF CONSEQUENTIALISM

DAVID O. BRINK

PERHAPS the most familiar form of consequentialism is classical hedonistic act utilitarianism, which claims, roughly, that an agent ought to perform that action, among the available alternatives, that produces the most net pleasure (pleasure, less pain) for everyone concerned. But this classical form of utilitarianism is thought by many to be just a special case of a more general or abstract class of consequentialist moral theories that make the moral assessment of alternatives depend in some way upon their value. How to understand and assess consequentialism depends on how one specifies this more general class of theories. I will understand consequentialism quite broadly, with the result that it is a large and heterogeneous family. This makes it difficult to get very far discussing the prospects for consequentialism as such. Different varieties of consequentialism will have different strengths and weaknesses. Of necessity, my discussion will be selective, concentrating on those varieties that seem to me to have a significant tradition or to be especially interesting.

1. Consequentialist Structure and Varieties

Classical hedonistic utilitarianism conceives of the good in terms of pleasure and identifies an agent's duty with his promoting pleasure. This makes the good explanatorily prior to the right, insofar as it defines right action in terms of promoting the good (see Rawls, 1971, sec. 5). Generalizing, we might understand consequentialism as the set of moral theories that make the good explanatorily primary, explaining other moral notions, such as duty or virtue, in terms of promoting value. For instance, a consequentialist conception of duty might identify an agent's duty as an action that promotes the good, whereas a consequentialist conception of virtue might identify virtuous dispositions as those with good consequences. We can construct consequentialist analyses of virtually any object of moral assessment, including actions, motives, individual lives, institutions, and moral codes. To be a consequentialist about the assessment of any of these things is to think that one's assessment of alternatives within that domain should be governed in a suitable way by the comparative value of the alternatives. Understanding consequentialism this way equates it with a teleological conception of ethics.

But consequentialism, as such, is neutral about a great many issues. To make discussion manageable, it will help to focus on one kind of consequentialist analysis. One traditional focus concerns the analysis of *duty* or *right action*. Many issues that arise in understanding and assessing consequentialist conceptions of right action apply *mutatis mutandis* to other kinds of consequentialist analysis.

Consequentialism takes the good to be primary and identifies right action as action that promotes value. As such, it contrasts with two different conceptions of right action. *Deontology* takes right action to be the primary evaluative notion; it recognizes various actions as obligatory, prohibited, or permitted on the basis of their intrinsic natures and independently of the value they produce. *Virtue ethics* takes the idea of a morally good character to be explanatorily primary in the account of right action; right action, on this view, is action performed by someone with a virtuous character or that expresses a virtuous character.[1]

The consequentialist conception of right action leaves several questions unanswered. One pertinent question concerns *what* is valuable. This is a question about what has intrinsic value. It is, in part, a question about the human good. What are the constituents of a good human life? One familiar conception is the *hedonistic* claim that pleasure is the one and only intrinsic good and that pain is the one and only intrinsic evil. Alternatively, one might understand the human good in *preference-satisfaction* terms, as consisting in the satisfaction of actual or suitably informed or idealized desire. Hedonism and preference-satisfaction views construe the human good as consisting in or depending upon an individual's contingent and variable psychological states. By contrast, one might understand the good in more objective terms, either as consisting in the *perfection* of one's essential capacities (e.g., one's rational or deliberative capacities) or as consisting in some *list* of disparate objective goods (e.g., knowledge, beauty, achievement, friendship, or equality).

Connected with these issues are other questions about the good. Who are the *bearers* of intrinsic good? Are there goods for all sentient creatures, or only for a more limited class of beings, such as human beings or persons?

Another question is whether some things are valuable independently of the contribution that they make to the lives of sentient creatures. If so, we might say that there are *impersonal* goods. Some people think that beauty and equality are impersonal goods. But even if they are intrinsic goods, it is debatable whether they have value independently of any contribution they make to sentient life. If there are no impersonal goods, we might say that all goods are *personal* or *sentient*.

Still another question is *Whose value matters?* Should an agent be concerned about all those that it is within her power to benefit, and among those that demand her concern, should they matter equally? At one extreme lies the *impartial* consequentialist view that an agent should be concerned to promote any and all kinds of value and, in particular, should have an equal concern to promote the well-being of all those that it is in her power to affect for better or worse. Utilitarianism is probably the most familiar form of impartial consequentialism. It instructs agents to promote human or sentient happiness generally. But a view that recognized impersonal values and instructed agents to promote these wherever possible would also be a form of impartial consequentialism. At the other extreme lies the *partial* consequentialist view that an agent should be intrinsically concerned with promoting only her own welfare. Such a view would be a form of ethical egoism. In between these extremes lie more *moderate* forms of consequentialism that demand intrinsic concern for others but that limit the scope or weight of such concern. One example of such a moderate view is the view that C. D. Broad called "self-referential altruism" and associated with common-sense morality (1971, esp. p. 279). Self-referential altruism claims that an agent's concerns should have wide scope, but variable weight. It says that an agent has an obligation to be concerned about anyone that it is in her power to benefit but that the weight of an agent's moral reasons is a function of the nature of the relationship in which the agent stands to potential beneficiaries. On this view, an agent has reason to be concerned for perfect strangers as well as intimate associates, but, all else being equal, she has more reason to be concerned about the well-being of an associate than a stranger.

These distinctions within consequentialism can also be made in terms of the distinction between agent-neutral and agent-relative reasons. The general form of *agent-relative* reasons makes essential reference to the agent in some way, whereas the general form of *agent-neutral* reasons does not (see Nagel, 1986, p. 152). Being under a duty to help children, as such, would involve an agent-neutral reason, whereas being under a duty to help one's own children would involve an agent-relative reason. Being under a duty to minimize suffering would be an agent-neutral reason, whereas the deontological duty never to be the cause of another's suffering, even if this is necessary to minimize total suffering, would be an agent-relative reason. Some writers have believed that this distinction between agent-neutral and agent-relative reasons is the way to distinguish between consequentialist and nonconsequentialist moral conceptions. But I do not share this view. Whereas only utilitarianism and other forms of impartial consequentialism will qualify as agent-neutral conceptions, some agent-relative conceptions are consequentialist. Ethical egoism and self-referential altruism both identify an agent's duty with promoting values, though they limit the scope or vary the weight of the values she ought to promote.

Consequentialists are concerned to promote the relevant values. This contrasts with the deontological response to value. To *honor* a value is to act on it or protect it at every opportunity. To *promote* a value is to take steps that lead to its greater realization overall. But promoting a value overall can require failing to honor it on some occasions, as it would, for example, if promoting and protecting freedom within a community required establishing a compulsory draft. And honoring a value on some occasion may involve failing to promote that value, as it would, for example, if saving an innocent life now could only be done in ways that prevented saving even more innocent lives at some later point in time. Whereas the consequentialist tells agents to promote the relevant values, the deontologist tells them to honor those values (see Pettit, 1991).

There are different ways of promoting values. Some ways of promoting values are *direct*, inasmuch as they assess alternative actions by the contribution that each alternative makes to the relevant values. The most traditional direct form of consequentialism is *act* consequentialism, which says that an agent should perform that action whose value (of the relevant sort) is at least as great as that of any alternative available to her (or at least one such action, if there are multiple actions meeting this condition). Act consequentialism tells the agent that it is her duty to maximize value. Some have found this act consequentialist claim too burdensome. In requiring agents always to do the best, act consequentialism seems unable to accommodate the idea of supererogatory actions—those actions that in some sense go beyond or are better than what is required by duty. Impressed by this worry, some direct consequentialists have looked for less demanding ways of promoting value. One such view is a *scalar* consequentialism. On this view, one alternative is morally better than another if it produces more of the relevant kind of value and morally worse if it produces less. The scalar view, as such, does not say what an agent's duty is. The scalar view is sometimes advanced as part of a *satisficing* view. The satisficer demands of the agent, not that she maximize value (the relevant values), but rather that she perform any of the alternatives that are good enough—that is, that lie above some specified threshold of value. Duty only requires that the agent perform an action above the relevant threshold. If she chooses an action far above the threshold, for instance, one that is at the top of the scale and maximizes the relevant values, then she has gone beyond her duty and done something supererogatory (see Slote, 1985, chs. 3, 5).

As we will see, there are other sorts of concerns about direct consequentialism. These are traditionally formulated about act or maximizing consequentialism, but I think that they apply, with suitable changes, to satisficing forms of consequentialism too. Roughly, the worry is that maximizing values will sometimes require agents to deviate from moral precepts that seem independently compelling. Perhaps honesty is generally the best policy for both egoists and utilitarians, but there must be cases in which the agent is better off or humanity is better off if the agent is dishonest. If honesty is an absolute moral demand, this spells trouble for direct consequentialism. And even if honesty is not an absolute demand, it may seem to be a more robust demand—less sensitive to consequences—than direct consequentialism would imply. Concerns such as these have led some to endorse *indirect* forms of consequentialism that assess actions not in terms of their values but rather in terms of the value of the rules or motives under which the action can be subsumed. So, for example, rule utilitarianism claims that an action is right just in case it conforms to a rule the general acceptance of which by humanity would have consequences at least as good for humanity as any alternative rule (see Brandt, 1963; Hooker, 2000). Rule egoism would say that an action is right just in case it conforms to a rule the general acceptance of which by the agent would promote his welfare at least as well as any alternative rule available to him. Just as rule consequentialisms identify duty with acting on optimal rules, motive consequentialisms identify duty with acting on optimal motives (see Adams, 1976; Gauthier, 1986). These forms of indirect consequentialism will be responsive to worries about direct consequentialism, insofar as the motives and rules recognized by common-sense morality have optimal acceptance value.

We can see how consequentialism, so conceived, forms a large and heterogeneous family of moral theories. Though some generalizations about consequentialism are more robust than others, it is difficult to assess the strengths and weaknesses of such a disparate set of claims. It will make discussion more profitable to focus on a few main forms of consequentialism.

2. MAXIMIZATION

First, I shall focus on maximizing versions of consequentialism. It will be easier to understand this focus within the framework of direct consequentialism, even if the debate between maximizers and satisficers cuts across the debate between direct and indirect consequentialism. One problem for the pure satisficer is that she seems to have no basis for choosing among or ranking options all of which are above the threshold of permissibility. If we discriminate only between options above and below the threshold, then it seems a matter of indifference how far above the threshold one is. But that is counterintuitive. Why should the value of options matter just up to the threshold and not at all above it? Indeed, the pure satisficer has a problem explaining why the best is typically supererogatory and deserving special praise. But these objections dissolve if satisficing is combined with the scalar view. For the scalar part of the view allows one to make moral discriminations among all options, both below and above the threshold, that track their value; the satisficing part of the view says that options below the threshold are impermissible and that all options above the threshold are permissible. So the scalar-satisficing view allows us to say why the best is supererogatory and deserves praise.

The main rationale for satisficing is that maximization seems too demanding. Performing the best option is typically permissible and admirable. But we might be reluctant to say that it is one's duty. For that would imply that all suboptimal actions, even very good ones, are wrong. And many such actions we would be reluctant to blame the agent for performing. It is tempting to say that duty only requires performing some action above a certain value threshold, that any action above the threshold is permissible, and that the very best action is, at least typically, supererogatory rather than obligatory. The scalar-satisficing view respects these intuitions. By contrast, maximizing act consequentialism seems to violate them, inasmuch it seems to imply that the optimal action is always obligatory, that all other actions, however good, are impermissible, and that there is no such thing as supererogatory action.

One reason the maximization may seem harsh is that it seems to require that we blame the agent for every suboptimal act, however good. But this does not follow. The maximizer must assess actions and responses to those actions separately. Even if suboptimal acts are wrong, it doesn't follow that it's good to blame them. They may be cases of *blameless wrongdoing* (see Parfit, 1984, ch. 1). Indeed, if sufficiently good, suboptimal actions not only need not be blameworthy but are likely to be praiseworthy. These would be cases of *praiseworthy wrongdoing*. These observations suggest a way in which the maximizer might try to capture the intuitions to which the scalar-satisficer appeals. Common-sense morality distinguishes among (1) the obligatory, (2) the permissible, and (3) the supererogatory. Though the maximizer makes the optimal obligatory, treats all suboptimal acts as impermissible, and does not strictly recognize actions that are morally better than one's duty, he can nonetheless draw a similar tripartite distinction among (1a) acts whose omission is blameworthy, (2a) acts whose omission is not blameworthy, and (2c) acts whose omission is not blameworthy and whose performance is praiseworthy (or perhaps deserving of special recognition and praise). Of course, these notions of praiseworthiness and blameworthiness must themselves be interpreted in maximizing consequentialist terms. While there is no a priori guarantee that the maximizer's tripartition will track perfectly the common-sense tripartition, there is reason to think that they will sort options in similar ways and to wonder whether the maximizer's tripartition might not provide reflectively acceptable guidance and correction where the common-sense tripartition provides uncertain or questionable guidance.[2]

Maximizing consequentialism is the more traditional form of that doctrine. Because it is not clear that its scalar-satisficing rival enjoys any real advantages, it will be simpler to focus on the traditional conception. However, much of what I say about the traditional conception applies, *mutatits mutandis,* to satisficing conceptions.

3. DIRECT CONSEQUENTIALISM

Second, I shall focus on direct, rather indirect, forms of consequentialism. Direct consequentialism assesses all things, including actions, in terms of the value of their consequences, whereas indirect consequentialisms assess actions in terms of their conformity to rules, motives, or dispositions with good or optimal acceptance value.

Indirect forms of consequentialism are worth discussing separately only if they have different implications from direct consequentialism. Will actions conforming to motives or rules with optimal acceptance value be different than the optimal actions? If we notice that motives can be very discriminating and rules can be fine-grained, we might wonder if the best motives and rules wouldn't always require the best actions. But it is often difficult to identify reliably the optimal action, and an agent may often do better overall by internalizing and acting on some fairly coarse-grained set of motives and rules than by attempting to optimize in each of her actions, even if this means performing some actions that are suboptimal. If so, it seems that acting on the best rules or with the best motives might not be the same as performing the best actions.

Even if indirect consequentialism is a genuine alternative to direct consequentialism, we may wonder whether it's superior. That may depend on which version we consider. For instance, rule utilitarianism, as traditionally conceived, defines right action as action that conforms to a rule the general acceptance of which by humanity would have consequences at least as good for humanity as any alternative rule. But what might be valuable *if* everyone else behaved similarly might not be especially valuable—indeed, could be quite bad—if everyone *actually* behaves quite differently. Driving fifty-five miles per hour might be best if everyone else did as well but not if everyone else is driving seventy-five miles per hour. So it may be a mistake for the indirect consequentialist to identify right action with action conforming to rules with optimal *general* acceptance value. Instead, he might identify right action with action in conformity with personal rules having optimal acceptance value, given the way others will actually behave.[3]

Even if the set of actions on the best motives or rules is different from the set of best actions and the former produces more value overall, this still does not favor indirect consequentialism. After all, the direct consequentialist assesses all sorts of things in addition to actions—including persons, policies, institutions, and, notably, motives and rules. Because she assesses all things according to their comparative value, she should prefer having and acting on the best motives or rules to performing the best actions, just in case these diverge and acting from the best motives is best overall. Indeed, any cases in which acting from the best motives or rules produces suboptimal actions would arguably count as cases of blameless wrongdoing.

If there aren't compelling advantages offered by indirect consequentialism, we might focus on more traditional direct forms of consequentialism. But doesn't the direct consequentialist assessment of actions imply that an agent's deliberations should always be guided by a comparative cost-benefit analysis of the alternatives? Whereas such consequentialist accounting may well be appropriate in special circumstances, it does not seem generally appropriate. For one thing, conscious attempts to optimize are often counterproductive. Optimizing deliberations are often inefficient when they are costly and time for deliberation is scarce. They are also subject to bias. Interpersonal maximization is often distorted by the agent's sense of his own interest, by his investing his own interests with normative significance out of proportion to their magnitude relative to the interests of others. Similarly, intrapersonal maximization is often distorted by the temporal proximity of benefits or harms, by agents investing near-term benefits and harms with normative significance out of proportion to their actual magnitude. Still more important, certain valuable activities and relations, including avocations and intimate associations, seem incompatible with regular scrutiny of their consequential value. As Bernard Williams suggests, the optimizer who pursues various projects or who provides aid and succor to his loved ones only after concluding that this is the optimal use of his resources, instead of merely consulting his passions or his loyalties, seems to "have one thought too many" (1976).[4]

There are several concerns here, but many of them rest on the assumption that the direct consequentialist should treat her consequentialism as a decision procedure, always deliberating as an optimizer. But a moral theory can supply a *standard* of right conduct, explaining what makes right acts right, without supplying a decision procedure. In *The Methods of Ethics,* Henry Sidgwick notes the so-called paradox of hedonistic egoism that one often better secures pleasure if one does not consciously aim at it (1966, pp. 48, 135–136). As Sidgwick notes, the paradox, if true, tells us something about how to satisfy the hedonistic egoist standard; it is not an objection to that doctrine. Similarly, he notes that satisfaction of the utilitarian standard may require that agents not always deliberate in explicitly consequentialist terms (1966, p. 413; see Bales, 1971; Brink, 1989, pp. 256–262; Railton, 1984). But if it was always counterproductive to reason with consequentialist principles or if it was best for the truth of consequentialism to be known only to a select philosophical elite, then, as Sidgwick notes, consequentialism would have the status of an "esoteric" morality (1966, pp. 489–490). This result would be worrisome, inasmuch as we expect moral principles to play some role in moral deliberation, especially about perplexing cases, and in moral education. But moral principles can play a significant role in moral deliberation without functioning as decision procedures. In particular, moral principles can *regulate* an agent's conduct in variety of ways without always figuring consciously in her deliberations or motivations. A principle will regulate an agent's conduct, even when she doesn't consult it, if she wouldn't act as she does unless her conduct satisfied the principle or might reasonably be thought to satisfy it. So an agent can act with a variety of motives and by consulting a variety of secondary precepts consistently with her conduct being regulated by a different master principle, provided that she so acts when doing so is clearly permissible (nonblameworthy) according to the principle, and provided that she refuses so to act when doing so would clearly be impermissible (blameworthy) according to the principle. However, if the principle does regulate her behavior, she will consult it when her motives and precepts that normally track the principle give uncertain or conflicting guidance, and she will periodically step back from her everyday motives and precepts and reassess their compatibility with the principle. In this way, the direct consequentialist can recognize that responsible and admirable agents need not and should not constantly consult the consequentialist principle or always engage in conscious consequentialist analysis, provided that their behavior is suitably regulated by consequentialist principles. If so, worries that consequentialism requires a mindset of moral accountancy that is inconsistent with spontaneity, authenticity, or fidelity appear misplaced or, at least, premature.[5]

4. PERFECTIONISM AND OTHER CONCEPTIONS OF THE GOOD

Direct consequentialism assesses actions, motives, persons, policies, and institutions in terms of the good they produce. But consequentialism, as such, does not tell us what is good. For that we need a theory of value. Though some of my discussion abstracts from different evaluative assumptions to focus on consequentialism as such, this agnosticism about the good is not always possible or helpful.

It is an interesting question whether there are any impersonal goods. I am somewhat skeptical that we would recognize anything as valuable independently of any contribution that it makes to improving lives, whether human, rational, or sentient. In any case, my discussion will focus on conceptions of a person's good. It is common to identify a person's good with his interests, well-being, or welfare. We can even identify a person's good with his happiness, provided that we do not assume at the outset that happiness is conceptually tied to satisfaction or contentment.[6] We can think of a person's good as what we ought to care about intrinsically, insofar as we are concerned about him for his own sake. We can then recognize different substantive conceptions of the good for a person (his interests, well-being, welfare, or happiness). Hedonism and preference-satisfaction views are subjectivist conceptions, whereas perfectionism and objective lists are objective conceptions. Conceptions of the good might also be mixed, containing both subjective and objective elements. My working assumption will be that pure subjectivist conceptions of the good are implausible and that some more objective conception in which perfectionist elements play a significant role is most promising. Let me briefly sketch this assumption.[7]

Hedonism is a form of *extreme subjectivism*; it says that happiness or value consists in mental states or sensations alone.[8] The desire-satisfaction theory, by contrast, is a form of *moderate subjectivism*, because it says that happiness depends upon a person's mental states—her desires—but consists in the satisfaction of her desires.

Familiar thought experiments show why it is difficult to maintain, as hedonism requires, the extreme subjectivist claim that happiness or value consists in psychological states alone. Robert Nozick questions whether we would really choose to hook up to an experience machine that provides experiences of any life we would enjoy; he assumes that we want to be the authors of our own lives, make real differences in the world, and sustain meaningful relations with others, and not merely have experiences as if we were doing these things, no matter how pleasant such experiences might be (1974, p. 42). In Aldous Huxley's *Brave New World* (1946), Deltas and Epsilons form the working classes, who are genetically engineered and psychologically programmed to acquiesce in and indeed embrace intellectually and emotionally limited lives that are liberally seasoned with mood–altering drugs. In such lives, pleasure and contentment are purchased at the price of dignity.

The experience machine raises problems for extreme subjectivism, but is not a direct threat to moderate subjectivism. For the desire–satisfaction theorist can note that the experience machine does not satisfy its clients' desires to be and do certain things (though it does, *ex hypothesi*, leave them satisfied). However, we sometimes judge that people who *are* satisfying their deepest desires nonetheless lead impoverished lives, because their desires are for unimportant or inappropriate things. Deltas and Epsilons lead contented lives precisely because they are satisfying their chief desires. While a certain amount of realism in one's ambitions and desires may be a good thing, we do not (in general) increase the value of our lives by lowering our sights, even if by doing so we increase the frequency of our successes.

Insofar as the goals of Deltas and Epsilons are based on false beliefs about their capacities or are the result of brainwashing, the moderate subjectivist may think that our concerns can be met by appealing, not to actual preferences, but to suitably *idealized* preferences that are fully informed and formed under conditions free from psychological manipulation by others. On this sort of view, what is good for someone is what his idealized self would want his (nonidealized) self to want.[9]

However, laundering people's preferences is an inadequate remedy. An ideal appraiser, like John Stuart Mill's competent judge, is supposed to be fully informed about all aspects of all the possibilities open to her. But there are various questions about the coherence and relevance of fully informed desire. Can one coherently combine wildly disparate possible experiences in one overall evaluative perspective (see Rosati, 1995; Sobel, 1994)? Moreover, one can't rule out the possibility that full confrontation with the facts wouldn't extinguish desire or shape it in ways that one would pretheoretically identify as pathological (see Gibbard, 1990, p. 20). Furthermore, we may wonder whether idealized desire satisfaction views don't confuse what's in our interest and what interests us (see Darwall, 1997). For it's not clear that everything that one might reasonably (or not unreasonably) desire would contribute to one's good.

The idealized desire-satisfaction view also faces a serious dilemma. If the process of idealization is purely formal or content-neutral, then it must remain a brute and contingent psychological fact whether suitably idealized subjects would care about things we are prepared, on reflection, to think valuable. But this is inadequate, inasmuch as we regard intellectually and emotionally rich lives as unconditionally good and intellectually and emotionally shallow lives as unconditionally bad. For a person with the normal range of intellectual, emotional, and physical capacities, it is a very bad thing to lead a simple and one-dimensional life with no opportunities for intellectual, emotional, and physical challenge or growth. One's life is made worse, not better, if, after informed and ideal deliberation, that is the sort of life to which one aspires.

Alternatively, we might conclude that anyone who would endorse shallow and undemanding lives simply could not count as ideal appraiser. We might agree with Mill, who claims in *Utilitarianism* that any competent judge, who has a proper sense of his own dignity, would never approve of contented but undemanding lives (1978b, chap. 2, para. 6). But if this is to explain how such lives are categorically bad, then it must be that one won't count as an ideal appraiser unless one possesses a sense of dignity that reflects a belief in the value of activities that exercise one's higher capacities. But such a notion of idealization carries substantive evaluative commitments. Suitably idealized desire, understood this way, presupposes, rather than explains, the nature of a person's good.

These worries about extreme and moderate subjectivism lend plausibility to objective conceptions of the good. One form of objectivism is a list of objective goods, such as knowledge, beauty, achievement, friendship, and equality.[10] Some such list may seem the only way to capture the variety of intrinsic goods. But if it is a mere list of goods, with no unifying strands, it begins to look like a disorganized *heap* of goods.[11] While we can't assume that there is a unified account of the good that is reflectively acceptable, we have reason to look for one and treat a mere list of objective goods as a kind of fallback position.

One promising objective conception that goes beyond a mere list of goods is *perfectionist*. There is a venerable perfectionist tradition, common to Aristotle, Mill, and T. H. Green, among others, that identifies a person's good with the perfection of her nature.[12] But human nature can be conceived of as a biological or normative category. It is hard to find capacities that we have as a biological species that are essential and whose exercise seems distinctively valuable.[13] A more promising avenue is to understand the appeal to human nature in normative terms. In *An Essay Concerning Human Understanding,* John Locke distinguishes between persons and men (or, as we might prefer to say, human beings) and claims that the concept of a person is a "forensic" or normative concept (1979, II.xxvii. secs. 8, 15, 17–21, 23, 26). Part of what Locke means is that only persons are accountable in law and morality, because only persons are responsible for their actions. Nonresponsible agents, such as brutes and small children, act on their strongest desires; if they deliberate, it is only about the instrumental means to the satisfaction of their desires. By contrast, responsible agents must be able to distinguish between the intensity and authority of their desires, deliberate about the value or authority of their desires, and regulate their actions in accordance with their deliberations. On this view, what is essential to persons are these capacities for practical deliberation and regulation of the will that mark one as a responsible agent. It is significant that the main figures in the perfectionist tradition understand the essentials of human nature in something like this normative way.

This kind of perfectionist view claims that a person's good consists in activities that exercise and express her capacities for practical deliberation. Such a view explains why we value lives of various sorts in which people are self-directed and engaged in activities that exercise their creative powers. In doing so, the perfectionist is able to accommodate an attractive kind of *pluralism* about the good, which recognizes a variety of different but equally or incommensurably good lives, without lapsing into an unsustainable *content-neutrality*, which places no substantive restrictions on the content of a good life. This sort of perfectionism also explains our reservations about shallow and undemanding lives, even when these are successful in meeting the agent's actual or reflective aims and aspirations. Finally, this sort of perfectionism is well suited to answer an important question about the normativity of the good. Though many people fail to care about what is actually good for them, it is common to think that people would, or at least should, care about their own good if they understood what it consisted in. If so, we can ask about any putative conception of an agent's good *why* he should care about it. Any account of the good should be able to explain why it is reasonable or makes sense for a person to care about his good, so conceived. It is not obvious why one should aim to experience pleasure or satisfy desires, regardless of the source of the pleasure or the object of desire. By contrast, a perfectionist conception that stresses the exercise of deliberative capacities ties the content of the good to the very capacities that make one a responsible agent, subject to reasons for action, in the first place. In pursuing this sort of perfectionist good, one is exercising the capacities that make one a rational agent. This kind of perfectionism, it seems, promises to explain the normativity of the good.

5. ACCOMMODATION AND REFORM

So far, I have examined various theoretical choices the consequentialist must make, expressing special interest in direct, maximizing conceptions of consequentialism that give an important role to perfectionist goods. However, I have not yet addressed the issues about whose well-being matters, and how it matters, that separate impartial (agent-neutral) and partial (agent-relative) consequentialists. I will examine these forms of consequentialism separately and in some detail.

My test of adequacy will be systematic comparative plausibility. Does the view in question recognize or violate plausible constraints on an adequate moral theory, and does it cohere well with other independently plausible philosophical commitments? In addition to various theoretical virtues, a plausible theory must cohere well with our independent moral judgments about actual and hypothetical cases. A good theory aims to subsume and explain familiar moral precepts, but the theory that does this best and has various theoretical virtues may well be morally revisionary. Ideally, we make tradeoffs among our theories, considered judgments, and other philosophical commitments, making adjustments here and there, as overall coherence seems to require, until our ethical views are in *dialectical equilibrium*.

Such a dialectical examination, therefore, involves both accommodation and reform of our preexisting moral outlook. When examining consequentialist conceptions, I will show that they sometimes appear to have counterintuitive implications. The consequentialist has two main responses available. He can respond by arguing that consequentialism can, after all, accommodate the allegedly recalcitrant intuition. Alternatively, where accommodation is impossible, the consequentialist can urge us to reform our intuitions, either because the intuitions lack an adequate philosophical rationale, or because the demands of global accommodation require local reforms. We will have to decide how much accommodation is possible and how much reform is reflectively acceptable.

6. UTILITARIANISM AND IMPARTIALITY

Contemporary discussions of consequentialism almost always focus on impartial or agent-neutral consequentialism, which tells agents to promote the good, as such, and not just the good of the agent or some other limited class of people. If we do not recognize impersonal goods, then impartial consequentialism directs us to what would most advance the well-being or happiness of all affected parties. This is the central claim of utilitarianism, though different conceptions of utilitarianism result from different conceptions of well-being or happiness.

Why take utilitarianism or any other form of impartial consequentialism seriously? Bentham and Moore seem to have thought that it is an analytic truth that one ought to do the action with the best consequences (Bentham, 1970, ch. 1, sec. 11; Moore, 1903, secs. 17, 89). But neither agent-neutral consequentialism nor utilitarianism passes Moore's own test for analytic truths—the Open Question Argument—because it is possible for competent speakers to doubt whether right action and action that maximizes value or happiness are the same. Others have thought that utilitarianism is attractive because it recognizes the central importance of benevolence as a virtue and the important role of sympathy in moral motivation (see Boyd, 1989, pp. 215–216; Scanlon, 1982, p. 115). But few think that benevolence is the only or the most important virtue.

My own view is that the chief attraction of utilitarianism lies in its interpretation of the concept of *impartiality*. It is a salient feature of modern conceptions of morality that they aim to overcome parochial concern. It is common to think of the moral point of view as one that asks an agent to transcend his own private concerns and allegiances. We might understand such transcendence in terms of adoption of a point of view that is impartial as among the interests of affected parties. The utilitarian conception of impartiality says that each is to count for one and none for more than one. When utilitarianism was first championed in the eighteenth and nineteenth centuries, its impartiality made it part of a revisionary moral and political theory that tended to undermine familiar institutions of class and privilege. This moral reform is now generally thought to have been a progressive influence, correcting an indefensible moral parochialism.

The utilitarian conception of impartiality assigns no moral importance, as such, to whom a benefit or burden befalls; it is the magnitude of the benefit or harm that matters morally. This conception of impartiality supports a maximizing moral standard. The utilitarian takes everyone's interests into account by aggregating their interests, balancing benefits to some against harm to others, as necessary, so as to produce the best total outcome.

Some critics object to the utilitarian conception of impartiality as requiring interpersonal balancing. Whereas balancing goods and harms may be acceptable *within a life*, many think that it is not acceptable to balance goods and harms *across lives*. On the aggregative conception, individual claims may simply be outvoted by a majority. In order to respect the separateness of persons, critics claim, our concern for each person must take a distributed, rather than an aggregative, form. One such distributed conception of impartiality is *contractualism*, which claims that distributions of benefits and harms must be acceptable, in the relevant sense, to *each*. One version of contractualism claims that actions and the way they distribute benefits and harms are right insofar as they conform to principles that no one can reasonably reject (Scanlon, 1998, p. 153). By giving each person in effect a veto, the contractualist seeks a kind of unanimity, in contrast to the majoritarianism of utilitarianism. The interpersonally best option may usually be acceptable to many, but it can fail to be acceptable to each.

How best to model impartiality is a large and important topic that goes beyond the scope of this study. But it is worth noting that utilitarian and contractualist conceptions of impartiality need not be treated as mutually exclusive alternatives. Given that people's actual talents, holdings, and prospects are often the product of arbitrary forces within natural and social lotteries, for which the individual has little responsibility, it would often be unfair in the distribution of benefits and burdens to give everyone a veto on the basis of his actual position and preferences. One needs to *moralize* the contract. One needs to replace the question "What arrangements could no one reject given knowledge of his actual endowments and preferences?" with something like the question "What arrangements could no one reject in fair circumstances that abstract from morally arbitrary facts about his endowments and preferences?" This arguably requires replacing the idea of an ex post agreement among different individuals with conflicting interests with an ex ante choice of a single self-interested individual under a veil of ignorance about his actual endowments and preferences. If we model contractualism this way, it is arguable that contractors would choose so as to maximize expected total or average welfare, for such a principle, in contrast with nonmajoritarian principles, is antecedently more likely to advance one's interests once the veil is lifted.[14] If so, contractualists need not reject the utilitarian conception of impartiality.

However, to say that the utilitarian conception of impartiality is compatible with contractualist conceptions is not to say that the utilitarian conception is unproblematic. We can group together several concerns about utilitarian impartiality under two main headings—*constraints* and *options* (see Kagan, 1989, ch. 1). Constraints are moral prohibitions, which are often thought to correlate with moral entitlements that individuals possess—such as rights—that limit what someone may do to them, even in the pursuit of good consequences. On such views, it can be wrong to do something, even though doing so might maximize value. Other critics have focused on options, rather than constraints, alleging not that the consequentialist demand for the agent to promote the good violates duties to others, but rather that it ignores prerogatives that the agent has to devote attention and resources to her own projects and those of others with whom she is associated out of proportion to their impersonal value.

7. IMPERSONAL CONSTRAINTS

One source of concern about utilitarian impartiality is its apparent failure to accommodate *impersonal* constraints. These are duties that an agent owes to anyone regardless of the relationship in which she stands to that person. Typically, these duties are correlated with claims or rights that a person has to be treated or not to be treated in certain ways. On one understanding, these duties are not to be violated, even if doing so produces more value overall. Nozick emphasizes this aspect of rights, when he insists that rights be understood as side constraints rather than as important goals; it is wrong for an agent to violate one person's right, even if so doing would minimize the total number of violations of such rights by others (1974, p. 29). To treat rights as side constraints is to recognize values that should be honored rather than promoted.

Most everyone recognizes rights, and the conception of rights as side constraints is quite appealing. But, on reflection, side constraints can appear paradoxical. As Nozick himself notes, if the nonviolation of a constraint is so important, shouldn't we take as our goal the minimization of violations of that constraint (1974, pp. 30–31)?

Nozick's own answer is to appeal to the separateness of persons and the Kantian demand that we treat all agents as *ends* and never merely as means. But the Kantian requirement does not obviously require side constraints. Suppose that only by causing harm to B can A prevent individually comparable harms to C, D, and E. If A harms B only in order to protect C, D, and E, perhaps A treats B as a means, but he need not treat her as a mere means. To do that would require viewing her as a mere instrument or tool, not as someone whose own agency is valuable. But A need not view her that way. He can take her agency into account; if so, he proceeds, but with reluctance that derives from a concern with her agency. If A could have protected C, D, and E without harming B, he certainly would have. If A acts impermissibly in acting so as to minimize harm, it is not because in so acting he must be treating those whom he harms as mere means.

Sometimes friends of side constraints appeal to a sort of *inviolability* that individuals possess if and only if their fundamental interests are protected by side constraints (Kamm, 1996, vol. 2, pp. 271–278; Nozick, 1974, p. 31; Rawls, 1971, pp. 3–4). But to make B inviolable in this way will require turning a deaf ear to the comparable interests of C, D, and E. This seems to deny them moral *considerability*. Though we want to take seriously the fundamental interests of each, it is not obvious that we should endorse inviolability, because ensuring the inviolability of each denies the moral considerability of others.[15]

Furthermore, we may wonder whether impersonal constraints would be acceptable within a suitably moralized contract. If we appeal to an ex ante self-interested choice subject to ignorance about whether one will be A, B, C, D, or E when the veil of ignorance is lifted, then there is every reason to believe that one would prefer a harm–minimization principle to one representing a side constraint upon causing harm. For, all else being equal, one clearly stands a better chance of avoiding harm under harm minimization than under a side constraint. If so, then impersonal constraints may seem problematic from the point of view of contractualist impartiality, as well as utilitarian impartiality.

So, despite the initial intuitive plausibility of impersonal constraints, they are not unproblematic. Absent an attractive rationale for such constraints, it would be premature to reject utilitarianism for its failure to accommodate them (see Kagan, 1989; Scheffler, 1982, ch. 4).

8. Personal Options

Whereas some critics of utilitarianism focus on constraints, others focus on options. Utilitarian impartiality demands that an agent always act so as to bring about the impersonally best outcome. But especially when we recognize the variety of grave imperfections in the world and the opportunities that these imperfections provide for contributing to a better world, utilitarianism can seem very demanding indeed. So much so that we may begin to wonder whether utilitarianism leaves the agent room to pursue those projects and associations that she cares most about and that give her life meaning. Williams has brought to our attention worries of this sort about the conflict between impartial moral conceptions, such as utilitarianism, and the personal point of view (1973, 1976). Responding to this conflict, Samuel Scheffler has proposed to *moderate* the demands of utilitarianism by recognizing moral options or *prerogatives* on the agent's part to devote time, energy, and resources to her own projects out of proportion to their impersonal value (1982, esp. chs. 1–3, 1992, esp. chs. 6–7).

Recognition of personal options is one way to recognize a limit on the sacrifices that morality can demand. And, unlike impersonal constraints, Scheffler argues, options are not inherently paradoxical. An important rationale for options is that they allow the agent to integrate morality into a reasonable life plan. In order for moral demands to be integrated into a reasonable and satisfying life plan, they must be motivationally accessible to agents. But, Scheffler argues, the "natural independence of the agent's point of view" means that agents have concerns for themselves, their own projects, and their intimates that is out of proportion to their impersonal value. But then impartiality without options won't be motivationally accessible to agents; only a form of impartiality moderated by options can be integrated into a reasonable and satisfying life plan.

One interesting question is whether one can have options without some sort of constraints, as Scheffler proposes. Scheffler seems to think of options or permissions as shielding the agent from the demands of impartial consequentialism. But if they are to provide a significant shield, it seems that an agent's options should correlate with duties of others to respect the agent's nonoptimizing personal choices (see Alexander, 1987). It is true we can imagine a system of permissions without any correlative duties in which each is free to pursue his own personal projects but no one is under a duty to refrain from interfering with the projects of others. But such unsupported options are not very attractive, especially to someone who saw options as a way of protecting the agent from demands by others. If so, then it is hard to defend options without constraints. Whether such constraints have to be understood as side constraints is, of course, a separate matter.

Should we recognize personal options? While I have no impossibility proof to offer, the arguments for them are not obviously compelling. It is not clear that utilitarianism fails the test of motivational accessibility. That may depend on how we understand the test. If motivational accessibility is relativized to people's actual motivations, then it may well be true that utilitarian demands are motivationally inaccessible to many, inasmuch as many, no doubt, do care about their own projects and commitments out of proportion to their impersonal value. But motivational accessibility, so understood, has potentially conservative implications, severely limiting the demands of moral reform. If this is how we interpret motivational accessibility, we may well decide to reject it as an acceptable constraint on moral theory. Alternatively, motivational accessibility might be relativized to possible or desirable motivations. But then a utilitarian morality may not be motivationally inaccessible. Motivation can be responsive to moral and other normative beliefs. But then if there are good arguments for an impartial morality, such as utilitarianism, acceptance of these arguments can help produce motivation congruent with such demands.[16] In short, it is hard to identify a conception of the motivational accessibility requirement that both yields a plausible requirement and clearly rules out utilitarian conceptions of impartiality.

9. Personal Constraints: Associative Duties

In some ways, what is most puzzling is the thought that the personal point of view limits the demands of impartiality by way of options. Insofar as common-sense morality recognizes limits on impartial demands, it recognizes duties, and not just permissions, of a personal nature. I am under duties of self-cultivation and duties toward associates that limit the impersonal good I can be expected to promote. I have in mind what are sometimes called *special obligations* that an agent has toward himself and toward others to whom he stands in various sorts of special relationships. Different kinds of special obligations are rooted in different sorts of relationships or associations—including parent-child relationships, marriage, friendships, and professional relations. Some of these relations are undertaken in a wholly voluntary way (as when I choose a spouse, friends, or colleagues), whereas others appear to have significant nonvoluntary aspects (I am unable to choose my parents). No doubt the nature and texture of such associations are quite variable. Nonetheless, there are common themes of shared experiences, learning from another, mutual trust, cooperation, common aims, and mutual concern pervading such associations. We might characterize associations as involving shared history between people that obtains when the beliefs, desires, intentions, experiences, emotions, and actions of each interact with and influence those of the other. Indeed, it would be natural to think that the strength of an association is proportional to the degree of psychological interaction and interdependence, with stronger and more intimate associations held together by greater psychological interdependence and influence. One might think of one's associational relations as forming a set of concentric circles in which my closer associates lie on the inner circles and more remote associates lie on the outer circles. But if special obligations are based on associational ties, then it would be natural for the strength of associational duties to be proportional to the strength of the underlying associational bonds.

How should I express concern for myself and my associates? That depends on which theory of the good is correct. If, as I have argued, perfectionist ingredients form the central elements of a person's good, then I should express my concern for my associates by doing things to further the proper development of their deliberative competence and their pursuit of projects and plans that they have reflectively endorsed and that exercise their deliberative capacities.

If we understand associational duties on this model, then such duties depend upon the right sort of interpersonal interaction and influence and do not automatically arise from all interpersonal relations. So, for example, children would owe no typical filial duties to biological parents who have played no role in their nurture and development. Similarly, estranged spouses would not have typical marital obligations toward each other. Hermits who live in physical proximity to each other would not be obligated as neighbors. Insofar as these restrictions on the scope of associative duties are reflectively acceptable, this makes the proposal to ground such duties in interpersonal interaction and influence more attractive.

On this view, associational relations ground special concern for the well-being of one's associates. Acting on this concern will often require modifying the roles that associates play in an association. This conception of associative duties contrasts with some strands within the communitarian tradition that find the content, as well as the ground, of associative duties in past associational relations and imply that associates have a duty to conform to the roles established by past association.[17] Past association may ground a duty of concern, but it does not settle the form that such concern should take. If our past association has not been mutually beneficial, then our shared history gives us special reasons to modify the terms of our relationship so as to be better adapted to the needs of one or both parties.[18] In the limiting case, special concern for the good of associates can provide reasons to discontinue an association, if that is what is best for associates.

In his article "Self and Others," Broad describes a moral theory that recognizes associative duties that he calls *self-referential altruism* and associates with common-sense morality. Like utilitarianism, it recognizes a reason to be concerned about anyone whom it is in the agent's power to affect for better or worse, but it insists that the weight or strength of the agent's obligations is a function of the relationship in which she stands to potential beneficiaries (1971, p. 280). Perhaps associational bonds also create options, but, as Broad recognizes, they characteristically generate obligations or duties. We have duties toward associates to enable and assist their development, to facilitate their projects and plans, to protect them from certain dangers, to console them in times of need, to provide constructive criticism, and so on. All else being equal, our duties toward associates take precedence over duties to nonassociates, and our duties to closer associates take precedence over duties to more remote associates. This aspect of self-referential altruism is hard to square with utilitarianism. The problem is that special obligations involve duties to associates whose normative strength appears to be out of proportion to the impersonal good that their fulfillment embodies.

Consider Sidgwick's admirably clear-headed attempt to accommodate special obligations within his hedonistic utilitarian framework. In the *Methods of Ethics*, he argues that the recognition of special obligations and a differentially greater concern for those to whom one stands in special relationships is in general optimal, because we derive more pleasure from interactions with associates, we often have better knowledge about how to benefit associates, and we are often better situated causally to confer benefits on associates (1966, pp. 431–439).

However, even if the demands of special concern and impartial concern often coincide, the coincidence is imperfect. I may derive more pleasure from interaction with my associates than with strangers, but those who are strangers to me have their own associates who derive special pleasure from them. If so, it is not clear how an impartial concern with happiness explains why I would have any reason to privilege the claims of *my* associates over those who are strangers to me but associates of others. Moreover, often—where the beneficiaries are near at hand and the benefits in question are fairly obvious—I am just as well positioned epistemically and causally to benefit strangers as to benefit my associates. When this is so, the classical utilitarian has no reason to regard an agent's investments in his friends as a more efficient use of his resources.

These accounts of special concern within an impartial or impersonal perspective appear to be unable to give a sufficiently robust account of special concern. The problem is that utilitarianism's impartiality assigns only *extrinsic* significance to special concern; special concern is valuable only so far as it tends causally to promote human happiness. By contrast, common sense attaches *intrinsic* significance to special relationships; the fact that A and B are friends gives A special reason to be concerned about B that he does not have to be concerned about C.[19]

Alternatively, we might put this point in terms of the distinction between agent-relative and agent-neutral reasons. Reasons to promote the good, as such, are agent-neutral reasons, whereas reasons to promote the good of those to whom the agent stands in special relationships are agent-relative reasons. Association seems normatively significant, because it seems to transform the reasons the agent has independently of the association. If so, one's reasons to be concerned about one's associates are agent-relative, not agent-neutral.

Because associational duties assign intrinsic and agent-relative significance to the shared history among associates, they resist capture within a utilitarian conception of impartiality. Special concern may not always trump impartial demands to promote happiness; but the former cannot be reduced to the latter. If so, we might entertain utilitarian or consequentialist views as revisionary challenges to the legitimacy of special concern but not, I think, as justifications of special concern.

10. Voluntarist and Distributive Concerns about Associative Duties

Many would think that this is reason to conclude that however adequate utilitarianism is as an account of impartiality, it represents an inadequate account of the sort of partiality characteristic of associational duties. However, while conceding the intuitive appeal of associative duties, some complain that such duties, like impersonal constraints, are paradoxical and require an adequate philosophical rationale that explains their normative significance. In particular, Scheffler has argued that associative duties are problematic on two fronts. Associative duties appear to be overly demanding of agents when, as in some familial relationships, they obligate agents to have special concern for associates they have not sought out. Recognizing such duties appears to violate the *voluntarist* assumption that all duties must be voluntarily undertaken by the agent. Whereas the voluntarist is worried about the *costs* of association for the agent, there is *distributive* concern about the *benefits* of association. Precisely insofar as associative duties give more urgency to the claims associates make on each other, they reduce the comparative urgency of the claims of nonassociates on associates. Associative duties privilege the claims of insiders against those of outsiders, and so might seem to give rise to legitimate complaints by outsiders. These objections render associative duties problematic and in need of an adequate philosophical rationale.[20]

But it is hard to see these as decisive objections to associative duties. First, we might not be as concerned by either the costs or the benefits of associative duties if we bear in mind that such duties involve *both* costs and benefits. Insider privileges may seem less significant when they are balanced against insider burdens, and insider burdens may seem less onerous when insider benefits are reckoned in. Moreover, it is not clear that associative duties, as understood here, violate the voluntarist assumption. Because associative duties, on this view, do not arise from just any interpersonal relations but require interpersonal interaction and influence (see section 9), they depend upon the voluntary actions of associates and so cannot be wholly nonvoluntary. Furthermore, the voluntarist assumption that duties can be generated only by the agent's voluntary undertakings itself stands in need of a rationale. Indeed, voluntarism is flatly inconsistent with utilitarianism and any other moral theory that recognizes various noncontractual duties toward others. So the utilitarian is in no position to complain that associative duties violate voluntarism. The distributive objection does focus on a way in which associative duties require a deviation from egalitarian or impartial concerns, but, of course, this is just the direct consequence of recognizing the demands of partiality. So I doubt that the associative duties that resist capture within the net of utilitarian impartiality are any more problematic than utilitarianism itself.[21]

11. PERSONAL IDENTITY, UTILITARIANISM, AND ASSOCIATIVE DUTIES

One way of defending utilitarianism against worries about constraints actually appeals to some of our claims about associative relations together with claims about personal identity. Several worries about utilitarianism's liability to violate rights focus on the *person neutrality* of utilitarianism. The utilitarian conception of impartiality assigns no moral importance, as such, to whom a benefit or burden befalls; it is the magnitude of the benefit or harm that matters morally. The utilitarian takes everyone's interests into account by aggregating their interests, balancing benefits to some against harm to others, as necessary, so as to produce the best total outcome. If the magnitude of benefits and harms is of moral importance as such, but their distribution across lives is not, then one should maximize net value, rather than seek any particular interpersonal distribution.

As such, person neutrality effects a kind of impartiality across lives akin to the impartiality that *temporal neutrality* effects within lives. It is a common view that the temporal location of a benefit or harm within a life should not, as such, have any rational significance. A person should only be concerned with the magnitude of the benefit or harm within her life, not its temporal location, which implies that she should be impartial among different stages of her own life and maximize her overall good, rather than achieve any particular intertemporal distribution.

Indeed, many have seen the motivation for utilitarianism as extending the familiar balancing and maximizing procedure from diachronic intrapersonal contexts into interpersonal contexts (Rawls, 1971, pp. 23–24; Sidgwick, 1966, p. 382). But, as I showed earlier (section 6), some critics of utilitarianism object to this assimilation of interpersonal balancing to intrapersonal balancing. Whereas balancing goods and harms may be acceptable *within a life*, many think that it is not acceptable to balance goods and harms *across lives*. To engage in interpersonal balancing, as utilitarianism does, is to fail to respect the *separateness of persons* (Nagel, 1970, pp. 134, 138–42; Nozick, 1974, pp. 31–34; Rawls, 1971, pp. 23–29, 187–188; Williams, 1976, p. 3).

This asymmetry between intrapersonal and interpersonal balancing is linked to concerns about *compensation*. In the case of intrapersonal balancing, the sacrifice of one's present good for one's later, greater good is compensated; benefactor and beneficiary are the same. But in the case of interpersonal balancing, benefactor and beneficiary are different people; unless the beneficiary reciprocates in some way, the benefactor's sacrifice will go uncompensated. Whereas intrapersonal balancing is automatically compensated, interpersonal balancing is not. This may make person neutrality problematic in a way that temporal neutrality is not.

If the compensation principle is interpreted so as to forbid all uncompensated sacrifices and all interpersonal balancing, then it apparently forbids all redistributions of resources from the superrich to the destitute—no matter how small a burden on the superrich and how great a benefit to the destitute. So interpreted, the compensation principle is hard to accept.

Derek Parfit has tried to defend utilitarianism against the separateness of persons objection in a different way. He has argued that if we accept a traditional conception of personal identity that analyzes personal identity into psychological relations, then we should deny that the separateness of persons is fundamental. If we reject the separateness of persons, then we can defend the utilitarian conception of interpersonal balancing (Parfit, 1984, ch. 15).

Parfit's view is similar to other views in the Lockean tradition of thinking about personal identity (Locke, 1979, II.xxvii), such as the views of Shoemaker (1963, 1984), Wiggins (1967), and Nozick (1980, ch. 1). Parfit calls his view a form of psychological reductionism. The psychological reductionist analyzes personal identity into relations of psychological *continuity* and *connectedness*. Roughly, two persons are psychologically connected insofar as the intentional states and actions of one influence the intentional states and actions of the other. Examples of intrapersonal psychological connections would include A's earlier decision to vote democratic and her subsequent casting her ballot for the democratic candidate, A's later memories of a disturbing childhood incident and her earlier childhood experiences, and A's later career change and her earlier reevaluation of her priorities. Two persons are psychologically continuous insofar as they are links in a chain or series of people in which contiguous links in the chain are psychologically connected. Both connectedness and continuity can be matters of degree. According to Parfit's form of psychological reductionism, it is the holding of many such relations of connectedness and continuity that unify the different stages in a single life. More specifically, on this view, personal identity consists in maximal (non-branching) psychological continuity.[22]

But psychological connectedness and continuity are one-many relations; there can be interpersonal, as well as intrapersonal, psychological connections and continuity. Though I am normally most strongly continuous with myself in the future, I can be psychologically continuous with others with whom I interact psychologically. Interpersonal, as well as intrapersonal, psychological continuity is quite common and can be found, to varying degrees, in all associative relations. Associates interact and help shape each other's mental life; in such relationships, the experiences, beliefs, desires, ideals, and actions of each depend in significant part upon those of the other.

According to psychological reductionism, what normally distinguishes intrapersonal continuity and interpersonal continuity is the *degree* of continuity.[23] There are more numerous and more direct psychological connections—between actions and intentions and among beliefs, desires, and values—in the intrapersonal case than in normal interpersonal cases. And where the connections among links in a chain are all weaker, continuity between any points in the chain will also be weaker. Different interpersonal associations exhibit different degrees of psychological connectedness and continuity.

Insofar as the difference between intrapersonal and interpersonal relations is a difference of degree, not kind, the separateness or diversity of persons is less fundamental than it would otherwise be. But if the separateness of person is not fundamental, and the same sort of glue that unifies a single life can be found, to a lesser degree, holding together different lives, then the asymmetry between intrapersonal balancing and interpersonal balancing may seem to disappear. If so, utilitarianism's interpersonal balancing may be no more objectionable than the sort of intrapersonal balancing demanded by temporal neutrality.

But while psychological reductionism may show that the separateness or diversity of persons is not fundamental, it does not vindicate utilitarianism. This is because there are real differences in degree of continuity and connectedness in the relations which a person bears to herself and others. We can think of the degrees of connectedness and continuity in terms of a set of concentric circles in which the person occupies the inner circle and her various associates stand in outer circles, depending on the strength and number of psychological interactions and interdependence she has with them. If one's reasons for concern track the degree of psychological interaction and interdependence, then, all else being equal, one has more reason to be concerned about closer associates than more distant associates or nonassociates. But this sort of *interpersonal discount rate* is incompatible with utilitarianism's person neutrality; it requires an agent-relative ethical theory that recognizes associative duties very similar in structure to self-referential altruism (see Jeske, 1993).

12. A RATIONALE FOR ASSOCIATIVE DUTIES

I can take this case for associative duties one step further by showing how reasonable assumptions about persons and personal identity provide a normative rationale for associative duties. We saw that Locke claimed that the concept of a person is a normative or "forensic" concept (section 4). In both morality and law, persons are responsible agents; it is only persons who are properly praised and blamed, because it is only persons who have the requisite capacities for practical deliberation. On this view, personhood requires responsibility, which requires deliberative capacities, which require a conception of oneself as a temporally extended self endowed with deliberative capacities. If we view persons from this Lockean perspective, then it is natural to endorse a version of psychological reductionism that understands the persistence of persons in terms that emphasize the continuous employment of deliberative faculties in the regulation of thought and action. If persons are essentially responsible agents, then an essential ingredient in psychological connectedness must be *deliberative* connections that hold among actions, intentions, and prior deliberations in the deliberate maintenance and modification of intentional states and in the performance of actions that reflect these prior deliberations.

While we normally find maximal continuity within single lives, we have seen that there are significant forms of continuity *across* individual lives within friendship and other forms of interpersonal association. If so, one's relations to associates are similar in kind to, if different in degree from, those that hold between oneself now and oneself in the future. But this suggests that one has the same sort of reasons to be concerned about associates as one does about one's own future self.

How does this help provide a rationale for associative duties? For one thing, it suggests that associative duties are no more problematic than the demands of prudence. Most people, even many utilitarians, recognize the requirements of prudence as normatively significant. But then associative duties have as strong a rationale as the demands of prudence do. We can go further. For we can ask about prudence, as we can about any putative normative standard, why we should care about its dictates. Why should I care about promoting my own good? Appeal to a deliberative conception of the person helps explain how prudence, conceived in perfectionist terms as exercising one's deliberative capacities, is a requirement of practical reason. For when prudence is understood in deliberative terms, it aims at the exercise of the very deliberative capacities that make one a responsible agent in the first place, capable of having and acting on reasons for action. Moreover, if my persistence depends upon the extension of my deliberative control into the future, we can see how the exercise of my deliberative capacities is part of my welfare. But insofar as associational relations involve interpersonal analogues of these psychological and deliberative connections, the resulting reasons to be concerned about the interests of associates will likewise depend upon the very deliberative capacities that make me a responsible agent, subject to reasons for action. On this view, associational bonds manifest the very same psychological relations that make one an agent, and this explains one's reasons to be concerned about associates. If so, we have the makings of a satisfying philosophical rationale for the normative significance of associational bonds. Whether there is any comparably satisfying rationale for utilitarianism remains to be seen.

13. Associative Duties and the Limits of Impartiality

Utilitarianism is plausible insofar as it provides a natural interpretation of the modern ideal of impartiality. But utilitarianism is doubly impartial. Christian and Enlightenment moral conceptions are impartial in the sense of insisting on the *wide scope* of moral concern. The utilitarian conception of impartiality embodies wide scope, because it insists that the scope of moral concern should be universal, extending to all human or rational (or sentient) beings. But utilitarianism is impartial in the further sense that it assigns *equal weight* to everyone's good. And it insists on this equal weighting of everyone's interests not just in special contexts—for instance, demanding that governments weigh the interests of their citizens equally—but of all agents in all contexts. The utilitarian can justify deviations from this second sort of impartiality only on pragmatic grounds as an effective strategy for actually better meeting the demands of equal concern.

The arguments on behalf of associative duties challenge any moral conception, such as utilitarianism, that is impartial in both senses. Associative duties show the need for a moral conception that embodies an agent-relative form of partiality. But to reject impartiality altogether would be to throw out the baby with the bath water. The interesting question is whether we can articulate a moral conception that combines wide-scope impartiality with the sort of partiality embodied in associative duties.

One attractive way to combine impartiality and partiality is self-referential altruism. Self-referential altruism is impartial and agent-neutral insofar as it insists that an agent has nonderivative reason to benefit anyone whom it is within her power to help. But it is partial and agent-relative insofar as it insists that the weight or strength of the agent's obligations is a function of the relationship in which she stands to potential beneficiaries. As Broad recognized, self-referential altruism combines impartiality and partiality in a way that resonates with common-sense morality.

But while self-referential altruism combines impartiality and partiality in an intuitively attractive way, it faces a problem about the normativity of its impartial demands. While the authority of any normative standard can be questioned, the question arises in an acute form for any impartial standard that has the potential to ask agents to make significant personal sacrifices to benefit others with whom they are not directly associated. Though self-referential altruism gives priority, other things being equal, to the claims of those to whom an agent stands in special relationships, it recognizes the claims of anyone, regardless of the relationship in which he stands to the agent. If my sacrifice can do enough good for strangers, then self-referential altruism may well claim that it is my duty to make such a sacrifice. It is not uncommon to interpret morality as requiring uncompensated sacrifices. This may just seem to be another aspect of the sort of transcendence of parochialism characteristic of modern moral conceptions. But we may wonder why we should regard such sacrifices as reasonable.

14. EGOISTIC CONSEQUENTIALISM

If a fundamental and underived commitment to impartiality raises difficult questions about the normativity of impartial requirements, one might explore the possibility of deriving impartial requirements within a fully agent-relative framework. In providing a rationale for associative duties, I showed how the normativity of associative duties might be grounded in interpersonal relations that extend an agent's rational capacities and, on perfectionist conceptions, contribute to the agent's good. That account of the normativity of associative duties was ultimately egoistic. The obvious challenge here is whether a sufficiently robust commitment to impartiality can be justified on egoist foundations.

Ethical egoism claims that it is an agent's moral obligation to do what promotes his own good or welfare. Such a view makes the agent's own good primary, defining other moral notions in terms of it. It represents an agent-relative form of consequentialism. As with agent-neutral forms, this sort of agent-relative consequentialism admits of different conceptions, depending on whether it takes maximizing or satisficing forms and on whether it takes a direct or indirect form. As before, we can focus on the more traditional direct, maximizing conceptions, inasmuch as the objections to such conceptions do not seem compelling and they seem to have resources to make the same distinctions and claims as their rivals. What this focus leaves open is the conception of the good. Much will depend on the conception of the good on which the egoist draws. As I will argue, perfectionist conceptions have the greatest resources for explaining the normative authority of prudential concern and for justifying other-regarding concern with wide scope. To appreciate these claims better, it will be helpful to look at the limitations in more familiar subjective forms of egoism.

15. STRATEGIC EGOISM

What account can we give of the morality of other-regarding concern within an egoist framework, if we employ hedonist or preference-satisfaction assumptions about the good? Of course, most of us have significant concerns for the well-being of associates and more generalized sympathies for other members of humanity that structure our desires and condition what we take pleasure in. Insofar as such other-regarding attitudes are strong and widespread, they provide the basis for an egoist justification of other-regarding conduct.

But this egoist justification of other-regarding action appeals to other-regarding attitudes without grounding them; as a result, it seems unable to explain why those who lack these attitudes should cultivate them or why those who do have them should maintain them. We need a more robust and counterfactually stable justification of other-regarding conduct and concern.

A traditional egoist defense of impartiality tries to argue that even those with more self-confined concerns have reason to broaden their concerns, because the demands of other-regarding morality and enlightened self-interest coincide. The main lines of this story are familiar enough. Much of impartial other-regarding morality involves norms of cooperation (e.g., fidelity and fair play), forbearance, and aid. Each individual has an interest in the fruits of interaction conducted according to these norms. Though it might be desirable to reap the benefits of other people's compliance with norms of forbearance and cooperation without incurring the burdens of one's own, the opportunities to do this are infrequent. Noncompliance is generally detectable, and others won't be forbearing and cooperative toward those who are known to be noncompliant. For this reason, compliance is typically necessary to enjoy the benefits of others' continued compliance. Moreover, because each has an interest in the cooperation and restraint of others, communities will tend to reinforce compliant behavior and discourage noncompliant behavior, with the result that well-socialized individuals will have internalized these norms. If so, compliance is often necessary to avoid the costs of external and internal sanctions. Whereas noncompliance may secure short-term benefits that compliance does not, compliance typically secures greater long-term benefits than noncompliance. In this way, compliance with other-regarding norms of cooperation, forbearance, and aid might be claimed to further the agent's interests. Insofar as this is true, the egoist can ground other-regarding sentiments and explain why those who do not have them should cultivate them and those who do have them should maintain them.[24]

The main problems with this strategic justification of other-regarding conduct and concern involve its scope and stability. The strategic egoist can justify other-regarding duties only toward partners in systems of mutual advantage. But it is a common modern view that morality has wide scope; it imposes obligations of restraint and aid where the agent stands to gain nothing strategically from the cooperation or restraint of the beneficiary. So, for instance, on this view a person can apparently have no reason to be concerned about future generations. And if the wealthy and talented have sufficient strength and resources so as to gain nothing by participating with the weak and handicapped in a system of mutual cooperation and forbearance, the former can have no reason, however modest, to assist the latter. When morality itself is interpreted in terms of strategic egoism, these are counterintuitive limitations in the scope of moral demands.

Moreover, serious limitations remain in the scope and stability of the concern that the strategic egoist can justify toward strategic partners. Sometimes noncompliance would go undetected; and even where noncompliance is detected, the benefits of noncompliance sometimes outweigh the costs of being excluded from future cooperative interaction. Furthermore, even if the coincidence between morality and self-interest were extensionally adequate, it would be counterfactually fragile. On this justification of compliance with other-regarding norms, compliance involves costs, as well as benefits. As a result, it must remain a second-best option, behind undetected noncompliance, in which one enjoys the benefits of others' compliance without the costs of one's own. So, as Glaucon and Adeimantus point out in Plato's *Republic*, if only I was able to enjoy the benefits of the compliance of others without the costs of my own compliance, then I would have no reason to comply (359b8–360d8). But moral norms seem counterfactually stable—they would continue to apply in these counterfactual circumstances—as other-regarding norms that the strategic egoist can justify are not. This counterfactual instability represents a further limitation in strategic egoism.

So, despite the promise of strategic egoism to justify impartial concern on agent-relative foundations, strategic egoism is unable to justify other-regarding demands with wide scope or stable significance. Such a view purchases normativity, if at all, at the price of failing to recognize impartiality and individual transcendence. Indeed, insofar as one may question the normative authority of pursuing pleasure or satisfying desire, independently of the sources of one's pleasure or the content of one's desires, one may doubt that strategic egoism can claim normative authority.

16. PERFECTIONIST EGOISM

We saw that a suitable perfectionist conception of the good promises to explain how prudence, so conceived, has normative authority (section 12). When prudence is understood to aim at the perfection of the agent's deliberative capacities, it aims at the exercise of the very capacities that make one a rational agent in the first place. If such a perfectionist conception of prudence has normative authority, it is worth asking how far such a perfectionist conception of egoism can go in accounting for impartial moral demands.

In addressing this issue, I should reiterate the most important of my earlier claims about persons, associative relations, and the reasons that persons have to care about their associates. If I endorse a version of psychological reductionism, then psychological interaction and interdependence is the glue that unifies disparate stages in a single life. Future directed self-concern involves being concerned about future selves that are uniquely continuous with my present and past selves. However, we saw that such uniqueness is really just a matter of degree of continuity and not a deep fact. Interpersonal, as well as intrapersonal, psychological continuity is not only possible but common. It is found, to different degrees, in all kinds of interpersonal associations in which the intentional states and actions of associates influence each other. Just as an agent should regard the good of his future self as part of his overall good, so too, I argued, should he regard the good of his associates as part of his overall good. This provides a prudential or egoist justification for an agent to be concerned about his associates.

Before examining the nature or scope of such other-regarding concern, we need to better understand the prudential value of interpersonal association. Once I have associates, my reasons to be concerned about them are, on this view, the same sort of reasons that I have to be concerned about my own future good. So perhaps I can see how a concern for my own good requires a concern for their good. But surely the nature and extent of my associations with others are matters that are, at least to some extent, within my control. What prudential reason do I have to cultivate associations with others in the first place?

The perfectionist answer must be that interpersonal association of the right sort makes for the fuller realization of my deliberative capacities. Though I am essentially a deliberative agent, I am not self-sufficient but am cognitively limited. Interpersonal association helps me transcend these limitations. Sharing thought and discussion with another diversifies my experiences by providing me with additional perspectives on the world. By enlarging my perspective, it gives me a more objective picture of the world, its possibilities, and my place in it. This echoes Plato's and Aristotle's claims that part of the value of friends, with whom one shares thought and conversation, consists in their providing a "mirror" on the self (*Phaedrus* 255d5, *Nicomachean Ethics* 1169b34–35). Insofar as my friend is like me, I can appreciate my own qualities from a different perspective, which promotes my self-understanding. But there are limits to the value of mirrors. Interaction with another just like me does not itself contribute to self-criticism. This is why there is deliberative value in interaction with diverse sorts of people many of whom are not mirror images of myself. This suggests another way in which I am not deliberatively self-sufficient. Sharing thought and discussion with others, especially about how to live, improves my own practical deliberations. It enlarges my menu of options, by identifying new options, and helps me better assess the merits of these options, by forcing on my attention new considerations and arguments about the comparative merits of the options. Here we should notice the deliberative value of open and vigorous discussion with diverse interlocutors. Moreover, cooperative interaction with others allows me to participate in larger, more complex projects and so extend the scope of my deliberative control over my environment. In this way, I spread my interests more widely than I could acting on my own. Here too diversity can be helpful; cooperation is improved and extends each person further when it draws on diverse talents and skills. In these ways, interpersonal associations arguably make for fuller realization of my deliberative capacities, and this explains the prudential importance of associative relations and concern.

17. The Scope of Other-Regarding Concern

An obvious concern about this perfectionist account of other-regarding concern is its *scope*. Restricted, as it seems to be, to explaining concern for intimates, friends, and other associates, it seems to fall well short of the wide or universal scope of concern on which modern moral conceptions insist.

The perfectionist egoist can begin to rebut the charge of parochialism by showing just how pervasive interpersonal association is. Associations, we have seen, are not restricted to regular interactions among like-minded people. They exist whenever there is psychological continuity among people. Psychological influence can be exerted between people, on each other, even when they have not had direct interactions, as when two people influence each other through their conversations with a common third party. The ripple effects on others of our conversations, plans, actions, and relationships can extend quite widely. Moreover, continuous selves need not be connected. Any elements in a series are continuous, just in case contiguous members in the series are well connected. This implies that noncontiguous members (e.g., the end-points) of such a series are continuous even if they are not well connected or connected at all. If so, people can be psychologically continuous who are not at all connected, provided they are members of a series of persons each of whom is connected to some degree with his neighbor in the series. There is room for debate about the comparative roles of continuity and connectedness within a psychological reductionist account of personal identity. Perhaps both relations matter and extend one's interests, but I think it is clear that continuity must matter.[25] If so, then the relations that justify other-regarding concern can extend far beyond the circle of those with whom one regularly interacts.

But can the scope of perfectionist concern be genuinely universal in scope if it is the result of interpersonal interaction? For then there must be someone—the proverbial remotest Mysian (Plato, *Theaetetus* 209b8)—with whom one has no previous relation, however indirect.[26] Should it somehow come within my power to help the remotest Mysian, at little or no cost to myself, it might seem the egoist cannot explain justified concern for him. This would represent a limitation in the scope of egoist concern.

If the remotest Mysian and I stand in no relations of connection or continuity, then his good is not already part of mine. So I can have no backward-looking reason to be concerned about him. But I can have forward-looking reasons. For it is now within my power to interact with him, and all the reasons for cultivating interpersonal association apply and provide a forward-looking rationale for concern. Even when the remotest Mysian and I have no prospect of further interaction, my assistance will enable or facilitate his pursuit of his own projects, and this will make his subsequent actions and mental states dependent upon my assistance. Indeed, other things being equal, the greater the assistance I provide, the greater is my involvement in his life. To the extent that another's actions and mental states are dependent upon my assistance, I can view the assistance as making his good a part of my own. Assistance to the remotest Mysian earns me a share, however small, of his good. If the perfectionist egoist can justify concern for the remotest Mysian, then the scope of such concern would seem to be genuinely universal.

18. Noninstrumental Concern for Others

But even if the scope of perfectionist concern is acceptable, perhaps its nature is not. Morality seems to require not just that we perform the actions it demands of us but also that we fulfill its demands from the right sort of motives, and sometimes morality seems to require not just that we benefit another but that we do so out of a concern for the other for her own sake. This is certainly true about the concern owed to intimates. But if justified concern for another is, as the perfectionist egoist claims, a special case of self-love, then mustn't such concern be at bottom instrumental?

The perfectionist can reply that if the good of another is a constituent part of her own good, and not just an instrumental means to the promotion of her own good, then she is justified in having intrinsic, and not merely instrumental, concern for another. When I undergo a present sacrifice for a future benefit, I do so because the interests of my future self are interests of mine. The on-balance rationality of the sacrifice depends upon its promoting my overall good. But because the good of my future self is part of this overall good, concern for my overall good requires, as a constituent part, a concern for the good of my future self. In this way, concern for my future self for its own sake seems compatible with and, indeed, essential to self-love. If psychological relations extend an agent's interests, then the good of others can be part of my overall good just as my own future good can be. Though the on-balance rationality of other-regarding action depends upon its promoting my overall good, concern for my overall good requires, as a constituent part, concern for the welfare of those to whom I am appropriately psychologically related.

19. THE VARIABLE WEIGHT OF OTHER-REGARDING CONCERN

Another issue concerns the *weight* of the reasons for other-regarding concern. Both connectedness and continuity are matters of degree. If we think of degrees of connectedness and continuity in terms of a set of concentric circles, with myself occupying the inner circle and the remotest Mysian occupying the outer circle, then, as we extend the scope of psychological interdependence, the strength of the relevant psychological relations appears to weaken, and the weight of one's reasons to give aid and refrain from harm presumably weakens proportionately. Despite the wide scope of justified concern, it must apparently have variable weight. Is such an interpersonal discount rate acceptable?[27]

An interpersonal discount rate of moral concern need not be a threat to our understanding of morality. For it is commonly thought that, even if morality has universal scope, the demands it imposes are a function not simply of the amount of benefit that one can confer but also of the nature of the relationship in which one stands to potential beneficiaries. Common–sense morality recognizes more stringent obligations toward those to whom one stands in special relationships—for instance, toward family and friends and toward partners in cooperative schemes—than toward others. It seems a reasonable hypothesis that the interpersonal relationships that have special moral significance are just those relationships of psychological interaction and interdependence that extend one's interests. If so, then there will be a moral discount rate that is isomorphic to the egoist interpersonal discount rate.

I have now sketched how within a form of perfectionist egoism one might derive other-regarding concern that is both universal in scope and variable in weight. Indeed, it would seem that we have succeeded in deriving the central claims of self-referential altruism from within a purely agent-relative form of egoism that does not recognize any underived demands of impartiality. Because the perfectionist conception of prudence appears to have normative authority, this is reason to take seriously its justification of moral concern with wide scope and variable weight.

20. CONSEQUENTIALISM'S PROSPECTS

If we identify consequentialism with agent-neutral conceptions of impartiality, such as utilitarianism, as many do, then I think that we must be skeptical of consequentialism. This sort of consequentialism cannot be the whole truth about morality. For while the agent-neutral conception of impartiality is attractive and surprisingly robust, such a conception of impartiality cannot do justice to associative obligations. These obligations resist capture within the intellectual net of agent-neutral consequentialism, and they admit of a philosophical rationale at least as plausible as anything the agent-neutral consequentialist has to offer. An adequate moral theory must recognize the demands of partiality, as well as those of impartiality.

But we can and should understand consequentialism more broadly, to include any view that takes the good to be explanatorily primary and understands other notions, such as duty and obligation, to supervene on the promotion of value. In particular, we can and should recognize forms of consequentialism that are not purely agent-neutral. One common–sensical form of consequentialism is self-referential altruism, which combines agent-neutral and agent-relative claims in a way that tries to capture both impartial and partial demands. While self-referential altruism has considerable intuitive plausibility, it leaves the normative authority of its commitment to agent-neutral impartiality unexplained. Why exactly should I be concerned about the weal and woe of others, regardless of their relationship to me? A related concern is that the self-referential altruist must answer the questions "Whom should I care about?" and "How much should I care about them?" in entirely different ways. Without some explanation of the normativity of its impartiality and some explanation for why these questions should be answered so differently, self-referential altruism may appear problematic.

These forms of consequentialism contrast with egoism, which is fully agent-relative, insisting that something is one's duty just insofar as it promotes one's own well-being or happiness. The obvious concern about egoistic consequentialism is with the stability and scope of its justification of other-regarding moral concern. These doubts are well founded when applied to forms of egoism employing traditional subjective conceptions of the good and relying on strategic arguments. Such strategic forms of egoism justify other-regarding concern that is limited in scope and counterfactually fragile. Moreover, subjective conceptions of the good fail to explain why the agent has reason to promote his own good. But a perfectionist conception of egoism fares better here. If we conceive of the good as consisting in the exercise of the very deliberative capacities that make someone an agent in the first place, we can see why he has reason to take an interest in his own good. But the relations that unify different parts of the agent's own life hold, to a significant degree, between the agent and others, which gives him reason to regard their good as part of his own good, in much the same way that the good of his future self is part of his own good. Such claims are not unfamiliar as applied to one's relationships with one's intimate associates. But the central claims apply much more widely. Indeed, because the act of benefiting another actually constitutes association, in the relevant sense, the scope of other-regarding concern that can be justified in this way is genuinely universal. On this view, the strength of one's reasons to be concerned about others is proportional to the strength of the associational bonds. It follows that this kind of perfectionist egoism can justify other-regarding concern with universal scope but variable weight. This means that we can derive the attractive mix of impartiality and partiality characteristic of self-referential altruism from purely agent-relative, indeed, egoistic foundations. In doing so, we appeal to foundations whose normative authority is clearer than it was in the case of self-referential altruism itself. We also provide a unified explanation of whom to care about and how much to care. We should care about others insofar as they are or will be psychologically connected to us in the right way and to an extent proportional to the degree to which we are or will be so connected.

There remain important questions about the structure and implications of these agent-relative conceptions of consequentialism, answers to which will affect the adequacy of such conceptions. Though these issues are beyond the scope of this study, they deserve mention. The main issue concerns how to combine the interests of different people within such views. This combinatorial issue will affect how demanding such views are.

Consider self-referential altruism. It recognizes the impartial demand to be concerned about anyone whom it is in one's power to benefit but claims that the strength or urgency of one's obligation to another is a function of the nature of the relationship between benefactor and beneficiary. This would treat associative relations as putting a sort of thumb in the scales of a utilitarian calculation so as to create a normative bias for associates. On this view, an agent is required to perform that action whose value is greatest after the consequences for everyone have been recorded and multiplied by the relevant factor (equal to or greater than one) corresponding to the strength of the relationships between the agent and beneficiaries. However, until we know how great the *associate-bias* is, it is hard to know or assess the consequences of accepting self-referential altruism.

One reason utilitarianism appears to be quite demanding of some people is that the world contains a great deal of suffering, some of which can be very efficiently relieved if the better-off make sacrifices. If others are not making their share of sacrifice (partial compliance), utilitarian demands for sacrifice will apparently increase. If each of us ought to give until the point that our sacrifices are as great as the benefits we confer, then, given the conditions of partial compliance, compliers ought to sacrifice a great deal. This sort of sacrifice would involve a very significant change in lifestyle for most of those living reasonably comfortable lives and would require sacrifices that would constrain the satisfaction of their associative duties.

Would the introduction of an associate-bias significantly reduce the amount of sacrifice required? Given the very high benefit-cost ratio of many relief operations—where I can save many lives by very small contributions—it is difficult to see how an associate-bias would significantly reduce utilitarianism's demands for aid under normal conditions of partial compliance, unless the bias is very large indeed. But self-referential altruism would then lose its main appeal in relation to agent-neutral conceptions of consequentialism, inasmuch as associative duties would never trump general duties of beneficence. Alternatively, if the bias is very large and is constant across different contexts, then associational demands are likely to defeat impartial demands in all contexts, including partial compliance. The resulting view would verge on a fairly complacent moral theory that involves very little transcendence. Insofar as perfectionist egoism implies self-referential altruism, the same issues arise for it. The only difference is that with perfectionist egoism the questions concern the combination of different aspects (more and less self-confined aspects) of the agent's own good, rather than the combination of the agent's own good and that of others.

This version of the combinatorial problem arises when we allow the demands of partial and full compliance to diverge. One way for the agent-neutral consequentialist to respond is to argue that the limits of beneficence under conditions of partial compliance should be set by the amount of beneficence that would be optimal under conditions of full compliance (see Hooker, 2000; Murphy, 2000). This would reduce the demands of beneficence in conditions of partial compliance, though it is unclear how far they would be reduced. The self-referential altruist or perfectionist egoist could presumably appeal to the same device to link the demands in partial compliance to those in full compliance. Because such views already constrain the duties of beneficence by duties to oneself and one's associates, linking the demands of partial compliance to those of full compliance would make the resulting demands of beneficence even more manageable than agent-neutral consequentialism would allow.

This strategy of response to the combinatorial problem holds some promise. But it appears to depart from traditional direct, maximizing consequentialism inasmuch as it employs indirection reminiscent of rule consequentialisms. Whether such a strategy can be housed within a defensible form of consequentialism is a matter for further study. What is certain is that the combinatorial problem, the demands of morality, and the relationship between the demands of partial and full compliance are issues that any moral theory must tackle.

NOTES

I thank David Copp for helpful comments on the penultimate version of this material. More general debts I owe to Dick Arneson and David Lyons. I have benefited from various discussions over the years with my colleague Dick Arneson about the forms and resources of consequentialism. The title of my essay is inspired by David Lyons's book

Forms and Limits of Utilitarianism (1965). Though my structural concerns with consequentialism are mostly different from David's, I have learned much from that work and his other writings on utilitarianism. The discussion here of utilitarianism and associative duties draws in part upon Brink, 1997c, 2001.

1. If good character is itself explained in terms of promotion of value, then this sort of virtue theory would itself be a special kind of consequentialist view, namely, motive consequentialism.

2. This defense of maximization is act consequentialist. Mill's view here is interesting. While many claims in *Utilitarianism* point toward act utilitarianism, an important strand in Mill's utilitarianism actually defines right action in terms of the utility of blaming the conduct in question. In particular, he claims that one is under an obligation to do something just in case failure to do it is wrong and that an action is wrong just in case some kind of external or internal sanction—punishment, social censure, or self-reproach—ought to be applied to its performance (1978b, ch. 5, para. 14). Whether sanctions ought to be applied to an action (hence whether it is wrong) depends on the utility of doing so (1978b, ch. 5, par. 25). This strand in Mill's theory ties wrongness to blame in a way that act utilitarianism does not. These aspects of Mill's theory are discussed in Lyons, 1994, and Brink, 1997a.

3. The issues here are complicated. In some such cases, it does seem pointless or even pernicious to conform to rules that would have optimal general acceptance value when others are not so conforming. But the appeal to general acceptance value may be an advantage in other cases of partial compliance. See the discussion in section 20.

4. Williams's concern is with impartial moralities, including, but not restricted to, utilitarianism. However, the worry seems to apply to a variety of optimizing theories, not just impartial conceptions.

5. Parts of this account of having one's conduct regulated by a principle, without constantly consulting it, can be found in Mill's claims in *Utilitarianism* (1978b, ch. 2, pars. 19, 23–25) and *A System of Logic* (1844, VI.xii.7) about the need for "secondary principles" that function in our practical reasoning in lieu of direct appeals to the utilitarian first principle. Scheffler, 1992, ch. 3, contains a nice discussion of the variety of roles that moral principles can play in moral deliberation.

6. So I do not distinguish, as some do, between happiness and well-being. Some distinguish the two, because, whereas they can entertain objective conceptions of well-being, they regard happiness as an inherently subjective concept that does not admit of objective conceptions. I am not persuaded of this contrast; I think that we can entertain and take seriously objective (including perfectionist) conceptions of happiness (see Kraut, 1979). Anyone who disagrees and thinks that subjectivism about happiness is true by definition can simply put happiness to the side and reinterpret the discussion solely in terms of well-being.

7. Thomas Hurka, chapter 13 in this volume, provides a more systematic discussion of the good and defends some related conclusions.

8. However, it should perhaps be noted that hedonism is objective, insofar as it claims that pleasure is a person's good whether or not the person realizes this or desires pleasure.

9. Ideal preference views sometimes trace their ancestry to Mill's appeal in *Utilitarianism* to the preferences of competent judges to identify higher pleasures, though I

think that Mill's claims can be given a consistent perfectionist reading. Important statements of the informed preference view include Brandt, 1979, and Griffin, 1986. The most sophisticated version of the view of which I am aware is Railton, 1986.

10. Moore endorses an objective list, 1903, ch. 6, as does Ross, 1930, p. 140. Parfit discusses such theories sympathetically (1984, pp. 493–502).

11. This is like the criticism, made by Joseph, among others, that the intuitionist's objective list of right-making factors amounts to nothing more than an "unconnected heap" of obligations (see Joseph, 1931, p. 67).

12. A vigorous contemporary statement of perfectionism is Hurka, 1993.

13. Kitcher, 1999, raises some relevant difficulties for Hurka's appeal to a biological essence.

14. Whereas unanimity may be the only decision rule acceptable to all ex post, majority-rule can be acceptable to all ex ante (see Mueller, 1979, ch. 11; Rae, 1969; M. Taylor, 1969). Harsanyi offers such a contractualist defense of utilitarianism (1978). For more discussion of the compatibility of contractualism and utilitarianism, see Brink, 1993.

15. Even Kamm does not think inviolability should be absolute (1996, 2: 274).

16. These thoughts may also suggest a reply to Rawls's argument that utilitarianism violates the strains of commitment within a well-ordered society (1971, esp. pp. 175–183, 496–502). If a well-ordered society is one in which citizens are regulated by a sense of justice, informed by a utilitarian conception of impartiality, then utilitarianism may not impose undue strains of commitment.

17. For communitarian conceptions that tie the content, as well as the ground, of associative duties to the terms of past association, see Bradley, 1927, esp. ch. 5; MacIntyre, 1981, esp. ch. 15; Sandel, 1982; C. Taylor, 1989; Walzer, 1983. The fact that my conception does not tie the content of associative duties to past association allows me to avoid Simmons's worries about grounding special obligations in morally imperfect associations (see Simmons, 1996, esp. p. 266).

18. This way of dealing with morally imperfect associations does not restrict the kind of interdependence and influence that generates associative duties but insists that associative duties enjoin concern for the associate's well-being. Alternatively, one might try to restrict the kind of interdependence and influence that generates associative duties in the first place, so that certain kinds of morally objectionable forms of association do not generate associative duties at all. One might insist that some degree of cooperative interaction and good will are essential ingredients of normatively significant association, much as some degree of diachronic cooperation and good will are arguably essential to unity within a single life. But just as intrapersonal unity must be compatible with some changes of mind and heart, so, too, normatively significant forms of interpersonal association cannot be limited to the virtuous. But then it becomes difficult to know how to restrict the normatively significant forms of association. However, this alternative deserves further study.

19. However, the intrinsic normative significance of special relations cannot be captured by recognizing the intrinsic value of associative relations within a utilitarian view. For instance, the utilitarian can assign special intrinsic value to friendship. But this won't allow her to claim that an agent has reasons to give priority to his own friend when he could provide comparable or greater benefits to the friend of someone who is a perfect stranger to him.

20. See Scheffler, 1995, 1997. In the latter work, Scheffler offers his own rationale for associative duties, which I won't discuss here.

21. Interestingly, whereas Kagan recognizes that any moral conception, including utilitarianism, must meet the demand for a philosophical rationale, he presses this demand only against friends of constraints and options, not against utilitarianism itself. See Kagan, 1989, pp. 18–19.

22. If we are to define identity, which is a one-to-one relation, in terms of psychological continuity, which can take a one-to-many form, we must define it in terms of *nonbranching* psychological continuity. But the reasoning that leads us to this conclusion may also lead us to the conclusion that it is continuity, rather than identity per se, that is what has primary normative significance. I discuss these matters in Brink, 1997b, 1997c.

23. Branching cases, such as fission, in which consciousness divides and psychological continuity is maximal but takes a one–many form, represent the limiting case of interpersonal psychological continuity. In fission cases, there is, by hypothesis, no less continuity than in normal intrapersonal cases. What makes the former interpersonal is simply that in them continuity takes a one–many form. Insofar as our primary concern is with psychological continuity, whether or not it takes a unique or nonbranching form, fission cases throw further doubt on the assumption that the separateness of persons is fundamental. See Brink, 1997c, pp. 138–143.

24. This is an act egoist justification of other-regarding moral norms. But its nature and limits bear comparison with Gauthier's (1986) motive egoist justification.

25. Continuity must figure in a reductionist account of identity if only to meet Reid's demand that any criterion of identity be transitive (see Reid, 1969, p. 358).

26. The introduction of the proverbial remotest Mysian into discussions of the scope of ethical concern is discussed by Annas, 1993, ch. 12.

27. The precise shape of the interpersonal discount rate is a matter for further investigation. As long as psychological continuity is one of the relations that matter, a significant threshold of concern can be justified well out into outer circles. But as long as psychological connectedness is also one of the psychological relations that matter, there will nonetheless be significant differences in the degree of concern that can be justified, above this threshold, in different circles, because an agent will be differentially psychologically connected to others.

REFERENCES

Adams, Robert. 1976. "Motive Utilitarianism." *Journal of Philosophy* 73: 467–481.

Alexander, Larry. 1987. "Scheffler on the Independence of Agent-Centered Restrictions." *Journal of Philosophy* 84: 277–283.

Annas, Julia. 1993. *The Morality of Happiness*. Oxford: Clarendon Press.

Bales, Eugene. 1971. "Act Utilitarianism: Account of Right-Making Characteristics or Decision-Making Procedures?" *American Philosophical Quarterly* 8: 257–265.

Bentham, Jeremy. [1789]. 1970. *An Introduction to the Principles of Morals and Legislation*. London: Athlone Press.

Boyd, Richard. 1989. "How to Be a Moral Realist." In *Essays on Moral Realism,* ed. G. Sayre-McCord, 181–228. Ithaca, N.Y.: Cornell University Press.

Bradley, F. H. [1876]. 1927. *Ethical Studies.* 2nd. ed. Oxford: Clarendon Press.

Brandt, Richard. 1963. "Toward a Credible Form of Utilitarianism." In Darwall, 2002, 207–235.

———. 1979. *A Theory of the Good and the Right.* Oxford: Clarendon Press.

Brink, David O. 1989. *Moral Realism and the Foundations of Ethics.* New York: Cambridge University Press.

———. 1993. "The Separateness of Persons, Distributive Norms, and Moral Theory." In *Value, Welfare, and Morality,* ed. R. Frey and C.Morris, 252–289. New York: Cambridge University Press.

———. 1997a. Critical notice of David Lyons, *Rights, Welfare, and Mill's Moral Theory. Philosophy and Phenomenological Research* 57: 713–717.

———. 1997b. "Rational Egoism and the Separateness of Persons." In *Reading Parfit,* ed. J. Dancy, 96–134. Oxford: Blackwell.

———. 1997c. "Self-Love and Altruism." *Social Philosophy* and *Policy* 14: 122–157.

———. 2001. "Impartiality and Associative Duties." *Utilitas* 13: 152–172.

Broad, C. D. [1953]. 1971. "Self and Others." In *Broad's Critical Essays in Moral Philosophy,* ed. D. Cheney, 262–282. London: Allen and Unwin.

Darwall, Stephen. 1997. "Self-Interest and Self-Concern." *Social Philosophy and Policy* 14: 158–178.

———, ed. 2002. *Consequentialism.* Oxford: Blackwell.

Gauthier, David. 1986. *Morals by Agreement.* New York: Oxford University Press.

Gibbard, Allan. 1990. *Wise Choices, Apt Feelings: A Theory of Normative Judgment.* Cambridge, Mass.: Harvard University Press.

Green, T. H. [1883]. 2003. *Prolegomena to Ethics.* Ed. D. Brink. Oxford: Clarendon Press.

Griffin, James. 1986. *Well-Being.* Oxford: Clarendon Press.

Harsanyi, John. 1978. "Bayesian Decision Theory and Utilitarian Ethics." In Darwall, 2002, 197–206.

Hooker, Brad. 2000. *Ideal Code, Real World: A Rule-Consequentialist Theory of Morality.* Oxford: Clarendon Press.

Hurka, Thomas. 1993. *Perfectionism.* Oxford: Clarendon Press.

Huxley, Aldous. 1946. *Brave New World.* 2nd ed. New York: Harper and Row.

Jeske, Diane. 1993. "Persons, Compensation, and Utilitarianism." *Philosophical Review* 102: 541–575.

Joseph, H.W.B. 1931. *Some Problems in Ethics.* Oxford: Clarendon Press.

Kagan, Shelly. 1989. *The Limits of Morality.* Oxford: Clarendon Press.

Kamm, Frances. 1996. *Morality, Mortality.* Oxford: Clarendon Press.

Kitcher, Philip. 1999. "Essence and Perfection." *Ethics* 110: 59–83.

Kraut, Richard. 1979. "Two Conceptions of Happiness." *Philosophical Review* 88: 176–196.

Locke, John. [1690]. 1979. *An Essay Concerning Human Understanding.* Ed. P. H. Nidditch. Oxford: Clarendon Press.

Lyons, David. 1965. *Forms and Limits of Utilitarianism.* Oxford: Clarendon Press.

———. 1994. *Rights, Welfare, and Mill's Moral Theory.* New York: Oxford University Press.

MacIntyre, Alasdair. 1981. *After Virtue.* London: Duckworth.

Mill, J. S. [1843]. 1844. *A System of Logic.* London: Longmans.

———. [1859]. 1978a. *On Liberty*. Indianapolis: Hackett.

———. [1861]. 1978b. *Utilitarianism*. Indianapolis: Hackett.

Moore, G. E. 1903. *Principia Ethica*. Cambridge: Cambridge University Press.

Mueller, Dennis. 1979. *Public Choice*. New York: Cambridge University Press.

Murphy, Liam. 2000. *Moral Demands in Nonideal Theory*. Oxford: Clarendon Press.

Nagel, Thomas. 1970. *The Possibility of Altruism*. Oxford: Clarendon Press.

———. 1986. *The View from Nowhere*. New York: Oxford University Press.

Nozick, Robert. 1974. *Anarchy, State, and Utopia*. New York: Basic Books.

———. 1980. *Philosophical Explanations*. Cambridge, Mass.: Harvard University Press.

Parfit, Derek. 1984. *Reasons and Persons*. Oxford: Clarendon Press.

Pettit, Philip. 1991. "Consequentialism." In Darwall, 2002, 95–107.

Rae, Douglas. 1969. "Decision-Rules and Individual Values in Constitutional Choice." *American Political Science Review* 63: 40–56.

Railton, Peter. 1984. "Alienation, Consequentialism, and the Demands of Morality." *Philosophy* and *Public Affairs* 13: 134–171.

———. 1986. "Facts and Values." *Philosophical Topics* 14: 5–31.

Rawls, John. 1971. *A Theory of Justice*. Cambridge, Mass.: Harvard University Press.

Reid, Thomas. [1785]. 1969. *Essays on the Intellectual Powers of Man*. Ed. B. Brody. Cambridge: MIT Press.

Rosati, Connie. 1995. "Persons, Perspectives, and Full Information Accounts of the Good." *Ethics* 105: 296–325.

Ross, W. D. 1930. *The Right and the Good*. Oxford: Clarendon Press.

Sandel, Michael. 1982. *Liberalism and the Limits of Justice*. Cambridge, Mass.: Harvard University Press.

Scanlon, T. M. 1982. "Contractualism and Utilitarianism." In *Utilitarianism and Beyond*, ed. A. Sen and B. Williams, 103–128. New York: Cambridge University Press,

———. 1998. *What We Owe to Each Other*. Cambridge, Mass.: Harvard University Press.

Scheffler, Samuel. 1982. *The Rejection of Consequentialism*. Oxford: Clarendon Press.

———. 1992. *Human Morality*. New York: Oxford University Press.

———. 1995. "Families, Nations, and Strangers." The Lindley Lecture. Lawrence: Department of Philosophy, University of Kansas.

———. 1997. "Relationships and Responsibilities." *Philosophy* and *Public Affairs* 26: 189–209.

Shoemaker, Sydney. 1963. *Self-Knowledge and Self-Identity*. Ithaca, N.Y.: Cornell University Press.

———. 1984. "Personal Identity: A Materialist's Account." In S. Shoemaker and R. Swinburne, *Personal Identity*, 67–132. Oxford: Blackwell.

Sidgwick, Henry. [1907]. 1966. *The Methods of Ethics*. New York: Dover.

Simmons, A. John. 1996. "Associative Political Obligations." *Ethics* 106: 247–273.

Slote, Michael. 1985. *Common-Sense Morality and Consequentialism*. London: Routledge and Kegan Paul.

Sobel, David. 1994. "Full Information Accounts of Well-Being." *Ethics* 104: 784–810.

Taylor, Charles. 1989. *Sources of the Self*. Cambridge, Mass.: Harvard University Press.

Taylor, Michael. 1969. "Proof of a Theorem on Majority Rule." *Behavioral Science* 14: 228–231.

Walzer, Michael. 1983. *Spheres of Justice*. New York: Basic Books.

Wiggins, David. 1967. *Identity and Spatio-Temporal Continuity*. Oxford: Blackwell.
Williams, Bernard. 1973. "A Critique of Utilitarianism." In J.J.C. Smart and B. Williams, *Utilitarianism: For and Against*, 75–155. New York: Cambridge University Press.
———. 1976. "Persons, Character, and Morality." In Williams, 1981, 1–19.
———. 1981. *Moral Luck*. Cambridge: Cambridge University Press.

CHAPTER 15

DEONTOLOGY

DAVID McNAUGHTON
PIERS RAWLING

WHAT determines which actions are morally required? According to act consequentialism (AC), the right action is the one that produces the most value (the
best state of affairs, which may include the act itself). Deontology denies this. One
of our foci is to contrast deontology with consequentialism, and clarify the debate
between them. Thus, in addition to defending our deontological view, we devote
attention to consequentialist positions.

Railton (1988, p. 113) refers to AC as "objective consequentialism."[1] He contrasts it with "subjective consequentialism":

> the view that whenever one faces a choice of actions, one should attempt to
> determine which act of those available would most promote the good, and
> should then try to act accordingly. One is behaving as subjective consequential-
> ism requires . . . to the extent that one uses and follows a distinctively conse-
> quentialist mode of decision making, consciously aiming at the overall good
> and conscientiously using the best available information with the greatest possi-
> ble rigor. (p. 113)

'Simple consequentialism' (SC) is our term for the combination of subjective and
objective consequentialisms. (In subsection 2.1 we discuss other varieties.)

Deontology, in contrast to SC, claims that the production of good is not the
only fundamental morally relevant consideration: agents may be permitted, and
even required, not to maximize the good. There is much debate about details,
but the basic distinguishing features of deontology standardly fall under three
rubrics.

1. Basic Features of Deontology

1.1. Constraints

Deontologists characteristically hold that we must not harm people in various ways. We should not lie, kill innocent people, or torture anyone. These prohibitions *constrain* us in what we may do, even in pursuit of good ends. Deontologists differ in how stringent these constraints are. Some think them absolute. Roman Catholic moral theology has traditionally held that one may never intentionally kill an innocent person. Kant infamously argued that it would be wrong to lie, even to prevent murder. Other deontologists have held that, though constraints are always a significant consideration, they may be overridden, especially if that is the only way to avoid catastrophe. Either way, deontology sometimes *requires* agents not to maximize the good. While, of course, any moral requirement restricts us in what we are permitted to do, we shall use the term 'constraints'[2] to refer to moral restrictions that may require one not to maximize the good, where these restrictions do not stem from our special relationships to others. The latter restrictions fall under a separate category: duties of special relationship.

1.2. Duties of Special Relationship

Many of our duties stem from special commitments to others. Some commitments are explicitly undertaken, such as promising. Some are tacit—as in commitments to friends. Some are not voluntarily acquired—consider commitments to parents. Like constraints, the responsibilities that come with relationships curtail our freedom of action, even when we could maximize the good by shirking them. John might benefit more from my help than will Jane, but if I have already promised Jane to help her, and I cannot help both, then it is Jane I ought to help. Duties of special relationship differ from constraints, in that they are owed, by their very nature, only to those to whom we stand in such relationships, whereas there are constraints against torturing or unjustly killing *anyone*.

1.3. Options

Given the amount of suffering in the world and the disparities in wealth, to follow SC and maximize the good would require enormous sacrifice from anyone with more than a minimal standard of living; SC may thus seem too demanding. Many deontologists suggest that our duty to help others is limited. There is some point, though its location is hard to determine, at which agents have done all that duty demands. At that point they have an *option* to decline to do more.[3] We admire those who make the extra sacrifice, but it is supererogatory—more than morality requires. Simple consequentialism leaves no conceptual space for supererogation.[4]

Deontologists don't deny that morality can be demanding. We may be obliged to make significant sacrifices—even of our lives—rather than breach a serious constraint or betray a friend. And we have a duty to do good. But, unlike SC, most deontologists see this latter duty as limited.

1.4. Agent-Relative and Agent-Neutral Theories

Traditionally, SC and deontology are distinguished by their differing accounts of the relation between the right and the good. Simple consequentialism holds that the good determines the right—the amount of goodness produced by an action is the sole determinant of its rightness—whereas the deontologist denies this, holding that other considerations are relevant. More recent writers distinguish between the two in terms of agent-relativity and agent-neutrality, claiming that SC is an agent-neutral theory, whereas deontology incorporates agent-relative elements.[5]

The distinction between the agent-neutral and the agent-relative may be introduced by reference to reasons for acting.[6] Roughly, someone's reason is agent-relative if, at base, there is reference within it to the agent. For example, egoists hold that each of us has reason to promote only *her own* welfare, whereas utilitarians believe each of us has reason to promote the general welfare. Note that both varieties of reason apply to us all, but agent-neutral reasons incorporate an added element of universality: To say that each of us has reason to promote the general welfare is to say that each of us has reason to pursue the *common* aim[7] of promoting the general welfare (and this requires that any person sacrifice her welfare if that will increase the general total), whereas according to egoism, each of us has a *distinct* aim: I have reason to pursue my welfare, you yours.

How does this distinction mesh with that between SC and deontology? SC holds that all moral reasons are agent-neutral, whereas deontology denies this. According to SC, we each have reason to maximize the good, and, morally speaking, this is all we have reason to do. We have one common moral aim: that things go as well as possible. Someone may object that we have distinct aims because my aim is that *I* maximize the good, and your aim is that *you* do so. Perhaps there are circumstances in which *my* maximizing the good does not result in the good being maximized. But this is to misread SC. Suppose I can directly produce ten units of good or five, and in the former case you will directly produce zero, whereas in the latter you will produce six. SC prescribes that I directly produce the five, since the total produced will then be greater. SC cares not about who produces what directly but about what is produced overall.

Deontology, by contrast, maintains that there are agent-relative moral reasons. Duties of special relationship are obviously agent-relative. That she is *your* daughter gives you special moral reason to further her interests. On this view, I am required to care for *my* family, you for *yours*: we have distinct aims. Contrast this with an SC view on which parental care-giving is valuable. On this view, we have the common aim of promoting parental care-giving—which requires that I neglect my own children if I can thereby increase the total amount of parental care-giving.

Constraints are also agent-relative. Suppose I can only prevent you killing two innocents by killing one myself. Those deontologists who advocate an absolute constraint against killing the innocent forbid my killing the one (they also forbid, of course, your killing the two, but we are assuming here that you will ignore this proscription): I have overriding moral reason (a distinct moral aim) not to kill anyone *myself* (as you should aim not to kill anyone *yourself*). Thus, although you will do wrong in killing the two, I should not kill the one in order to prevent you. By contrast, SC holds that, *ceteris paribus*, I should kill the one: killing innocents is bad, so I have an agent-neutral moral reason to contribute to the common aim of minimizing the killing of innocents.

Options need not be agent-relative in their formulation. They simply permit us not to maximize the good. But their standard rationale is agent-relative. Each of us is morally permitted to give special weight to *his own* interests.

There seem to be two ways of distinguishing between agent-relative and agent-neutral moral theories. On the one hand, theories prescribe aims, and these can be common or distinct. By this criterion, a moral theory is agent-neutral exactly if it prescribes common aims, and is agent-relative otherwise. On the other hand, a theory is agent-neutral just in case it countenances only agent-neutral moral reasons, and is agent-relative otherwise. Simple consequentialism is agent-neutral, and deontology agent-relative, on either account.

Common-sense morality[8] (CSM) acknowledges special obligations, constraints, and options. Thus deontology is closer to CSM than SC in this regard. Those advocates of SC who are radical reformers[9] claim that CSM is mistaken here. But many moral theorists hold that we cannot ignore our common-sense moral intuitions, seeing them as a key source of evidence. Other nondeontological theories, then, including other forms of consequentialism, endeavor to achieve a closer fit with our moral intuitions by allowing room for agent-relative considerations. We turn next to discussing some of these theories.

2. Nondeontological Theories

2.1. Consequentialisms

According to AC, the right action is the one that maximizes good ("right equals best"). SC supplements this with a decision procedure that has us "consciously aiming at the overall good" (Railton, 1988, p. 113). SC, then, is apparently direct in the sense that one should employ the criterion of right action in deciding what one ought to do.

But there is a complication. Regan (1980, pp. 264–265 n. 1) offers the following example. You must choose between acts f and g, where f has an even chance of producing zero or ten (objective) utiles, and g is sure to produce 9 utiles. Unbeknownst to you, f will produce 10 utiles, and is thus best, and hence the right act by AC's criterion. But surely you ought to g. We shall interpret "consciously aim at the overall good" as "consciously aim at maximizing expected objective utility." We think of "ought" as action-guiding; thus when we speak of what the agent ought to do, we are referring to the output of the recommended decision procedure when correctly followed. Thus what the agent ought to do, according to SC, is what, on the basis of the information available to her, she calculates will maximize expected objective utility, where no calculation error is made but where her information may be less than full. We shall leave in place the AC criterion of rightness. Thus in Regan's case, according to SC, what you ought to do is the wrong thing. You cannot, however, know in advance that it is wrong. According to SC, then, "right equals best," even where you cannot know what is best. What you ought to do is epistemically accessible; thus what you ought to do may be wrong. But what you ought to do is never something that you know at the time to be wrong.

Some authors refer to a consequentialist theory as "direct," just in case it is a form of AC.[10] Rule consequentialism (RC) is an example of a consequentialist theory that is not direct in this sense. According to RC: "An act is wrong if and only if it is forbidden by the code of rules whose internalization by the overwhelming majority . . . has maximum expected value" (Hooker, 2000, p. 32). RC assesses rules, but not acts, in terms of their contribution to the good. Wrong actions are those that violate the rules. Thus an act may not be wrong and yet fail to produce the best ("right does not equal best") since the optimal rules must be, for example, simple enough to learn and sufficiently appealing that people will generally follow them. So they will often lead us to do less good than we could. Rules that would be fine for angels might be disastrous for humans. And even if humans could be trained to follow them, the cost of inculcating them might be too high.

Act consequentialist theories, while direct in the foregoing sense, may be psychologically indirect: they may tell you not always to think about the (expected) good in deciding what to do (i.e., they may not be subjective consequentialisms in Railton's sense) because you may produce less good if you are obsessively concerned with its production.

Railton is an act consequentialist who advocates such psychological indirection. His "sophisticated consequentialist is someone who has a standing commitment to leading an objectively consequentialist [i.e., AC] life, but who need not set special stock in any particular form of decision making and therefore does not necessarily seek to lead a subjectively consequentialist life" (1998, p. 114). Indeed, it may be that a sophisticated consequentialist "should have (should develop, encourage, and so on) a character such that he sometimes knowingly and deliberately acts contrary to his objectively consequentialist duty" (p. 121)—that is, unlike the simple consequentialist, the sophisticated consequentialist *can* know in a particular case that what she ought to do is the wrong thing.[11]

Consequentialist theories may be indirect in both senses. Consider RC. Given that the optimal code has been internalized as part of a "shared conscience" (Hooker, 2000, p. 2), the agent should, it seems, generally follow her conscience rather than worry about the rules. In the case of RC, we interpret the question of psychological indirection as asking whether we ought to worry about right and wrong when deciding what to do;[12] hence RC is psychologically indirect: the agent should not always consciously employ the criterion of right action in deciding what to do.

Although RC and sophisticated consequentialism (Sophisticated C) are both psychologically indirect, they may differ on how to think in morally tricky cases. According to Sophisticated C, when faced with a morally tricky decision where deliberation is in order, you should often *not* focus upon the right (but upon, say, your spouse). But for RC, in such cases, it is plausible to maintain that you *should* focus upon the right—either by wondering what your current rules tell you to do in this case, or by wondering whether your current rules are the best set.

Motive consequentialism (MC), as we shall understand it,[13] is similar to RC vis-à-vis indirection.[14] The right act need not be best, but is in conformity with the best set of motives.[15] And, assuming one has internalized this set, one should in general simply follow it without worrying about rightness. MC and Sophisticated C differ in their criteria of right action, although both claim that virtuous agents act in accord with the best motives.

Our classificatory efforts are summarized in the following table.

	Act is wrong if not best (AC theories)	Suboptimal act need not be wrong
Psychologically direct	SC	
Psychologically indirect	Sophisticated C	MC, RC

In subsection 1.4, we characterized agent-relative moral theories in terms both of reasons and aims. We noted that deontology is agent-relative on both accounts, and SC agent-neutral. How are MC, RC, and Sophisticated C to be classified? If we think of aims as the outputs of decision procedures, all three are agent-relative by the aim criterion.

RC incorporates, for example, a fairly simple rule against killing the innocent, because the adoption of a more complicated rule that allowed killing in pursuit of the good would be harder to follow and would undermine our valuable reluctance to kill. (Such prohibitions will not be absolute. Agents are permitted to breach them when catastrophe threatens.) There will also be rules that require us to devote time and energy to looking after friends and family.[16] These rules give each agent a distinct aim. I have the aim that *I* not kill the innocent, and look after *my* family, and so on; you have the aim that *you* not kill the innocent, and look after *your* family. And these rules do not permit their own violation in order to promote greater conformity to them.

Similar remarks apply, *mutatis mutandis,* to MC and Sophisticated C.

Turning to the reason criterion, we assume that, for MC and RC, one has most reason to do the right thing. Thus MC and RC are agent-relative by this criterion also: a rule (motive) against killing the innocent is part of the best set (where, recall, this is determinative of rightness); thus I have strong moral reason not to kill the innocent *myself* (even to minimize the number of such actions).

The case of Sophisticated C is not so straightforward. Does one have most reason to do the right thing or to follow the best motives? If the former, Sophisticated C is agent-neutral by the reason criterion (one has moral reason only to maximize the good); if the latter, agent-relative (the sophisticated consequentialist has the same best motives as the motive consequentialist).

If, then, these theories are genuinely consequentialist, it might appear that the agent-relative/agent-neutral distinction is not the apt way to draw the distinction between deontology and consequentialism. On the traditional distinction, by which consequentialism, but not deontology, claims that the right is determined solely by the good, at least AC (and hence Sophisticated C), although not RC or MC, is consequentialist.

There is another sense, however, in which all three theories are agent-neutral. We can assess an action's value from some particular person's perspective—we can ask, for example, whether it is bad for him. But we can also assess its value impersonally. For instance, pain is bad, regardless of whose it is. Claims about impersonal value make no fundamental reference to any particular agent, and so, in this sense, impersonal value is agent-neutral. Each form of consequentialism assesses something, at its base, in terms of impersonal value. But what they assess varies. AC assesses acts; MC assesses motives; Sophisticated C assesses both acts and motives; and RC assesses rules. As Hooker notes, "the agent-relativity in RC is derivative. Agent-relative rules are justified by their role in promoting agent-neutral value" (2000, p. 110). Similarly, the agent-relativity in Sophisticated C and MC is derived from considerations of agent-neutral value. Deontology, by contrast, holds that some agent-relative considerations are *underivatively* relevant. They have weight in their own right, not merely in virtue of their serving some further purpose.[17]

2.2. Nonconsequentialist Nondeontological Theories

Some nonconsequentialist theories have the same structure as RC but offer nonconsequentialist criteria for selecting the rules. Copp's society-centered theory, for example, sees a rule as "justified in relation to a society just in case the rule is included in the moral code that the society would be rationally required to select, in preference to any other code, to serve as its social moral code" (1997, p. 190). It is practically rational for individuals or societies to select, roughly, what would best satisfy their needs and further their values. Such a theory will generate rules rather similar to those endorsed by RC. However, since the test for what rules are acceptable does not appeal to agent-neutral value, the theory is not consequentialist. But that does not make it deontological, since the moral force of any agent-relative considerations is only derivative.[18]

Unlike Copp's theory, Scheffler's (1994) theory makes room for underivative agent-relativity. It agrees with SC's rejection of constraints but incorporates options, and justifies these by appeal to the cost to *the agent* of maximizing the good. In refusing to give the personal perspective any *moral* weight, consequentialism does not reflect the *natural* weight that agents give to *their own* projects, friends, family, and so on. Scheffler's theory is thus not consequentialist: it allows that agent-relative considerations have fundamental moral weight in justifying options. Yet arguably it is not a deontology. The latter, strikingly, sometimes *requires* us not to maximize the good, but Scheffler merely *permits* this, when it would significantly damage our concerns.

Having classified various nondeontological theories, we turn now to classifying deontologies.

3. ROSSIAN DEONTOLOGY

Ross (1930, ch. 2) claims that there are several distinct underivative agent-relative moral considerations, which he formulates as a list of basic principles or duties. These include agent-relative duties of promise-keeping, gratitude, reparation, and not harming others.[19] In addition, he agrees with SC that there is an agent-neutral requirement to promote the good (which includes, for Ross, justice). These duties are only prima facie (or, as we prefer, *pro tanto*) since, though each is relevant to determining what is right, they can conflict. If keeping a promise will harm someone, for example, to determine what is right, the duty to keep the promise must be weighed against the duty not to harm, where this weighing is governed by no higher rule—it requires discernment and judgment.

While other deontologists, such as Kant and Scanlon (see hereafter), agree with Ross that there are a number of basic principles, they see them as basic only in the sense that they are not instances of some more general principle. For instance, all three might agree that the duty to pay one's debts is not basic because it is an instance of the duty to keep promises, whereas the latter is basic since it is not itself an instance of some more general duty. For Kant and Scanlon, however, but not Ross, even such basic principles rest on a common foundation (although Kant and Scanlon disagree as to what this is): There is a test that principles must pass—a test, furthermore, that is claimed to be in some sense definitive of morality. Ross denies that there is such a test. (SC agrees with Ross in this: There is no test that SC's fundamental principle, maximize the good, must pass.)

Ross also claims that the prima facie duties are self-evident. By this he means (roughly) that they stand in no need of justification,[20] and we can see their truth directly, without reasoning from further premises.

In formulating his principles, Ross assumes that if a consideration is fundamentally morally relevant in one case, it is relevant in the same way in all cases. If we have a fundamental prima facie duty not to harm, then the fact that an act will cause harm is invariably a moral reason not to do it, though not necessarily an overriding one. Harmfulness has invariably negative moral valence. Apparently Ross reasons thus. Any feature of an action may be morally relevant to its rightness, but many features are merely derivatively relevant. That it is Tuesday is morally relevant if I have promised to do something on Tuesday, but its relevance derives from the content of my promise. What is fundamentally relevant, however, cannot derive its moral force from elsewhere, and so must have it essentially. Its valence will not vary.

This argument is, however, invalid. A moral consideration may be basic, in that wherever it counts its moral force is underivative. Yet its force may be conditional on the presence of other features—it might not count in all cases. Take promise-keeping. Ross claims that my having promised to do an act always counts in favor of doing it. But this is mistaken. Promises extracted by fraud or force are null and void, as are promises to do something immoral. Suppose I promise to perform a contract killing. It is implausible to hold that, though I ought not to do it, all things considered, the fact that I promised gives me *some* moral reason to do it. The duty to keep promises is not derivative—when we have reason to keep a promise, there is no more basic moral reason that explains why—but it is conditional.[21]

It may seem, however, that Ross can address this concern. We could arrive at a consideration that has invariant valence by simply adding the relevant conditions. Particularists (who hate a principle), however, disagree.

4. PARTICULARISM

To what extent is morality codifiable? Some hold that moral theory should refine and qualify our moral principles so that a verdict can always be "read off" from them. Ross and the particularist agree that there are no such verdictive principles. What of nonverdictive principles? Are there, for example, nonnormative features with invariant valence? The particularist says not. For example, it might be claimed that there is always a moral reason not to lie. But Dancy (1993b, pp. 60–61) raises the case of children's games in which lying is part of the fun. Lying in these contexts, he claims, does not carry negative weight. The particularist's general claim here is that any nonnormative feature varies in valence according to context.

One response to this general claim is to increase the complexity of the nonnormative features. Perhaps lying has universally negative valence except in contexts in which all relevant parties tacitly acknowledge its acceptability. One worry here, however, is that acceptability is itself a normative notion. Second, there may be other exceptions to the principle that lying counts negatively—indeed, there may be no finite list of exceptions that suffices.

But Ross, we think, largely accepts this line, at least tacitly: apart from the case of (perhaps) promise-keeping, his principles claim invariant valence only for normative notions such as justice, gratitude, loyalty, and reparation. Ross's principles, then, are usually couched in normative terms, and thus it requires moral sensitivity to determine whether an act falls under them.

Principlists might retort, however, that (1) there must be nonnormative features with invariant valence because we cannot make moral judgments without appeal to them, and (2) consistency is essential to morality, and to be consistent is to follow principles or rules.[22]

The response to (1) is to note that we test whether, say, lying under certain conditions has universally negative valence by searching for counterinstances. But the very possibility of such a search shows that we can tell whether lying is relevant in a particular case without appeal to our principle about lying. When we come across circumstances, real or imagined, that force us to qualify a principle, we recognize that the qualification is required. And this recognition, on pain of regress, is not achieved by appeal to some further principle. Furthermore, even if there are principles with finite numbers of exception clauses, the particularist claims that we can never know that we have listed them all. Principles are epistemically redundant.

The response to (2) is to recall one of the Wittgensteinian rule-following considerations. Suppose the principle is "Lying has universally negative valence"; then, in order to apply it, one must be able to determine whether a novel case is a case of lying. But to do so consistently, according to the view that consistency requires appeal to principles or rules, requires appeal to some further rule. Even if such can be formulated, its consistent application will require appeal to further rules, and so on. Eventually, there must be brute application without appeal to rules. And this will vitiate claims to consistency (on this view of consistency). Thus either we are inevitably inconsistent, or consistency is not a matter of rule-following.

According to the particularist, then, reasons function holistically: no consideration is uninfluenced by its surroundings—the relevance of any feature may vary according to context. Do we, as Rossians, agree? Not if the particularist maintains that *all normative* features have variable valence. If the notion of a promise is a normative notion, then we might agree that promise-keeping is a normative feature that can vary from having positive valence to being irrelevant (though we doubt that there are cases where the fact that I made a promise counts *against* keeping it); but we find it implausible that there are cases in which features such as justice or loyalty are morally irrelevant or even negative. Justice and loyalty are thick moral concepts. These are, roughly, those associated with the virtues and vices. And these, we contend, have invariant valence.[23] The particularist view that anything may count (or not), and in ways that cannot be specified in advance, seems to have no way of accounting for the moral centrality of the thick moral concepts, beyond noting that they are more frequently relevant than others.

But have we not conceded too much to the particularist? It might appear that not only are there nonnormative considerations that have invariant valence but also there are actually such considerations that always make an act, say, wrong. We agree, for example, that gratuitous torture is always wrong. But we claim that the notion of gratuitous torture cannot be spelt out nonnormatively. One might try: inflicting pain on another for no reason. But the difficulty is that reason is a normative notion. So how about: Inflicting pain on others solely for one's own pleasure is always wrong. Again, we agree. But the proscription is tantamount to: Inflicting pain on others where the only reason for doing so is one's own pleasure. And, again, this adverts to the normative notion of a reason.

Some form of Rossian deontology seems to us to strike the correct balance between principlism and particularism. Having defended Ross from the particularist, we now turn to alternative foundations for deontology and the attack from principlism.

5. ALTERNATIVE FOUNDATIONS FOR DEONTOLOGY

Rossian deontology seems to have a number of drawbacks. First, there is a diversity challenge: In uncovering the fundamental moral principles, Ross appeals solely to our reflective convictions, so what do we say to those whose reflective moral beliefs differ significantly from ours? Second, we have a reasons hurdle: How do we argue with those who doubt that moral considerations are reasons? Third, there is the no-algorithm difficulty. There are disagreements about what is right, both because people cannot agree about the weight to be given to competing considerations and because there are disagreements about how to apply a principle. We may agree that harming others is *pro tanto* wrong but disagree both about how this weighs against other considerations in a particular case and about what constitutes harm. Ross offers no algorithms for deciding difficult cases. Finally, rather than a unified account of the nature of obligation, Ross offers an irreducible list of disparate fundamental considerations—the unity problem.

Other deontological theories might appear to do better in addressing these difficulties. Some, such as Scanlon's (see subsection 5.2), arrive at the content of morality by considering what principles people have reason to agree to. Others, such as Kantianism, ask what principles could be universally accepted.

5.1. Kant

Kant sees morality as a species of practical rationality, and offers a test of the latter: the Categorical Imperative (CI) test.[24] Actions that fail this test are, he claims, wrong. Crucial to the test is the notion of a maxim. We act with certain aims (which we might not have consciously formulated), and these can be specific or general. Maxims are general aims. Thus my maxim may be: Make lying promises (i.e., ones I intend not to keep) whenever it benefits me. The CI test asks first on what maxim I propose to act, and then enquires whether this maxim is one that I could will to be a universal law. Here is a rough illustration:[25] The maxim to make lying promises whenever it benefits me cannot be universally willed, because its universal adoption would lead to the demise of the very practice on which it relies—namely, the practice of promising. Hence, making lying promises for my own benefit is wrong. (One issue here is whether the fact that the maxim on which you acted cannot be universally willed is even relevant to the issue of why the action is wrong.)

How exactly the CI test is to be understood and what it would rule out are matters of scholarly dispute.[26] But there is general agreement that Kant's ethics has a deontological structure. The test yields constraints, for agents are forbidden, on an alternative formulation of the test, to treat others *merely* as a means. Exactly what this entails is again in dispute, but it is intended to rule out such things as lying and killing the innocent even to minimize lying and the killing of innocents by others. To kill an innocent yourself to prevent other killings, for example, would be to use your victim as a means to minimize victimization. From SC's perspective, these constraints forbid one to maximize the good. Kant's system also admits options: We have only a limited duty to help others.[27]

The rationale for Kant's test lies in a certain conception of rationality. If something is a reason for one agent, then it must be capable of being a reason for all. Thus a maxim is not a good reason for action unless it is one on which all agents can act. Any maxim that could not consistently be followed by all, or could not consistently be willed as one that all should follow, is not rationally acceptable—it fails to show respect for the autonomy of all other rational agents.

Kant's theory seems to overcome the supposed drawbacks of Rossian deontology. It meets the diversity challenge, because Kant's test for right action is a purely formal one, appealing only to what can be willed consistently. It does not presuppose any substantive evaluative or deontic claims. It leaps the reason hurdle by claiming that it would be irrational to act on a maxim that could not be universally adopted. It avoids the unity problem because the test offers a unified underpinning to our disparate duties. Finally, it goes some way to surmount the algorithm difficulty, in claiming that certain kinds of consideration are morally decisive. Some duties—the duty not to lie[28] or kill the innocent, for example— are held to be absolute; that is, they can never be overridden by other moral considerations. Clear and unequivocal moral guidance is, however, here bought at a high price. For the claim that it is always wrong to lie, even to save a life, runs counter to most people's moral intuitions.

Equally counterintuitive is Kant's claim that only other persons have moral claims on us—nonrational creatures have no independent moral standing (for instance, the fact that an action would cause suffering to an animal is itself no reason not to do it, according to Kant). These and other well-known objections to Kant's theory prevent it from fulfilling its ambitious program.

5.2. Scanlon

Whereas Kant asks of a principle whether rational agents could universally will it, Scanlon asks whether reasonable persons could reject it. (Scanlon sees his position as continuing the social contract tradition, hence the name "contractualism.") On Scanlon's view: "An act is wrong if its performance under the circumstances would be disallowed by any set of principles for the general regulation of behavior that no one could reasonably reject as a basis for informed, unforced general agreement" (1998, p. 153). Our aim is "to find principles [for the general regulation of behavior] that others who share this aim also could not reasonably reject" (Scanlon, 2002, p. 519), where someone may only object to some proposed principle if its general acceptance would place excessive or arbitrary burdens on her. Whether the objection constitutes grounds for reasonable rejection depends on whether there is a comparable principle available that is not subject to similar objection (1998, p. 205).

Scanlon distinguishes between narrow and broad morality (1998, pp. 6–7, 171–177). Narrow morality is his central focus: it is this that concerns wrongness as defined above, and is captured by the phrase "what we owe to each other" (p. 7). While Scanlon agrees, for instance, that "pain—whether that of rational creatures or nonrational ones—is something we have prima facie reason to prevent, and stronger reason not to cause" (p. 181), there is (*ceteris paribus*) more reason to respond to the pain of a rational creature: Not only is the rational creature's pain bad, but in addition "we may owe it to him to help relieve it." The fact that A-ing is wrong is a reason not to A that augments the other reasons against A-ing (p. 11) (where wrongdoing cannot be committed against nonrational creatures).

Scanlon is sympathetic to deontology,[29] so how does his view differ from SC? SC requires us to aggregate value across persons, which requires significant sacrifice on the part of a few in order to produce a relatively small benefit for each of the many if more good is produced thereby. Contractualism, by contrast, holds that "the justifiability of a moral principle depends only on various *individuals'* reasons for objecting to that principle and alternatives to it" (1998, p. 229; italics in original). And this, Scanlon thinks, is sufficient to block objectionable aggregation.

Aggregation is counterintuitive if values are not on a par, and contractualism captures this. Suppose we can rescue an electrician in a television transmitter station, but only by switching off the transmitter and depriving millions of World Cup football. No viewer could reasonably reject the principle that one must "save a person from serious pain and injury at the cost of inconveniencing others or interfering with their amusement . . . no matter how numerous these others may be" (1998, p. 235). Each viewer's complaint is so trivial that, no matter how many are affected, the electrician should be rescued.

A consequentialist who sees values as lexically ordered, however, would aggregate only when values are on a par. But Scanlon denies any appeal to aggregation. Suppose there are two groups of people, the second more numerous than the first. Suppose, further, that I am morally required to save at least one group but cannot save both. On aggregative grounds, I should obviously save the second group. However, since all the individuals apparently have the same complaint, none of them, it seems, can reasonably reject a principle that permits the saving of either group. Scanlon rightly sees this as counterintuitive. But he cannot appeal directly to aggregation, on pain of turning consequentialist and rejecting the central importance of individual complaints: "It therefore seems that as long as it confines itself to reasons for rejection arising from individual standpoints contractualism will be unable to explain how the number of people affected by an action can ever make a moral difference" (1998, p. 230). Scanlon saves contractualism here by noting that a person from the second group can protest against a principle permitting the saving of either group that, were she not present, it would still be permissible to save either group. Thus her presence apparently makes no difference—it is as if her life has no "moral significance" (p. 232). But her life, she protests, has the same moral significance as everyone else's. And this is a complaint from an individual standpoint.

Does this appeal to individual standpoints make Scanlon's system deontological? Scanlon intends that the individual complaints for rejecting principles be agent-relative (for instance, a complaint that the adoption of a principle would not maximize the good is not an individual complaint); thus the theory acknowledges underivative agent-relative considerations. On the other hand, Scanlon's theory has agent-neutral elements. Given several competing principles, Scanlon's theory would presumably require us to rank-order the complaints against them in accord with their seriousness, and then select the principle that suffers the fewest complaints at the most serious rank: we have the common aim of minimizing the number of complaints at the most serious rank. We can also ask, of course, whether the principles that are so selected will be agent-relative or agent-neutral.

For example, each of us has reason to want a principle concerning the wrongness of taking of human life.[30] But what form should this principle take? We might begin with "killing people is wrong." But, as Scanlon notes, "what about self-defense, suicide, and certain acts of killing by police officers and by soldiers in wartime? And is euthanasia always strictly forbidden?" (1998, p. 199). He continues:

> The parts of this principle that are clearest are better put in terms of reasons: the fact that a course of action can be foreseen to lead to someone's death is normally a conclusive reason against it; the fact that someone's death would be to my personal advantage is no justification for aiming at it; but one may use deadly force when this seems the only defense against a person who threatens one's life; and so on.

Perhaps Scanlon has in mind a principle along the following lines.

Principle K: If A sees that X can be foreseen to lead to someone's death, then, in the absence of special justification (such as self-defense), A must not do X.

Whether K is reasonably rejectable depends, of course, on what counts as "special justification." This is a phrase lifted from Scanlon's principle F (1998, p. 304), and a key question is whether the fact that my killing one would save several others from being killed by another is such a justification. If so, then K is not a deontological constraint but is, rather, consistent with an agent-neutral prescription to minimize killing—ordinarily the best way to do this is not to kill anyone yourself, but there are exceptional circumstances where this is not so.

There are parallels here with the case of saving the more numerous of two groups. Suppose by killing Jane I can thwart your effort to kill John and Joe. And suppose K is interpreted as forbidding this. Then John (or Joe) can complain that it is as if his life has no "moral significance." There is some question, then, as to whether Scanlon's theory incorporates a deontological constraint against killing. And to the extent this "moral significance" argument can be generalized, there may be similar questions raised about other principles. In addition, Scanlon departs from traditional deontology in not seeing special obligations to one's friends and family as *moral* obligations (1998, p. 162).

Suppose, however, that Scanlon's contractualism is a deontology: how does it compare with Rossian deontology? The Rossian agrees that "[p]rinciples . . . are general conclusions about the status of various kinds of reasons for action. So understood, principles may rule out some actions by ruling out the reasons on which they would be based, but they also leave wide room for interpretation and judgment" (Scanlon, 1998, p. 199). So, for example, the Rossian concurs that killing solely for personal gain is wrong. And Scanlon manifests particularist tendencies when he notes (p. 51) that some feature may be a reason in one context, but not in another.

Furthermore, Scanlon appeals to Rossian reasons in his discussion of broad morality: as we have seen, he thinks that "pain—whether that of rational creatures or nonrational ones—is something we have prima facie reason to prevent, and stronger reason not to cause" (1998, p. 181). But what about narrow morality? In Scanlon's view: "What is basic to contractualism . . . is the idea of justifiability to each person (on grounds that he or she could not reasonably reject)" (p. 390 n. 8). But what does the claim that justifiability on reasonable grounds is central add to the claim that reasons are central? Any rejection that is reasonable must be supported by reasons. Hence the digression through reasonable rejectability appears unnecessary.[31] Scanlon maintains: "What *makes* an act wrong are the properties that would make any principle that allow it one that it would be reasonable to reject ([such as] the needless suffering and death of [a] baby)" (p. 391 n. 21). But why can't we appeal, in Rossian fashion, to the reasons directly? A-ing would be wrong because it would result in the needless suffering and death of a baby, as opposed to: A-ing would be wrong because it would be reasonable to reject any principle that would permit it; and such rejection would be reasonable because any such principle would permit the needless suffering and death of babies.

Scanlon and the Rossian differ on their views concerning whether wrongness is itself a reason. The Rossian identifies wrongness with the presence of decisive negative moral reasons, whereas Scanlon thinks that wrongness is itself a decisive negative reason: "The fact that an act is wrong seems itself to provide us with a reason not to do it, rather than merely indicating the presence of other reasons (although it may do that as well)" (1998, p. 11). Indeed, "the fact that an action would be wrong constitutes sufficient reason not to do it (almost?) no matter what other considerations there might be in its favor" (p. 148). We do not see this difference as redounding to Scanlon's advantage, however.

One worry is that Scanlon's account might lead to 'double-counting'. Suppose it would be wrong for A to kill B. Then the wrongness is a reason against the killing. But Scanlon acknowledges that there will be other reasons against the killing (such as B's reasonable complaint that it would unfairly harm him). The danger is that these other reasons against the killing will also be part of the reason why the killing is wrong and thereby get counted twice.

In his favor, perhaps Scanlon makes progress on the unity problem—at least when it comes to narrow morality.[32] Moral agents have the unifying aim of seeking principles of a certain kind. And narrow morality concerns "what we owe each other," which is cashed out in terms of reasonable rejectability. But as we have shown, reasonable rejectability appeals to a wide range of reasons: Scanlon seems to allow an irreducible list of disparate fundamental considerations. We doubt, then, that Scanlon's claim to unity is any stronger than the Rossian's, particularly in light of the fact that the Rossian is considering broad morality.

On the issue of a decision algorithm for testing or generating moral verdicts, Scanlon readily allows that his "principles . . . leave wide room for interpretation and judgment" (1998, p. 199).

Concerning the reasons hurdle, Scanlon takes it as given that "everyone has reason to seek and be guided by . . . principles [for the general regulation of behavior that no-one who shares the aim of finding such principles could reasonably reject]" (2002, p. 519) But this is not going to be accepted by those who doubt that moral considerations are reasons. Like the Rossian, Scanlon does not present arguments against such a skeptic.

Such objections only appear worrying, however, if we judge moral theories by more stringent standards than we deploy elsewhere. First, are there decision procedures in all other areas of knowledge? Second, the Rossian contends that there are a variety of moral considerations, and faces the apparent challenge of explaining what makes them all moral—but is there some underlying feature that explains what makes, say, all logical considerations logical? Third, the diversity challenge is no more of a problem in ethics than it is in many areas of inquiry. Finally, all normative enquiries face the reasons hurdle, including theoretical reason and logic. We can explore the status of any consideration's claim to be a reason. Why think the status of moral considerations is especially dubious?[33]

6. DEFENDING DEONTOLOGY

In this section, we turn to the defense of our Rossian deontology against its two main contenders: consequentialism and virtue ethics. The latter we address briefly in subsection 6.4. There are many well-known objections to the former. Simple consequentialism, it is claimed, would over-burden us with calculations, and would demand too many sacrifices of us. MC and Sophisticated C may also seem unreasonably demanding in the latter sense: given the dispositions that others actually have, the best disposition for you to have might be to make continuous significant sacrifice on behalf of those in poverty. RC gets around this by asking not what rules I should follow in the current situation but what rules would be best if (almost) everyone accepted them—in which case (provided that those who accept rules tend to follow them), quite a modest level of self-sacrifice would eliminate avoidable suffering.[34] But RC suffers the charge of irrational rule-worship:[35] if the rules rest on considerations of value, how can it be insisted that it is wrong to override the rules in pursuit of value?[36] And the list of objections continues. In subsections 6.1 and 6.2, we focus on social relations and autonomy, respectively, and maintain that deontology does better than consequentialism with regard to them, in subsection 6.3, however, we are concessive to consequentialism in our discussion of constraints, but we maintain that our view remains, nevertheless, distinctively deontological.

6.1. Special Relationships

Deontology holds that there are underivative agent-relative moral ties between those who stand in certain social relationships to each other. *Agent-relative*, because reference to the fact that *I* am in the relationship is an ineliminable part of the reason why I should do something for the other person: "I owe it to her because she is *my* colleague, child, virtue fellow citizen, and so on." *Underivative*, because that reason does not rest on considerations about the general value of people being in such relationships, or behaving in certain ways when they are. You have a right, for example, to expect that I will give you a ride because I promised you, and not because of the general utility of supporting the useful institution of promise-keeping. *Moral*, because it is *pro tanto* wrong to be in breach of your special obligations to others.

On this matter, common sense concurs with deontology. Consider loyalty between friends. It is not just that friends spend time with each other, support each other, and so on. In addition, a friend has the right to expect *your* loyalty and support because she is *your* friend. If you betray her, she has a moral complaint against you that no one else has. Moreover, the (tacit) acknowledgment of a moral tie between friends appears essential to friendship (as placing oneself under an obligation is essential to "successful" promising—i.e., promising where none of the countervailing conditions are in play). Friends come through for one another; someone who neither came through for you, nor believed she should, would not be loyal and so would not be a friend.

If this is right, then consequentialism has a serious strike against it. Loyalty is essential to friendship. Loyalty involves the recognition of an underivative agent-relative obligation to my friends. Consequentialism has no place for underivative agent-relative obligations; thus it has no room for friendship. But friendship, as is generally acknowledged by consequentialists, is an important intrinsic good. Consequentialism holds that the good is to be promoted; but here is a good that it apparently cannot accommodate.

We have posed this as a problem for consequentialism generally, because although consequentialists of different stripes can respond differentially to this objection, they all deny the existence of agent-relative, underivative, moral obligations. SC simply denies that there are agent-relative obligations. RC, MC, and Sophisticated C deny that they are underivative. And self-effacing theories, which we introduce hereafter, share SC's denial that there really are such obligations, while maintaining that it would be better if people believed there were. Let us look in more detail.

SC has no room for moral ties, hence for friendship, because it has no place for agent-relative moral reasons. But can it accommodate a different account of friendship based on the idea that there are special psychological (and nonmoral) bonds of affection between friends? We contend not. Even if we abandon the thought that we are *required* to favor friends, surely we must be *permitted* to favor them, if our bonds to them are to be special. That is, we must be permitted to favor our friends even when we could do more good overall by not doing so. But SC denies us this permission: An act is wrong if it fails to maximize the good. All bonds are of equal importance: Your bonds to your friends are of no more importance than bonds between others and their friends. You might have reasons of efficiency to tend to those nearest to you: It does more good for less effort to give flowers to *your* spouse. But reasons of efficiency do not allow room for *special* bonds of affection. Your spouse would not be heartened to discover that you, being conscientious in following SC, have given him flowers only because love relationships are good, and this is the most efficient way to promote such relationships.

Does Sophisticated C do better? Assuming that a disposition to be loyal to those for whom one has special affection forms part of the motivational set that produces the best results, Sophisticated C requires loyalty, in the sense that following its recommended decision procedure will result in loyal behavior. Thus virtuous agents are disposed to act loyally—even in some circumstances when disloyalty would produce more good. By Sophisticated C's lights, however, loyal action in such circumstances is wrong (there can be occasions when the virtuous agent knowingly does the wrong thing). Hence, like SC (both being forms of AC), Sophisticated C not only rules out moral obligations to friends, but acts of friendship are morally permitted only when they maximize the good. Sophisticated C might leave room for friendship, but only at the expense of endorsing immoral action.

How does MC fare? By MC's lights, one is permitted not to maximize value if that failure is in accord with the best motivations. Thus if the best motivational set contains friendly dispositions, it is permissible to favor friends. But if the motive consequentialist asks herself why the fact that someone is her friend has moral significance, she will find herself ultimately appealing to considerations of the general good: she has a disposition to be loyal to Mary because the disposition to be loyal to friends is a good general disposition to have, not because of her particular relation to Mary—this relationship has no special moral importance for her.

Like MC, RC acknowledges that nonoptimific acts need not be wrong, but, like MC, it fails to capture friendship because it maintains that preferential treatment of friends can be justified only by appeal to the general good:

> Moral requirements of loyalty are . . . needed . . . when affection isn't up to the job. . . . [S]pecial moral obligations towards family and friends can then be justified on the ground that internalization of these obligations gives people some assurance that some others will consistently take a special interest in them. Such assurance answers a powerful psychological need. (Hooker, 2000, p. 141)

This does not yield genuine loyalty. Friends have moral reason not to let us down, and assurance is engendered in part by a belief that they will respond to this reason. (This is not to say that the only reasons here are moral.) But on RC, the *moral* reason for John not to let Mary down is the assurance that results from the internalization of a rule requiring the special treatment of "friends," not anything special about his relationship with Mary.

RC's position is: Given human psychology, it is best if each of us has special others who can be relied upon to reciprocate, thus the best set of rules takes account of this. And given the human tendency to feel special psychological connections to certain others, the least costly option is to inculcate a rule requiring their preferential treatment. However, if we now contemplate our reasons to favor them, we see that these reasons rest not on our putative special relationships with those others but on the impersonal calculus of costs and needs.[37]

Some of our objections thus far have hinged on the possibility of an agent reflecting on his reasons for being loyal to friends and finding that these ultimately rest on considerations of the general good. Psychological indirection is of some help in addressing this concern: the virtuous agent does not consult the relevant theory each time he acts, be it toward friends or otherwise. But, we contend, were an agent to ask himself why he should be loyal to his friends, he would have to abandon his psychological indirection and would then see that his relationships with his friends are of no special moral importance to him.

At this point a further move is possible: The theory's psychological indirection could be strengthened so that the theory directs us not to believe it, thus placing the considerations we are directed to ignore permanently and completely out of reach. This would be to make the theory self-effacing.[38] Thus, even though you should behave loyally to friends because, ultimately, this is a good thing, you never see this far, and falsely believe that there are genuine reasons of loyalty. And this might be the best state of affairs.

Why is this objectionable? Williams[39] objects that, if self-effacing consequentialism were true, then nobody ought to believe it. Self-effacing consequentialism tells us to see certain considerations as practical reasons when they are, by its lights, not. And it tells us to deny that certain factors are practical reasons when, by its lights, they are. We take it that moral reasoning is a species of practical reasoning concerning moral rectitude. And we have a picture of practical reasoning according to which practical reasoning involves determining which considerations are practical reasons. A self-effacing consequentialism is inconsistent with this conception in the sense that, by the lights of the theory, things go best only if we remain ignorant of (many of) our fundamental practical reasons. We are debarred from being robust practical reasoners.

Is this coherent? Self-effacing consequentialisms give practical grounds for our having false beliefs about our practical reasons (grounds of which we must, of course, remain ignorant, lest we lose the false beliefs). But there are cases where this seems quite coherent. If you knew about the lurking lion, this would cause you to sweat, thereby enabling it to smell you. Thus there is a practical ground for remaining ignorant. You have a reason for believing in the absence of lions that has no bearing on the claim that they are absent. Self-effacing consequentialisms simply embrace such beneficial ignorance on a larger scale. But while this may be coherent, there are theoretical costs. In the case of the lurking lion, there is a backdrop of practical ends (not being devoured being a prominent one) of which the agent is aware and toward the achievement of which the ignorance contributes. But self-effacing consequentialisms require general false beliefs about practical ends, and it seems less plausible that adept practical reasoners could be *generally* mistaken about their practical *ends*.

Rossian deontology does not have to bear such theoretical costs. It gives a straightforward account of our obligations toward our friends: There are basic agent-relative reasons to favor friends, some of which are of sufficient exigency in certain circumstances to constitute obligations.

But are these special obligations unacceptably partial? No. In our view, we show partiality in allocating goods only if we give the claims of one person or group more weight than we are *warranted* in doing (partiality is an irreducibly normative notion). The different theories all respect the need to be impartial, but offer competing conceptions of what features are relevant in assessing whether one person's claim is weightier than another's. If, as welfare consequentialism maintains, people's claims are proportional to the effect on their interests, then we would show partiality if we gave greater weight to the interests of some particular person(s). Unlike consequentialism, Kantianism and contractualism put obligations to other people center stage. But they treat persons impartially by making no distinction among persons: Each owes the same to every other, simply in virtue of all being persons. Thus Korsgaard, a leading Kantian, (1996b, pp. 126–128) and Scanlon (1998, pp. 160–162), while admitting that friendship has many of the structural features of morality, deny that it is a basis of *moral* obligation. If, however, as we are claiming, we have moral ties to friends and family, we are not showing partiality to them merely in virtue of putting their interests above those of others. We act partially only if, like the clannist, we give *undue* weight to those interests, more than is warranted by the relationship.

Must the Rossian deny that friendship is valuable? No. Friendship is valuable, and there are reasons to promote friendship in general, but your reasons to favor your own friends do not derive from these. And that you could better promote friendship by abandoning your friends would not furnish you with sufficient reason to do so.

Nor does the Rossian see duties of special obligation as inexplicable. But the explanation does not appeal to the value. Rather, reasons of friendship, such as reasons to be loyal, cannot be derived from anything more fundamental, just as for the consequentialist the proposition that, say, human welfare is a good, cannot be derived. But basic reasons of friendship, like fundamental propositions about what is valuable, can be explained by incorporating them into a well-articulated account of morality. The choice is ultimately between differing overall such accounts. We have suggested that consequentialist accounts fare worse than Rossian accounts when it comes to special relationships.

We are not wholly in agreement with Ross, however. On his view, there is a duty to be beneficent provided that one is not subject, in the circumstances, to a more stringent duty. Thus all reasons to favor friends must be moral, lest they carry no weight against the duty to be beneficent. On our view, there is a duty to be beneficent on occasion, but it is not pervasive. Thus there is room for nonmoral reasons to favor friends. More generally, Ross's duty of beneficence rules out options—our next topic.

6.2. Options

Suppose pleasure is a good. And suppose that on some occasion Al receives some pleasure and Betty experiences pain, with the result that the net amount of pleasure in the world is increased. On one view, perhaps, the amount of good in the world is increased, but Al does not receive a benefit that Betty is denied. Benefits cannot go to individuals, and thus the debate about distribution cannot get off the ground. We set aside this position, however, on the grounds that most consequentialists would find it as counterintuitive as we do (one of the initial attractions of consequentialism is the thought that we should make as many lives as possible go as well as possible; but to make a life go well is to provide its liver with benefits).

On the assumption that benefits can go to individuals, we can ask whether each person has special reason to pursue her own benefit. We think she does. But on SC, it seems, she does not: She only has reason to pursue her own benefit insofar as its pursuit will contribute to her maximization of the general good, and this is not a special reason that she has and others lack.

SC, then, leaves no room for the pursuit of, say, personal projects, unless their pursuit maximizes the good. However, there seems to be a rationale for their pursuit even in the face of their suboptimality. Each of us has special 'personal reason' to care about our own interests and concerns just because they are ours. These agent-relative personal reasons arise because each of us has our own point of view. I have a personal reason to care about my pain that I cannot have to care about yours, namely, that it is mine. This does not mean that I have no reason to care about your pain, nor does it commit me to denying that pain is equally bad whoever has it. Personal reasons, then (to put matters in consequentialist terms) give each agent moral permission—that is, the option—not to maximize the good when the cost to *her* would be significant.[40] An agent is allowed, in determining what she is morally required to do, to accord greater weight to the cost borne by her than is warranted by its impersonal disvalue.

How can this be? Since I am a creature with a personal point of view, who has personal reasons, a morality that required me to transcend that point of view and think of the world as if I had no particular place in it would not merely be unreasonably demanding, it would deny all moral significance to the fact that my life is, in a sense, all I have. There has, therefore, to be some balance between the demands that the needs of others put on us and our right to live our own lives. Determining where that balance lies is notoriously difficult. No doubt, we are inclined to suppose that morality is less demanding than it is. But this does not entail that there is no balance to be struck.

SC cannot accommodate personal reasons if it sees all reasons as stemming from agent-neutral value—it can then at best hold that, since people care disproportionately about their own good (though they have no reason to), their failure to maximize good is understandable when the cost to them is high. But to understand is not to justify.

A weaker thesis is that all *moral* reasons are agent-neutral. SC might allow that personal reasons can mount up to give us sufficient reason not to do the right act. That concession, however, will not give us options, for we will not have *moral* permission to bring about less good than we could. Sophisticated C may appear to give us such moral permission, since it tells agents that they *should* develop dispositions that may lead them to do wrong. However, the justification for that advice lies not in the moral significance of personal reasons but in the claim that giving some priority to our own concerns will bring about better long-term results than if we try to act rightly on each occasion.

AC, then, cannot accommodate the moral significance of personal reasons. Given the AC framework, this denies room for supererogation (acting beyond the call of duty): The person who bears great personal cost in maximizing the good, although admirable in the extreme, would be doing something morally wrong if he did otherwise.

RC does better. An agent who follows the rules does not act wrongly: She does enough good—it is meritorious but not required to do more. The presence of this personal space, however, stems from impersonal costs: We are psychologically resistant to making significant sacrifices, and this makes it too expensive to inculcate a more demanding rule. But this resistance is a regrettable flaw, not a mark of personal reasons. Even if RC concedes that the resistance has a rational basis, it is still committed to denying the *moral* significance of personal reasons at the fundamental level. They matter morally only because of the cost of training people to ignore them.

On one deontological view, in deciding what to do the virtuous agent balances the good to be achieved, and for whom, against his cost. Although his cost makes no moral claim on him, personal reasons are nevertheless morally significant because he is morally permitted not to bear the cost if it is disproportionately heavy. On this picture, the agent may not be morally required to satisfy the weightiest moral claim—but if, under these circumstances, he does, he is praiseworthy not only for doing good but also for doing it supererogatorily.

Deontology also permits us to choose how to exercise our beneficence, if no other obligations are in play. People are free to take up causes dear to their hearts, without this being part of a strategy for maximizing the good.

Supererogatory acts do not require either saintly or heroic qualities. Small sacrifices can be supererogatory. Many quite trivial acts of kindness are like this. Whether helping others is supererogatory, as opposed to morally required, depends on, among other things, the relative size of the benefit and the sacrifice, and the relation in which you stand to the beneficiary.

Most contemporary defenses of supererogation rest on the claim that agents cannot be required to do good if the cost would be disproportionately great. Some believe that this concedes too much to consequentialism from the start. It implies that we would have a duty to do as much good as we could, if it were cost free. Traditional theology[41] has denied this. God has a duty, perhaps, to grant us lives worth living, but not to grant anything more, even though to him it is cost free.

6.3. Constraints

Constraints, though often regarded as the most distinctive feature of deontology, seem hard to justify. Consider an absolute constraint (C) against (intentionally) killing an innocent person. Suppose Anne and several other innocents are about to be shot by Bert, but he agrees to let the others go if you shoot Anne. (C) forbids you to do it. Yet, as Scheffler[42] points out, this appears inexplicable: Anne is going to be shot, but at least you can prevent the other shootings. The standard objection to constraints is that they forbid their own violation *even to minimize such violation.* Another difficult case is one in which violation will result in some other good that outweighs the bad of the violation. The general SC complaint against constraints, be they absolute or *pro tanto*, is that they can *forbid* you to do good.

There are proscriptions acceptable to both SC and us—but they are not constraints. Recall Scanlon's remark that "the fact that a course of action can be foreseen to lead to someone's death is normally a conclusive reason against it; [and] the fact that someone's death would be to my personal advantage is no justification for aiming at it" (1998, p. 199). This implies that there is an absolute prohibition against killing purely for personal gain. That is, there is an absolute prohibition against killing another person when one's only motivation is personal gain, and when, in fact, there are no (other) reasons to kill.[43] Such a ban is acceptable to us, since one could only violate it for reason of one's own personal gain, which is no reason to kill someone. And since killing someone purely for personal gain does not increase the good, one cannot violate the ban in order to do so; hence it is acceptable to SC. Constraints, on the other hand, are proscriptions that admit the possibility of, and forbid, their own violation to good effect.

Another important feature of constraints as understood by traditional deontology is that they are underivative. RC, for example, incorporates proscriptions, but these are "justified by their role in promoting agent-neutral value" (Hooker, 2000, p. 110).

We have defended special obligations and options by contending that, in addition to the amount of good we do, positional facts—that the good would accrue to *my* friend or to *me*—are also morally relevant. Constraints, however, cannot be similarly defended. What justifies constraints? That their violation is bad is no answer, for then how could it be forbidden for someone to violate a constraint in order to prevent worse actions by others? The strategy of introducing morally relevant positional facts does not help. Constraints single out no group on the basis of my relationship to its members, thus they cannot rest on my being more closely related to some than others. Hence, the only positional possibility is to claim that my violating a constraint, even to prevent worse actions by others, is a bad *for me*. But although such a violation may matter to me, since I have a perfectly understandable, if perhaps not always commendable, reluctance to get my hands dirty, this, at best, *might* ground a *permission* not to violate the constraint under these conditions. It cannot ground a *requirement* not to do so. It is implausible to suppose that a constraint violation is wrong because we have an aversion to it; and to say that we have an aversion to it because it is wrong does nothing to explain why it is wrong.

Constraints embody as fundamental the fact of my agency. I should not, claims the defender of a constraint against killing, aim directly at someone's death myself, even when my ultimate goal in doing so is to thwart the similar killing aims of several others. But why, SC asks, should this disposition of the will matter, from the moral point of view, when my ultimate goal is good (fewer killings)? One response is simply to claim that, in addition to doing good, I should respect constraints, and the latter takes priority. Constraints are fundamental, so we should not expect to find a deeper justification for them. Their being fundamental does not, however, preclude our defending constraints, as we did with special obligations and options, by explicating their nature in ways that make their force clearer. The problem is that we can find no explication of constraints that dispels their air of irrationality in light of cases such as that of Anne and Bert.

Many deontological attempts to explain why agency matters, for example, seem to presuppose the very point at issue.[44] Thus it is said (in a Kantian vein) that persons deserve respect in view of their unique importance as rational moral agents. But why does such respect forbid you to harm others rather than requiring you to minimize harm? It may be said that, just as we owe particular duties to others in view of our special relationships with them, so we owe to everyone else a duty not to harm them because of our general relationship with them. But what is that relationship? Perhaps that of being fellow humans, or fellow persons. Whatever the answer, the problem remains: Why does our standing in that relationship to all ground a *constraint* against harming them, as opposed to a duty to minimize harm? Similarly, natural law theorists move from the claim that there are certain basic values, including life, to the claim that we should never act directly against a basic value, even in seeking to protect that value elsewhere. But how is that move to be justified?

Another Kantian line is to claim that we cannot be responsible for another's will. Thus, even though you may prevent others, say, killing innocents by killing one yourself, you would not thereby have prevented those others from harboring evil intent. And you are neither responsible for those intentions nor for their fulfillment. While we have some sympathy with this line, nevertheless, standing idly by when you could achieve an overall net saving of human life on the grounds that its loss is not your responsibility suggests a squeamish desire to keep *your* hands clean.

Some defenders of constraints[45] have complained that, in seeing constraints as *agent*-relative, recent attempts to ground constraints have wrongly focused on agency. Rather, they claim, we should focus on a *patient*-centered justification—on what it is about innocents that entails the existence of constraints against harming them. But this does not seem to help. By the nature of innocence, innocents do not deserve to be harmed, so that, ideally, we should not harm them. But what are we to do in our nonideal world in which innocents are under threat?

Quinn, Kamm, and Nagel[46] suggest that it is impermissible to kill the innocent (even to prevent further such killings) because the world is better for having such an innocence-respecting constraint. Fewer innocents might be killed in a world where such a constraint is lacking—it being permissible to kill innocents there to minimize the number of innocents killed. But, the claim runs, the reduction in the amount of killing in the latter world notwithstanding, our constrained world is better because innocent life is more valuable here due to the impermissibility of its sacrifice. Even if this is correct, however, why is the constrained world actual? It is not valid to argue from betterness to truth (for instance, our longevity does not follow from the premise that it would be better if we all lived longer). Nagel sees the difficulty, but thinks that such reasoning "may have a place in ethical theory, where its conclusion is not factual but moral" (1995, p. 92). In our view, however, this is to justify constraints at the expense of standards of justification.

If we deny the existence of constraints, however, won't we have to abandon many of our intuitions? No. First, as we have shown, certain proscriptions are acceptable: they are bans on doing things *for inappropriate reasons*. Second, many intuitions that appear to be based on constraints are actually based on other features. We may, for example, think it wrong to take ten dollars from one person in order to enrich another by twenty dollars. But our grounds for that (depending on the circumstances) might be that the harm of taking ten dollars *honestly possessed* outweighs the benefit of bestowing twenty dollars *unearned*. Or we may think it wrong to do considerable harm to one person in order to prevent small harms to a large number. But that may be because harms are lexically ordered. Finally, acts that are considered by traditional deontologists to be violations of serious constraints will increase good only in dire circumstances.

We are tentatively proposing, then, a morality devoid of constraints (as traditionally understood) but incorporating duties of special obligation and options. Hence, we must answer arguments to the effect that constraints are required to "protect" our relations with our friends and family, and our option, say, to limit our charitable donations.[47]

Suppose I am proposing to buy a house, and you note, correctly, that I could do more good by buying a cheaper house and donating the savings to Oxfam. I reply that doing so would be supererogatory. You then argue that you are permitted to maximize the good, and will set about frustrating my attempt to purchase the more expensive house. Or suppose that I refuse to be disloyal to a friend. You see that my loyalty here is not maximizing the good, and set about undermining it.

We have argued that each of us has reasons, say, to favor friends and pursue personal projects. I can acknowledge that your friendships are valuable, and that at least some of your personal projects are worthwhile. Thus, insofar as I have reason to promote the good, I have reason to promote your friendships and your pursuit of those projects of yours that are worthwhile. But perhaps I can do more good by interfering with your friendships and your projects. What reason is there to desist, unless there are constraints against my so interfering?

However, the standard difficulty with constraints applies here also. Suppose there is a constraint against interfering with another's pursuit of his friendships. Then I am forbidden to interfere with your friendships even to prevent much greater such interference by someone else. It seems to us more plausible to maintain that noninterference is itself valuable; so that, in addition to the general value of your friendships and worthwhile pursuits, there is an additional reason for my noninterference. This even affords some protection for your trivial pursuits. But in no case is the protection absolute, of course: There can be greater values at stake, for example.

Kagan[48] mounts a different argument against Scheffler's attempt to have options without constraints. Suppose there is an option to forego saving the life of a stranger if it will cost you $10,000. Then why are you not permitted to kill a stranger to gain $10,000?[49] The former permission seems reasonable, but the latter is not. Thus, it appears, any moral system that incorporates the first option must incorporate a constraint against killing.

If one notes that it is not a constraint against killing *simpliciter* that is required, but an acceptable ban against killing for personal gain, one must face the issue of why there is not also an acceptable ban against refusing to save the life of a stranger for selfish reasons. (Note that there is an acceptable ban against doing nothing to save the lives of strangers for selfish reasons—that is, there is a requirement to do something for charity.) Kagan's opponent might argue that refusing to save here can be outweighed by the relevant personal reasons, whereas the proposed killing cannot. There are at least three potentially relevant differences (whether they are actually relevant depends upon the circumstances) that support this. First, killing may be in itself worse than not saving. Second, there may be a morally relevant difference between donating a sum of significance to you and not gaining that sum. Both these claims of moral difference are hotly contested,[50] but our position is that they can be relevant on occasion.

The third difference is that, in the case of the killing, you would be solely responsible, whereas in the case of not saving, you would typically share responsibility with all the others who could have contributed but didn't. Where you would not share responsibility, and there are no other relevant differences between the killing and the refusal to save, we suspect that there is no option not to save. Suppose, say, that, by no fault of yours, your life savings are about to be burned at the local incinerator, and you are rushing to retrieve the money. If you delay, you know you will lose it. In case (1), you must stop if you are not to kill a stranger lying unconscious in the road. In case (2), you are the only person capable of saving a stranger from being killed by an oncoming vehicle, but you must stop if you are to do it. Are we committed to saying that you are morally required to stop in case (1) but not case (2)? No. Our view is that you must stop in both cases. The fact that you are the *only* person capable of saving this life is a crucial morally relevant consideration in case (2): It is one of the factors that here renders irrelevant the difference between harming and failing to prevent harm. But to conclude from this that such a difference is never relevant is to overgeneralize.

We are not, then, in Kagan-like examples, generally committed to the permissibility of harming to gain a benefit *b* in cases that are analogous to cases in which it is permissible to fail to prevent a similar harm in order to save oneself from a cost of *b*, because there may be relevant differences between harming and failing to prevent harm, or between gaining a benefit and saving oneself from a cost, that disrupt the purported analogy.

A theory with special obligations and options, but without constraints, is still deontology: Agent-relative considerations are underivatively relevant, and agents are forbidden in certain circumstances to maximize the good. On Ross's view, there are, of course, no *absolute* constraints. But Ross may nevertheless be interpreted as claiming that there is a constraint against harming. If so, we tentatively disagree with him. On our alternative, personal reasons and those stemming from special relationships carry significant weight on the moral scales, but mere reluctance to harm in the service of good that outweighs that harm carries none.

6.4. Virtue Ethics

Consequentialism and deontology do not exhaust the options for a moral theory. Virtue ethics rejects what it sees as serious defects in both approaches, particularly their focus on the deontic status of acts, and their belief that moral theory should formulate precise moral principles from which to read off conclusions about what to do. Good moral judgment requires sensitivity, experience, and discernment, rather than slavish adherence to predetermined rules. The virtues are valuable in their own right, and not just as a guarantor of reliably choosing the right act. And only those who possess them can discern what is morally salient in any particular situation. The moral emotions play a crucial role not only in determining how one should act but also in motivating the agent; the sense of duty is to be harnessed only when better motives fail. Moral philosophy should focus more, therefore, on what kind of person it is best to be, rather than on what principles we should invoke to solve artificially constructed moral dilemmas.

There are two views concerning the purport of virtue ethics. On the less radical, virtue ethics is proposed as a welcome corrective to various distortions that have afflicted many versions of both deontology and consequentialism. On the more radical, it is put forward as an alternative theory in its own right. With the less radical approach, we are entirely in sympathy. The deontological theory we favor, which is broadly Rossian in spirit, takes the foregoing points on board. We see overly principled approaches as distorting moral thinking by downplaying the need for judgment and imagination in discerning, in a particular case, which features are relevant, how they interact with each other, and what weight should be given to each. And it has often been pointed out that deontology and virtue ethics make common cause against consequentialism.[51] But we are skeptical of the more radical approach, which maintains that the right is metaphysically dependent upon the judgments of the virtuous. In difficult cases, we may have no *epistemic* access to which act is right, other than via the judgment of virtuous agents.

But the virtuous agent judges an act right because it is right, not the other way around. Otherwise, on what does he base his judgment? It must be responsive to reasons, and those reasons, if he is appropriately sensitive, lead him to the truth. The latter is there for him to find; he does not construct it. Virtue ethics is thus best seen as a crucial part of the best deontological theory.[52]

NOTES

We are grateful to members of the Florida Philosophical Association, and to members of a graduate seminar on consequentialism and deontology at Florida State University, for comments on earlier versions of some of this work. We are also grateful to Eve Garrard for discussion of some of the issues here raised, and especially to David Copp, who commented selflessly and extensively on a number of drafts.

1. For a careful statement of this position, see Arneson, 2003, p. 382.
2. For this terminology, see, e.g., Nagel, 1986, ch. 9, and Kagan, 1989.
3. Note that some deontologists, such as W. D. Ross, 1930, reject options, maintaining that we ought to do as much good as we can, limited only by duties of special obligation and constraints.
4. This is not true of all forms of consequentialism: see hereafter.
5. Darwall, 1986; McNaughton and Rawling, 1991; Nagel, 1986; Parfit, 1987; Scheffler, 1994.
6. But see McNaughton and Rawling, 1991, for discussion of some problems for this approach.
7. Parfit, 1987, p. 27.
8. Parfit, 1987, p. 40, notes that Sidgwick coined this phrase.
9. See for instance Kagan, 1989; Smart, 1998, pp. 288–289.
10. E.g., chapter 14 in this volume.
11. Parfit sees such actions as cases of "blameless wrongdoing":

If we have one of the best possible sets of motives, we shall sometimes knowingly act wrongly according to our own theory [namely, sophisticated consequentialism]. But, given the special reason why we are acting wrongly, we need not regard ourselves, when so acting, as morally bad. We can believe these to be cases of *blameless wrongdoing*. We can believe this because we are acting on a set of motives that it would be wrong for us to cause ourselves to lose. (Parfit, 1987, p. 49, italics in original)

12. This issue perhaps does not arise if RC is seen as merely laying down a criterion of wrong action in terms of rules, where these rules need never have been formulated or internalized. But we shall assume that "the rules are to be *public*" (Hooker, 2000, p. 85, italics in original) and are "inculcated . . . by family, teachers, and the broader culture" (p. 79).
13. See Adams, 1976.
14. Copp's Mill may be another case in point. On this interpretation of Mill, "S's

doing A would be wrong if, and only if, (a) there is a maximal alternative to S's doing A, and (b) it would be maximally expedient that if S did A, S would feel regret for this to some degree" (Copp, 1979, p. 84). Thus, if an act is wrong it is not best, but its failure to be best does not entail its wrongness. And, we suspect, Copp's Mill would not advocate that agents employ thoughts about clauses (a) and (b) in deliberating about what to do in every case.

15. The best motives, it is claimed, need not produce the best acts—we set aside here discussion of the coherence of this claim (see Parfit, 1987, pp. 31–35, 37–40, for discussion of this sort of issue); a similar worry about coherence might also arise in the case of Sophisticated C.

16. RC incorporates options, but their justification is not agent-relative—it appeals, rather, to the cost of inculcating a rule that requires consistent significant sacrifice. (And, perhaps, to the value of people being permitted to pursue personal projects?)

17. For a dissenting voice on the issue of whether RC is genuinely consequentialist, see Howard-Snyder, 1993. For Hooker's reply, see Hooker, 1994.

18. For a full exposition of Copp's view, see Copp, 1995.

19. This last is, we think, agent-relative for Ross: He does not appear to countenance doing harm oneself in order to minimize the total amount of harm. (For a rebuttal of the complaint that this is an unsystematic list see McNaughton, 1996.)

20. Audi, 1996, points out that someone can know a self-evident truth without knowing that it is self-evident. Moreover, from the fact that a claim needs no justification it does not follow that it has none.

21. Ross's equation of the unconditional with the underivative might explain why he sees prima facie duties as on a par with simple mathematical truths. In the mathematical and the ethical cases one can see that certain truths are basic. Thus, thinks Ross, like the mathematical truth, the ethical truth is unconditional. Unfortunately for Ross, however, the ethical case, unlike the mathematical, may be conditional.

22. A view stoutly maintained by R. M. Hare. See, for example, Hare, 1963, ch. 2, esp. p. 7.

23. See McNaughton and Rawling, 2000.

24. Since Kant is so adequately covered elsewhere in this volume (see chapters 11 and 17 here) our discussion of Kant will be brief.

25. Of one version of the CI test—contradiction in the world. There is also contradiction in willing.

26. See chapter 17 in this volume.

27. This interpretation of Kant is disputed (see chapter 17 in this volume, esp. n. 2). Kant does not appear to take this line in the *Grounding of the Metaphysics of Morals*. In discussing the second formulation of the Categorical Imperative, which requires us to treat others always as ends in themselves and never simply as means, he writes—"concerning meritorious duty to others"—that merely refraining from impairing the happiness of others is not sufficient. For

> this, after all, would harmonize only negatively and not positively with humanity as an end in itself, if everyone does not also strive, *as much as he can*, to further the ends of others. For the ends of any subject who is an end in himself must *as far as possible* be my ends also, if that conception of an end in itself is to have its full effect in me. (1993, p. 37, emphasis added)

28. Korsgaard suggests that we can read Kant in a slightly less rigoristic manner in "The Right to Lie: Kant on Dealing with Evil," in Korsgaard, 1996a, pp. 135–158. See also "Two Arguments against Lying," in the same volume, pp. 335–362.

29. See his discussion of constraints, Scanlon, 1998, pp. 81–86.

30. We are modeling this discussion on Scanlon's discussion of his principle F of fidelity (1998, p. 304) where he speaks of reasons to want a principle. Scanlon's principles lay out what is right and wrong; and the fact that some act would be, say, wrong, is itself a reason not to do it, on Scanlon's account. Thus, on this account it seems, we have reason to want there to be certain further reasons, and this is relevant in determining whether there are such further reasons. On our view, by contrast, you might have reason to want, say, that I give you money, because my doing so will benefit you; but whether the fact that my act will benefit you is a reason for me to do it is not dependent on whether you want it to be a reason.

31. There has been much discussion of what has come to be called "the redundancy objection," first raised by Pettit, 1993, p. 302. See, for example, Blackburn, 1999; McGinn, 1999; McNaughton and Rawling, 2003a; Ridge, 2001; Stratton-Lake, 2003.

32. Scanlon, 1998, p. 7, thinks that "it is not clear that morality in the broader sense is a single subject that has a similar unity."

33. On this last point, we agree with Scanlon; see also McNaughton and Rawling, 2003b.

34. MC and Sophisticated C might respond by arguing that, given the tendencies many of us have to resentment and other forms of psychological resistance to altruism, the best disposition *for such individuals* might not be to make continuous significant sacrifice on behalf of those in poverty. RC, however, does not rely in this way on contingent empirical facts about differences in individual psychology. RC might maintain that the right act accords with those motives that are such that *if everyone had them*, things would go best.

35. Smart, 1998, 292, accuses RC of "superstitious rule-worship."

36. Hooker, 2000, endeavors to circumvent this objection by resting the theory on value *plus impartiality*.

37. Copp's Mill does not escape this sort of objection: According to him, it is not wrong to favor friends at the expense of failing to maximize the good because it would not be maximally expedient to feel regret for doing so. But surely, rather, it is permissible to favor friends at the expense of failing to maximize the good because they are your friends.

38. Parfit, 1987, pp. 40–43.

39. In Smart and Williams, 1973, p. 135.

40. For an extended defense of this approach, see Scheffler, 1994.

41. See, e.g., Adams, 1972.

42. Scheffler, 1994.

43. This is not quite our final position on this issue; but laying out our final position would take us too far afield from the concerns of this essay.

44. A point made with force by Scheffler, 1994, ch. 4.

45. See for instance Brook, 1991; Kamm, 2000. For discussion see McNaughton and Rawling, 1993.

46. Kamm, 1989, 1992; Quinn, 1993; Nagel, 1995. For a longer discussion of this point see McNaughton and Rawling, 1998.

47. Of course, the defender of constraints might buy the arguments hereafter to the effect that special relationships and options entail constraints, and see these arguments as arguments for constraints.

48. See Kagan, 1984. Scheffler responds in Scheffler, 1994, pp. 167–192.

49. Kagan's original example (1984) contrasts saving a stranger with killing one's uncle. We have modified it to avoid considerations of special relationships.

50. For a sustained and vigorous attack see Kagan, 1989.

51. Recent writers (e.g., Driver, 2001; Hurka, 2001) have argued that consequentialism can incorporate many of the claims of virtue ethics in its less radical version. For a helpful collection of articles on virtue ethics see Crisp and Slote, 1997. For an exposition and defense, see Hursthouse, 1999.

REFERENCES

Adams, R. 1976. "Motive Utilitarianism." *Journal of Philosophy* 73: 467–481.

Arneson, R. 2003. "Consequentialism versus Special-Ties Partiality." *Monist* 86: 382–401.

Audi, R. 1996. "Intuitionism, Pluralism, and the Foundations of Ethics." In Sinnott-Armstrong and Timmons, 1996, 101–136.

Blackburn, S. 1999. "Am I Right?" *New York Times,* February 21.

Brook, R. 1991. "Agency and Morality." *Journal of Philosophy*88: 190–212.

Crisp, R., and M. Slote, eds. 1997. *Virtue Ethics.* Oxford: Oxford University Press.

Copp, D. 1979. "The Iterated-Utilitarianism of J. S. Mill." *Canadian Journal of Philosophy,* supp., 5: 75–98.

———. 1995. *Morality, Normativity and Society.* Oxford: Oxford University Press.

———. 1997. "Does Moral Theory Need the Concept of Society?" *Analyse und Kritik* 19: 189–212.

Dancy, J. 1983. "Ethical Particularism and Morally Relevant Properties." *Mind* 92: 530–547.

———. 1993a. "An Ethic of Prima Facie Duties." In Singer, 1993, 230–240.

———. 1993b. *Moral Reasons.* Oxford: Blackwell.

Darwall, S. 1986. "Agent-Centered Restrictions from the Inside Out." *Philosophical Studies* 50: 291–319.

Driver, J. 2001. *Uneasy Virtue.* Cambridge: Cambridge University Press.

Hare, R. M. 1963. *Freedom and Reason.* Oxford: Clarendon Press.

———. 1981. *Moral Thinking: Its Levels, Method, and Point.* Oxford: Clarendon Press.

Hooker, B. 2000. *Ideal Code, Real World.* Oxford: Clarendon Press.

———. 1994. "Is Rule-Consequentialism a Rubber Duck?" *Analysis* 54: 62–67.

Hooker, B., and M. Little, eds. 2000. *Moral Particularism.* Oxford: Clarendon Press.

Howard-Snyder, F. 1993. "Rule Consequentialism Is a Rubber Duck." *American Philosophical Quarterly* 30: 271–278.

Hurka, T. 2001. *Virtue, Vice and Value.* New York: Oxford University Press.

Hursthouse, R. 1999. *On Virtue Ethics.* Oxford: Oxford University Press.

Kagan, S. 1984. "Does Consequentialism Demand Too Much?" *Philosophy and Public Affairs* 13: 239–254.

———. 1989. *The Limits of Morality.* Oxford: Clarendon Press.

Kamm, F. 1989. "Harming Some to Save Others." *Philosophical Studies* 57: 227–260.

———. 1992. "Non-Consequentialism, the Person as an End-in-Itself, and the Significance of Status." *Philosophy and Public Affairs* 21: 381–389.

———. 2000. "Nonconsequentialism." In Lafollette, 2000, 205–226.

Kant, I. [1785]. 1993. *Grounding of the Metaphysics of Morals* Trans. J. Ellington. Indianapolis: Hackett.

Korsgaard, C. M. 1996a. *Creating the Kingdom of Ends.* Cambridge: Cambridge University Press.

———. 1996b. *The Sources of Normativity.* Cambridge: Cambridge University Press.

Lafollette, H. 2000. *The Blackwell Guide to Ethical Theory.* Oxford: Blackwell.

McGinn, C. 1999. "Reasons and Unreasons." *New Republic,* May 24, 34–38.

McNaughton, D. 1988. *Moral Vision.* Oxford: Blackwell.

———. 1996. "An Unconnected Heap of Duties?" *Philosophical Quarterly* 46: 433–447.

McNaughton, D., and P. Rawling. 1991. "Agent-Relativity and the Doing-Happening Distinction." *Philosophical Studies* 63: 167–185.

———. 1993. "Deontology and Agency." *Monist* 76: 81–100.

———. 1998. "On Defending Deontology." *Ratio* 11: 37–54.

———. 2000. "Unprincipled Ethics." In Hooker and Little, 2000, 256–275.

———. 2003a. "Can Scanlon Avoid Redundancy by Passing the Buck?" *Analysis*63: 328–331.

———. 2003b. "Naturalism and Normativity." *Proceedings of the Aristotelian Society,* supp., 77: 23–45.

Nagel, T. 1986. *The View from Nowhere.* Oxford: Oxford University Press.

———. 1995. "Personal Rights and Public Space." *Philosophy and Public Affairs* 24: 83–107.

Parfit, D. 1987. *Reasons and Persons.* Rev. ed. Oxford: Clarendon Press.

Pettit, Philip. 1993. *The Common Mind.* New York: Oxford University Press.

Quinn, W. 1993. *Morality and Action.* Cambridge: Cambridge University Press.

Rachels, J., ed. 1998. *Ethical Theory.* Oxford: Oxford University Press.

Railton, P. 1988. "Alienation, Consequentialism, and the Demands of Morality." In Scheffler, 1988, 93–133.

Regan, D. 1980. *Utilitarianism and Cooperation.* Oxford: Clarendon Press.

Ridge, M. 2001. "Saving Scanlon: Contractualism and Agent-Relativity." *Journal of Political Philosophy* 9: 472–581.

Ross, W. D. 1930. *The Right and the Good.* Oxford: Clarendon Press.

Scanlon, T. 1998. *What We Owe to Each Other.* Cambridge, Mass.: Harvard University Press.

———. 2002. "Reasons, Responsibility, and Reliance." *Ethics* 112: 507–528.

Scheffler, S. 1994. *The Rejection of Consequentialism.* Rev. ed. Oxford: Clarendon Press.

———, ed. 1988. *Consequentialism and Its Critics.* Oxford: Oxford University Press.

Singer, P., ed. 1993. *A Companion to Ethics.* Oxford: Blackwell.

Sinnott-Armstrong, W., and M. Timmons, eds. 1996. *Moral Knowledge: New Readings in Moral Epistemology.* Oxford: Oxford University Press.

Smart, J. J. C. 1998. "Extreme and Restricted Utilitarianism." In Rachels, 1998, 286–297.

Smart, J. J. C., and B. Williams. 1973. *Utilitarianism: For and Against.* Cambridge: Cambridge University Press.

Stratton-Lake, P. 2003. "Scanlon's Contractualism and the Redundancy Objection." *Analysis* 63: 70–76.

CHAPTER 16

MORAL RIGHTS

HILLEL STEINER

1. "NONSENSE UPON STILTS"?

DOES morality have to contain rights? Most accounts of morality present it as
fundamentally concerned with the quality of persons' intentions in acting and/or
the qualities of the reasonably foreseeable consequences of their actions. Neither
of these considerations necessarily signifies a role for rights in our moral thinking.
The view that morally desirable actions are either ones motivated by good intentions, or ones presumed likely to secure desirable outcomes, in no way implies
that such actions include respect for others' rights. It is entirely consistent with
this view that others might not have rights or, indeed, that there might not be
any others. To paraphrase a recent writer, "[t]here might not have been moral
rights" (Coyle, 2002, p. 21).

For rights are essentially about who is owed what by whom. They presuppose
the presence of at least two persons and, moreover, persons who can interact with
one another: that is, whose actions can affect one another's well-being or freedom.
In this sense, rights are concerned with *interpersonal distribution*—the interpersonal distribution of valued things or, more specifically, the ways persons' conduct
can affect that distribution.

And yet, even if morality does reflect a concern for such interpersonal distribution, that would still be insufficient grounds for claiming that rights occupy
a fundamental position in morality. This, because such a concern might be a
purely instrumental one: Conduct that is respectful of persons' rights might simply

be the best *means* for acknowledging the moral status of those persons, or for securing independently desirable outcomes of action. The interpersonal distribution ordained by a set of rights might thus lack any intrinsic moral desirability.

This, indeed, is Bentham's view of the matter, as expressed in his famous dismissal of *natural rights* as "nonsense upon stilts." For him and many others, the idea of moral rights is strictly superfluous, even pernicious. Rights can register no distinctive set of moral demands and, hence, the highly structured logic of rights language is appropriately confined to describing the design of legal rules and institutions (see Waldron, 1987).

I believe that Bentham is mistaken, and that he is led to this erroneous view of the concept of moral rights by several aspects of his utilitarianism. More will be said later, by way of explanation and justification for this claim. But, for now, it is equally important to note that Bentham is correct in affirming both the highly structured form of rights language and its applicability to the realm of law.[1] For what is distinctive of that realm is that it is one of enforceable rules: Rules that assign enforceable duties and that render persons liable to that enforcement. Correspondingly, sets of rights determine who is owed such duties and who is empowered to secure their enforcement.

Theories of *moral* rights are inherently theories about what the basic content of those legal rules *should* be: Their accounts have constitutional reference. A standard form of complaint against a legal rule is that it fails to advance or protect persons' moral rights—it fails to be *just*—whereas its failure to satisfy other moral requirements, for example, benevolence, is not commonly seen as being equally damning. While we do not expect legal systems to enforce generosity, we do expect them to uphold our moral rights. Implicitly or explicitly, then, theories of moral rights advance views about how specific other persons' valued services[2] should be interpersonally distributed by enforceable systems of rules. We could do worse than to think of rights as parcels of such services, with the morally prescribed contents and destinations of those parcels being determined by principles of justice. Moral rights are, so to speak, the instantiating progeny of justice. By attending to the general characteristics of moral rights, we can learn something about the demands of justice—about how the legal realm must be in order to be just.

These general characteristics inhabit different levels of generality and, not surprisingly, the contestedness of claims advanced at each such level varies inversely with the degree of generality it reflects. Most general—least contested—are accounts concerning the logical *structure* of rights. Next come theories about the broad *content* of rights. And then we encounter debates about the *status* of rights in our moral thinking. Rival answers to content and status questions have a very direct bearing on such familiar issues as those concerning who or what can be a right-holder, whether moral rights can conflict with one another, whether moral rights must be permissibly enforceable, and whether there are positive as well as negative moral rights. It therefore seems sensible to proceed by looking at each of these levels in turn, and to start with the most general one.

2. THE STRUCTURE OF RIGHTS

There are at least six features that have been attributed to rights or presupposed about them in virtually all legal and moral discussions of rights.

1. Rights are constituted by rules. (The rules constituting *moral* rights are standardly taken to be those of *justice*.)
2. Rights signify a bilateral normative relation between those who hold them (their *subjects*) and those against whom they are held (their *objects*).
3. These relations entail the presence or absence of prescribed encumbrances on the conduct (performances and forbearances) of objects.
4. These encumbrances consist either in objects' duties, or in their lack of capacity to alter those or other encumbrances.
5. Rights are exercisable.
6. This exercisability consists in the capacity to control objects' encumbrances by either extinguishing them or enforcing them.

The leading systematic incorporation of these features, into an analytical schema of deontic relationships, is due to Wesley N. Hohfeld (1919). Complaining of the imprecision with which both lawyers and the general public have tended to use the word "rights" when referring to the conduct-constraining implications of legal rules, Hohfeld distinguished no fewer than four quite different entitlements, any one of which might be held by persons commonly and indiscriminately described as right-holders: claims, liberties, powers, and immunities. Holders of any one of these entitlements are placed, by the rules constituting them, in certain bilateral relations to specifiable other persons. And these other persons thereby hold correlatively entailed encumbrances with regard to the conduct governed by those rules.

Only a brief rehearsal of the basic aspects of the Hohfeldian classification of prescriptive relations will be needed here. Among the more recent analytical discussions of it, those supplied by Wellman (1985, chs. 1, 2), Sumner (1987, ch. 2), and Kramer (1998, pp. 7–60) are especially illuminating and repay careful study.[3] The reason why this classification is important and not restricted in its interest to the technical concerns of lawyers is that only some of these positions (or combinations of them) imply the presence of constraints on others' conduct. Since such constraint is an uncontested feature of rights, it is the holding of only some of these positions, or some combinations of them, that amounts to having rights, in the sense explored in this essay.[4]

The position most commonly identified with having a right is what Hohfeld calls a *claim*. If Red has a claim that Blue pay him five pounds, that claim correlatively entails that Blue has a *duty* to pay Red five pounds. Claims are regarded by Hohfeld as rights 'in the strictest sense'. Almost equally common, however, are misleading assertions that one has a right to do things that one has no duty not to do: "I have a right to wear mis-matched socks" or "I have a right to publish my opinions." What is actually being asserted here is more precisely denoted as a *liberty*.[5] Other terms sometimes used to refer to this absence of a duty include *privilege, license,* and *permission*.[6] If Red has no claim that Blue pay him five pounds, Blue has a liberty not to pay him five pounds, and Red has what is called (for lack of an idiomatic term) a *no-claim* that Blue pay him five pounds.

These paired relationships between Red and Blue—claim/duty and no-claim/liberty—hold in respect of some specified act on the part of Blue (the act of paying Red five pounds) and determine the permissibility of its performance or forbearance. Red's having a claim and Blue a duty with respect to this act entail that Blue's not paying is impermissible. Conversely, Blue's having a liberty and Red a no-claim with respect to it entail that Blue's not paying is permissible.

These deontic modalities of acts—permissible and impermissible—are, however, insufficient to distinguish moral duties correlative to moral claim-rights from other kinds of moral duty that have nothing to do with rights. For it is true of *any* moral duty that forbearing from its performance is impermissible. And it is correspondingly true of any act not required by a moral duty that its forbearance is permissible. What is distinctive, then, about the duties that figure in rights language is that, within the rules constituting them, they are permissibly *alterable* or alternatively *enforceable* by virtue of certain choices to that effect. Thus, sets of rules constituting the aforesaid Hohfeldian relationships also create normative relationships that have to do with that alterability and enforceability. Although Blue may have no duty—may have a liberty not—to pay Red five pounds, Red or someone else may have the authority, or what is often called a *power*, to impose (i.e., create and, if necessary, enforce) such a duty on her. In which case, she is describable as having a *liability* to be subjected to this duty.[7] But if Red or everyone lacks this power, Blue enjoys an *immunity* against being subjected to this duty by any of them and they, correspondingly, each have a *disability* to subject her to it.[8] Conversely, although Blue may have a duty—may lack a liberty not—to pay Red five pounds, Red or someone else may have the power to waive (i.e., extinguish) that duty and/or to waive its enforcement.

In general, we may regard the latter set of positions and the relationships between them as 'second-order' or 'procedural' ones. They are so because they signify rule-constituted capacities and incapacities to alter 'first-order' (claim/duty, liberty/no-claim) relationships and, indeed, other second-order relationships as well. Second-order positions are of particular significance, since it is these that come into play when we consider opposing theoretical views concerning the broad content of rights. In order to clarify our understanding of those views, I shall hereafter confine my attention primarily to claims (and immunities).[9]

3. The Content of Rights

Evidently, the content of moral rights can vary enormously. It is true that, inasmuch as they constitute moral standards for the design of legal systems, there is fairly general theoretical agreement that such rights—that is, the duties and disabilities correlative to them—are permissibly enforceable.[10] Nevertheless, what acts persons can have moral claims to, or immunities against, must depend not only on the fundamental requirements of justice but also on the details of particular agreements or special relationships that some individuals may have with others. However, and that diversity notwithstanding, most literature on rights—especially moral rights—has tended to advance or presuppose some factor that is common to all the duties correlative to such rights. The thought here is that something more, more than the mere structural fact of their entailing permissibly waivable or enforceable duties, is true of all rights.

Historically, since at least the mediaeval period, writers have advanced two opposing theories—or, more precisely, families of theories—as attempts to identify this common factor: the *interest* (or *benefit*) *theory* and the *will* (or *choice*) *theory*. That long-running controversy has persisted to this day.[11]

What exactly is at issue here? As a first approximation, the central thesis of the interest theory is that all duties correlatively entailed by claims are ones the fulfilment of which benefits the claim-holders, whereas the counterpart thesis of the will theory is that such fulfilment is a compliance with the claim-holders' wishes.

On the face of it, these two theses do not seem very far apart from one another. However, this initial impression of similarity is quickly dispelled by their more precise formulations. For, according to the interest theory, the necessary and sufficient condition of a duty's being a correlative one—of its implying another person's claim—is that its fulfilment can generally be expected to serve that person's important interests.[12] For the will theory, on the other hand, a duty correlatively entails someone's having a claim if (and only if) that same person is vested with the powers to *control* that duty: the power to waive it *and* the power to demand/secure compliance with it.[13] While interest theory rights may sometimes vest such control over duties in claim-holders themselves, they need not do so: Control may be vested in others. Correspondingly, while duties correlative to will theory rights may serve claim-holders' important interests, they need not do so: Those duties may serve only the interests of others. Interest theory rights confer important benefits; will theory rights confer choices or, perhaps, freedoms.

These rival accounts each have far-reaching implications, not only for what can and cannot count as a right but also for who is the holder of the right entailed by any permissibly enforceable duty and, indeed, for who can count as a possible right-holder. In the latter regard, the will theory, in restricting rights to power-holders, evidently cannot ascribe rights to beings who are inherently incapable of exercising powers. A standard view is that will theory right-holders must be *moral agents*: beings to whom it makes sense to attribute choice-making capacities and, thereby, who are capable of giving or withholding consent. Living sane adult human beings are typically taken to exhaust the membership of the club of will theory right-holders. The interest theory, by way of contrast, can vest rights in anyone to whom it makes sense to attribute interests. And while I cannot here enter into an exhaustive discussion of how inclusive that class of beings might be, it evidently extends far beyond living sane adult humans and has been held to encompass such unempowerable beings as fetuses, the dead, members of future generations, and nonhuman animals. Since duties to protect the interests of those unempowerable beings are controllable—waivable or enforceable—only by living sane adult humans, the claims correlative to them can, according to the will theory, be held only by the latter; whereas the interest theory vests such claims directly in those *unempowerables* themselves, entrusting only the powers to control them to the latter.

Does this difference make a difference? The short answer is yes. For if the duty not to kill me is controllable by me, then an act of voluntary euthanasia that brings about my death will not be a violation of my rights. Whereas if that duty is not controllable by me—if I lack the power to waive it—then my consent to that act is insufficient to preclude its being a right-violation. Current environment-degrading activities, that jeopardize the vital interests of persons who will exist only two hundred years hence, are violations of their rights, according to the interest theory, but not according to the will theory. Abortion is not a violation of a will theory right but may be a violation of an interest theory right. The same is true of appropriation of decedents' estates (see Steiner, 1994, pp. 249–261).

As is suggested by the voluntary euthanasia example, the practical differences between these two theories of the general content of rights are also evident in their respective construals of *paternalistic* measures. Thus enforceable duties to refrain from gambling, addictive drug consumption, dangerous sports, or any other self-endangering activities might appear to be more readily interpreted as correlative to interest theory rights than to will theory ones, insofar as they protect those persons' vital interests. In fact, the matter is somewhat more complicated than that. For the persons bearing these duties are the very persons whose interests are being thereby protected and who would, under the interest theory, therefore also be the correlative claim-holders. But the idea that one can have rights against oneself is not only contrary to the Hohfeldian schema, which holds that correlative relations hold only between *different* persons, but also contrary to ordinary usage, whereby one's claims are claims against others. An alternative interpretation of such duties—one that *is* consistent with Hohfeld and ordinary usage—would be that the holder of the claims correlative to them is some collective entity, such as the state or the community.[14] If that collective entity can be said to have vital interests that are protected by such duties, then those claims can indeed be interpreted as interest theory rights. What's also true, however, is that if that collective entity is empowered to waive or demand fulfilment of those duties, then those claims can equally be interpreted as will theory rights. Much the same may be said about enforceable duties regulating voluntary relationships between members of the same sex or different racial and ethnic groups.

Finally, a further difference between the two theories has sometimes been thought to arise in respect of the idea of *inalienable rights*. That idea entails the possibility of rights that simply cannot be waived—neither by their holders nor by anyone else. Quite clearly, the will theory is incapable of accounting for such rights. Does the interest theory fare better, in this regard? Here, we need to consider what a right's being inalienable would imply. Hohfeld's schema indicates that someone's being disempowered to waive Blue's right entails that person's having a disability. Accordingly, someone holds the immunity correlative to that disability. Moreover, if that right is unwaivable, so too must be that immunity: otherwise, its holder would be empowered to waive it, thereby rendering Blue's right itself waivable. But if that immunity is indeed unwaivable, then its holder— being in turn disempowered—must hold a disability that correlatively entails yet another immunity. Accordingly, this chain of unwaivable immunities must either extend into an unacceptable infinite regress or terminate in an immunity that *is* waivable, thereby rendering Blue's right waivable, that is, alienable (see Steiner, 1994, pp. 71–72, 1998, pp. 253–255). In short, the idea of inalienable rights proves, on closer inspection, to be problematic in itself, regardless of whether we employ the interest theory or will theory of rights.

4. THE STATUS OF RIGHTS

Concerns about the status of moral rights, like concerns about the status of other moral norms, are typically motivated by the possibility of *conflict.* That is, we worry about such matters because we imagine or actually encounter circumstances in which two (or more) duties, though each separately performable, are not jointly performable. There is now a growing philosophical literature on the subject of whether duty-conflicts—dilemmas—signify the presence of contradictions in the moral code that generates them: that is, whether such conflicts are real or merely the apparent results of a code whose provisions are remediably incomplete or otherwise underspecified.[15]

Whatever may be the correct answer to that question, it is generally agreed that such conflicts are both theoretically and practically undesirable. We want our set of moral norms to deliver a definitive answer to the question of whether a particular person's performance of a particular act, A, in a particular circumstance, C, is permissible or impermissible. And this desire seems to be an especially strong one when it comes to issues of moral rights. The reason for its special strength has very much to do with the status of such rights.

For, as previously noted, a set of moral rights—as embodiments of justice—is presumed to constitute the relevant standard for the moral appraisal of legal rules. Since one of the distinguishing empirical features of legal rules is their *dominant enforceability*—since their demands in fact enjoy enforceable priority over any competing demands—it seems to follow that the moral standard to which legal rules *should* conform must itself enjoy priority over all other practical (including moral) requirements. In a conflict of duties, only one of which is correlative to a right, it is the fulfilment of that duty that morality requires. This kind of prioritization of correlative moral duties—of moral rights or, simply, justice—over the demands of other moral rules or values, has been variously expressed: John Rawls (1971, pp. 42–44) assigns *lexical priority* to the demands of justice; Robert Nozick (1974, pp. 28–33) describes moral rights as *side-constraints* on the pursuit of our ends; Ronald Dworkin (1977, ch. 4) has argued that rights are *trumps.*

The view of morality presupposed by such claims is decidedly *not,* as some writers have erroneously suggested, that it is 'right-based' (see Mackie, 1978). It does not imply that all moral duties are, in some sense or other, derivative from the duties correlative to moral rights. Rather, what such claims presuppose is that morality is *pluralistic:* that it consists of several primary rules or values (including one for justice or moral rights) that are mutually independent in the sense of not being reducible one to another.[16] And what such claims assert is that, within this plurality of norms, the demands of justice or moral rights enjoy primacy. In circumstances where a duty generated by any of these other primary norms conflicts—is jointly unperformable—with a duty correlative to a moral right, compliance with the latter is what morality requires.

Although the assignment of this status to moral rights has not gone unchallenged, it does seem to conform to widely held views. Such an assignment does, for instance, appear to be a necessary condition for making sense of the common notion of 'having a right to do wrong' (see Waldron, 1981). Of course, and following Hohfeld, no one can ever be strictly said to have a *right* to do anything: At most, persons have *liberties* to act, and having a liberty to do something does not entail a duty in anyone else. But we can have rights—claims—that others not interfere with our acting in certain ways, and those persons would thereby hold correlative duties of noninterference. Among the ways of acting that are protected by such claims may be ones that, in certain circumstances, are wrong on grounds other than justice. Thus, one of morality's primary rules or values may well be *charity*—a norm that vests me with duties to transfer some of my resources to those more in need of them than I am. Assuming that I am justly entitled to those resources—that I hold moral rights that others not interfere with my disposition of them—this does *not* entail that I do no wrong in refusing to act charitably and insist on withholding those resources from needier persons. All that is entailed by assigning primacy to moral rights is that others would be committing a *worse* wrong by forcing me to make that transfer. In other words, morality's assigning such primacy entails that the following three alternatives are listed in descending order of desirability: (1) my choosing to transfer my resources to the needy; (2) my withholding those resources; and (3) my attempting to withhold those resources but being forced by others to transfer them. It is outcome (2) that represents having (i.e., exercising) a right to do wrong. The fact that my withholding is an exercise of my rights is insufficient morally to justify that act. All that it would suffice to justify are whatever actions might be necessary to prevent or remedy my being forced to transfer (see Steiner, 1996).

There is another, and related, feature of our moral thinking that suggests primacy status for moral rights. In everyday moral discussions, we standardly don't invoke rights to resolve our disagreements, except as a last resort. Thus, as members of a newspaper's editorial staff, we might disagree with one another about which candidate the paper should support in a current electoral contest. Typically, the way we would argue about the relative merits of each of the candidates is by ascertaining facts, clarifying conceptual ambiguities, and appealing to one or another of the more fundamental moral rules or values that might severally be associated with each alternative. In other words, we would do our best to reach a consensus on which option is the morally optimal one. It's only when we find ourselves unable to reach that consensus that I might fall back on asserting "Look, I'm the managing editor here—I'm the one with the moral right to decide whom the paper supports." For me to offer that argument at the *outset* of our discussion would be not only churlish but also beside the point, since what that discussion is about is how best I can exercise my right: that it *is* my right is not in dispute. In other words, the resolving role of moral rights in moral disputes is not to dissolve disagreement but rather to determine *who*—in the face of indissoluble disagreement—ought to decide what is to be done. And it seems clear that moral rights can play this adjudicating role only if their status is one of having priority over whatever other moral norms may be in mutual contention in such disputes.

5. THE COMPOSSIBILITY OF RIGHTS

This primacy of moral rights is very far, however, from exhausting all the issues surrounding their status. For, on the face of it, it looks like duty-conflicts can occur not only between correlative and noncorrelative moral duties but also between different correlative duties themselves (see Rowan, 1999; Wellman, 1999). If rights are indeed *trumps*, then conflicts between two (or more) correlative duties would be akin to what might happen in card games played with two decks of cards! In a world where all sorts of moral demands are increasingly presented as moral rights, the problem of conflicting—*incompossible*—rights has been much noted and, as we'll see, sheds important light on another aspect of the status, as well as the content, of moral rights.

Duty-conflicts, as was previously noted, are both theoretically and practically undesirable. But they are especially undesirable if the moral duties in conflict are correlative ones, that is, are ones each entailing a moral right. Why? One reason has to do with the aforementioned fact that moral rights are presumed to constitute the relevant standard for the moral appraisal of legal systems. And legal systems, through the pyramidically hierarchical structure of their judicial institutions, are intolerant of conflicts between legal duties, resolving them by deeming only one of the mutually conflicting duties to be legally valid. Hence, a set of moral rights that is *not* similarly univocal—that sustains conflicts between its correlative duties—is less able to perform that aforementioned adjudicating role, and would thereby be impaired as a standard for the moral appraisal of legal systems. Invoking its authority would be somewhat like using an elastic string as a device for measuring distances. It would leave judicial institutions free—indeed, obliged—to make their decisions on grounds other than ones based on litigants' moral rights. For many writers, such judicial powers are seen as antithetical to the idea of 'the rule of law' (see Hart, 1985).

Of course, the fact that a set of correlative moral duties *may* generate such conflicts does not imply that it will actually do so. Sometimes, we can suppose, there is more than one way of complying with a moral duty. And in many such cases, it may well be true that at least one of these alternatively compliant actions would be such as *not* to amount to a breach of another duty. That said, however, our everyday experience of moral dilemmas strongly suggests that the occurrence of duty-conflicts is far from being merely a conceivable possibility.

So the question we need to ask ourselves is: What characteristics must a set of rights possess, if its entailed set of correlative duties is to be incapable of generating conflicts? As a first approximation, we can say that it must, at least implicitly, divide action-space into discretely demarcated portions. Since the fulfilment of each duty consists of a performance or a forbearance, it involves its subject in occupying certain spatio-temporal locations and using certain material objects: These are the physical elements of the conduct required by that duty. For two duties not to be in conflict, it's necessary that their respective sets of physical elements do not *intersect* with one another, for example, that these duties do not respectively require the same person or thing to be in two different places at the same time. A set of duties that fails to satisfy this condition is one that suffers from what I've elsewhere called 'extensional overlap': two (or more) of its required pieces of conduct are separately but not jointly performable, because their respective sets of physical components are partly but not wholly identical.[17]

In this sense, a set of compossible rights is one in which each right vests its holder with a unique *domain*, within which the duty correlative to that right is to be fulfilled. Hence, the traditional Lockean view—that all rights are essentially property rights—far from being merely a piece of bourgeois ideology, actually embodies an important conceptual truth. In this vein, H.L.A Hart correctly observes: "Rights are typically conceived of as *possessed* or *owned* or *belonging to* individuals, and these expressions reflect the conception of moral rules as not only prescribing conduct but as forming a kind of moral property of individuals to which they are as individuals entitled" (1955, p. 182). What this amounts to is simply a claim that, in a compossible set of rights, all rights are *funded*. The sets of resources respectively required for the fulfilment of each of their entailed duties are specifiable as extensionally distinct from one another.

None of this should be taken to deny what is obviously true: Namely, that intensional descriptions of duty-required actions—descriptions formulated in terms of their aims or purposes—usually serve as perfectly adequate *surrogates* for extensional specifications. But they can do so precisely because, and to the extent that, duties to do those actions exist against a background of reasonably well-partitioned domains. Certainly a world devoid of the linguistic and other conventions that facilitate such surrogacy would, to say the least, be cumbersome in the extreme. So all that is being argued here is that these intensional descriptions *must be* such surrogates: in the event of litigation, they must be transformable, however tediously, into extensional specifications. For insofar as they are not, insofar as a set of moral rights contains incompossibilities, it will fail to serve as a moral standard for legal decision-making.

In this respect, the will theory of rights enjoys an obvious advantage over the interest theory.

For even the latter's proponents acknowledge: "If rights are understood along the lines of the Interest Theory . . . then conflicts of rights must be regarded as more or less inevitable" (Waldron, 1989, p. 503). This is not surprising. Recall that, according to this theory, persons have a right if and only if some aspect of their well–being (some interest of theirs) is sufficiently important in itself to justify holding other persons to be under a duty. Whereas will theory duties are identifiable solely by virtue of their controllability, what is distinctive of interest theory duties is that they all have the same general intensional content: All actions enjoined by them have the purpose of servicing these important interests. And there are evidently no reasons to suppose that any two such services need be jointly performable, as well as many reasons to suppose that frequently they are not. The important interests persons have, both in privacy and in free expression, are, as we know, ones that cannot invariably be jointly serviced. Nor, tragically, can the vital interests several persons may each have in gaining access to some scarce medical resource. Accordingly, it would appear that any conflict between duties to service those interests can be adjudicated only by reference either to moral values other than that of rights themselves, or to what would—in that particular case—most increase the socially aggregated amount of interest-service. The problem with the first of these is its implication that rights register no independent set of moral demands, while the second excludes the distinctly *distributive* function of rights. In contrast, will theory rights, as domains over which claim-holders have controlling powers, more readily lend themselves to the sort of discrete partitioning of action-space that was previously indicated to be a necessary condition of their compossibility (see Simmonds, 1998, pp. 196 ff.).

6. THE ENFORCEABILITY OF RIGHTS

Important aspects of the status of moral rights are also implicit in their property of being permissibly *enforceable*. This permissible enforceability is, indeed, readily inferable from the aforementioned fact that moral rights constitute the standard for the moral assessment of legal rules that are, *ex hypothesi,* enforceable. To say that a right is permissibly enforceable is to say that the breach of its correlative duty may be forcibly prevented or redressed. However, perplexing problems arise in this regard when, as is often the case, the only way of preventing or redressing such a breach involves violating another right. Such situations have been analysed by some writers as yet another form of rights-conflict, inasmuch as they presume that the person whose right is threatened with, or suffers, a violation has a consequent right to that enforcement—a right that is thereby in conflict with the right whose violation is necessary in order to enforce the former one.

Thus Amartya Sen has proposed cases involving *multilateral interdependences:* Donna can prevent Amanda's being killed by a time bomb planted by Brian, but only by commandeering Charles's telephone to warn Amanda of the danger awaiting her. Sen contends that any moral theory that takes rights seriously—that assigns them nonderivative independent moral value—must be a consequentialist one that vests Donna with a duty to commandeer Charles's telephone. That is, such a moral theory must mandate tradeoffs of less valuable rights (Charles's rights with respect to his telephone) for more valuable ones (Amanda's right not to be killed).[18]

Nozick objects to such claims, arguing that they foster a 'utilitarianism of rights' that, in failing to reflect the deontological side-constraint function of rights, is inconsistent with the inviolable *status* of persons that moral rights are supposed to express. Moral rights, he maintains, "reflect the underlying Kantian principle that individuals are ends and not merely means; they may not be sacrificed or used for the achieving of other ends without their consent" (1974, pp. 30–31). A moral theory embodying a utilitarianism of rights would allow, indeed require, us to violate a person's right if that were necessary to minimize total rights-violation in society (pp. 28–32). Arguing in considerable detail along similar lines, Frances Kamm suggests that "[n]ot permitting minimising violations is . . . to show maximal concern for the right and the status [of that person], *consistent with* the right and the status existing at all" (1996, p. 267).

Can persons have moral rights to the enforcement of their moral rights? A possible resolution of the Sen versus Nozick-Kamm debate might go like this. Recall that the enforcement of rights can consist in either the ex ante prevention of right-violations or the ex post redress of them. So we might say that Donna does indeed have a correlative duty to violate Charles's right, in order to prevent the violation of Amanda's right. But rather than that trade-off being the end of the matter—as some consequentialists would allow—we add two further provisions: (1) that Donna also has a correlative duty to make redress to Charles for that violation; and (2) that Brian has a correlative duty to make redress to Donna for imposing on her a situation in which she is (enforceably) obliged to violate Charles's right.[19]

More generally, what this proposed resolution suggests is that the difference, between consequentialist views of rights and the view of them as deontological side-constraints, may be less than is often assumed. A pluralist consequentialism of the sort advanced by Sen, in acknowledging (as some consequentialisms do not) a multiplicity of primary values, need not be committed to mandating tradeoffs between those several values, even if (like all consequentialisms) it must mandate tradeoffs between competing instances of the *same* value.[20] For it can immunize any of those values against the former kind of tradeoff by according it a lexically prior status in relation to the others. That is, it can consistently hold, as Nozick-Kamm do, that any duty of justice *trumps* or *side-constrains* the pursuit of all other values and the performance of whatever duties that pursuit entails. Nor is this side-constraining property lost in the case of rights to the enforcement of rights. For as we've seen, the tradeoff between Amanda's right and that of Charles does not entail that the latter is overridden. Rather, and due to the aforesaid dual nature of enforcement, it entails only that Charles's right can be enforced by other means (see Steiner, 1994, pp. 203–206; 2005).

7. NEGATIVE AND POSITIVE RIGHTS

The issue of whether moral rights are negative or positive—whether our correlative duties require forbearances or performances—is essentially a question about the more specific content of *justice* as a moral principle. However, because the literature advancing various rival theories of justice has, since the 1971 publication of Rawls's work *A Theory of Justice*, proliferated enormously and shows no sign of abating, it would be impossible here to summarize—or even simply list—all the diverse contributions that have been made to the discussion of this issue.[21] Hence, the treatment of this issue here must, perforce, be limited to an examination of several of the more general aspects of rights that are implicit in it.

Despite some impressions to the contrary, virtually all theories of moral rights allow that these can be *both* negative and positive. That is, our correlative duties can consist of both acts that we must not perform and acts that we must perform. Thus, I can have correlative duties not to assault you and correlative duties to pay you five pounds. Where controversy arises in this regard is more perspicuously located in the issue of whether negative and positive moral rights are equally fundamental or *foundational*. Most theories embrace the view that our foundational rights include negative ones, but some theories maintain that they include *only* negative ones, and that whatever positive moral rights we may have must be nonfoundational or *derivative* ones. To grasp the core of what is at stake in this controversy, we need first to attend to the notions of foundational and derivative rights.

A foundational right is one that is not inferable from any other right and from which other rights—derivative ones—are inferable. One way of understanding the present controversy is in terms of *how* derivative rights are inferred from foundational (or other derivative) rights. Thus a right to Y might be derived from a right to X by virtue of the fact that Y is a form or *instance* of X. This is plainly evident if Y is physical health and X is well-being, or if Y is nonincarceration and X is freedom. Another mode of derivation is *instrumental:* Thus, say, Y is medical treatment and X is physical health. Instantiating and instrumental derivations, respectively, conjoin conceptual and causal premises with the statement that there is a right to X, in order to derive their conclusion that there is a right to Y. That is, the duty to do Y is either a constitutive element of the correlative duty to do X, or doing Y is a means to doing X.

Still other modes of derivation invoke Hohfeldian considerations. One way a right to Y can be derived from a right to X is through the exercise of *powers* attached to the right to X. Your current Y right to that car is created by my exercising my antecedent X right to that car: that is, by my exercising the power to transfer the ownership of the car to you. In exercising that power, I extinguish my X right that you (and others) not interfere with my use of the car, and I create your Y right that others (and I) not interfere with your use of it. Another kind of derivation involves the exercise of *liberties*. Thus my X rights to (others' noninterference with) my use of my supply of paper and my paper-shredding machine standardly give me a Y right to their noninterference with my use of the shredded paper. Such 'Hohfeldian derivations' combine the statement asserting the X right with statements asserting (1) the existence of those powers or liberties, and (2) the fact of their having been exercised, in order to infer the right to Y.

Theories of moral rights that regard foundational rights as *solely* negative are predominantly ones in which whatever positive rights they sustain are ones that exist by virtue of such Hohfeldian derivations. Your positive right to my services—teaching, for example—is derived from my consent to provide them to you. In the absence of that consent, your compelling me to provide them[22] would not count as an enforcement of a correlative duty, that is, as an enforcement of your positive right, for you would have *no* such right. Rather, such compulsion would amount to a breach of *your* negative correlative duty not to interfere with me in that way.[23] Such theories deploy, as their foundation, either an array of rights against various specified forms of interference or some single general right to freedom—often more precisely formulated as a right to *equal* freedom (see George, 1931, ch. 9; Hart, 1955; Kant, 1991, pp. 56–58; Pollock, 1981; Spencer, 1851, ch. 6; Steiner, 1994, pp. 216–223). Sometimes this general right to freedom is used, implicitly or explicitly, to derive—as an instantiation of it—a right of *self-ownership* (see Kant, 1991, p. 63; Nozick, 1974, pt. 2). It has further been argued that self-ownership, though necessary, is insufficient to instantiate a right to equal freedom, inasmuch as no partitioning of action-space—beyond the confines of right-holders' bodies—can be derived from it.[24] Accordingly, each person's right of self-ownership must be conjoined with an entitlement to part of the external world, if each is to be possessed of that foundational right. The latter entitlement can itself be construed as a negative right: a right that others forbear from appropriating more than an equal per capita share of land or natural resources. And in a world where land and natural resources have been fully appropriated by only some persons, the latter right entitles its holders to redress in the form of an equal per capita share of the *value* of what has been appropriated.[25]

There is an abundance of theories advancing the view that foundational rights are positive as well as negative ones. Almost all contemporary nonlibertarian theories of justice do so, as do most standard (less-theorized) accounts of human rights. Some of these theories deploy forms of contractarian reasoning to support this view; others seek to sustain it through teleological accounts of human nature. Such basic positive rights, in less-theorized accounts, are presented simply as an array of diverse kinds of entitlement that are each presumed to be self-evidently essential for right-holders to have. In more-theorized accounts, they typically derive from one unifying or underlying right entitling its holders to be secured in a certain broadly designated personal condition: well-being, autonomy, self-respect, and agency are among those most favoured. Accordingly, the correlative duties derived from these, while including many forms of noninterference, also extend to the provision of what are reasonably conceived to be the necessary political, economic, and social means for obtaining them. In this regard, the set of rights generated by such theories is more readily associated with the interest theory model of rights than with its will theory counterpart, since the immediate content of their correlative duties is dependent not on right-holders' choices but rather on what would best bring about that designated personal condition. And here some of these theories encounter the aforementioned problem of incompossibility, inasmuch as they often fail to incorporate a strictly distributive requirement in their reasoning. For there is no a priori reason why the means, needed to enhance some persons' well-being, autonomy, self-respect, or agency, may not be such as to diminish that of others: Rival claims to those means can be adjudicated only by reference either to values other than the right to that designated condition or to which assignment of those means would achieve the greater amount of it.

NOTES

I'm very grateful to David Copp for his extensive comments on an earlier draft of this article.

1. So, in the latter regard, his error lies in claiming that rights discourse has no application *outside* the realm of law, that is, in a state of nature.

2. The term 'services' simply and generally refers to persons' actions. A right is an entitlement to another person's performance or forbearance.

3. A considerably more elaborate scheme is presented in Kocourek, 1928.

4. See note 9.

5. Liberty, in this *normative* or *evaluative* or *rule-constituted* sense, is to be distinguished from the *descriptive* or *empirical* concept—absence of prevention—which is equally signified by the word 'freedom'.

6. As various writers have noted, these terms may have slightly different additional connotations, depending on the other contents of the set of rules implying this absence of duty: A privilege or a license is typically an exceptional absence of a duty of a type that is normally present. Nevertheless, all of them refer to an absence of duty.

7. A further—though somewhat disputed—aspect of having a power is that, within the rules assigning that power, it entails having the liberty to exercise it. Thus Red can be said to have the power to subject Blue to a duty to pay him five pounds only if Red has the liberty to do so and Blue the correlative no-claim that Red not do so. If, on the contrary, Red lacks this liberty and thus has a duty not to subject Blue to the duty of paying him five pounds, he would also lack the power to subject her to that payment duty. So powers and their correlative liabilities, respectively, entail liberties and their correlative no-claims; see Steiner, 1998, pp. 242–243, 268.

8. Following the previous note's reasoning, we can see that since Red's disability is his lack of a power, this entails his lack of a liberty and thus his having a duty that, in turn, correlatively entails that someone (as the holder of the immunity correlative to Red's disability), usually Blue, has a claim. On the reducibility of power/liability and immunity/disability relations to liberty/no-claim and claim/duty relations, see Ross, 1968, pp. 118–120, and Lindahl, 1977, p. 212 ff.

9. Much ink has been needlessly spilt in disputes over whether all rights entail the presence of correlative constraints. To some great extent, the issue is purely terminological. The view that some rights don't entail constraints trades on the undiscriminating use of the term 'rights' noted by Hohfeld. Clearly, neither no-claims nor liabilities are in themselves constraints on the conduct of those who have them: They do not imply, of any act, that it is impermissible. Hence, no clear analytical purpose is served by treating their correlatives—liberties and powers—as rights. Since only duties and disabilities are constraints, clarity and precision tell in favor of counting only their correlatives (claims, immunities) as rights. For a contrary view supporting the inclusion of liberties and powers as rights, on grounds of both common usage and analytical utility, see Wenar, forthcoming.

10. 'Enforcement of a disability' is, at best, an awkward formulation and not a little opaque in terms of both ordinary and legal usage. What such enforcement amounts to is securing the nullification of someone's presumed exercise of a power that, having that disability, she in fact lacks. Canceling a sale of stolen property is a standard example.

11. The classic statement of modern will theory is Hart's 1973 essay "Bentham on Legal Rights," republished in Hart, 1982; see also Hart, 1955. Some of the more influential presentations of the modern interest theory include: Raz, 1984, 1986, pt. 3; MacCormick, 1977; and Lyons, 1969. On aspects of the early modern origins of this controversy, see Tuck, 1979. The most recent and extensive presentations of these rival theories are to be found in Kramer, Simmonds, and Steiner, 1998.

12. See Raz, 1984, p. 166, who suggests that persons may be said to have a right if

and only if some aspect of their well–being (some interest of theirs) is sufficiently important in itself to justify holding other persons to be under a duty.

13. That is, a will theory claim-holder is the person who is empowered *both* to extinguish that duty ex ante (or forgive its nonfulfilment ex post) *and* alternatively to demand fulfilment of it ex ante (or secure redress for its nonfulfilment ex post).

14. The question of whether and, if so, in what sense collectivities can be moral right-holders—whether there can be *group rights*—is a complex one. Among the issues it seems to turn on is that of whether either agency or interests can be irreducibly attributed to collectivities: that is, agency or interests that are not disaggregateable into the respective agencies or interests of their individual members. In the burgeoning literature on the topic of collectivities as right-holders, see Kramer, 1998, pp. 49–60; Kymlicka, 1995; MacDonald, 1989; Jones, 1999.

15. What amounts to no more than a woefully incomplete sample of the relevant leading work here includes the following items, listed in no particular order: Von Wright, 1963, 1972; Hilpinen, 1971, 1981; Porn, 1970; Rescher, 1967; Williams, 1973; Korner, 1974; Raz, 1978, 1990; Levi, 1986; Gowans, 1987; Sinnott-Armstrong, 1988; Vallentyne, 1989; Stocker, 1990; Steiner, 1994, ch. 4; Mason, 1996; Forrester, 1996; Nozick, 1997.

16. Hence the possibility, mentioned at the outset, that morality might not contain rights. For morality might be pluralistic and yet not include justice/moral rights among its set of primary rules or values. Or alternatively, it might be *monistic*, enjoining obedience to only one rule or the maximized achievement of only one valued state of affairs, with all of its other injunctions amounting to no more than particular instantiations of— or instrumental derivations from—that single norm.

17. If they—including the respective bearers of those duties—were wholly identical, there would be no joint unperformability, inasmuch as one piece of conduct would suffice to discharge both duties. The conditions for the absence of extensional overlap evidently need further refinement. For while someone (or some object) cannot be in two places at the same time, that person (or it) can be in one place at two different times, or at two places at two different times, and so on. Equally, two persons cannot occupy exactly the same spatio-temporal location. For a fuller elaboration of those conditions, see Steiner, 1994, pp. 74–101, 1998, pp. 262–274.

18. See Sen, 1982, pp. 4–19, 1985, p. 15; also Thomson, 1990, chs. 4–7. It should be noted that it is unclear whether Sen himself believes that Donna's moral duty to commandeer the telephone is a correlative one, i.e. is one entailing a right in Amanda.

19. And presumably Brian's redress duty would thereby consist in compensating Donna for the redress she owes to Charles. Readers are strongly advised to consult Kamm's text for a full statement of the reasons why she would *not* accept the validity of this proposed resolution.

20. Indeed, it is unclear to me how *deontological* theories can avoid mandating such tradeoffs.

21. Prominent among these contributions, apart from works previously mentioned, are: Barry, 1995; Scanlon, 1998; Dworkin, 2000; Van Parijs, 1995; Rakowski, 1991; Gauthier, 1986; Cohen, 1995; Lomasky, 1987; Ackerman, 1980; Murphy and Nagel, 2002; Walzer, 1983; Sen, 1992; Roemer, 1998; Gewirth, 1996.

22. Or your penalizing me for failing to provide them.

23. Of course, most such theories also include provisions for the creation of positive rights to redress of right-violations, regardless of whether the rights violated are

themselves negative or positive. In the event of my failing to provide you with my agreed teaching services, or of my assaulting you, you have a power to create a positive right to my compensating you.

24. It's worth noting that, in the case of "Siamese twins," even such a minimal right as self-ownership can generate incompossible duties.

25. Anthologies tracing the history and current accounts of this view are Vallentyne and Steiner, 2000a, 2000b.

REFERENCES

Ackerman, Bruce. 1980. *Social Justice in the Liberal State.* New Haven, Conn.: Yale University Press.

Barry, Brian. 1995. *Justice as Impartiality.* Oxford: Oxford University Press.

Cohen, G. A. 1995. *Self-Ownership, Freedom and Equality.* Cambridge: Cambridge University Press.

Coyle, Sean. 2002. "Are There Necessary Truths about Rights?" *Canadian Journal of Law and Jurisprudence* 15: 21–49.

Dworkin, Ronald. 1977. *Taking Rights Seriously.* London: Duckworth.

———. 2000. *Sovereign Virtue.* Cambridge, Mass.: Harvard University Press.

Forrester, James. 1996. *Being Good and Being Logical.* New York: M. E. Sharpe.

Gauthier, David. 1986. *Morals by Agreement.* Oxford: Oxford University Press.

George, Henry. 1931. *Social Problems.* London: Henry George Foundation.

Gewirth, Alan. 1996. *The Community of Rights.* Chicago: University of Chicago Press.

Gowans, Christopher, ed. 1987. *Moral Dilemmas.* New York: Oxford University Press.

Hacker, P.M.S., and J. Raz, eds. 1977. *Law, Morality and Society.* Oxford: Oxford University Press.

Hart, H.L.A. 1955. "Are There Any Natural Rights?" *Philosophical Review* 64: 175–191.

———. 1982. *Essays on Bentham.* Oxford: Oxford University Press.

———. 1985. "The Nightmare and the Noble Dream." In *Essays in Jurisprudence and Philosophy,* 123–144. Oxford: Oxford University Press.

Hilpinen, Risto, ed. 1971. *Deontic Logic: Introductory and Systematic Readings.* Dordrecht: Reidel.

———. 1981. *New Studies in Deontic Logic.* Dordrecht: Reidel.

Hohfeld, Wesley N. 1919. *Fundamental Legal Conceptions.* W. W. Cook, ed. New Haven, Conn.: Yale University Press.

Jones, Peter. 1994. *Rights.* Houndmills, England: Palgrave.

———. 1999. "Group Rights and Group Oppression." *Journal of Political Philosophy* 7: 353–377.

Kamm, F. M. 1996. *Morality, Mortality.* Vol. 2. *Rights, Duties and Status.* Oxford: Oxford University Press.

Kant, Immanuel. 1991. *The Metaphysics of Morals.* Trans. and ed. Mary Gregor. Cambridge: Cambridge University Press.

Kocourek, Albert. 1928. *Jural Relations.* Indianapolis: Bobbs-Merrill.

Korner, Stephan, ed. 1974. *Practical Reason.* Oxford: Blackwell.

Kramer, Matthew. 1998. "Rights without Trimmings." In Kramer, Simmonds, and Steiner, 1998, 7–111.

Kramer, Matthew, Nigel Simmonds, and Hillel Steiner. 1998. *A Debate over Rights: Philosophical Enquiries.* Oxford: Oxford University Press.

Kymlicka, Will, ed. 1995. *The Rights of Minority Cultures.* Oxford: Oxford University Press.

Levi, Isaac. 1986. *Hard Choices.* Cambridge: Cambridge University Press.

Lindahl, Lars. 1977. *Position and Change.* Dordrecht: Reidel.

Lomasky, Loren. 1987. *Persons, Rights and the Moral Community.* Oxford: Oxford University Press.

Lyons, David. 1969. "Rights, Claimants and Beneficiaries." *American Philosophical Quarterly* 6: 153–185.

MacCormick, D. N. 1977. "Rights in Legislation." In Hacker and Raz, 1977, 189–209.

MacDonald, Ian. 1989. "Group Rights." *Philosophical Papers* 28: 117–136.

Mackie, J. L. 1978. "Can There be a Right-Based Moral Theory?" *Midwest Studies in Philosophy* 3: 350–359.

Mason, H. E., ed. 1996. *Moral Dilemmas and Moral Theory.* New York: Oxford University Press.

Murphy, Liam, and Thomas Nagel. 2002. *The Myth of Ownership.* Oxford: Oxford University Press.

Nozick, Robert. 1974. *Anarchy, State and Utopia.* New York: Basic Books.

———. 1997. "Moral Complications and Moral Structures." In *Socratic Puzzles,* 201–248. Cambridge, Mass.: Harvard University Press .

Pollock, Lansing. 1981. *The Freedom Principle.* Buffalo, N.Y.: Prometheus Books.

Porn, Ingmar. 1970. *The Logic of Power.* Oxford: Blackwell.

Rakowski, Eric. 1991. *Equal Justice.* Oxford: Oxford University Press.

Rawls, John. 1971. *A Theory of Justice.* Cambridge, Mass.: Harvard University Press.

Raz, Joseph, ed. 1978. *Practical Reasoning.* Oxford: Oxford University Press.

———. 1984. "On the Nature of Rights." *Mind* 93: 194–214.

———. 1986. *The Morality of Freedom.* Oxford: Oxford University Press.

———. 1990. *Practical Reason and Norms.* Princeton, N.J.: Princeton University Press.

Rescher, Nicholas, ed. 1967. *The Logic of Decision and Action.* Pittsburgh: University of Pittsburgh Press.

Roemer, John. 1998. *Equality of Opportunity.* Cambridge, Mass.: Harvard University Press.

Ross, Alf. 1968. *Directives and Norms.* London: Routledge and Kegan Paul.

Rowan, John. 1999. *Conflicts of Rights.* Boulder, Colo.: Westview.

Scanlon, T. M. 1998. *What We Owe to Each Other.* Cambridge, Mass.: Harvard University Press.

Sen, Amartya. 1982. "Rights and Agency." *Philosophy and Public Affairs* 11: 3–39.

———. 1985. "Rights as Goals." Austin Lecture 1984. In *Equality and Discrimination: Essays in Freedom and Justice,* ed. Stephen Guest and Alan Milne, 11–25. Stuttgart: Franz Steiner.

———. 1992. *Inequality Reexamined.* Oxford: Oxford University Press.

Simmonds, Nigel. 1998. "Rights at the Cutting Edge." In Kramer, Simmonds, and Steiner, 1998, 113–232.

Sinnott-Armstrong, Walter. 1988. *Moral Dilemmas.* Oxford: Blackwell.

Spencer, Herbert. 1851. *Social Statics.* London: John Chapman.

Steiner, Hillel. 1994. *An Essay on Rights.* Oxford: Blackwell.

———. 1996. "Duty-Free Zones." *Aristotelian Society Proceedings* 96: 231–244.

———. 1998. "Working Rights." In Kramer, Simmonds, and Steiner, 1998, 233–301.

———. 2005. "Conscription." In *The Egalitarian Conscience: Essays in Honour of G. A. Cohen,* ed. Christine Sypnowich. Oxford: Oxford University Press.

Stocker, Michael. 1990. *Plural and Conflicting Values.* Oxford: Oxford University Press.

Sumner, L. W. 1987. *The Moral Foundation of Rights.* Oxford: Oxford University Press.

Thomson, Judith Jarvis. 1990. *The Realm of Rights.* Cambridge, Mass.: Harvard University Press.

Tuck, Richard. 1979. *Natural Rights Theories.* Cambridge: Cambridge University Press.

Vallentyne, Peter. 1989. "Two Types of Moral Dilemmas." *Erkenntnis* 30: 301–318.

Vallentyne, Peter, and Hillel Steiner, eds. 2000a. *Left-Libertarianism and Its Critics.* Houndmills, England: Palgrave, 2000.

———. 2000b. *The Origins of Left-Libertarianism.* Houndmills, England: Palgrave.

Van Parijs, Philippe. 1995. *Real Freedom for All.* Oxford: Oxford University Press.

Von Wright, G. H. 1963. *Norm and Action.* London: Routledge and Kegan Paul.

———. 1972. *An Essay in Deontic Logic and the General Theory of Action.* Amsterdam: North-Holland.

Waldron, Jeremy. 1981. "A Right to Do Wrong." *Ethics* 92: 21–39.

———. 1987. *"Nonsense upon Stilts": Bentham, Burke and Marx on the Rights of Man.* London: Methuen.

———. 1989. "Rights in Conflict." *Ethics* 99: 503–519.

Walzer, Michael. 1983. *Spheres of Justice.* New York: Basic Books.

Wellman, Carl. 1985. *A Theory of Rights.* Totowa, N.J.: Rowman and Allanheld.

———. 1999. *The Proliferation of Rights.* Boulder, Colo.: Westview Press.

Wenar, Leif. Forthcoming. "The Nature of Rights."

Williams, Bernard. 1973. "Ethical Consistency." In *Problems of the Self,* 166–186. Cambridge: Cambridge University Press.

CHAPTER 17

KANTIAN NORMATIVE ETHICS

THOMAS E. HILL, JR.

KANT is often studied for his contribution to debates that today might be classified as metaethical,[1] but my concern here is with questions of normative ethics. In particular, I want to focus on how certain basic normative questions are addressed by Kant and various contemporary Kantians who interpret and extend Kant's theory. The main questions are familiar ones: Are there many basic moral principles or only one? How are we to articulate and interpret the basic principle or principles? How do they, or does it, function as an action-guide for particular moral problems? Are the basic Kantian principles really (as Kant thought) the norms underlying common moral judgments?

My discussion will be wide-ranging, but still limited in several ways. Kant's ethical writings are open to different interpretations, and the literature devoted to interpreting and extending his ideas is vast, diverse, and of mixed quality. Although I draw from several prominent contemporary Kantians, I cannot survey all of the good literature in this area. When illustrating the action-guiding use of Kant's basic principles, I limit my discussion by concentrating primarily on cases of beneficence and mutual aid rather than addressing a full range of moral problems. Because I review many different interpretations, my description and illustration of each, including the ones that I find most promising, must be quite brief. My primary aim is to call attention to a variety of different ways in which contemporary Kantians are attempting to develop Kant's normative ethics. I hope that this will encourage further investigation and development of the views only sketched here.

A secondary aim is to illustrate these different developments by relating them to a particular task that any normative ethical theory needs to address. This is to determine, at least in broad terms, when and why we are morally required to help others. Kant's theory is justly famous for its insistence that pursuit of happiness, for both oneself and others, is constrained by moral requirements of justice and respect for human dignity. Kant also insists, however, that it is categorically imperative for us to make it our maxim to promote the happiness of others. It is currently a matter of controversy how much latitude this requirement is supposed to leave us to pursue nonobligatory projects of our own.[2] Focusing on beneficence to illustrate various contemporary developments in Kantian ethical theory should bring out similarities and differences among them. It may also reveal some of their relative strengths and weaknesses.

1. WILLING MAXIMS AS UNIVERSAL LAWS

1.1. The Formulas of Universal Law

Kant's interpreters have most often taken as his primary action-guiding principle the first formulation of the Categorical Imperative, the formula of universal law. The initial expression of this in *Groundwork* I is: "I ought never to act in such a way *that I could not also will that my maxim should become a universal law*" (Kant, 2002, p. 203 [4:402]).[3] Kant's first formula of the Categorical Imperative in *Groundwork* II is commonly thought to express the same idea: "Act only on that maxim by which you can at the same time will that it should become a universal law" (p. 222 [4:421]). Kant then offers a variant of the formula: "Act as though the maxim of your action were to become by your will a universal law of nature" (p. 222 [4:421]). Following tradition, we can label the first two quotations as expressions of the *formula of universal law (FUL)* and the third as an expression of the *formula of universal law of nature (FULN)*. Kant repeats these formulas with variations in wording throughout his ethical writings.[4]

All of these are supposed to express the only principle that can be, in the strictest sense, a "categorical imperative," and so it is called a formulation of *the Categorical Imperative* (Kant, 2002, p. 214 [4:413]). This implies that it expresses in the form of an imperative an unconditional basic requirement of practical

reason. An *imperative*, in Kant's technical terminology, expresses an objective principle as a *constraint* on imperfectly rational persons. An *objective principle* is one
that any *fully rational* person would follow—but human beings (who are imperfectly rational) might not (p. 214 [4:401]). Kant later states several other formulas
of the Categorical Imperative, but he claims that these are simply different ways
of expressing fundamentally the same principle—the supreme principle of morality (p. 237 [4:436]). He sometimes refers to more specific moral principles as
"categorical imperatives." This may cause confusion, because he says explicitly
that there can only be one categorical imperative (p. 222 [4:421]). We can understand his view as consistent if we take the Categorical Imperative, expressed in
various formulas, as the only imperative that is categorical *in a strict sense* but
then add that more specific moral principles can be called "categorical imperatives" *in an extended sense* if they are derived from the Categorical Imperative and
hold without exception.

Commentators differ significantly about how Kant's formulas are supposed
to work as action-guides, but some points seem clear enough.

First, to determine whether a proposed act would be right, we must identify
"the maxim" of the act. Maxims are "subjective principles" on which we act (Kant,
2002, p. 202 n. [4:401 n.]).[5] The fullest statements of them describe the act, its
purpose, and the underlying reason (at least as the agent understands these).[6]
They can be expressed as policy statements with the form "In conditions C, I
shall do X in order to E from the motive M." They may be very general, such as
"I shall always do what best serves my own interests," or quite specific, such as
"When in need and aware that I cannot repay loans, I shall borrow money anyway
with a (false) promise to repay."[7] Some maxims are morally bad, some are good,
and many are morally indifferent. Kant offers the universal law formulas as a way
of testing whether acting on our proposed maxim would be wrong.[8] Of course,
it may actually be rare that we have in mind an explicitly articulated maxim when
we act. If, however, we sincerely question whether a proposed act would be morally permissible, we can reflect on what we are about to do, and why, and from
this try to construct the relevant maxim to test by the universal law formulas.
How exactly this should be done remains a problem, but certain guidelines seem
implicit in the aim to deliberate conscientiously. For example, our maxim can
only refer to facts of which we are aware, and it should reflect honestly our beliefs
about what is morally relevant in the situation. Apart from this, it should not
include details that are irrelevant to our policy, purpose, and reasons for acting
as we propose to do.[9] If our first attempts to articulate our maxim fail the test,
it may be that, on honest refection, we can rephrase the maxim in way that more
aptly describes what we propose to do, our purpose, our reasons, and the limits
of the policy that we mean to endorse.[10] Since the practical purpose of the formula
is to guide conscientious deliberation about whether it is permissible to act as we

are inclined to do, it would be both dishonest and self-defeating to try to rig the statement of our maxim so that Kant's tests will "justify" what we really believe is wrong. Philosophers sympathetic to Kant's project also may be suspected of rigging maxims in a dishonest and self-serving way if, *whenever* faced with counterexamples, they keep redescribing the maxim until Kant's texts yield the intuitive result that they want. If that is necessary, the formula is not really serving as a decision guide.

Second, Kant distinguishes between two kinds of maxims that fail the test posed in the universal law formulas. Some maxims cannot be *conceived* as universal law[11] without contradiction; others can be, but cannot be consistently *willed* as universal law. Thus, in effect, our maxims must meet two requirements. The first is that we must be able to *conceive* our maxim as a universal law without contradiction. If we cannot, then it is wrong to act on the maxim. If we can conceive our maxim as a universal law without contradiction, we must then still ask whether we can *will* our maxim as a universal law. Maxims that satisfy both requirements are supposed to be permissible to act on; those that fail either requirement are supposed to be wrong to act on. In the *Groundwork,* Kant gives two examples of maxims that fail the first test and two examples of maxims that fail the second test.[12]

Third, although Kant presents these requirements as tests of the *permissibility* of acting on a proposed maxim, they could lead us to the conclusion that we have a positive *duty* to act in certain ways. If we wonder whether it is also duty to act on a given permissible maxim, then we must consider what our maxim would be if we chose to do otherwise. If we could not consistently conceive and will that alternative maxim as a universal law, then it is wrong to act on the alternative maxim. Whenever it is wrong to act on the only alternative to a permissible maxim, it is a positive duty to act on the permissible maxim. There may, of course, be many alternatives, but at least we can say that it is a positive duty to act on the initial permissible maxim, unless at least one of the alternatives can be conceived and willed as a universal law. Consider, for example, a maxim to aid persons in distress, at least when one can at little cost to oneself or others.[13] Presumably, this can be conceived and willed as a universal law, and so it is permissible to act on this maxim. When confronted with a particular case, we need to consider what our maxim would be if we did not act on this maxim to help the distressed person. There are obviously many other things we could do instead, but presumably the maxims we would be acting on if we did not help would need to make reference to the morally salient fact that we would be refusing to help someone in distress even though we could easily aid the person without harm to ourselves or others.[14] If these alternative maxims cannot be conceived and willed as universal laws, then not to give aid in the circumstances would be wrong, and so giving aid would be a positive duty.

1.2. Questions of Interpretation

This is not the place to try to evaluate all interpretations with regard to either their fidelity to texts or their plausibility as moral standards, but here are a few of the variations on Kant's theme.

A preliminary question concerns the relation between FUL and FULN. Do both of these offer procedures for testing the morality of maxims? If so, do they propose exactly the same test or different ones? On one reading, the more abstract FUL is not a practical action-guide by itself but expresses an idea that can be applied to human conditions only when "universal law" is replaced with the more specific concept "universal laws of nature."[15] On another reading, FULN simply specifies what was implicitly intended in FUL, and so the two formulas offer exactly the same test for maxims. A third possibility is that the FUL and FULN offer slightly different tests. In one version, FUL is concerned with *laws of freedom,* while FULN is concerned with *teleological laws of nature.* Thus the first asks us whether we can will that everyone freely choose to act on our maxims, and the second asks us whether we could consistently conceive and will our maxims as teleological laws in a harmonious system of natural purposes.[16] A more promising variation, in my view, is this: FUL asks us whether we can consistently conceive and will our maxim as *permissible* for everyone to act on,[17] and FULN asks us to whether we can consistently conceive and (if we had the power) will that, as if by a law of nature, everyone adopts and acts on the maxim.[18]

Other questions arise about what might, in a relevant sense, prevent us from conceiving a maxim as a law, or law of nature, for everyone. Most obviously, if everyone's acting (or being permitted to act) on a given maxim is logically impossible, then the maxim cannot be conceived as a universal law in the relevant sense. Kant's examples, however, suggest that they be ruled out if, *assuming some general background facts* about the human condition, it is logically impossible for everyone to act on them.[19] On another interpretation, they are excluded if it is logically impossible for a harmonious system of nature to include everyone's acting in the manner *and for the purpose* indicated in the maxim.[20] A more promising suggestion, perhaps, is that maxims cannot be conceived as universal laws (or laws of nature) if it is logically impossible to will simultaneously the following set of intentions: (1) to act on the maxim, (2) to bring it about (if one had the power) that everyone else act on the maxim, and (3) the normal foreseeable consequences of everyone's acting on the maxim.[21] This is a particular version of the idea that we cannot conceive of a maxim without contradiction if the maxim "would be self-defeating if universalized: [Our] action would become ineffectual for [our] purpose if everyone (tried to) use it for that purpose" (Korsgaard, 1996b, p. 78).

There are also different ways of understanding the relevant impossibility of *willing* maxims that can be conceived as universal laws. I cannot review them all, but here is a sample. The least plausible, but all too common, idea is this means simply *being unwilling, for any reason, to choose* that our maxim be adopted by everyone. If, for example, racial bigots, because of their prejudice, would not be willing to for everyone to work for racial equality, then they could argue that by Kant's principle they would be wrong to do so. Even worse, they could argue that because they are willing for everyone to adhere to their policy of strict racial segregation, it is morally permissible for them to pursue it.[22] Equally, but less obviously, implausible is the assumption that *any contingent inability* (in our nature or circumstances) to will our maxims as universal law means that we would be wrong to act on them. Especially when we consider rather specific maxims, this would mean that all sorts of morally irrelevant factors would rule out actions that are quite innocent. If there were not enough of some trivial commercial product for everyone to buy it, the test would apparently show that it is wrong for anyone to buy the product. If, because of dizziness, some people cannot climb high ladders, it would seem that no one should.

Now, by reformulating the maxims and adding ad hoc stipulations to the test, we might circumvent these and other particular counterexamples; but arguably the interpretation in question is mistaken in principle. What should be relevant under the universal law tests is whether we can *rationally* endorse a maxim as a universal law.[23] The fact that not everyone *can* act in certain ways is often no reason for others to refrain, and all sorts of morally irrelevant quirks and prejudices may determine whether we are willing to endorse policies for everyone. What we need to consider is whether endorsing our maxims as universal laws is *contrary to reason* in some relevant way.[24] Obviously, maxims that cannot be *conceived* as universal laws without contradiction cannot be *rationally willed* as universal law, but beyond this, the relevant standards of rational willing are more controversial. A standard of logical consistency and coherence among one's intentions is unlikely to be sufficient by itself to generate appropriate results from the universal law tests. In a Kantian theory, however, these standards should not be intuitive moral norms that have no basis at all in Kant's moral theory, at least if we accept the common view that all other moral norms are derivative, in some sense, from Kant's basic moral principles.[25] In applying Kant's formulas, however, we should be able to rely on whatever specific moral norms we have already confirmed, or could confirm (on Kantian grounds) as rational requirements.[26]

Readers will need to assess the various interpretations for themselves, but a particularly important further controversy should be mentioned. In assessing whether we can *reasonably* will our maxims as universal laws, can we rely on the other formulas of the Categorical Imperative? To try to do so would be useless if, as some think, the later formulas add nothing new and action-guiding beyond what the universal law formulas say.[27] If, however, as others claim, the later formulas articulate basic moral standards apart from (or at least not explicit in) the universal law formulas, then they would provide resources for arguments that certain maxims cannot be reasonably willed as universal laws. For example, if we exclude the later formulas, a rich miser who abhors charity for anyone might argue that he can will his maxim of refusing to help the needy as a universal law because he is prepared to die before accepting charity. If, however, we accept as a rational requirement that we treat humanity in each person as an end-in-itself, then arguably the miser could not reasonably endorse his "no charity" policy as a universal law.[28] Kantians take different positions on whether later formulas can supplement the universal law formulas, depending on their different interpretations of the textual evidence regarding Kant's intentions and their philosophical judgment as to what makes most sense.

1.3. Illustration: Helping Others in Distress

Kant's project in the *Groundwork* and *Critique of Practical Reason*, where the formula of universal law figures prominently, was not primarily to explain and illustrate how to apply his formulas to particular problems. In both works, and especially the latter, more attention is devoted to discovering and defending the basic presuppositions of the use of practical reason—finding its constitutive principles and their relation to freedom of the will (in several senses). *The Metaphysics of Morals* is the work where Kant turns explicitly to the task of working out intermediate principles for guiding ethical judgment in various areas of human life, and here the universal law formulas play a more modest role. In fact the idea of humanity as an end-in-itself is what Kant's arguments most often appeal to. Nevertheless, in the *Groundwork* Kant expresses great confidence that the universal law formulas can serve as guide to moral judgment, enabling us to distinguish right from wrong in every case (Kant, 2002, pp. 204–206 [4:403–4], pp. 224–226 [4:424–425]). Moreover, he suggests that, although ordinary people can become confused, they implicitly respect and rely on the universal law formulas as a standard (pp. 204–207 [4:403–405], 1997, p. 7 n. [5:8 n.]). Not surprisingly, not all readers have shared Kant's confidence in the formulas as an action-guide. For centuries now, critics have pointed out problems in applying them, and Kant's supporters have developed subtle defenses of his basic idea beyond anything that we can find explicitly in Kant's texts.

Let us consider how the universal law formulas might guide our moral reflection about helping others. First, we must acknowledge that many ways of helping others are morally impermissible. Justice, respect for others, and certain "perfect duties to oneself" set limits to what we may do to aid and promote the happiness of others. These constraints call for justification, by the either universal law formulas or later formulas, but let us assume for now that these restrictions can be justified. The general question is, if we fulfill our duties of justice, respect, and so on, what more must we do for others? To apply the universal law tests, we must look at the problem initially from the point of view of a particular agent in a particular context. Suppose, then, you are inclined to refuse an appeal to give to famine relief, but you wonder if this is morally permissible. The first thing to consider is what maxim honestly and accurately reflects what you propose to do. Cases will vary, but suppose you are inclined not to help anyone beyond what justice demands, though you could easily make a gift that would help to relieve someone's distress (Kant, 2002, pp. 224–225 [4:424–425]). Your maxim might be "From self-interest I will always refuse to help others in need except when they have a right to my aid, even though I could easily help without significant harm to myself or others." Presumably, you can consistently conceive a world in which everyone adopts and acts on this maxim. If everyone did so, however, and you should fall into dire need, by your policy others would help you only if you could demand help as a matter of justice (your rights). This, in most cases, would be contrary to your self-interest, and, by hypothesis, your purpose in adopting your maxim was to advance your self-interest. So willing that everyone adopt and act on your maxim would be willing a situation incompatible with your aim in adopting your maxim. You cannot rationally will both, and so, it seems, you would be wrong to act on your maxim.

Suppose now that you are an unusually wealthy, secure, independence-loving miser. You might object to the previous argument, saying that you would prefer to die rather than accept aid from others. Then, you might argue, you can consistently act on your personal preferences (expressed in your maxim) while also willing your maxim for yourself *and everyone else,* for in this case your purpose in adopting your maxim was to satisfy a personal preference that you *and everyone else* refuse to give to charity. To meet this objection, one might argue that you cannot *rationally* chose that you would forego the means to your survival if you should happen to fall into dire need.[29] Arguably, the issue here is not the odds of your falling into dire need but rather what you can rationally will for the *possible* circumstance in which it happens, whatever the odds against it. As a *rational* person, one might argue, you necessarily value your existence as a rational agent over inclination-based preferences, and therefore you must treat the means to your survival as having a value of higher priority than your disinclination to accept charity. If so, it would be contrary to reason to will your maxim as one for everyone to follow. The upshot is that it is wrong for you to act on your maxim; and so unless you can honestly say that your refusal to give aid is based on some other, morally acceptable ground, you have a positive duty to give aid on the occasion in question. Furthermore, assuming you will have normal opportunities and abilities in the future, arguably you can ensure that you will not act on your impermissible maxim (or similar bad maxims) in the future only if you make it your principle generally to help others in need when you can at little cost to yourself or others.[30] None of this implies, however, that you must try to maximize happiness or to work for the happiness of others *whenever you have no conflicting duties*.[31]

1.4. Problems and Doubts

The most persistent worry about Kant's universal law formulas is that they often seem to lead to intuitively unacceptable conclusions. They apparently condemn some maxims that we regard as innocent and fail to condemn maxims that we regard as immoral. Frequently, revising the description of the maxim leads to more acceptable results, but there seems no principled way to tell before applying the tests what the "correct" description should be.[32] Even if we can always find some apt maxim description that allows us to reach common-sense conclusions, we are not really being guided by the formulas if we need to rely on our understanding of the right conclusion in order to find the best statement of the maxim. Even if the tests appropriately show that acting on certain maxims is *wrong* and acting on others is *permissible*, they can generate a *positive duty* to do something only indirectly by showing that it is wrong not to do it. Since there are usually many ways of *not doing* something, we would need to identify and test all of the many maxims that we might follow if we did not do as the alleged positive duty would prescribe. Defenders of Kant's universal law formulas have devised many subtle supplements to these as maxim-testing procedures, but arguably the proposals are merely ad hoc devices to patch up a flawed procedure or else they amount to an admission that the universal law formulas alone are not sufficient for determining particular moral requirements.

Another recurrent concern about treating the universal law formulas as the sole, or primary, moral action-guide is that the recommended test procedure, by itself, seems not to reflect what is most central to moral deliberation. As many Kantians now admit, even if the universal law formulas can flag certain maxims as morally wrong, or at least suspect, they do not adequately explain *why* acting on those maxims is wrong. What is wrong with slavery, for example, is not adequately explained by saying that it is impossible for everyone to act the maxim of a would-be slave-owner. It may be that those who rob banks and commit murder cannot consistently will both their maxim and that everyone act on that maxim, but this inconsistency seems at best only part of the story why such acts are wrong. Although Kant's formulas do not work well as precise decision procedures for particular moral cases, they should at least reflect, in a general way, essential features of a Kantian moral perspective for thinking about particular problems. Taken by themselves, the universal law formulas seem inadequate for this purpose. Arguably, Kant himself thought that the full import of the moral law becomes clear only when all of the formulas are fully taken into account.

2. TREATING HUMANITY AS AN END-IN-ITSELF

2.1. The Formula of Humanity

Kant's next formulation of the Categorical Imperative is this: "*Act in such a way that you treat humanity, whether in your own person or in any other person, always at the same time as an end, never merely as a means*" (Kant, 2002, pp. 229–230 [4: 429]).[33] He elaborates this formula in various ways. He says both that *persons* are ends-in-themselves and that *humanity, or rational nature*, in persons is an end-in-itself.[34] An *end*, in Kant's broad sense, is "what serves the will as the objective ground of its self-determining"; that is, it gives us a *reason* to do or refrain from doing various things (p. 228 [4:427]). Ordinarily we think of an end as something we aim to achieve or promote, but Kant says that an end-in-itself in his sense is a "self-sufficient" or independently existing end, rather than an end to be produced (p. 238 [4:437]). An end-in-itself is necessarily an end for every rational being: That is, its existence is an objective reason for doing or refraining from certain acts, independently of our inclinations. To value rational persons as ends, we must not use them for ends that, in some sense, they cannot share (pp. 230–231 [4:430]). Kant adds that persons, conceived as members of a kingdom of ends, have a *dignity*, which is grounded in their *autonomy* of will (pp. 234–237 [4:434–436]).[35] Dignity is an "unconditional and incomparable worth," above all *price* and "without equivalent." Thus dignity is a value that is independent of a person's social status and utility, and it is not to be exchanged for anything with merely conditional value.[36] Negatively, it is a value against which we must never act; and yet, positively, we take the conception of humanity as an end-in-itself fully to heart only if we try to make the (permissible) ends of others our own (pp. 230–231 [4:430], pp. 237–238 [4:437–438]).[37]

2.2. Questions of Interpretation

The humanity formula, like the previous ones, has been interpreted in a variety of ways. One question is whether the formula has any independent action-guiding content. Obviously, it would not if the test for our treating humanity as an end were simply that we could will the maxim of such treatment as universal law.[38] Similarly, if the formula meant no more than "Respect persons' rights and give them moral consideration due to human beings," then it would obviously give no guidance unless supplemented with an independent account of rights and due consideration. Some commentators maintain that the formula offers nothing substantial beyond the formula of universal law.[39] Others take the humanity formula to be Kant's basic action-guiding principle, the first principle of morals from which all duties are derivable.[40] Most commentators, however, take an intermediate position, granting that the humanity formula at least adds significantly to our understanding of Kant's basic criteria or procedures for deciding what is right.[41]

Some accounts focus on whether our *purposes can be shared* by those affected by our acts;[42] but others take the key to be a relatively substantive idea of *human dignity*;[43] and still others construe the formula as primarily an imperative to *respect persons*.[44] The apparent differences here are no doubt to some extent matters of emphasis, but some not entirely.

More specifically, the first line of interpretation draws heavily from Kant's claim that we must treat ends-in-themselves as "beings who must themselves be able to share in" our end in acting (Kant, 2002, p. 230 [4:430]). The point, surely, is not that we may do something to others only if they actually share our purpose in doing it, for (as Kant suggests) on this basis a criminal could object to the just sentence a judge imposes. The idea, instead, may be that, before acting in ways that seriously affect others, we must look at our proposed act and purpose from the point of view of a reasonable recipient. We should not act as we propose if the recipient of our act *could not* will for us so to act, that is, could not endorse our so acting without contravening (presupposed) appropriate rational standards for endorsing others' treatment of oneself. On this reading, both the universal law formulas and the humanity formulas ask us, in effect, to assess whether a person could (reasonably, by some appropriate standard) endorse a maxim as a general policy. The universal law formulas focus attention on the perspective of a reasonable agent; the humanity formula directs us to the perspective of a reasonable recipient; but neither sort of reflection is simply about our actual preferences, as agents or recipients.[45]

The second type of interpretation treats the main point of the humanity formula to be an attribution of a special value (*dignity*) to *humanity*, or *rational nature* in human beings. When dignity is treated as a substantive value, this means placing a high priority (above "price") on the preservation, development, exercise, and honoring of our rational capacities.[46] One radical version of this idea treats dignity simply as a high-priority value in a "Kantian consequentialism" devoted to maximizing value.[47] More traditional readings treat dignity as a status of inviolability, not a value that can be quantified and weighed, but a worth to be respected, esteemed, and honored in all our actions. In one version, discussed hereafter, the reasons for acting based on the idea of human dignity are *expressive reasons*, concerned with what our acts *say* and *mean*.[48]

In *The Theory of Morality*, Alan Donagan develops the idea that the humanity formula is a comprehensive principle of respect for persons. Donagan dismisses

Kant's universal law formula as a nonsubstantive requirement of impartiality: That is, for a moral system legitimately to treat something as permissible for some persons and not others, there must be "a reasonable ground" in differences between the two groups or their circumstances (1977, pp. 58–59). The highest moral principle, he maintains, is his version of the humanity formula: "[I]t is impermissible not to respect every human being, oneself or any other, as a rational creature" (p. 66). Although granting that judgment is needed to determine specifically what such respect requires, Donagan argues we have enough common understanding of the phrase "respect . . . as rational" that, without appeal to independent moral principles, we can see that the formula condemns some acts and requires others. In fact, Donagan develops a system of fairly specific moral principles that, he claims, can be derived from the fundamental principle of respect. These draw from Kant's *Metaphysics of Morals*, but modify it considerably.[49] The principles express quite stringent requirements regarding promise-keeping, truthtelling, suicide, murder, use of force, development of talents, beneficence, and various institutional obligations. These principles contain qualifications within them but are not merely prima facie duties. To treat human beings with due respect, we must strictly comply with all the principles. Even to promote a very good end, we must never use means that violate the principles. We may, however, find ourselves in a moral dilemma because of previous wrongdoing, and then, though we will be acting wrongly no matter what we do, we must do the lesser of evils (pp. 143–149; 1984, pp. 291–309; 1993, pp. 7–21). The humanity formula, Donagan argues, sharply opposes the consequentialist doctrine of negative responsibility: that is, the idea that we are just as responsible for not preventing bad outcomes as for bringing them about directly through our actions. In fact, regarding Bernard Williams's famous story, Donagan thought it absolutely wrong for Jim to kill one innocent Indian to prevent Pedro from killing nineteen others.[50]

Alan Wood also understands the humanity formula as a principle of respect, though Wood holds that all of Kant's formulas should be taken together as a system. He agrees with Donagan that the humanity formula serves a crucial guide for moral judgment and that it is superior, in several ways, to the universal law formulas.[51] Like Donagan, Wood also thinks that some specific act-guiding principles can be derived deductively from the humanity formula when it is understood as a principle of respect for human dignity. We need intermediate premises specifying what it is to respect dignity in different contexts, but he argues that these are empirical and hermeneutical premises, not independent moral principles (1999, p. 154). Since the basic requirement is always to respect humanity in persons, we need intermediate premises specifying the *meaning* expressed by acts in various circumstances. The premises needed in Kant's arguments against suicide and false promises, for example, say that, for various reasons, suicide expresses disrespect for humanity in oneself and making false promises expresses disrespect for another person. Typically, we express disrespect, not by altogether ignoring

the dignity of other persons, but by considering our own worth superior to others'
or by valuing things of mere *price* above human *dignity*. In Wood's view, there
are no algorithms or decision procedures for interpreting the expressive meaning
of acts, but we can give reasons for our judgments about this. Kant's humanity
formula was not intended to resolve all moral problems directly but to provide a
"correct framework" for deliberating about and discussing moral problems
(pp. 154–155).

2.3. Illustration Regarding Helping Others

Donagan's treatment of beneficence is typical of his Kantian theory. If we respect
persons as rational creatures, we will "take satisfaction in their achieving the well-
being they seek, and will further their efforts" as far as we prudently can. So "it
is impermissible not to promote the well-being of others by actions in themselves
permissible, inasmuch as we can do so without proportionate inconvenience"
(Donagan, 1977, p. 85). The ground is not that they deserve it, but that to refuse
would be to fail to respect for them as rational creatures. Proper respect, in
Donagan's view, requires us to promote the well being or "human flourishing" of
others,[52] especially those who, for various reasons, cannot help themselves.[53] Two
qualifications are important: it is wrong to promote others' well-being by means
that are disrespectful of any rational person, and to promote others' well-being
by sacrificing equal or greater goods for ourselves is not required but supererogatory (p. 86). Beneficence, based on respect, also requires "preventing what might
harm others or frustrate their permissible projects, and abstaining from actions
that would foreseeably elicit responses by which others would be injured" (p. 85).
In general, we are required to make it our policy to promote permissible ends of
others when there is no disproportionate inconvenience; but in those cases where
only we can help another in serious need, without disproportionate sacrifice, then
helping that person is morally mandatory.

Wood's treatment of beneficence is similar in some respects, but emphasizes
the *meaning expressed* by helping or not helping others. In his view, "the reason
that we should help others in need is that we thereby *exhibit* proper esteem for
their worth as rational beings" (1999, p. 149, emphasis added). Because of this, he
argues, "rugged individualists" who want no one to be charitable cannot rationally
will this as a universal policy, because this would entail willing that others "show
contempt" for their humanity if they should fall into dire need (p. 150). Presumably, not helping others in many circumstances would not show contempt for
them, and so the duty to aid others is limited in various ways. Only when not
helping is disrespectful of their humanity is it morally mandatory, and this is a
matter of interpretation.

2.4. Problems and Doubts

Disputes about which interpretations best explain Kant's texts may be endless. For present purposes, I want merely to call attention a few potential problems in different ways of developing and relying on Kant's humanity formula.

First, and perhaps most obviously, the formula presents an ideal that is important and inspiring but far from a determinate, precise decision procedure. Virtually all commentators acknowledge this to some extent, but some (for example, Donagan) may have more confidence than warranted in our ability to agree on what specifically "respecting a person as rational" implies for a wide range of cases. This becomes more of a problem the more the humanity formula is taken to be a self-standing guide to decision in all particular cases or by itself a fully determinate first premise for justifying strict moral rules.

Second, if we treat the humanity formula, as Donagan and others do, as primarily about relatively simple, self-contained interpersonal exchanges, we risk missing relevant moral considerations that arise from the larger context. What seems on the surface to be a disrespectful way to treat one person (e.g., a lie) may have ramifications regarding others that could justify it from a perspective that is concerned with how best to express equal respect for all persons. From that perspective, even the person deceived might approve the general policy that would allow exceptions to the duty of truth-telling for that occasion. Exclusive focus on what is intuitively respectful in the narrower context of person-to-person interactions leads readily to apparent dilemmas in which, so far as we can tell, all of our options are forbidden.[54] Arguably, however, we can make progress on some of these problems if we treat the humanity formula as an evaluative attitude mandated first and foremost for our deliberations about general moral principles and policies in the light of the many complex factors that may be relevant.[55]

Third, the more the humanity formula is understood to express substantive, "thick," and controversial values, the harder will be the task of arguing convincingly that everyone, despite cultural and individual differences, has good reasons to accept it. Sometimes, of course, it is hard to convince everyone of propositions that are nevertheless true and backed by good reasons, and so a strong burden of proof is not the same as disproof. Nevertheless, arguably, both Donagan's stringent nonconsequentialist "Kantian" rules and Cummiskey's "Kantian" consequentialism present the humanity formula as essentially committed to (opposite) sides of some issues about which reasonable persons disagree. For example, even with its (Kant-inspired) value priorities, Cummiskey's Kantian consequentialism seems open to the familiar objection that there are conflicts between justice and what promotes the best consequences. Similarly, Donagan's (relatively) inflexible principles apparently would require, in certain emergency situations, refusal to protect lives and other Kantian values by extraordinary means that reasonable persons might rightly (but reluctantly) approve. Donagan more nearly captures Kant's own particular moral beliefs, but these are not necessarily implicit in the humanity formula or correctly derivable from it. Both substantive theories have the burden of defending *why* some apparently reasonable common moral judgments are wrong.

Finally, apart from this, there is philosophical reason, as well as textual evidence, for treating Kant's supreme moral principle (in all its versions) as describing an essential framework for moral deliberation and discussion rather than as an independent and determinate guide, as some have assumed.[56] In a world of tragic cultural and individual conflicts, moral philosophy needs to articulate a point of view from which, despite substantial differences, human beings can work together toward reasonable, mutually acceptable principles and policies. This purpose is defeated if a theory *too readily* renders judgment on a wide range of controversial moral issues. This is not to say that a moral theory should not in the end sharply condemn certain conventional moralities. The point is that moral theorists should be careful not to unduly allow their own strong moral convictions about particular issues to shape their ideas about what is essential to a moral point of view. If, as Kant thought, morality concerns what reasonable persons can accept, despite diversities, then accounts of the basics of morality should leave room for diversity and reasonable disagreement regarding many particular situations.

3. A Kantian Legislative Perspective

3.1. The Formulas of Autonomy and a Kingdom of Ends

Kant's next two formulas are closely related. In fact, Kant did not even distinguish them in his review of formulas. The *first*, commonly called the formula of autonomy, is initially characterized as "the Idea of *the will of every rational being as a will that legislates universal law*" (Kant, 2002, p. 232 [4:431]). The point, evidently, is that we must *always act in ways compatible* with this idea. The context makes clear that Kant conceives the rational law giving in question as not motivated by inclinations and desires. There are some differences of interpretation among commentators, especially as the abstract formula of autonomy is reexpressed through the somewhat fuller idea of a kingdom of ends (pp. 233–234 [4:433]). The following points, however, seem fairly clear.

The independence of desires and inclinations that the formula attributes to rational lawmakers is not a total lack of motivating dispositions. It would be absurd to think of them as legislating while "caring" about nothing. All rational agents have ends; this is inherent in the very idea of a rational agent. In addition to whatever (rationally) contingent ends they may have as individuals, rational agents as such are (allegedly) disposed to acknowledge a rationally necessary ("objective") end-in-itself, which is "humanity" or "rational nature." In Kant's view, unlike Hume's, reason is not "inert." Kant holds that "pure reason can be practical": That is, rational agents as such, independently of contingent inclinations, are supposed to be necessarily committed to basic noninstrumental, action-guiding principles, expressed in the formulas of the Categorical Imperative. The values inherent in this commitment can be a motivating factor, independently of our desire-based ends.[57]

In addition, although Kant's claim that there can be rational law-giving not motivated by inclinations is controversial, it does not imply the process takes place in complete *ignorance* of human inclinations. Rational agents with autonomy are lawmakers in some respects like ideal secular or divine legislators, though their "laws" are not legal requirements backed by threats of punishment but rather moral principles endorsed for themselves (as well as for others). Rational legislators of universal laws do not choose their laws as a means to satisfying their own special inclinations, but, at some stage, they must take into account the conditions under which the laws will be applied. All of the formulas of the Categorical Imperative are supposed to express basic objective principles the rationality of which does not depend on contingent human conditions, but none can be applied to particular human situations without some knowledge of that situation and general facts about our world. Many particular facts may prove to be irrelevant to a given judgment, but the formulas cannot guide us to any particular judgment until we consider the context of application.

Rational lawmakers are supposed to give themselves laws as rational wills with *autonomy*. This implies that they are committed to standards of rational choice beyond hypothetical imperatives. They do not merely acknowledge the rationality of taking necessary means to their desired ends; they have over-riding rational standards of the form "One ought to do X, and not just because it promotes one's desire-based ends." They have the capacity and predisposition to act on principles that are not based on their desires as individuals. Further, all such principles are ultimately grounded in rational requirements (expressed in the Categorical Imperative) that are independent of all rationally contingent features of human nature. Human moral agents, being imperfectly rational, do not always live up to these principles that express their autonomy of will, but inevitably, Kant thought, they at least implicitly acknowledge the principles as standards that should override any conflicting claims of inclination. In extremely immoral persons, this acknowledgement may be more evident in their pangs of conscience than in any resolution to reform; but if some people lack it completely, this (in Kant's view) would indicate that either they lack the capacity for practical reason or (like very young children) they have not developed it.[58]

The idea of autonomy implies further that the legislators' laws are, in a sense, *self-imposed*. We need to distinguish here basic principles that are constitutive of rational agency from the more specific "laws" that the rational legislators are supposed to give to themselves. The former presumably include the other forms of the Categorical Imperative, the hypothetical imperative, and any other principles necessary to rationally consistent and coherent choice. The latter are the more specific moral principles that, given appropriate facts, rational legislators (who are committed to those basic standards) would adopt for specified (e.g., human) conditions. (The *Groundwork* is primarily devoted to the basic principles, and *The Metaphysics of Morals* is primarily devoted to intermediate level principles or "laws" for human conditions.) We cannot coherently think of the rational legislators as "making" and "giving themselves" the basic rational standards that constitute their rationality. Nevertheless, their autonomy implies that they *identify* themselves with these constitutive standards rather than seeing them as externally imposed and alien. When their reasoning according to the standards leads to a particular judgment, then they regard it as the result of their own judgment. The more specific "laws" that the legislators make can be understood as *given to themselves by themselves* in a further sense that is represented in the idea of a kingdom of ends. Here for good reasons, all rational legislators endorse the same general laws for everyone, and they are subject only to laws that they all endorse as legislators. In a sense, then, they legislate for themselves rather seeing laws as given to them by nature, tradition, or divine command.[59]

Kant does not give examples to show how the formula of autonomy might be applied. Instead, he develops its core idea into a *second* formula expanding the idea of autonomy, the kingdom-of-ends formula. This appears in his review of the formulas as a "complete determination of all maxims": "*All maxims which stem from autonomous lawgiving are to harmonize with a possible kingdom of ends as with a kingdom of nature*" (Kant, 2002, p. 237 [4:436]). A kingdom of ends is "a systematic union of different rational beings under common laws" (p. 234 [4: 433]). It is an ideal analogue of a political state or commonwealth in which rational members make all of the laws to which they are subject. The members have "private ends," but in conceiving of the kingdom of ends we "abstract" from their content as well as from other "personal differences" among the members (p. 234 [4:433]). The kingdom has a nominal sovereign or head that makes the same laws without being subject to them. Because the sovereign (a "holy will") lacks needs and inclinations that might interfere with rational choice, the laws of the kingdom do not appear as *imperatives* or *obligations* for the sovereign (p. 240 [4:439]).[60] Other (human) members are subject to obligation because, though subject to contrary inclinations, they too are committed to the same rational principles. The sovereign is conceived as having "unlimited resources adequate to his will." It may help to motivate us, Kant thought, to think of the kingdom of ends and the kingdom of nature as united under this same sovereign (pp. 234–235 [4:434], pp. 239–240 [4:439]). The kingdom of ends, Kant says, would become actual if everyone always followed its laws, but we are still obligated to follow the laws of a possible kingdom of ends in our world, where obviously not everyone does so (pp. 238–239 [4:438]).

3.2. Interpretative Issues

There are a number of questions about how to interpret these formulas. For example, how are they related to the preceding formulas? In his review of formulas, Kant suggests that the universal law formula is the best to use in judging maxims. The later formulas help to provide "access" to the moral law by bringing it "closer to intuition" and "feeling" (Kant, 2002, pp. 236–238, [4:436–437]). He also suggests, however, that the kingdom–of–ends formula combines ideas in the preceding ones and so provides the most "complete determination" of moral requirements on maxims (p. 237 [4:436]).[61] The former suggests that the main function of the kingdom–of–ends formula is to inspire and motivate us, but the latter suggests that it gives Kant's fullest characterization of the moral requirements on maxims and so, presumably, our most comprehensive action-guide.

Again, are we to think of all moral agents as members of the kingdom, or only those who show themselves worthy of it by acting morally? At one point, Kant suggests that the possible kingdom would become actual only if we all did our duty; but later he suggests that it would become a "true reality" only if God were sovereign of both nature and the kingdom of ends, thereby ensuring that the permissible ends of the virtuous would be fulfilled (Kant, 2002, pp. 238–240 [4:438–439]). For practical purposes, however, what matters is *what we as rational members would legislate*, not whether we think of ourselves and others as actually or merely possibly belonging to the kingdom of ends.

The most important interpretative question, especially for later development of Kantian ethics, concerns how the members in the kingdom make their laws. Kant's political metaphors suggest an ideal legislature in which all citizens are free and rational legislators and (except for the sovereign) bound by the laws that they make. As legislators, they share the same rational dispositions and values (e.g., humanity as an end-in-itself). Since the model abstracts from their personal differences and the content of their private ends, the laws that one legislator would endorse are just the same as the laws that each other would endorse. Nonetheless, the picture is that of joint legislation by and for all members. Their agreement results, as it were, from the fact that they acknowledge the same reasons and cannot be sidetracked by private concerns not shared or recognized by others. Here "abstracting" from differences functions, rather like Rawls's "veil of ignorance," to guarantee impartiality at the highest level of moral deliberation (1971, pp. 11, 17, 188–223). On this reading, the kingdom-of-ends formula would tell us always to conform to those laws that we would make as members of this ideal moral legislature. The legislature would differ in significant ways from real legislatures. For example, the legislators do not make coercive laws backed by sanctions; their jurisdiction includes (at least initially) all rational agents;[62] the legislators are not bound by independent obligations or subject to external pressures; they never legislate irrationally; and so on.

Some passages, however, suggest a different picture. Here we imagine a possible world in which everyone conforms to the universal law formula, acting only on maxims that they can will as universal law. The outcome, we are to suppose, would be a harmonious system of ends, with no one being treated as a mere means and everyone having a chance to pursue their permissible ends without undue interference. Since there is no legislature in this picture, arguably there is no need to ignore personal differences to ensure impartiality. The "laws" of the kingdom would be identified as individuals tested their maxims and found that certain ones could not be willed as universal law. "Never kill people for profit," for example, would be a law if no one could will a proposed maxim of killing for profit as a universal law. This interpretation allows the universal law formula to do the work of moral assessment, leaving for the kingdom-of-ends formula the role of an inspiring idea of the outcome if we all would do our part.[63]

3.3. A Legislative Model for Deliberation about Moral Rules

On close examination, the texts remain ambiguous, and they leave many questions open. On the last interpretation, however, the kingdom of ends offers no new practical guide to deliberation and it inherits all of the problems of applying the universal law formulas. Arguably, however, by construing the kingdom of ends instead as an idealized model of moral legislation and then extending this idea, we can take Kantian ethics (broadly conceived) in a different, and perhaps more promising direction. The inspiration for the project comes from John Rawls's theory of justice, although Rawls himself interprets Kant rather differently.[64]

The project presupposes that we can distinguish fundamental Kantian values from less basic rules and principles concerned with particular areas of the moral life. From the former, drawn primarily from versions of the Categorical Imperative, we would try to construct a conception of the perspective from which we should reflect about more specific rules and principles, how to articulate them, what qualifications they should contain, and so on. We would think of more basic values as constituting, for purposes of the theory, the essentials of an ideal point of view for trying to work out with others what moral demands and limits should be included in our principles concerned, for example, with obedience to the law, property rights, just punishment, gratitude, beneficence, respect, and friendship. It should not be assumed, of course, that we need specific principles or rules for all areas of life. Working toward common, well-defined standards is important in some areas; but in others, we may do better simply to approach problems with a good attitude and sensitivity to the context. In addition, the principles, if any, that we can justify as reasonable independently of historical context may be few and indeterminate in ways that leave much room for interpretation and judgment. In any case, despite what Kant himself thought, the best we can do may be to use the basic deliberative perspective to work on problems that arise in the more circumscribed conditions in which we now live.[65] Reasonable principles for familiar circumstances may be applicable more generally, but extending them is impossible unless we understand the other contexts well enough to see that there are no relevant differences.

Although we might expect that actual people who take up the deliberative perspective could agree on some general principles that rather directly reflect their constitutive values, we cannot expect that they would always agree. Agreement on fundamental values does not ensure unanimity on how these can be best implemented in various situations. Differences in judgment and in understanding of background facts are bound to result in disagreements on particular moral issues. The legislative perspective may still be useful, however, as a standard for conscientious action. That is, we can think of conscientious action as doing whatever, after due deliberation and dialogue with others, we judge should be required by principles adopted from the legislative perspective. We would need to consider what we would recommend for universal approval if we were debating the matter from the legislative perspective. Then, as conscientious persons, we should follow this, keeping in mind that others may reasonably disagree.

The Kantian legislative perspective suggested by the kingdom-of-ends formula combines ideas from Kant's other formulas. *First*, as legislators, we deliberate by assessing whether we can reasonably endorse various general policies, considered as principles for everyone. Thus we must move beyond the narrower point of view that we take when first inclined to act in a certain way and consider how things would be if we endorsed moral principles permitting everyone to act that way. In doing, so we need not identify precisely "the maxim" of each act, but instead can review systematically sets of permissive, prohibitive, and obligatory principles together. Although our maxim might be described in any of several ways, our act will be wrong if, under any description, it is incompatible with the principles that we would endorse from the legislative perspective.

Second, legislators who acknowledge each other as ends-in-themselves would have to deliberate with the constraints and values, whatever these may be, inherent in the idea of humanity as an end-in-itself. Because the legislators have "private ends" but "abstract from differences," they must generally favor conditions that further the members' ends, but their law-making should not be influenced by partiality for their own ends in particular. In addition, arguably, the value of humanity as an end motivates them to place a high priority on members' survival, development, and opportunities to live as rational agents. More abstractly, the value of humanity is reflected in their unwillingness to engage in conduct that they could not, from the legislative perspective, justify to other members. This motivating disposition to treat humanity in each person as an end would be considered not merely a contingent desire but rather a disposition inherent in rational nature.

Third, the idea of autonomy is reflected in the stipulation that the legislators are subject to no laws or principles other than those they themselves rationally endorse. They do not endorse principles merely because tradition, the state, or God sanctions them. They endorse some fundamental rational constraints and values, such as humanity as an end, simply because these express their nature as rational persons. They endorse more specific moral principles, such as beneficence and fidelity, because these principles prescribe conduct that expresses, secures, or promotes their basic values in the context of our complex empirical world. The idea of autonomy is also reflected in the stipulation that, when deliberating, legislators set aside inappropriate partiality toward their own special ends. Further, valuing other persons as (at least potentially) autonomous colegislators of the moral standards that govern our mutual relations has implications regarding specifically how we are to respect them as persons.

3.4. Illustration: Meeting Needs and Doing Favors

The Kantian legislative perspective sketched here is obviously not yet an adequate normative ethical theory, much less a complete one. Let us, however, overlook for now remaining gaps and problems and return, instead, to the example of beneficence. From a Kantian legislative perspective, how might we think about grounds and limits of our obligation to help others? Let us consider what general duty we should attribute to everyone, acknowledging that special circumstances are likely to call for more or less than any general principles can anticipate.[66]

Consider several candidates regarding the general obligation to help others in need. (1) We should always help those in need when we can, whether they have a right to it or not. (2) Helping others in need is morally optional, except when they have a right to demand it. (3) We should help others with basic needs, at least when their need is great and the cost to us is proportionately small. As legislators concerned to work out a reasonable system of moral principles, we might at once see that all of the principles need to be qualified by adding (a) *except that helping is generally wrong when their need is for resources to complete immoral projects and* (b) *except that it is wrong when we can only help by immoral means.* "Immoral" here would have to be determined by other, higher priority principles that the legislators have adopted. On further reflection, we might see that what others need to survive, develop, and thrive as rational autonomous agents (i.e., "basic needs") should take priority over what they need to accomplish projects based only on personal preference. This seems implicit in valuing rational nature as an end-in-itself, at least on substantive interpretations. Especially within the first category, it seems that the greater the need, other things equal, the more reason to help. Given this, we might realize that the same priority applies equally well to the agent's own needs. Thus, we should not in general disregard our urgent basic needs merely to help others in minor, optional projects. Thus the first candidate (1), even amended with (a) and (b), would be unacceptable, because it ignores the agent's own needs and potential differences in the kind and degree of need. If amended to take these factors into account, (1) would look more like (3).

We cannot evaluate (2) properly without first deciding what help persons can demand as their right. This would have to be a prior issue to take up from the legislative perspective, but let us assume for now that familiar intuitions about this are right. In general, since rights are enforceable claims, presumably moral legislators would want to express and promote their values not only by assigning individual rights but also by adopting principles that call upon conscientious persons to do more for others than they can demand by right.[67] If so, candidate principle (2) would be unacceptable. It implies that, beyond doing what we can rightfully be coerced to do, we may do as we please, ignoring all the needs of others, no matter how great these are and no matter how little it would cost us to help. If everyone, even everyone so inclined, were to act that way, then the prospects of everyone to live a full life as a rational, autonomous person would be diminished. Secure, wealthy individuals might calculate that they are likely to be better off under (2) than (3), but they could not justify that idea to others, or themselves, if they took up the legislative point of view that abstracts from personal differences and views humanity in each person as an end.

The third candidate (3), by contrast, seems quite promising. If this principle (at least) is endorsed, then, given the uncertainties of human life, the prospects of every representative person are better in ways that matter to rational legislators. The main question about (3) is whether it is too minimal a requirement, and so needs to be supplemented with further principles regarding helping.

Two supplements, at least, seem to be appropriate from the legislative perspective. First, because (3) addresses only cases where we could help others whose needs are great and basic to rational, autonomous living, we need some general principle about helping others whose needs are not as urgent and fundamental. We need to consider helping others in their personal projects: for example, doing favors rather than attempting to meet basic needs. As before, legislators will want to qualify any principle in this area by ruling out helping others in their immoral projects or by using immoral means, where immorality is defined by incompatibility with higher priority principles, already endorsed. Consider three candidate principles concerning helping others where great basic needs are not involved: (4) Help others whenever you can, unless fulfilling some other duty. (5) Helping others is entirely optional, assuming that you fulfill your other duties. (6) Make it an end of yours that others realize their (permissible) ends; and so, to some significant extent, contribute to others' (permissible) ends as well as your own.

A problem with (4) is that it fails to acknowledge the importance, from the legislative perspective, of the agent's own personal ends. To be sure, (4) implies that others should help the helper, and so the helper's ends are not totally ignored. However, (4) also unreasonably implies that, other duties aside, each person should help to promote others' ends, irrespective of the cost to the person's own projects. Thus, everyone would have to sacrifice their very important projects whenever they could permissibly help someone else on a relatively minor project. The principle must at least be adjusted to require only sacrificing opportunities to promote one's own projects when, all considered, helping others instead would contribute proportionately more to others' equally or more highly valued projects. Even amended this way, (4) is still a far more demanding requirement than most people could accept. Unless we are working to satisfy other duties, it requires us to drop whatever we are doing whenever an opportunity presents itself to work on another person's personal project, provided only the other person cares slightly more about his or her project than we care about ours. A readiness to do so might seem saintly, in some respects, but, given the limits of human nature, it seems more than could reasonably be expected of everyone. In addition, being constantly "on call" to help others who are not in urgent or vital need would make it difficult, if not impossible, to structure a life with meaningful personal projects of one's own, which is something that presumably rational autonomous agents would value.

Given that rational agents necessarily set themselves and pursue ends, candidate principle (5) arguably expresses an attitude incompatible with valuing rational agency in each person as an end-in-itself. It implies that we may ignore the (permissible) projects of others, no matter how much the others care about them and no matter how insignificant the inconvenience of helping would be to ourselves. If everyone, or even those so inclined, always acted in this way, everyone's prospects, considered from the legislative perspective, would be worse than if they adopted candidate principle (6). Some fortunately situated individuals might prosper, but legislators respecting humanity in each person equally would not cater to their special advantages. Arguably they would acknowledge the worth of all as rational, autonomous persons by requiring everyone to aid others in personal projects, to some significant extent, but leaving a wide latitude for choice (apart from the requirement regarding basic needs) as to when, how, and exactly how much to help. Principle (6) is just this sort of requirement, for it tells us to include it among our important ends that others also fulfill their (permissible) personal ends.

From the Kantian perspective, persons have a status of "unconditional and incomparable worth" that is acknowledged in practice by conforming to the "laws" to which they all, as rational and autonomous legislators, would agree. They are "equal," in that they have the same status under the moral law, no one being intrinsically more important than any other, and each person being inviolable in ways determined by the principles everyone mutually endorses. This equal standing under the moral law is quite different from the sort of equality that classic utilitarians prescribe. Equality for them is equal consideration (or "weight") for equal pleasures and pains, no matter whose they are. That idea is not part of the Kantian picture, and, as is often noted, following it could lead to exploiting and oppressing a few for the greater pleasure of many. Kantian legislators are not utility-maximizing legislators but are constrained by their acknowledgment of a worth of individual persons that cannot be quantified, weighed, or traded for "more" value. The specific implications of this idea still need to be worked out, but it clearly implies that Kantian legislators do not have the authority to prescribe *whatever* is predicted to produce a maximum quantity of some comparable and conditional value, such as pleasure, satisfaction, and the like. Further, rejecting the idea that they must measure, compare, and produce the greatest quantity of happiness, Kantian legislators need not even require the qualified principle "You must always help others whenever other duties allow and others would gain more happiness than you would lose by helping." By contrast, the more indeterminate principle (6) expresses respect for all persons by valuing their (permissible) ends without so restrictively dictating precisely when and how much time and energy to devote to helping others, beyond the requirement regarding basic needs (3).

3.5. Remaining Problems

These last comments are meant merely to illustrate how reflection on a Kantian legislative perspective might proceed. Further considerations are no doubt relevant, and in any case the legislative perspective has not been defined fully enough to permit more than rather loose, informal argument. In addition, my discussion has concerned only the general principle of beneficence, not special requirements in specific circumstances. All attempts to reconstruct Kant's basic normative standard must work out remaining problems and address various objections. The proposed idea of a Kantian legislative perspective is obviously no exception. For example, we need to consider further the importance and limits of rules and principles for a moral life. The appropriate degree and kind of "abstracting from personal differences" needs to be clarified, especially as this may vary with the context and scope of the problem to be addressed. Different ways of understanding the central value of humanity as an end-in-itself need to be clarified and assessed. Any other presupposed standards of "rational" and "reasonable" willing need to be articulated explicitly. Special problems are raised when we try to use and adjust principles for different social and economic conditions. If we insist on quite simple, inflexible principles appropriate for an idealized world, we may unreasonably ignore morally relevant differences between those conditions and the real world. If we bend and adjust principles too readily to accommodate special circumstances, there would be no point in having principles. It would be madness to insist that the consequences of adopting a principle never matter, but it must be clear how and within what limits reflection on consequences is appropriate from a Kantian legislative perspective. We also need to address suspicions that trying to construct principles from an ideal perspective complicates moral judgment needlessly and alienates us from our more particular moral perspective in daily life.[68] Much can be said in response to these problems, but whether the problems ultimately undermine the promise of this approach to Kantian normative theory remains to be seen.

NOTES

1. For example, are moral judgments based on reason or sentiment? What does it mean to say that something *ought* to be done? What distinguishes moral from nonmoral "ought" claims? Do moral predicates refer to properties that are objective and real? Are they empirically accessible natural properties or constructs of some kind? The terms we use in our contemporary discussions are often different from Kant's, but Kant clearly had positions and arguments that are relevant to these issues. Some may doubt that metaethical and normative questions can be separated and answered independently, but I will proceed as if they can be usefully addressed, at least to some extent, as separate matters. My project, then, is to survey Kantian answers to the normative questions, leaving aside for now questions about how these are related to other issues.

2. My discussion of beneficence here, though inevitably sketchy, may help in a small way to fill a gap in my previous accounts of the duty of beneficence in Kantian ethics. See my *Human Welfare and Moral Worth: Kantian Perspectives*, 2002, chs. 3, 5, 7. The last of these essays, "Meeting Needs and Doing Favors," addresses the recent controversy over whether this duty to promote others' happiness should be interpreted as a very stringent ("rigoristic" or "robust") requirement or as a quite limited ("minimal" or "anemic") requirement. Following H. J. Paton and Mary Gregor, I argued earlier that the duty to promote the happiness of others, at least as presented in Kant's fullest account of it in *The Metaphysics of Morals*, 1991a, is a minimal requirement. David Cummiskey and, to some extent, Marcia Baron have argued that the requirement is more

stringent. My contention is that, unsurprisingly, we find a modest beneficence requirement in *The Metaphysics of Morals*, for that work is supposed to describe duties in the most general way appropriate for all human conditions. A modest general requirement makes good moral sense, however, only if there is a plausible way to argue from basic principles that in various special circumstances helping others is not optional. By using beneficence as my example when I survey applications of Kant's basic moral principle(s), I can show various ways in which Kantians can argue from the Categorical Imperative to this conclusion. These arguments may help to fill the gap in my previous defense of the minimal interpretation of the general principle of beneficence, for, if successful, they would supplement Kant's minimal general principle with Kantian grounds for judging that in many cases, giving aid to others is strictly required. See Baron, 1995, and Cummiskey, 1996.

3. Numbers in brackets refer to the corresponding volume and page numbers in the standard Prussian Academy edition.

4. Wood, 1999, pp. 363–365 plausibly suggests that some of Kant's statements that are commonly taken to be versions of FUL are in fact expressions of his later formula of autonomy.

5. Later Kant restricts the term to the "material principles" that agents act on, i.e., principles based on their (nonrational) desires. See Kant, *Critique of Practical Reason* (hereafter abbreviated CPrR), 1997, pp. 17–19 (5:19–22).

6. Kant's own examples are not uniform in structure. They usually describe the act and indicate its purpose but only sometimes state a separate reason or motive. In Kant's suicide example, 2002, p. 223 (4:422), the act is suicide, the purpose to end pain (when life promises no more compensating pleasures), and the underlying reason or motive is "self-love."

7. O'Neill, 1989, p. 84, makes a case that the maxims that should be tested are "underlying principles or intentions by which we guide and control our more specific intentions." This suggestion that they express our more general, fundamental life commitments is in line with Kant's suggestion in CPrR that all nonmoral maxims fall under "the general principle of self-love or one's happiness" (O'Neill, 1989, p. 84; Kant, 1997, p. 19 [5:22]). Kant himself does, however, use the universal law formulas to test examples that are more specific.

8. Here I set aside controversies about whether FUL proposes a test for maxims different from that proposed in FULN.

9. The reason for the first point is that, for purposes of her deliberation, the maxim must reflect the agent's understanding of what she is doing (and why). (Kant often suggests that we cannot know with certainty what maxims we were really acting on in the past, but in deliberating about what to do next we must assume that we will act on whatever maxim that we adopt after due reflection.) The second point stems from the fact the very purpose of trying to articulate our maxims is to determine for ourselves whether it is morally all right to act as we are inclined to. It would defeat our purpose to work with a phony maxim that not even we ourselves see as accurately reflecting what we intend to do, our reasons, and factors we count as morally relevant. Suppose you plan to gain political power to serve your ethnic community but you know that taking the necessary means will harm many innocent people. A maxim that omitted reference to the fact that your act would harm innocent people would not be the morally appropriate one to test. (This fact should turn out to be salient anyway,

when you try to conceive and will the world where everyone acts on your *unqualified* maxim to take the available means to help your ethnic community.) If the third point were ignored, the reasons we could will certain maxims as universal law might have nothing to do with their moral status. For example, one might (mistakenly) argue that because irrelevant details make unwelcome recurrences of the case unlikely, you might will as universal law the maxim "To convenience myself, I shall tell a lie to a bald, skinny, diabetic man on a Tuesday night with a full moon." If we dishonestly include morally irrelevant detail or omit salient moral considerations, the universal law tests are likely to give morally inappropriate results. However, the apparent need to make judgments of moral relevance before applying the universal law tests poses a problem for those who think that the tests are sufficient by themselves to determine right and wrong. Herman, 1993, addresses this problem at length.

10. The sort of limits I have in mind may be expressed, for example, in the maxim "I will refuse a government order to do something *if what was ordered was contrary to an already established perfect ethical duty* (such as to bear false witness in court)." This is a qualification or limit that Kant acknowledged (1991a, p. 98 [6:322], pp. 136–137 [6:371]; 1998, p. 153 n. [6:154 n.]). Despite what Kant himself thought, it seems only reasonable that the maxim of person who wants to help an innocent friend escape from a murderer might be "I will tell a lie *if it is told to someone who is threatening the life of an innocent person and if it is the only way, as far as I can tell, to prevent a murder.*"

11. That is, cannot be conceived as either a universal law or as a universal law of nature (if that is different). For present purposes, I am setting aside the question whether the formulas offer two tests or only one.

12. Kant suggests that failure to pass the first (contradiction in conception) test indicates a violation of strict or "perfect" duty. Maxims that fail the second (contradiction in willing) test are bad maxims that we should not act on, but the general principles that we would violate by doing so are principles of "imperfect" duty. These require us, for example, to adopt the maxims to promote as ends the happiness of others and our own perfection. It is strictly a duty to adopt these maxims, but what we must do toward the prescribed ends is not specified in a determinate way.

13. The maxim as stated here is perhaps too simple and unqualified to be reasonably willed as a law for all circumstances. We may, for example, have conflicting obligations; others may be better positioned to provide the aid; etc. For now, I set aside such complications. For any explicit maxim, there will presumably be background conditions implicitly understood. Any attempt to defend the universal law formulas as satisfactory determinants of right and wrong would have to confront the problems these implicit background assumptions raise.

14. Suppose, instead, in considering not aiding accident victims (even though only I am available to help them), I describe my proposed maxim merely as "To save time, I will not make stops on my drives to work." Because this omits the morally salient fact that not stopping now may result in the death of innocent persons, the maxim may seem quite innocent, that is, one that we can conceive and will as universal law. Nevertheless, it seems clear that it would be wrong not to aid the injured persons. (Arguably, if the maxim I stated is intended as an inflexible policy, we should be able to see that it cannot be reasonably willed as a universal law, despite its innocent look; for, if we reflected carefully, we should be able to anticipate emergencies that will require exceptions.)

15. In favor of this interpretation is the fact that in the *Critique of Practical Reason* Kant suggests that the universal law formula can only be applied through a "typic," the idea of a natural order, that mediates between the abstract moral law and our concrete situation (1997, pp. 59–60 [5:69–70]). In addition, Kant's examples in the *Groundwork* all refer to laws of nature. Some evidence to the contrary is that Kant does not refer to laws of nature in the formula that (in his review of formulas, 2002, p. 237 [4:436–437]) he says is best to use in moral assessment. In addition, Kant sometimes gives examples that suggest that the relevant question is whether we can conceive and will our maxim as one that it is permissible for everyone to act on. (p. 204 [4:403]).

16. See Paton, 1958, chs. 14, 15. Under FUL, Paton says, we ask whether "we can will our maxim as an instance of a principle valid for all rational beings and not merely adopted arbitrarily for ourselves" (p. 146). With FULN, by contrast, "we put ourselves imaginatively in the position of the Creator and suppose that we are making a world of nature [i.e., a system of natural purposes] of which we are apart" (p. 146).

17. An example of this type of interpretation is developed by Pogge, 1998.

18. We must try to conceive everyone adopting the maxim and acting on it *in conditions where it is applicable.* The conditions should be given in the maxim, which has the form "In conditions C, I shall do X . . ." Presumably, when we conceive a maxim as a *universal law of nature*, we assume that some appropriate conditions will occur and so the maxim will be acted on. Otherwise, a maxim would pass the first test if, though no one could act on it, everyone could "adopt it" (perhaps in the form "In C, I shall X if I can"). To understand the test that way would undermine Kant's most persuasive example, that of a lying promise to repay a loan (Kant, 2002, p. 223 [4:422]).

19. Brandt, 1959, pp. 27–35, among others, noted this. An example would be the fact that people would generally remember those who did not repay loans and would be reluctant to trust those persons again.

20. Paton, 1958, pp. 146–156.

21. See Nell, 1975. In this early work, she maintains that one who wills a maxim thereby, if rational, wills the normal foreseeable consequences of what she wills. For example, if I will for everyone to adopt and act on my maxim to rob a bank for personal enrichment, then, if rational, I thereby also will the normal foreseeable consequence that bank security will become prohibitively tight. To will this, of course, is inconsistent with my original intention to enrich myself by bank robbery. I express some doubts about whether this account is satisfactory in my review of *Acting on Principle* (Hill, 1979).

22. Their argument would assume that the universal law formulas provide a sufficient, not merely necessary, condition of moral rightness. Wood, 1999, pp. 76–110, for one, argues that they do not provide such a criterion and were not meant to.

23. The term "rationally" has apparently acquired a narrower sense in our times than Kant's sense, which arguably encompasses more broadly what we might prefer to call "reasonable." Thus, in my view, Kant's test should be construed as about what we can rationally *and reasonably* endorse as universal policies. Adding the term suggests, not inappropriately in my view, that the reasons relevant to whether we can will maxims as universal law are not restricted to logical inconsistency and formally incompatible intentions. However, it would be contrary to the structure of Kant's moral theory simply to rely on intuition unrelated to any version of the Categorical Imperative for the standards of what can be reasonably willed as universal law.

24. Although as human beings we do not always "will" what we would if perfectly rational, Kant identifies our "will" with certain practical capacities we have as rational beings. He repeatedly says that acting on maxims that we cannot will as universal law implies "contradiction" or "conflict" in the will that would be absent if we were more fully rational.

25. For example, to argue that it is unreasonable to will a certain policy as universal law because that would undermine certain traditional values, we must independently show (by Kantian principles) that we ought to preserve those traditional values. Most contemporary Kantians seem to accept that all other moral norms must be "derived," at least in a broad sense, from the Categorical Imperative and noncontroversial principles of instrumental rationality, but one could treat Kant's principles as a merely as framework of general moral considerations that constrain all other moral considerations but need to be supplemented by them. We would naturally wonder, of course, what is the source of these other moral considerations, why we should accept them, and whether disagreements about them can be resolved.

26. Kant himself suggests that in ordinary cases we come to our moral problem already having a stock of relevant moral beliefs, and if so, what reflection on the universal law formulas may do is simply to highlight the discrepancy between these general beliefs (that we readily apply to others) and our own proposed action (Kant, 2002, pp. 224–225 [4:424]). Here, asking whether we can will our maxims as universal laws is a way of considering whether our proposed act fits ideas that we already have about what everyone may, and may not, do. Clearly, there is a "contradiction the will" of someone who, without good reason, makes herself an exception to general principles that she accepts as reasonable.

27. Singer, 1961, p. 235, for example, argues this.

28. Herman, as we shall see, has an argument against the miser that does not rely on the humanity formula, but I am not convinced that contemporary Kantians should follow her in this.

29. Here I follow roughly Herman's line of argument (1984, pp. 577–602).

30. Kant holds that it is a duty to adopt the maxim, not merely to aid those in distress, but more generally to promote the (permissible) ends of others. Regarding how much one must do to promote others' happiness, and when and to whom one must do it, however, the duty is not determinate. Beneficence is a "wide, imperfect" duty.

31. The latter implausibly stringent principle is a little-noticed consequence of Ross's famous system (1930, ch. 2) of "prima facie duties," at least as long you think of your own happiness as *yours* rather than thinking of it impartially as merely the good of some person. Cummiskey, 1996, esp. chs. 5, 6, argues that Kant is committed to a slightly weaker, but still incredibly stringent, principle of beneficence, namely, that, absent other duties, we must maximize the general good (including happiness and rational development), taking all persons (including yourself as one) into account.

32. Earlier I mentioned a few guidelines for constructing a maxim that may help to set aside certain counterexamples, but I doubt that, even if supplemented with other suggestions, such guidelines are sufficient.

33. To derive this more general duty from universal law formulas, it seems that we would need to show that unless we adopted a maxim of promoting the (permissible) ends of others, we would act on some maxims that we cannot will as universal law.

34. Kant apparently treated these expressions as equivalent, but it may matter

which expression is taken as primary. Kant frequently contrasts our humanity (or rational nature) with our animality, as different aspects of our nature as human beings. In his *Religion within the Boundaries of Mere Reason,* 1991b, he contrasts our animality with both our personality (or moral predisposition) and our humanity (other features of rational agency). Earlier I argued that we should understand the expression "treat rational nature in persons as an end in itself" as simply as saying more specifically what is meant by "treat persons as ends in themselves." It would be a mistake, however, to equate these with a command to do whatever promotes the greatest possible development and use of reason, for Kant is clear that an end-in-itself is not an end in the sense of a goal or something to be produced. See my 1980.

35. Not all commentators agree about whether the autonomy that grounds human dignity is our capacity and disposition to morality (i.e., giving ourselves moral laws as standards) or the actual realization of this capacity (i.e., willing always to conform to the moral law). Most commentators favor the former interpretation, but some passages suggest the latter. See Dean, 1996, pp. 266–288.

36. Since dignity is "above price," it obviously cannot be legitimately exchanged or sacrificed for commodities or pleasures; but, apparently though less obviously, Kant means that dignity has no "equivalent" even among other things with dignity. Thus, insofar as persons have dignity, they have an incalculable value that prohibits justifying one violation of human dignity by the thought that it would prevent two or more similar violations. This does not necessarily imply, however, that when we cannot save everyone's life in an emergency it would be wrong to do what would save more rather than fewer lives. I discuss this problem in my 1992c.

37. There is an often-noted tension between these passages, because the first tells us that ends-in-themselves are to be conceived only negatively, while the second prescribes a "positive agreement" with the idea.

38. See Singer, 1961.

39. See Singer, 1961, p. 235. See also Wolff, 1973, p. 176.

40. This is the position of Donagan, 1977, pp. 57–74. Donagan, however, does not claim that the first principle is self-evident or indubitable. In a rational ethical theory principles can be presented in hierarchical form, representing more specific principles as deductive conclusions from more abstract and comprehensive higher level principles; but, in considering reasons to accept the system, we may have initially more confidence in the more specific intermediate principles. Thus we may treat the fact that the "first principle" leads to just these principles, and not to conclusions we find unacceptable, as some confirmation that the first principle, as stated, is correct. See Donagan, 1993. Wood gives the humanity formula a crucial "grounding" role in his interpretation of Kant's basic ethical theory, but does not give it as exclusive a role as Donagan does. See Wood, 1999, pp. 111–155.

41. There are as variety of possible views of this sort. For example, one may think that the humanity formula only makes explicit what was presupposed in the formula of universal law, thus helping to clarify or interpret it. One may think that they are independent principles that are at best practically equivalent, in that they yield the same conclusions about cases. Or one may think that these two formulas each express certain aspects of a more comprehensive principle that is expressed in a later formula (or must be constructed from all of the formulas). The latter is more or less the position I propose as a reconstruction, but not strict interpretation, of Kant's views.

42. See O'Neill, 1989, pp. 137–140.

43. This was the theme of my early essay "Humanity as an End in Itself," 1980. Cummiskey, 1996, also begins from an interpretation of the humanity formula based on the idea that to be an end-in-itself is to have dignity, as opposed to price.

44. Donagan's account, 1977, treats the formula as a principle of respect, but in *The Metaphysics of Morals*, 199a, Kant's discussion of respect for others is concerned only with certain aspects of morality (contrasted with beneficence, gratitude, etc.), not as a comprehensive moral guide. Similarly, Kant seems to treat self-respect as a more specific requirement than the Categorical Imperative, though one could argue that all duties to oneself are "really" requirements of self-respect.

45. Although for purposes of developing Kantian ethics I suggest that an alternative interpretation in terms of dignity is more promising, I think that the account proposed here has some merit, at least as an interpretation of Kant's remark that ends must be valued *as able to share our end.* In "Donagan's Kant," 1993, I suggest this leads to a "thin" reading of the humanity formula, in contrast with an earlier "thick" reading that emphasized the incomparable value of rational agency. See my *Respect, Pluralism, Justice: Kantian Perspectives*, 2000, pp. 148–151.

46. For example, my "Humanity as an End in Itself," 1980.

47. See Cummiskey, 1996.

48. See Wood, 1999, p. 141. I turn to Wood's view shortly. See also Korsgaard, 1996a, pp. 106–132, esp. 275. Both Korsgaard and Wood emphasize our value-conferring status as beings who rationally set ends for ourselves.

49. For example, Donagan's principle regarding lying is this: "Even for a good end, it is impermissible for anybody, in conditions of free communications between responsible persons, to express an opinion that he does not hold" (1977, p. 89).

50. See Williams, 1973, pp. 77–155.

51. For example, the humanity formula can ground positive duties, express the basic value that "grounds" our moral judgments, and is not liable to generate the bizarre, counterintuitive results that the universal law formulas may yield when maxims are described in certain ways.

52. Kant says that we have a duty to promote the *happiness* of others, and he typically understands happiness as a subjective idea of lasting contentment or realizing all one's desire-based ends (not the same idea as the classic idea of human flourishing). I discuss the contrast in my 1999.

53. Donagan, 1977, p. 85, includes persons orphaned, grieving, injured, chronically ill, blind, deaf, senile, etc.

54. See my 1993, pp. 46–49.

55. This idea is proposed and illustrated in my 1992c.

56. This suggestion is developed further in the next section and in my *Dignity and Practical Reason in Kant's Moral Theory*, 1992a, chs. 2, 10, 11, and *Respect, Pluralism, and Justice*, 2000, chs. 2, 4, 8.

57. In the kingdom of ends, the lawmakers are conceived as having a system of personal ends, even though in thinking of the kingdom we "abstract" from their content. Having ends that one sets oneself is a necessary feature of being a rational agent, though these ends can vary among different kinds of rational beings (e.g., human and nonhuman) and among individuals of the same kind. This has implications about the

motivations of the rational legislators, even when (as if behind a "veil") they abstract from the content of their ends. For example, they would tend to favor whatever promotes everyone's ends and frustrates no one's, and whatever establishes conditions under which all can effectively pursue their ends. Because, as members of the kingdom of ends, they regard the humanity of each member as an end-in-itself, then they have a general motivational stance that will encourage promoting others' ends but rule out certain kinds of ends as unworthy.

58. Kant's belief, or perhaps faith, that virtually all competent adult human beings implicitly acknowledge his noninstrumental moral principles may be hard to sustain in our times, but it can be seen at least as a morally reasonable working presumption in the absence of compelling evidence regarding particular cases. In addition, we may see Kant as offering a model of rational agency (with related conceptions of "reasons," "reasonable," etc.) that (arguably) is presupposed in common thought, and this can be valuable, even if not every member of our species turns out to satisfy its criteria for being a "rational agent." Kant's claim that *rational* agents at least implicitly acknowledge his basic moral principles, I take it, is a substantive normative thesis, not an empirical hypothesis and not a proposition "analytically" true by virtue of the ordinary meaning of the word "rational" (or a special meaning that Kant stipulates). Contrary to some influential Kant scholars, I think that Kant's primary argument for his thesis is that *common moral consciousness* (especially the idea of "duty") *presupposes* that we are practically rational agents who, as such, acknowledge his basic principles. This, of course, is not an argument that would move anyone who lacked the sort of moral consciousness that Kant took for granted.

59. The kingdom of ends is said to have a "head" or "sovereign" who apparently legislates the same laws for the same reasons as the members. The head is not "bound" by the laws, presumably because, lacking in all needs and inclinations, the head is never tempted to deviate from rational principles. As Kant earlier says of a "holy will," the language of imperatives, necessitation, and "ought" is inappropriate when there is no possibility of misconduct.

60. The "sovereign" or head (*Oberhaupt*) of the kingdom is technically like a state sovereign as traditionally conceived, in that the sovereign makes laws but is not *bound* by them, *subject* to them, or under *obligation* to follow them. This does not mean, however, that the sovereign may, or even can, act contrary to the laws that all members, including the sovereign, legislate. The point is that the sovereign, a "holy will," necessarily does whatever is rational by the sovereign's own nature, and so talk of the sovereign's obligations is out of place. Importantly, the members would legislate the same laws (because they are rational) and have the same obligations even if there were no sovereign.

61. The text is ambiguous at several relevant points. For example, it is not clear whether Kant means that "each of [the three main formulas] by itself uniting the other two within it" (Kant, 2002, pp. 236–237 [4:436]) or "one of them by itself containing a combination of the other two" (Kant, 1964, p. 103 [4:436]). If the latter were right, the one that combines the others would clearly be the kingdom-of-ends formula. Again, after Kant says that "[a]ll maxims have . . . a form, . . . a matter, . . . and a complete determination," it is not entirely clear whether the subsequent expressions of the moral law are meant as characterizations of the form, matter, and complete characterization of the

moral law (the *maxim* of a good will) or requirements regarding the form, matter, and complete determination of ordinary maxims of action (Kant, 2002, p. 237 [4:436]).

62. A reasonable extension of Kant's idea, I think, would have to view its application as proceeding in several stages, in a way to be explained later. At the first stage, we would imagine all rational agents legislating for all rational agents and so not tailoring their principles for any local circumstances.

63. Wolf, 1973, p. 183, for one, endorses this interpretation.

64. The primary similarity to note between Kant and Rawls here is in the "constructivist" structure of the theories. There are other significant similarities, of course, but there are also very substantial and important differences. I have discussed the proposed legislative model, its relation to Rawls's work, and the problems it raises in several essays, and only a few basic points will be sketched here. See my *Dignity and Practical Reason in Kant's Moral Theory*, 1992a, chs. 3, 4, 11, and *Respect, Pluralism, and Justice*, 2000, chs. 2, 4, 8.

65. This is not to say that we take our moral standards from our historical circumstances. The point is that in using our basic standards to reach particular conclusions, we need to take into account the facts about our historical condition, at least insofar as they are relevant under those basic standards. We should not assume at the outset that we know the scope of the principles we can justify from basic values, how much they are open to exception, and even whether they are general enough to be useful guides. This is part of what would need to be worked out.

66. I discuss this question in more detail in "Meeting Needs and Doing Favors," in my 2002, ch. 7.

67. This, in any case, is how Kant views wide imperfect duties, such as beneficence, in *The Metaphysics of Morals*, 1991a.

68. I discuss these and some other objections in *Respect, Pluralism, and Justice*, 2000), esp. ch. 2, and *Human Welfare and Moral Worth*, 2002, ch. 3.

REFERENCES

Baron, Marcia. 1995. *Kantian Ethics (Almost) without Apology*. Ithaca, N.Y.: Cornell University Press.

Brandt, Richard. 1959. *Ethical Theory*. Englewood Cliffs, N.J.: Prentice Hall.

Cummiskey, David. 1996. *Kantian Consequentialism*. New York: Oxford University Press.

Dean, Richard. 1996. "What Should We Treat as an End-in-Itself?" *Pacific Philosophical Quarterly* 77: 266–288.

Donagan, Alan, 1977. *The Theory of Morality*. Chicago: Chicago University Press.

———. 1984. "Consistency in Rationalist Moral Systems." *Journal of Philosophy* 81: 291–309.

———. 1993. "Moral Dilemmas, Genuine and Spurious: A Comparative Anatomy." *Ethics* 104: 7–21.

Guyer, Paul, ed. 1998. *Kant's Groundwork of the Metaphysics of Morals: Critical Essays*. Lanham, Md.: Rowman and Littlefield.

Herman, Barbara. 1984. "Mutual Aid and Respect for Persons." *Ethics* 94: 577–602. Reprinted in Herman, 1993, 45–72.

———. 1993. *The Practice of Moral Judgment.* Cambridge, Mass.: Harvard University Press.

Hill, Thomas E., Jr. 1979. "A Review of *Acting on Principle* by Onora Nell." *Ethics* 89: 306–311.

———. 1980. "Humanity as an End in Itself." *Ethics* 91: 84–90. Reprinted in Hill, 1992a, 38–57.

———. 1992a. *Dignity and Practical Reason in Kant's Moral Theory.* Ithaca, N.Y.: Cornell University Press.

———. 1992b. "A Kantian Perspective on Moral Rules." In *Philosophical Perspectives,* vol. 6, *Ethics,* ed. James E. Tomberlin, 285–304. Atascadero, Calif.: Ridgeview. Reprinted in Hill, 2000, 33–56.

———. 1992c. "Making Exceptions without Abandoning the Principle: Or How a Kantian Might Think about Terrorism." In Hill, 1992a, 196–225.

———. 1993. "Donagan's Kant." *Ethics* 104: 22–52. Reprinted in Hill, 2000, 119–152.

———. 1997. "A Kantian Perspective on Political Violence." *Journal of Ethics* 1: 105–140. Reprinted in Hill, 2000, 200–236.

———. 1999. "Happiness and Human Flourishing in Kant's Ethics." *Social Philosophy and Policy* 16: 143–175. Reprinted in Hill, 2002, 164–200.

———. 2000. *Respect, Pluralism, and Justice: Kantian Perspectives.* Oxford: Oxford University Press.

———. 2001. "Hypothetical Consent in Kantian Constructivism." *Social Philosophy and Policy* 18: 300–329. Reprinted in Hill, 2002, 61–98.

———. 2002. *Human Welfare and Moral Worth: Kantian Perspectives.* Oxford: Oxford University Press.

Kant, Immanuel. [1785]. 1964. *Groundwork of the Metaphysics of Morals.* Trans. and ed. H. J. Paton. New York: Harper and Row.

———. [1797–98]. 1991a. *The Metaphysics of Morals.* Trans. and ed. Mary Gregor. Cambridge: Cambridge University Press.

———. [1793–94]. 1991b. *Religion within the Boundaries of Mere Reason.* Trans. and ed. Allen Wood. Cambridge: Cambridge University Press.

———. [1788]. 1997. *Critique of Practical Reason.* Trans. and ed. Mary Gregor. Cambridge: Cambridge University Press.

———. [1785]. 2002. *Grounding for the Metaphysics of Morals.* Trans. and ed. Thomas E. Hill, Jr., and Arnulf Zweig. Oxford: Oxford University Press.

Korsgaard, Christine. 1996a. *Creating the Kingdom of Ends.* Cambridge: Cambridge University Press.

———. 1996b. "Kant's Formula of Universal Law." In Korsgaard, 1996a, 77–105. Originally published in *Pacific Philosophical Quarterly* 66: 24–47.

Nell, Onora (O'Neill). 1975. *Acting on Principle.* New York: Columbia University Press.

O'Neill, Onora. 1989. *Constructions of Reason.* Cambridge: Cambridge University Press.

Paton, H. J. 1958. *The Categorical Imperative.* London: Hutchison.

Pogge, Thomas. 1998. "The Categorical Imperative." In Guyer, 1998, 189–214.

Rawls, John. 1971. *A Theory of Justice.* Cambridge, Mass.: Harvard University Press.

Ross, W. D. 1930. *The Right and the Good.* Oxford: Clarendon Press.

Singer, Marcus G. 1961. *Generalization in Ethics.* New York: Knopf.

Williams, Bernard. 1973. "A Critique of Utilitarianism." In *Utilitarianism: For and Against*, ed. J.J.C. Smart and Bernard Williams, 77–155. New York: Cambridge University Press.

Wolf, Robert Paul. 1973. *The Autonomy of Reason*. New York: Harper and Row.

Wood, Allen W. 1999. *Kant's Ethical Thought*. Cambridge: Cambridge University Press.

CHAPTER 18

VIRTUE ETHICS

JULIA ANNAS

In the tradition of Western philosophy since the fifth century B.C., the default form of ethical theory has been some version of what is nowadays called virtue ethics; real theoretical alternatives emerge only with Kant and with consequentialism. This continued dominance is not very surprising, given that concern with virtue is a concern with the kind of person you are, and that this has always been important to real-life ethical matters in Western societies. (And, as is becoming increasingly familiar, this is also true of some non-Western societies and philosophical traditions, particularly Asian ones.)

The tradition has taken several different forms, and sorting these out is useful for finding the underlying structure. I shall also say a little about the way that virtue ethics has been ignored or trivialized by analytical ethical philosophy for about a hundred years, only to reemerge vigorously during the last forty.

Virtue ethics is best approached by looking at the central features of what I shall call the classical version of the tradition. Its theoretical structure is first clearly stated by Aristotle, but it is wrong to think of it as peculiarly Aristotelian, since it underlies all of ancient ethical theory (Annas, 1993, 1999). The classical version is our best entry-point into the subject, because we have a large amount of material that was developed and refined over hundreds of years by extensive debate and that contains resources for establishing the whole theoretical structure, and for understanding what in it is basic and what more parochial. Modern virtue ethical theories have not yet achieved such a critical mass of argument and theory, and most are as yet partial or fragmentary. As I will show, it is only when we have this whole picture in view that we can understand other theories that call themselves virtue ethics. So I shall first build up, cumulatively, a picture of the entire structure of classical virtue ethics, and then see how different versions of it result from ignoring or rejecting parts of that structure. The result, while unavoidably schematic, should help to clarify the various debates that are growing up in virtue ethics, and help to orient those who are less familiar with the terrain and are sometimes puzzled by the recent proliferation of theories with the name *virtue ethics*.

1. Virtue Ethics: The Whole Picture

1.1. The Central Role of Practical Reasoning

A virtue is a state or disposition of a person. This is a reasonable intuitive claim; if someone is generous, say, then she has a character of a certain sort; she is dispositionally, that is, habitually and reliably, generous. A virtue, though, is not a habit in the sense in which habits can be mindless, sources of action in the agent that bypass her practical reasoning. A virtue is a disposition *to act*, not an entity built up within me and productive of behavior; it is my disposition to act in certain ways and not others. A virtue, unlike a mere habit, is a disposition to act *for reasons*, and so a disposition that is exercised through the agent's practical reasoning; it is built up by making choices and exercised in the making of further choices. When an honest person decides not to take something to which he is not entitled, this is not the upshot of a causal buildup from previous actions but a *decision*, a choice that endorses his disposition to be honest.

The exercise of the agent's practical reasoning is thus essential to the way a virtue is both built up and exercised. Because of this feature, classical virtue ethics has been criticized as being overly intellectualist (even "elitist") on this basis (Driver, 2001). However, the reasoning in question is just what everyone does, so it is hard to see how a theory that appeals to what is available to everyone is elitist. Different virtue theories offer us differing ways of making our reflections more theoretically sophisticated, but virtue ethics tries to improve the reasoning we all share, rather than replacing it by a different kind.

What is the role of the agent's practical reasoning? Virtue is the disposition to do the right thing for the right reason, in the appropriate way—honestly, courageously, and so on. This involves two aspects, the affective and the intellectual.

What is the affective aspect of virtue? The agent may do the right thing and have a variety of feelings and reactions to it. She may hate doing the right thing but do it anyway; do the right thing but with conflicted feelings or with difficulty; do the right thing effortlessly and with no internal opposition. One feature of the classical version of virtue ethics is to regard doing the right thing with no contrary inclination as a mark of the virtuous person, as opposed to the merely self-controlled. Mere performance of the right action still leaves open the issue of the agent's overall attitude; virtue requires doing the right thing for the right reason without serious internal opposition, as a matter of character. This is, after all, just one implication of the thought that in an ethics of virtue it matters what kind of person you are. Of course, what it takes to develop your character in such a way that you are wholehearted about being generous, act fairly without regrets, and so on is a large matter. There is no single unified theory of our affective nature that all virtue theories share, and so there is a variety of views as to how we are to become virtuous, rather than merely doing the right thing for the right reason. All theories in the classical tradition, however, accept and emphasize the point, familiar from common sense, that there is an important moral difference between the person who merely acts rightly and the person who is wholehearted in what she does. Some modern theories implicitly deny the importance of this distinction, without giving a reason for this.

The virtuous agent, then, does the right thing, undividedly, for the right reason—he understands, that is, that this is the right thing to do. What is this understanding? In classical virtue ethics, we start our moral education by learning from others, both in making particular judgments about right and wrong, and in adopting some people as role models or teachers or following certain rules. At first, as pupils, we adopt these views because we were told to, or they seemed obvious, and we acquire a collection of moral views that are fragmented and accepted on the authority of others. For virtue ethics, the purpose of good moral education is to get the pupil to think for himself about the reasons on which he acts, and so the content of what he has been taught. Ideally, then, the learner will begin to reflect for himself on what he has accepted, will detect and deal with inconsistencies, and will try to make his judgments and practice coherent in terms of a wider understanding which enables him to unify, explain and justify the particular decisions he makes. This is a process that requires the agent at every stage to use his mind, to think about what he is doing and to try to achieve understanding of it (Annas, 2001).

We can see this from an example. In many modern societies, the obvious models for courage are macho ones focusing on sports and war movies. A boy may grow up thinking that these are the paradigmatic contexts for courage, and have various views about courage and cowardice that presuppose this. But if he reflects about the matter, he may come to think that he is also prepared to call people in other, quite different contexts brave—a child struggling with cancer, someone standing up for an unpopular person in high school, and so on. Further reflection will show that the macho grasp of courage was inadequate, and will drive him to ask what links all these very diverse cases of bravery; this will lead him to ask what the reasons are on which brave people act, rather than to continue uncritically with the views and attitudes he initially found obvious.

The development of ethical understanding, leading the agent to develop a disposition that is a virtue, is in the classical tradition standardly taken to proceed like the acquisition of a practical skill or expertise. As Aristotle says, becoming just is like becoming a builder. With a practical skill, there is something to learn, something conveyable by teaching; the expert is the person who understands through reflection what she has been taught, and thinks for herself about it. We are familiar with the notion of practical expertise in mundane contexts like that of car repair, plumbing, and so on. In the classical tradition of virtue ethics, this is an important analogy, because ethical development displays something that we can see more clearly in these more limited contexts: There is a progress from the mechanical rule- or model-following of the learner to the greater understanding of the expert, whose responses are sensitive to the particularities of situations, as well as expressing learning and general reflection.

The skill analogy brings out two important points about ethical understanding: It requires both that you learn from others and that you come to think and understand for yourself. (The all-important progress from the learner to the expert is lost in the modern tendency to reduce all practical knowledge to 'knowing how', as opposed to 'knowing that'.) Ethical reflection begins from what you have learned in your society; but it requires you to progress from that. Virtue begins from following rules or models in your social and cultural context; but it requires that you develop a disposition to decide and act that involves the kind of understanding that only you can achieve in your own case.

Virtue is like a skill in its structure. But the skill analogy, of course, has limits. One is that practical skills are devoted to achieving ends from which we can detach ourselves if we cease to want them, whereas virtue is devoted to achieving our final end, which, as I will show, is not in this way an end we can just cease to want. Another limit is that the development of practical understanding in a skill can be relatively independent of emotion and feeling, whereas the development of practical understanding goes along with a development in the virtuous person's affect and response.

Some modern theorists have difficulty grasping the role of practical reasoning in the classical version of virtue ethics because it offends against a common modern dogma to the effect that reason functions only instrumentally, to fulfill whatever desires we happen to have. The issue is too large to discuss here, but it is important to notice that the classical theory of practical reasoning is a theoretical rival to this account, so that assuming it against the classical version of virtue ethics is begging the question. (One of the most interesting and fruitful modern debates in ethics is opening up the question of the tenability of the instrumentalist account.) The classical account can be shown to be empirically well supported, and this makes it easier to show that virtue ethics of the classical kind is not vulnerable to some criticisms that assume the truth of an account of practical reasoning that it rejects (Annas, 2001).

The classical account has also been criticized because of the notions of disposition and character that are central to it. Some modern theories object to making character basic to ethical discourse, as opposed to single actions; this reflects a difference between types of ethical theory that focus on actions in isolation and types that emphasize the importance of the agent's life as a whole, and, relatedly, the importance of moral education and development. Recently, virtue ethics of the classical kind has been attacked on the ground that its notion of a disposition is unrealistic. These attacks rely on some work in 'situationist' social psychology that claims that unobvious aspects of particular situations have a large role in explaining our actions. Some philosophers have claimed from this that we are not justified in thinking that people have robust character traits; for, if they did, these would explain their actions reliably and across a wide variety of types of situation, excluding this kind of influence (Doris, 2002; Harman, 1999).

However, these studies assume a notion of disposition that is defined solely in terms of frequency of actions, where the actions in question are defined with no reference to the agent's own reasons for acting. For virtue ethics, however, a virtue is a disposition to act *for reasons*, and claims about frequency of action are irrelevant to this, until some plausible connection is established with the agent's reasons, something none of the situationists have done (Sreenivasan, 2002).

1.2. Virtues and My Flourishing

Virtues, then, are character traits of the kind discussed. There are character traits, however, which are not virtues. To qualify as a virtue, a character trait must embody a commitment to some ethical *value*, such as justice, or benevolence. Moreover, this commitment is not merely a matter of performing actions that happen to be just, benevolent or whatever; a disposition, as already stressed, works through the agent's practical reasoning. The virtues are dispositions *to be* just, benevolent and so on, to give others their fair share, treat others in considerate ways, stand up for others' rights.

So far I have talked of virtue, but of course in everyday life we encounter a number of different virtues—fairness, generosity, courage and so on. The virtues, as we ordinarily think of them, embody commitments to a number of values, and this comes out in the ways in which different kinds of situation are typically thought of as requiring different virtues.

What makes such diverse virtues as courage and generosity *virtues*, dispositions that it is ethically admirable to have? Any theory of virtue will have something to say about the way the different virtues are valuable. Since the virtues are dispositions of me, they are ways that I am, traits of my character; so they contribute to my living my life as a whole in a certain way. So thinking about the virtues leads to thinking of *my life as a whole*. This notion is crucial, and is prominent in all forms of classical virtue ethics, because the virtues make sense only within a conception of living that takes the life I live to be an overall unity, rather than a succession of more or less unconnected states. And further, cultivating the virtues is worthwhile because living virtuously will constitute my living my life as a whole in a way that lives it *well*, in a way that it is valuable to live.

The final end to which the virtues contribute is often called *eudaimonia*, since this is the term found in ancient Greek theories (that are hence, unsurprisingly, called eudaimonist). The least unsatisfactory modern English equivalent is *flourishing*, which I shall use. *Happiness* would be in many ways better, but unfortunately runs into two problems. One is that the modern philosophical notion of happiness has been influenced by utilitarian ideas, leading easily to the trivializing thought that happiness is pleasure. And while the idea that happiness is flourishing—a well-lived life—does have a place in everyday ideas of happiness, it is often held together with implicitly conflicting ideas, such as that happiness is having a good time, or being prosperous. Modern analogues of ancient eudaimonist theories have, moreover, come to be called virtue ethics, not happiness ethics. Virtue is the concept that has become the central one in recent philosophy, sometimes obscuring the importance of the idea of the agent's overall flourishing to which the virtues contribute.

Do we have such a final end? It is important to note here that the idea is not a philosophers' demand brought in from outside everyday ethical reasoning. It is just a very ordinary and everyday way of thinking of our lives. We get to it simply by reflecting that our actions can be thought of not just in a linear way, as we perform one action after another: They can also be thought of in a nested way, as happens whenever we ask *why* we are doing something, for the answer will typically make reference to some broader concern, and this in turn to one even broader. Given that I have only one life to lead, I will eventually come up with some very broad conception of my life as a whole, as what makes sense of all my actions at any given point. I cannot escape the fact that at any given point, my actions reflect and express the kind of person I am, and the nature of my ends and priorities. This is a very ordinary way of thinking, one in which everybody engages. (People who are severely conflicted about their aims, or in denial about the way their actions fit into broader patterns in their lives, appear to be exceptions to this; but note that we think of them as having *damaged* lives, not as showing us alternative ways of living *well*.)

Thinking in this way, we come up with the notion of my living my life as a whole, and living it well. This is not yet specific as to its content. (For Aristotle, it is trivial that my final end is *eudaimonia* or happiness, but this link is not obvious for us, and even for Aristotle this was the start, not the finish, of debate as to what living well consists in.) But it is not a trivial result. For one thing, my final end must meet the formal constraint of being *complete*—all my actions are done for its sake, while I do not seek it for the sake of anything further. This at once rules out some instrumental ends, such as money or fame, which always raise the question of what they are sought *for*, what part they play in the living of a flourishing life. For another thing, my final end, flourishing, cannot consist in things, stuff, or passive states like pleasure. I am aiming at *living* in a certain way, being active where my life is concerned rather than letting it drift along. One major difference from many modern theories is that I am aiming at living my life in a way that only I can do, by developing the way I reason about it; I am not aiming at stuff, or states that other people could just as well provide for me.

How do the virtues contribute to my flourishing? Classical theories of virtue ethics claim that virtue is, more weakly, necessary, or, more strongly, sufficient for flourishing. How is this to be understood? Classical virtue theories reject the idea that flourishing can be specified right at the start, in a way that is both substantive and makes no reference to the virtues. Someone who supposes that flourishing can be defined as feeling good, or getting whatever you want, has given an account of it that is unacceptable to a virtue theory even before we get to the virtues. Rather, virtue ethics tells us that a life lived in accordance with the virtues is the *best specification* of what flourishing is. This claim in turn is not neutral ground between the virtue ethicist and the person who thinks that flourishing is getting whatever you want. Rather, we have already got *rival specifications* of what it is to flourish, to lead a good life. And this is exactly what we would expect, given that the issue of what it is to lead a flourishing life is not one that we could expect to be decided at the *start* of ethical investigation, *before* we try to spell out what is involved in living a life in which you try to live fairly, courageously, and so on, as opposed to living a life in which you aim to get whatever you want. It is a theoretical advantage of classical virtue ethics that it respects a fundamental point about our ethical discussions. When people disagree as to whether someone did or did not ruin his life by performing an action that is honest but loses him a job he has aimed for, we do not expect them to resolve the dispute by appeal to some neutral list of indicators that a way of life is worth living. We recognize that this kind of dispute is not a simple disagreement about rival means to an agreed-upon end. It is a complex kind of dispute that brings in a wide range of issues, because what is in dispute just is what kind of life constitutes a flourishing one, as opposed to a failure.

Many modern critics have objected to the claim that virtue is even necessary for flourishing, on the grounds that not everybody thinks that it matters to be fair or brave, and that some of these people appear to be flourishing by conventional standards. It is clear, however, that this kind of objection misses the point that virtue ethics does not begin from any specification of flourishing that is substantive and independent of the virtues. Virtue ethicists are often accused of naivete in thinking that being virtuous is a good bet if you want to flourish, where flourishing is understood independently of the virtues; but virtue ethics rejects this conception of flourishing. Each of us begins with an unspecific notion of living his life well as a whole, and different theories within virtue ethics give us differing answers as to the importance of virtue in giving us a right specification of living well, and so of flourishing. Virtue ethics begins from the point that we do attach value to being virtuous, as well as to having money, a family life, and so on. (It is exceptional, not standard, as some modern critics think, to be cynical about the value of the virtues in life; this is not what we teach our children, or assume in most ethical discourse.) The argument proceeds by getting us to see that virtue is not just one value in life, which could reasonably be outweighed by others, such as money; it has a special status such that, on the weaker version, those without it do not flourish, whatever else they have, and, on the stronger version, virtue is necessary and sufficient for a flourishing life. Different theories press different points, and no complete range of positive arguments can be given here, but it can be stressed that most classical theories emphasize the point that virtue is like a skill exercised on the materials of your life. Acting virtuously is not an *alternative* to making money, for example. Rather, making money is one of the things you have to do, one of the circumstances of your life, and you can do this either virtuously or not; which of the two it is makes all the difference to the place and significance in your life of making money.

The point that flourishing, as the aim of the virtues, is not antecedently specified independently of living virtuously is also important in defusing various objections to the effect that classical virtue ethics is egoistic. Sometimes it is claimed that someone who lives virtuously as a way of aiming at flourishing is acting for egoistic reasons. But this is a confusion. The person who aims at living a flourishing life by living in a fair, generous, and brave way is not aiming at *her* good, as opposed to the good of others. Still less is she aiming at some *state* of herself. Living in a flourishing way is an activity, the ongoing activity of a life, and living in a brave, generous, and so on way is a specification of what that is.

Hence it is a mistake to claim that the virtuous person's motivation is egoistic because it is aimed at her flourishing and not mine, or yours. She aims at her own flourishing and not mine just in the sense that she is living her life and not mine. There is no implication that she is furthering her own interests at the expense of mine. It would be odd to do this by acting fairly, being generous, courageously standing up for others! Still less is it plausible to think that the agent who thinks that living virtuously is the best specification of a flourishing life will be acting for egoistic reasons. This objection simply misconstrues what a virtue is. Courage, for example, is the disposition to stand up for what is right, among other things, whether or not this benefits me or others. Courage is not a disposition that can be switched off when my own interests, as opposed to those of others, are not at stake. Someone who has dispositions that further only his own interests in a way that could conflict with those of others is not even a minimal candidate for being virtuous.

The complaint that virtue ethics is egoistic is surprisingly stubborn. It seems to depend partly on the assumption that flourishing must be specified independently of the practice of the virtues, so that they are just means to it as an independently agreed end, and partly on the assumption that ethical disputes about lives are disputes about alternative means to agreed-upon ends. But neither assumption is shared by virtue ethics, so these objections miss their target. And in any case, they are false.

1.3. Living Virtuously

How does virtue ethics explicate the notion that I have just made use of so far, of the *right thing to do*? It is clearly important for the theory, since a virtue is a disposition built up by doing the right thing and acquiring increasing understanding of what this is, and why.

Virtue ethics makes the realistic assumption that by the time you come to think about ethics and want to develop or improve your life as a whole, you already *have a life*. You already have a social position, a cultural education, a family, a job, and so on. These are all factors that have contributed to your ethical development, for good or for ill. Because for virtue ethics it matters what kind of person you are, it takes into account the importance of the person you already are when you begin to think about being virtuous. It is unrealistic to think that your ethical views are all completely disposable, and that you can come to be a better person by overnight conversion. By the time you think for yourself about what it is to be brave, just, and so on, you already have developed views and attitudes.

However, classical virtue ethics always assumes that reflection about our ethical views will reveal them to be inadequate to the way we want to be. As Aristotle says, "In general everyone seeks not the traditional but the good" (*Politics* 1269a3–4). All classical virtue ethics assumes, in a way oddly absent from many modern theories, that ethical thought essentially includes an *aspiration* to be better than we are. Classical virtue theories are marked both by realistic recognition of the socially embedded nature of our ethical life, and by insistence that if we are thinking ethically, we are striving to be better, to reach an ideal that is not already attained. And all classical virtue theories are very demanding in this regard (Annas, 2002). It is therefore irrelevant to point out that the specific classical theories were produced for audiences in societies very different from ours. Virtue ethics gets a grip whenever we realize that the ethical beliefs we live by are inadequate, that, for example, they may imply sexist and racist attitudes, and that we need to become *better people.* Virtue ethics develops from the reasonable thought that *I* have to improve myself; no teacher or book can do the job.

None of this is incompatible with our recognizing that there are some judgments about action that are not only widely shared but not negotiable when we think about virtue and the good life. This is just part of the background from which we all begin. What is important, however, is that this cannot be developed into a theory telling people what it is right and wrong to do in a way that pays no attention to the fact that they are aspiring to ideals from within different contexts and at very different stages of their own ethical development. Some modern theories have thought that there is such a thing as a 'theory of right action', which will tell us which actions are right, or give us an account of what makes an action right, and can be used by anyone, at any stage of moral development, with any level of interest in being a good person. This would make ethical thinking about how to act like using a computer manual. As has been forcefully pointed out (Hursthouse, 1991, 1999), this is a completely unrealistic view of ethical thinking. It is not plausible to suppose that a bright eighteen-year-old could by reading a book become an ethically wise person, an excellent source of ethical advice as to what to do. Nor can we realistically separate the questions of whether we respect someone's advice as to what to do, and our attitude to what they find admirable in life. We cannot take someone's 'theory of right action' seriously if they have appalling priorities in their life—even if they claim, on theoretical grounds, that the two are unrelated.

The answer that virtue ethics offers to the question what is the right thing to do denies that there is any such thing as a 'theory of right action' in this abstract sense. In explaining what is the right thing to do, virtue ethics appeals to the idea of what would be done by the virtuous person. This is not a definition in which the virtuous person is independently defined and right actions derived from this. For virtue ethics appreciates that 'the virtuous person' cannot be defined in a void and then used to derive right actions in a void. Rather, the thought is that what I should do, in my situation, is what I would do if I were brave (generous, fair, etc.), where this is taken to mean: braver than I am, nearer the ideal of the brave person. Working out the answer is complex, because, as we have seen, it requires thinking about both what matters in this situation, and what bravery demands. This in turn requires reflection on what the relevant factors in question are, and whether the conception of bravery I have acquired thus far is adequate; perhaps I need now to think harder about the brave person's reasoning. Obviously, no simple universally applicable formula will result from this.

Virtue ethics' commitment to the position that acting rightly should be understood as acting as the virtuous person acts has led to a number of different objections. One simply restates that this is not a 'theory of right action' available to all, regardless of what they are like. We can see by now that there is no way that virtue ethics could produce such a theory, so the issue moves to whether this is an advantage or not. So far, advocates of such a 'theory of right action' have failed to produce any arguments for thinking that this is the form that ethics should take, mostly because it has been until recently an unchallenged assumption. Here the recent resurgence of virtue ethics has opened up a much-needed debate.

Another objection, increasingly fading as virtue ethics becomes better understood, is that it is ethically conservative, since it begins from our embedded lives, rather than assuming that we are blank slates receptive of a 'theory of right action' telling us what to do. These charges come from noticing only half the theory's concern with action, its recognition of embeddedness. They ignore the theory's commitment to virtue as an *ideal*, and the insistence that ethics involves *aspiration* to an ideal. In the classical tradition, different theories make more or less stringent demands on us as we aspire to the ideal. The most stringent demand, that of the Stoics, is that to be virtuous I must think of myself as just one among other rational humans, one member of the moral community, with no special standing because of my individual achievements and relationships. Other theories make less stringent demands. No classical virtue theory takes seriously the idea that virtue could be achieved by conforming to your society's conventions; this would leave out what ethics is all about—aspiration to an ideal, trying to live better.

At the beginning of its recent revival, virtue ethics was sometimes accused of not being "applicable" to moral problems; telling us what kind of person to be, it was thought, would not help us with problems like the ethical status of abortion and euthanasia and other difficult moral problems that we would expect ethical theory to help us with. At this point, it is clear that all that virtue ethics cannot provide is an all-purpose 'theory of right action' that will mechanically give anybody the answers to these problems in any context. But it is also clear that virtue ethics rejects this view of a 'theory of right action' in favor of an account that does more justice to our moral discourse and moral psychology. Meanwhile, virtue ethics has been applied to a gamut of such problems, with spectacular effectiveness, judging by the level of interest. There is now a wealth of virtue ethical approaches in every branch of applied ethics, so the facts are by now on the ground. A virtue ethics approach to abortion in particular has been extremely influential.[1]

1.4. Virtue and Nature

It is often assumed that virtue ethics is naturalistic—that is, that its claims about our final end and virtues depend on a particular view of nature, especially human nature, understood in a broadly scientific way independent of the ethical claims themselves. Sometimes this theory is called 'Aristotelian'.

It is actually not true that virtue ethics is bound to be naturalistic. In the ancient world, we find versions of virtue ethics that incorporate Jewish and Christian beliefs, and Christian virtue theories were standard during the mediaeval period and, in a different form, in the eighteenth century. Even among the ancient pagans there is a minority tradition, deriving from passages in Plato, taking virtue to be 'becoming like God'. Thus aspiring to the ideal of virtue may be understood in terms of a radically otherworldly theory, metaphysical or religious, that tells us to find out about our human nature only to transcend it.

However, the most developed and influential classical theories of virtue were naturalistic, and so are most modern versions (with the exception of a revival of Christian virtue ethics, as in Porter, 2001). The best known modern virtue theories, Foot's and Hursthouse's, characterize themselves as neo-Aristotelian, and this is the form of naturalism most commonly associated with classical virtue ethics. It is Aristotelian in spirit, in that the claim that the virtues benefit me, by constituting my flourishing, is supported by the claim that having the virtues benefits me as a human being. I flourish only if I am virtuous, because human nature is such that flourishing, for humans, requires us humans to live in a virtuous way.

This is, obviously, a definite and bold claim. It has often been criticized on mistaken grounds. It is sometimes, for example, thought that it depends on a 'metaphysical biology' peculiar to Aristotle and long since refuted. However, classical virtue theory does not depend on biology, or any science, in the way that modern philosophers have often demanded of a theory that is naturalistic. Virtue ethics is not derived from science or any other field; as we have seen, it emerges as a theoretical version (ultimately, several theoretical versions) of reflective thoughts that we all have. There is no question of ethics being "reduced" to some nonethical level, or emerging as the result of the analysis of the vocabulary of some other field. Ethics, in this tradition, emerges from our reflections on how to live, and, when developed in a theoretically rigorous way, guides us in how to live better.

Nonetheless, an ethical theory is weakened if the best contemporary science conflicts with its claims or makes it hard to see how they could be true. In the ancient world, classical forms of virtue ethics appealed to what they considered to be the best science available, which is why Aristotle reasonably thinks that his ethics is supported by his biological account of human nature: It explains and supports the moral psychology that the ethics presupposes. However, can contemporary forms of virtue ethics appeal to human nature, scientifically considered, in the same way? Some have tried to resuscitate particular features of Aristotle's own biological outlook, such as teleology, but this has not been found very convincing.

Contemporary virtue ethics with the ambitions of the classical theories, of which the most powerful example is that of Hursthouse, does in contemporary terms what the classical theories do in theirs. It looks at human nature as we find out about that from the best contemporary science. Here the relevant sciences are biology, ethology, and psychology, studies of humans and other animals as parts of the life on our planet. When we look at other species, it has long been clear that we can discern patterns of flourishing particular to the species. There has been reluctance to extend this to humans, on the grounds that we, unlike other animals, can choose and create different patterns of living, and evaluate them, sometimes rejecting and changing them as a result. It is only recently that it has been realized that this is not a reason for rejecting naturalism. For this fact about our species is, precisely, a *fact* about our *species*. It is because we are rational beings that we can create and evaluate different ways of living, rather than carrying on in the set patterns that members of other species follow. And this is a fact about us of the same sort as the facts about other species on the basis of which we study them. Human rationality is not something that cuts us off from the rest of the biological universe; it is just what is most distinctive about us as a species. If we take this point seriously, then a naturalistic account of humans needs to come up with patterns of flourishing as we do for other species, but specific to humans, thus taking account of the way our life patterns are dominated by the fact that we are rational beings. Virtue theory takes advantage of the fact that human rationality has been the subject of scientific study by psychologists for quite some time now, though it has only recently been recognized that it is this, rather than some outdated Aristotelian ideas, that forms the basis of a naturalistic support for virtue theory.

Neo-Aristotelian kinds of virtue theory claim not only that it benefits me as an individual to be virtuous, but also that it benefits humans to have the virtues because of the kind of animals that we are. This is obviously a large claim, and it has been found contentious. But it is important to note that it is a claim based on accepting and studying the best science. It does not depend on ignoring biology, or on 'moralizing' biological claims. It comes from taking seriously the fact that we are rational animals, *as a natural fact*. Here, again, virtue ethics has opened up a fruitful new set of issues. One of them is whether, when we do give due weight to our rationality as determining the way we live, we will end up with something nearer to a Stoic than to an Aristotelian view; this is explored by Becker (1998).

This has been a highly schematic and bare account of the major structural features of classical virtue ethics. I have not been able even to touch on some of the many rich areas that have been explored by modern as well as ancient writers. To mention but a few: The importance of practical reasoning in a virtue raises the issue of the degree to which the virtues are unified by the reasoning they share. This in turn highlights the importance of the affective element in virtue, and of exploring the moral psychology of the emotions, and of pleasure. The social embeddedness of the virtues raises issues of social and political cooperation, and the kind of theory of justice a virtue ethics requires. It also foregrounds the kind of demand that the ideal of virtue must make if a virtue ethics is to have the kind of universality that we commonly demand from an ethical theory. All these issues are now reemerging as subjects of lively discussion.

2. REDUCED VERSIONS OF VIRTUE ETHICS

2.1. Weakening the Centrality of Practical Reasoning

While all the aforementioned features of virtue ethics in its classical version are important, perhaps the most crucial is the central role of the agent's practical reasoning. I am not virtuous unless I have thought through and understood for myself the reasons on which I act, even if I have originally picked them up from teachers and parents. If we omit this point, we get the idea of a virtue just as a disposition to act. It need not be a disposition that I have endorsed for myself in thinking through the reasons on which I decide to act bravely, justly, or whatever.

What would be the point of such a disposition? A common line of thought is that I have reason to have such a disposition, to act bravely or whatever, if it does some good, either to me or to others. For why ever should I be motivated to have the disposition, if it did no good to me or others? Hence we get a 'Humean' kind of virtue ethics.[2] On this view, a virtue is a disposition that is, broadly, useful to me or to others, a disposition that, in general, does good. On this view, why should it matter whether I endorse the disposition in my own reflective reasoning? The moderate version of this position holds that I can have a virtue even if reflection reveals that I have it purely as a result of the influence of others, without my own reflective endorsement (Merritt, 2000). The radical version holds that I need not put reflective thought into the matter at all; I can have a virtue even if my having that disposition requires me to be ignorant or thoughtless (Driver, 2001).

Once we have weakened the requirement that the disposition develop and be exercised through the agent's practical reasoning, virtues can be seen as merely dispositions to act that are productive of good (the agent's good, or good in general), and this is the part assigned to them in those forms of consequentialism that recognize a role for the virtues. Their value for a consequentialist is an instrumental one, and since they get their value from being productive of consequentialist good, it is this good-productivity that will determine their shape.[3]

Hence, for a consequentialist, virtues will be plastic dispositions that take their changing shape from the shifting circumstances of good-productivity. This line of thought is taken to comic extremes in Bentham. However, some more recent consequentialists have realized that this takes us rapidly far away from any ordinary understanding of the virtues, making the exercise arguably pointless. They have therefore also explored the idea of taking the virtues in their full classical version, and asking how these can be *indirectly* productive of good within a consequentialist framework (Slote, 1988).

All these varieties of virtue are clearly trivial by comparison with the full classical account, and theories that include virtue in any of these roles are not generally taken to be types of virtue ethics. This is because the centrality of practical reasoning in the classical version links a virtue as a disposition to the agent's reflective reasoning and thus to her character; virtue is not just a disposition in the sense of a reliable habit productive of something, but is the way the agent is, constitutive of the way she is living her life as a result of her own decisions. It is no accident that theories that talk about virtue but omit this element try to fit virtue into a framework that is fundamentally centered on something other than the agent: usually production of consequentialist good. Virtue in these theories is trivialized, since its links have been cut to the importance of the agent's living a certain kind of life in accordance with his own reflective reasoning rather than values he happens to have picked up. For this latter is the point of classical virtue ethics.

Kantian theories have also been accused of trivializing virtue, but this is a more complex situation. When discussing virtue, Kant regards it as strength of will to do your duty, and he has been interpreted as holding that virtue is nothing more than a disposition instrumentally valuable for its role in enabling the agent to do what is independently recognized as being what he ought to do. This impression is strengthened by Kant's imperceptive attacks on classical theories of virtue that see it as constituting our final end (Irwin, 1996). Yet other interpretations of Kant insist that his theory does not cut the rightness of action off sharply from the agent's life and overall patterns of emotional response. Recent richer interpretations of Kant that take into account all of his ethical works give us a more nuanced picture of the place of virtue in his thought (Engstrom, 2002; Sherman, 1997; Wood, 2002). This harmonizes with recent Kantian interpretation and neo-Kantian theories that place less stress on the deontological aspect of obeying rules and give more importance to the role of respect for persons and the 'kingdom of ends' (Herman, 1993; Korsgaard, 1996). The relation of Kantian ethics to classical virtue ethics is still in the process of discovery (Engstrom and Whiting, 1996; Hursthouse, 1997).

2.2. Narrowing Our Conception of Flourishing

The idea that our final end is defined by formal constraints rather than by content is still relatively unfamiliar in modern ethical philosophy. We are also unfamiliar with the thought that we begin from a vague specification of flourishing, but then, via ethical reflection, achieve the understanding that flourishing requires living virtuously (at which point there are different theoretical options as to the place of virtue in a flourishing life). Modern theories tend to assume that any conception of flourishing that has a role in ethical theory must be defined at the start in a way that is independent of the virtues. (This tendency has been encouraged by utilitarianism, which thinks of happiness passively, in terms of a pleasant state, rather than as the active living of a life.) This has the immediate result that the virtues appear to have an egoistic role, being seen as merely instrumental to the acquisition of the agent's final end, and their being seen in this reduced role has encouraged the widespread rejection of virtue as an ethical notion in the twentieth century. Virtue ethics has also been seen as implausible in holding that being virtuous is the best way to achieve flourishing independently defined. Many critics see virtue ethics as this unattractive combination of high-mindedness and selfishness. But their target is only the reduced form of virtue that results when our conception of flourishing is narrowed in advance by being defined independently of virtue. And it is no surprise that it has been hostile critics who have constructed this easy target.

Seeing the virtues as merely means to an independently specified end has appealed to consequentialists who try to attach the virtues to an end other than the agent's own flourishing. But, as we have seen, either the virtues become plastic dispositions pushed and pulled around by the demands of producing consequentialist good, or they have to be defended in a merely indirect way. If this result is seen as problematic, then a consequentialist has either to reject the virtues altogether as part of ethical theory (a move that is becoming increasingly implausible) or find a way of giving them a noninstrumental role in the production of good, where this is defined independently of the agent's life and concerns. But this is hard to do, as long as the point of having the virtue is unconnected to the agent's concern with his own life; if the role of practical reasoning is also eliminated, then no connection is established between virtue and the agent's priorities in living, and this leaves virtue with a reduced and trivialized role.[4]

2.3. Rejecting a Final End

What happens if we reject the idea that we have a final end, or, less radically, reject the idea that the virtues are connected to it if we have one? It is possible to hold that our lives are given shape by our having a final end but to deny that the virtues contribute to that end. Perhaps the virtues are focused on such different values that practicing them does not unify my life by contributing to my living my life overall. Or perhaps they do, but the result is not to benefit me, in which case the notion of flourishing will come apart from the way the virtues enable me to live a specific kind of life (Swanton, 1997).

It is more common, however, to reject, or just ignore, the notion of flourishing and indeed of a final end altogether. This does not in itself imply rejecting or ignoring the virtues, but it does imply the rejection of a unified rationale for them. It is compatible with either accepting or rejecting a central role in the virtues for practical reasoning, but it commits the theory to the idea that the agent's practical reasoning develops in the different areas of the virtues in a way that is not unified over her life as a whole. This in turn puts severe constraints on the extent to which practice of the virtues can be taken to be part of aspiration to an ideal of living a better life as a whole.

In recent years, there has been a revival of interest in the virtues, sometimes unaccompanied by any interest in the notion of the agent's life as a whole as providing a unifying rationale for them. One form this has taken has been study of the particular virtues in a consciously piecemeal way. This has gone with a deliberately atheoretical, or even antitheoretical, approach to them (Pincoffs, 1986).

Other approaches have been more theoretical but have limited themselves to discussing virtues in the absence of any eudaimonist framework. As a result, it has been uncertain what the relation of virtue is to other ethically important notions, particularly those concerned with action, and there has been much debate. One version argues that the rightness of actions can in fact be based in the quality of the agent's virtuous motivation (Slote, 2001). Another goes to the other extreme in locating virtue entirely in the performance of virtuous actions, dispensing with the character aspect of virtue (Thomson, 1997). Unsurprisingly, this has been held to collapse into 'Rossian pluralism', the view that various kinds of acts just are right or wrong in a piecemeal way.

2.4. Keeping Embeddedness and Neglecting Aspiration

Some theories calling themselves virtue ethics that have been developed in recent years have stressed the social embeddedness of virtue to the neglect of the aspirational side, the point that virtue is an ideal that virtue ethics demands that we try to achieve. (The early work of Alasdair MacIntyre [1984] has been interpreted in a one-sided way, but his later work provides a balance.) Such theories have put emphasis on the point that virtues are developed within existing traditions and societies. Over-emphasis on this, however, risks falling into relativism, the view that different virtues are developed within contexts that cannot be meaningfully compared and thus are removed from mutual discussion and criticism. (This has resulted in much unfair criticism of the classical view, which always stresses virtue as an ideal not limited to particular social contexts.) These versions of virtue ethics have been both attacked and defended for being ethically conservative, stressing the importance of our social embeddedness at the expense of reflection about the ethical tenability of many aspects of that embeddedness.

Failure to stress the ideal aspiration side of virtue also tends to lead to a lessened emphasis on the role of practical reasoning within the virtues. Indeed, culturally conservative theories reduce their conception of virtue by stressing the position of the learner as someone who must acquire the virtues within a social and cultural context, but neglecting the stages of increasing understanding and independent thought that are crucial to the classical versions. Culturally conservative theories of this kind may stress the importance of the agent's final end as the point of the virtues, but will put reduced emphasis on the extent to which the agent's own reflection can rethink and reorder her priorities.

Since the classical theory is made up of several different important elements, there are obviously a large number of ways in which modern theories can produce reduced accounts of virtue by minimizing or omitting these elements in various combinations. I have just tried to present, in a way I hope is illuminating about them and their mutual relationships, the commonest ways in which modern theories do diverge from the model of full virtue in the classical tradition.

3. UNREDUCED MODERN VIRTUE

Not all modern versions of virtue ethics do work with reduced versions of virtue, however. Most promising here is the work of Foot and Hursthouse in developing a 'neo-Aristotelian' theory of virtue, and of Becker in developing a 'neo-Stoic' theory. These theories recognize the importance of the agent's own reasoning in the practice of virtue; claim that the virtues benefit the agent by leading to flourishing; and stress that the virtuous person does far more than conform to the conventions of her society. Moreover, they explore a form of naturalism that locates humans in the biological universe in a scientifically sound way. These theories, of course, differ from ancient eudaimonist theories in many ways, but this is exactly what we would expect. They rethink the full structure of classical virtue ethics in distinctively modern ways.

4. Conclusion

Why has virtue ethics been so neglected for so much of the last hundred years? One influence has been consequentialism, which has recognized only a reduced notion of virtue as instrumental to the achievement of some independently defined good. There has also been a general focus on actions at the expense of agents; the dominant forms of Kantian ethics have until recently been narrowly obsessed by rules and principles. Indeed, until recently, it was assumed that the only two major forms of ethical theory were consequentialism and deontology—an assumption that clearly takes it for granted that the central concern of ethics is action in isolation from agents. The resurgence of virtue ethics has not merely provided a "third way"; it has challenged this underlying assumption, and thus it not only provides an alternative to the other forms of theory but provides resources from which they have been enriched.

A role has also been played by narrow and metaphysics-driven 'metaethics', which has argued, from metaphysical premises that have little to do with ethics, that any form of naturalism is problematic. This has for some time been thought to provide problems for virtue ethics. But this is doubly mistaken: virtue ethics is not by definition naturalistic, and those forms of it that are take their start from the actual state of knowledge in biology, ethology, and psychology rather than from metaphysics. Indeed, the growth of virtue ethics has provided one challenge to the idea that metaphysics is somehow privileged with regard to ethics; many workers in ethics are impatient of the idea that metaphysics is 'first philosophy' that can lay down rules for ethics prior to any work in ethics. The rapid growth of modern virtue ethics has gone along with an explosion of interest in applied ethics that likewise takes it that our first task is to get the ethics right and then ask about metaphysical implications, rather than vice versa.[5]

We are now emerging from a period of piecemeal understanding of virtue ethics, and a variety of theories focused on one or other form of reduced virtue. It is obvious from this chapter that I think that the future belongs to theories that do in modern terms what the classical theories did in theirs. This is not because of any reverence for the past, but simply because these theories deal with the full range of issues that virtue brings up, and thus provide for virtue, as an ethical notion, a structure adequate to show how and why it is the central concept in ethical theory as well as ethical discourse. The more discussion brings the major issues to the fore, the sooner we will emerge from some still–current criticisms that treat objections to reduced versions of virtue as though they were objections to the full theory. In the last thirty to forty years, we have seen virtue reemerge as a theoretical notion in ethical discussion and have progressed to the point where virtue ethics is once more a recognized ethical approach. We are getting to the point of being able to develop some of the major issues of the classical theories in modern terms—for example, the kind of naturalism we need to ground a theory that, as virtue ethics does, makes substantial appeal to the rationality of our human nature. What is most needed is more clarity as to the relation of virtue to flourishing and to practical reasoning, issues that are prominent in current discussion.

Virtue ethics receives far more bitter and hostile criticism than other forms of ethical theory, and this seems to be because it challenges assumptions that have grounded ethics for much of the last hundred years, and thus is rightly perceived to be a radical and unsettling force. Once we look beyond reduced conceptions of virtue, we can see why virtue ethics has been so uncomfortable for the previous settled academic orthodoxy. Ethics now has to consider rival accounts of practical reasoning; pay attention to moral psychology; ask seriously what is involved in giving a unifying justification to our uses of a moral concept; question whether an ethical theory can churn out a one-size-fits-all decision procedure to settle all ethical problems; take seriously the ethical role of our lives as wholes and the living of a life as activity rather than passive state. There is enough here to keep the pot boiling for years.

NOTES

1. Hursthouse, 1991, has been reprinted in a large number of anthologies.
2. Baier, 1994; see also Foot, 1978. (Contrast Foot's later work, in Foot, 2002, where her views on the role of practical reasoning and virtue are far closer to the classical view.)
3. Hurka, 2001, follows G. E. Moore in allowing virtue a limited noninstrumental role within consequentialism. Hurka's idiosyncratic definition of virtue as a positive attitude to intrinsic good produces a reduced account; it omits the dispositional aspect of virtue, the role of practical reasoning, and the role of a final end.
4. See note 3.
5. The work of John McDowell, however, is influenced by metaethical concerns: see McDowell, 1979 (frequently reprinted).

REFERENCES

Annas, Julia. 1993. *The Morality of Happiness.* Oxford: Oxford University Press.
———. 1999. *Platonic Ethics Old and New.* Ithaca, N.Y.: Cornell University Press.

———. 2001. "Moral Knowledge as Practical Knowledge." In *Moral Knowledge,* ed. E. E. Paul, F. D. Miller and J. Paul, 236–256. Cambridge: Cambridge University Press.

———. 2002. "My Station and Its Duties: Ideal and the Social Embeddedness of Virtue." *Proceedings of the Aristotelian Society* n.s., 102: 109–123.

Baier, Annette. 1994. *Moral Prejudices.* Cambridge, Mass.: Harvard University Press.

Becker, Lawrence. 1998. *A New Stoicism.* Princeton, N.J.: Princeton University Press.

Crisp, Roger, ed. 1996. *How Should One Live?* Oxford: Oxford University Press.

Crisp, Roger, and Michael Slote, eds. 1997. *Virtue Ethics.* Oxford: Oxford University Press.

Doris, John M. 1998. "Persons, Situations and Virtue Ethics." *Nous* 32: 504–530.

———. 2002. *Lack of Character.* Cambridge: Cambridge University Press.

Driver, Julia. 2001. *Uneasy Virtue.* Cambridge: Cambridge University Press.

Engstrom, S. 2002. "The Inner Freedom of Virtue." In *Kant's Metaphysics of Morals: Interpretative Essays,* ed. Mark Timmons, 289–315. Oxford: Oxford University Press.

Engstrom, S., and J. Whiting, eds. 1996. *Aristotle, Kant and the Stoics.* Cambridge: Cambridge University Press.

Foot, Philippa. 1978. *Virtues and Vices.* Oxford: Blackwell.

———. 2001. *Natural Goodness.* Oxford: Oxford University Press.

———. 2002. *Moral Dilemmas.* Oxford: Oxford University Press.

Harman, Gilbert. 1999. "Moral Philosophy Meets Social Psychology: Virtue Ethics and the Fundamental Attribution Error." *Proceedings of the Aristotelian Society,* new series, 119: 315–331.

Herman, Barbara. 1993. *The Practice of Moral Judgement.* Cambridge, Mass.: Harvard University Press.

Hurka, Thomas. 2001. *Virtue, Vice and Value.* Oxford: Oxford University Press.

Hursthouse, Rosalind. 1991. "Virtue Theory and Abortion." *Philosophy and Public Affairs* 20: 223–246.

———. 1997. "Virtue Ethics and the Emotions." In *Virtue Ethics,* ed. Daniel Statman, 99–117. Edinburgh: Edinburgh University Press.

———. 1999. *On Virtue Ethics.* Oxford: Oxford University Press.

Irwin, Terence. 1996. "Kant's Criticisms of Eudaemonism." In Engstrom and Whiting, 1996, 63–101.

Korsgaard, Christine. 1996. *Creating the Kingdom of Ends.* Cambridge: Cambridge University Press.

MacIntyre, Alasdair. 1984. *After Virtue.* Notre Dame, Ind.: University of Notre Dame Press.

McDowell, John. 1979. "Virtue and Reason." *Monist* 62: 331–350.

Merritt, Maria. 2000. "Virtue Ethics and Situationist Personalist Psychology." *Ethical Theory and Moral Practice* 3: 365–383.

Pincoffs, E. 1986. *Quandaries and Virtues.* Lawrence: University of Kansas Press.

Porter, Jean. 2001. "Virtue Ethics." In *The Cambridge Companion to Christian Ethics,* ed. Robin Gill, 96–111. Cambridge: Cambridge University Press.

Sherman, Nancy. 1997. *Making a Necessity of Virtue: Aristotle and Kant on Virtue.* Cambridge: Cambridge University Press.

Slote, Michael. 1988. "Utilitarian Virtue." In *Midwest Studies in Philosophy,* vol. 13, *Ethical Theory: Character and Virtue,* ed. Peter French, T. Uehling, and H. Wettstein, 384–397. Notre Dame, Ind.: University of Notre Dame Press.

————. 2001. *Morals from Motives*. Oxford: Oxford University Press.

Sreenivasan, Gopal. 2002. "Errors about Errors: Virtue Theory and Trait Attribution." *Mind* 111: 47–68.

Statman, D., ed. 1997. *Virtue Ethics*. Edinburgh: Edinburgh University Press.

Swanton, Christine. 1997. "Virtue Ethics and the Problem of Indirection: A Pluralistic Value-Centred Approach." *Utilitas* 9: 167–181.

Thomson, J. J. 1997. "The Right and the Good." *Journal of Philosophy* 94: 273–298.

Wood, Allen. 2002. "The Final Form of Kant's Practical Philosophy." In *Kant's Metaphysics of Morals: Interpretative Essays*, ed. Mark Timmons, 1–21. Oxford: Oxford University Press.

CHAPTER 19

THE ETHICS OF CARE

VIRGINIA HELD

THE ethics of care is only a few decades old.[1] Some theorists do not like the term "care" to designate this approach to moral issues and have tried substituting "the ethic of love," or "relational ethics," but the discourse keeps returning to "care" as, so far, the more satisfactory of the terms considered, though dissatisfactions with it remain. "Care" has the advantage of not losing sight of the work involved in caring for people, and of not lending itself to the ideal-but-impractical interpretation of morality to which advocates of the ethics of care often object. Care is both value and practice.

By now, the ethics of care has moved far beyond its original formulations, and any attempt to evaluate it should consider much more than the one or two early works so frequently cited. It has been developed as a moral theory that is relevant not only to the so-called private realms of family and friendship but to medical practice, law, political life, the organization of society, war, and international relations.

The ethics of care is sometimes seen as a potential moral theory to be substituted for such dominant moral theories as Kantian ethics, utilitarianism, or Aristotelian virtue ethics. It is sometimes seen as a form of virtue ethics. It is almost always seen as emphasizing neglected moral considerations of at least as much importance as the considerations central to moralities of justice and rights, or of utility and preference satisfaction. And many who contribute to the development of the ethics of care seek to integrate the moral considerations, such as justice, that other moral theories have clarified, satisfactorily with those of care, though they often see the need to reconceptualize these considerations.

1. FEATURES OF THE ETHICS OF CARE

Some advocates of the ethics of care resist generalizing this approach into something that can be fitted into the form of a moral theory. They see it as a mosaic of insights, and value the way it is sensitive to contextual nuance and particular narratives rather than making the abstract and universal claims of more familiar moral theories (Baier, 1994, esp. ch. 1; Bowden, 1997; M. Walker, 1992). Still, I think one can discern among various versions of the ethics of care a number of major features.

First, its central focus is on the compelling moral salience of attending to and meeting the needs of the particular others for whom we take responsibility. Caring for her child, for instance, may well and defensibly be at the forefront of a person's moral concerns. The ethics of care recognizes that human beings are for many years of their lives dependent, that the moral claim of those dependent on us for the care they need is pressing, and that there are highly important moral aspects in developing the relations of caring that enable human beings to live and to progress. Every person needs care for at least her early years. Prospects for human progress and flourishing hinge fundamentally on the care that those needing it receive, and the ethics of care stresses the moral force of the responsibility to respond to the needs of the dependent. Most persons will become ill and dependent for some periods of their later lives, including in frail old age, and some who are permanently disabled will need care the whole of their lives. Moralities built on the image of the independent, autonomous, rational individual largely overlook the reality of human dependence and the morality it calls for. The ethics of care attends to this central concern of human life and delineates the moral values involved. It refuses to relegate care to a realm "outside morality." How caring for particular others should be reconciled with the claims of, for instance, universal justice, is an issue that needs to be addressed. But the ethics of care starts with the moral claims of particular others, for instance, of one's child, whose claims can be compelling regardless of universal principles.

Second, in the epistemological process of trying to understand what morality would recommend and what it would be morally best for us to do and to be, the ethics of care values emotion rather than rejects it. Not all emotion is valued, of course, but in contrast with the dominant rationalist approaches, such emotions as sympathy, empathy, sensitivity, and responsiveness are seen as the kind of moral emotions that need to be cultivated, not only to help in the implementation of the dictates of reason but also to better ascertain what morality recommends (see, e.g., Baier, 1994; Held, 1993; Meyers, 1994; M. Walker, 1998). Even anger may be a component of the moral indignation that should be felt when people are treated unjustly or inhumanely, and it may contribute to rather than interfere with an appropriate interpretation of the moral wrong. This is not to say that raw emotion can be a guide to morality; feelings need to be reflected on and educated. But from the care perspective, moral inquiries that rely entirely on reason and rationalistic deductions or calculations are seen as deficient.

The emotions that are typically considered and rejected in rationalistic moral theories are the egoistic feelings that undermine universal moral norms, the favoritism that interferes with impartiality, and the aggressive and vengeful impulses for which morality is to provide restraints. The ethics of care, in contrast, typically appreciates the emotions and relational capabilities that enable morally concerned persons in actual interpersonal contexts to understand what would be best. Since even the helpful emotions can often become misguided or worse, as when excessive empathy with others leads to a wrongful degree of self-denial or when benevolent concern crosses over into controlling domination, we need an *ethics* of care, not just care itself. The various aspects and expressions of care and caring relations need to be subjected to moral scrutiny and *evaluated*, not just observed and described.

Third, the ethics of care rejects the view of the dominant moral theories that the more abstract the reasoning about a moral problem the better, since the more likely to avoid bias and arbitrariness, and the more nearly to achieve impartiality. The ethics of care respects rather than removes itself from the claims of particular others with whom we share actual relationships (see, e.g., Benhabib, 1992; Friedman, 1993; Held, 1993; Kittay, 1999). It calls into question the universalistic and abstract rules of the dominant theories. When the latter consider such actual relations as between a parent and child, if they say anything about them at all, they may see them as permitted, and cultivating them a preference a person may have. Or they may recognize a universal obligation for all parents to care for their children. But they do not permit actual relations ever to take priority over the requirements of impartiality. As Brian Barry expresses this view, there can be universal rules permitting people to favor their friends in certain contexts, such as deciding to whom to give holiday gifts, but the latter partiality is morally acceptable only because universal rules have already so judged it (see Barry, 1995; Bubeck, 1995, pp. 239–240; Held, 2001; Mendus, 2002). The ethics of care, in contrast, is skeptical of such abstraction and reliance on universal rules, and questions the priority given to them. To most advocates of the ethics of care, the compelling moral claim of the particular other may be valid even when it conflicts with the requirement usually made by moral theories that moral judgments be universalizable, and this is of fundamental moral importance.[2] Hence the potential conflict between care and justice, friendship and impartiality, loyalty and universality. To others, however, there need be no conflict if universal judgments come to incorporate appropriately the norms of care previously disregarded.

Annette Baier considers how a feminist approach to morality differs from a Kantian one, and Kant's claim that women are incapable of being fully moral because of their reliance on emotion rather than reason. She writes: "Where Kant concludes 'so much the worse for women,' we can conclude 'so much the worse for the male fixation on the special skill of drafting legislation, for the bureaucratic mentality of rule worship, and for the male exaggeration of the importance of independence over mutual interdependence' " (1994, p. 26).

Margaret Walker contrasts what she sees as feminist "moral understanding" with what has traditionally been thought of as moral "knowledge." She sees the moral understanding she advocates as involving "attention, contextual and narrative appreciation, and communication in the event of moral deliberation." This alternative moral epistemology holds that "the adequacy of moral understanding decreases as its form approaches generality through abstraction" (1989, pp. 19–20).

The ethics of care may seek to limit the applicability of universal rules to certain domains where they are more appropriate, like the domain of law, and resist their extension to other domains. Such rules may simply be inappropriate in, for instance, the contexts of family and friendship, yet relations in these domains should certainly be *evaluated*, not merely described, hence morality should not be limited to abstract rules. We should be able to give moral guidance concerning actual relations that are trusting, considerate, and caring and concerning those that are not.

Dominant moral theories tend to interpret moral problems as if they were conflicts between egoistic individual interests on the one hand and universal moral principles on the other. The extremes of "selfish individual" and "humanity" are recognized, but what lies between these is often lost sight of. The ethics of care, in contrast, focuses especially on the area between these extremes. Those who conscientiously care for others are not seeking primarily to further their own *individual* interests; their interests are intertwined with the persons they care for. Neither are they acting for the sake of *all others* or *humanity in general;* they seek instead to preserve or promote an actual human relation between themselves and *particular others.* Persons in caring relations are acting for self-and-other-together. Their characteristic stance is neither egoistic nor altruistic; these are the options in a conflictual situation, but the well-being of a caring relation involves the cooperative well-being of those in the relation, and the well-being of the relation itself.

In trying to overcome the attitudes and problems of tribalism and religious intolerance, dominant moralities have tended to assimilate the domains of family and friendship to the tribal, or to a source of the unfair favoring of one's own. Or they have seen the attachments people have in these areas as among the nonmoral private preferences people are permitted to pursue if restrained by impartial moral norms. The ethics of care recognizes the *moral* value and importance of relations of family and friendship, and the need for *moral* guidance in these domains to understand how existing relations should often be changed and new ones developed. Having grasped the value of caring relations in such contexts as these more personal ones, the ethics of care then often examines social and political arrangements in the light of these values. In its more developed forms, the ethics of care as a feminist ethic offers suggestions for the radical transformation of society. It demands not just equality for women in existing structures of society, but equal consideration for the experience that reveals the values, importance, and moral significance, of caring.

A fourth characteristic of the ethics of care is that, like much feminist thought in many areas, it reconceptualizes traditional notions about the public and the private. The traditional view, built into the dominant moral theories, is that the household is a private sphere beyond politics into which government, based on consent, should not intrude. Feminists have shown how the greater social, political, economic, and cultural power of men has structured this "private" sphere to the disadvantage of women and children, rendering them vulnerable to domestic violence without outside interference, leaving women economically dependent on men and subject to a highly inequitable division of labor in the family. The law has not hesitated to intervene into women's "private" decisions concerning reproduction but has been highly reluctant to intrude on men's exercise of coercive power within the "castles" of their homes.

Dominant moral theories have seen "public" life as relevant to morality, while missing the moral significance of the "private" domains of family and friendship. Thus the dominant theories have assumed that morality should be sought for unrelated, independent, and mutually indifferent individuals assumed to be equal. They have posited an abstract, fully rational "agent as such" from which to construct morality (good examples are Darwall, 1983; Gauthier, 1986), while missing the moral issues that arise between interconnected persons in the contexts of family, friendship, and social groups. In the context of the family, it is typical for relations to be between persons with highly unequal power who did not choose the ties and obligations in which they find themselves enmeshed. For instance, no child can choose his parents, yet he may well have obligations to care for them. Relations of this kind are standardly noncontractual, and conceptualizing them as contractual would often undermine or at least obscure the trust on which their worth depends. The ethics of care addresses rather than neglects moral issues arising in relations among the unequal and dependent, relations that are often emotion-laden and involuntary, and then notices how often these attributes apply not only in the household but in the wider society as well. For instance, persons do not choose which gender, racial, class, ethnic, religious, national, or cultural groups to be brought up in, yet these sorts of ties may be important aspects of who they are and how their experience can contribute to moral understanding.

A fifth characteristic of the ethics of care is the conception of persons with which it begins. This will be dealt with in the next section.

2. THE CRITIQUE OF LIBERAL INDIVIDUALISM

The ethics of care usually works with a conception of persons as relational, rather than as the self-sufficient, independent individuals of the dominant moral theories. The dominant theories can be interpreted as importing into moral theory a concept of the person developed primarily for liberal political theory, seeing the person as a rational, autonomous agent, or a self-interested individual. On this view, society is made up of "independent, autonomous units who cooperate only when the terms of cooperation are such as to make it further the ends of each of the parties," in Brian Barry's words (1973, p. 166). Or, if they are Kantians, they refrain from actions that they could not will to be universal laws to which all fully rational and autonomous individual agents could agree. What such views hold, in Michael Sandel's critique of them, is that "what separates us is in some important sense prior to what connects us—epistemologically prior as well as morally prior. We are distinct individuals first and *then* we form relationships" (1982, p. 133; other examples of the communitarian critique that ran parallel to the feminist one are MacIntyre, 1981, 1988; Taylor, 1979; Unger, 1975). In Martha Nussbaum's liberal feminist morality, "the flourishing of human beings taken one by one is both analytically and normatively prior to the flourishing" of any group (1999, p. 62).

The ethics of care, in contrast, characteristically sees persons as relational and interdependent, morally and epistemologically. Every person starts out as a child dependent on those providing care to this child, and we remain interdependent with others in thoroughly fundamental ways throughout our lives. That we can think and act as if we were independent depends on a network of social relations making it possible for us to do so. And our relations are part of what constitute our identity. This is not to say that we cannot become autonomous; feminists have done much interesting work developing an alternative conception of autonomy in place of the liberal individualist one (see, e.g., Clement, 1996; MacKenzie and Stoljar, 2000; Meyers, 1989, 1997; see also Oshana, 1998). And feminists have much experience rejecting or reconstituting relational ties that are oppressive. But it means that from the perspective of an ethics of care, to construct morality *as if* we were Robinson Crusoes, or, to use Hobbes's image, mushrooms sprung from nowhere, is misleading. (This image is in Hobbes, 1972, p. 205; for a contrasting view see Schwarzenbach, 1996.)

As Eva Kittay writes, the liberal individualist conception fosters the illusion that society is composed of free, equal, and independent individuals who can choose to associate with one another or not. It obscures the very real facts of dependency, for everyone when young, for most people at various periods in their lives when they are ill or old and infirm, for some who are disabled, and for those engaged in unpaid "dependency work" (Kittay, 1999).

Not only does the liberal individualist conception of the person foster a false picture of society and the persons in it but also it is, from the perspective of the ethics of care, impoverished also as an ideal. The ethics of care values the ties we have with particular other persons and the actual relationships that partly constitute our identity. Although persons often may and should reshape their relations with others, distancing themselves from some persons and groups and developing or stengthening ties with others, the autonomy sought within the ethics of care is a capacity to reshape and cultivate new relations, not to ever more closely resemble the unencumbered abstract rational self of liberal political and moral theories. Those motivated by the ethics of care would seek to become more admirable relational persons in better caring relations.

Even if the liberal ideal is meant only to instruct us on what would be rational in the terms of its ideal model, thinking of persons as the model presents them has effects that should not be welcomed. As Annette Baier writes: "Liberal morality, if unsupplemented, may *unfit* people to be anything other than what its justifying theories suppose them to be, ones who have no interest in each others' interests" (1994, p. 29). And there is strong empirical evidence on how adopting a theoretical model can lead to behavior that mirrors it. Various studies show that studying economics, with its "repeated and intensive exposure to a model whose unequivocal prediction" is that people will decide what to do on the basis of self-interest, leads economics students to be less cooperative and more inclined to free ride than other students (Frank, Gilovich, and Regan, 1993; Marwell and Ames, 1981).

The conception of the person adopted by the dominant moral theories provides moralities at best suitable for legal, political, and economic interactions between relative strangers, once adequate trust exists for them to form a political entity (Held, 1984, ch. 5). The ethics of care is, instead, hospitable to the relatedness of persons. It sees many of our responsibilities as not freely entered into but presented to us by the accidents of our embeddedness in familial and social and historical contexts. It often calls on us to *take* responsibility, while liberal individualist morality focuses on how we should leave each other alone.

This view of persons seems fundamental to much feminist thinking about morality and especially to the ethics of care. As Jean Keller writes, whatever shape feminist ethics takes, "the insight that the moral agent is an 'encumbered self,' who is always embedded in relations with flesh and blood others and is partly constituted by these relations, is here to stay"(1997, p. 152).

3. What Is Care?

As with many exploratory inquiries, definitions have often been less than precise, or have been rather hastily assumed, or postponed, in the growing discourse of the ethics of care. Some have attempted clarity, with mixed results, while others have proceeded with the tacit understanding that of course we know what we are talking about when we speak of taking care of a child, or providing care for the ill.

There has been some agreement that care at least refers to an activity, as in taking care of someone. That it involves work and the expenditure of energy on the part of the person doing the caring has usually not been lost sight of. That engaging in care is not merely caring *about* something or someone has been acknowledged. But there are many forms of care, and there have been different emphases.

Noddings focuses especially on caring as an attitude that typically accompanies the activity. Central to caring are close attention to the feelings, needs, desires, and thoughts of those cared for, and a skill in understanding a situation from that person's point of view (Noddings, 1986, esp. pp. 14–19). Carers act in behalf of others' interests, but they also care for themselves. The cognitive aspect of the carer's attitude is 'receptive-intuitive' rather than 'objective-analytic', and understanding the needs of those cared for is, in Noddings's view, more a matter of feeling with them than of rational cognition. Abstract rules are of limited use in caring. Sometimes persons have a natural impulse to care for others, but sustaining this calls for a moral commitment to the ideal of caring (pp. 42, 80). Care is for Noddings an attitude and an ideal manifest in activities of care in concrete situations.

For Joan Tronto, care is much more explicitly labor. She and Berenice Fisher define it as activity that includes everything we do to maintain, continue, and repair our world so that we may live in it as well as possible (Fisher and Tronto, 1990, p. 40). This definition is so broad that most economic activity would be included, losing sight of the distinctive features of caring labor, including what Noddings calls the needed "engrossment" with the other. Alternatively, if one accepts Marx's distinction between productive and reproductive labor, and thinks of caring as reproductive labor, one misses the way that caring, especially for children, can be transformative. It is not only production that transforms human life, while elsewhere biology repeats itself. Care includes the creative nurturing that occurs in the household and in child care, and in education generally, and care has the potential to shape new and ever–changing *persons*. Care can impart and express increasingly more advanced levels of meaning and culture and society. The idea that what is new and creative and distinctively human must occur outside the realm of care is a familiar but biased misconception.

Diemut Bubeck offers a precise but problematic definition of care. She suggests that "[c]aring for is the meeting of the needs of one person by another person, where face-to-face interaction between carer and cared for is a crucial element of the overall activity and where the need is of such a nature that it cannot possibly be met by the person in need herself" (1995, p. 129). She distinguishes caring for someone from providing a service, so that a wife who cooks for her husband when he could perfectly well cook for himself is not engaging in care but providing a service to him, whereas cooking a meal for a small child would be care. Care, she asserts, is "a response to a particular subset of basic human needs, i.e. those which make us dependent on others" (p. 133). To Bubeck, care does not require any particular emotional bond between carer and cared–for, and it is important to her general view that it can and often should be publicly provided, as in public health care. Care for her is constituted almost entirely by the objective fact of needs being met, rather than by the attitude or ideal with which the carer is acting. This opens her conception to the criticism that, as long as the objective outcome for the child is the same, providing care with the least admirable of motives would have as much moral worth as taking care of a child out of affection and because one sought what is best for the child. This would miss how care can express morally valuable social relations.

For Bubeck, as for Noddings in her early work, the face-to-face aspect of care is central, making it questionable whether we can think of our concern for more distant others in terms of caring. But Bubeck does not see her view as implying that care is then limited to the context of the relatively personal, for Bubeck includes the activities of the welfare state in the purview of the ethics of care. She thinks that in child–care centers and facilities for the elderly, care will be face-to-face, but that it should receive generous and widely supported public funding. And in her later work, Noddings agrees (Noddings, 2002).

In his elaboration of caring as a virtue, Michael Slote thinks it entirely suitable that our benevolent feelings for distant others be conceptualized as caring. He thinks "an ethic of caring can take the well-being of all humanity into consideration"; to him, caring is a "motivational attitude" (2001, pp. ix, 30). And several contributors to the volume *Feminists Doing Ethics* also see care as a virtue (DesAutels and Waugh, 2001). But some feminists would object, I think, to seeing care entirely as a motive, since this may lose sight of it as work, and encouragement should not be given to the tendency to overlook the question of who does most of this work.

My own view is that care should be thought of as both a practice and a value (Held, 2004). Care is a practice of responding to needs—material, psychological, cultural—but it is not a series of unrelated actions, it is a practice that develops, that has attributes and standards, and that should be continually improved. Care should be carried out with the appropriate attitudes; motives, and what we express in our caring activities, are important, along with outcomes. Adequate care can come progressively closer to being good care, able to express the caring relations that hold persons together and that can transform children into increasingly more morally admirable human beings.

Care is also a value. We value caring persons and caring attitudes, and can organize many evaluations of how persons are interrelated around a constellation of moral considerations associated with care or its absence. We can ask of a relation, for instance, whether it is trusting and mutually considerate, or hostile and vindictive. Care is not, I think, the same as benevolence, because care is more the characterization of a social relation than the description of an individual disposition, such as the disposition of a benevolent person. What caring societies ought to cultivate are caring relations, often reciprocal over time, if not at given times. It is caring relations, rather than persons as individuals, that especially exemplify the values of caring. Caring relations form the small societies of family and friendship on which larger societies depend. Weaker but still–evident caring relations between more distant persons allow them to trust one another enough to live in peace, to respect each others' rights, and to care together for the well-being of their members and of their environment.

4. Justice and Care

Some conceptions of the ethics of care see it as contrasting with an ethic of justice in ways that suggest one must choose between them. Carol Gilligan's suggestion of alternative perspectives in interpreting and organizing the elements of a moral problem lent itself to this implication; she herself used the metaphor of the ambiguous figure of the vase and the faces, from psychological research on perception, to illustrate how one could see a problem as either a problem of justice or a problem of care but not as both simultaneously (Gilligan, 1982, 1987).

An ethic of justice focuses on questions of fairness, equality, individual rights, abstract principles, and the consistent application of them. An ethic of care focuses on attentiveness, trust, responsiveness to need, narrative nuance, and cultivating caring relations. Whereas an ethic of justice seeks a fair solution between competing individual interests and rights, an ethic of care sees the interests of carers and cared-for as importantly intertwined rather than as simply competing. Whereas justice protects equality and freedom, care fosters social bonds and cooperation.

These are very different emphases in what morality should consider. Yet both deal with what seems of great moral importance. This has led many to explore how they might be combined in a satisfactory morality. One can persuasively argue, for instance, that justice is needed in such contexts of care as the family, to protect against violence and the unfair division of labor or treatment of children. And one can persuasively argue that care is needed in such contexts of justice as the streets and the courts, where persons should be treated humanely. Both care and justice are needed in the way education and health and welfare should be dealt with as social responsibilities. The implication may be that justice and care should not be separated into different "ethics"—that, in Sara Ruddick's proposed approach, "justice [should] always [be] seen in tandem with care" (1995, p. 217).

Few would hold that considerations of justice have no place at all in care. One would not be caring well for two children, for instance, if one persistently favored one of them in a way that could not be justified on the basis of some such factor as greater need. The issues are rather what constellation of values have priority, and which predominate in the practices of the ethics of care and the ethics of justice. And it is quite possible to delineate significant differences between them. In the dominant moral theories of the ethics of justice, the values of equality, impartiality, fair distribution, and noninterference have priority; in practices of justice, individual rights are protected, impartial judgments are arrived at, punishments are deserved, and equal treatment is sought. In contrast, in the ethics of care, the values of trust, solidarity, mutual concern, and empathetic responsiveness have priority; in practices of care, relationships are cultivated, needs are responded to, and sensitivity is demonstrated.

An extended effort to integrate care and justice is offered by Bubeck. She makes clear that she "endorse[s] the ethic of care as a system of concepts, values, and ideas, arising from the practice of care as an organic part of this practice and responding to its material requirements, notably the meeting of needs" (1995, p. 11). Yet her primary interest is in understanding the exploitation of women, which she sees as tied to the way women do most of the unpaid work of caring. She argues that such principles as the minimization of harm, and of equality in care, are tacitly if not explicitly embedded in the practice of care, as carers whose capacities and time for engaging in caring labor are limited must decide how to respond to various others in need of being cared for. She writes that "far from being extraneous impositions . . . considerations of justice arise from within the practice of care itself and therefore are an important part of the ethic of care, properly understood" (p. 206). The ethics of care must thus also concern itself with the justice, or lack of it, of the ways the tasks of caring are distributed in society. Traditionally, women have been expected to do most of the caring work that needs to be done; the sexual division of labor exploits women by extracting unpaid care labor from them, making women less able than men to engage in paid work. "Femininity" constructs women as carers, contributing to the constraints by which women are pressed into accepting the sexual division of labor. An ethic of care that extols caring but fails to be concerned with how the burdens of caring are distributed contributes to the exploitation of women, and of the minority groups whose members perform much of the paid but ill-paid work of caring in affluent households, daycare centers, hospitals, nursing homes, and the like.

The question remains, however, whether justice should be thought to be incorporated into any ethic of care that will be adequate, or whether we should keep the notions of justice and care and their associated ethics conceptually distinct. I think there is much to be said for recognizing how the ethics of care values interrelatedness and responsiveness to the needs of particular others, and how the ethics of justice values fairness and rights, and how these are different emphases.[3] Too much integration will lose sight of these valid differences. I am more inclined to say that an adequate, comprehensive moral theory will have to include the insights of both the ethics of care and the ethics of justice, among other insights, rather than that either of these can be incorporated into the other in the sense of supposing that it can provide the grounds for the judgments characteristically found in the other. Equitable caring is not necessarily better *caring*, it is fairer caring. And humane justice is not necessarily better *justice*, it is more caring justice.

Almost no advocates of the ethics of care are willing to see it as a moral outlook less valuable than the dominant ethics of justice (see Clement, 1996). To imagine that the concerns of care can merely be added on to the dominant theories, as, for instance, Stephen Darwall suggests (1998, ch. 19), is seen as unsatisfactory. Confining the ethics of care to the private sphere while holding it unsuitable for public life is also to be rejected. But how care and justice are to be meshed without losing sight of their differing priorities is a task still being worked on.

My own suggestions for integrating care and justice are to keep these concepts conceptually distinct, and to delineate the domains in which they should have priority (Held, 1984). In the realm of law, for instance, justice and the assurance of rights should have priority, though the humane considerations of care should not be absent. In the realm of the family and among friends, priority should be given to expansive care, though the basic requirements of justice surely should also be met. But these are the clearest cases; others will combine moral urgencies.

Universal human rights, including the social and economic ones as well as the political and civil, should certainly be respected, but promoting care across continents may be a more promising way to achieve this than mere rational recognition. When needs are desperate, justice may be a lessened requirement on shared responsibility for meeting needs, though this rarely excuses violations of rights. At the level of what constitutes a society in the first place, a domain within which rights are to be assured and care provided, appeal must be made to something like the often weak but not negligible caring relations among persons that enable them to recognize each other as members of the same society. Such recognition must eventually be global; in the meantime, the civil society without which the liberal institutions of justice cannot function presumes a background of some degree of caring relations rather than of merely competing individuals (Held, 2000). Further, considerations of care provide a more fruitful basis than considerations of justice for deciding much about how society should be structured, for instance how extensive or how restricted markets should be (Held, 2002). And in the course of protecting the rights that ought to be recognized, such as those to basic necessities, policies that express the caring of the community for all its members will be better policies than those that grudgingly, though fairly, issue an allotment to those deemed unfit.

Care is probably the most deeply fundamental value. There can be care without justice: there has historically been little justice in the family, but care and life have gone on without it. There can be no justice without care, however, for without care no child would survive, and there would be no persons to respect.

Care may thus provide the wider and deeper ethics within which justice should be sought, as when persons in caring relations may sometimes compete and in doing so should treat each other fairly, or, at the level of society, within caring relations of the thinner kind, we can agree to treat each other for limited purposes as if we were the abstract individuals of liberal theory. But though care may be the more fundamental value, it may well be that the ethics of care does not itself provide adequate theoretical resources for dealing with issues of justice. Within its appropriate sphere and for its relevant questions, the ethics of justice may be best for what we seek. What should be resisted is the traditional inclination to expand the reach of justice in such a way that it is mistakenly imagined to be able to give us a comprehensive morality suitable for all moral questions.

5. IMPLICATIONS FOR SOCIETY

Many advocates of the ethics of care argue for its relevance in social and political and economic life. Sara Ruddick shows its implications for efforts to achieve peace (Ruddick, 1989). I argue that as we see the deficiencies of the contractual model of human relations within the household, we can see them also in the world beyond, and begin to think about how society should be reorganized to be hospitable to care, rather than continuing to marginalize it. We can see how not only does every domain of society need transformation in light of the values of care, but so would the relations between such domains, if we took care seriously, as care would move to the center of our attention and become a primary concern of society. Instead of a society dominated by conflict restrained by law, and preoccupied with economic gain, we might have a society that saw as its most important task the flourishing of children and the development of caring relations, not only in personal contexts but among citizens, and using governmental institutions. And we would see that instead of abandoning culture to the dictates of the marketplace, we should make it possible for culture to develop in ways best able to enlighten and enrich human life (Held, 1993).

Joan Tronto argues for the political implications of the ethics of care, seeing care as a political as well as moral ideal advocating the meeting of needs for care as "the highest social goal" (1993, p. 175). She shows how unacceptable current arrangements are for providing care: "[C]aring activities are devalued, underpaid, and disproportionately occupied by the relatively powerless in society" (p. 113). Nancy Fraser showed that how needs are defined are public and contested issues (Fraser, 1987). Diemut Bubeck, Eva Kittay, and many others argue forcefully that care must be seen as a public concern, not relegated to the private responsibility of women, the inadequacy and arbitrariness of private charities, or the vagaries and distortions of the market (Bubeck, 1995; Folbre, 2001; Harrington, 1999; Kittay, 1999). In her recent book *Starting At Home*, Nel Noddings explores what a caring society would be like (2002).

When we concern ourselves with caring relations between more distant others, this care should not be thought to reduce to the mere "caring about" that has little to do with the face-to-face interactions of caring labor and can easily become paternalistic or patronizing. The same characteristics of attentiveness, responsiveness to needs, and understanding situations from the points of view of others should characterize caring when the participants are more distant. This also requires the work of understanding and of expending varieties of effort (see, e.g., Lugones, 1991).

Given how care is a value with the widest possible social implications, it is unfortunate that many who look at the ethics of care continue to suppose it is a "family ethics," confined to the "private" sphere. Although some of its earliest formulations suggested this, and some of its related values are to be seen most clearly in personal contexts, an adequate understanding of the ethics of care should recognize that it elaborates values as fundamental and as relevant to political institutions and to how society is organized as those of justice. Perhaps its values are even more fundamental and more relevant to life in society than those traditionally relied on.

Instead of seeing the corporate sector, and military strength, and government and law as the most important segments of society deserving the highest levels of wealth and power, a caring society might see the tasks of bringing up children, educating its members, meeting the needs of all, achieving peace and treasuring the environment, and doing these in the best ways possible to be those to which the greatest social efforts of all should be devoted. One can recognize that something comparable to legal constraints and police enforcement, including at a global level, may always be necessary for special cases but also that caring societies could greatly decrease the need for them. The social changes a focus on care would require would be as profound as can be imagined.

The ethics of care as it has developed is most certainly not limited to the "private" sphere of family and personal relations. When its social and political implications are understood, it is a radical ethic calling for a profound restructuring of society.

6. THE ETHICS OF CARE AND VIRTUE ETHICS

To some philosophers, the ethics of care is a form of virtue ethics. Several of the contributors to the volume *Feminists Doing Ethics* adopt this view (see Andrew, 2001; McLaren, 2001; Potter, 2001; Tessman, 2001). The important virtue theorist Michael Slote argues extensively for the position that caring is the primary virtue and that a morality based on the motive of caring can offer a general account of right and wrong action and political justice (Slote, 2001).

In my view, although there are similarities between them, and although to be caring is no doubt a virtue, the ethics of care is not simply a kind of virtue ethics. Virtue ethics focuses especially on the states of character of individuals, whereas the ethics of care concerns itself especially with caring *relations*. It is caring relations that have primary value.

If virtue ethics is interpreted, as with Slote, as primarily a matter of motives, it may neglect unduly the labor and objective results of caring, as Bubeck's emphasis on actually meeting needs well highlights. Caring is not only a question of motive or attitude or virtue. On the other hand, Bubeck's account is unduly close to a utilitarian interpretation of meeting needs, neglecting that care *also* has an aspect of motive and virtue. If virtue ethics is interpreted as less restricted to motives, and if it takes adequate account of the results of the virtuous person's activities for the persons cared for, it may better include the concerns of the ethic of care. It would still, however, focus on the dispositions of individuals, whereas the ethics of care focuses on social relations, and the social practices and values that sustain them. The traditional Man of Virtue may be almost as haunted by his patriarchal past as The Man of Reason. The work of care has certainly not been among the virtuous activities to which he has adequately attended.

The ethics of care, in my view, is a distinctive ethical outlook, distinct even from virtue ethics. Certainly it has precursors, and such virtue theorists as Aristotle, Hume, and the moral sentimentalists can contribute importantly to it. As a feminist ethic, the ethics of care is certainly not a mere description or generalization of women's attitudes and activities as developed under patriarchal conditions. To be acceptable, it must be a *feminist* ethic, open to both women and men to adopt. But in being feminist, it is different from the ethics of its precursors, and different, as well, from virtue ethics.

The ethics of care is sometimes thought inadequate because of its inability to provide definite answers in cases of conflicting moral demands. Virtue theory has similarly been criticized for offering no more than what detractors call a "bag of virtues," with no clear indication of how to prioritize the virtues, or apply their requirements, especially when they seem to conflict. Defenders of the ethics of care respond that the adequacy of the definite answers provided by, for instance, utilitarian and Kantian moral theories is illusory. Cost-benefit analysis is a good example of a form of utilitarian calculation that purports to provide clear answers to questions about what we ought to do, but from the point of view of moral understanding, its answers are notoriously dubious. So too, often, are casuistic reasonings about deontological rules. To advocates of the ethics of care, its alternative moral epistemology seems better. It stresses sensitivity to the multiple relevant considerations in particular contexts, cultivating the traits of character and of relationship that sustain caring, and promoting the dialogue that corrects and enriches the perspective of any one individual (for another view, see Campbell, 1998). The ethics of care is hospitable to the methods of discourse ethics, though with an emphasis on actual dialogue that empowers its participants to express themselves rather than on discourse so ideal that actual differences of viewpoint fall away (see Benhabib, 1992; Habermas, 1995; Young, 1990).

7. CARE, CULTURE, AND RELIGION

Questions that may be raised are whether the ethics of care resembles other kinds of ethical theory that are not feminist, and whether there can be nonfeminist forms of the ethics of care. Some think the ethics of care is close to Hume's ethics (see especially Baier, 1994). Others have debated whether the ethics of care resembles Confucian ethics. Chenyang Li argues that it does. He holds that the concept of care is similar to the concept of jen or ren that is central to Confucian ethics, and that although the Confucian tradition did maintain that women were inferior to men, this is not a necessary feature of Confucian thought (Li, 1994, 2002). Daniel Star thinks that Confucian ethics is a kind of virtue ethics, always interested in role-based categories of relationships, such as father/son and ruler/subject, and that because of this it will not be able to prioritize *particular* relationships, such as that between a particular parent and a particular child, as does the ethics of care (Star, 2002).

Lijun Yuan argues that Confucian ethics is so inherently patriarchal that it cannot be acceptable to feminists (Yuan, 2002). But other interpretations are also being developed.[4] One way the ethics of care does resemble Confucian ethics is in its rejection of the sharp split between public and private. The ethics of care rejects the model that became dominant in the West in the seventeenth and eighteenth centuries as democratic states replaced feudal society: a public sphere of mutually disinterested equals coexisting with a private sphere of female caring and male rule. The ethics of care advocates care as a value for society as well as household. In this there are some resemblances to the Confucian view of public morality as an extension of private morality.

It may be suggested that the ethics of care bears some resemblance to a Christian ethic of love, counseling us to love our neighbors and care for those in need. But when a morality depends on a given religion, it has little persuasiveness for those who do not share that religion. Moralities based on reason, in contrast, can succeed in gaining support around the world and across cultures. The growth of the human rights movement is strong evidence. One of the strengths of the dominant, rationalistic moral theories such as Kantian ethics and utilitarianism, in contrast with which the ethics of care developed, is their independence from religion. They aim to appeal only to universal reason (though in practice they may fall woefully short of doing so).

Virtue ethics is sometimes based on religion, but need not be. The universal appeal of virtue ethics, however, has been less than that of ethics based on reason, given the enormous amount of cultural variation in what have been thought of as the virtues, in comparison to such basic moral prohibitions based on reason as those against murder, theft, and assault, thought to be able to provide the basis for any acceptable legal system.

The ethics of care, it should be noted, has potential comparable to that of rationalistic moral theories. It appeals to the universal experience of caring. Every conscious human being has been cared for as a child and can see the value in the care that shaped her; every thinking person can recognize the moral worth of the caring relations that gave him a future. The ethics of care builds on experience that all persons share, though they have often been unaware of its embedded values and implications.

Various feminist critics hold that the ethics of care can be hostile to feminist objectives. A traditional Confucian ethic, if seen as an ethic of care, might be an example on an ethic of care unacceptable to feminists; traditional communitarian views that appreciate care but hold that women ought to confine themselves to caring for their families while leaving "public" concerns to men might be others. Liberal feminist critics of the ethics of care charge it with reinforcing the stereotypical image of women as selfless nurturers and with encouraging the unjust assignment of caring work to women. They think it lacks the prioritizing of equality that feminism must demand (see, e.g., Nussbaum, 1999; Okin, 1989). Other feminist critics find women's experience of mothering as it has occurred under patriarchal conditions suspect, or fear that an ethics of care will deflect attention from the oppressive social structures in which it takes place (see, e.g., Card, 1995; Houston, 1987; Jaggar, 1995; but see also Willett, 1995).

Feminist defenders of the ethics of care argue that it should be understood as a feminist ethic. It makes clear, in their view, why men as well as women should value caring relations, and should share equally in cultivating them. It does not take the practices of caring as developed under patriarchal conditions as satisfactory, but does explore the neglected values discernible through attention to and reflection on them. And it seeks to extend these values as appropriate throughout society, along with justice. If one wishes to count any view that prioritizes care as a version of the ethics of care, one must be careful to distinguish between acceptable and unacceptable versions.

My own view is that to include nonfeminist versions of valuing care among the moral approaches called "the ethics of care" is to unduly disregard the history of how this ethics has developed and come to be a candidate for serious consideration among contemporary moral theories. The history of the development of the contemporary ethics of care is the history of recent feminist progress.

8. THE FEMINIST BACKGROUND

The ethics of care has grown out of the constructive turmoil of the phase of feminist thought and the rethinking of almost all fields of inquiry that began in the United States and Europe in the late 1960s. At this time, the bias against women in society and in what was taken to be knowledge became a focus of attention.

Feminism is a revolutionary movement. It aims to overturn what many consider the most entrenched hierarchy there is: the hierarchy of gender. Its fundamental commitment is to the equality of women, though that may be interpreted in various ways. A most important achievement of feminism has been to establish that the experience of women is as important, relevant, and philosophically interesting as the experience of men. The feminism of the late twentieth century was built on women's experience.

Experience is central to feminist thought, but what is meant by experience is not mere empirical observation, as so much of the history of modern philosophy and as analytic philosophy tend to construe it. Feminist experience is what art and literature as well as science deal with. It is the lived experience of feeling as well as thinking, of performing actions as well as receiving impressions, and of being aware of our connections with other persons as well as of our own sensations. And by now, for feminists, it is not the experience of what can be thought of as women as such, which would be an abstraction, but the experience of actual women in all their racial and cultural and other diversity (see, e.g., Collins, 1990; Hoagland, 1989; Narayan, 1997; Spelman, 1988; P. Williams, 1991).

The feminist validation of women's experience has had important consequences in ethics. It has led to a fundamental critique of the moral theories that were and to a large extent still are dominant, and to the development of alternative, feminist approaches to morality. For instance, in the long history of thinking about the human as Man, the public sphere from which women were excluded was seen as the source of the distinctively human and moral and creative. The Greek conception of the polis illustrated this view, later reflected strongly in social contract theories. As the realm of economic activity was added after industrialization to that of the political to compose what was seen as human, transformative, and progressive, the private sphere of the household continued to be thought of as natural, a realm where the species is reproduced, repetitively replenishing the biological basis of life.

The dominant moral theories when the feminism of the late twentieth century appeared on the scene were Kantian moral theory and utilitarianism. These were the theories that, along with their relevant metaethical questions, dominated the literature in moral philosophy and the courses taught to students.[5] They were also the moral outlooks that continued to have a significant influence outside philosophy in the field of law, one of the few areas that had not banished moral questions in favor of purportedly value-free psychology and social science.

These dominant moral theories can be seen to be modeled on the experience of men in public life and in the marketplace. When women's experience is thought to be as relevant to morality as men's, a position whose denial would seem to be biased, these moralities can be seen to fit very inadequately the morally relevant experience of women in the household. Women's experience has typically included cultivating special relationships with family and friends rather than primarily dealing impartially with strangers, and providing large amounts of caring labor for children and often for ill or elderly family members. Affectionate sensitivity and responsiveness to need may seem to provide better moral guidance for what should be done in these contexts than do abstract rules or rational calculations of individual utilities.

At around the same time that feminists began questioning the adequacy of the dominant moral theories, other voices were doing so also, which increased the ability of the feminist critiques to gain a hearing. With the work of Alasdair MacIntyre and others, there began to be a revival of the virtue theory that had been largely eclipsed.⁶ Larry Blum's work on how friendship had been neglected by the dominant theories and Bernard Williams's skepticism about how such theories could handle some of the most important questions human beings face contributed to the critical discourse (Blum, 1980; B. Williams, 1985). Arguments about how knowledge is historically situated, and about the plurality of values, further opened the way for feminist rethinking of moral theory (see, e.g., Anderson, 1993; Stocker, 1990; Taylor, 1985).

Within traditional moral philosophy, debates have been extensive and complex concerning the relative merits of deontological or Kantian moral theory, as compared with the merits of the various kinds of utilitarian or consequentialist theory, and of the contractualism that can take a more Kantian or a more utilitarian form. But from the newly asserted point of view of women's experience of moral issues, what may be most striking about all of these is their similarity. All are theories of right action. Both Kantian moralities of universal, abstract moral laws, and utilitarian versions of the ethics of Bentham and Mill advocating impartial calculations to determine what will produce the most happiness for the most people have been developed for interactions between relative strangers. Contractualism treats interactions between mutually disinterested individuals. All require impartiality and make no room at the foundational level for the partiality that connects us to those we care for and to those who care for us. Relations of family, friendship, and group identity have largely been missing from these theories, though recent attempts, which I believe to be unsuccessful, have been made to handle such relations within them.

Although their conceptions of reason differ significantly, with Kantian theory rejecting the morality of instrumental reasoning and utilitarian theory embracing it, both types of theory are rationalistic. Both rely on one very simple supreme and universal moral principle: the Kantian Categorical Imperative, or the utilitarian principle of utility, in accordance with which everyone ought always to act. Both ask us to be entirely impartial and to reject emotion in determining what we ought to do. Though Kantian ethics enlists emotion in carrying out the dictates of reason, and utilitarianism allows each of us to count ourselves as one among all whose pain or pleasure will be affected by an action, for both kinds of theory we are to disregard our emotions in the epistemological process of figuring out what we ought to do. These characterizations hold also of contractualism.

These theories generalize from the ideal contexts of the state and the market, addressing the moral decisions of judges, legislators, policy-makers, and citizens. But since they are *moral* theories rather than merely political or legal or economic theories, they extend their recommendations to what they take to be *all* moral decisions about how we ought to act in any context in which moral problems arise.

In Margaret Walker's assessment, these are idealized "theoretical-juridical" accounts of actual moral practices. They invoke the image of "a fraternity of independent peers invoking laws to deliver verdicts with authority" (1998, p. 1). Fiona Robinson asserts that in dominant moral theories, values such as autonomy, independence, noninterference, self-determination, fairness, and rights are given priority, and there is a "systematic devaluing of notions of interdependence, relatedness, and positive involvement" in the lives of others (1999, p. 10). The theoretical-juridical accounts, Walker shows, are presented as appropriate for "the" moral agent, as recommendations for how "we" ought to act, but their canonical forms of moral judgment are the judgments of those who resemble "a judge, manager, bureaucrat, or gamesman" (1998, p. 21). They are abstract and idealized forms of the judgments made by persons who are dominant in an established social order. They do not represent the moral experiences of women caring for children or their aged parents, or of minority service workers providing care for minimal wages. And they do not deal with the judgments of groups who must rely on communal solidarity for survival.

9. FEMINIST ALTERNATIVES

In place of the dominant moral theories found inadequate, feminists have offered a variety of alternatives. There is not any single "feminist moral theory" but a number of approaches sharing a basic commitment to eliminate gender bias in moral theorizing as well as elsewhere (see esp. Jaggar, 1989).

Some feminists defend versions of Kantian moral theory (e.g. Baron, 1995; Herman, 1993) or utilitarianism (e.g. Purdy, 1996) or of such related theories as contractualism (e.g. Hampton, 1993; Okin, 1989) and liberal individualist moral theory (e.g., Nussbaum, 1999). But they respond to different concerns and interpret and apply these theories in ways that none or few of their leading nonfeminist defenders do. For instance, taking a liberal contractualist approach and focusing on justice, equality, and freedom, many argue that the principles of justice should be met in the division of labor and availability of opportunities within the family and not only in public life. Of course this will require an end to the domestic violence, marital rape, patriarchal dominance, and female disadvantage in opportunities for health, education, and occupational development that still afflict many millions of women around the world, as it will require that the burdens of child care and housework not fall disproportionately on women. Achieving such aims as these would produce very radical change at the global level.

The most influential nonfeminist advocates of dominant moral theories have paid almost no attention to feminist critiques (see Okin, 1989), but when these theories are extended in the ways feminists suggest, they can be significantly improved as theories.

Other feminist theorists, at the same time, have gone much further in a distinctive direction. Rather than limiting themselves to extending traditional theories in nontraditional ways, they have developed a more distinctively different ethics: the ethics of care. Although most working within this approach share the goals of justice and equality for women that can be dealt with using traditional theories, they see the potential of a quite different set of values for a more adequate treatment of moral problems, not only within the family but in the wider society as well. The ethics of care is a deep challenge to other moral theories. It takes the experience of women in caring activities such as mothering as central, interprets and emphasizes the values inherent in caring practices, shows the inadequacies of other theories for dealing with the moral aspects of caring activity, and then considers generalizing the insights of caring to other questions of morality.

I will locate the beginnings of the ethics of care with a pioneering essay called "Maternal Thinking," by the philosopher Sara Ruddick, published in 1980. In it, Ruddick attended to the caring practice of mothering, the characteristic and distinctive thinking to which it gives rise, and the standards and values that can be discerned in this practice. Mothering aims to preserve the life and foster the growth of particular children and to have these children develop into acceptable persons. The actual feelings of mothers are highly ambivalent and often hostile toward the children for whom they care, but a commitment to the practice and goals of mothering provides standards to be heeded. Virtues such as humility and resilient good humor emerge as values in the practice of mothering; self-effacement and destructive self-denial can be seen as the "degenerative forms" of these virtues and should be avoided. Her essay showed how women's experience in an activity such as mothering could yield a distinctive moral outlook, and how the values that emerged from within it could be relevant beyond the practice itself, for instance, in promoting peace.

Ludicrous as it now seems in the twenty-first century, at the time this essay appeared, the practice of mothering had been virtually absent from all nonfeminist moral theorizing; there was no philosophical acknowledgment that mothers *think* or *reason* or encounter moral problems, or that one can find moral values in this practice. (For some early feminist theorizing about mothering, see Trebilcot, 1983.) Women were imagined to think or to face moral problems only when they ventured beyond the household into the world of men. The characteristic image was one of human mothers raising their young much as animal mothers raise theirs. Philosophical thinking about women or mothers had incorporated them into a natural biological or evolutionary framework. Or, if women were portrayed in a psychological or psychoanalytic framework, they might be seen as reacting emotionally, but again, they were not associated with reasoning and thinking, and certainly not with the possibility that there might be distinctive and valid forms of moral thought to which they have privileged access through their extensive experience with caring.

Other caring activities such as caring for the sick or elderly were similarly dismissed as irrelevant for the construction of moral theory, though existing theory, for instance a Kantian respect for persons, might be applied to a problem in medical ethics such as whether a doctor should tell his patient that she is dying, or a Rawlsian view of justice might be used to evaluate how health care should be distributed.

Ruddick's essay showed that attending to the experience of women in a caring practice could change how we think about morality, and could change our view of the values appropriate for given activities. Though men can also engage in caring practices, if they do not, they may fail to understand the morality embedded in these practices.

In 1982, Carol Gilligan's book *In a Different Voice* provided impetus for the development of the ethics of care. Gilligan, a developmental psychologist, aimed for findings that would be empirical and descriptive of the psychological outlooks of girls as they become more mature in their thinking about morality. Gilligan was suspicious of the test results obtained by Lawrence Kohlberg, a psychologist with whom she worked, which seemed to show that girls progress more slowly than boys in acquiring moral maturity. She noted that all the children studied in the construction of the "stages" that were taken to indicate advancement in moral reasoning were boys; she decided to study how girls and women approach moral problems. To moral philosophers it was striking that the "highest stage" of Kohlberg's account of moral maturity closely resembled Kantian moral reasoning, presupposing such difficult questions as whether maturity in ethics really is primarily a matter of reasoning, and whether a Kantian morality really is superior to all others.

Gilligan thought from her inquiries that it is possible to discern a "different voice" in the way many girls and women interpret, reflect on, and speak about moral problems: They are more concerned with context and actual relationships between persons, and less inclined to rely on abstract rules and individual conscience. Gilligan asserted that although only some of the women studied adopted this different voice, almost no men did. As she put it in a later essay, this meant that "if women were eliminated from the research sample, care focus in moral reasoning would virtually disappear" (1987, p. 25).

Gilligan's findings, to the extent that they were claims about men and women as such, have been questioned on empirical grounds, since African men showed some of the same tendencies in interpreting moral problems as the women she studied, and when education and occupation were comparable, the differences between women and men were to some researchers unclear (see, e.g., Harding,

1987; J. Walker, 1984). But the importance of Gilligan's work for moral theory has not been what it showed about how men and women brought up under patriarchy in fact think about morality, whether social position is as or more important than gender in influencing such thinking, or whether women who advance occupationally learn to think like men. It has been its suggestion of alternative perspectives through which moral problems can be interpreted: a "justice perspective," which emphasizes universal moral principles and how they can be applied to particular cases and values rational argument about these; and a "care perspective," which pays more attention to people's needs, to how actual relations between people can be maintained or repaired, and values narrative and sensitivity to context in arriving at moral judgments. Gilligan herself thought that for a person to have an adequate morality, both perspectives are needed, as men overcome their difficulties with attachment and become more caring, and as women overcome their reluctance to be independent and become more concerned with justice. But she did not indicate how, within moral theory, care and justice are to be integrated.

Feminist philosophers reading Gilligan's work found that it resonated with many of their own dissatisfactions with dominant moral theories (see, e.g., Kittay and Meyers, 1987; Morgan, 1987). Whether or not women were in fact more likely to adopt the "care perspective," the history of philosophy had virtually excluded women's experiences. An "ethic of care" that could be contrasted with an "ethic of justice" might, many thought, better address their concerns as they understood how the contexts of mothering, of family responsibilities, of friendship, of caring in society, were in need of moral evaluation and guidance by moral theories more appropriate to them than the dominant theories seemed capable of being. Theories developed for the polis and the marketplace were ill suited, these feminists thought, for application to the contexts of experience they were no longer willing to disregard as morally insignificant.

Soon after, Nel Noddings's book *Caring* (1984) provided a more phenomenological account of what is involved in activities of care. It examined the virtues of close attention to the feelings and needs of others, and the identification with another's reality that is central to care. The collections *Women and Moral Theory* (1987), edited by Eva Kittay and Diana T. Meyers, and *Science, Morality and Feminist Theory* (1987), edited by Marsha Hanen and Kai Nielsen, contributed significantly to the further development of the ethics of care. Annette Baier's important work on trust, and her appreciation of Hume's ethics as a precursor of feminist ethics, added further strength to the new outlook on care.[7] Many other articles and books contributed to this discourse, some criticizing the ethics of care and some defending and elaborating it. During and after the 1990s, the numbers expanded rapidly.[8] The ethics of care now has a central, though not exclusive, place in feminist moral theorizing, and it has drawn increasing interest from moral philosophers of all kinds.

The ethics of care builds concern and mutual responsiveness to need on both the personal and wider social level. Within social relations in which we care enough about each other to form a social entity, we may agree for limited purposes to imagine each other as liberal individuals, and to adopt liberal policies to maximize individual benefits. But we should not lose sight of the restricted and artificial aspects of such conceptions. The ethics of care offers a view of both the more immediate and the more distant human relations on which satisfactory societies can be built. It provides new theory with which to develop new practices, and can perhaps offer greater potential for moral progress than is contained in the views of traditional moral theory.

NOTES

I am grateful to Elizabeth Anderson, Richmond Campbell, and David Copp for very helpful comments on earlier versions of this essay.

1. I use the term 'ethics' to suggest that there are multiple versions of this ethic, though they all have much in common, making it understandable that some prefer 'the ethic of care'. I use 'the ethics of care' as a collective and singular term. Some moral philosophers have tried to establish a definitional distinction between 'ethics' and 'morality'; I think such efforts fail, and I use the terms more or less interchangeably, though I certainly distinguish between the moral or ethical beliefs that groups of people in fact have and moral or ethical recommendations that are justifiable.

2. It is often asserted that to count as moral a judgment must be universalizable: If we hold that it would be right (or wrong) for one person to do something, then we are committed to holding that it would be right (or wrong) for anyone similar in similar circumstances to do it. The subject-terms in moral judgments must thus be universally quantified variables and the predicates universal. "I ought to take care of Jane because she is my child" is not universal; "all parents ought to take care of their children" is. The former judgment could be universalizable if it were derived from the latter, but if, as many advocates of the ethics of care think, it is taken as a *starting* moral commitment, rather than as dependent on universal moral judgments, it might not be universalizable.

3. This is not to deny that justice includes responding to needs in the general sense. For instance, any decent list of human rights should include rights to basic necessities, despite the peculiar backwardness of the United States in recognizing this. Most of the world rightly accepts, at least in theory, that economic and social rights are real human rights along with civil and political rights. But justice and fairness require such rights because it is unfair as a matter of general principle for some to have more than they need of the means to live and to act, while others lack such means. See, e.g., Held, 1984; Henkin, 1990; Nickel, 1987; Shue, 1980. See also Copp, 1998. Care, in contrast, responds to the particular needs of particular persons regardless of general principles.

4. Chan Sin Yee, examining Confucian texts, finds the traditional neo-Confucian

denigration of women a misinterpretation. She acknowledges that even a reformed Confucian ethics might subscribe to a gender essentialism in which appropriate though not necessarily unequal roles based on gender would be promoted, but suggests how a return to early Confucianism could avoid this (Yee, 2003).

5. I share Stephen Darwall's view that normative ethics and metaethics are highly interrelated and cannot be clearly separated. See Darwall, 1998, esp. ch. 1.

6. See MacIntyre, 1981. A virtue theorist who was fairly widely read in the period before this was Foot, 1978. See also Rorty, 1980. Other work contributing to the revival of virtue ethics includes Slote, 1983, 1992. See also Flanagan and Rorty, 1992. Nussbaum's work (e.g., 1986) has contributed to virtue theory, but she is critical of the ethics of care.

7. Annette Baier's influential essay "Trust and Anti-Trust" appeared in 1986; it and other essays on trust and other matters are collected in Baier, 1994.

8. In addition to the titles mentioned in the text, others include: Addelson, 1991; Bell, 1993; Blustein, 1991; Card, 1991, 1999; Cole and McQuin, 1992; Hanigsberg and Ruddick, 1999; Hekman, 1995; Koehn, 1998; Larrabee, 1993; Manning, 1992; Meyers, 2002; Sevenhuijsen, 1998; Sherwin, 1992; Tong, 1993; M. Walker, 1999, 2003; White, 2000.

REFERENCES

Addelson, Kathryn Pyne. 1991. *Impure Thoughts: Essays on Philosophy, Feminism, and Ethics.* Philadelphia: Temple University Press.
Anderson, Elizabeth. 1993. *Value in Ethics and Economics.* Cambridge, Mass.: Harvard University Press.
Andrew, Barbara S. 2001. "Angels, Rubbish Collectors, and Pursuers of Erotic Joy: The Image of the Ethical Woman." In DesAutels and Waugh, 2001, 119–133.
Baier, Annette C. 1986. "Trust and Anti-Trust." *Ethics* 96: 231–260.
———. 1994. *Moral Prejudices: Essays on Ethics.* Cambridge, Mass.: Harvard University Press
Baron, Marcia. 1995. *Kantian Ethics Almost without Apology.* Ithaca, N.Y.: Cornell University Press.
Barry, Brian. 1973. *The Liberal Theory of Justice.* London: Oxford University Press.
———. 1995. *Justice as Impartiality.* Oxford: Oxford University Press.
Bell, Linda A. 1993. *Rethinking Ethics in the Midst of Violence: A Feminist Approach to Freedom.* Lanham, Md.: Rowman and Littlefield.
Benhabib, Seyla. 1992. *Situating the Self: Gender, Community, and Postmodernism in Contemporary Ethics.* New York: Routledge.
Blum, Lawrence A. 1980. *Friendship, Altruism and Morality.* London: Routledge, 1980.
Blustein, Jeffrey. 1991. *Care and Commitment.* New York: Oxford University Press.
Bowden, Peta. 1997. *Caring: Gender Sensitive Ethics.* London: Routledge.
Bubeck, Diemut. 1995. *Care, Gender, and Justice.* Oxford: Oxford University Press.
Campbell, Richmond. 1998. *Illusions of Paradox: A Feminist Epistemology Naturalized.* Lanham, Md.: Rowman and Littlefield.
Card, Claudia. 1995. "Gender and Moral Luck." In Held, 1995, 79–98.

————. 1999. *On Feminist Ethics and Politics.* Lawrence: University Press of Kansas.

————, ed. *Feminist Ethics.* 1991. Lawrence: University Press of Kansas.

Clement, Grace. 1996. *Care, Autonomy, and Justice.* Boulder, Colo.: Westview Press.

Cole, Eve Browning, and Susan Coultrap McQuin, eds. 1992. *Explorations in Feminist Ethics: Theory and Practice.* Indianapolis: Indiana University Press.

Collins, Patricia Hill. 1990. *Black Feminist Thought: Knowledge, Consciousness, and the Politics of Empowerment.* Boston: Unwin Hyman.

Copp, David. 1998. "Equality, Justice, and the Basic Needs." In *Necessary Goods,* ed. Gillian Brock, 113–133. Lanham, Md.: Rowman and Littlefield.

Darwall, Stephen L. 1983. *Impartial Reason.* Ithaca, N.Y.: Cornell University Press.

————. 1998. *Philosophical Ethics.* Boulder, Colo.: Westview Press.

DesAutels, Peggy, and Joanne Waugh, eds. 2001. *Feminists Doing Ethics.* Lanham, Md.: Rowman and Littlefield.

Fisher, Berenice, and Joan Tronto. 1990. "Toward a Feminist Theory of Caring." In *Circles of Care,* ed. E. Abel and M. Nelson, 35–62. Albany: State University of New York Press.

Flanagan, Owen, and Amelie Oksenberg Rorty, eds. 1992. *Identity, Character, and Morality: Essays in Moral Psychology.* Cambridge, Mass.: MIT Press.

Folbre, Nancy. 2001. *The Invisible Heart: Economics and Family Values.* New York: New Press.

Foot, Philippa. 1978. *Virtues and Vices.* Berkeley: University of California Press.

Frank, Robert A., Thomas Gilovich, and Dennis T. Regan. 1993. "Does Studying Economics Inhibit Cooperation?" *Journal of Economic Perspectives* 7, 2: 159–171.

Fraser, Nancy. 1987. "Women, Welfare and the Politics of Need Interpretation." *Hypatia* 2, 1: 103–121.

Friedman, Marilyn. 1993. *What Are Friends For? Feminist Perspectives on Personal Relationships.* Ithaca, N.Y.: Cornell University Press.

Gauthier, David. 1986. *Morals by Agreement.* Oxford: Oxford University Press.

Gilligan, Carol. 1982. *In a Different Voice: Psychological Theory and Women's Development.* Cambridge, Mass.: Harvard University Press.

————. 1987. "Moral Orientation and Moral Development." In Kittay and Meyers, 1987, 19–33.

Habermas, Jurgen. 1995. "Discourse Ethics." In *Moral Consciousness and Communicative Action.* Cambridge, Mass.: MIT Press.

Hampton, Jean. 1993. "Feminist Contractarianism." In *A Mind of One's Own: Feminist Essays on Reason and Objectivity,* ed. Louise M. Antony and Charlotte Witt, 227–255. Boulder, Colo.: Westview Press.

Hanen, Marsha, and Nielsen, Kai. 1987. *Science, Morality and Feminist Theory.* Calgary, Alberta: University of Calgary Press.

Hanigsberg, Julia E., and Sara Ruddick, eds. 1999. *Mother Troubles: Rethinking Contemporary Maternal Dilemmas.* Boston: Beacon Press.

Harding, Sandra. 1987. "The Curious Coincidence of Feminine and African Moralities." In Kittay and Meyers, 1987, 296–315.

Harrington, Mona. 1999. *Care and Equality: Inventing a New Family Politics.* New York: Knopf.

Hekman, Susan J. 1995. *Moral Voices, Moral Selves.* University Park: Pennsylvania State University Press.

Held, Virginia. 1984. *Rights and Goods: Justifying Social Action.* New York: Free Press.
———. 1993. *Feminist Morality: Transforming Culture, Society, and Politics.* Chicago: University of Chicago Press.
———. 2000. "Rights and the Presumption of Care." In *Rights and Reason: Essays in Honor of Carl Wellman,* ed. Marilyn Friedman, Larry May, Kate Parsons, and Jennifer Stiff, 65–78. Dordrecht: Kluwer.
———. 2001. "Caring Relations and Principles of Justice." In *Controversies in Feminism,* ed. James P. Sterba, 67–81. Lanham, Md.: Rowman and Littlefield.
———. 2002. "Care and the Extension of Markets." *Hypatia* 17, 2: 19–33.
———. 2004. "Taking Care: Care as Practice and Value." In *Setting The Moral Compass,* ed. Cheshire Calhoun, 59–71. New York: Oxford University Press.
———, ed. 1995. *Justice and Care: Essential Readings in Feminist Ethics.* Boulder, Colo.: Westview Press.
Henkin, Louis. 1990. *The Age of Rights.* New York: Columbia University Press.
Herman, Barbara. 1993. *The Practice of Moral Judgment.* Cambridge, Mass.: Harvard University Press.
Hoagland, Sara Lucia. 1989. *Lesbian Ethics: Toward New Value.* Palo Alto, Calif.: Institute of Lesbian Studies.
Hobbes, Thomas. 1972. *The Citizen: Philosophical Rudiments Concerning Government and Society.* Ed. B. Gert. Garden City, N.Y.: Doubleday.
Houston, Barbara. 1987. "Rescuing Womanly Virtues: Some Dangers of Moral Reclamation." In Hanen and Nielsen, 1987, 237–262.
Jaggar, Alison M. 1989. "Feminist Ethics: Some Issues for the Nineties." *Journal of Social Philosophy* 20: 91–107.
———. 1995. "Caring as a Feminist Practice of Moral Reason." In Held, 1995, 179–202.
Keller, Jean. 1997. "Autonomy, Relationality, and Feminist Ethics." *Hypatia* 12, 2: 152–165.
Kittay, Eva Feder. 1999. *Love's Labor: Essays on Women, Equality, and Dependency.* New York: Routledge.
Kittay, Eva Feder, and Diana T. Meyers, eds. 1987. Women and *Moral Theory.* Lanham, Md.: Rowman and Littlefield.
Koehn, Daryl. 1998. *Rethinking Feminist Ethics: Care, Trust and Empathy.* London: Routledge.
Larrabee, Mary Jeanne, ed. 1993. *An Ethic of Care: Feminist and Interdisciplinary Perspectives.* New York: Routledge.
Li, Chenyang. 1994. "The Confucian Concept of *Jen* and the Feminist Ethics of Care: A Comparative Study." *Hypatia* 9, 1: 70–89.
———. 2002. "Revisiting Confucian *Jen* Ethics and Feminist Care Ethics: A Reply to Daniel Star and Lijun Yuan." *Hypatia* 17, 1: 130–140.
Lugones, Maria C. 1991. "On The Logic of Pluralist Feminism." In Card, 1991, 35–44. Lawrence: University Press of Kansas.
MacIntyre, Alasdair. 1981. *After Virtue: A Study in Moral Theory.* Notre Dame, Ind.: University of Notre Dame Press.
———. 1988. *Whose Justice? Which Rationality?* Notre Dame, Ind.: University of Notre Dame Press.
MacKenzie, Catriona, and Natalie Stoljar, eds. 2000. *Relational Autonomy: Feminist Perspectives on Autonomy, Agency, and the Social Self.* New York: Oxford University Press.

Manning, Rita. 1992. *Speaking From the Heart: A Feminist Perspective on Ethics.* Lanham, MD: Rowman and Littlefield.

Marwell, Gerald, and Ruth Ames. 1981. "Economists Free Ride, Does Anyone Else? Experiments on the Provision of Public Goods." Pt. 4. *Journal of Public Economics* 15, 3: 295–310.

McLaren, Margaret A. 2001. "Feminist Ethics: Care as a Virtue." In DesAutels and Waugh, 2001, 101–117.

Mendus, Susan. 2002. *Impartiality in Moral and Political Philosophy.* Oxford: Oxford University Press.

Meyers, Diana T. 1989. *Self, Society, and Personal Choice.* New York: Columbia University Press.

———. 1994. *Subjection and Subjectivity.* New York: Routledge.

———. 2002. *Gender in the Mirror: Cultural Imagery and Women's Agency.* New York: Oxford University Press.

———, ed. 1997. *Feminists Rethink the Self.* Boulder, Colo.: Westview Press.

Morgan, Kathryn Pauly. 1987. "Women and Moral Madness." In Hanen and Nielsen, 1987, 201–226.

Narayan, Uma. 1997. *Dislocating Cultures: Identities, Traditions and Third World Women.* New York: Routledge.

Nickel, James W. 1987. *Making Sense of Human Rights.* Berkeley: University of California Press.

Noddings, Nel. 1986. *Caring: A Feminine Approach to Ethics and Moral Education.* Berkeley: University of California Press.

———. 2002. *Starting at Home: Caring and Social Policy.* Berkeley: University of California Press.

Nussbaum, Martha C. 1986. *The Fragility of Goodness.* Cambridge: Cambridge University Press.

———. 1999. *Sex and Social Justice.* New York: Oxford University Press.

Okin, Susan Moller. 1989. *Justice, Gender, and the Family.* New York: Basic Books.

Oshana, Marina. 1998. "Personal Autonomy and Society." *Journal of Social Philosophy* 24, 1: 81–102.

Potter, Nancy. 2001. "Is Refusing to Forgive a Vice?" In DesAutels and Waugh, 135–150.

Purdy, Laura M. 1996. *Reproducing Persons: Issues in Feminist Bioethics.* Ithaca, N.Y.: Cornell University Press.

Robinson, Fiona. 1999. *Globalizing Care: Ethics, Feminist Theory, and International Affairs.* Boulder, Colo.: Westview Press.

Rorty, Amelie, ed. 1980. *Essays on Aristotle's Ethics.* Berkeley: University of California Press.

Ruddick, Sara. 1980. "Maternal Thinking." *Feminist Studies* 6: 342–367.

———. 1989. *Maternal Thinking: Toward a Politics of Peace.* Boston: Beacon Press.

———. 1995. "Injustice in Families: Assault and Domination." In Held, 1995, 203–223. Boulder, Colo.:

Sandel, Michael. 1982. *Liberalism and the Limits of Justice.* Cambridge: Cambridge University Press.

Schwarzenbach, Sibyl. 1996. "On Civic Friendship." *Ethics* 107, 1: 97–128.

Sevenhuijsen, Selma. 1998. *Citizenship and the Ethics of Care.* London: Routledge.

Sherwin, Susan. 1992. *No Longer Patient: Feminist Ethics and Health Care.* Philadelphia: Temple University Press.

Shue, Henry. 1980. *Basic Rights.* Princeton, N.J.: Princeton University Press.

Slote, Michael. 1983. *Goods and Virtues.* Oxford: Oxford University Press.

———. 1992. *From Morality to Virtue.* New York: Oxford University.

———. 2001. *Morals from Motives.* Oxford: Oxford University Press.

Spelman, Elizabeth V. 1988. *Inessential Woman.* Boston: Beacon Press.

Star, Daniel. 2002. "Do Confucians Really Care? A Defense of the Distinctiveness of Care Ethics: A Reply to Chenyang Li." *Hypatia* 17, 1: 77–106.

Stocker, Michael. 1990. *Plural and Conflicting Values.* New York: Oxford University Press.

Taylor, Charles. 1979. *Hegel and Modern Society.* Cambridge: Cambridge University Press.

———. 1985. *Philosophical Papers.* Cambridge: Cambridge University Press.

Tessman, Lisa. 2001 "Critical Virtue Ethics: Understanding Oppression as Morally Damaging." In DesAutels and Waugh, 2001, 79–99.

Tong, Rosemarie. 1993. *Feminine and Feminist Ethics.* Belmont, Calif.: Wadsworth.

Trebilcot, Joyce, ed. 1983. *Mothering: Essays in Feminist Theory.* Totowa, N.J.: Rowman and Allanheld.

Tronto, Joan C. 1993. *Moral Boundaries: A Political Argument for an Ethic of Care.* New York: Routledge.

Unger, Roberto Mangabeire. 1975. *Knowledge and Politics.* New York: Free Press.

Walker, Lawrence J. 1984. "Sex Differences in the Development of Moral Reasoning: A Critical Review." *Child Development* 55: 677–691.

Walker, Margaret Urban. 1989. "Moral Understandings: Alternative 'Epistemology' for a Feminist Ethics." *Hypatia* 4: 15–28.

———. 1992. "Feminism, Ethics, and the Question of Theory." *Hypatia* 7: 23–38.

———. 1998. *Moral Understandings: A Feminist Study in Ethics.* New York: Routledge.

———. 2003. *Moral Contexts.* Lanham, Md.: Rowman and Littlefield.

———, ed. 1999. *Mother Time: Women, Aging, and Ethics.* Lanham, Md.: Rowman and Littlefield.

White, Julie Anne. 2000. *Democracy, Justice, and The Welfare State: Reconstructing Public Care.* University Park: Pennsylvania State University Press.

Willett, Cynthia. 1995. *Maternal Ethics and Other Slave Moralities.* New York: Routledge.

Williams, Bernard. 1985. *Ethics and the Limits of Philosophy.* Cambridge, Mass.: Harvard University Press.

Williams, Patricia J. 1991. *The Alchemy of Race and Rights.* Cambridge, Mass.: Harvard University Press.

Yee, Chan Sin. 2003. "The Confucian Conception of Gender in the Twenty-First Century." In *Confucianism for the Modern World,* ed. Hahm Chaibong and Daniel A. Bell, 312–333. Cambridge: Cambridge University Press.

Young, Iris Marion. 1990. *Justice and the Politics of Difference.* Princeton, N.J.: Princeton University Press.

Yuan, Lijun. 2002. "Ethics of Care and Concept of *Jen*: A Reply to Chenyang Li." *Hypatia* 17, 1: 107–129.

CHAPTER 20

PARTICULARISM AND ANTITHEORY

MARK LANCE
MARGARET LITTLE

A veritable chorus of voices in moral philosophy has lately been raised in protest against ethical theorists' recurrent tendency to ignore the importance of context. Objections have been directed, for instance, against theorists whose love of simplicity and order blinds them to the rich diversity of the moral landscape. Theory, we're reminded, isn't supposed to straitjacket everything into a few favorite categories; proposals that prune and consolidate the explanatory concepts of ethics too radically will end up leaving out important phenomena or rendering them unrecognizable. Other objections have been levied against the conceit that mere *possession* of a moral theory is sufficient for moral knowledge. However adequate a set of moral principles might be, after all, someone who doesn't notice what is salient in a situation won't know what to apply the principles to. Those who are morally obtuse will stumble about blindly, like novice hikers outfitted with Global Positioning Systems who discover (to their rescuers' deep irritation) that they are in fact poorly if expensively equipped to find their way. However good your map, it can't keep you from getting lost if you don't know where you are.

These sorts of points, deservedly influential as they've been, are in an important sense remedial education for philosophers. If they underscore points too often forgotten or mislaid in the history of moral theory, they are claims no one, once reminded, will object to. Everyone should agree: Crude theory is bad theory, and no theory deploys itself.

Another set of objections to moral theory's tendency to ignore context, in contrast, is altogether more ambitious—and controversial. *Moral particularists* have urged us to see as misguided the very goal of constructing an edifice of exceptionless moral generalizations. Working from a number of camps, but most centrally from neo-Aristotelianism, narrative ethics, and modern British moral realism, these philosophers have argued that attempts to codify the moral landscape are bound to be disappointed. As Jonathan Dancy puts it: "There are lots of reasons, there are no principles" (unpublished, p. 2). Or, as David McNaughton (1988, p. 190) once put it, "moral principles are at best useless, and at worst a hindrance, in trying to find out which is the right action."[1] It's not just that moral principles are more complicated and their understanding less mechanistic than we might have suspected; they *do not exist*, or at least are far less central to the moral enterprise than is typically thought.

Questions come fast and furious. What motivates such a seemingly pessimistic view of moral reflection? Is it a certain picture of moral phenomenology, a special view of the metaphysics in question, an alternative conception of moral explanation? And again, what aspect of moral reflection is meant to be its target? Is the primary idea to urge a revisionary account of everyday moral epistemology and deliberation, or to comment on the underlying structure—or lack thereof—that moral philosophers have searched for? Most centrally, perhaps, and for either such level, just how radical are its implications for moral theory meant to be? Do particularists really mean to imply that inference from theoretical generalizations forms *no* part of everyday epistemology or that morality as a domain is not governed by laws?

Some deny that much remains of the doctrine once these questions are carefully answered. Particularism, it has been argued, either reverts to the less radical reminders about the moral landscape or remains distinct but wildly implausible. Particularists, in their turn, insist that the doctrine is both distinctive and insightful, but present their favored lessons in remarkably different ways. Discussion of the doctrine has thus been increasingly marked by confusion, with proponents and opponents alike talking past one another.

If there's confusion about the motivations for and implications of particularism, the explanation for this is, in part, that two quite different agendas get grouped together under the particularist label. Some who get cast as particularist are animated first and foremost by suspicion of the justificatory role of theoretical generalizations in morality. Emphasizing the importance of discernment, nonexplicit skill, or the narrative quality of moral understanding, their central concern is to reject the idea that moral inquiry is a theory-building project. Another group of particularists, though, are animated centrally by denial of a specific model of how reasons work—namely, in virtue of being subsumable under exceptionless explanatory generalizations. For this group, it turns out, implications for moral theory remain tantalizingly open: Everything turns on the details of the account replacing that more traditional conception.

In this essay, we survey the current debate over particularism. Distinguishing motives, targets, and positions, we attempt to recast the crucial issues that divide different approaches and lay out the implications of various sorts of particularism for the possibility of moral theory. We ourselves believe that, in its most interesting form, moral particularism is both more insightful and less hostile to theory than many suppose: The upshot of particularism, as we see it, is not to dispatch explanatory generalizations in morality, but to offer a fundamentally different view of what they are and how they do their job. Our main goal, though, is to provide a map through the complex terrain of moral particularism to more properly situate its various claims—and its controversies—in moral philosophy.

1. Classical Principles and Their Functions

We start by exploring the notion of a moral principle. If particularism is to hang its hat on rejecting "moral principles," we had better know what sort of creatures they would be.

The term "moral principle" is bandied about loosely: It can sound as though any list of broad moral injunctions count, which makes it difficult to isolate particularism's target. That difficulty is probably reinforced by the doctrine's name (not to mention the rhetorical flourishes its proponents sometimes favor); "particularism," after all, sounds as though it must stand in opposition to "generalism"—a position, presumably, that attests to the existence or usefulness of generality in morality. But there are some forms of generality—for example, subsumption under concepts, or, again, everyday generalizations about, say, the frequency of unfair elections—that no one would eschew. In fact, though, the conception of moral principle that forms particularism's target is meant to be something quite specific. Let's take a look.

We can begin by distinguishing two different tasks that purported principles have been asked to play in morality. Broadly put, *normative principles* purport to articulate which considerations count as good- or bad-making, right- or wrong-making. In contrast to ontological claims about what, as it were, *make* good-making features good-making—a divine commandment, a Platonic Reality, the output of some idealized contract—normative principles aim to set forth those that do so count. A deontologist's list of duties, the utilitarian's injunction to maximize net aggregate utility, the Ten Commandments would all qualify—together with theoretical generalizations that try to elucidate the concepts therein (understanding, say, what makes an act count as consent, a gesture as generous).

Deliberative principles are generalizations that purport to give us advice on what procedures mere mortals should follow in order to arrive at good moral verdicts. These principles lay out directions to agents about what to *do* with a given set of inputs in order to move from uncertainty to clarity, disagreement to resolution. For many, of course, the correct deliberative principles piggyback fairly straightforwardly on the correct normative principles: The best procedure is to apply one's understanding of the normative principles to the inputs at hand. The two sorts of principles needn't go hand in hand, though.[2] After all, one might think the moral landscape susceptible to all manner of interesting methods of divination—kicking the Blarney stone three times, following instructions to achieve the requisite meditative epiphany, doing whatever one's wise friend Fred does. Less fancifully, many utilitarians famously distinguish their normative and deliberative principles: The utilitarian calculus determines what actions are in fact good or bad, but it isn't as if one is meant to engage in expected utility calculations when deciding how to react to an abusive boyfriend. Here local rules of thumb are advised, precisely because employing them has higher utility than attempting a utility calculation.

Kant's moral philosophy was complex in part because he provided both sorts of principles. Part of his task was to outline a principle that marks a deliberative procedure for deciding what is permissible—namely, identify one's maxim, see if it could be a natural law, and then see if it could be willed as such. This is a principle that doesn't itself state contentful moral injunctives. But he also, familiarly, pulled back from that first-personal test to defend a set of normative injunctions, including directives not to lie, not to treat others as mere means (or wear wigs).[3]

We have, then, two agendas that are at least conceptually separable: sorting out the nature of moral reality and figuring out procedures to make our moral way.

Now obviously, a great many people, from Ann Landers to Aristotle, think there's *something* to be said by way of filling in our understanding of the normative terrain and of giving suggestions for helpful procedures. At the core of an enormously wide range of Western ethical theory, though, is a certain conception of the sort of generalization we can—and should—find in answer to these questions. The conception is sufficiently dominant, indeed, that it might fairly be called the *classical conception* of moral Principles (hence hereafter awarded capitalization). It is this sort of Principle that forms the target of particularism.

A classical Principle is marked by the following three features.

1. Classical Principles are universal, exceptionless, law-like moral generaliza-

tions that mark the moral import of considerations. Normative such Principles purport to *illuminate* something's moral status, or again to set forth the conditions for *understanding* its moral status, by making explicit a necessary and nontrivial connection. Deliberative such Principles, where distinct from invocations to use the former, purport to set forth procedures that, if ideally executed, *guarantee* hitting their mark, by capturing something essential about the nature of good deliberation (think of Kant's Categorical Imperative test rather than the utilitarian's locally useful rules of thumb). This implies that while such Principles can be rendered as universal conditionals of the form

$$(\forall x)(Fx \rightarrow Gx) \text{—or perhaps } \Box(\forall x)(Fx \rightarrow Gx)\text{—}$$

where G picks out some recognizable moral property,[4] the conditional must assert some sort of a substantive and law-like connection between F and G. The $\rightarrow$ is not, that is, the $\supset$ of material implication: Surface grammar does not a Principle make.

2. The conditionals implicit in classical Principles serve genuine inferential roles in determining, criticizing, or justifying particular moral claims. They are supposed to name a genuinely possible *move* from noting that something is F to concluding it is G: They concern the import, that is, of features whose moral import—for instance, whether it counts as a reason for or against the action—is in principle questionable. Crucially, then, agreement on a given Principle can serve as epistemic leverage on beliefs, hunches, or conjectures about individual cases. Hence, $\rightarrow$ is also not expressing merely the sort of self-evident entailment of obvious analyticity that, however helpful it might be for housekeeping and regimenting our language, is without possibility of substantive controversy.

3. Classical Principles are members of theoretical systems. A system, as the name implies, is meant to be more than simply an aggregate—or "unconnected heap," as David McNaughton (1996) nicely puts it—of true generalizations. A system is a set of interanimating propositions whose cross-connections themselves serve to illuminate the subject matter. Crucially, then, commitment to one Principle can serve as leverage when discussing, deliberating, or disputing commitment to another such generalization. Such inter-Principle leverage can be achieved either through simplification—as when we corral otherwise disparate phenomena under a few common and elegantly interrelated categories, or by articulating a complex web whose multiplicity of inferential connections between Principles helps to tighten our understanding of each. Whatever account one prefers, something isn't a classical Principle unless it fits into a structure of other Principles that purport to systematic illumination.

Classical Principles, then, are exceptionless, explanatory, interrelated moral generalizations that are capable of serving key epistemic functions.

Highlighting these various features begins to show why there is something substantive in contention with their denial. It's sometimes argued that particularism's objection to Principles, far from being radical, is more a tempest in a teapot. Everyone, surely, is a generalist, once we go sufficiently far up in abstraction or far down in detail. After all, even particularists agree that the moral supervenes on the natural—two situations cannot be alike in every natural respect and differ in their moral features. This means that there must be *some* exceptionless generalizations that express the moral as a function of the natural. Such "supervenience functions," as we might call them, may of course be enormously complex; but that's just a difference in degree, not kind. Moving to the other end of the spectrum, even the most committed particularist, it's said, will admit that there is *some* level of abstraction where moral generalizations are safe from exception, if only principles such as 'pursue the good' or 'do the right thing'. This means, though, that they are not rejecting principles, just squabbling over their concreteness. Particularists, in short, don't reject moral principles; they just relocate them.

But admitting the existence of exceptionless moral generalizations is not equivalent to admitting to the existence of Principles. As the foregoing criteria make clear, the latter must be explanatory, ensconced in a surrounding theory, and epistemically useful. This means, for one, that acknowledgement of mere supervenience functions does not go far toward acknowledgement of a Principle. As John McDowell (1979) points out, supervenience can be admitted so readily because doing so admits to so little: it doesn't mean that there are any useful patterns to the way in which the dependencies line up (see also Little, 2000, sec. 3; Jackson, Pettit, and Smith, 2000). While situations can't differ in their moral properties without also differing in their natural properties, that is, this does not imply that a given moral difference (say, the difference between being just and unjust) need always be found in the same natural differences. Instead, stringing together the situations in which an action is cruel rather than kind, for example, may yield groupings that would simply look gerrymandered to anyone who does not have an independent competency with the moral concepts. On such a picture, the complicated sets of properties mentioned in supervenience functions will not constitute anything recognizably explanatory; they are too disjointed—"too indiscriminate," as Jonathan Dancy (1999, p. 26) puts it—to serve.

Similarly for abstraction. It's certainly true that no one will abjure the existence of exceptionless heady abstractions in morality—at the limit, we can *invent* a predicate whose application entails invariant moral import (we could dub 'lighing', say, as the term to pick out those cases of lying that are wrong-making). But this doesn't yet mean we have on hand anything explanatory or procedurally useful. If classification as such simply reflects judgment of its objectionable nature definitionally, no substantive explanatory work will be done by the generalization that lighings are wrong. The predicate may still be useful—say, in marking off moral from pragmatic or again legal reasons; but expression of the generalization won't serve as check on one's specific intuitions. Similarly for deliberative principles. "Choose well, grasshopper," may be a pragmatically helpful inspiration, but it hardly offers substantive guidance.

Finally, since classical Principles are meant to be pieces of theory, one cannot determine the status of a given generalization as such in isolation from its relation to other theoretical generalizations. This excludes one otherwise innocuous use of the "principlist" label as off topic here.[5] Someone who avows a particular list of injunctions as "principles to live by" may count in one sense as strongly principlist; if those principles, though, are a disconnected list, or involve concepts, such as Justice Stewart's conception of 'obscenity', about which no further theorizing can be done, one does not thereby count as advocating a set of Principles of the sort particularists want to reject.

2. BEYOND MECHANICAL PRINCIPLES

There is another source for the widespread sense that particularism is not as radical as its proponents fancy. This is the presumption that the notion of Principle being attacked actually smuggles in substantially more than our three constraints. And there are indeed conceptions of principles and the way they function in theory that are far stronger. One conception in particular—what for some has been the Holy Grail of Principles—adds a requirement of very strong context-independence. We might call it the Enlightenment model of morality—not because most Enlightenment moral philosophers espoused it, but because the Enlightenmental model of explanation and perception prevalent in its philosophy of science has proved enticing to so many in the Anglo-American tradition as a picture of what moral theorists should aspire to.

On this picture, the central task of moral theory is to articulate a catalogue of moral Principles and their interactions that can take us from a highly concrete and evaluatively neutral description of a situation to a conclusion about what to do. Moral theory is supposed to offer us up various morally salient "forces"—akin to Newtonian forces of motion—each of which pushes in the direction of one of the moral verdicts, and to provide us with some sort of algorithm or moral calculus—akin to Newtonian vector analysis—for combining these moral forces into a resultant moral verdict. Further, the task is to find forces that can be rendered in morally neutral terms (say, 'caused pain') whose instantiation can be agreed upon by those engaged in moral disputes. On this model, then, moral theory consists of identifying a set of transparent forces that can be combined algorithmically to yield all-things-considered moral verdicts.

Much of recent moral philosophy has been marked by arguments protesting this model. Such a view, it's been urged, undersells by half the complexity of the moral landscape—and moral deliberation. Any number of philosophers have argued, for instance, that the inputs relevant to moral deliberation aren't features that can be picked up in this way (see, for instance, Nussbaum, 1985; Blum, 1991). If there are epistemically basic moral forces, so the objection goes, they stop a good way short of the brutely physical. How we know when infliction of pain counts as *cruelty*, or empirical disparity as *unfairness*, is simply not something for which mechanistic explanations are in order. Instead, what is required is *interpretation*—a term that is meant to signal a nonmechanistic skill not itself reducible to our ability to see physical traits of actions. There is no way to gain competence in the application of the concepts one needs to get moral deliberation going without being trained to see the moral *point* of things.

It has further been argued that the interrelationship between moral forces can't be reduced to any algorithmic principle (e.g., McDowell, 1979; Nussbaum, 1985; Sherman, 1989). There is no setting out once and for all how to balance these principles when they conflict, as all too often they do: sometimes fidelity trumps fairness, and sometimes it's the other way around. Instead, what is required is *judgment*—a term that is meant to signal a comparison not subsumable under a calculative principle. Wise moral agents know how to assess an action in light of the various good- and bad-making features of it, but their judgment can be passed on only by training and immersion in the particulars of moral experience.

Now these moves remain controversial in some circles. The ineliminability of interpretation is a position of vulnerability, according to some. How, it's asked, can we judge consistency of application, let alone measure justification, if there is no specifying a property's instantiation in morally neutral terms? The ineliminability of judgment, in turn, requires a philosophy of mind and epistemology that allows moves to be reasonable without being subsumable under concrete deductive laws. That, too, will raise a skeptical eyebrow or two. How, it will be asked, can we judge consistency of application, or have any hope of resolving disagreements, if there is no such law to appeal to?

If the objections are familiar, though, so, too, by now, are the rejoinders offered in their defense. Our philosophies of mind and epistemology, it's pointed out, have long had to deal with properties, such as 'being a chair', whose instantiation cannot be given in scientific terms. It is only when we demand that semantic competence and justification be reduced to machinations on what are essentially brute susceptibilities to causal influences of natural properties that dealing with them seems precarious. As McDowell (1979, 1981) says, consistency need not be found at the natural level to count as consistency; we can learn "how to go on" with patterns that look gerrymandered from the natural point of view without resorting to a spooky sort of perception, perhaps based in some modular or specially individuated faculty (see also the discussion in Dancy, 1993, ch. 5).

Further, it is simply prejudice, as Martha Nussbaum (1985) puts it, that counts only quantitative judgments as judgments backed by reason. A variety of other models of understanding have been forwarded that allow us to see judgment as nontheoretical, yet reasonable: Aristotle's phronesis, Heidegger's involvement in the ready–to–hand, Wittgensteinian forms of life, and Dreyfus and Dreyfus's (1992) conception of skill all provide attempts to understand such noncalculative rational judgment (see Garfield [2000] for an explicit such application).

Now whether these arguments are in the end satisfying is, of course, a matter of continued debate. And, indeed, much of particularism's energy has been devoted to their fortification. But these moves, important as they are to the particularist, are not the particularist's claim to fame (or infamy). For while it may be a mistake to think that explanation of moral import can somehow be extricated once and for all from reliance on interpretation and judgment, that's a lesson that any number of self-declared generalists have long pressed.

Take, for example, the contextualist principlism of W. D. Ross (1930; current expositors include Crisp, 2000; McNaughton and Rawlings, 2000; Pietrowski, 1993). Ross developed and defended a list of Principles that represented the duties of morality. He urged, though, that the subject of such Principles were morally rich concepts, such as 'fidelity' and 'beneficence', that resisted reduction to bluntly naturalistic specification such as 'telling the truth' and 'decreasing pain'; and he insisted that there was no way to codify how to balance them when they conflict. Instead, the job of moral theory, on his view, is to develop a list of prima facie or "pro tanto" duties, which are understood, in the first instance, by reference to what we should do if no other such duties were present. Morally salient features of actions, then, are still governed by laws—fidelity and beneficence are always "good-making," dishonesty is necessarily "bad-making"; but there is no mechanical way to identify when those features are instantiated, and no principled or theoretically tractable way to move from a list of the morally salient forces to an overall verdict.

They are lessons that Kant, too, would endorse. Unlike Ross, Kant thought there were some Principles, both deliberative and normative, capable of delivering all-things-considered verdicts. Nonetheless, as modern-day Kant scholars such as Onora O'Neill (2001) and Barbara Herman (1993) are wont to point out, he would have shuddered at the thought that moral judgment can function mechanistically. For one thing, there was no thought that those Principles could be applied without interpretation; just as important, he insisted that only certain aspects of morality—namely, the arena of the impermissible—were amenable to such powerful Principles. Decisions about imperfect duties and exercise of the virtues, just as essential to moral worth, were never claimed to be subsumable under them.

In short, the sort of context-dependency just insisted upon is not antiprinciplist. It simply—and importantly—insists that not all the moves we make from input to output can be modeled as even tacitly subsumable under independently understandable deductive principles. It argues that moral interpretation and judgment are inexpungible elements of moral knowledge.

What further claims, then, mark off the move to something deserving the name particularism? In fact, different claims are at issue for different stripes of particularist. In the following, we distinguish two broad camps, which we'll call—for reasons we explain—*epistemological* and *holistic* particularism, and urge that the latter further cleaves between what we'll call *metaphysical* and *defeasibility-based* holism.

3. EPISTEMOLOGICAL AND DELIBERATIVE PARTICULARISTS

The first, and perhaps most familiar, sort of particularism works to reject the epistemic or deliberative usefulness of moral Principles. We've already conceded that such generalizations don't capture the entirety of moral epistemology and deliberation—that's just what it is to agree that Principles aren't mechanical. These philosophers go further (how much further depending on how radical their views) to say that *little to none* of the work we do in trying to determine, question, understand, or justify is done with Principles, even nonmechanically understood. There is no Kantian or Rawlsian procedure to follow or neat checklist of inputs to scour situations for. To a much greater extent than is appreciated by theory-loving philosophers, moral knowledge is not about inference and application of explanatory generalizations but rather about mastering concepts and discerning their instances.

Some such antitheorists are *antistructuralists*. They focus, in essence, in denying condition 3 of moral Principles. There may be individual explanatory generalizations that help us find our way around the moral world, but they form no illuminating structure. Perhaps God offers a series of isolated injunctions that add up to no coherent or inferentially rich conception of the good: They are simply scattered orders, and the morally acceptable life is one that follows them.[6] The more usual basis, of course, is rather more secular, with most such commentators tracing the lack of structure to the very multiplicity of exceptionless generalizations. The moral landscape, they urge, is *irreducibly* rich. There is a veritable plethora of, there are even unboundedly many, good-making properties, and no thought they can be helpfully systematized. Strains of this sort of antitheory appear in Annette Baier (1985) and Iris Murdoch (1970; for an excellent discussion of Murdoch, see Millgram, 2002). There is no theoretical unification of the moral realm to be had: No smaller set of generalizations accounts for the broader multiplicity; no purchase is gained on moral confusion or dispute by way of substantive and nontrivial inferential connections between exceptionless generalizations. On this view, then, *inter-principle* epistemic leverage is radically reduced: For the most part, one simply has to come to know each explanatory generalization one by one. We may make use of individual theoretical generalizations—a definition of consent here, a commitment to the evil of gossip there—but we shouldn't hope for anything remotely resembling a theory.

A different set of moves aims to question the justificatory usefulness of the individual principles themselves. "Discernment" antitheorists urge that verdicts on cases are reached, not by applying theoretical generalizations, but by seeing what moral meaning the various saliences in a case form together. These philosophers focus, in essence, on rejecting condition 2. What theoretical generalizations we recognize in morality do not mark epistemically significant moves from premise to conclusion. While we may agree that gratuitous cruelty is always bad-making, this is because competent grasp of the very concept involves seeing the bad in all such actions.

To some, this is because moral principles are merely *summaries* of past judgments—potent in discursive justification because they represent a concentrated way to represent that history, but summaries nonetheless (see, e.g., Garfield, 2000). They cannot budge intuitions about instances, only reflect them. For others, it is because they involve concepts whose meaning is dominated by their noninferential role. Coming to understand 'cruelty,' like coming to understand 'red', is fundamentally a matter of coming to be able to see it. Thus, while there can be theoretical moral generalizations like "Cruelty is 'bad-making," they are like the "principle" that "Red objects are colored," belief in which is an utterly minimal condition of competency with the concept. Such principles are of no epistemic help in getting an otherwise empirically confused person to see that something is cruel or again red, for one not already knowing this principle has no grasp at all of the concept.

Exceptionless generalizations, on either of these views, merely make explicit content implicit in the noninferential judgment of the moral expert. (All moral generalizations are, in this sense, analytic.) Such generalizations may be useful as crutches for the moral novice, in regimenting moral language, or again as reminders for someone momentarily confused; but genuine epistemic reliance on generalizations shows a lack of understanding. This sort of antitheory, then, is not based in a denial of meaningful structure (indeed, one could think that these analytic principles form a tight unified structure, akin to that found among the definitional postulates of abstract mathematics). Rather, it denies the sort of explanatory or justificatory role necessary for these generalizations to deserve the name "law-like."

For some antitheorists—including, arguably, Baier and Murdoch—the complexity of moral deliberation reflects the complexity of the underlying nature of morality. Many who are skeptical of theory, though, are more restricted in their agenda. Such commentators may well think that, at its ultimate level (what Wilfrid Sellars [1956] would call the "scientific image"),[7] morality is indeed governed by Principles forming a neat theoretical structure. What they are concerned to reject is the belief that this structure has much direct contact with the way a competent moral agent reasons:[8] Such Principles provide no justificatory or deliberative guide at the level of everyday decision-making and assessment (at the "moral manifest level," as it were). For these more restricted particularists, one important epistemic function of Principles could then remain: It may be that deep *understanding* of morality—as Aristotle would put it, knowing the 'why'—may consist in knowledge of Principles. For those who reject Principles at both levels, in contrast, knowing the 'why' is a matter, pure and simple, of concept mastery (for more here, see Little, 2001).

Whatever their other differences, the central idea common to epistemological particularists is that inferential justification—of theoretical generalizations or of particular verdicts, at the manifest or the scientific level—plays a far smaller role than ethical theorists have supposed. Moral principles can serve pedagogic and heuristic roles—they can help us to develop mastery of moral concepts and discern their instances; but they do not mark epistemically or explanatorily rich inferential relationships between propositions.

Now many have found plausible the claim that inferential justification via moral Principles is *less* central than traditional theory-loving philosophers have believed: A large part of moral life consists in noninferential uptake of moral significance. Controversy surfaces, though, when the claim's scope extends more radically. After all, it will be pointed out, however much we rely on discernment and judgment, it certainly *looks* as though an important part of how we justify, convince, teach, deliberate, and clarify is by pointing to explanatory generalizations whose truth we seem to endorse.[9] Sometimes we convert by showing a film; then again, sometimes we do it by giving an argument (say, that one shouldn't discriminate on the basis of sex). Sometimes we teach by modeling behavior; but sometimes we do it by articulating a generalization (say, that wrongful interference is measured by lack of consent). And when we want to understand what someone means when he invokes a contested concept (say, 'equality'), sometimes we ask for his verdict on a test case, but sometimes (if only to control for differing factual interpretations) we ask him to give us his definition. In short, we seem to theorize—to appeal to interrelated explanatory generalizations—all over the place. Debate over this brand of particularism, then, is in large part a matter of debating how many of these phenomena can be appropriately accounted for as heuristic rather than justificatory.

4. Valence-Switching and the Holism of Moral Reasons

Another camp of particularists is concerned with quite a different issue. These philosophers direct their attention to the first condition of classical Principles outlined earlier—their status as exceptionless explanatory generalizations. The epistemological particularists just surveyed, however otherwise radical, do allow that there are true exceptionless moral generalizations in virtue of which considerations count as reasons—there are just too many, or they merely reflect, rather than lead to, verdicts about individual cases. For another group of particularists, though, it is just this remaining concession that is rejected. Let's take a look.

A number of particularists, most prominently Jonathan Dancy (1993, 2004), have argued that considerations carry their moral import only *holistically*. A consideration that in one context counts for an action can in another count against it or be irrelevant, and all in a way that cannot be cashed out in finite or helpful terms. Pain is prima facie to be avoided—well, except when it's constitutive of athletic accomplishment; intentionally telling a falsehood is at least prima facie wrong—well, but not when playing the game Diplomacy or responding to the demands of Nazi guards, to whom the truth is not owed. Pleasure always counts in favor of a situation—well, except when it's the sadist's delight in her victim's agony, where her pleasure is precisely part of what is wrong with the situation, not its "moral silver lining."[10]

To be sure, moral reasons, as opposed to garden-variety practical reasons, are meant to be universalizable. But this only commits us to the claim that a consideration must function as a reason in all relevantly similar situations, and the claim is that "relevantly similar" cannot be cashed out. Exceptions lurk, however carefully matters are specified. For moral considerations contribute to an action's moral status in the way that a given dab of paint on the canvas carries its contribution to the aesthetic status of a painting: The bold stroke of red that helps balance one painting would be the ruin of another; and there is no way to specify the conditions in which it will help and the conditions in which it will detract.[11] Just so, whether a given feature counts as any moral reason at all—and if so, in what direction—is itself irreducibly dependent on the background context.

The claim, then, is not just that the moral contribution made by these considerations gets *outweighed* by others (as when the pain of a measles shot is justified by the utility it brings); the claim is that the moral "valence" of the consideration—its positive or negative contribution to overall moral status—itself depends irreducibly on the background context in which it appears. Thus, not only can't one codify how the moral weight of a given feature stacks up against other moral considerations, it need not have any moral weight to begin with, and certainly none of any given direction.

Now of course, everyone thinks there are *some* sorts of considerations whose import varies wildly by context: The utilitarian can agree that wiggling one's thumb can, in the right context, constitute disutility while constituting utility in another. But moral holists claim not just that incidentals can vary in this way, but that valence can switch *at the level of explanation*. That is, the holist claims that a consideration can itself function as a reason—a full, complete, and genuine reason—while acting fully otherwise in another circumstance. To be sure, there must be further differences to be found if a consideration that counts in one case as a reason does not in another, but it's a mistake, Dancy (1993, p. 81) argues, to think that those differences must then be mentioned as part of what makes the action right or wrong.[12] Not all features that make an extensional difference to moral status qualify as reasons. Some function as the context in virtue of which others are reasons: They are "enabling conditions"—necessary conditions for others to function as reasons but not themselves amongst the material or substantive considerations that make something good or bad; others may be, variously, "defeators," "underminers," and the like. What sets moral holists apart—for better or worse—is the claim that valence can switch at the level of the property doing the work of constituting a reason. Such a view, then, is meant to come squarely up against the traditional view that explanation must involve subsumption under exceptionless generalization.

Moral holists vary in how broadly they cast their claim. Some believe it is only so-called naturalistic reasons (those describable without obvious use of evaluative language) that function holistically; moral considerations so identified are granted invariant reason-giving force—that an action is just always counts in its favor, that it causes pleasure does not. For others, it's in for a penny, in for a pound: Even 'cruelty' is said to switch valence, depending on the context in which it appears, and the aphorism that you sometimes have to be cruel to be kind is to be taken at face value. Once we see that reasons need not function atomistically in order to be reasons, we see that many of the so-called thick moral properties that so impress others as invariant can themselves switch valence depending on the context—as Elijah Millgram (2002) puts it, the "defusing move" can work on just about anything. Jonathan Dancy (1995), in particular, has urged that there is no ex ante reason to believe moral properties must be univalent, in part because he regards the division between 'natural' and 'moral' predicates as fraught: There is simply no reason to draw a semantic line in the sand.

But this isn't to say that holists must believe that *all* moral reasons are multivariant. Indeed, Dancy himself agrees that there may well be nontrivial univalent moral reasons (he gives the example of causing gratuitous pain to unwilling victims [2004, p. 77]). For after all, there's also no ex ante reason to think there *can't* be such reasons. Philosophers are deserving of the name 'holist' just so long as they think *there are* reasons that irreducibly function holistically—just so long as they think, that is, that there are some moral reasons that do not function as such in virtue of substantive, exceptionless moral generalizations.

5. OBJECTIONS TO HOLISM

Claims of moral holism have generated intense objections across a range of theorists otherwise divided in their approaches. Frank Jackson, Philip Pettit, and Michael Smith (2000) for example, have been forceful critics of particularism on semantic grounds. They agree that particularism is consistent with morality's supervenience on the natural; but precisely because supervenience functions do not count as useful patterns, they urge, those functions aren't enough to connect us in needed ways to the natural. More specifically, such a view makes it difficult to see how we could come to learn to discriminate and classify according to moral predicates—"how we could have mastered that language"—since such predicates have no patterned relationship to natural properties. If particularists mean simply to return to some form of blunt intuitionism, according to which we are credited with a special, modular faculty that allows us to pick up on 'cruelty' in some causally direct way, then we'd at least have a replacement view of how the semantics story can be built. But most would consider that a high price to pay; more to the point, particularism looked like it meant to offer something more than a return to the not-so-golden oldies.

In response, holists agree that an account is needed of how we learn moral concepts. They are skeptical, though, of the assumption that the task is more difficult in the moral case than the natural one. The thought that it is seems to involve a presupposition. If one supposed that perception and conceptual understanding were fundamentally a matter of standing in a particular causal relation to the object responsible for the production of a percept, then one would well think that natural objects and properties enjoy an epistemic advantage over all others, since they are the most natural candidate causal relata.[13] Once we have moved beyond this sort of epistemology, though, such an asymmetry will strike one as unfounded. Following Sellars again, rejecting the idea that inferential relations are causal relations, after all, is part and parcel of the whole approach to epistemology consonant with holism. As before, the attractive epistemological positions for the particularist will be those of Heidegger, the pragmatists, Wittgenstein, Sellars, and Dreyfus and Dreyfus; and on these approaches, while an account is called for, there is no reason to think it any harder for moral semantic competence than for any other sort.

Others have protested from a perspective that allows moral discourse a more robust independence from the natural. A number of theorists who happily subscribe to the view that competencies with nonnatural concepts are not beholden to those with natural ones nonetheless reject holism as an account of reasons. In their view, such a move simply mislocates the lessons we should take from the importance of context. It is certainly true that natural properties switch moral valence in ways that defy helpful codification: As long as we confine our attention to naturalistically specified considerations, that is, we will find exceptions to generalizations about what is good-making. But all this shows is that good-making features aren't located at the natural level. They are found, instead, at the level of so-called thick moral properties—properties such as courage and cruelty, which are contentful but seem to wear their moral valence on their sleeve.

Thus Roger Crisp (2000) argues that, while we'll often begin an explanation of why an action was wrong by pointing to features such as the lie that was involved, examples such as lying in the board game Diplomacy show that the real reason the action was wrong was its *dishonesty*. If it isn't always wrong-making to refuse to return a borrowed book—as when it turns out to be stolen property— it is always wrong-making when refusing to do so in an instance of *injustice*. David McNaughton and Piers Rawling (2000) similarly argue that a great many of the countervalence cases pointed to by particularists are best understood as cases in which genuine explanation for an action's moral import is located at the level of morally rich properties that don't switch valence. If the concept of injury, for instance, seems not to switch valence, it's because it is equivalent, in fact, not to mere "infliction of pain" but to *unfair* infliction of pain—and that's something that is always wrong-making. Understanding when such properties are instantiated, of course, takes a good deal of interpretation; exceptionless Principles are recovered, though, once we realize they need to include "evaluative riders" to any more naturalistically specified considerations (McNaughton and Rawling, 2000, pp. 268–269).

According to these theorists, then, once we make the distinction between "primary and secondary," or "proximate and ultimate," reasons, and once we're willing to be good nonnaturalists, we will see that atomism survives intact as the best theory, either writ large or at least for large swaths of the moral landscape. It's a mistake—the naturalist mistake—to think that we can construct bridge laws or even useful sufficiency conditions that can guide us in deciding what we should do; but that doesn't mean we should abandon atomism. What it means, instead, is that we must ascend to the moral level to find good- and right-making considerations.

Finally, even for those otherwise attracted to the view, there is the worry that the position proves too much. In unqualified form, moral holism of the sort just outlined seems to imply that lying, killing, and the infliction of pain have no more intimate connection to wrongness than do truth-telling, healing, and the giving of pleasure. After all, each, against the right context, can have a positive, negative, or neutral moral import. But the morally wise person, one might have thought, is someone who understands that there is a deep difference in moral status between infliction of pain and shoelace color, even if both can, against the right narrative, be bad-making. It is not just that infliction of pain *can* be, or in our local neighborhood *usually is,* wrong-making; we feel that there is an *intimate* connection here, one having something to do with the nature of the consideration, even if there are exceptions.

In response to these objections, holists have argued that once we are freed of the epistemological and metaphysical biases that tried to force us toward atomism, we lose the motivation to *insist* on univalence in every case. There will be cases in which ascending to a univalent property *lessens* explanatory potency, cases in which the real work of illuminating—rather than regimenting—is done by the thick, rich, and messy world of the multivalent. Once we realize that atomism isn't the only legitimate model of explanation, it would then be odd to insist that all explanatory moral generalizations just *must be* univalent. Thus, while it remains a crucial question whether particularism is the right substantive view of ethics—whether ethical considerations do in fact function in a holistic valence-switching manner—once one understands that genuine justificatory and explanatory work *can* be done holistically, the important war has been won.

It's one thing, though, to insist that atomism is not the only alternative, another to spell out what the better one is. Atomism is nothing if not familiar, both in morality and in the philosophy of science, in which reason is tied to explanation, which is, in turn, tied to subsumption under laws, which are typically presumed to be exceptionless. The holist, then, must do more than make gestures to nondiscursive skills, forms of life, or the "ready to hand." In the end, the plausibility—or lack thereof—of holism turns on what replacement picture is offered of how reasons *do* function, a picture that must vindicate the genuine moral difference between lying and shoelace color.

And it is here that we come to the last, and in many ways deepest, divide among particularists. On the one side are holists who want to reject the idea of subsumption under generalization altogether. For these philosophers, one thing can be a reason for another without there being any generalization connecting them at all. For others, the lesson is that we must reconceive our idea of a principle: must find a way to see principles as both exception-laden and law-like. We begin with the first approach.

6. METAPHYSICAL HOLISM: EXPLANATION WITHOUT GENERALIZATION

Jonathan Dancy, whose work has done the most to revive interest in particularism, argues that considerations function as reasons when they stand in a particular metaphysical relationship he dubs "resultance" (1993, pp. 73–79). One of the ways we explain in everyday life, he urges, is by pointing out such a relationship. That white is winning in a given position is a result of the passed pawn on the Queenside; that the painting is beautiful is a result of its colors' pensive juxtaposition. Such examples, he agrees, make it tempting to accept a *constitution* theory of resultance, according to which what it is for this object now to be G is constituted here by its being F. In the end, though, the relationship is simply hard to say much about: It is, he argues, a primitive but thoroughly familiar relationship.

At any rate, a key point is that it is a relationship that does not issue in type-type identities. "The [resultance] tree for the same property of a different object will quite probably be different, because the way in which that object gets to be F (where F-ness is a resultant property) will probably be different from the way in which this one got to be F" (Dancy, 1993, p. 74). So there is no assumption that winning in general results from passed pawns, or that passed pawns generally result in winning positions; the same color juxtaposition in another painting might well result in ugliness. Of course, this point does not itself entail that there are no type–type relations, since it is possible that there is some exhaustive list of (type-specified) ways in which something could get to be F (the relation would be "If P_1 or, . . . or P_n then F"). But Dancy's view is that once one begins down this road—once one recognizes that there are multiple ways to instantiate the salient moral resultant properties—there will be no reason to think that, in general, you can stop anywhere short of the particular token instance of a given property. As he says, claims of resultance are for "this property of this object now" (p. 74).

This isn't to say that all properties (understood now as types) are moral equals. Some properties, Dancy (1993, p. 103) argues, are "moral defaults." Metaphorically put, they come to a situation already "turned on"; more formally, they are properties that need no *enabler* in order for them to function as reasons of a certain direction, though they may, of course, be "turned off" in all manner of contexts by the presence of defeaters or underminers. (By contrast, Ross thought that they could be overridden, but always must push in the same direction. Lying may be an overall good thing to do, but that is always despite the fact that its character as a lying counts against it. For Dancy, other features may change the nature of the contribution lying itself makes to the status of the whole act.) The central claim is one of explanatory asymmetry: There are some properties with a default valence—one that itself needs no explanation; it can, like any import, shift to another, but its doing so demands explanation. One thus may need to explain why pain is, in this case, good-making, but not why in another it is bad-making.

Moral epistemology, on this view, is quite radically antitheoretic. The account of explanation is, broadly put, not one of subsumption but of narrative. As with describing a building, we characterize the situation in ways that will get others to interpret and see it as we do (Dancy, 1993, p. 112). To be sure, moral Principles familiar from theory are helpful devices to remind us of what moral import various considerations *can* have, but they serve no independent justificatory function. Adducing Principles can thus be useful in pedagogy or in helping others to see things as one ought; but they carry no more justificatory weight than that. And, while we can come to know which properties count as moral defaults, this crucially doesn't mean such properties count as *epistemic defaults*—it doesn't mean one is entitled to presume that the property carries that valence in the case at hand, absent evidence to the contrary.

All of this helps to make clear what Dancy has in mind when he says there are no moral principles. He agrees that there are true exceptionless moral generalizations; indeed, as we showed, he agrees that there can be nontrivial univalent properties—why not? Such generalizations are not yet principles in his sense, though. Principles have to state explanatorily substantive, not merely formal, connections; more than that, they are supposed to be *that in virtue of which reasons function* (see Dancy, 2000, sec. 1, 2004, ch. 5). It is the latter condition that is never met. For if genuinely variable considerations can genuinely serve as reasons, he says, they are functioning qua reasons in the same way that features with invariant valence so function—namely, by serving as the resultance base of the moral import. It can't be essential to the reason-giving relation that it instantiate a principle. Even if there are universal exceptionless generalizations about certain good-making properties, then, principlism is no good as an account of how reasons work.

For Dancy, then, the issue is less about whether or how many moral reasons are univalent; it's about relocating the concept of a reason away from the space of epistemology to a metaphysical relationship. It's in this sense that we call him a "metaphysical" particularist—a label he also gives himself (2004, ch. 8)—rather than because he is uninterested in the epistemological fallout. (This also explains why he puts so much weight on maintaining the category split between what count as reasons and what as context, rather than on claims about uncodifiability; for what matters to him in reason claims is what stands in a particular metaphysical relationship.)[14]

According to Dancy (1993, p. 106), the lesson of all this is clear: "Reasons do not function in virtue of generalizations; they are about the ways things add up here." He wants to "deny that the explanation [of specific moral truths] has any need to be run in terms of general moral truths. The explanation will be given

in terms of the properties from which the thin properties of rightness and wrongness result. This has no need to be generalized." Dancy's replacement view of
reasons, in short, severs their connection to generalization. The epistemic upshot
of this is that understanding the reason that something is good or bad is not a
function of uncovering generalizations. For Dancy, indeed, apprehending that a
consideration is a reason is far more like a sort of discrete perception, of seeing
how things add up here. The very idea of a generalization is otiose for notions
of reason.

This is certainly a view that will leave some uneasy. For many, explanation is
neither something to be stipulated as a brute metaphysical fact nor something
that *could* be, as Dancy puts it at one point, "stubbornly particular" (1993, p. 104).
It has *something* to do with generalization, even if not a deductive one.

To show this, let's return to constitution, that claimed close cousin to resultance. Citing something as constitutive of another is explanatory in a way that,
say, citing a simple token–token identity is not.[15] The whole point of constitution
is that there are multiple paths or criteria by which something might be an individual of the type, and citing which path is the actual one is both illuminatingly
what "makes it" of the type and what explains its being so (that the chess position's strength here is due to the pawn's position and not, say, to the rook's).
Constitution (and resultance), then, is able to be explanatory in a way that mere
identity is not because different things could serve as the constitutor.

Taken as a purely metaphysical relationship, though, there are any number
of different things that could be counted as "constituting" something's being phi.
We could mention the position of the passed pawn; then again, we could say the
position's strength is constituted here by the complex fact of the entire tree of
legal game continuations, or any number of levels in between. Similarly, in the
case of the painting, we could say that the beauty is constituted by the distribution
of red and green, or again or that it is constituted by the distribution of atomic
particles across a given region. What allows us to pick, from among these various
possible levels, which one is a favored, *explanatory* relationship? How do we go
about determining the level at which resultance is said to hold?

At times, Dancy seems to appeal to his narrativist epistemology to provide
the answer. But whatever the pluses or minuses of narrative as an epistemology,
it won't serve to locate resultance. "Narrative bases" are neither unique nor "in
nature"—what is heuristically useful depends on a great number of subjective
factors.[16] We can always imagine two different stories, each of which leaves out
elements of the other, and each of which successfully enables a given listener to
gestalt what there is morally to see in the situation; there is thus no unique set
of properties that count, as a matter of brute metaphysical fact, as a narrative
base.

Most of the time, though, this is simply of limited worry for Dancy; after all, according to him, resultance is primitive. He takes our intuition about which level of description is the one that "really" counts and dubs it as pointing to a special metaphysical relationship. For many, though, there is more of an answer that can—and should—be given. Whatever the details, something counts as explanatory—as a "resultance base," if you like—when it serves a particular *epistemic function*, namely, when it can serve in particularly robust ways (with 'robust' interpreted differently by different theorists) as the basis of an inference to the conclusion. This, after all, is what ties the idea of something being a reason to something that can serve in reasoning. But to play *this* role requires hooking in to generalization. To be committed to the propriety of an inference *is* to be committed to its propriety in some set of other contexts. Imagine Smith, a moral novice, who is told by Jones, the moral expert, that the reason the action they just witnessed is bad is because it is cruel. Imagine further that, when Smith again witnesses cruelty and thinks it a basis for believing, or perhaps presuming, or at least hypothesizing (all epistemic attitudes) that it is bad-making, she is met with absolute and utter befuddlement by Jones: "Whyever would you think *that*?" Surely, one loses touch of what is meant by "reason" in the face of such a reaction. As Alan Goldman (2001) puts it, the difference that stands as a reason can't just be a "one-off."

Similarly, the narrativist account Dancy gives—an intentionally metaphoric account in which the saliences assume a shape—is not in fact equivalent to adducing reasons. There is a difference between adducing a set of facts as a reason for something and telling a story. The first gives an explanation; the second tells enough of the supervenience base to allow someone to gestalt or perceive the resultant property on her own.

This isn't to deny that the relationship of resultance is a metaphysical one. Rather, it's to say that we get to *classify* any candidate as standing in such a relationship only in virtue of the candidate's epistemic relevance. (That is, even if one could directly perceive the resultant—that this act is cruel—the proper explanation of why the relation between that property and its base counts as resultance is in virtue of the epistemic work the connection can do for us—that we can explain why this act is cruel in terms of the fact that it caused harm, etc.) Similarly with the categories of defaults, enablers, disablers, and underminers: It is not that such distinctions make no sense, or that one can't regard them as "metaphysical," but that the criteria for counting as a member of that class must concern its ability to play an epistemological role.

Finally, Dancy's view requires that quite a lot of weight be put on moral perception. As we've seen, every brand of particularist countenances the existence of moral discernment. For Dancy, though, our talents of discernment extend to knowledge of something's counting as a reason—not to mention enabler and disabler. Something's "being a reason"—this brute metaphysical relationship in no way tied to generality or theory—is now just one more atomic observable, akin to "being white." Not a few philosophers will wonder whether this is a plausible candidate for such a treatment.

7. DEFEASIBLE GENERALIZATIONS

Another set of particularists takes a very different tack. These philosophers insist that reasons, as explanations, cannot be unmoored from generalizations. Instead, the lesson of particularism is to challenge the first condition of classic Principles— the condition that generalizations, to be explanatory, must be exceptionless. Put differently, the lesson of valence switching is not to deny the role of theoretical generalizations in morality, but to give a different picture of what those generalizations must look like if they're to do the work asked of them.

When we reflect on the sorts of explanatory generalizations deployed in various theoretical enterprises, a notable feature emerges: Disciplines from epistemology to biology or semantics are rife with claims that seem explanatory even while they are porous—shot through with exceptions that cannot be usefully eliminated. As a rule, matches light when struck; for the most, appearances are warrant-conferring; absent defeators, fish eggs turn into fish. Those drawn to holism will be skeptical of finding any tractable, concrete way to fill in the conditions in which the effects actually occur (of demarcating all the circumstances in which, say, fish eggs don't turn into fish). Yet the statements don't thereby seem empty—claiming simply that such effects *can* happen, or do unless they don't. Instead, the point of the generalizations seems to involve isolating a connection that is, for one reason or another, particularly telling of something's nature.

Aristotle called them "for the most part" generalizations. Such an expression is misleading, though, since the generalizations at issue aren't merely statistical reports of what usually happens. Indeed, they can concern an effect that in fact rarely happens—as with fish eggs, whose usual fate, after all, is to end up in another creature's belly. Further, except in arenas such as quantum mechanics that are ruled by genuinely statistical laws, statements about what is "usual" are contingent expressions of local happenings, not principles with significant explanatory import. One might call them 'ceteris paribus' generalizations, but this expression, too, can be a misleading way to pick out the sorts of generalizations here at issue. Literally meaning "other things being equal," the qualifier 'ceteris paribus' includes enthymematic cases in which what is held equal is fully specifiable (think Boyle's gas laws), or again, can be used to isolate a specific force that always pushes in the same direction (think the forces of physics or, again, Ross's prima facie duties), and that, hence, doesn't allow exceptions to claims about the direction-*pushing* or good-*making* nature of the object. In contrast, the present generalizations are meant to tell us about the nature of something, not by standing in for better versions that would be free of exceptions to the isolated connection but by demarcating what has status *of* exception. We might call them "defeasible generalizations" to mark the point.

We have elsewhere urged that the semantic content of such qualified generalizations is best understood as one that unpacks the notion in explicitly normative terms, by reference to various notions of "privileged conditions" (Lance and Little, 2004, forthcoming). The core content of a defeasible generalization on this approach is the claim that "in privileged conditions," all As are B: Understanding such a conditional is a matter *both* of understanding what, for its purposes, count as privileged conditions, *and* what compensatory moves are required by various deviations from those conditions. Such privileging, we've argued, is a genus with different species, including the privileging of paradigm over riff, of normal conditions over interfering ones, and of certain features as justificatorily prior to certain others. A great deal of the nuance of such claims, indeed, lies in unpacking which is at stake in a given claim.

Whether one is drawn to this semantics or another, though, such generalizations, if meaningful, offer a different way of reading the lesson of moral holism. The exceptions pointed to by the particularist need not stand in the way of genuinely explanatory generalizations; they can, instead, be marks that the explanations in question are ones offered by defeasible generalizations. The features of an act that are genuinely explanatory of its moral status—as opposed to random details of a narrative, or, again, contingently relevant features—are subjects of defeasible explanatory generalizations. In saying that defeasibly, lying is wrong-making, we are neither saying that these features always carry this valence nor merely asserting that it usually does in our neck of the woods; we are saying, instead, that where lying lacks this valence, as it sometimes or even often may do, it is in virtue of the ways it deviates from what are classified as paradigm or somehow illustrative conditions. In our view, again, this is best parsed out in terms of the notion of privileging maneuvers. Infliction of pain is defeasibly bad-making: It can be good-making, bad-making, or neutral, but its status in each case is understood by the way in which that given case relates to conditions that are in some appropriate sense privileged.

Moral defeasible generalizations, we believe, exhibit the full range of the privileging typology. Sometimes, the privileging is meant to mark out that something is morally *amiss* in cases where the countervalence holds. Take the moral status of killing. Killing is always wrong-making in privileged conditions; but in certain others—one's favorite postapocalyptic scenario, say, where the world is infested with vicious and unreasoning brutes intent on killing one's family—it may be a good-making feature of one's act that one shoot first and ask questions later. In such a case, though, the very fact that killing is not right-making is a signal that something in the situation (namely, the prevalence of vicious and unreasoning brutes) is morally defective—*would* that killing were here wrong-making! In these sorts of cases, privileged conditions are morally superior situations; the counter-valence cases bear the "trace" that they are worse to the extent, and in the way, that they depart from those superior situations.

In another central sort of privileging, the priority of the privileged condition is an explanatory or justificatory one. Defeasibly, lying is wrong-making; but there are morally innocuous cases of reversed valence—as when lying while playing the game Diplomacy. Here, the priority of the privileged condition is constituted not by its moral superiority but by its explanatory primacy: We can understand a situation in which lying is wrong-making without resort to any context in which it has the opposite valence; but to understand the moral status of lying in Diplomacy, one must understand the players as having agreed to play a game with these rules in a context in which lying does have its typical valence. Without such an agreement, or without its having been made in a situation in which lying has the normal valence, it would not be thusly moral to lie during the play of the game.

According to such a view, moral understanding essentially involves skill at "navigating the normal." It requires understanding not just the various sorts of privileged conditions and notions of privilege, but where one is in relationship to them, what compensatory moves that relationship urges, and an ability to rec-ognize the trace left by the necessary defeasible generalization in nonprivileged conditions.

Such a view can maintain a radical position on the valence-switching pro-pensity of moral considerations without flattening the moral field in such a way as to render shoelace color and infliction of pain moral equals. Shoelace color and the infliction of pain can both be bad-making, but the similarity ends there. For while shoelace color can have various moral imports in various contexts, it has none of them defeasibly. In contrast, lying not only can have a negative moral import, but also, always, and necessarily, it has the property of being defeasibly bad-making.

In this way, note, the view can agree with Dancy that some properties con-stitute moral "defaults" in the metaphoric sense of "coming already with" a particular valence; but the notion of a default is no longer understood as some brute metaphysical feature unconnected to the giving of reasons and explanations. Rather, to say that some features have a default valence simply means that they defeasibly have that valence—that they have that valence, that is, in situations that are fundamental in one of the various senses.[17] It also makes clear the sense in which this notion of "default" is not equivalent to the notion of *epistemic* default—of the import one may presume the feature has until presented with evidence to the contrary. Lying will have an epistemic default status of being wrong-making in many contexts, but it precisely won't in deviant circumstances.

Now some who are attracted to this broad approach retain the antitheoretic stance common to so many particularists.[18] Defeasible moral generalizations, it is argued, while illuminating of underlying moral reality, are of no help in daily epistemology, for they are, once again, mere summaries of prior specific knowledge. One's conception of illustrative conditions, and again of the compensatory moves required by a situation's relation to them, is simply and entirely filled in by first-order verdicts of particular cases. Others, though—ourselves included—believe that moral experience can help give us a relatively independent grasp of the defeasible generalizations themselves. Even if one's understandings of defeasible generalizations and particular moral verdicts are inextricably *intertwined*, that is, one's skill at appreciating the generalizations can often be developed with some degree of independence from particular verdicts one might reach. The former can thus exert leverage on one's commitments about particular instances and can stand as serious epistemic checks on one's other moral intuitions. In such cases, understandings of defeasible generalizations can function, much as traditional theory was meant to, as both argument for moral conclusions and unifying explanation of moral phenomena.

Such a view is nonetheless loyal to certain fundamental particularist claims. Just so long as one's epistemic grasp of the shape of the illustrative conditions, and of the difference that a departure from them makes, is not itself capturable as a set of Principles, the holism the particularist cherishes will be preserved. Further, and crucially, the view retains the core particularist claim that no moral verdict is guaranteed by any substantive explanatory considerations, conceived of independently of the particular case. It simply argues that such an insight does not stand in contrast to all generality, or even theoretical generalizations as laws; it stands in contrast to conceptions of those laws that obscure the centrality of our skills of navigating the space of privilege and exception. It is radical, if radical it seems, not because it is eliminativist of the epistemic use of explanatory laws but because it challenges so fundamentally a certain picture of how those laws must function.

NOTES

1. Note that McNaughton's view has interestingly changed; see McNaughton and Rawling, 2002.

2. Richardson, 1995, offers an excellent exposition of the difference. On analogy, he

points out, one might believe that revealed preference theory counts as the correct theory of what practical reasons there are, while thinking that such a theory would be a dreadful guide for deliberation.

3. Modern Kantians differ according to which aspect receives emphasis in their own version of the theory. Some find Kant's method incapable of yielding meaningful directives but find wisdom in his respect-based normative ethics; some who resist much that is said at the level of emergent normative principles find most wisdom in the method—and then there are those who think them too intricately tied to be judged independently.

4. Which doesn't mean the predicate need be recognizably a moral one.

5. The conversation over "principlism" in bioethics has been dogged by just this confusion. Objections to Beauchamp and Childress's classic *Principles of Biomedical Ethics*, 2001, are a mixture of what are, by this essay's lights, genuine particularist worries and worries that the four principles they make use of are simply too abstract, or again too few, to be the most perspicuous such list to use.

6. There are interpreters of the Old Testament who maintain that this was the common understanding of early Hebrew scripture. God is not presenting us a theory—even an infallible one—or even a picture of goodness that can be understood as a coherent whole. He is merely giving orders, ones we would do well to follow.

7. The manifest image is the conceptual space of ordinary objects, properties, and relations, most of which are noninferentially observable. The scientific image is the conceptual space of theoretical posits and the laws that govern them. This image is populated by purely theoretical entities—that is, by entities belief in whose existence is justifiable only inferentially. ('Scientific', in this sense, need have nothing to do with 'science' understood as a naturalistic enterprise.)

8. An example would be a utilitarian who endorsed a virtue theoretic moral epistemology, perhaps on the ground that the greatest utility in worlds reasonably close to ours would always be achieved by agents who trusted the judgments of virtuous moral experts. See again Richardson, 1995.

9. This paragraph is taken from Little, 2001.

10. The pain example is from Millgram, the Diplomacy example a variant of one of McNaughton's, and the pleasure example from Dancy.

11. This nice example is David McNaughton's, personal communication.

12. It is worth noting that just this move is made in epistemology by Wilfrid Sellars. One of the key points urged in "Empiricism and the Philosophy of Mind," 1956, is that there are many forms of epistemic dependence. A claim, according to Sellars, can be genuinely noninferentially justified, and yet its status as such depend on the existence of other beliefs of the agent. That is, a claim Q can depend for its status on another claim P, without P being a reason (or evidence) for Q. P is, to put it in Dancy's terms, an enabler of the noninferential status of Q. The same goes for inferential beliefs. It may be that P is good reason for Q only in the context of R, without this implying that it is really P and R that form the reason for Q.

13. So, if it is assumed that things are straightforward in the natural case, that learning the concept dog, say, is a matter of learning to perceive and identify dogs, and that this latter ability is merely coming to be in a particular sort of causal relation with dogs, then one would indeed find nonnaturalistically reducible moral concepts especially problematic.

14. Others argue that what matters most deeply is the anticodification theme made famous in McDowell's writings. After all, if there were crisply codifiable generalizations about which conditions count as enabling, we could accept the category split between reasons and "context" without needing to shift our underlying view of how moral explanation or epistemology works.

15. Jon may well be Uncle Bud, but there is a clear sense in which being Uncle Bud isn't the reason why he is Jon.

16. At times of course also with the relation of constitution, as when the picture is made up of dots.

17. If the privilege is justificatory, then these precisely are cases not calling for justification. One can rely on a noninferential assumption that lying is bad-making.

18. Jay Garfield, 2000, is perhaps a good example. He seems to be drawn to what would broadly qualify as a defeasibility-based particularism, in our sense; yet he argues that the resulting moral generalizations, "suitably festooned with ceteris paribus clauses" (p. 200), are mere summaries of prior case verdicts. Hence they still serve no justificatory roles—only (valuable) heuristic and pedagogic ones.

REFERENCES

Baier, Annette. 1985. "Theory and Reflective Practices." In *Postures of the Mind,* 207–227. Minneapolis: University of Minnesota Press.

Beauchamp, Tom, and Jim Childress. 2001. *Principles of Biomedical Ethics.* New York: Oxford University Press.

Blum, Lawrence. 1991. "Moral Perception and Particularity." *Ethics* 101: 701–725.

Crisp, Roger. 2000. "Particularizing Particularism." In *Moral Particularism,* ed. Brad Hooker and Margaret Little, 23–47. Oxford: Oxford University Press.

Dancy, Jonathan. 1993. *Moral Reasons.* Oxford: Oxford University Press.

———. 1995. "In Defense of Thick Concepts." In *Midwest Studies in Philosophy,* ed. P. French, T. E. Uehling, Jr., and H. K. Wettstein, 20: 263–279.

———. 1999. "Defending Particularism." *Metaphilosophy* 30: 25–32.

———. 2000. "The Particularist's Progress." In *Moral Particularism,* ed. Brad Hooker and Margaret Little, 130–156. Oxford: Oxford University Press.

———. 2004. *Ethics without Principles.* Oxford: Oxford University Press.

———. Unpublished. "An Unprincipled Morality."

Dreyfus, Hubert, and Stuart Dreyfus. 1992. "What Is Moral Maturity? Towards a Phenomenology of Ethical Enterprise." In *Revisioning Philosophy,* ed. James Ogilvey, 111–131. Albany: State University of New York Press.

Garfield, Jay. 2000. "Particularity and Principle: The Structure of Moral Knowledge." In *Moral Particularism,* ed. Brad Hooker and Margaret Little, 178–204. Oxford: Oxford University Press.

Goldman, Alan. 2001. *Practical Rules: When We Need Them and When We Don't.* Cambridge: Cambridge University Press.

Herman, Barbara. 1993. "Obligation and Performance." In *The Practice of Moral Judgment,* 159–183. Cambridge, Mass.: Harvard University Press.

Jackson, Frank, Philip Pettit, and Michael Smith. 2000. "Ethical Particularism and Patterns." In *Moral Particularism,* ed. Brad Hooker and Margaret Little, 79–99. Oxford: Oxford University Press.

Lance, Mark, and Margaret Little. 2004. "Defeasibility and the Normative Grasp of Context." *Erkenntnis* 61: 435–455.

———. Forthcoming. "Defending Moral Particularism." In *Moral Theories,* ed. James Dwyer. Oxford: Blackwell.

Little, Margaret. 2000. "Moral Generalities Revisited." In *Moral Particularism,* ed. Brad Hooker and Margaret Little, 276–304. Oxford: Oxford University Press.

———. 2001. "On Knowing the 'Why': Particularism and Moral Theory." *Hastings Center Report* 31, 4: 32–40.

McDowell, John. 1979. "Virtue and Reason." *Monist* 62: 331–350.

———. 1981. "Non-Cognitivism and Rule-Following." In *Wittgenstein: To Follow a Rule,* ed. Steven Holtzman and Christopher Leich, 141–162. London: Routledge and Kegan Paul.

McNaughton, David. 1988. *Moral Vision: An Introduction to Ethics.* Oxford: Blackwell.

———. 1996. "An Unconnected Heap of Duties?" *Philosophical Quarterly* 46: 433–447.

McNaughton, David, and Piers Rawling. 2000. "Unprincipled Ethics." In *Moral Particularism,* ed. Brad Hooker and Margaret Little, 256–275. Oxford: Oxford University Press.

———. 2002. "Conditional and Conditioned Reasons." *Utilitas* 14: 240–248.

Millgram, Elijah. 2002. "Murdoch, Practical Reasoning, and Particularism." *Notizie di Politeia* 18: 64–87.

Murdoch, Iris. 1970. *The Sovereignty of Good.* London: Routledge and Kegan Paul.

Nussbaum, Martha. 1985. "Finely Aware and Richly Responsible: Moral Attention and the Moral Task of Literature." *Journal of Philosophy* 82, 10: 516–529.

O'Neill, Onora. 2001. "Practical Principles and Practical Judgment." *Hastings Center Report* 31, 4: 15–23.

Pietrowski, Paul. 1993. "Prima Facie Obligations, *Ceteris Paribus* Laws in Moral Theory." *Ethics* 103: 489–515.

Richardson, Henry. 1995. "Beyond Good and Right: Toward a Constructive Ethical Pragmatism." *Philosophy and Public Affairs* 24: 108–141.

Ross, W. D. 1930. *The Right and the Good.* Oxford: Clarendon Press.

Sellars, Wilfrid. 1956. "Empiricism and the Philosophy of Mind." In *The Foundations of Science and the Concepts of Psychoanalysis,* Minnesota Studies in the Philosophy of Science, vol. 1, ed. H. Feigl and M. Scriven, 127–196. Minneapolis: University of Minnesota Press.

Sherman, Nancy. 1989. *The Fabric of Character: Aristotle's Theory of Virtue.* Oxford: Clarendon Press.

CHAPTER 21

INTUITIONS IN MORAL INQUIRY

MICHAEL R. DEPAUL

THE mention of intuition in a discussion of moral inquiry will lead many readers to think of intuitionism, the view of H. A. Prichard (1912) and W. D. Ross (1930). Their eyes will glaze over as they conjure up images of England in the first part of the twentieth century, of stuffy men in tweed discussing the requirements of duty while taking their port. Stereotypes aside, it is easy to think intuitionism was justly charged and convicted of dressing up what is at best one man's personal morality, and at worst his class prejudices, to try to pass them off as the self-evident truth about the right and the good. No doubt many moral philosophers find it comforting to think that, despite the many shortcomings of their discipline, they have at least been able to get past such silliness. My aim in this essay is not to defend intuitionism. I wish to focus more narrowly on the use of intuitive judgments in moral inquiry. This was a prominent element of intuitionism, but it can be isolated from the rest of intuitionism, and it is not an element only of intuitionism.[1]

Let's adopt a weak, mostly negative understanding of intuitions: An intuition is just a belief in a proposition[2] that (1) the person does not currently hold because of perception or introspection or memory or testimony or because the person has explicitly inferred the proposition, but (2) the person now holds simply because the proposition seems true[3] to the person upon due consideration.[4] It is now easy to distinguish different strands in intuitionist thinking. There is a methodological element that claims that moral inquiry ought to be guided, in a way to be specified, by our intuitions; there are epistemological elements, for example, the claim that some moral propositions are self-evident or that moral intuitions are certain, and there are structural theses, for example, that the only general moral truths concern prima facie duties. We should then recognize that the intuitionists have had plenty of company when it comes to the core methodological element of their view. Henry Sidgwick and G. E. Moore advocated versions of utilitarianism rather than intuitionism, but both made use of intuitions.[5] Use of intuition isn't just a Brit thing. Think for example of Kant's discussion of moral worth, where he describes cases such as that of a prudent merchant who does not overcharge a young client because it is good for business to maintain a reputation for honesty, expecting it to be intuitively obvious that such an action has no real moral worth (Kant, 1993, p. 10). Neither is appealing to intuitions an Enlightenment thing—the practice goes way back. It is easy to find the ancients doing it. Plato, for example, begins the *Republic* by rejecting the principle that it is just to return what one owes on the basis of the intuitive judgment that it would be wrong to return borrowed weapons to a person who is raving mad (Plato, 1992, p. 6).

Intuitions are not merely a disused artifact from the history of moral thought. Contemporary moral debates, particularly in applied ethics, are chock full of them. In fact, there are so many intuitions driving contemporary discussions that any choice of an example is bound to seem arbitrary, but let me mention Judith Thomson's case of the famous violinist with kidney disease. In the night and without your consent, the Society of Music Lovers has kidnapped you and connected the violinist's circulatory system to yours so that your kidneys can keep him alive. You are informed that the violinist will die unless he remains connected to you for nine months. Thomson expects us to make the intuitive judgment that it would not be wrong for you to disconnect the violinist, and seeks to use this judgment to undermine a familiar argument for the immorality of abortion (Thomson, 1971, pp. 48–49).

It would seem, then, that we should not allow ourselves to be too smug when we think of those musty old intuitionists, at least where reliance on intuitive judgments is concerned. Given our continuing widespread use of intuitive judgments in moral inquiry, there is a danger that we are just as silly as they were ever thought to be, that we too are dressing up nothing more than our own personal views and prejudices as intuitions, and then strutting them out to take command of our own moral inquiries. Personally, I do not believe that our practice of using intuitions in our moral inquiries is silly. I will try to defend this practice. But I should caution here at the outset that my defense will be modest. There is a good chance that what can be said, or at any rate what I can say, in behalf of intuition-driven moral inquiry will strike many as not nearly good enough.

1. Intuition-Driven Moral Inquiry and the Epistemology of Intuitions

The central claim of the methodological element of intuitionism is that intuitions play a special guiding role in moral inquiry. Various views regarding the precise nature of this role are possible. One might hold that all intuitions should be used or that only certain intuitions should be used. If one takes the second option, there are various ways of restricting the intuitions that count. One might do so on the basis of the nature of the persons who have the intuitions, for example, by trying to distinguish competent from incompetent judges, or one might look to the nature of the object of the intuition, for example, by employing only intuitions regarding the morality of actual particular actions or by limiting oneself to intuitions regarding general moral principles. Once one has decided which intuitions are to be employed in moral inquiry, there are many possible views about how one should use them. According to one stereotype, intuitionists hold that intuitions are absolutely unrevisable, providing a totally secure bedrock that moral inquiry need do no more than generalize from, if the intuitions concern particular cases, or apply to particular cases, if we intuit general principles. However, not even W. D. Ross conformed to this stereotype, since he held that intuitions are revisable.[6] Any sensible view will agree with him, and will therefore have to accord a more complex role to intuitions, part of which will involve a specification of the conditions under which intuitions are to be revised in the course of moral inquiry.

Although it would be misleading to suggest that there is no controversy about it, there is nevertheless a substantial consensus about how we should conduct moral inquiry. Very many philosophers explicitly endorse the method known as reflective equilibrium, and even more end up conducting their moral inquiries in ways that can easily been seen to fall under the description of reflective equilibrium. Moreover, it is, I think, quite clear that reflective equilibrium grants intuitions a leading role in moral inquiry. The method is clearly the most sophisticated intuitionistic approach to moral inquiry described to date, and, more significant, I believe that when properly understood, it constitutes the only reasonable way to conduct inquiry. So rather than canvassing possible alternative intuitionistic methods, I shall move directly to a consideration of reflective equilibrium. Unless this notion can be defended, I doubt that much can be said in behalf of any alternative intuitionistic approach to moral inquiry and, indeed, that much can be said in behalf of any sort of philosophical inquiry into morality.

Before moving into a discussion of reflective equilibrium, I would like to call attention to an important distinction. It is easy to run methodological views regarding the use of intuitions in moral inquiry together with views regarding the epistemic status of intuitions. One reason might be that positions regarding the epistemic status of intuitions often have methodological consequences. For example, if moral intuitions are certain and infallible, and we can easily identify these intuitions, then we should always revise anything found to be in conflict with an intuition and should never revise an intuition. Another reason might be that some people are unable to imagine any reason for employing intuitions other than their having a strong positive epistemic status. But it is important to recognize that even methodological positions that grant a significant role to intuitions need not hold them to have a strong epistemic status. It is even possible for those irrealists who hold that moral "beliefs" are not subject to epistemic evaluation at all to think that moral inquiry ought to be guided by intuitions. One might, for example, hold that morals are nothing more than a reflection of a person's preferences regarding how others conduct themselves, and still think that the proper way to determine a particular person's morality is by taking the person's intuitive moral judgments and trying to work out the most simple system of principles that captures these intuitive judgments. It is also important to notice that even if some intuitions regarding basic moral propositions have a very high epistemological status, this might not provide much guidance regarding the conduct of moral inquiry. Assuming that moral judgments are truth apt, it is possible that there are some specially propitious circumstances and certain special characteristics of persons such that the moral intuitions formed in those circumstances by persons with those characteristics are highly or even perfectly reliable. But if we do not know what these special circumstances or characteristics are or we cannot determine when people are in the circumstances or which persons have the characteristics, it is not clear how we could make use of these highly reliable intuitions in moral inquiry. The methodological role and epistemic status of intuitions are, therefore, two different things. The connections between them can be more complicated and circuitous than one might think. It will be useful to bear this in mind as I proceed.

2. REFLECTIVE EQUILIBRIUM

We owe the term 'reflective equilibrium' to John Rawls (1971), who provided a description of the method and proceeded to employ it in *A Theory of Justice*. Nelson Goodman (1955, pp. 65–68) had earlier advocated this approach as the way to work out and justify a theory of inductive logic. But once you have an abstract characterization of the method, it is plausible to think that philosophers have been using it, in ethics and elsewhere, all along.

2.1. Narrow Reflective Equilibrium

I find it useful to think of reflective equilibrium as though one were to follow the method in a stepwise fashion.[7] The method recognizes that each of us begins the process of moral inquiry with a fair number of intuitive moral beliefs already in hand.[8] Some will be about the rightness or wrongness of particular actions, for example, my belief that it was wrong to take so long to get graded papers back to my class last semester. Others will likely concern mid-level moral rules, for example, that it is wrong to copy term papers from web sites. Some will have to do with our rights, for example, that we all have a right to bodily integrity, and some with virtues and vices, for example, that courage is a virtue and gluttony a vice. Other intuitive beliefs might concern the appropriateness or inappropriateness of moral feelings such as guilt or remorse, for example, my belief that it is appropriate that I am grateful to a colleague who provided comments that helped me to improve an article. And so on. Most likely, not all these initial beliefs deserve a role in moral inquiry. The inquirer might be rather unsure of some, or have no settled conviction about others. Still others will have been formed in circumstances the inquirer recognizes as ones in which error is very likely, for example, where the inquirer was ignorant of the facts of a case, stands to gain or lose in some way, or was emotionally distraught. The inquirer's considered moral judgments are those beliefs that remain after she has eliminated the beliefs where there are these kinds of obvious grounds for doubting both the accuracy of any such belief and that the belief represents the inquirer's real moral convictions.

The next and first important step of the method is for the inquirer to formulate a moral theory that explicates her considered moral judgments. The most significant feature of reflective equilibrium emerges at this point: The inquirer attempts to construct a moral theory by a process of *mutual* adjustment to the principles that make up the moral theory and her considered judgments. Early on in the process, we might expect the inquirer to hold her considered judgments constant while she formulates principles, tests them against considered judgments, and reformulates the principles accordingly. But a principle or theory can come to seem plausible in its own right, apart from its entailing desired judgments about particular cases when combined with the facts about those cases.[9] Indeed, since a person's set of considered moral judgments can include general principles as well as particular judgments, it is possible that an inquirer's initial efforts at a moral theory will be drawn from the more general of her considered judgments, in which case the general principle will have considerable intuitive plausibility for the inquirer at the outset.[10] Because elements of a person's moral theory can enjoy their own intuitive plausibility, when the inquirer becomes aware of conflicts between her provisional moral theory and her considered judgments it is an open question whether she will revise the theory or the considered judgments. All she can do in such a case is reflect upon the conflicting judgments and theory. She must decide which to revise on the basis of which seems more likely to be correct to her upon reflection, or, in other words, on the basis of which seems intuitively more plausible to her after reflection.

2.2. Clarifications

Before completing the description of reflective equilibrium, it is worth pausing to clarify some features of the method. The first concerns what I mean by a moral theory. A single moral principle (such as the utilitarian greatest happiness principle or one of Kant's formulations of the Categorical Imperative) that, when conjoined with relevant facts, entailed all the inquirer's considered moral judgments would provide a paradigm case of a moral theory. A moral theory might take the form of a small number of general principles, perhaps along with instructions, such as a rank-ordering, that determined which principle to employ in cases to which more than one principle could be applied. But I also want to allow the possibility that the inquirer is unable to formulate a set of one or more principles that entail all of his considered moral judgments. In such a case, the moral theory will consist of as much in the way of principles organizing considered judgments as is possible. I would even want to allow extreme moral particularism, the view that there are no valid general moral principles at all, no matter how limited their scope, as a possible outcome.[11] So, to repeat, as I understand a moral theory here, it will be a set of principles that entails or organizes the inquirer's considered moral judgments as much as this is possible. I leave the precise shape of these principles entirely open. Specifically, I allow that the set of principles may be incomplete, because it does not entail all of the inquirer's considered judgments. I even leave open the possibility that the set might be empty, or equivalently, contain only the principle to the effect that there are no general moral principles.

One might, therefore, be led to ask what the point of this first stage of the method is supposed to be. To answer this question, let's forget about reflective equilibrium for a moment and consider the beginnings of an actual course of moral reflection. I have already described Thomson's case of the violinist with renal failure, so I might as well continue with it as my example. Thomson was concerned with a familiar argument against abortion: The fetus is a person; as a person, the fetus has a right to life; hence abortion is morally impermissible. There has been a great deal of debate regarding the first premise of this argument, but most people apparently take it to be intuitively obvious that the conclusion follows if the premise is true. Thomson granted this premise in order to question whether the conclusion actually follows. Her example is clearly pertinent. The violinist is undoubtedly a person who has a right to life, but it is not at all clear that it would be immoral to disconnect the violinist, even though the violinist will die as a result just as surely as fetuses "disconnected" from women by abortion die.

There are obviously many dissimilarities between the case of the violinist and a case of pregnancy. For one thing, in the violinist case, you have been kidnapped and the violinist is connected to you against your will. You did not choose to do anything that you had any reason to believe might have put you in such a position. In the usual case of pregnancy, the woman did choose to engage in an activity that she knew might put her in a position where another person would be dependent upon the use of her body for survival.[12] Many think that for this reason, the pregnant woman has a special responsibility to the fetus, and the fetus has special rights against the woman. Hence, they might reply that even though it is morally permissible to disconnect the violinist, it is not permissible for a fetus to be "disconnected."

A part of Thomson's response to this argument makes use of a series of examples, which run from the ordinary to the bizarre.

> If the room is stuffy, and I therefore open a window to air it, and a burglar climbs in, it would be absurd to say, "Ah, now he can stay, she's given him a right to the use of her house—for she is partially responsible for his presence there, having voluntarily done what enabled him to get in, in full knowledge that there are such things as burglars, and that burglars burgle." It would be still more absurd to say this if I had had bars installed outside my windows, precisely to prevent burglars from getting in, and a burglar got in only because of a defect in the bars. It remains equally absurd if we imagine it is not a burglar who climbs in, but an innocent person who blunders or falls in. Again, suppose it were like this: people-seeds drift about in the air like pollen, and if you open your windows, one may drift in and take root in your carpets or upholstery. You don't want children, so you fix up your windows with fine mesh screens, the very best you can buy. As can happen, however, one of the screens is defective; and a seed drifts in and takes root. Does the person-plant who now develops have a right to the use of your house? Surely not. (1971, pp. 58–59)

This series of examples obviously is not sufficient to settle the issue regarding abortion, but I think it serves well to illustrate how intuitions about hypothetical cases are used to test arguments or principles that might be thought to settle real moral questions, and, more significant, the back-and-forth movement from intuitive judgment to general principle. The general principles are not always explicitly formulated, but whenever one takes note of a possibly relevant dissimilarity between a hypothetical case presented as a counterexample and the real case that is at issue, a refinement of the original principle is there in the background. It should be clear that the sort of inquiry exemplified in this segment of Thomson's argument is exactly what is involved in reaching narrow reflective equilibrium—it just is (1) less broad, since it is employed to investigate the morality of a particular type of action rather than to develop a fully general moral theory, and (2) not followed through to a point of stability, where there are no further cases to be considered and no further revisions to be made.

Now the first point I would like to make is that this sort of effort to attain a small portion of reflective equilibrium clearly makes sense in spite of the fact that it is not aimed at the construction of a full-blown moral theory. In essence, the inquiry strives to avoid contrary intuitive judgments about cases between which the inquirer can find no morally relevant difference, and this is obviously a good thing to avoid. The second point is that this sort of inquiry makes good sense in spite of the fact that it is not followed through even to a narrow equilibrium limited to abortion. Such a limited equilibrium is an ideal state, just as full narrow reflective equilibrium is. It would be a huge undertaking to bring one's beliefs into a state of such equilibrium, and given the limited time and energy we have to devote to it, not to mention our limited intellectual capacities, we cannot expect ever to complete the task. But we needn't react with pessimism; it still makes good sense to do the best we can, to bring our beliefs as close to the ideal as we can, given our various limitations and the various constraints within which we must work.

2.3. Wide Reflective Equilibrium

Even if, after a series of revisions to her considered moral judgments and her moral theory, an inquirer reached a point of stability, where the judgments and theory were perfectly coherent and no further revisions to either were necessary, the inquirer's work would not be finished. She would only have attained what is known as narrow reflective equilibrium. To bring her beliefs into wide reflective equilibrium, she must consider alternatives to her narrow equilibrium theory and the arguments that might be constructed for and against the alternative theories and her own theory. In an influential essay, Norman Daniels (1979) suggested that we think of this process as an effort to attain coherence among the inquirer's considered moral judgments, moral theory, and the background theories she accepts. The idea seems to be that the philosophical arguments for and against the various moral theories, or at least those that have some purchase with the inquirer, will draw their premises from her broader views, for example, philosophical or psychological beliefs regarding the nature of persons or rational decision-making, or sociological views about such things as the role of morality in society. If, for example, an argument against the theory she accepted in narrow equilibrium seems compelling to the inquirer, what this shows is that this theory together with her considered judgments do not cohere with some of the other views she holds. The inquirer must revise something to eliminate the conflict, but, as in the effort to attain a narrow equilibrium, no type of belief gets special treatment. The method directs the inquirer to reflect upon the conflicting beliefs, and decide whether to revise her moral theory and considered moral judgments or to revise her background theory on the basis of what seems intuitively most plausible to her after reflection.

I certainly would not want to disagree that things can go as Daniels suggests. But I think he sells short the power of moral theories, background theories, and philosophical arguments. It is not the case that we only change our minds about moral and philosophical matters when such a change is required by something else that we already believe. When confronted with an alternative moral or philosophical conception, a person can find that conception intuitively attractive on its own—and this can happen even though the new conception is in conflict with the inquirer's previously settled convictions. Consideration of alternative moral theories, background theories, and philosophical arguments for and against such theories does not merely serve to make one aware of the consequences of one's existing views and possible conflicts inherent within one's current system of belief. It can present for one's consideration ideas, propositions, principles, theories, outlooks, and so on that one has not previously thought about, or it can present such things that one has previously thought about in a new way. Upon consideration, these things can come to seem intuitively plausible on their own. And they can come to seem intuitively plausible even though they do not fit in with what one has previously thought. When this happens, the inquirer will likely have to do a considerable amount of reflecting and revising to bring her beliefs into equilibrium again. And when the inquirer manages to reestablish a stable equilibrium, we can expect that it will mark a radical break with what she had previously thought, in the sense that the new set of views is not determined by the propositions the inquirer previously believed, how likely these propositions seem to the inquirer to be true, and the logical and evidential relations among them.

One might be tempted to think of a radical shift in view as one that involves an alteration in a large number of beliefs, but the alteration of large numbers of beliefs is not the defining feature of the kind of shift in view I have in mind. A large number of beliefs can be altered in a nonradical way. For example, a person might come to realize that a large number of his particular moral judgments are in conflict with a moral principle of which he is very certain—that is, one that seems much more likely to be true to the inquirer than any of the particular judgments with which it conflicts—and then revise all the particular judgments accordingly. In such a case, the change in belief, large though it may be, is straightforwardly required by the person's antecedent beliefs and degrees of belief or commitment.[13] This is not a radical change. What makes a change radical, in the sense that concerns me here, has to do with what requires the change. When beliefs are changed to resolve a conflict and the changes made are in accord with one's previous beliefs and degrees of belief, the change is not radical. But when one alters one's judgment of the intuitive plausibility of something in a way that is not dictated by one's previous beliefs and degrees of belief, the change is what I call radical, and it is radical even if the change involves only a relatively small number of beliefs.

In effect, by stressing this radical element of wide reflective equilibrium, I put the accent on 'reflective' rather than 'equilibrium'. I do not conceive of moral inquiry as a mechanical process where the inquirer begins with a list of moral propositions believed to various degrees and must merely bring these beliefs into equilibrium by (1) searching out conflicts and revising the belief that intuitively seems less likely to be true and (2) formulating general principles that nicely systematize the beliefs she retains. I instead conceive of the inquirer as seeking to bring her beliefs into equilibrium in this way, but doing it while also continually reflecting on what she already believes, as well as new propositions encountered along the way, and revising her beliefs when these reflections lead to a sufficient alteration in how likely to be true some propositions seem. According to the mechanical conception, another person could work out an inquirer's equilibrium point just as well as the inquirer could herself, provided this person could be given the inquirer's initial beliefs and degrees of belief. According to the conception of moral inquiry I favor, the job must be done by the individual inquirer herself, since the direction of the inquiry is determined by the inquirer's own, perhaps constantly changing, assessments of intuitive plausibility.[14]

I believe the more radical understanding of reflective equilibrium is in fact what Rawls intended. He pointed out that reflective equilibrium is open to several interpretations, and then commented:

> [T]he notion varies depending upon whether one is to be presented with only those descriptions which more or less match one's existing judgments except for minor discrepancies, or whether one is to be presented with all possible descriptions to which one might plausibly conform one's judgments together with all relevant philosophical arguments for them. In the first case we would be describing a person's sense of justice more or less as it is although allowing for the smoothing out of certain irregularities; in the second case a person's sense of justice may or may not undergo a radical shift. Clearly it is the second kind of reflective equilibrium that one is concerned with in moral philosophy. (1971, p. 49)

3. Enriching Reflection

The account of reflective equilibrium I have provided to this point is more or less standard. I will now introduce a nonstandard element into the conception of reflective equilibrium. I believe that including this element is consistent with the general spirit of reflective equilibrium, so I hope that my amendment to the standard view can be accepted as friendly.

Twenty years before the publication of *A Theory of Justice*, Rawls argued that we should take the considered moral judgments of competent moral judges as data for moral theory construction (1951, pp. 184–186). As we have seen, the method of reflective equilibrium still employs the notion of considered moral judgments.[15] However, reflective equilibrium no longer employs the notion of the competent judge. According to Rawls, the characteristics defining the competent judge are those "which, in the light of experience, show themselves as necessary conditions for the reasonable expectation that a given person may come to know something" (p. 179). We might expect that any normal adult would have some of the characteristics Rawls explicitly cites, for example, that the judge would have average intelligence and know those things about the world and the consequences of various kinds of actions that we would expect the average person to know. But other characteristics go well beyond those we can count on any mature person to possess. They also seem to be more than would be required for a reasonable expectation that the person know just anything; they seem to be characteristics that are particularly relevant to forming moral judgments. The competent judge, for example, "knows, or tries to know, his own emotional, intellectual, and moral predilections and makes a conscientious effort to take them into account in weighing the merits of any question" (p. 179) and has a sympathetic knowledge of the human interests that are relevant to moral decisions, a knowledge that must often be acquired imaginatively.

Why did Rawls drop the notion of the competent moral judge from his characterization of reflective equilibrium? He seems to have been thinking that anyone is competent to engage in moral inquiry. Indeed, when he introduced reflective equilibrium, Rawls claimed that "for the purposes of this book, the views of the reader and the author are the only ones that count" (1971, p. 50). Perhaps this makes sense, given Rawls's purposes. He supposed that "everyone has in himself the whole form of a moral conception" and aimed to characterize a part of this, the person's "sense of justice" or "conception of justice," by working out the part of the moral theory the person accepts in reflective equilibrium that concerns justice (pp. 49–50). I will critically examine this idea later, but what I want to note here is this: While it is hard to disagree with the idea that a method of moral inquiry ought to be something that any person can take up and follow, there is something awfully appealing about the idea of a competent moral judge. There certainly are various characteristics that lead us to trust, or distrust, the moral views of the persons who have them. I am, however, focusing on methodological issues at this point. It may be reasonable to deny that any strong positive epistemic status is had by the moral views of incompetent moral judges, even the views that are in reflective equilibrium for such judges, and reasonable also to claim a high epistemic status only for the views of judges who have attained a certain level of competence. But what follows methodologically? Suppose we admit that inquirers differ with respect to their moral competence, with some failing to be competent at all; what changes to the method of reflective equilibrium are required by this admission?

To see what might follow with respect to the method of moral inquiry, let's consider one specific characteristic plausibly associated with competent judges: having a sympathetic understanding of the interests of other human beings, including especially those interests one does not share. As Rawls pointed out, one must often acquire this understanding through extensive exercise of the imagination. I am here inclined to chime in by stressing the role that literature, particularly novels, movies, and plays, can have both in the development of our general imaginative and sympathetic capacities and in helping us to gain a sympathetic understanding of specific human interests we do not share. But as tyrants in particular know well, literature, film, and the theatre are powerful weapons that can be used for good or ill; they can damage as well as develop imagination and sympathetic understanding. So what are we to do?

As the name implies, the method of reflective equilibrium involves a great deal of reflection. As an inquirer attempts to construct a moral theory that accounts for her considered moral judgments, he must reflect upon the moral beliefs he already holds, moral principles that might provide all or part of a systematic account of his particular moral judgments, background theories of all sorts that might be relevant to his moral views, and even alternative moral theories, along with philosophical arguments for and against such alternatives. It is significant that the focus of all this reflection is propositions the inquirer believes or might believe, and the logical and evidential connections that hold among various such propositions. Through the course of all these reflections, what the inquirer seemingly need not reflect upon is himself. Specifically, he need not reflect upon his ability to imagine the interests of others or his level of sympathetic understanding of such interests. He need not reflect about whether any experiences he has had, either in the first person or by way of his reading, viewing plays or films, or even listening to music, might have impaired his capacity to understand certain interests sympathetically. He need not reflect upon how he might try to enhance his ability to imagine the lives of others or acquire more sympathetic understanding of their interests. Surely, if it made any sense at all to include sympathetic understanding as one of the characteristics of a competent moral judge, it makes sense to require people to reflect about such things in the course of their efforts to construct a moral theory, and, depending upon the upshot of these reflections, to seek to develop their imaginations and their sympathetic understanding.

More generally, I maintain that it is only reasonable to modify reflective equilibrium by requiring inquirers to reflect upon, and to try to formulate a view about, what characteristics are required to be a competent moral judge. As a part of such reflection, inquirers should of course consider what others have taken to be required for one to be a competent judge and adjust their own views of competence according to the outcome of this consideration. Inquirers should then give careful consideration to how they fare with respect to the characteristics of a competent judge and how they can acquire the characteristics they seem to lack. Finally, and before placing any confidence in their own intuitive judgments, inquirers should take whatever actions their reflections indicate are necessary to become a competent moral judge.

I would like to make two comments about the amended version of reflective equilibrium before proceeding. First, depending upon just how wide one understands the usual conception of reflective equilibrium to be, the amendment I've proposed may not be terribly significant. It may merely focus attention on a neglected element of the method that was there all along. This is because there are various ways in which reflection on one's background theories could be expected to lead one to undertake the kind of reflection upon one's own capacity for making moral judgments that I have stressed. If epistemological theories are included within the background theories one must reflect upon, for example, then to bring one's beliefs into wide reflective equilibrium even as it is ordinarily understood, one will need to consider what characteristics a person must have to be competent to make the sorts of moral judgments that play a pivotal role in the process and whether one has those characteristics one's self. If it turns out that one does not, then one's system of beliefs will not be coherent, because certain moral beliefs, indeed, beliefs that are playing a significant role in determining the overall shape of one's system of moral beliefs, will fall short of one's own epistemic standards. There seem to be only two ways to remedy the situation. (1) One might simply jettison the moral judgments that don't satisfy one's epistemological standards. But of course, since they are being jettisoned because one is not competent to make moral judgments, one cannot very well replace them with other moral judgments. Therefore, this way of addressing the problem amounts to abandoning engaging in any sort of moral inquiry for one's self. (2) One will have to try to live up to one's own epistemic standards by considering how to make one's self into a competent moral judge and undertaking the appropriate course of personal development.

Second, there obviously is no guarantee that every inquirer will become competent as a result of undertaking the kind of reflection I have proposed and striving to attain competence in the way this reflection indicates. This is particularly clear where such reflection and striving are most needed. Suppose an inquirer lacks one or more of the characteristics of a competent judge. Why trust such an inquirer, of all people, to be able to figure out that she is incompetent, why she is incompetent, and what best to do about it, and then to follow through effectively? Given that there is no good answer to this question, why bother incorporating the enriched type of reflection I have described into our understanding of reflective equilibrium? Wouldn't it be better to follow the course Rawls took in his earlier work? If we had a good account of what makes a competent moral judge, we could either restrict reflective equilibrium to persons who already are competent, or supplement the method with directions for attaining such competence. I do not think following either of these approaches would be better than enhancing reflective equilibrium as I have proposed. To take one of these approaches, we would have to either abandon the idea that moral inquiry is something everyone can engage in or abandon what I take to be the essence of reflective equilibrium—the idea that the course of moral inquiry should be shaped by what seems most likely to be true to the inquirer himself, that is, by the inquirer's intuitive judgments. Hence, even though I must admit that there is no guarantee that the enhanced version of reflective equilibrium I have proposed will mold all inquirers into competent moral judges, I do not think any more can be done while remaining true to the spirit of reflective equilibrium.

4. THE RELIABILITY OF MORAL INTUITIONS

When I first mentioned reflective equilibrium, I admitted that it is controversial, even though there is something of a consensus about its being the correct method for moral inquiry. From the beginning, this sophisticated version of intuitive moral inquiry has been criticized for the same reason as other more simple understandings of intuition-driven moral inquiry. Critics do not believe intuitive judgments have the epistemic credentials to justify their playing the significant role in shaping moral inquiry granted them by intuitionist methodologies.[16] One natural way of presenting this criticism is in terms of reliability, specifically, by claiming that moral intuitions must be shown to be reliable before they can be used as reflective equilibrium proposes.

One important point to make in response to this version of the criticism is that other types of beliefs that clearly have a positive epistemic status and are legitimately employed in theory construction, such as ordinary perceptual beliefs, cannot meet the standard being imposed on moral intuitions. Let's grant that we can now explain some of the processes by which ordinary perceptual beliefs are produced and that this allows us to offer interesting "scientific" arguments for the reliability of these beliefs. The problem is, such explanations, and hence such arguments, are a relatively recent development. The ordinary perceptual beliefs of ordinary human beings had a positive epistemic status—indeed, I would think a very strong positive epistemic status—for hundreds of thousands of years before these arguments for the reliability of perceptual beliefs became available.[17] Moreover, we certainly could never have developed the arguments without relying on perceptual beliefs. Finally, we do not, to this day, have such "scientific" arguments for the reliability of other types of beliefs that clearly have a strong positive epistemic status and can legitimately be used in inquiry, for example, beliefs arising from introspection or memory or about simple mathematical propositions.[18]

The critic might reply that arguments for the reliability of a type of belief that rely upon a scientific understanding of how that belief is produced are not at issue—ordinary inductive arguments for reliability are good enough, and these must have been available for a very long time. However, such arguments are more problematic than one might think. They seem to be circular, since they rely upon perception to establish the reliability of perception.[19] In addition, while they may have been available to human beings for more than the last few centuries, does it really make sense to suppose that, within the course of a single life, the individual's perceptual beliefs had no positive epistemic status until she put together such arguments? Finally, introspective beliefs still provide a counterexample to the standard being forced on moral intuition. A person may be able to look again or more closely or ask another observer to verify a perceptual belief and thereby begin to put together some sort of an inductive argument for the reliability of perceptual beliefs, but one can hardly do this sort of thing for beliefs about the contents of one's own stream of consciousness.

There is more to be said on both sides regarding this line of argument, but rather than giving further consideration to whether it is too stringent to require that intuitions be shown reliable prior to being used in moral inquiry, let's simply ask whether there is any reason to think that they are reliable. No one could deny that it would be a very good thing if we could come up with a decent account of the reliability of moral intuitions—and such an argument is on offer. Seeking to defend the use of intuitive judgments for philosophical inquiry in general, some philosophers have tried to establish the reliability of intuitions by construing the targets of philosophical theories to be our concepts, where concepts are understood as in-the-head mental or psychological entities (Bealer, 1998; Goldman and Pust, 1998). More specifically, as Alvin Goldman and Joel Pust explain in their presentation of this position, which I will follow them in calling "mentalism," concepts are

> a psychological structure or state that underpins a cognizer's deployment of a natural-language predicate. Thus, Jones's concept of apple is the psychological structure that underlies her deployment of the predicate 'apple', and Jones's concept of knowledge is the psychological structure that underlies her deployment of the predicate 'knows' (or 'has knowledge'). (1998, pp. 187–188)[20]

Given the mentalist construal of the target of philosophical inquiry, the reliability of intuitive judgments comes as no surprise. Goldman and Pust explain:

The concept associated with a predicate 'F' will have many dispositions, but among them are dispositions to give rise to intuitive classificational judgments such as "example e is (is not) an instance of F." Thus, it is not only possible, but almost a matter of *definition*, that if the concept possessor were fully informed about the relevant features of e, then if e satisfied the concept he expresses through 'F', his intuitive response to the question of whether e satisfies this concept would be affirmative; and if e did not satisfy the concept he expresses through 'F', then his intuitive response to the question of whether e satisfies this concept would be negative. In other words, a concept tends to be manifested by intuitions that reflect or express its content. . . . Moreover, although we do not currently know the precise causal route that connects concept structures with their conscious manifestations, it is extremely plausible, from any reasonable cognitive-science perspective, that there should be such a causal route. (1998, p. 188)

It does not follow, of course, that all intuitive beliefs are reliable or that intuitions can be used in any sort of inquiry. Intuitive beliefs about the motion of bodies, for example, do not provide good evidence for theories of mechanics, because such theories concern the behavior of bodies in the real world, and unfortunately there is not the same kind of close link between the actual behavior of such bodies and our intuitive beliefs about their behavior. But mentalism seems to provide a reason for trusting the sorts of intuitions that do the bulk of the work in philosophical inquiries, that is, intuitions about whether various real and hypothetical things are, or are not, knowledge, justified, right, just, good, and so on.

Much of what Rawls himself had to say about reflective equilibrium when he introduced it suggests that he would find mentalism congenial. Recall the passage I quoted earlier where he claimed that "everyone has in himself the whole form of a moral conception" and went on to say that the point of a theory of justice is to characterize a part of this conception (1971, p. 50). Rawls also suggested one significant variation on mentalism that construes moral theory as similar to the theory of grammaticality developed by linguists (p. 47).[21] Explicit application of the rules or principles that make up a theory of grammaticality allow us to specify which sentences of a language are meaningful. We do not have explicit knowledge of these rules even for our own native language, but, presumably, we somehow employ them to form our own meaningful sentences and to understand the meaningful sentences produced by others using our language. Our intuitive judgments about whether or not purported sentences of our language are grammatical or meaningful can provide evidence for or against a theory of grammaticality, because our disposition to make such judgments is another manifestation of our linguistic competence, which is constituted by an implicit grasp of the rules.

Although mentalism may provide reason for thinking that intuitive judgments are reliable, it is significant that mentalism is not committed to holding that intuitive judgments are perfectly reliable, and hence, unrevisable. Even in hypothetical cases where all the facts are stipulated, the person's concept is not the sole determinant of the intuitive belief. Various factors can interfere with a person's performance, for example, he may be tired or distracted or the case may be too complicated for him to remember all the relevant features.[22] Nevertheless, given that such factors are not that commonly present, we can expect intuitive beliefs to be generally reliable, and in favorable circumstances, where pains have been taken to ensure that no interfering factors are present, we can expect them to be very reliable indeed. And so it seems that mentalism is able to legitimize the use of intuitions in philosophical inquiry, and to do so without getting involved in any kind of extravagant metaphysics or absurdly optimistic epistemology.

Very neat, but, I'm afraid, too neat. Perhaps mentalism will work for areas of philosophical inquiry where intuitions are used in a simpler way, but I do not think it will do for moral theorizing or other areas of philosophical inquiry where *wide* reflective equilibrium is employed.[23] Wide reflective equilibrium, as I have explained it, simply requires too much critical reflection about intuitive moral beliefs and the moral principles used to account for them, and allows too many different kinds of grounds for the revision of intuitive beliefs for us to construe it merely as a method for constructing a theory that accounts for our existing concepts.[24] A number of features of wide reflective equilibrium just do not make sense if we understand the target of moral inquiry and the nature of intuitive beliefs as mentalism proposes. I will address two such features.

I have already explained that mentalism can allow for some revision of intuitive judgments. But if mentalism were true, it would be correct to revise an intuitive judgment only if the intuitive belief did not accurately reflect the shape of the relevant concept. We ordinarily would not think a judgment's accurately reflecting the shape of a concept is the same thing as a judgment's being accurate, which ordinarily requires being in accord with some portion of reality that goes beyond that concept. A racist's immediate intuitive judgment about a member of a minority may well accurately reflect the racist's concept of the relevant minority, but it would not accurately reflect the nature of the person who is the object of the belief. In part for this reason, we would not expect the conditions that must be met—by the believer, the circumstances of belief formation, or both—for it to be likely that an intuitive belief will accurately reflect a concept to be the same as the conditions that must be met for it to be likely that an intuitive belief will accurately reflect some portion of extra-conceptual reality. Hence, we should expect that the kinds of revisions of intuitive beliefs that will be justified will differ, depending on whether those beliefs are taken to indicate the shapes of concepts, or whether they are taken to indicate the nature of some portion of reality that goes beyond the relevant concepts. This is not to say that some revisions might not be justified either way. If I form an intuitive belief when I am extremely tired or distracted, I would have reason to doubt both that it accurately reflects my concepts and that it accurately reflects the nature of reality. Not so for other revisions. If I have little or no experience dealing with horses, there still might be no reason to doubt that my intuitive belief about how a horse will behave accurately reflects my concept of a horse, but there would be reason to doubt that it accurately reflects how horses actually behave.

Think now about revisions of beliefs, including intuitive beliefs, that occur as a result of the consideration of alternatives to the system of moral beliefs one would hold in narrow reflective equilibrium. Let's consider a specific example. Imagine an exceptionally thoughtful person who comes from a conservative religious environment. This person has a very conventional set of intuitive moral beliefs and accounts for these with a simple divine command view of ethics combined with a belief that the Bible should be interpreted literally and that it informs us of God's commands. The person's intuitive moral beliefs and moral theory are in a very stable equilibrium. The person then considers alternative moral theories, in particular, versions of consequentialism and eudaimonism. Although initially these views seem mistaken and counterintuitive to the person, consideration of them gets her thinking about the nature of human happiness and the connection between morality and happiness. It comes to seem intuitively obvious to the person that morality cannot be totally disconnected from happiness, but try as she might, she just cannot avoid the conclusion that some of her previous moral views primarily serve only to increase human misery. This brings her to reject the now offending, but previously intuitive, moral judgments. She sets about trying to attain a new equilibrium, but she cannot to do so while retaining her old divine command views. In the end, she comes to accept a consequentialist moral theory combined with a more naturalistic understanding of human happiness.

This kind of example may not be absolutely decisive against mentalism. A defender could well come up with something to say to save the theory. But it is hard to come up with a convincing reason to think that the person's initial intuitive beliefs failed to reflect her moral concepts. It is much more plausible to suppose that in such a case the intuitive moral beliefs she started out with accurately reflected her moral concepts and that she came to doubt and then revise these beliefs not because they did not accurately reflect those concepts but because she came to think that at least some of these beliefs are just plain wrong. One might perhaps make a case for saying that the person ends up constructing a new set of moral concepts and that her new intuitive beliefs accurately reflect the nature of these new concepts. But even if this story of concept construction were true as far as it goes, it would leave out a most significant element. If the person does change her moral concepts, the change is not some sort of willy-nilly change she makes just for the hell of it. She would be attempting to construct new moral concepts that are adequate to capture some element of reality that involves something more than her own system of concepts. So whether we take it that the person in my example revises intuitive moral beliefs because of doubts that they are accurate, as is most straightforward, or we interpret the person as constructing a new set of moral concepts, I think it is clear that such a case shows that we cannot understand wide reflective equilibrium to be a method merely for constructing theories of our own moral concepts.

If I was right to enrich the type of reflection involved in reflective equilibrium by requiring the inquirer to consider whether he is a competent moral judge and how to acquire or enhance such competence, this provides a second indication that mentalism and reflective equilibrium do not fit together. It is odd to think of a competent moral judge merely as one whose intuitive moral beliefs accurately reflect the shape of his moral concepts. Indeed, one wonders whether anyone lacks such competence, although I suppose it is possible for a person to be so chronically tired or distracted or confused or distraught that his intuitive moral judgments fail to indicate the nature of his own moral concepts. It makes much more sense to think of moral competence in terms of the characteristics a person needs to have in order to be in a good position to form intuitive moral beliefs that are correct or true, where whatever moral correctness or truth turns out to be, it is more than some sort of mere correspondence with the believer's own concepts. When reflecting about one's own moral competence, it is most natural, in my opinion, to consider whether one is sufficiently attuned or sensitive to all the right things. One will ask one's self such questions as: Am I capable of appreciating all the things of value that might be at stake in a situation that requires a moral judgment? Do I have a sympathetic understanding of the human interests that can come into conflict? Have I been corrupted in some way so that I take things to be valuable that in fact have no real value? It would be unreasonable to refuse to entertain such questions about one's self in the course of any serious philosophical inquiry into morality. Thus, I have tried to make an important place for the consideration of such questions in the conception of wide reflective equilibrium I have offered. But it does not seem that mentalism can allow room for such questions.

If I can conclude that reflective equilibrium does not merely generate theories that explicate our own moral concepts, I would like to go on to say that this is a good thing. If it did not do more, or more modestly, try to do more, it would very obviously be an inadequate method of moral inquiry. The reason is that some people have odd, misguided, or even downright vicious moral concepts. Consider, for example, the concepts racists, sexists, and bigots of all sorts have of the groups against which they are prejudiced. These concepts are morally loaded; they are likely to entail, for example, that the members of these groups have lower moral worth than members of the bigot's group and that members of the bigot's group are morally justified in treating members of these groups in various ways we would consider seriously immoral. The bigot's intuitive moral beliefs will reflect all this, so a method of inquiry that sought a moral theory that characterized the nature of the bigot's moral concepts would produce moral principles that endorsed the bigot's behavior. Hence we should not accept a method of moral inquiry that merely produces theories of a person's current moral concepts. An acceptable method must subject such concepts, and our moral beliefs more generally, to critical reflection. It is undoubtedly too much to expect philosophical inquiry, on its own, to be able to correct the moral concepts and moral views of every person with faulty concepts or views who engages in such inquiry. But an acceptable method of philosophical inquiry must do as much as possible to force such correction. A method that merely generates a theory of existing concepts does nothing at all.

It would be very easy to misunderstand the point I have just made. One might complain, "But look, with all the examination of intuitive judgments and principles and alternative moral theories and background theories and arguments regarding those theories and even all the self criticism and soul-searching you have built into wide reflective equilibrium, it still cannot guarantee that bigots or others who have morally reprehensible views will not continue to hold such views at the end of their moral inquiries. Or to put the point another way, for all you have said, it is possible for a person to hold racist or sexist or other sorts of bigoted views in wide reflective equilibrium. Given the right intuitive judgments and background beliefs, the judgment that female circumcision is morally right could be in reflective equilibrium for a person. So could the judgment that one has a duty to perform a suicide bombing against infidels or even the judgment that it is morally required that we sacrifice a virgin when there is a total eclipse of the sun. Why then is the existence of people with distorted moral concepts supposed to pose a special problem for those who propose that the point of moral inquiry is to explicate moral concepts? It seems you have the same problem." I'll admit I have a problem, but I do not have the *same* problem. Indeed, the fact that I can admit I have a problem is the reason I do not have the same problem. The problem with construing moral inquiry as capable of producing nothing more than an analysis or explication of a person's moral concepts is this: When it produces an analysis that is adequate to all the person's intuitive moral judgments, but some of these judgments and some of the judgments attained by applying the analysis are morally repugnant—or at least we feel certain they are morally repugnant; the person whose concept is analyzed will of course see nothing wrong with them—everything will nonetheless have gone perfectly. The judgments have to be seen as accurate and the analysis or moral theory that entails them as established. I need say no such thing about the moral views a person holds in reflective equilibrium. I can allow that such views are mistaken, and even morally repugnant. Much as I might not like it, I would have to admit that in such a case, a properly conducted philosophical inquiry was powerless to expose and eliminate that particular inquirer's mistaken moral views to that particular inquirer. But, as I hope to show in section 6, I think I could console myself with the thought that the philosophical inquiry had done all that could rationally be done.

If I am right that mentalism won't work, that leaves us with no account of the reliability of moral intuitions. We are left with the claim that we need no such argument for moral intuitions to play the role reflective equilibrium grants them. But of course, if they are not in fact reliable, it would not seem to be legitimate to make such unabashed use of them in the construction of moral theories. And some objectors do not offer the argument I considered earlier, which claims that we need an argument for reliability up front; they simply argue that moral intuitions are unreliable. The number one reason for claiming that moral intuitions are not reliable is that there is so much disagreement about morality. With all that disagreement, someone has got to be mistaken, and that means that all of our moral intuitions cannot be reliable. I admit that I cannot adequately respond to this argument, but let me mention a few things. First, it is easy to exaggerate the amount of disagreement regarding morality and to underestimate the vast amount of agreement. We tend to disagree about a few things, for example, abortion, euthanasia, the death penalty, the treatment of animals, and so on, that naturally become very salient precisely because we do disagree. But we agree about very many more things; you can easily construct your own long list of examples. Second, it is also easy to exaggerate how reliable we must be about something for our beliefs to have a strong positive epistemic status. We are not uncommonly victims of lies, but beliefs based on testimony surely have a strong positive status. We often make mistakes even about what those closest to us are thinking and feeling, but our beliefs about "other minds" can have a positive status. And our ordinary perceptual beliefs are often incorrect—think about reports from witnesses at the scene of an accident—but they are still sufficiently reliable to have a positive epistemic status. Can we really say that the amount of disagreement regarding morality indicates that moral intuitions are significantly less reliable than these other types of beliefs? I think not. Finally, what have got to be reliable for the type of moral inquiry I defend to be legitimate are the intuitive moral beliefs held by competent judges who are well on their way down the road to reflective equilibrium. I suppose it is possible that moral disagreement is so pervasive that even competent judges will disagree about these intuitive beliefs to such a great extent that they cannot be reliable. But it certainly is not obvious that there will be a high level of disagreement about these intuitions; indeed, I am not aware of any particularly strong reason for expecting to find such disagreement.[25]

5. Why Reflective Equilibrium?

I will close by offering a defense of reflective equilibrium that takes a somewhat different tack. I'll try to argue that there simply is no reasonable alternative to reflective equilibrium.[26]

To see that there is no reasonable alternative, it is useful to boil reflective equilibrium down to its essence. Basically, the method tells us to do three things as we attempt to construct a moral theory: (1) reflect on the interconnections among our beliefs, (2) leave nothing relevant out of these reflections, where this means both that we do not leave any of our own beliefs that might be relevant out of consideration and that, ideally, we are to consider all alternatives to our views, and (3) settle any conflicts that emerge, and more generally decide what to believe, on the basis of what intuitively seems most likely to be correct upon reflection. What real alternative is there to these directives? There have been thinkers who have opposed reflection, but this is the stuff of authoritarianism and dogmatism, not philosophy, so I do not think I need to defend (1).

It might seem that there is more to be said in behalf of leaving certain beliefs out of our reflections. One might think, for example, that science provides an example of a mode of inquiry that has made great strides only by constructing theories on the limited basis of observation. We all know how accurate mechanics was when it was constructed on the basis of our intuitive judgments about the motions of bodies. Drawing the obvious lesson from this example, we should follow the lead of science and exclude intuitive judgments from our inquiries. The example does not establish the lesson, however. In the first place, we do not limit the data for empirical inquiry to observations for no reason at all. This procedure is required by other things we believe—some of them on the basis of intuition. Far from having a counterexample to reflective equilibrium, therefore, we have an example of it working very successfully. In the second place, it is not as though successful empirical inquiry proceeds without any intuitive judgments. Intuitive judgments regarding things that can be observed may be so thoroughly overturned in favor of observations that such intuitions seem to have dropped entirely out of consideration, but all sorts of other intuitions continue to play an active role. For one thing, scientific inquiry obviously conforms to all sorts of epistemic principles: At the most basic level, these principles will concern perception, and they will run the gamut all the way to technical principles of inductive reasoning. According to reflective equilibrium, intuitive judgments play a crucial role in the development and justification of these epistemic principles.[27] Notice that when we favor observation over mere intuitive judgments regarding observable things, we are conforming to such epistemic principles. From the point of view of reflective equilibrium, then, in such cases the appearance that we are going against our intuitions is superficial; we are in fact conforming to our stronger intuitions, which in this case are those that underlie our epistemic principles. Other intuitive judgments might concern how decisions between competing empirically equivalent theories should be made, for example, on the basis of such factors as simplicity and elegance, and the comparative simplicity and elegance of competing theories.

The important point to remember with respect to (2) is that including beliefs in our reflections does not necessarily mean that those beliefs will determine the outcome. The broad, inclusive sort of reflection envisioned by reflective equilibrium can just as easily lead us to reject beliefs as to construct theories on their basis. The idea behind (2) is that we start out with everything we believe and think about all that we believe, which will involve subjecting these beliefs to critical examination. Beliefs will be dropped when we uncover problems. A real alternative to reflective equilibrium would have to ignore certain beliefs before we even begin reflecting, which is to say that we would have to drop the beliefs before we have any reason for doing so. With respect to the consideration of all alternatives, it is important to recognize that this is an ideal. In real life, where we have limited resources, there can be all sorts of good reasons for not considering certain alternatives, starting with the simple fact that we may not have the time to do so. But it is hard to see what reason could be given for denying that the ideal should be openness to the consideration of any alternative.

This brings us to the distinctively intuitionistic element of reflective equilibrium, the idea that the shape of one's moral view is to be determined by what comes to seem right intuitively as a result of one's reflections. It is not hard to adopt a perspective from which this looks highly questionable. If the system of moral beliefs an individual accepts in reflective equilibrium is determined by nothing more than what seems likely to be true to that person, then surely this system must be flimsy in the extreme. To find a perspective that puts the procedure i a better light, a perspective that, in my opinion, affords us a more accurate vi it is once again useful to think about what the alternatives to (3) might Reflective equilibrium does not direct an inquirer simply to believe what to be true. The inquirer is to believe what seems intuitively correct *after* fully reflected, that is, after she has considered everything else that she be well as the alternatives to what she believes. At such a point it will not $_n$, the case that the proposition in question seems true to the inquirer. I,$_{28}$ the rest of what she believes will not count against believing the p$_{led}$ and she will have considered each alternative to the proposition$_{son}$ against it. What, other than believing the proposition that is intui$_{lieve}$ in such a position supposed to believe? There are only two possib$_{ition}$ the intuitive proposition, that is, believe its negation or some $_{elieve}$ that is incompatible with it, or withhold the intuitive proposit$_{ct the}$ neither it nor its negation. It certainly would make no sense $_{other}$ person to believe the negation of the proposition in que incompatible alternative to it, for a person who has thought things all the way through will have fully considered such an alternative and decided it is not likely to be true. And why on earth think the person should withhold belief? She will have thought through all the considerations relevant to the proposition, so there will not be any reason one could give her for withholding, at least none that would find purchase with the inquirer and not be defeated or outweighed by other considerations the inquirer finds more compelling.

At the end of the day, then, there really isn't any sensible alternative to going along with the intuitions we have after full reflection. It is surely natural to worry about this. It is natural to want certainty or something else that is more secure than what seems true upon reflection. But we are not destined to have such things, at least not for very much of what we believe. The best we can do is think things through and trust the conclusions we reach. The defender of reflective equilibrium calls it like it is and says that is good enough. No more hankering after what cannot be.

NOTES

Many thanks to Christian Miller and David Copp, most patient of editors, for comments on an earlier version of this chapter.

1. For a contemporary defense of intuitionism, or at least a more substantial portion of it than concerns me here, see Robert Audi, 1997, 2004.

2. I may already have built too much into the understanding of intuitions. According to the standard philosophical understandings, propositions are essentially truth apt, and to believe a proposition is in some way to accept it as true. Hence, it would seem that many metaethical positions, for example, prescriptivism and expressivism, are inconsistent with the existence of any moral intuitions. I do not want this to be a consequence of this minimal characterization of intuitions, so I mean to be using 'belief' and 'proposition' in a way that is looser than the standard philosophical usage. In ordinary conversation, it is perfectly appropriate for a person to say (1) "I believe that abortion is [...]" or (2) "I believe that women should have a right to choose," just as it is perfectly appropriate to say (3) "I believe that human beings evolved from some more [...]e species" or (4) "I believe that there is life on other planets." I want to be [...]lief' as it is used in such statements and to use 'proposition' to refer to what[...]at-clause in such statements refers to. That's all I mean to commit myself to [...]her the philosophical analysis that ultimately proves correct will hold 'belief' [...]) to refer to the same sort of state as it refers to in (3) and (4) does not [...] does it matter whether this analysis regards the referents of the that-clauses [...] to be the same sorts of things as the referents of the that-clauses in (3)

[...] seems true' to be understood in a philosophically noncommittal way, a way that allows that it might seem true to a person that it is wrong to behave in some way even though, in the final analysis, it is neither true nor false that it is wrong to behave in that way.

4. For an excellent discussion of such a sense of intuition and its importance for philosophical inquiry in general, see Sosa, 1998.

5. Sidgwick, 1874, held intuitionism, understood as the view that there is a multiplicity of distinct moral principles, to be less plausible than either utilitarianism or egoism, between which he could not decide on philosophical grounds alone. But when he considered how utilitarianism and egoism were justified, Sidgwick fell back on the claim that there are certain fundamental moral truths that we can see, intuitively, to be true, some of which support utilitarianism, others of which support egoism. G. E. Moore, 1903, advocated a nonmonistic form of utilitarianism that recognized a number of distinct things as being intrinsically good. But he maintained that propositions regarding the intrinsic values of things cannot be proved and can only be known via intuition.

6. Ross claims that the moral convictions of thoughtful, well-educated people are the data that the moral theorist must use to build theories, but he admits that these convictions can conflict. In cases of conflict, he says the theorist must retain the conflicting conviction that "better stands the test of reflection" and throw out the other (Ross, 1930, pp. 40–41). Assuming that the moral convictions of thoughtful, well-educated people are intuitions, it follows that intuitions are revisable.

7. This obviously idealizes or abstracts from actual practice, which mixes the various steps together.

8. Why this initial limitation to *intuitive* beliefs? Presumably, moral beliefs do not arise from sense perception or introspection. It strikes me as somewhat an odd case, but I suppose it is possible for a person to hold a moral belief as a result of memory. However, if the proposition believed does not also seem true to the believer on its own, that is, if it is not also intuitive, so that it really is believed solely on the basis of memory, in the way one might remember, for example, one's phone number, then I do not think it makes much sense to grant the belief a serious role in moral inquiry. That leaves moral beliefs formed on the basis of testimony or via inference. There is nothing odd about moral beliefs formed in these ways, but it makes sense to set them aside for methodological reasons. In the case of moral beliefs formed via inference, it is best to focus on the noninferential premises from which they, ultimately, must have been inferred. Provided these premises are retained as the moral inquiry proceeds, the beliefs excluded now can be included as inquiry proceeds because they will cohere within the believer's system of belief. In the case of moral beliefs formed on the basis of testimony, it is best to focus on the intuitive reasons why the believer accepts the testimony, for example, the reasons the believer takes another person to be authoritative with respect to morality or some aspect of morality. Once again, provided that these reasons hold up, the beliefs accepted on the basis of testimony can be included later on in the inquiry, again because they will cohere.

9. Notice, this is to say that a principle originally formulated via inference from a number of intuitive judgments about particular cases can come to be an intuition itself. In such a case, the principle would at first, and perhaps for some time, have been believed on the basis of its best explaining a range of intuitive judgments. But at some point the principle would come to seem true in its own right, and would be believed on the basis of its seeming true rather than on the basis of inference.

10. Earlier I characterized intuitions as beliefs that do not arise from any of the more usual sources, such as sense perception or introspection, but instead are formed simply because the proposition believed seems true to the believer upon reflection. When I say such things as that a principle is intuitively plausible, I mean to indicate that it seems true in this way.

11. See Dancy, 2004, for a presentation and defense of extreme particularism and the essays in Hooker and Little, 2000, for critical evaluation of particularism.

12. Not all pregnant women made such a choice; and so Thomson is led to consider pregnancy resulting from rape as something possibly more nearly similar to the violinist case.

13. I use 'degree of belief' and 'degree of commitment' to refer to how likely it seems to the person that the proposition believed is true. This is not the standard way of using these terms, but I risk possible confusions because it often allows me to say things in a much simpler way.

14. For more on the radical, nonmechanical conception of reflective equilibrium see DePaul, 1987, 1993.

15. The notion of considered moral judgments employed in reflective equilibrium is, however, more liberal than the notion employed in the earlier work, which imposed the following conditions on considered moral judgments: (1) the judge does not stand to be punished for making the judgment, (2) the judge does not stand to gain by making the judgment, (3) the judgment concerns a real case where real interests are in conflict, not a merely hypothetical case, (4) the judgment was preceded by careful inquiry into facts and fair opportunity for all concerned to state their side, (5) the judge feels sure of the judgment, (6) the judgement is stable for the judge across time and shared by other competent judges, and (7) the judgment is intuitive, in the sense that it was not formed as a result of the conscious application of moral principles (Rawls, 1951, pp. 181–183).

16. In his review of *A Theory of Justice*, Hare, 1973, criticized Rawls on this ground, and shortly thereafter Singer, 1974, raised it. They have been followed by many others.

17. I am assuming that creatures classified as members of the species *Homo sapiens* should be counted as ordinary human beings, and that all such creatures have ordinary perceptual beliefs. If one thinks either that only more recent members of the species *Homo sapiens* count as ordinary human beings or that a creature must have a language in order to be capable of having beliefs and that not all creatures classified as *Homo sapiens* had language, then "for upward of a hundred thousand years" would be more accurate.

18. This line of response is old and familiar. See Daniels, 1979.

19. On the inability to provide a noncircular defense of perception see Alston, 1993. For a nice explanation of the way in which externalist theories in epistemology seem to allow troublingly easy arguments that employ a belief forming faculty to establish the reliability of that very belief forming faculty, see Fumerton, 1995, pp. 173–180.

20. In a note to this passage, they expand: "More generally, the target of philosophical analysis may be a (tacit) folk *scheme* or folk *theory*, not just a folk *concept*; the psychological unit, in other words, may be larger than that of a concept" (Goldman and Pust, 1998, pp. 196–197).

One might object straightaway that this approach misunderstands the nature of concepts. It confuses what philosophers have traditionally taken a concept to be, that is, something like the meaning of a term, with some sort of psychological structure that underpins a particular person's use of the term. The issues raised by this objection are deep and complicated. For one thing, I am not at all sure that there really is one traditional philosophical understanding of concepts. To be perfectly honest, I am not sure I'm capable of sorting out all the relevant issues regarding concepts. I am sure, however, that I could not begin to do so in the space I have available here. So let me get away with a warning that Goldman and Pust's understanding of concepts may very well be different from your own and even nonstandard. I might also mention that Rey, 1983, provides a good initial formulation of the objection that the psychological understanding of concepts is significantly different from the traditional philosophical understanding.

21. Harman, 1999, provides a more recent sympathetic exploration of this view.

22. See Goldman and Pust, 1998, p. 189, for a brief discussion of this issue. Compare Daniels, 1980, and Harman, 1999, for a discussion of the related issue of the performance/competence distinction in linguistics. Both consider various factors that might lead a person to make intuitive judgments of grammaticality (performance) that do not correspond to the rules of the person's implicit grammar (competence).

23. In fairness to Goldman and Pust, I must note that they propose mentalism in order to defend the evidential status of intuitions as they are used in philosophical analysis. They allow that there might be other legitimate types of philosophical inquiry. What follows should therefore not be seen as a direct response to, or criticism of, what they explicitly assert. Strictly speaking, my comments should be viewed as an effort to forestall any effort to co-opt mentalism to defend a broad sort of philosophical inquiry into morality that goes beyond the analysis of moral concepts. I think it would be fair for me to note, however, that Goldman and Pust do explicitly mention justice and the good as examples of targets for philosophical inquiry and go so far as to express doubts about whether such things have "essences or natures independent of our conception of them" (1998, p. 187). Hence, to the extent that I defend a type of philosophical inquiry into such things that goes beyond mere conceptual analysis, that is, to the degree that I can defend wide reflective equilibrium, I probably am taking a position that will end up conflicting with theirs.

24. In his very fine discussion of Rawls's suggestion that moral inquiry is importantly similar to linguistics, Daniels, 1980, makes the same point.

25. Returning to the issues I addressed in the previous paragraph, while I have to admit that it is possible for a person to hold morally repugnant moral views in reflective equilibrium, it is open to me to hope, and to believe, that this would be a very rare occurrence. If I'm right, it remains possible that intuitive moral judgments are reliable.

26. For a somewhat more thorough presentation of this line of defense see DePaul, 1998.

27. Recall that reflective equilibrium was originally proposed as a method for the justification of inductive principles in Goodman, 1955.

28. What I mean here is that the rest of her beliefs, in total, will not provide a reason for not believing the proposition. She may have another belief, or beliefs, that, when taken in isolation, provide a reason against believing the proposition. But in such a case, there will be other things she believes that defeat these reasons for not believing. And within her total system of belief, there will be no reason for not believing for which there is not a defeater. Another way of putting the point, then, is to say that she

will have no other belief that provides an undefeated reason for not believing. For more on defeaters, a good place to begin is Pollock, 1986, pp. 37–39.

REFERENCES

Alston, W. 1993. *The Reliability of Sense Perception.* Ithaca, N.Y.: Cornell University Press.

Audi, R. 1997. "Intuitionism, Pluralism, and the Foundations of Ethics." In *Moral Knowledge and Ethical Character,* 32–65. Oxford: Oxford University Press.

———. 2004. *The Good in the Right: A Theory of Intuition and Intrinsic Value.* Princeton, N.J.: Princeton University Press.

Bealer, G. 1998. "Intuition and the Autonomy of Philosophy." In *Rethinking Intuition: The Psychology of Intuitions and Their Role in Philosophical Inquiry,* ed. M. DePaul and W. Ramsey, 201–239. Lanham, Md.: Rowman and Littlefield.

Dancy, J. 2004. *Ethics without Principles.* Oxford: Oxford University Press.

Daniels, N. 1979. "Wide Reflective Equilibrium and Theory Acceptance in Ethics." *Journal of Philosophy* 76: 256–282.

———. 1980. "On Some Methods of Ethics and Linguistics." *Philosophical Studies* 37: 21–36.

DePaul, M. 1987. "Two Conceptions of Coherence Methods in Ethics." *Mind* 96: 463–481.

———. 1993. *Balance and Refinement: Beyond Coherentism in Moral Inquiry.* London: Routledge.

———. 1998. "Why Bother with Reflective Equilibrium?" In *Rethinking Intuition: The Psychology of Intuitions and Their Role in Philosophical Inquiry,* ed. M. DePaul and W. Ramsey, 293–309. Lanham, Md.: Rowman and Littlefield.

Fumerton, R. 1995. *Metaepistemology and Skepticism.* Lanham, Md.: Rowman and Littlefield.

Goldman, A., and J. Pust. 1998. "Philosophical Theory and Intuitional Evidence." In *Rethinking Intuition: The Psychology of Intuitions and Their Role in Philosophical Inquiry,* ed. M. DePaul and W. Ramsey, 179–197. Lanham, Md.: Rowman and Littlefield.

Goodman, N. 1955. *Fact, Fiction and Forecast.* Cambridge, Mass.: Harvard University Press.

Hare, R. 1973. "Rawls' Theory of Justice." Pt. 1. *Philosophical Quarterly* 23: 144–155.

Harman, G. 1999. "Moral Philosophy and Linguistics." In *Proceedings of the Twentieth World Congress of Philosophy,* vol. 1, *Ethics,* ed. Klaus Brinkmann, 107–115. Bowling Green, Ohio: Philosophy Documentation Center, Bowling Green State University.

Hooker, B., and M. Little, eds. 2000. *Moral Particularism.* Oxford: Clarendon Press.

Kant, I. 1993. *Grounding for the Metaphysics of Morals with On a Supposed Right to Lie Because of Philanthropic Concerns.* 3rd ed. Trans. J. Ellington. Indianapolis: Hackett.

Moore, G. 1903. *Principia Ethica.* Cambridge: Cambridge University Press.

Prichard, H. 1912. "Does Moral Philosophy Rest on a Mistake?" *Mind* 21: 21–37.

Plato. 1992. *Republic.* Trans. G. M. A. Grube and C. D. C. Reeve. Indianapolis: Hackett.

Pollock, J. 1986. *Contemporary Theories of Knowledge.* Totowa, N.J.: Rowman and Littlefield.

Rawls, J. 1951. "Outline of a Decision Procedure for Ethics." *Philosophical Review* 60: 184–186.

―――. 1971. *A Theory of Justice.* Cambridge, Mass.: Harvard University Press.

Rey, G. 1983. "Concepts and Stereotypes." *Cognition* 15: 237–262.

Ross, W. 1930. *The Right and the Good.* Oxford: Oxford University Press.

Sidgwick, H. 1874. *The Methods of Ethics.* London: Macmillan.

Singer, P. 1974. "Sidgwick and Reflective Equilibrium." *Monist* 58: 490–517.

Sosa, E. 1998. "Minimal Intuition." In *Rethinking Intuition: The Psychology of Intuitions and Their Role in Philosophical Inquiry,* ed. M. DePaul and W. Ramsey, 257–269. Lanham, Md.: Rowman and Littlefield.

Thomson, J. 1971. "A Defense of Abortion." *Philosophy and Public Affairs* 1: 47–66.

CHAPTER 22

THEORY, PRACTICE, AND MORAL REASONING

GERALD DWORKIN

The study of moral philosophy, how exceedingly beneficial may
it be to us, suggesting to us the dictates of reason, concerning
the nature and faculties of our soul, the chief good and end of
our life, the ways and means of attaining happiness, the best
methods and rules of practice; the distinctions between good
and evil, the nature of each virtue, and motives to embrace it;
the rank wherein we stand in the world, and the duties proper
to our relations:by rightly understanding and estimating which
things we may know how to behave ourselves decently and
soberly toward ourselves, justly and prudently towards our
neighbors; we may learn to correct our inclinations, to regulate
our appetites, to moderate our passions, to govern our actions,
to conduct and wield all our practice well in prosecution of our
end; so as to enjoy our being and conveniences of life in
constant quiet and peace, with tranquility and satisfaction of
mind.

Isaac Barrow

We can no more learn to act rightly by appealing to the ethical
theory of right action than we can play golf well by appealing
to the mathematical theory of the flight of the golf-ball. The

interest of ethics is thus almost wholly theoretical, as is the
interest of the mathematical theory of golf or billiards.

C. D. Broad, *Five Types of Ethical Theory*

A philosopher is someone who seeing something work in
practice, wonders whether it will work in theory.

Unknown

IN recent years there has been a steady flow of skeptical reactions to the very idea
of an ethical theory. The doubts take various forms but include, at least, the
question of whether our ethical beliefs or judgments can be codified or captured
by any structure that deserves the name of a theory. My topic is a different one.
Even if such structures were possible, there are additional doubts about the relationship, if any, of such a theory to our moral practices of judging, evaluating,
and determining how we ought to act. It is clear that if we are to understand and
evaluate such doubts, we need some fairly clear understanding of what an ethical
theory might be.

Bernard Williams, one of the skeptics, suggests the following conception of
an ethical theory. "An ethical theory is a theoretical account of what ethical
thought and practice are, which account either implies a general test for the
correctness of basic ethical beliefs and principles or else implies that there cannot
be such a test" (1985, p. 72). Jonathan Dancy suggests a similar conception: "a list
of basic moral principles, a justification of each item on the list, and some account
of how to derive more ordinary principles from the ones we started with" (1991,
p. 219).

The first thing to note is that moral theories include at least two distinctive
types of theory—to use Scanlon's terminology—Moral Inquiry and Philosophical
Inquiry. The first "has the aim of clarifying our first order moral concepts and
judgments, clarifying the grounds of the judgments we make . . . and clarifying
the relations between various moral concepts such as rights, justice, welfare and
responsibility." Philosophical inquiry, on the other hand,

> [a]ims not at establishing which claims merit acceptance as moral truths but
> rather at explaining what it means for there to be such truth at all. What kinds
> of claims do moral judgments make? How can we best understand the distinc-
> tive importance and authority that they seem to have for us. (1995, p. 344)

So, if we ask about the relationship of moral theory to moral practice we have to
ask, at least, about the relation of moral inquiry and philosophical inquiry separately, as these are theories developed to satisfy different aims, and may have
different relations to practice. One would expect, for example, that the former
has more relevance than the latter.

The next thing to note is what I have in mind by moral practice. Sometimes
thinking about right and wrong in particular cases is called applied ethics. In

particular, bioethics, business ethics, environmental ethics, and legal ethics are
included as branches of applied ethics. I certainly mean to include these under
moral practice, but I am using the term more broadly so as to include any attempt
to determine what is morally permissible, forbidden, or obligatory in particular
circumstances. Such contexts are mainly informal and routine matters that do
not come under the heading of a particular discipline such as medical ethics.

What I shall mean by moral practice is to be distinguished from the attempt
to justify very general moral principles, for example, the principle of utility, and
also the attempt to justify moral assessments of act types, for example, it is wrong
to lie. I shall be concerned primarily with the attempt to justify moral assessments
of act tokens, for example, it is wrong for me to lie to my student about his
philosophical abilities in order to avoid an uncomfortable situation. These all-
things-considered judgments have been called "verdictives" by Philippa Foot, and
I will use her terminology (Foot, 1978, p. 182).

1. POSSIBLE INTERPRETATIONS

In this section, I will canvass the various interpretations that have been advanced
concerning the relation between moral theory and practice. Some of these are not
directly relevant to my topic but are mentioned for the sake of completeness. For
example, there is a considerable literature devoted to what might be thought of
as the converse of my topic—how do we develop ethical theory in light of our
particular moral judgments? Do we test our moral theories in terms of their
implications for our considered moral judgments? Can a coherence between our
theories and judgments validate our theories, or does this beg the question of
whether our judgments can be considered reliable?

The main set of claims concerns the ways in which theory enters into the
determinations of practice. It should be noted that there are two kinds of claims
at issue. The first is a normative one. The relation between theory and practice
ought to be the following: For example, theories provide principles that, in connection with particular facts, allow deductions of what to do, and are the proper
way of justifying such particular judgments. The second is a descriptive claim. If
we observe the way people reason to particular moral judgments, we see that they
deduce them from general principles (which are supplied by moral theories). If I
do not explicitly refer to a descriptive claim, I should be understood as examining
normative claims about the proper use of theories.

Such claims include the following views.

Deductive: Moral theory is related to practice as premises are to conclusions. A moral theory contains rules or principles that, together with the details of the particular circumstances, allows us to deduce the right thing to do.

Balancing: Theory provides us with a list of relevant factors, or a set of prima facie principles. But we get from these to particular judgments by a process of intuitive balancing.

Norm specification: We start with the norms of theory, but rather than deduce the conclusions of practice, we engage in a process of making the norms more specific. We replace general norms by ones that reflect more accurately the details of our case until we arrive at a norm that, by deductive reasoning, settles the case.

Virtue theory: The virtue theorist defines right action as the action that a (perfectly) virtuous agent would (characteristically) do in the particular circumstances we are faced with. Therefore, to determine what to do in a particular case one must determine what the virtuous agent would do.

Reflective equilibrium: This is best thought of as a way of justifying principles that could then be used in any of the ways already listed.

All of these suggest some role for moral theory. A number of views deny that theory plays any significant role in determining particular moral judgments. These include:

Particularism: There are no general principles, or even lists of factors, that enable us to determine what to do. A factor that has weight and direction in a particular set of circumstances may have a different weight or direction depending upon the circumstances of another case. As already mentioned, particularism is the denial that moral theories are true and, therefore, the claim that they can play no role in moral practice. But the theory leaves open how we ought to arrive at particular moral judgments.

Casuistry: We start from particular cases in which we are confident of our judgments and then reason by analogy to new cases. Like particularism, this theory denies that moral theories ought to play a role in justifying particular moral judgments. Unlike particularism, it need not deny that moral theories are true and play some other role.

A distinct set of claims concerns the issue of whether a theory is supposed to be used to inform practice or whether it has some other role. This is the issue of two-level theories, such as indirect consequentialism (one version of which has rules validated by utility and cases settled by rules). These are views that some theory stands in an indirect relationship to our moral practice. A distinct question is whether a theory provides us with an explanation or account of what makes an action right but does not claim to be useful in thinking about what to do (Bales, 1971).

2. DEDUCTIVE REASONING

The brunt of skepticism about the use of moral theory to moral practice has been borne by the claim that the relation between the two is one of deductive inference. The claim is that there are quite abstract principles about act types that, together with the premise that the act at issue falls under one of these principles, determines deductively that the act is permissible or not. So, if we have a theory among whose principles is "It is always wrong to take the life of an innocent person," then when faced with the example of whether it is permissible, while driving five badly injured persons to the nearest emergency room, to drive over someone trapped in the middle of the road, we deduce the conclusion that we must not drive over her. For surely the person in the road is an innocent person.

It has seemed to some that the relation between ethical theory and determining what to do in particular circumstances must be deductive, for what else could it be? In principle, one might think that one could reason inductively, that is, from the belief that in past cases like this, the right thing to do was X, and therefore it is likely that the thing to do in this case is X. But, as the foregoing example shows, we are at least hypothetically, and sometimes actually, faced with cases that we have never encountered before; not even cases roughly similar. And, in any case, even when faced with a case similar to those encountered before, we must have reason to think that the past generalization is correct, that is, X was the right thing to do. But, at least for the first of those cases encountered, we could not have used induction from the past.

If the relevant reasoning is to be deductive, then we must have principles available that are absolute in form. That is, they must be of the form "All acts of type A are forbidden, obligatory, or permissible." The antideductivist claim is that we don't have such principles, or, more cautiously, that any such principles we do have are very unlikely to figure in any decision we might have to make. It is true that the infliction of pain on babies for the amusement of those present is always wrong. But what quandary about our own acts is it supposed to help resolve? Who might we be dealing with who needs to be told this?

The obvious riposte is that we do have such principles but they are much more complicated than the example of killing innocent persons supposes. The principle governing the taking of innocent life is of the form "It is always wrong to take the life of an innocent person, unless (a), (b), . . . (w)." For example, (a) might be the case in which no matter what we do, innocent persons will be killed, and in such a case we may kill the fewer number, as in the case of a pilot whose plane is doomed to crash and who has a choice between a more populated and a less populated area, aiming his plane at the less populated area.

But it is not at all clear that we have principles of this type either. For the list of exceptions cannot be known to be closed, or even, if closed, of manageable computational length. It has been suggested that the principles might be always attached to an "other things being equal" condition. But, as Brandom and others have suggested, "the function of ceteris paribus clauses . . . is not to mark something else that might be equal, and that when filled in would make the inference deductive rather than defeasible; it is, rather, to mark nonmonotonicity in inference" (2001, p. 468).[1]

There is also the issue of monism or pluralism. Assuming that deductive inference were available, it is crucial whether there is (ultimately) only one principle or many in the best or true theory. For if there are multiple principles, then the possibility arises of conflicts between them. More than one might apply to a set of particular circumstances and give conflicting results. So, to use an example made famous by Thomson (1971)—that of the kidnapped violinist, in which the kidnap victim is forced to give life support to a stranger by having her organs hooked up with his, and in which, although she can unhook him, doing so will kill him—we may believe that it is always wrong to take the life of an innocent person but also that no person is required to make large sacrifices (particularly those involving the use of her body) to preserve the life of another person who has not been given the right to use her body. If, in these circumstances, to deprive the person of life support *is* to kill an innocent person, then we cannot deduce the correct thing to do. If we had priority rules for the multiple principles, this would be different, but no system currently available has such an ordering.

As to the systems, such as monistic utilitarianism, that do have a single principle, they are scarcely credible, and if they were, they rely on empirical determinations (what action would maximize human well-being or preferences into the [foreseeable?] future), which rule out deductive inference, because we can never be confident about the truth of the premises.

However slim the evidence for deduction from one principle, or a ranked list of principles, the view remains dominant because of the "What else?" claim. Unless, and until, some other convincing account is presented about how we can make, or ought to make, our particular moral judgments, it will remain the default position.[2]

3. BALANCING

The model of balancing does not seem to involve deduction, for its whole point is that there are no priority rules by which to order multiple norms. The position, called "intuitionism" by Rawls, has been defined by him as follows: "[a] plurality of first principles, which may conflict to give contrary directives in particular types of cases . . . and no explicit method, no priority rules, for weighing these principles against one another: we are simply to strike a balance by intuition" (1971, p. 34).

The main objection to balancing is that it seems to leave the agent incapable of giving reasons for his decision other than to say that is how it strikes him, and that there does not seem to be a way of determining after the decision whether it was correct or not.

It is obvious that in other kinds of practical reasoning we do something like the balancing of plural and incommensurable factors. The student deciding which college to attend, the physician diagnosing a patient on the basis of various symptoms, the person deciding how to allocate financial assets for retirement do not operate on an algorithm. They accumulate information about the various options, they use various value criteria, and then they choose. "On balance," they say, it seems the right thing to do, and they can point to various factors that seemed to them the "more important" ones.

In addition, in such cases, there are criteria for whether the outcome was mistaken. The student will find out whether he is satisfied with his choice, and he may have indirect evidence (from friends who made other choices) that he would not have been as satisfied with another choice. The physician will find out whether the treatment based on his diagnosis improves the patient, and may have subsequent tests that confirm his diagnosis. The woman who arrives at retirement will see whether her accumulated assets allow her to live the kind of life she wanted to.

The issue is whether something analogous takes place in the case of moral reasoning. For, after all, the agent does have views as to what are the relevant factors in the case, why some of them seem to be more important (given the particular mix) than others, and uses her best judgment to determine the proper outcome. It is not as if nothing can be said on behalf of the particular determination that was reached.

What about the issue of whether there are tests for the correctness of the decision? As Hare put this point, "I do not object to rational weighing or judging, in which there is a way of telling whether it is done well or ill" (1988, p. 224).

I think it is reasonable to think that there are these kinds of considerations with respect to moral decisions as well. Having made a particular decision, we have to see whether we can adhere to it and live by it. Is the decision one that, because of consistency requirements, creates more moral dilemmas for us than we were faced with originally? Are the cooperative relations with our fellows made more difficult or more congenial? Do we find that a life lived in accordance with this decision is more or less meaningful than previously, or than one that would have been led if we had made another decision? Does the precedent of this decision lead to new decisions that seem reasonable to us, or do the new decisions based on this precedent seem sufficiently distasteful that we are led to reconsider. In short, "Try it; you'll like it" is not a bad way of determining whether we were mistaken or not.

Still, there remains the suspicion that balancing can be used in arbitrary and inconsistent ways. How can we prevent the person who distinguishes the case before him from similar ones in which he has decided differently by pointing to some feature x, simply declaring that the addition of x seemed to him to be so important that it changed the nature of his decision? In the absence of something like a general reason, does balancing simply become fiat?

A different approach to the task of balancing is to claim that all such weighing must be in terms of values, that is, some feature that is good or bad, or casts a favorable or unfavorable light on the alternatives being weighed. Such an evaluation may be particularistic in character. In each case of conflict, there is some value that provides a means of evaluation of the choices. The choice that comes out highest on that value scale is the one that should be chosen. Whether such a strategy will prove successful cannot be settled a priori. It is a hypothesis that must be tested by first seeing if some of the choices that we are confident are correct are resolved in that fashion—and whether that strategy can be projected onto new cases and provide solutions that stand up over time.

Those who defend the role of theory believe that it is the only way to avoid mere fiat in the balancing of reasons or values. Again, the issue can be resolved only by comparison of the use of theory to alternative structures.

4. NORM SPECIFICATION

One attempt to go beyond the first two models—deduction and balancing—is the idea of norm specification. Associated with Henry Richardson (1990), the idea is that when we have plural norms, we attempt neither to introduce priority rules (enabling deduction) nor to simply balance conflicting norms and weigh them against one another—the first because there are no such rules available, the second because the metaphor of weighing is misleading in assuming that there are independent weights which the balance measures. The idea of norm specification is that we start with a set of norms considered as typically qualified by "generally" or "for the most part." When faced with cases of conflicting norms, we attempt to specify one or more of the norms until the point at which it becomes obvious that the case before us falls under it and that no other conflicting norms cover it. The specified norm does not replace the original norm, in the way in which if we find an exception to an "absolute" norm, we build it into a revised norm. The specified norm remains alongside of the original norm, both honoring the point of that norm, and, in some cases, allowing the original norm to dictate actions of compensation or apology (Richardson, 1990).

As an example, suppose we are faced with the case of the Nazi storm trooper inquiring as to the whereabouts of Anne Frank, when we know where she is. Our only alternatives are to speak truly or to lie. We have a norm: For most actions, the fact that it is a lie makes it forbidden. We also have a norm: For most actions, the fact that it would save an innocent person from being murdered, without comparable cost to the agent, makes it required.

The idea is to modify the norm against lying by supplying particular circumstances so that it does not apply to the case before us. In this case: For most actions, the fact that it is a lie told to someone who is not going to use the information to violate the rights of others makes it forbidden.

It is clear that this procedure does not allow us to arrive at verdictives by deduction. For one thing, a norm preceded by a "for the most part" cannot yield any conclusion about a particular case. In any case, it is not merely a balancing of one norm against another, since it is possible that only one norm is at issue. Finally, we are to arrive at a new norm, which balancing does not do.

The specified norm will be controversial, but that is not problematic. What is at issue is how one can defend the new norm—precisely the point that is supposed to improve the situation over balancing. The idea is that we are to engage in a process of reasoning about the new norm and its relation to the old, and to evaluate the new system by seeking reflective equilibrium. What is the point of the original norm, and is it preserved in the new? Do the particular circumstances built into the specified norm seem relevant to the issue? Are there assumptions built into the original norm that may be legitimately questioned and revised in the specified norm, for example, does the prohibition against lying assume that those being lied to are themselves willing to abide by norms of cooperation? Does the new system of norms produce decisions that we are able to abide by and commit ourselves to?

As James Wallace puts it, "[when moral considerations conflict], the aim [of deliberation] must be to modify one or more considerations so that it applies, so that its original point is to some degree preserved, and so that one can live with the way [of proceeding] so modified" (1988, p. 86). While all this seems perfectly plausible, it is not clear how it diverges fundamentally from the deductive model. It looks very much as if the specified norm (if it had a universal quantifier) would function like an exception to a (universally quantified) original norm. The advantage, of course, is that we are not open to counterexamples, since it is only a "for the most part" norm.

The corresponding disadvantage is that we do not know that the norm does (not) apply to the case in question. To take my example, maybe this is one of those exceptions in which although the person being lied to would use the information wickedly, one is still not allowed to lie.[3]

The claim is that we must use judgment in the final step. But then this view faces the objection to balancing I have already considered, that is, that all we can say is that this case does not seem to be an exception.

5. CASUISTRY

I turn now to the tradition in moral philosophy, associated with Catholic theology, known as "casuistry." The most comprehensive modern treatment of the subject defines the term as

> the analysis of moral issues, using procedures of reasoning based on paradigms and analogies, leading to the formulation of expert opinion about the existence and stringency of particular moral obligations, framed in terms of rules or maxims that are general but not universal or invariable, since they hold good with certainty only in the typical conditions of the agent and circumstances of actions. (Jonsen and Toulmin, 1988, p. 257)[4]

The essence of this mode of reasoning is to start with some general principle (Thou shalt not kill), to present a series of paradigmatic cases that clearly fall under the prohibition (a direct unprovoked attack on an innocent person causing her death), and then to move away from the paradigm in small steps, introducing various circumstances that make the case more problematic. The traditional list of circumstances was "who, what, where, when, why, how, and by what means." This was also usually accompanied by various moral maxims (a lesser evil can be tolerated to prevent a greater; what is not explicitly granted should be considered forbidden) that served as additional argumentative material. The conclusion was that the case at issue was sufficiently like or unlike the paradigmatic cases, supplemented by maxims, so that it warranted being decided one way rather than another.

Consider, for example, the question "May you kill someone who insults you by beating and slapping him?" One argument proceeded by drawing the analogy with the theft of money. If defense of one's money is permitted, then so was defense of honor, since honor is more valuable than money. But against this analogy it was objected that the stolen goods still existed and might be recaptured by pursuit, whereas honor is gone for good. To this it was replied that honor can be recovered. In addition, it was argued, if pursuit and punishment were not permitted, license would be given to wicked persons to insult anyone and run away (Jonsen and Toulmin, 1988, pp. 224–225).

Casuistry is essentially tied to arguments from analogy, which are certainly present in most legal reasoning and clearly occur in many moral contexts as well. Again, in a trivial sense, they can be put into deductive form.

(1)   We judge that P in case Y because of features a and b.
(2)   Case Z has features a, b, and d.
(3)   Feature d does not play a significant moral role in how we should judge case Z, and no other feature of Z is morally relevant.
      Therefore, we ought, if we are consistent, to judge that P in case Z.

But (3) is clearly not a general principle of moral theory.

This process of reasoning can at most show that we are consistent with our original judgment(s). But, by itself, it cannot show that we are right to judge P. That depends on whether we were right to judge P in case Y. But the same is true of all deductive arguments. We either have to accept the conclusion or abandon one of the premises.

A more troubling problem, as Bernard Williams has noted, is that "the repertory of substantive ethical concepts differs between cultures, changes over time, and is open to criticism. . . . It has no claim that there are preferred ethical categories that are not purely local" (1985, p. 96).

Since everything depends on the initial starting point, as well as a shared sense of similarity, and both of these are culturally variable, the issue of whether this leads to an objectionable form of relativism arises. It may be that there is nothing better than the Wittgensteinian point that a community shares a sense of similarity, of knowing how to go on, that has no deeper foundation.

6. PARTICULARISM

It might seem that the method of casuistry is as antigeneral as one can get. We start from particular cases, we proceed to particular judgments, and we do so by making use of claims about the relevance and similarity of the cases in question. It is true that, as always, we are dealing with types of cases, but the only generalization seems to be: "Cases such as B are sufficiently similar to cases such as A that we ought to judge them similarly." But there is a view that is even more radically antigeneral, which goes by the name of particularism. It is, perhaps, most associated with Jonathan Dancy. What is unique about this doctrine is its denial that a morally relevant consideration, if it has positive (or negative) weight in one case, has the same weight wherever it appears. Some particularists believe that a property that counts in favor of an act in some circumstances may count against it in others. Far from being at least close to casuistry, this would make all casuistry impossible. For the casuist focuses on feature X and says that since it leads to a judgment in one case, it ought to lead to a similar judgment in another (provided there are not other dissimilarities). The idea is that since our initial judgment is made *because* of the presence of X, we would be inconsistent, *ceteris paribus,* in not making the same judgment whenever X is present. This idea is present in all the theories we have considered and seems to be a necessary feature of moral argument. As Blackburn points out:

> In trying to discover what to do, we imagine different actions, and register their good and bad features. It is essential to this process that these features are reliably extracted from any contexts or total situations in which we have come across them and carry some moral import when translated into the new hypo-thetical situation. (1996, p. 97)

Dancy denies this. Consider "pleasure," for example. Most theorists assume that pleasure always contributes positively to the goodness of a state of affairs, even though on many accessions it may be outweighed by other considerations. The particularist, among others, claims that if we consider the pleasure that people take in the torturing of others, then the pleasure actually contributes negatively to the goodness of the total state of affairs. It is not that it is outweighed by the means used to produce the pleasure; it is that its contribution to the total good-ness of the state of affairs is negative. It would be a better state of affairs (though still horrible) if the torturers were not to derive pleasure from the actions. Note that this thesis is similar to Shelly Kagan's denial of what he calls the ubiquity thesis. This is the claim that if a factor makes a difference anywhere, it makes a difference everywhere. Now this claim is consistent with the particularist thesis, that is, a given factor could always makes a difference, but the difference could vary from case to case. Nevertheless, the particularist, like Kagan, denies the ubiq-uity thesis. Where they differ is that Kagan believes that there is some finite list of principles (undoubtedly very complicated) that determines the moral status of an act, based on the particular features of the act. The function from features to moral status of the act may very well be nonadditive, that is, it is not the sum of independent right- and wrong-making features, and undoubtedly very compli-cated, but it is there waiting to be discovered. It is this claim that the particularist denies.

How then does a particularist decide what to do? For surely she does not think that the fact that we are presented with a new case means that we must start completely afresh, or that there is no story to be told about how the factors interact in the new case. One must make a careful, detailed, and sensitive assessment of each individual case with all of its particulars.

This view is similar to Rossian balancing, except that we do not have the luxury of being able to assume that if the case can be brought under a certain description, for example, is a lie, then we at least know that counts against doing the act. We cannot know in advance whether the property of being a lie counts for, counts against, or is neutral concerning our reasons for doing the act.

Some have insisted that morally relevant factors are univalent, that is, always have the same moral direction. The kinds of counterexamples presented by the particularist are either incorporated into the relevant statement of the principle—for example, all pleasures that are not taken in the suffering of others are good—or it is claimed that the factors remain relevant but are overridden.

If the particularist is correct about valency, there are obvious worries about such a view. One is how it accounts for a crucial feature of moral argument—the appeal to consistency. Often we get people to change their minds by showing that they are committed to making a certain judgment in a case with features A, B, and C, and therefore ought to do the same with a different case which also has A, B, and C. But it is always open to the particularist to say that because of feature D in the latter case, A no longer counts for (against) the act. Of course, it is always possible for the nonparticularist to say that although A, B, and C retain their polarity, their force is altered by the presence of D (nonadditivity) or that even if they retain the same force, the presence of D changes the nature of the judgment that should be made about the new case. Consistency can always be achieved. Like postulation, according to Russell, it sometimes has the advantages of theft over honest toil. But, like theft, it may carry costs—in particular, of seeming to be arbitrary and ad hoc.

7. VIRTUE THEORY

The next view to be considered is that of virtue theory. It has been thought by many that virtue theory is not a competitor to other theories such as consequentialism or Kantianism, in that it is agent-centered rather than act-centered. It is interested in the role of character, not that of right action. It is concerned with the concept of acting well, as opposed to acting rightly. If all this were correct, then there would be no role for such a theory to play in providing action guidance, and I should not consider such a theory in my survey.

A number of philosophers have argued that this view is incorrect. While there may be problems with virtue theory as an action-guide, it seems to have the right form to count. The virtue theorist defines right action as the action that a (perfectly) virtuous agent would (characteristically) do in the particular circumstances one is faced with. Therefore, to determine what to do in a particular case, one must determine what the virtuous agent would do. Of course, if "perfectly virtuous agent" were defined in terms of an agent who does the right thing, this would be viciously circular. But this is not the case. A virtuous agent is one who possesses and exercises the virtues. And the virtues are those traits of character that (typically) benefit the agent and others.[5]

If we are faced with a moral issue, such as, for example, whether a doctor should lie and tell the wife of a drowning victim trapped in his car that he died instantly (when in fact he died after a painful struggle), then we are to think about what an agent who is honest and kind would do. And, again, we are not to determine that by figuring out in some other way what the right thing to do is and then imputing that decision to the virtuous agent. The difficulty, however, lies in how we are supposed to figure out what the virtuous agent would do. I suppose, if we knew of one, we could simply ask her.

There are two problems. One is that no real person is perfectly virtuous. The second is that perfectly virtuous agents would not find themselves in many of the situations we do. For example, a perfectly virtuous agent would not make two promises to different people that cannot both be kept. We could substitute the idea of what the virtuous agent would advise us to do in situations that she would never find herself in. But this is quite a different theory. The right action is what the virtuous agent would advise us to do, not what the virtuous agent characteristically would do.

There is also difficulty with the idea that we can try to determine for ourselves how an agent possessed of the appropriate virtues would think about the matter before us. In the aforementioned case, we can ask ourselves whether an honest agent would lie in order to spare the wife terrible thoughts, that is, to be kind?

But this suggestion is not like the contractualist view that we try and determine what principles would be agreed upon by suitably motivated agents. In that case, we have to supplement the theory in various ways before we can think about what are the correct principles. We have to have some notion of human interests, and some normative conception of what agreements are reasonable (Scanlon, 1998).

In the case of virtue theory, what would be necessary to supplement the advice to do as the virtuous would do? At the least, some guidance about what it means to act as the virtuous do, for example, what it is to act honestly or kindly. Is acting honestly compatible with telling lies to those who have no right to know your views on certain matters? Is acting justly compatible with doing something that will harm someone, for example, giving a student the grade she deserves, knowing that ruins her chances for being admitted to law school? Hursthouse makes claims such as that the explanation for "why agents do not know the answer to 'What should I do in these circumstances?' arises from an inadequate grasp of what is involved in doing what is *kind* or *unkind,* in being *honest,* or in general, of how the virtue (and vice) terms are to be correctly applied" (1999, p. 60). How does she know this? What kind of reasoning or perception gives this result?

One might say that some things are built into the definition of a virtue. The courageous person is prepared to risk harm to himself. But it is not built into the concept of courage that the courageous person does not risk harm to himself by Russian roulette. In the case where different virtues seem to call for different acts (conflicts of virtues), there must be some way of thinking about how to resolve the conflict. It is not enough to reply that any nonmonistic theory is faced with the same question. For other theories either maintain that such conflicts cannot arise (Kantians) or that such conflicts must give rise to priority rules (Rawls) or that such conflicts are resolved by perception of the particulars (Ross). Virtue theory denies the first, denies that the virtues can be ranked lexically, and if it takes the Rossian tack, since it is the perceptions of the virtuous that are decisive, we are thrown back to our original doubts about how to determine what those are.

A common defense of virtue theory is to maintain that it is in no worse condition than alternatives. Kantians have to exercise judgment in determining the level of description for the maxims to be universalized. The particularist cannot do more than tell us to look carefully at the particular facts. Consequentialists, if they are pluralists in their value theory, have to provide tradeoff rules among the values. But what seems distinctive about virtue theorists is that the crucial step is resistant to further illumination. If it's not compatible with honesty to spare the wife her ghastly thoughts about how her husband died, we need to know why. But providing such information seems to itself provide the action-guidance without going through the virtuous agent.

Finally, there is some epistemological difficulty about the idea that nonvirtuous agents such as ourselves can think sensibly about what the perfectly virtuous agent would do (or advise). It's like the character in a Mamet movie who figures out something clever but denies that he is very smart. How did he do it? "By imagining a very clever person, and then figuring out what he would do."

I am not denying that thinking about the virtues is an important part of any comprehensive moral theory. Acting well is as significant a topic as doing the right thing. But as a competitor to the theories I have been considering, virtue theory is a nonstarter.

8. REFLECTIVE EQUILIBRIUM

The last suggestion about the nature of the reasoning for determining what to do in particular cases is the method of reflective equilibrium. This methodology, most frequently associated with Rawls, is a broadly coherentist method of justification. The idea is that we start *in medias res* with a variety of judgments that we accept. These range from judgments about particular cases (it's wrong to lie to Jones about his cancer) to judgments about which rules are correct (one should avoid cruelty) to convictions about what kind of reasoning is inadequate (the fact that a rule would have good consequences—only if it were kept secret—is not a justification for the rule) to views about human motivation (the strains of commitment). We seek coherence among these by revising and refining them. Our initial judgments serve as the starting point for reflection, but no judgment need be held free from revision. We test principles by seeing what their implications are for particular cases; we revise our views about particular cases in light of principles that have theoretical support and explain our judgments in a wide variety of other cases.

It seems to me, however, that this methodology does not provide us with a distinct way of reasoning about particular cases. Rather, it is a way of providing support for general reasons and principles that are then used to reason about particular cases in ways I have already discussed. We reason about a new case in terms of rules or principles that we have reason to accept in light of our search for reflective equilibrium. But the route from these rules or principles is either a case of straightforward deduction, or some process of balancing, or a process of specification, and so on.[6]

Another way of seeing this is to look at arguments from analogy. Here, again, one might say that we are searching for consistency or coherence in our moral views. Since one made judgment J in a case with features a, b, c, and Y, one either must make the same judgment in a new case with the same features or differentiate the two cases. And one may also bring in low-level principles that have guided one in other cases. One seeks to make a coherent whole of one's past practice and judgments. In that sense, one is seeking reflective equilibrium. But in that sense, all methods of reasoning about particular cases seek coherence. What distinguishes them is the different modes of reasoning about particular cases.

9. ESOTERIC THEORY

One of the important issues about the relation of theory to practice is whether the correct moral theory can be "esoteric." By this is meant the idea that the correct theory may not be the one that should be learned and used by agents in reaching their decisions. The correct theory may specify that it is best for agents (as judged by the theory) to use an incorrect theory in their decision-making and to remain in ignorance of the correct theory.

While the first appearance of such an idea may be in Plato—the noble lie—it has its most notable exposition in Sidgwick.

> Thus, on Utilitarian principles, it may be right to do and privately recommend, under certain circumstances, what it would not be right to advocate openly; it may be right to teach openly to one set of persons what it would be wrong to teach to others; it may be conceivably right to do, if it can be done with comparative secrecy, what it would be wrong to do in the face of the world. (1966, 489–490)

In the contemporary literature, the two poles on this issue are taken by Rawls and Parfit. The former believes that any adequate moral theory must satisfy what he calls the "publicity condition," that is, it must be a theory that everyone ought to accept, and that is publicly recognized as the code that everyone ought to accept. Parfit, on the other hand, believes that we can distinguish between the questions of which theory ought to be promulgated and accepted and which theory is *true*. A true theory may be what he calls "self-effacing," that is, the theory itself may call for taking steps to see that it is not believed (1984, p. 43).

It is somewhat unclear what Parfit thinks a theory is or is for. He seems to think that a theory gives us "aims." So a consequentialist theory gives us the aim "that outcomes be as good as possible." But what aims does the theory of common-sense morality, what Parfit calls M, give us? He seems to think that if I am a doctor, then my M-given aim is the welfare of my patient.

But this is quite unclear. Is it the welfare of my patient, the autonomy of my patient, the welfare of my patient as brought about by my not lying, my being an ally of my patient, or something else again? And how is the aim of the theory related to what it directs us to do? A consequentialist theory tells us what it would be good or rational to bring about, that is, maximally good outcomes, so deriv atively it may say that it would be best for us to have certain dispositions. But does it tell us to try and develop those dispositions? It might be, after all, as Parfit recognizes, that trying to do that would be counterproductive. So, perhaps, it tells us to do whatever will, in fact, develop such dispositions.

How is one to think about the issue of whether a correct moral theory is one that is itself to be used, and publicly recognized as such, in reasoning about particular moral issues? There are two separate issues. One is that a moral theory may tell us to go about things in an indirect way. This is simply an issue of efficiency. But it remains the case that we can all recognize and acknowledge that this is what our theory tells us. It is a distinct question what the theory tells us ought to be the theory that is publicly acknowledged and advocated. A view such as Sidgwick's or Parfit's is only contradictory if one views morality, by definition, as a public code to be used by all moral agents capable of moral reasoning.

This is exactly the view of contractualist schemes, such as Scanlon's, that tie a moral code to a prior conception of what morality is supposed to be. On their view, the point of morality is to enable us to justify our actions to one another in ways that mutually recognize our desire to do so. Does this beg the question against those who view morality as a special kind of practical reasoning that enables persons to solve certain coordination problems and to reach desirable outcomes? It does not beg the question if some defense is given by the contractualist as to why their conception of morality is superior. This may be in terms of the conception giving us a better explanation of various moral phenomena, or being closer to the moral phenomenology of everyday life, or in terms of the overall superiority of a theory that takes morality as so defined. It is ultimately, then, a philosophical question of what conception of morality is most fruitful for which purposes.

10. CONCLUSION

I have canvassed a number of different views about the ways in which theory may relate to practice. Are there any tentative conclusions we can draw? Rather than attempting to judge winners and losers, let me suggest an approach to the general issue of the relation between theory and practice. Whether we need something like a theory to guide practice is related to the role of principles. If we need principles, if moral reasoning requires general principles, then we need some body of analysis to clarify the nature of, and provide grounds for, the principles. This can be thought of as a theory.

Why might we need principles? There are several possible answers to this, but I want to focus on one in particular. We need principles because we want to impose a constraint on our moral reasoning, that is, that of consistency. Consider the following from Justice Scalia: "[I]t is no more possible to demonstrate the inconsistency of two opinions based upon a 'totality of the circumstances test' than it is to demonstrate the inconsistency of two jury verdicts. Only by announcing rules do we hedge ourselves in" (1989, p. 1179).

This idea can be thought of as pragmatic in nature, that is, it is not a claim about the necessary nature of moral reasoning, or even the contingent claim that we, in fact, cannot get along without principles. It is a claim about how we should regulate our moral discourse. The need for principles is not one that emerges from normative inquiry. It is something we impose to regulate, and make possible, such inquiry. This means that the justification for the requirement of principled action must answer to our best conception of what the point of such inquiry is. Only after we understand that can we see whether the imposition is conducive to that point.[7]

Having justified that much on pragmatic grounds, there are two important issues. The first is the exact nature of the principles. The second is whether principles of that nature can be used to determine verdictives.

As to the first question, my hypothesis is that we can have *pro tanto* principles that are understood to hold only within certain contexts and under certain conditions. Thus, a principle about promising does not build in as an exception the condition that the promise is not coerced or immoral. Rather, it is only under those conditions that a promise has the normal force favoring its being kept. How are these conditions discovered? By examining the kind of thing a promise is, and the value that having such a practice serves.

As to the use of such principles as "One ought to keep promises" to provide answers to particular moral questions, here, I think, the particularist idea has greater merit. The answers to particular questions of what to do when there are competing reasons must be based on the understanding of the particular factors as they occur in the particular case. To show how such judgments are possible, that they are not arbitrary, and what story to tell about how to make such judgments is the most important task for normative theory. But it remains possible that the answer will be that we do not use theory to make such judgments.

NOTES

1. Monotonicity is the property of an argument such that its validity is not affected by the addition of new premises.
2. It is important to emphasize that this section is neutral on the issue of whether there are alternatives to deductive reasoning. The criticism is addressed to the existence of relevant premises, not to the relevance of deduction.
3. Leaving aside the Kantian view, an interesting essay by W. G. MacLagan, 1968, argues that although it may be just to kill a POW camp guard in order to escape, it would not be just to bribe him, thus corrupting his will.
4. The last bit seems distinctly consequential in nature.
5. See Hursthouse, 1999, pp. 28–29. There are alternative ways of defining right ac-

tion that would also have to be considered, for example, the right action expresses virtuous states of character.

6. The alternative, suggested by Brock, 1995, is that we actually try to reach reflective equilibrium when we are determining what to do in a particular case. This is very implausible, given the enormous task that this involves. Do we really have to wonder how our particular views about, for example, lying, cohere with the best social science available, or what we believe the best metaethical view is?

7. This approach, obviously, avoids the issue of whether we want our principles to be "true," not merely useful for some purpose. To defend this pragmatic view would require an article in itself.

REFERENCES

Bales, R. Eugene. 1971. "Act-Utilitarianism: Account of Right-Making Characteristics or Decision-Making Procedure?" *American Philosophical Quarterly* 8: 257–265.

Blackburn, Simon. 1996. "Securing the Nots: Moral Epistemology for the Quasi-Realist." In *Moral Knowledge? New Readings in Moral Epistemology,* ed. Walter Sinnott-Armstrong and Mark Timmons, 82–100. New York: Oxford University Press,

Brandom, Robert. 2001. "Actions, Norms and Practical Reasoning." In *Varieties of Practical Reasoning,* ed. Elijah Millgram, 465–479. Cambridge, Mass.: MIT Press.

Broad, C. D. 1930. *Five Types of Ethical Theory.* London: Kegan Paul, Trench, Trubner.

Brock, Dan. 1995. "Public Moral Discourse." In *Society's Choices: Social and Ethical Decision making in Biomedicine,* ed. Ruth Ellen Bulger, Elizabeth Meyer Bobby, and Harvey V. Fineberg, 215–240. Washington, D.C.: National Academy Press.

Dancy, Jonathan. 1991. "An Ethic of Prima Facie Duties." In *A Companion to Ethics,* ed. Peter Singer, 219–229. Oxford: Blackwell.

Foot, Philippa. 1978. *Virtues and Vices.* Berkeley: University of California Press.

Hare, R. M. 1988. "Comments." In *Hare and His Critics: Essays on Moral Thinking,* ed. Douglas Seanor and Nicholas Fotion, 199–293. Oxford: Clarendon Press.

Hursthouse, Rosalind. 1999. *On Virtue Ethics.* Oxford: Oxford University Press.

Jonsen, Albert R., and Stephen Toulmin. 1988. *The Abuse of Casuistry.* Berkeley: University of California Press.

MacLagan, W. G. 1968. "How Important Is Moral Goodness?" In *Ethics,* ed. Judith Jarvis Thomson and Gerald Dworkin, 512–526. New York: Harper and Row.

Parfit, Derek. 1984. *Reasons and Persons.* Oxford: Clarendon Press, 1984.

Rawls, John. 1971. *A Theory of Justice.* Cambridge, Mass.: Harvard University Press.

Richardson, Henry. 1990. "Specifying Norms as a Way to Resolve Concrete Ethical Problems." *Philosophy and Public Affairs* 19: 279–310.

Scalia, Antonin. 1989. "The Rule of Law as a Law of Rules." *University of Chicago Law Review* 56: 1175–1188.

Scanlon, T. M. 1995. "Moral Theory: Understanding and Disagreement." *Philosophy and Phenomenological Research* 55: 343–356.

———. 1998. *What We Owe to Others.* Cambridge, Mass.: Harvard University Press.

Sidgwick, Henry. [1907]. 1966. *Methods of Ethics.* 7th ed. New York: Dover.

Thomson, Judith Jarvis. 1971. "A Defense of Abortion." *Philosophy and Public Affairs* 1: 47–66.

Wallace, R. Jay. 1988. *Moral Relevance and Moral Conflict.* Ithaca, N.Y.: Cornell University Press.

Williams, Bernard. 1985. *Ethics and the Limits of Philosophy.* London: Collins, 1985.

INDEX

....

Value
  adjustment of, 58
  balancing and, 631
  care as, 546
  definition of, 358–59
  dispositionalism and, 201
  environmental, 375–77
  ethical, 519
  ethical naturalism and, 92
  fundamental, 499
  of humanity formula, 493
  perception of, 186–93
  philosophy of, 148
  promoting, 383
  reality of, 202
  reasons and, 208–12
  sentiment and, 196
  variety of, 204–8
Value theory, 21–22, 357–59
  hedonism and, 359–61
Value-facts, 137–38
Value-judgments, 197
  hedonism and, 360
van Inwagen, Peter, 350
  on judgments, 343
  on PAP, 334–35
  practical reasoning and, 324–26
Verdictives, 626
Virtue
  artificial, 223–24, 232
  conceiving, 638
  definition of, 516, 638
  examples of, 517–18
  faux, 210–11
  final end and, 530–31
  flourishing and, 519–23
  living by, 523–25
  natural, 220, 222
  nature and, 525–28
  perfectionism and, 365
  reasons and, 585
  self-interest and, 30
  sensibility theory and, 193
  skill model of, 209
  unreduced modern, 532
Virtue consequentialism, 20
Virtue ethics, 20, 29–30, 158, 516–28, 636–38
  Aristotle and, 29, 515
  assumptions of, 523
  caring v., 225
  consequentialism and, 381, 533
  criticism of, 534

  deontology and, 453–54
  evolution of, 526–27
  features of, 515–16
  flourishing and, 521–22
  future of, 533–34
  Humean theory and, 528
  practical reasoning in, 518
  reduced versions of, 528–32
  weak, 531–32
Virtue theory, 20, 627, 636–38
  ethics of care and, 29, 551–52
  feminism and, 551–52
Virtuous actions, 91
Voluntarism. *See also* Theological
    voluntarism
  associative duties and, 401–2
  utilitarianism v., 402

Walker, Margaret, 540
  feminism and, 556–57
Wallace, James, 632
Walzer, Michael, 263*n*11
Welfare-maximizing, 129
Well-being, 418*n*6
Wierenga, Edward R., 69–70, 75
Wiggins, David
  on evaluative concepts, 206–7
  sensibility theory and, 191
  on sentimentalism, 196
  on univocity, 215–16*n*32
Will
  act of, 275
  autonomy of, 489
  Kant on, 508*n*24
  weakness of, 150–51
Will theory, 463
Williams, Bernard, 71, 114*n*9
  casuistry and, 634
  on ethical theory, 625
  moral psychology and, 220
  on relativism, 253–54
  sensibility theory and, 191
  sentimentalism and, 206
Willing maxims, 481–88
Wittgenstein, Ludwig, 158–59, 300
Women. *See also* Feminism
  ethics of care and, 539–40
  exploitation of, 547–48
  moral theory and, 555
Wood, Alan, 491–92
Wrangham, Richard, 169
Wright, Crispin, 215*n*24